.

Zev Farber
Images of Joshua in the Bible and Their Reception

Beihefte zur Zeitschrift für die alttestamentliche Wissenschaft

Edited by
John Barton, Reinhard G. Kratz
and Markus Witte

Volume 457

Zev Farber

Images of Joshua in the Bible and Their Reception

—

DE GRUYTER

G

ISBN 978-3-11-033888-1
e-ISBN (PDF) 978-3-11-034336-6
e-ISBN (EPUB) 978-3-11-038366-9
ISSN 0934-2575

Library of Congress Cataloging-in-Publication Data
A CIP catalog record for this book has been applied for at the Library of Congress.

Bibliographic Information published by the Deutsche Nationalbibliothek
The Deutsche Nationalbibliothek lists this publication in the Deutsche Nationalbibliografie;
detailed bibliographic data are available on the Internet at http://dnb.dnb.de.

© 2016 Walter de Gruyter GmbH, Berlin/Boston
Printing and binding: CPI books GmbH, Leck
♾ Printed on acid-free paper
Printed in Germany

www.degruyter.com

Dedicated to my wife, Channie.

ACKNOWLEDGMENTS

This book began as a Ph.D. dissertation at Emory University, and thus, I must first acknowledge my dissertation advisor, Jacob Wright, for guiding me through the process, as well as the rest of the committee—William Gilders, Luke Timothy Johnson, Ed Noort, Carol Bakhos, and Michael Segal—for their comments and critiques, all of which helped me improve the book. I also want to mention my M.A. advisor of long ago, Mordechai Cogan; his seminar in Joshua peaked my interest in this topic in the first place. I further wish to thank De Gruyter and the editors of the BZAW series for working with me on this project, specifically Reinhard Kratz for his initial feedback, and Sabina Dabrowski and Sophie Wagenhofer for carrying the project through. I would also like to thank Angela Roskop Erisman for putting together the index, as well as my friend Jeffrey Sokolow for proofreading the manuscript. Even with all this assistance, there will still be errors and linguistic infelicities, all of which are my own.

Contents

Introduction

In this book I trace the development and reinvention of the image of the prominent biblical character of Joshua (יהושע בן נון) over time and through a variety of traditions. Focusing on the literary character of Joshua, with a particular emphasis on how these depictions of Joshua relate to the societies that reinvent him, this study endeavors to contribute a greater understanding of the interaction between reception history and mnemohistory (i.e., cultural memory studies) in the identity formation and internal narrative of a culture. Additionally, by focusing the lens on multiple religious traditions and periods, my hope is to improve our understanding of the continuities and discontinuities of religious traditions that differ radically but, nevertheless, maintain certain figures and ideals in common.

Outline

This book explores the mnemohistory of Joshua as expressed by groups who venerate him as part of their cultural memory. I discuss two related questions about mnemohistory, both focusing on how the construction of cultural memory affects the way a group speaks about figures from its past. First, how much does the inherited story define the nature of the discourse about the character? Conversely, how much do each culture's values, even if different from those of the earlier sources, define its discourse about the received character? The give and take between these two foci forms the basis of the question and research in this project.

The book's six chapters can be divided roughly into three parts: Biblical Joshua (chs. 1 and 2), Rewritten Joshua (chs. 3 and 4), and Interpretations of Joshua (chs. 5 and 6). The first chapter is dedicated to a literary analysis of Joshua's character from a synchronic perspective. The Bible is the main source for all descriptions of Joshua that follow. For this reason, it is important to understand what was available to the later receivers of Joshua. Whether an interpreter veered from the biblical image greatly or hardly at all, the biblical Joshua is the starting point for all later traditions. Since the method of reading Bible before the advent of modern biblical criticism was to see the text synchronically, as one linear presentation of Joshua's "actual" story, the book begins with this approach. Chapter 1 catalogues and isolates the images of Joshua in the Bible and offers an overall impression of Joshua's multifaceted character.

As useful as this synchronic approach may be, however, it is insufficient for understanding the biblical text. Modern methods of biblical study, such as redaction criticism, source criticism, and tradition-historical criticism, demonstrate that the biblical text of the Primary History cannot really be read as a literary (or a historical) composition written by an author or school of authors from beginning to end in a consistent fashion.[1] Rather, the text was most likely put together piecemeal and chapter 2 traces the contours of this development.

These two chapters work in tandem. Analyzing the text synchronically uncovers a Joshua who grows and changes over time and who cannot be described two-dimensionally. It is this complex biblical character who inspires generations of readers to interpret and reinterpret the story of Joshua from multiple hermeneutic perspectives. The opening chapter approaches the material from this vantage point.

At the same time, isolating the discontinuities in the received text facilitates diachronic readings. Although the editors do their best to smooth out the tensions in Joshua's story and his character, most scholars agree that real discontinuity lies beneath. The best explanation for this discontinuity is that multiple Joshua traditions developed in different communities during different periods. Since important cultural markers and values inevitably shift among various communities, it is hardly surprising that a number of tailor-made Joshuas appeared among the ancient Israelites and Judahites, eventually being woven together into one complex character by the biblical editors.

Unfortunately, if there were pre-biblical documents discussing Joshua—I believe there were—they are lost to us, and any suggestion of what they may have contained needs to be reconstructed. For oral traditions, the matter is even more daunting. As part of my diachronic analysis, I will offer some suggestions for the origins of the various biblical images of Joshua. The goal is to understand when and where these images of Joshua emerged, what communities they resonated with and what function—religious, polemic, nationalist—they may have served before they were smoothed over by the biblical editors. As part of this project,

---

[1] I have chosen the term Primary History over alternatives such as Enneateuch, or Deuteronomistic History, since it seems the most innocuous and least presumptuous of the terms. Without taking a position on authorship or how to divide the accounts, the term "Primary History" is meant to convey the idea that the stories found in Genesis/Exodus through Kings represents the older, hence "primary," account of Israel's origins found in the Bible. I am aware that some, such as A. Graeme Auld, might challenge this assertion, but I think it is a reasonable consensus position, and, in the end, some term must be chosen. For more details on Auld's contention that both, Chronicles and Samuel-Kings are independently derivative works of an earlier Urtext, see: A. Graeme Auld, *Kings without Privilege: David and Moses in the Story of the Bible's Kings* (Edinburg: T&T Clark, 1994).

tradition historical, source critical and redaction critical strategies will be brought to bear on the question.[2]

Chapter 3 explores the many retellings of the Joshua story which were written during Second Temple times: Josephus, *Liber Antiquitatem Biblicarum (L.A.B.* or Pseudo-Philo), *Assumptio Mosis* and *Apocryphon of Joshua*.[3] As these retellings of the Joshua story come from very different contexts, it is not surprising that their perspectives are very different as well. The chapter evaluates which images of Joshua each retelling focuses upon and looks for correlation between this reception of Joshua and the overall project of the author whenever possible.

The fourth chapter jumps more than a millennium to the Samaritan community in the 14th century and the Arabic *Samaritan Book of Joshua*. Although this work is clearly a composite of a number of legends or traditions, the earliest known written version dates from this period. The work is primarily a retelling of the biblical Joshua story, including an introduction which retells parts of the Pentateuch with a focus on Joshua's role in certain stories. Although very distant in time to the texts explored in chapter three, it partakes of the same genre as many of them (especially *L.A.B.*).

Chapter 5 examines the early Christian use of Joshua as a prefiguring of Jesus. The first half of the chapter concentrates on the creation of the Joshua-Jesus typology, and the rest traces the ebb and flow of the usage of this typology through the fourth century CE.

The sixth and final chapter addresss Joshua as he is understood in rabbinic literature. Although the Rabbis have a multiplicity of interpretations and images of Joshua, many of which contradict each other, the relationship of Joshua to Moses features prominently in many of the rabbinic interpretations. The possibility (or probability) that the rabbis were aware of the Christian understanding of Joshua as a Jesus figure will be explored as well.

Finally, the book concludes with a synthesis of the data from the six chapters, in which I consider how the various continuities and discontinuities in Joshua's character as presented in these texts reflect on the groups who tell these stories. The goal is to appreciate the extent to which each group's unique reception of this "one" character bears a relationship to its own cultural values and, con-

---

2 Nevertheless, I will not attempt a full timeline of all Joshua traditions or a full redaction critical/source critical analysis of the book of Joshua, since this would take this project too far afield.

3 Also included in this chapter are a few small subsections dealing with references to Joshua during Second Temple times that are not part of a rewritten biblical text (Ben Sira, 1 and 2 Maccabees, 4 Ezra, and Philo).

versely, to what extent it creates continuity with different groups and with a (perceived) shared past.

Scope of the Book

In determining the scope of the book, I took into account three limiting factors were at play. One guiding principle has been to maintain focus on Joshua's image. The question driving the research is how his image was constructed in the memories of various groups. For this reason certain topics generally discussed when analyzing Joshua have been avoided.

For example, in the second chapter, textual reconstructions have been proposed and carried only as far as was necessary to delineate possible stages in the development of the Joshua traditions. Although a full attempt at reconstructing the stages of the literary development of the text would be a desideratum, such a project would be a book in and of itself.

Additionally, the book does not examine the difficult questions surrounding the Joshua account and the morality of war. The book of Joshua presents the modern reader with serious moral questions about wars of conquest, annihilation of local populations, and the rhetoric of power, but these issues are outside the scope of this book, which discusses the image of Joshua as presented and understood in pre-modern times. Hence, even though Joshua as warrior will be discussed, no critique of his character and position in Israelite—and Western—mnemohistory is raised unless the critique appears in one of the ancient or medieval sources under discussion.

A second limiting factor was determining the periods, places and cultures the study would cover. From the time the biblical story of Joshua was formed —if not before then—Joshua has been a central figure of memory and historiography among people or groups of people who identify themselves as being in continuity with Israelite tradition in some way. In this book, I chose only a few examples; many others could have been added but this would have made the work unwieldy.[4]

Nevertheless, I will take this opportunity to note two of the most interesting and significant usages of Joshua from pre-modern times I encountered during my research. The first is the use of Joshua in Islamic tradition. Although there is no

---

4 I chose to deal with ancient sources because this is my expertise. I hope to be able to follow through with other images of Joshua in future publications.

reference to Joshua in the Quran,[5] there is an entire section devoted to him in Abu Jafar al-Ṭabari's *History of the Prophets and Kings* (تاريخ الرسل والملوك, popularly referred to as *Tarikh al-Ṭabari*), which depicts Joshua as a great warrior and defeater of giants.[6] The second is the portrayal of Joshua in the work of the Hasidic and Qabbalistic thinker, R. Mordecai Joseph Leiner of Izbitz. Leiner paints Moses and Joshua as structural opposites. Moses conquered lust and brought the people out of Egypt to Mount Sinai (=law) but could not bring them into the land of Israel (=grace) because he was angry.[7]

Additionally, during the course of my research on Joshua I encountered a number of remarkable modern usages of Joshua. For example Joshua, as the conqueror of the land, has become an iconic figure in the Zionist and post-Zionist camps. One American rabbi, known for his right-wing political leanings, wrote a book about Joshua, envisioning him as "a prophet for today."[8] In Israel, the right-wing politician Moshe Feiglin has said that to solve Israel's problems, he is "searching for the Joshua bin Nun of our day."[9] David Ben Gurion used to hold a study session in his house on the book of Joshua, which eventually led to a published volume,[10] and the celebrated general and defense minister, Moshe Dayan, explicitly compared himself to Joshua.[11] There is even an image of Moses handing over the leadership to Herzl in place of Joshua.[12]

---

5 There is a possible allusion to him in a passage about the scouts.

6 I struggled with whether to include an analysis of this work. In the end, I decided that due to time contraints and my limited experience with Islamic sources, including my lack of familiarity with other Islamic treatments of Joshua less famous and accessible than that of al-Ṭabari, this material would best be handled separately in a future publication.

7 In Leiner's view, anger is the natural consequence of law; the relationship between this view and that of Christian exegesis (described in ch. 5) seems evident. For more discussion, see: Don Seeman, "Martyrdom, Emotion and the Work of Ritual in R. Mordecai Joseph Leiner's *Mei Ha-Shiloah*," *AJS Review* 27.2 (2003): 253–280 [277–279]. I thank Don Seeman for making me aware of this source.

8 Steven Pruzansky, *A Prophet for Today: Contemporary Lessons from the Book of Yehoshua* (Jerusalem: Gefen, 2006).

9 Quoted in: Tomer Persico, "The Messianic Fervor that Revamped Gush Emunim," *Mussaf-Shabbat* (July 1 2012): http://musaf-shabbat.com/2012/07/01/המשיחיות-שהחליפה-את-גוש-אמונים-תומר-פר/ [Hebrew].

10 *Studies in Tanakh by the Study Group in the House of David Ben-Gurion* (Hayim Rabin, Yehuda Elitzur, Hayim Gevaryahu, and Ben Tzion Luria, eds.; Jerusalem: Kiryat Sefer, 1971) [Hebrew]. For more on this, see: Rachel Havrelock, "The Joshua Generation: Conquest and the Promised Land," *CRR* 1.3 (2013): 308–326.

11 Moshe Dayan, *Living with the Bible* (illus. Gemma Levine; New York: William Morrow, 1978), 225–226.

On the other hand, the post-Zionist camp points to Joshua and his story as a precursor to all the wrong they believe the State of Israel has done.[13] Shlomo Sand, the well known post-Zionist scholar, speaks about his experience as a child with an atheist Bible teacher who still "felt the need" to defend Joshua's "behavior" as a conqueror. He uses this example to illustrate how important it is—in his opinion—to deconstruct such mythological figures as Joshua.[14]

Joshua also continues to be a figure that resonates among contemporary Christian scholars. Francis Schaeffer, for instance, has a monograph on Joshua, in which he envisions Joshua as the biblical figure who represents choice.[15] This is a key concept in the "post-Christian world," says Schaeffer. Schaeffer analogizes the modern world to the period of the Judges, a time filled with lawlessness and debauchery, and suggests to his readers that they should follow the path of Joshua and choose a life dedicated to God. Another example is the monograph of Douglas Earl, who offers a Christian reading strategy to counter the claims of post-colonialist readers who see Joshua simply as a biblical precedent for colonialism and genocide.[16] Earl suggests that readers can focus on passages like that of Rahab to interpret Joshua as someone who was open to like-minded people joining the community of believers.

Joshua has also found his place in American politics. In a famous speech towards the beginning of his candidacy, Barack Obama referred to his generation of African Americans as "The Joshua Generation."[17] Joshua was the leader of the second generation of Israelites, those who inherited the land. Similarly, Obama declared, his generation of African Americans have inherited a place in American society after the "fighting" of the previous generation.

Stories about Joshua have also been used by modern-day military figures. An example of this was pointed out to me by my brother-in-law, Lawrence Kaplan, a former visiting professor at the U.S. Army War College and a writer on military

---

12 I thank Asher Bieman for this reference, who came across this image during his research. Unfortunately, neither of us has been able to locate the image again by the time of this publishing.

13 See, for example, the discussion in Nur Masalha, *The Bible and Zionism: Invented Traditions, Archaeology and Post-Colonialism in Palestine- Israel* (London: Zed Books, 2007), 273–274.

14 Shlomo Sand, *The Invention of the Jewish People* (trans. Yael Lotan; London: Verso, 2009), 14.

15 Francis A. Schaeffer, *Joshua and the Flow of Biblical History* (2nd ed.; Wheaton, IL: Crossway Books, 2004; originally pub. 1975), see especially pp. 219–223.

16 See: Douglas S. Earl, *Reading Joshua as Christian Scripture* (JTIsupp. 2; Eisenbrauns: Winona Lake, 2010).

17 See: David Remnick, "The Joshua Generation," *The New Yorker* (Nov. 17, 2008); http://www.newyorker.com/reporting/2008/11/17/081117fa_fact_remnick.

matters. After suffering a certain defeat in Iraq, versions of the following email message circulated among officers:

> The Bible recounts that, after conquering Jericho, Joshua sent a party to reconnoiter toward Ai. Upon returning, the scouts assured their commander that this quarter of the Promised Land would fall easily. There would be no need to use the entire army. "Spare the whole people such a toil," the scouts urged. "The enemy are not many." Joshua detached only a token force to subdue the region and then deployed it clumsily. The people of Ai, unimpressed with the reputation of Joshua's army, resisted fiercely and turned back the attackers. They pursued the Israelites to a place called Shebarim, where "they made havoc of them."[18]

The arrogance of Joshua and his "officer corps" is being compared here heuristically to a mistake made by the higher-ups in the American army, which, by implication, is believed also to result from overconfidence. The generals should have learned from "The General" par excellence never to underestimate the enemy. This brief survey should demonstrate the rich possibilities that exist for a survey of the use of Joshua in modern times.

A third limitation has to do with secondary literature. This study traverses a massive amount of texts. Beyond the biblical literature on Joshua and the Second Temple literature on Joshua, where I attempted to be exhaustive, the study covers Samaritan literature, Rabbinic literature and early Christian literature. Each group of texts quoted has its own scholarly literature and debate. Considering the time and size constraints on any project, I felt that an attempt to fully survey the various approaches to these texts in secondary literature would have forced me to make the project much smaller in scope. Instead, I have chosen to keep the scope of the study relatively wide and focus on direct analysis of the texts themselves.

For this reason, the book discusses secondary literature only when it directly pertains to the questions being asked. I have tried to directly engage those scholars that are conversation partners in the endeavor to study the character or image of Joshua in any given text, and I try to footnote only these and a handful of other key studies that shed light on the discussion. Given that such choices are difficult to make, I beg the reader's indulgence in cases where I referenced either too little or too much.

The wide scope of the book make it very long. One of the reasons for this is the amount of primary sources I quote, both in the original and in translation,

---

18 The quote is included as part of the introduction to Kaplan's forthcoming book on the Iraq war.

especially in chapters 3–6.[19] Since the material in these chapters comes from a wide variety of sources, are written in different languages, and reflect expertise in very different fields, I felt that it would be unfair to my readers to make them search out the sources if they wish to evaluate my claims. Therefore, I generally quoted the relevant passage in full—in the original language and in translation—to make things easier on the reader, even though this makes the book much longer.[20] On the other hand, I have written the sections in such a way that these sources need not be read thoroughly to understand the argument.

Models of this Sort of Study

The study of a particular biblical figure's place, both in biblical literature as well as reception history, has become a burgeoning field of research over the last few decades. Although each study has its own parameters and goals, I have used several such studies as comparative models for my own work. Five examples stand out.

A) In an article on Abraham, Annette Yoshiko Reed studies the early formation of what would later characterize this character's reception in Western religious thought: Abraham the paragon of faith and virtue.[21] She points out that one would hardly have chosen this characteristic to summarize the biblical Abraham corpus as a whole. Nevertheless, during the Hellenistic period, and under the influence of Hellenistic thinking about what makes a heroic figure worthy of emulation, authors such as Philo, Josephus, and the author of the *Testament of Abraham* crafted a new and improved version of Abraham, albeit using some of the stories about him as the starting point.

B) In a monograph on the reception of the character of Ishmael in rabbinic literature, Carol Bakhos notes the sea change in the Rabbinic descriptions of Ishmael that occurs after the rise of Islam.[22] Before this period, although Ishmael

---

19 The first to chapters are based upon analysis of biblical passages and are more accessible. I quote two in those sections as well, but not nearly as much as in the other chapters.

20 I always include the original language in my quotes when possible, in order to allow the reader to check my translation and evaluate my argument on his or her own. Although I do feel that this is the best approach to presenting a study such as this, I apologize in advance for the length.

21 See: Annette Yoshiko Reed, "The Construction and Subversion of Patriarchal Perfection: Abraham and Exemplarity in Philo, Josephus, and the *Testament of Abraham*," *JSJ* 40 (2009): 185–212.

22 See: Carol Bakhos, *Ishmael on the Border: Rabbinic Portrayals of the First Arab* (SUNY Series in Judaica: Hermeneutics, Mysticism, and Religion; Albany: State Univ. of New York Press, 2007).

still represents the "other"—the son of Abraham that was banished—he is portrayed in more than one way. After the rise of Islam, however, Ishmael comes to represent the ancestor of the Muslims and is portrayed almost exclusively in the light in which the Rabbis wished to portray Islam. Bakhos ends her book with a fascinating comparison of the Muslim and Jewish versions of the story of Abraham visiting Ishmael, demonstrating the reality of cultural interchange and mutual borrowing which helped shape both traditions' understanding of these characters.

C) In a recent monograph, also on Abraham, Jon Levenson attempts to do two things.[23] He focuses mainly on the development of the image of Abraham in Jewish tradition and how this reflects the development of Judaism itself.[24] Levenson, nonetheless, also explores Abraham's function as a pivotal character, one who is associated with three distinct religious traditions. Contrary to the more popular claim that Abraham is a consensus figure, Levenson prefers to focus on the differences in the reception and conception of Abraham in these traditions:

> Given these conflicting interpretations of the supposedly common figure, the claim that Abraham is a source of reconciliation among the three traditions increasingly called 'Abrahamic' is as simplistic as it is now widespread. Historically, Abraham has functioned much more as a point of differentiation among the three religious communities than as a node of commonality (Levenson, *Inheriting Abraham*, 8–9).

Although Levenson appears correct that the figure illustrates the differences between the various religious traditions, I think he overstates the case. The very fact that all three religions desire to express *continuity* with this figure of Israelite and Judahite cultural memory is itself a fact worthy of note and demonstrates some level of continuity or perceived continuity between these traditions. A balanced study of the function of a mnemohistorical character must take into account both the differences between the traditions that the reinvention of the character demonstrates and the implications of the attempt to maintain continuity with this character and how this is achieved.

This last point brings up an issue of methodology. This book contains very different kinds of texts and genres, each of which requires its own methodology. Instead of declaring the type of method I will employ at the outset, I have decided that it is best to let each text dictate the appropriate methodological tool. Nev-

---

23 See: Jon D. Levenson, *Inheriting Abraham: The Legacy of the Patriarch in Judaism, Christianity and Islam* (Princeton: Princeton University Press, 2012).
24 "The evolution of the figure of Abraham in Jewish sources reflects the evolution of Judaism itself over the centuries," (Levenson, *Inheriting Abraham*, 3).

ertheless, since the book does have one overarching analytical goal—to study the development of the character of Joshua as it emerges over time and in different cultural settings—the one methodological lens through which every chapter has been refracted is that of cultural memory studies or, as Jan Assmann calls it, mnemohistory.[25]

D) Jan Assmann applies his mnemohistorical method mostly to the study of ancient Egypt, but he also wrote a monograph on Moses.[26] By tracing the reception of Moses through history (primarily Enlightenment Europe), Assmann shows how the culturally constructed concepts of "Egypt" and "Mosaic religion" were developed over time, despite the extremely loose connection to historical Egypt. This work serves as a model for how the study of the reception of a biblical character in a given society can demonstrate a great deal about that society's values and cultural identity.

E) Rachel Havrelock's study differs from the previous four since she is not actually studying a character but the Promised Land itself.[27] Specifically, Havrelock is interested in the various constructions of the map of the Promised Land found in the biblical texts and how these maps both shaped and were shaped by the cultural contexts that produced them. She then traces the reception of these various maps into the modern period, showing how they affect political and religious discourse to this day by shaping the cultural memory of the various groups (Israelis and Palestinians) vying for the land. What is particularly significant and resonant in Havrelock's work is her argument that despite the editor's attempt to smooth over the contradictory views in his sources and redactional layers about the map of the Promised Land, nevertheless, the traditions actually continue independently with one or another being the primary influence on a

---

25 The field of cultural memory studies was "invented" by Maurice Halbwachs, but has come into its own as a methodological lens for the interpretation of religion and ancient history through the work of Jan Assmann. See: Maurice Halbwachs, *On Collective Memory* (trans. and ed. Lewis A. Coser; Chicago: University of Chicago Press, 1992 [original French pub. 1941, 1952]); Jan Assmann, *Religion and Cultural Memory: Ten Studies* (Stanford: Stanford University Press, 2006). The field has also been applied to the study of modern Jewish history and identity. This was first done in the pioneering work of Yerushalmi, which focused on the problem of history replacing memory: Yosef Hayim Yerushalmi, *Zakhor: Jewish History and Jewish Memory* (Samuel and Althea Stroum Lectures in Jewish studies; Seattle: University of Washington Press, 1982). See also the work of Yehuda Kurtzer, who constructively engages Yerushalmi's dilemma: Yehuda Kurtzer, *Shuva: The Future of the Jewish Past* (Waltham, Mass.: Brandeis University Press, 2012).
26 Jan Assmann, *Moses the Egyptian: The Memory of Egypt in Western Monotheism* (Cambridge: Harvard University Press, 1997).
27 See: Rachel Havrelock, *River Jordan: The Mythology of a Dividing Line* (Chicago: University of Chicago Press, 2011).

given culture's worldview. I will make a similar argument about certain Joshua traditions having resonance with particular groups irrespective of the "whole" Joshua of the biblical editor.[28]

Earlier Surveys of Joshua in Reception History

There are a myriad of works written about Joshua, including some about his function in a given piece of literature. However, there have been few surveys of Joshua's character or image as it develops over time. There are five, in particular, that should be foregrounded before proceeding fruther.

A) Thomas Elßner has written the only book-length study on the reception of Joshua of which I am aware.[29] In this book, which is divided into eleven sections, Elßner traces the reception of Joshua into the late Old Testament/Apocryphal books, New Testament books, Philo and Josephus, Rabbinic literature (including Maimonides) and Christian literature (through the 17th century). Nevertheless, Elßner's focus is not on Joshua's image or on his function as a constellation of memory for various groups, but rather on the ethics of war. Elßner focuses on how traditions that venerate Joshua contend with the problematic reality of his story—the story of a killer who wipes out entire nations in the name of his deity. Although this is an exceedingly important question, it is well beyond the purview of this book. Thus, my engagement with Elßner's work is limited.

B) Ed Noort has published more than one study on Joshua in reception history. In his first article on Joshua and reception, Noort focuses on the development of the image of Joshua as a prophet. More significantly for this study, he presents a key methodological claim about reception history studies.[30] Noort argues (following Gadamer) that uncovering the latent possibilities in the text upon which the various receptions were based is part of studying the history of reception.[31] This methodological insight informs the organization of this

---

28 Israel Knohl makes a similar argument about his Priestly Torah (PT) and Holiness School (HS). Knohl belives that both schools of thought extended their reach well into the Second Temple period, despite HS's aggressive rewriting of PT. See, Israel Knohl, *The Sanctuary of Silence: The Priestly Torah and the Holiness School*, (Minneapolis: Fortress, 1995).

29 Thomas R. Elßner, *Josua und seine Kriege in jüdischer und christlicher Rezeptionsgeschichte*, (Theologie und Frieden 37; Stuttgart: W. Kohlhammer, 2008).

30 See: Ed Noort, "Joshua: The History of Reception and Hermeneutics," in *Past, Present, Future: The Deuteronomistic History and the Prophets* (eds. Johannes C. De Moor and Harry F. Van Rooy; Oudtestamentische Studiën 44; Leiden: Brill, 2000), 199–215.

31 For more on reception history in general, see: Hans-Georg Gadamer, *Truth and Method* (2nd revised ed.; trans. Joel Weinsheimer and Donald G. Marshall; New York: Continuum, 1999);

book as encompassing both an analysis of the biblical text itself as well as a study of reception.[32]

C) In an article on Joshua, Katell Barthelot offers an overview of the reception of Joshua in Second Temple literature, focusing on Joshua's image.[33] The first part of her article focuses on the fact that biblical texts (other than the verse in Kings) do not emphasize the image of Joshua as a predictor of the future, but that in Second Temple literature from Qumran, this image of Joshua emerges strongly.[34] This does not mean, Barthelot points out, that Joshua was a particularly popular figure in Qumran literature. In fact, he is a marginal figure in Qumran literature.

Outside of Qumran, Barthelot notes, Joshua is also rather marginal, except in the *Antiquities* of Josephus, *Liber Antiquitatem Biblicarum L.A.B*, and *Assumptio Mosis*, all of which are retellings of biblical stories that focus on Joshua. In these texts there is no evidence that Joshua's image developed in any specific direction, but rather each text has its own version of Joshua.

D) Alexander Rofé concentrates on the development of Joshua's persona in the biblical text itself.[35] Using a diachronic approach to the biblical text, Rofé peels back layer after layer of supplemental material in an attempt to draw a timeline for the development of biblical texts about Joshua. He isolates a number

---

Robert C. Holub, *Reception Theory: A Critical Introduction* (New Accents; London: Methuen, 1984); Wolfgang Iser, *The Act of Reading: A Theory of Aesthetic Response* (Baltimore: Johns Hopkins University Press, 1978); and Hans Robert Jauss, *Toward an Aesthetic of Reception* (trans. Timothy Bahti; Theory and History of Literature 2; Minneapolis: University of Minnesota Press, 1982).

32 Noort wrote a further study of Joshua and reception which focuses mostly on the position of Joshua in the Samaritan book of Joshua, although it also includes a short survey of Joshua's position in biblical and post-biblical literature. See: Ed Noort, "Der Reißende Wolf – Josua in Überlieferung und Geschichte," in *Congress Volume Leiden 2004*, (VTSup 109; Leiden: Brill, 2006), 153–173. The title of this article is taken from Shaubak's taunt to Joshua, where he calls him "the tearing (or murdering) wolf." Noort also wrote a third historical survey of Joshua, but this essay focuses mostly on the history of scholarship on the book of Joshua, beginning in the medieval period, which is outside the scope of this book. See: Ed Noort, "Josua im Wandel der Zeiten: Zu Stand und Perspektiven der Forschung am Buch Joshua," in *The Book of Joshua* (ed. Ed Noort; BETL 250 – Proceedings of the CBL; Leuven: Leuven University Press, 2010), 21–47.

33 See: Katell Barthelot, "The Image of Joshua in Jewish Sources from the Second Temple Period," *Meghillot* 8–9 (2010): 97–112 [Hebrew]. I thank Atar Livneh for drawing my attention to this article.

34 Barthelot argues that Noort's claim, that Joshua is a "prophet" in Qumran literature, is too broad, as he does not bring God's messages to the people, as prophets generally do, but only predicts the future.

35 Alexander Rofé, "Joshua son of Nun in the History of Biblical Tradition," *Tarbiz* 73.3 (2004): 333–364 [Hebrew]. I thank Michael Segal for drawing my attention to this article.

of stages and attempts to explain the appeal of each image to a given society. Although I do not adopt all of Rofé's conclusions in my chapter on the development of biblical Joshua (ch. 2), Rofé's method serves as one of the core models for this part of my study, and his article is my chief—although not my only—conversation partner throughout the second chapter.

E) Although much of his work is well beyond the scope of this book, Elchanan Reiner's two studies of Joshua are excellent models for how to get behind the details of hero legends and explore larger sociological questions.[36] In his studies of Joshua as a Galilean hero, Reiner explores how certain uniquely Galilean traditions about Joshua in the medieval period, whether geographic or legendary in nature, relate to an ancient Galilean tradition about a messiah figure name Joshua. Reiner then explores how these traditions merge Joshua, Jesus, Joshua the high priest, and Rabbi Joshua ben Peraḥia, creating a constellation of legendary material that forms the basis of a uniquely Galilean messianic tradition. Since most of Reiner's texts and evidence come from the medieval period, I can make only sparse use of his findings. Nevertheless, I will summarize some of his ideas in the final chapter of the book, which explores Rabbinic literature.

What is New about this Study?

As the reader can appreciate from this introduction, following Joshua—or any biblical character—from his biblical roots to his eventual flowering in the literature of various religious traditions is hardly a novel idea. Most of the previous studies of this nature, however, have been either cursory surveys, limited in scope, or (in the case of Elßner) focused on the ethics of war and genocide. This study is the first attempt to survey Joshua's development in detail through a large swath of literature spanning multiple religious traditions and time periods.

By following Noort's suggestion that one should put the reception of a biblical character in conversation with the possible meanings of the biblical text it-

---

36 Elchanan Reiner, "From Joshua to Jesus: The Transformation of a Biblical Story to a Local Myth: A Chapter in the Religious Life of the Galilean Jew," in *Sharing the Sacred: Religious Contacts and Conflicts in the Holy Land: First-Fifteenth Centuries CE* (eds. Arieh Kofsky and Guy G. Stroumsa; Jerusalem: Yad Izhak Ben Zvi, 1998), 233–271; Elchanan Reiner, "From Joshua through Jesus to Simeon bar Yohai: Towards a Typology of Galilean Heroes," in *Jesus Among the Jews: Representation and Thought* (ed. Neta Stahl; Routledge Jewish Studies Series; London: Routledge, 2012), 94–105. I thank Yair Furstenberg, John Mandsager, and Geoffrey Herman for drawing my attention to Reiner's work.

self, I have been able to incorporate a study of biblical literature as a part of this reception history. I believe that doing so will help correct the artificial divide between biblical literature and post-biblical literature, which puts the biblical text in the unfair position of being a sort of *ex nihilo* creation, "the beginning before which there was nothing."

Finally, by examining how four different post-biblical traditions received Joshua, this study aims to sharpen the understanding of the different values held by these religious traditions, to uncover hidden conversations and points of agreement and disagreement between them, and to clarify what is at stake for each in their continued veneration of the ancient Israelite hero, Yehoshua bin Nun.

Note on translations: All translations in this book from Hebrew, Aramaic, Syriac, Greek, Latin, and Arabic are mine unless otherwise noted.

Chapter 1 – Biblical Joshua(s)

> There are too many distinctive features of
> Joshua's characterization to read it as
> exclusively paradigmatic or idealized.
>
> Sarah Lebhar Hall [37]

As the biblical text is the earliest written introduction to the character of Yehoshua bin Nun (Joshua), a detailed survey of his images in the Bible seems the proper place to start. In this chapter, the biblical text(s) will be analyzed to get a sense for how the Bible as a whole—or, more accurately, the Primary History as a whole—presents Joshua to its readers. To do so, literary analysis of the final forms of the text—even in final form criticism textual variants and multiple editions must be taken into account—wil be deployed. As will be seen, Joshua is presented as a complex and multifaceted character in the biblical texts—one that cannot be captured in one image or one sentence.

Exodus and Numbers

Battle with Amalek: Joshua as Warrior

Joshua appears in the Bible without a proper introduction.[38] He is given no patronymic and no tribal affiliation, only a sword and orders to muster the troops and engage the enemy. The orders come directly from Moses and leave the reader wondering what the basis for Joshua's selection had been. Had Joshua demonstrated military prowess or leadership skills in prior, unreported contexts? The text of the Torah offers no answer. Nevertheless, in the course of the story, Joshua does demonstrate that Moses' faith in him was well-placed. The Amalekites are handily defeated, Joshua having "weakened them by the sword."

Despite Joshua's obvious importance in this account, his position contrasts with that of two other characters that appear to outrank him, namely Aaron and Hur.[39] While Joshua must take charge of the "mundane task" of organizing an

---

37 Sarah Lebhar Hall, *Conquering Character: The Characterization of Joshua in Joshua 1 – 11* (The Library of Hebrew Bible/Old Testament Studies 512; New York: T&T Clark International, 2010), 9.
38 Exod 17
39 Although the reader is already familiar with Moses' older brother Aaron, Hur appears in this story just as abruptly as Joshua does. However, unlike Joshua, Hur disappears as mysteriously as

army and doing battle with the enemy, Aaron and Hur are to accompany Moses to the top of a mountain. There Moses will stand with his arms in the air, the staff of God in his hand; Moses' raised arms are the key to an Israelite victory. Aaron and Hur's role begins as ceremonial. As the battle rages on, however, and Moses' arms begin to tire, it falls to his two attendants to prop them up.

The story ends with an important twist. God commands Moses to write on a scroll that God swears to annihilate Amalek in the future. Further, Moses is instructed to read this scroll aloud, but only to Joshua. As this command comes directly from Yhwh, the reader understands that Joshua has more than succeeded in his task as military commander, and that God has chosen him to continue the struggle against the hated Amalekites.[40]

Joshua as Moses' Attendant – Part One

When next we meet Joshua (Exod 24), he has earned the title of Moses' attendant (משרת משה). This time, Joshua will accompany the master up the mountain, while Moses informs the elders that any Israelite with an urgent matter (בעל דברים) should approach Aaron and Hur. The term בעל דברים invokes for the reader the newly created legal hierarchy described in Exodus 18.[41] In that account, Moses stands at the pinnacle of the legal structure, dealing with only the most difficult matters. In his absence, this will be the job of Aaron and Hur.

The choice of Joshua to accompany Moses up the mountain may indicate Moses' intention to groom Joshua for a future leadership position. Nevertheless,

---

he appears; a fact which inspires the Rabbinic suggestion, that Hur was murdered by the mob when he refused to comply with their request to make them a new god (b. *Sanhedrin* 7a).

40 Interestingly, Joshua does not deliver the ultimate crushing blow to the Amalekites, rather Saul, the first king of Israel (according to Samuel) accomplishes this. The relationship between the Saul accounts and the Joshua accounts will be touched upon in the next chapter.

41 See Exod 18:22, for example:

וְהָיָה כָּל הַדָּבָר הַגָּדֹל יָבִיאוּ אֵלֶיךָ וְכָל   And it will be that any difficult <u>matter</u> they will bring to you,

הַדָּבָר הַקָּטֹן יִשְׁפְּטוּ הֵם.   and any small <u>matter</u> they will judge themselves.

Nevertheless, the intertextual resonances between these two stories are weakened by the fact that the main verb for bringing a case forward to a judge differ in the stories (בוא in ch. 18 but נגש here in 24).

at this point in the narrative, Joshua has not yet attained a senior position, as he was not part of the meal with Yhwh recorded earlier in the chapter.[42]

The reader next encounters Joshua on the mountain, although apparently not all the way up top with Moses.[43] Having just been informed of the Israelite apostasy, Moses encounters Joshua on his way down the mountain. Joshua does not yet know what is happening in the camp. Nonetheless, perhaps due to his proximity to it, Joshua hears the noise in the camp and speculates on what was occurring. Joshua's speculation turns out to be incorrect, but, for this very reason, is telling. Joshua assumes that the Israelites have been attacked and the noises he hears are the cries of battle.

Joshua's inclination towards a military interpretation reflects the aspect of his character that first brings him to prominence; he is a general at heart. Moses takes note of this in his response, which has strong intertextual resonances with the account of the battle of Amalek in chapter 17, where Joshua features prominently.

---

42 Neither was Hur, for that matter. To some extent, the tension between the first part of chapter 24 and the second part is a good example of where the synchronic "literary analysis" approach to the Pentateuch breaks down. When one looks at the leadership described in the chapter in its entirety, the choice of invitee seems inexplicable. If the meeting was meant only for older and more seasoned leadership, Nadab and Abihu should not have been there and Hur should have. If it was meant for the up-and-coming leadership as well, Joshua should have been there. In the end, it makes the most sense to posit that the stories from the first and second half of the chapter come from different sources or traditions, one of which had Aaron and his sons as the leaders and one of which had Aaron, Hur and Joshua as leaders. The only satisfying explanation for why Hur was not at that meeting is, that the author of that source never heard of Hur. (This is not surprising if one assumes that Hur is a Judahite hero, added into a Northern account.) Other explanations are possible – perhaps Hur was needed to watch over the people while the rest of the leaders were at the meal – but, in the end, such explanations reflect the logic of a redactor, trying to combine disparate sources, not of an author, who holds a consistent view of the Israelite hierarchy of the period.

43 Again, without taking a source or redaction critical approach this makes little sense. Why would Moses bring his attendant half way up the mountain? Most probably, the discussion between God and Moses—where Moses is informed of what the Israelites were doing and he begs God for mercy—was spliced into an (earlier) account, in which Joshua was the first to inform Moses of the noise in the camp. Nevertheless, for the purposes of a synchronic reading, one is to assume that Moses singled out Joshua to be on the mountain but he was not permitted to meet with God together with Moses.

שמות לב:יז Exod 32:17		שמות יז:יא Exod 17:11	
אֵין קוֹל עֲנוֹת גְּבוּרָה,	This is not the sound of cries of <u>triumph</u>,	וְהָיָה כַּאֲשֶׁר יָרִים מֹשֶׁה יָדוֹ וְגָבַר יִשְׂרָאֵל וְכַאֲשֶׁר יָנִיחַ יָדוֹ וְגָבַר עֲמָלֵק.	And it happened that as Moses raised his arm Israel <u>triumphed</u> but as he lowered his arm Amalek <u>triumphed</u>.
וְאֵין קוֹל עֲנוֹת חֲלוּשָׁה.	And this is not the sound of cries of <u>defeat</u>.	וַיַּחֲלֹשׁ יְהוֹשֻׁעַ אֶת עֲמָלֵק וְאֶת עַמּוֹ לְפִי חָרֶב.	So Joshua <u>defeated</u> Amalek and his people with the sword.

The resonances between the two stories do not appear fortuitous, but seem designed to underscore a significant disparity between the two accounts. When Aaron and Hur accompany Moses to the top of a mountain, leaving Joshua responsible for the people, everything goes smoothly. However, when Joshua accompanies Moses to the top of a mountain and Aaron and Hur are left responsible, the entire camp falls apart.[44] This unstated comparison foreshadows the eventual choice of Joshua as the next leader of Israel.

The final mention of Joshua in Exodus (33:11) contrasts powerfully with his image in chapter 17. In this account, Moses, having slaughtered the golden-calf worshipers, sets up a tent—the Tent of Meeting (*ohel mo'ed*)—outside the camp. The tent would function as a sort of sanctuary for God to manifest God's presence at a safe distance from the apostate Israelites. Moses frequents this tent, where he converses with Yhwh face to face. In many ways, the tent parallels the mountains in the previous stories. Earlier, Moses was required to climb a mountain to meet with God now God will descend to meet with Moses. Moses would spend his time travelling between the Israelite camp and the tent sanctuary, whereas "his young attendant Joshua son of Nun was never absent from the tent" (Exod 33:11). This is the first time the Torah uses Joshua's patronymic and references his youth.[45]

In the context of the story, the contrast between Joshua and the people of Israel in general could not be more pronounced. Yhwh refuses to dwell with the people. They can only watch as Moses exits their camp and enters the tent where God's glory resides. Even so, God grants Joshua permission to dwell in God's tent. The reader cannot help but guess that God will eventually choose Joshua as the only worthy successor to Moses.

---

44 Although Aaron's failure of leadership is dealt with explicitly in the story, Hur is never mentioned again. This leads to the rabbinic speculation (referenced above) that Hur was actually faithful to Yhwh, refusing to fashion a golden calf for the people, and that the people murdered him for this reason. This gives the rabbis a plausible defense of Aaron as well: he was afraid for his life (see *Lev. Rab. Tzav* 10:3).

45 *Na'ar* doesn't necessarily mean "young;" this will be discussed later.

Joshua as Moses' Attendant – Part Two

In the book of Numbers, the biblical description of Joshua picks up where it left off (Joshua does not appear in Leviticus at all), with Joshua as Moses' attendant (11:28). Moses feels overwhelmed as the sole leader of Israel and begs God to give him some prophetic partners with whom he can share the burden of leadership. God agrees to these terms and organizes a group of 70 elders to meet outside the camp and receive a piece of Moses' "prophetic spirit."

Two of the intended recipients of this divine grace, Eldad and Medad, do not make it to the meeting, and begin to prophesy in the camp. A young messenger runs to tell Moses what is occurring in the camp, and the message is overheard by "Joshua son of Nun, attendant of Moses, one of his hand-picked (men)."[46] This description of Joshua contains some internal tension. On one hand, Joshua is Moses' attendant, i.e. the only one, but on the other hand, he is also one of his hand-picked men, i.e. one of many.

Joshua reacts to the news of Eldad's and Medad's public prophesying by blurting out the suggestion: "My master, Moses, restrain them!" Moses shrugs off the impetuous advice, berating Joshua for being overzealous. In fact, Moses states, he would be more than happy if God would share his spirit with all of Israel.

This exchange expresses well the unique position of Joshua. Joshua is one of Moses' picked men and Moses' attendant. Joshua's position in the narrative is conspicuously important. He is one of the few named characters other than Moses. Furthermore, he clearly feels comfortable offering his own opinions to Moses bluntly, albeit respectfully, in "full court." Nevertheless, Joshua does not appear on the list of the 70 men chosen to share the burden of leadership with Moses.

The exchange between Joshua and Moses in this account has much in common with their exchange on Mount Sinai recorded in Exodus 34. Again Joshua jumps to a military evaluation of the situation, understanding the public prophesying of Eldad and Medad as a type of rebellion against Moses' authority requiring a forceful reaction. The Torah demonstrates the close relationship between Joshua and Moses by having Moses respond with gentle censure, recasting the situation in a different light.

---

46 The new JPS translates this as "from his youth."

Joshua as Loyal Scout

In Numbers chapter 12, as preparation for the invasion of Canaan, Yнwн commands Moses to send scouts to traverse the land and deliver a report. The scouts are to be leaders in their respective tribes (נשיאים), although, presumably, younger than the tribal chieftains, considering the nature of the task.[47] The scout chosen for the tribe of Ephraim is Hoshea son of Nun, whom, the reader is informed, Moses renamed Joshua (Num 13:8, 16).

From this short introduction, the reader learns some important information about Joshua. First, and perhaps most surprisingly, his name isn't actually Joshua; that name was given him by Moses. Since the text never informs the reader of when this occurred, one is left wondering whether the renaming occurred before the battle with Amalek, or whether the name used in that story should be understood as a retrojection.[48]

Second, we learn of Joshua's tribal affiliation for the first time. Up until this point, Joshua has been more of a national figure, an understudy to Moses and chief of the army. Picturing Joshua as an Ephraimite and an up-and-coming leader of his own tribe adds a new dimension to his character. Whether there will ever be tension between his tribal and national allegiances is a question the reader is left to ponder as he or she reads further on into the primary history.[49]

Joshua's speaking part comes late in the narrative, only after an initial interchange between the ten "rogue scouts" and the scout from Judah, Caleb ben Jephuneh. In their first report, the majority of the scouts proclaim publicly that the inhabitants of Canaan are simply too powerful to overcome. Caleb responds to his colleagues that the conquest of the land is eminently doable, and that the Israelites should commence with the invasion forthwith. Caleb's enthusiasm only exacerbates the situation, causing the remaining scouts to exaggerate the physical prowess of the natives even further. Panic strikes. A suggestion is floated by an anonymous faction that the Israelites should appoint a new leader and return to Egypt. Moses and Aaron fall on their faces, powerless and dispirited.

---

47 There is no overlap whatsoever in names between the list of chieftains who bring offerings at the dedication of the tabernacle in chapter 7 and the list of spies in chapter 13.
48 From a source-critical perspective, the simplest argument is to posit that the redactor of the book of Numbers is combining two different accounts of the origins of Joshua. In one account, Joshua begins as Moses' attendant and is eventually proclaimed to be his successor. In the other account, Joshua begins his career as one of only two spies who maintain their faithfulness to God. This tension between Joshua accounts will be discussed at length in the next chapter.
49 This question of inter-tribal conflict looms large in the narrative accounts of a number of biblical figures, such as Gideon, Jephtah, and David.

Throughout this narrative, the attentive reader is bothered by the conspicuous absence of Joshua's voice. How can it be that only Caleb has spoken up until now? The reader has been justifiably impressed with Caleb's unexpected lone stance. Caleb is a new character, an unknown quantity. Joshua, in contrast, has a history as a loyal disciple of Moses, as a military chief, as well as a lad, who spends the majority of his time dwelling in the tent of YHWH! Has the tent-dwelling attendant of Moses turned his back on God? Is the military general afraid to speak up against the mob?[50]

The reader can breathe a sigh of relief when Joshua finally adds his voice to that of Caleb's (14:6), speaking out in defense of the land and the plan for conquest. In their speech, Caleb and Joshua emphasize the lushness of Canaan, the power of YHWH, the evil of rebellion and the comparative weakness of the enemy. The speech succeeds only in making the Israelite mob furious enough to pelt them with stones, a crisis which finally brings the presence of YHWH into the camp.

Why does Joshua wait so long to respond, and what made him finally cast his lot in with Caleb? Although Joshua is not especially afraid of Amalekites or Canaanites, he seems to be afraid of Israelites.[51] This will be a theme that comes up again when Joshua is named Moses' successor. Perhaps what forces Joshua to finally respond is the sight of his master, Moses, falling face down on the ground in public, helpless against the wave of rebellion crashing through the Israelite camp.

YHWH's response to the rebellion is swift and brutal. The treacherous spies are condemned to death, and the remaining Israelites are forced to wander the desert until all who witnessed the Exodus from Egypt have perished. God allows for only two exceptions: Joshua and Caleb, the loyal scouts (Num 14:30, 38; 26:65).

---

50 A source critic would answer this question by saying that this story is a classic example of a doublet, with two different spy accounts being combined into one. In the first account, the loyal spy is Caleb, and there is no mention of Joshua. In the second account, both loyal spies, Caleb and Joshua, respond together. A supplementarian would answer by saying that the doublets were added into a preexisting story that did not have Joshua. Although some version of the documentary or supplementary hypothesis is clearly correct in this case, nevertheless, if one takes redaction criticism seriously, one still needs to account for the final form of the story, which places Joshua in a questionable light for some time before he speaks.

51 By way of analogy, in Ariel Sharon's autobiography, he describes his mentor Moshe Dayan as "the most courageous man on any battlefield, the least courageous at taking a stand in public." See Ariel Sharon and David Chanoff, *Warrior: An Autobiography* (New York: Touchstone, 2001), 222 (cf. 230, 329).

Joshua as Successor of Moses

In chapter 27, YHWH informs Moses that the time has come for him to die. Moses replies in alarm that if he is to die now there would be no one left to lead the Israelites. Certainly, YHWH does not intend to abandon the children of Israel to their fate like a flock of sheep without a shepherd!

YHWH is ready for this response. He informs Moses that a successor has already been chosen, Joshua bin Nun. Moses is to stand Joshua before Elazar the priest and the Israelite people and put his hands upon his successor's head. This will transfer some of Moses' spirit to Joshua and will encourage the people to obey him. With this command, Joshua has come full circle.

In chapter 11, a young Joshua witnessed the appointment of 70 elders, all of whom received a part of Moses' spirit. Now, almost 40 years later, Joshua will receive some of Moses' "glory" as well as the mantle of leadership. Unlike the elders, however, Joshua is not in need of Moses' spirit. YHWH has already stated that Joshua bin Nun is a man with "spirit in him" (Num 27:18).

One problematic aspect of this narrative is that YHWH's response appears to pull Joshua's name out of the thin air. Wasn't Joshua being groomed as Moses' successor for well-nigh 40 years by this point? Why does Moses act as if there was no obvious solution to the question of succession? Why doesn't he suggest Joshua himself?

If the omission has any significance, one must imagine that in part, Moses does not feel that Joshua is up to the task. Possibly Joshua's fear of the mob could be understood as a factor, although Moses never explicitly takes note of this in the text.[52] A more compelling interpretation can be adduced from the two previous accounts in which Moses censures Joshua.[53] Perhaps Moses fears that Joshua, with his tendency to paint situations in military colors, is more general than statesman.[54]

Joshua's position appears less lofty than one might have expected, considering the unexpected prominence of another character: Elazar the priest. When comparing the Joshua-Elazar structure to that of Moses and Aaron, we see that the power of Elazar is greater than expected. Despite Aaron's obvious importance, there is never any doubt that he was completely subservient to Moses.

---

52 On the other hand, in Deuteronomy Moses will give Joshua a number of peptalks, so one may speculate wether the reader is to assume, that Moses did, in fact, notice Joshua's confidence issue.

53 In the golden calf and Eldad and Medad episodes

54 I thank one of my early mentors, David Silber, for this observation and for the emphasis on the martial character of Joshua in the Pentateuch as a whole.

Like Elazar, Aaron holds the *Urim ve-Tumim*, the priestly oracle stones, but there is no mention of his ever having used them, and certainly none of Moses having need of their use. Now, for the first time, YHWH explicitly states that the next leader, despite his "spirit", will be in need of constant oracular advice from the high priest.

In an ironic twist on Moses' request for a leader who will "come and go before them", God informs him that the new leader, Joshua, will himself, along with the people "come and go" before the high priest, following his oracular advice. Joshua will not really share Moses' spirit after all.[55]

Joshua as Administrator

As Moses' administration winds down, Joshua and Elazar are placed in charge of overseeing certain projects that Moses will not live to complete.

The first instance of this is the participation of the Transjordanian tribes in the conquest of Cisjordan. Initially shocked at the request of Reuben and Gad to settle Transjordan and forgo their claim to land in Cisjordan, Moses eventually strikes a deal with the tribes. They may build pens for their livestock and cities for their families in Transjordan, if the men of the tribe promise to cross over into Cisjordan and assist with the conquest. They are to remain militarily active until such time as the entire land is conquered and all of the other tribes have received their respective inheritances.

Having made this agreement and received the assurances of the tribes of Reuben and Gad that they would be faithful to this agreement, Moses puts the maintenance of this pact under the jurisdiction of Joshua and Elazar (Num 32:28–30). They are to be the arbiters of this agreement since they are to be the conquerors of the land.

The second instance is the explicit appointment of Joshua and Elazar by YHWH as the chief functionaries in charge of dividing the Cisjordan among the remaining ten tribes. In chapter 34, YHWH describes to Moses the appropriate hierarchy for the division of land. Joshua and Elazar will be the chief executives in charge, with a representative of each tribe (including Ephraim!) underneath, ostensibly to represent their respective tribe's interest.

---

55 From a redaction-critical perspective, the references to Elazar the priest seem later than the core text here, which originally commanded the appointment of Joshua as the undisputed leader of Israel. This will be discussed more fully in the next chapter.

On one hand, this list, more than anything else, emphasizes the national character of Joshua bin Nun. Although he is a member of the tribe of Ephraim, and has represented them in the past (i.e., during the scout story), he is now so distanced from his tribal affiliation that another representative, Kemuel ben Shiftan, must be appointed to represent the tribe's interests. This contrasts well with the position of his former comrade Caleb, who is put forward in YHWH's list as the appropriate representative of the tribe of Judah.[56]

The element that stands out most in the above accounts of Joshua's administration is that he is consistently mentioned together with Elazar the priest in what seems to be a type of co-chieftaincy. As YHWH expresses in chapter 27, Joshua will not be the sole leader of Israel.

Perhaps the most surprising element of Joshua's position in the latter half of the book of Numbers is where he is not mentioned. Although he is side by side with Elazar the priest in his future administrative assignments, he is conspicuously absent during the account of the war with Midian, an account in which Elazar plays a strong role. What happened to Joshua the warrior?[57]

Book of Deuteronomy

Joshua as Moses' Successor

References to Joshua bookend Deuteronomy. In chapter 1, Moses recounts the story of the scouts, albeit with details that are in significant tension with the account in Numbers.[58] In this telling, the people first beseech Moses to send scouts, and then ignore the positive report they receive for fear of the natives. God reacts in fury against the people, condemning the entire exodus generation to die in the wilderness. The only exception is to be Caleb, as a reward for his steadfastness. Everyone else is included in this curse, even Moses.

---

56 This appointment takes on new meaning in this chapter, since in 32:12, Moses, in his anger, blurts out a fact that the reader was not aware of until that point: Caleb is not actually Israelite, but Kenizite. Nevertheless, he has been appointed by YHWH himself to represent the tribe of Judah.

57 As will be seen in chapter 4, the Samaritan book of Joshua fixes this anomaly by placing Joshua in the battle, and in a leadership role.

58 The retelling of the wilderness period's history in Deuteronomy 1–3(4) is a conspicuous feature of this section of the book. Although a source-critical study of this section is beyond the scope of this project, I would merely suggest that it seems to be an older source, not originally attached to Deuteronomy, which was added as a sort of introduction and heavily reworked.

Considering the above, the reader cannot help but be surprised when, in the same breath, YHWH is reported to say that Joshua bin Nun is to lead the people into Canaan. Why has he not been grouped with the rest of the generation together with his master? If it is because he was a loyal scout like Caleb, why is this not mentioned in the verse describing Caleb's reward?

The possibility that most recommends itself is the consideration of Joshua's youth; only a lad, Joshua was too young to be subject to the collective punishment of the previous generation. Instead, YHWH groups him with the generation of the children of the Exodus. Since he is Moses' attendant, he is the perfect person to be chosen as this generation's natural leader.

Despite the above, the tension between this narrative and that of Numbers is palpable. If Joshua was appointed leader immediately after the desert generation is condemned, why would Moses react in panic 40 years later and accuse God of leaving the people of Israel leaderless? So too, it is hard to accept that Joshua's loyalty as a scout would be skipped over in Moses' recounting when Caleb's was not. Although this tension will be explored through source/redaction critically in the next chapter, from the perspective of synchronic analysis, one can suggest that this speech represents the "creative memories" of the elderly Moses, whose perspectives on events of the past are colored by his own experiences.

Moses next references Joshua twice towards the end of this same speech. The problematic nature of the references becomes apparent when one looks at their order and context. At this point in the speech, Moses has just described the conquest of the Transjordanian territories and his conditional land-grant to the Transjordanian tribes.[59] In this context, Moses reports that he "commanded" Joshua not to fear the Amorites of the Cisjordan. Joshua has seen all that God did to the Amorites of the Transjordan, Moses claims, and he should assume that God will do the same again during the next phase of the conquest under his (Joshua's) leadership.

Although one wonders why Moses was under the impression that Joshua was afraid of the upcoming battles,[60] it would seem that Moses has made his

---

59 Again, the discord between this account and that of Numbers cannot be overlooked. According to this speech, it was Moses' idea to give the land to the tribes of Reuben and Gad. Furthermore, one senses that Moses thinks of this as part of the conquest and not just a fortuitous addition to the real conquest. Moses' only concern is that the two and a half tribes assist their brothers in conquering their own land, i.e., he wants the entire conquest to be the result of a joint Israelite coalition and not to have tribes drop out of the war when their respective lands are conquered.

60 Perhaps one can chalk this up to Moses' paternal feelings for his long-time understudy.

peace with God's decision and is now attempting to help his successor along. For this reason, Moses' very next sentence may take the reader by surprise.

Encouraged by his successful conquest of the Transjordan, Moses suddenly beseeches YHWH to allow him to cross over to the Cisjordan. YHWH angrily dismisses Moses' request, commanding him never to bring it up again. Rather, Moses should spend his final hours preparing and encouraging Joshua.[61]

YHWH's response confirms Moses' own concerns about Joshua's fear. Whereas Moses has already "commanded" Joshua not to be afraid, YHWH has now commanded Moses to encourage and strengthen Joshua. Apparently, Joshua's pluck is a live concern. The importance of the theme of "strengthening Joshua" cannot be overemphasized. This motif dominates the description of Joshua's transition into leadership, both at the end of Deuteronomy as well as at the beginning of Joshua.

Although Joshua is not mentioned again until the end of Deuteronomy, the narrative very clearly "picks up where it left off." Joshua is mentioned by name seven times in chapter 31. Moses first mentions him in a brief address to the Israelites. He tells them that he is now 120 years old and can no longer "come and go."[62] Therefore, Joshua will lead them into Israel.[63]

Immediately after the speech, Moses summons Joshua to stand before him and the Israelites. Moses then delivers a short version of this same address, this time directed at Joshua. The speech begins with an injunction to be strong and ends with "do not fear." During the short address, Joshua is told that he will bring the Israelites into the Cisjordan and that God will be with him. The word for bring (תבוא) yet again invokes Moses' original concern about leadership. However, as opposed to YHWH's implication that the real "comer-and-goer" would be Elazar the priest, Moses says it will be Joshua.[64]

At this point, the narrative of "leadership transfer" is interrupted. Moses proceeds to write down the Torah on a scroll. The scroll is given to Levitical priests

---

61 The most YHWH will grant is that Moses can climb a local mountain and allow himself a distant glimpse of the Cisjordan.

62 It sounds as if Moses is implying that the reason he will not lead Israel into Canaan is because he is too old. This would then be a third explanation for Moses' death in the Transjordan.

63 The words "come and go" are highly reminiscent of Moses' panicked response to God in Numbers 27 where he says that the Israelites will require someone to "come and go" before them. From a source critical perspective, one must ask whether this section is a continuation of that story or a later (redactional?) intertextual reference to it.

64 As mentioned earlier, the next chapter will argue that in the unredacted source behind Numbers 27, Elazar the priest is not mentioned, and Joshua is to be the "comer and goer" according to YHWH as well.

who carry the ark, along with a commandment to read the scroll to the entire nation every seven years, as they gather to the holy precinct during the Sukkot festival. The contrast between this account and Exodus 17 is manifest. After the battle with Amalek, Moses wrote God's words on a scroll. That scroll was to be placed "in the ears of Joshua." Here the scroll is to be placed by the side of the ark, in the keeping of the Levitical priests, and read to the entire nation. One cannot help feeling again that, although Joshua has ostensibly won the leadership of Israel, he has lost something in the process as well.

The narrative of leader-transfer picks up again in verse 14, when Yhwh commands Moses to bring Joshua to the Tent of Meeting and await God's presence there. Once God arrives, the transfer-narrative is yet again interrupted with a message to Moses detailing the Israelites' future apostasy and God's abandonment of them. God has written a song about this, which he wants Moses and Joshua to write down and teach to the people as a type of forewarning.

Only after Moses writes down the song does Yhwh continue with the appointment of Joshua. This appointment lasts all of one verse, in which God tells Joshua to be strong since he will bring the people into the Promised Land, and that God will be with him for this process.

Following this short, one-sentence ceremony, the spotlight returns to Moses as he exhorts the Levites to treat the scroll he has just given them as a witness to their future apostasy. He then turns to the Israelites as a whole and proceeds to teach them the song he learned from Yhwh. Only after the song has been recited, does the text mention that Joshua actually sang along with Moses (32:44).[65]

The scroll-account and song-account minimize the position of Joshua; he is barely an afterthought. Although there is no suggestion that the people will apostatize during the tenure of Joshua as leader, nevertheless, both accounts divide the epochs into Moses and post-Moses. In neither account does God say that the people will actually apostatize after the death of Joshua, as opposed to Moses. Again, Moses so completely overshadows Joshua here that the latter's tenure is hardly worth mentioning when discussing the future of Israel.

After the song is complete, Yhwh tells Moses to climb the mountain where he is destined to die. Before he does so, however, the account is once more interrupted, this time with Moses' final blessing to the tribes.[66] After the blessing, Moses climbs Mount Nebo, looks upon the Cisjordan and, in the presence of Yhwh alone, dies.

---

65 Oddly, the MT reads here הוא <u>יהושע</u> בן נון. One is hard-pressed to know whether this was intentional or a scribal error.

66 This is a much nicer song than the one Moses has just sung to them. Perhaps he does not want to leave the Israelites on a sour note.

Before continuing on to end the book with the statement that no prophet ever arose in the history of Israel as great as Moses, the text offers one verse about Joshua's elevation to the mantle of leadership. The verse states that Joshua bin Nun was filled with the spirit of wisdom, *since Moses placed his hands upon him*, and that the people of Israel acknowledged his leadership, *acting as God had commanded Moses for them to do.*

Looking at this account carefully, one cannot help but notice the less than fully flattering position in which it places Joshua. This becomes particularly conspicuous when the verse is compared with the scene of Aaron's death in Numbers 20. In this scene, Aaron is accompanied by Moses as well as his son and successor Elazar to the top of Mount Hor. There, Elazar is dressed in Aaron's garments before his eyes. Only then does Aaron die. This ceremony demonstrates symbolically that Elazar is the worthy successor of his father Aaron.

In the account of Moses' death on Mount Nebo, however, Moses is alone with YHWH. This is especially striking considering the fact that Joshua accompanies Moses onto Mount Sinai as well as into the Tent of Meeting in Exodus. One would have expected him to be with Moses at the moment of his passing, but this was not to be.

The end of Deuteronomy underlines the point that although Joshua will be the next leader of Israel, he cannot really replace Moses. In the eyes of the Torah, this is not an accident of history or a condemnation of Joshua, but rather an important axiom of Israelite theological history. Joshua does not replace Moses because Moses is irreplaceable; he is the best there ever was and the best there ever will be, which is why his book and his laws are the final and authoritative word in all matters.[67] It is no wonder that Joshua is nervous.

Book of Joshua

Introduction (Ch. 1)

The book of Joshua opens with the image of Joshua as the successor to Moses.[68] It begins with the implicit comparison of the two characters by describing their

---

[67] In an article on the formation of the Pentatuch, Marc Brettler and Thomas Römer argue that this point was central in changing the organizing principle from an Israel/conquest-focused Hexateuch to a revelation/Torah-focused Pentateuch. See: Thomas Römer and Marc Zvi Brettler, "Deuteronomy 34 and the Case for a Persian Hexateuch," *JBL* 119 (2000), 401–419.

[68] A detailed analysis of the image or character of Joshua in chapters 1–11 of the book of Joshua was undertaken recently in two different works. See: Elie Assis, *From Moses to Joshua and from*

previous titles. Moses was the "servant of YHWH" whereas Joshua was the "attendant of Moses." As if this message were not clear enough, the first address of YHWH to Joshua begins by reminding Joshua of why he is now the leader: "Moses, my servant, is dead."[69]

YHWH tells Joshua to cross the river along with the people and enter the land, which YHWH will give them. They will be given every spot upon which their feet trod, as YHWH promised Moses. This is followed by an expansive description of the land's borders. No one will even stand up to Joshua throughout his life, as YHWH promises to be with him as he was with Moses, and never to abandon him.

This first description of Joshua's task paints an ideal picture. The conquest, if one could call it that, seems purely pro forma. Joshua only has to walk upon the land and it will be his. The natives have all but vanished! Perhaps the most tiring ordeal Joshua faces is the vast amount of land he and his followers will have to walk, as they are to inherit not only the Cisjordan, but all of the (former) Hittite lands to the north, even up to the Euphrates itself.

Why such a rosy hue? Reading between the lines, one thought presents itself: God need not promise never to abandon Joshua if Joshua were not afraid of being abandoned. The latter part of the address strengthens this point. The structure of this latter half of the speech (except for verses 7–8) closely parallels

---

the Miraculous to the Ordinary: A Literary Analysis of the Conquest Narrative in the Book of Joshua (Jerusalem: Magnes Press, 2005 [Hebrew]); and Hall, *Conquering Character.* Both works limit their literary analyses to the first part of Joshua. This is a common approach, due to the very different style of most of the second half of the book (13–21). A recent article on Joshua by André Wénin does this as well, albeit including ch. 12 in the mix. See: André Wénin, "Josué 1–12 Comme Récit," in *The Book of Joshua* (ed. Ed Noort; BETL 250 – Proceedings of the CBL; Leuven: Leuven University Press, 2010), 109–135.

My approach in this chapter is similar to that of Hall's, as she does a section by section reading and catalogues the various images she finds. It would be overly zealous, and not a little tedious, to compare all the myriad of images she catalogues with the ones I catalogue in this section, since there is tremendous overlap. For this reason, I will limit my references to Hall's work to places where she makes a significant or novel point or places where we disagree.

69 In an article on Joshua, much of which dovetails with his book, Elie Assis writes:

> The presentation of Joshua as a second Moses serves to bridge between the ideological reservation against appointing a leader after Moses and the practical need for one.

Elie Assis, "Divine Versus Human Leadership: Joshua's Succession," in *Saints and Role Models in Judaism and Christianity* (eds. Marcel Poorthuis and Joshua Berman; Jewish and Christian Perspectives Series 7; Leiden: Brill, 2004), 25–47 [37]. Although I think Assis exaggerates how much Joshua appears as a second Moses (as will be discussed in a later footnote), I agree that there is a certain reluctance in the biblical text to speak about a successor to Moses (How can someone succeed Moses?)

the three speeches regarding Joshua and the conquest of Cisjordan in Deuteronomy 31:

יהושע פרק א:ה-ו,ט Josh 1:5 – 6, 9	דברים לא:ז-ח Deut 31:7 – 8	דברים פרק לא:ו Deut 31:6	דברים לא: כג Deut 31:23
ה) לֹא יִתְיַצֵּב אִישׁ לְפָנֶיךָ כֹּל יְמֵי חַיֶּיךָ כַּאֲשֶׁר הָיִיתִי עִם מֹשֶׁה אֶהְיֶה עִמָּךְ 5 No man will stand before you all the days of your life; as I was with Moses I will be with you לֹא אַרְפְּךָ וְלֹא אֶעֶזְבֶךָּ.70 I will not forsake you and I will not abandon you.			
ו) חֲזַק וֶאֱמָץ, 6 Be strong and brave,	ז) חֲזַק וֶאֱמָץ 7 Be strong and brave,	חִזְקוּ וְאִמְצוּ 6 Be strong and brave,	כג) חֲזַק וֶאֱמָץ 6 Be strong and brave,
כִּי אַתָּה תַּנְחִיל אֶת הָעָם הַזֶּה אֶת הָאָרֶץ אֲשֶׁר נִשְׁבַּעְתִּי לַאֲבוֹתָם לָתֵת לָהֶם... For you will settle this nation on the land which I swore to their ancestors to give to them...	כִּי אַתָּה תָּבוֹא אֶת הָעָם הַזֶּה אֶל הָאָרֶץ אֲשֶׁר נִשְׁבַּע יְהוָה לַאֲבֹתָם לָתֵת לָהֶם וְאַתָּה תַּנְחִילֶנָּה אוֹתָם. For you will bring this nation into the land which YHWH swore to their ancestors to give to them and you will cause it to be settled by them.		כִּי אַתָּה תָּבִיא אֶת בְּנֵי יִשְׂרָאֵל אֶל הָאָרֶץ אֲשֶׁר נִשְׁבַּעְתִּי לָהֶם. For you will bring the children of Israel into the land which I swore to [give to] them.
ט) 71 הֲלוֹא צִוִּיתִיךָ חֲזַק וֶאֱמָץ? 9 Have I not commanded you to be strong and brave?			
אַל תַּעֲרֹץ וְאַל תֵּחָת Do not be frightened or dismayed	ח) לֹא תִירָא וְלֹא תֵחָת 8 Do not be scared or dismayed	אַל תִּירְאוּ וְאַל תַּעַרְצוּ מִפְּנֵיהֶם Do not be scared or frightened before them	

---

70 Although it is in a different spot, this phrase parallels the endings of Moses' two speeches in Deuteronomy.

71 This superfluous phrase is a resumptive-repetition of the beginning of the speech, due to the interruption of the Torah study theme.

וְאָנֹכִי אֶהְיֶה עִמָּךְ.	כִּי יְהוָה אֱלֹהֶיךָ הוּא הַהֹלֵךְ עִמָּךְ	וַיהוָה הוּא הַהֹלֵךְ לְפָנֶיךָ הוּא יִהְיֶה עִמָּךְ	כִּי עִמְּךָ יְהוָה אֱלֹהֶיךָ בְּכֹל אֲשֶׁר תֵּלֵךְ.
And I will be with you.	For YHWH your God—it is he who walks with you.	And YHWH walks before you and he will be with you.	For YHWH your God is with you in every path you walk.
	לֹא יַרְפְּךָ וְלֹא יַעַזְבֶךָּ.	לֹא יַרְפְּךָ וְלֹא יַעַזְבֶךָּ.	
	He will not forsake you and he will not abandon you.	He will not forsake you and he will not abandon you.	

Despite the variations, the basic structure of the speech can be outlined as a five-part address:

1. Be brave
2. You (Joshua) will bring the people into the Promise Land
3. Do not fear
4. YHWH will be with you
5. YHWH will not abandon you

Joshua's apparent anxiety stands out in this address. Bravery and lack of fear punctuate the two central points of the speech.[72]

Joshua's response to this speech is to make two commands. First, he tells the leaders of the people to have the people ready in three days to cross the river and inherit the land. Again, the term inheritance echoes YHWH's sanguine presentation of the upcoming conquest. Second, Joshua speaks privately with the Transjordanian tribes, reminding them of the deal they made with Moses. Here, although the same benign term "inherit" is used, Joshua's speech hints at the realities of this inheritance, by reminding the Transjordanian tribes that they will be crossing "armed."[73]

The response of the Transjordanian tribes reinforces the earlier impression of the reader that Joshua feels insecure.[74] They promise to do anything that Joshua says and go wherever he commands. Nevertheless, in their response, they subtly place seeds of doubt. For example, they promise to listen to him as they listened to Moses "as long as" or "since" YHWH will be with Joshua the

---

72 A. Joshua is the leader and, B. YHWH will be with him.

73 Hebrew: חמושים. This unusual term is the same used in Exodus 13:18, in reference to the Israelites fleeing Egypt, and there is much scholarly debate about what the precise translation should be.

74 From a redaction-critical perspective, Joshua's speech to the Transjordanian tribes appears to be a supplement; the response was originally that of the tribal administrators.

way he was with Moses. Is this meant to be a condition? Furthermore, they promise to put anyone who disobeys Joshua to death. But YHWH had already promised Joshua that no one would stand up to Joshua throughout his life. Does this mean someone will stand up to him?

The speech ends with a familiar phrase: "just be strong and have courage." Coming from the people it strikes a strange cord. YHWH knows Joshua is nervous, and Moses suspects it as well. Now, it seems, even the people are feeling Joshua's strain. Instead of feeling encouraged, the reader is left wondering whether Joshua will succeed after all.

Two additional but interrelated points should be made in the context of this chapter. First, considering the amount of rebellions that occur during Moses' tenure as leader of Israel, one wonders how seriously this ideal picture of the wilderness period is meant. Does Joshua not remember the scout incident or the golden calf incident? Second, there appears to be a subtle shift in emphasis regarding what Joshua should "not be afraid of." Whereas during YHWH's speech one would imagine that Joshua was being reassured that the war would go smoothly, by the end of the chapter one feels that the reassurance is really about his own position among the Israelites. From the response of the Transjordanian tribes, one can reinterpret YHWH's original message. Perhaps Joshua wasn't being told that no Canaanite will stand up to his might but rather that no Israelite will challenge his authority.

Joshua as Torah Scholar (Ch. 1)

Chapter 1 also introduces a relatively new image of Joshua: Joshua the Torah scholar. During the latter half of his speech to Joshua, YHWH tells him to keep the Torah that Moses commanded him and not to veer from it at all. Only then will Joshua be wise in all that he does. Furthermore, this "book of the Torah" should never leave his lips. He should study it day and night, which will allow him to keep the commandments, leading to his success and wisdom.[75]

The picture of Joshua studying all day and night has some resonance with the young neophyte Joshua, who spent all his days in the Tent of Meeting. However, the "wisdom" feel of the exhortation seems entirely new. Suddenly, in the midst of a speech about the need to cross over the Jordan and inherit the land of

───────

75 From a redaction-critical perspective, these two verses appear to have been added to the speech at a later date. The *Wiederaufnahme* at the beginning of verse 9 strengthens this possibility.

the Amorites, YHWH exhorts Joshua to spend all of his time reading and speaking words of Torah, perfecting his mitzvah performance and increasing his wisdom.[76]

Joshua's character makes a dramatic shift in this image. When first we meet Joshua, he is given a scroll, which describes the future battle that must be fought with Amalek. Now he is given a scroll, which demands constant meditation and wisdom; all this while Joshua's essential job description remains the same. After all, Joshua has just been given the go-ahead to cross the river and take the Cisjordan. Despite YHWH's circumlocutions in this chapter, the reader is well aware that Joshua will have to annihilate the inhabitants.

Additionally, the fact that YHWH prefaces this exhortation with the usual "be strong and brave" is striking. Is Joshua nervous that he is not learned or wise enough, or that his performance of YHWH's commands is imperfect, such that YHWH must reassure him that he can, indeed, successfully comply with this directive?

Finally, it must be admitted that this image of Joshua is used sparsely. Joshua the wise Torah scholar is introduced here and returns in his final speech to the people before his death. The book uses this image of Joshua as a framing of his overall stature as God's chosen leader, but not as a consistent factor to explain or motivate his actions.[77]

The Scouts (Ch. 2)

The crossing of the Jordan represents Joshua's first action as an independent leader. As such, the many resonances between this river crossing and that of Moses at the Sea of Reeds are significant.

---

76 Despite the relative abruptness of this command, seeds for it can be seen in chapter 31 of Deuteronomy. As noted earlier, the transfer of power from Moses to Joshua was interrupted with the writing of the Torah and the handing of it over to the priests. Perhaps YHWH is rectifying this somewhat here, by allowing Joshua access to the Torah scroll as well. If so, one wonders if one is supposed to picture Joshua going to the high priest and borrowing "this Torah scroll" or whether he had access to a copy already. The last the reader heard about said scroll it was leaning upon the side of the Ark of the Covenant.

77 From a redaction critical perspective, this is best explained by the phenomenon of reframing supplements being added to the beginning and end of narratives but not to the middle. This phenomenon is related to that which Sara Milstein has dubbed "revision through introduction," which is the subject of her dissertation and her forthcoming book, *Tracking the Master Scribe: Revision through Introduction in Biblical and Mesopotamian Literature.*

Before crossing the river, Joshua, like Moses before him, sends scouts. The mention of scouts should give the reader pause, as he or she recalls what occurred when Moses sent scouts and that Joshua himself was one of those scouts.[78] Nevertheless, a number of differences stand out between the two stories.

a. Moses appoints twelve scouts whereas Joshua appoints only two.
b. Moses' scouts are important and named individuals, Joshua's seem to be unknowns.
c. Moses' scouts represent their respective tribes whereas Joshua's represent nobody.
d. Moses' scouting mission is public and the report is delivered in public; Joshua's mission seems to be private, and the report is delivered directly to him.

Overall, Joshua's plan is more cautious. The number of scouts is manageable; they have little power, and they are to report directly to Joshua. In this case, it seems that Joshua's martial personality is an improvement upon Moses' more egalitarian spirit. Joshua's scouting mission ends well, with the scouts returning with confidence in their upcoming victory.[79]

The Crossing of the Jordan (Chs. 3 – 5:1)

The crossing of the river represents another success. The presentation of Joshua's image in this story cuts in two directions. On one hand, there are many intertextual hints at Joshua's being another Moses, as well as a number of explicit statements to this effect. On the other hand, certain aspects of the story seem to push the priests and the ark into the forefront, making Joshua look almost secondary. This latter point is reminiscent of Joshua's relationship with Elazar the priest.[80]

---

78 Perhaps Joshua's previous experience causes him to plan the mission differently than Moses.
79 Yair Zakovitch understands this story as a spoof or parody, emphasizing the fact that the scouts bring back no real intelligence, the natives notice them the very day they enter the city, and they spend their entire trip in a brothel. There may be some element of the comic here, but I think that Zakovitch exaggerates this. The overall story seems positive not negative in valence. See: Yair Zakovitch, "Humor and Theology or the Successful Failure of Israelite Intelligence: A Literary-Folklore Approach to Joshua 2," in *Text and Tradition: The Hebrew Bible and Folklore* (ed. Susan Niditch; Atlanta: Scholars Press, 1990), 75 – 98. See also the critique of this position: Frank Moore Cross, "A Response to Zakovitch's 'Successful Failure of Israelite Intelligence,'" in *Text and Tradition: The Hebrew Bible and Folklore* (ed. Susan Niditch; Atlanta: Scholars Press, 1990), 99 – 104.
80 This is just one of many examples of narrative tension in this text. In general, my preferred solution is to assume multiple layers or sources. For an attempt to solve the tension by assuming

Joshua awakens early in the morning, a sign of enthusiasm, and brings the people to the banks of the river. The people are then told by the officials to follow the ark into Canaan. Although neither Joshua nor the people have yet been informed how they are to cross the Jordan, Joshua seems to have an inkling. He announces that the people should purify themselves since on the following day YHWH will perform a wonder. This announcement has intertextual resonances with the story of YHWH's revelation at Mt. Sinai as well as with the story of the quail in the wilderness:

במדבר יא:טז-יח	שמות יט:י-יא	יהושע ג:ה
וַיֹּאמֶר יְהוָה אֶל מֹשֶׁה: "אֶסְפָה לִי שִׁבְעִים אִישׁ מִזִּקְנֵי יִשְׂרָאֵל... וְיָרַדְתִּי וְדִבַּרְתִּי עִמְּךָ שָׁם... וְאֶל הָעָם תֹּאמַר <u>הִתְקַדְּשׁוּ לְמָחָר</u> וַאֲכַלְתֶּם בָּשָׂר..."	וַיֹּאמֶר יְהוָה אֶל מֹשֶׁה: "לֵךְ אֶל הָעָם <u>וְקִדַּשְׁתָּם</u> הַיּוֹם <u>וּמָחָר</u> וְכִבְּסוּ שִׂמְלֹתָם. וְהָיוּ נְכֹנִים לַיּוֹם הַשְּׁלִישִׁי כִּי בַּיּוֹם הַשְּׁלִישִׁי יֵרֵד יְהוָה לְעֵינֵי כָל הָעָם עַל הַר סִינַי."	וַיֹּאמֶר יְהוֹשֻׁעַ אֶל הָעָם: "<u>הִתְקַדָּשׁוּ</u> כִּי <u>מָחָר</u> יַעֲשֶׂה יְהוָה בְּקִרְבְּכֶם נִפְלָאוֹת."
Num 11:16–18	Exod 19:10–11	Josh 3:5
YHWH said to Moses: "Gather for me 70 men from the elders of Israel... and *I will descend* and speak with you there... and to the people say: '<u>Sanctify</u> <u>[yourselves] for the morrow</u> and you will eat meat...'"	YHWH said to Moses: "Go to the people and <u>sanctify them</u> today, and <u>tomorrow</u> they shall wash their clothing. They should be ready by the third day, for on the third day YHWH *will descend* before the eyes of the entire nation upon Mount Sinai."	Joshua said to the people: "<u>Sanctify [yourselves]</u>, for <u>tomorrow</u> YHWH will do wonders in your midst."

Since there seems to be no reason to connect the crossing of the river with the account of the quail, the mostly likely explanation of this resonance is that both stories use the Sinai revelation account as a paradigm. As Joshua will not preside over a revelatory experience on his own, painting one of his big miracles in Sinaitic colors strengthens his image as a new Moses and a central figure in Israelite tradition.

YHWH's first speech to Joshua in this section further paints him in Mosaic colors. The connection to Moses is both explicit as well as intertextual:

---

one literary layer, see: Elie Assis, "A Literary Approach to Complex Narratives: An Examination of Joshua 3–4," in *The Book of Joshua* (ed. Ed Noort; BETL 250 – Proceedings of the CBL; Leuven: Leuven University Press, 2010), 401–413.

יהושע פרק ג:ז	Josh 3:7	דברים ב:יז, כה	Deut 2:17, 25
וַיֹּאמֶר יְהוָה אֶל יְהוֹשֻׁעַ:	YHWH said to Joshua:	וַיְדַבֵּר יְהוָה אֵלַי לֵאמֹר: "..."	YHWH said to me: "...
"הַיּוֹם הַזֶּה אָחֵל גַּדֶּלְךָ בְּעֵינֵי	"This day I will begin	הַיּוֹם הַזֶּה אָחֵל תֵּת פַּחְדְּךָ	this day I will begin
כָּל יִשְׂרָאֵל אֲשֶׁר יֵדְעוּן כִּי	to make you great in	וְיִרְאָתְךָ עַל פְּנֵי הָעַמִּים תַּחַת	to place fear and
כַּאֲשֶׁר הָיִיתִי עִם מֹשֶׁה	the eyes of all Israel,	כָּל הַשָּׁמָיִם אֲשֶׁר יִשְׁמְעוּן	dread of you upon
אֶהְיֶה עִמָּךְ."	who will know that just as I was with Moses I will be with you."	שִׁמְעֲךָ וְרָגְזוּ וְחָלוּ מִפָּנֶיךָ."	the nations under the heavens, who will hear accounts of you and tremble and shake before you."

The repetition of this point later in this section has a Mosaic resonance as well:

יהושע ד:יד	Josh 4:14	שמות פרק יא:ג	Exod 11:3
בַּיּוֹם הַהוּא גִּדַּל יְהוָה	On that day, YHWH made	וַיִּתֵּן יְהוָה אֶת חֵן הָעָם בְּעֵינֵי	YHWH placed the charm
אֶת יְהוֹשֻׁעַ בְּעֵינֵי כָּל	Joshua great in the eyes	מִצְרָיִם גַּם הָאִישׁ מֹשֶׁה	of the people in the eyes
יִשְׂרָאֵל וַיִּרְאוּ אֹתוֹ	of all Israel, and they	גָּדוֹל מְאֹד בְּאֶרֶץ מִצְרַיִם	of Egypt; Moses himself
כַּאֲשֶׁר יָרְאוּ אֶת מֹשֶׁה	were in awe of him, just	בְּעֵינֵי עַבְדֵי פַרְעֹה וּבְעֵינֵי	became very great in the
כָּל יְמֵי חַיָּיו.	as they were in awe of Moses all the days of his life.	הָעָם.	Land of Egypt in the eyes of Pharaoh's servants and in the eyes of the people.

In the first quote, YHWH explicitly tells Joshua that he will be with him as he was with Moses. The second quote affirms that the people fear Joshua the way they feared Moses. Moreover, in each verse, there is a further intertextual resonance with a passage about Moses.

Joshua 3:7 resonates with Deuteronomy 2:25, in which YHWH tells Moses that "on this day I will begin" to make the nations fear you. This was YHWH's introduction to Moses' conquest of the Transjordan. YHWH now delivers a similar message to Joshua at the opening of his conquest of the Cisjordan. The difference between these two verses is telling. Whereas YHWH assures Moses that the nations will fear him, YHWH tells Joshua that the Israelites (not the nations) will respect him. Joshua's aforementioned insecurity as leader again finds expression in this subtle shift.

The same trend can be seen when comparing Joshua 4:14 with Exodus 11:3. In Exodus 11, Moses becomes great in the eyes of the Egyptians, but in Joshua 4, Joshua becomes great in the eyes of Israel. Again, Joshua needs to be propped up as a leader of Israel whereas Moses is granted status vis-à-vis the other nations, in this case Egypt.

The most obvious connection to Moses, however, is the nature of the miracle itself. Both leaders miraculously split a body of water and cross it. The two accounts share imagery, with the two miraculously disconnected pieces of the river or sea being pictured as standing like walls on either side of the crossing Israelites. There is also some shared vocabulary, particularly the terms חרבה (Josh 3:17 and Exod 14:21) and the more unusual term נד (Josh 3:13,16 and Exod 15:8).

Thematically, the two "crossing" accounts are inverses of each other, directionally. Moses splits the Sea of Reeds in order to facilitate the *escape* of the Israelites *from* the rapidly approaching Egyptian army. Joshua, on the other hand, splits the Jordan River in order to allow the invading army of Israelites to *enter into* Canaan and eliminate the inhabitants. Moses escapes a battle and Joshua begins one. Moses runs to the wilderness and Joshua leaves it. Moses' miracle is done in panic whereas Joshua's occurs in perfect calm.

To some extent, these differences emphasize the connection between the two leaders. Moses and Joshua complement each other as do their missions. In between these two seminal moments is the period of the wilderness wandering, the period in which the people were formed and Moses and Joshua worked together.

One final parallel between the two leaders with regard to crossing appears in the description of the reaction of the nations. In the Joshua account (Josh 5:1), when the Amorite kings and the Canaanite kings on the coast hear about the drying of the Jordan, their hearts melt and they lose their spirit. In the Song of the Sea (Exod 15:14–16), the Philistines, Canaanites, Edomites, and Moabites all panic, tremble, and melt away.

Another set of differences between the two water-splitting accounts points in an alternative direction. Whereas Moses is the only named actor (other than the Israelites) in the splitting of the Sea of Reeds narrative, and his staff is the only prop, Joshua must share the stage with the priests, twelve representatives of the tribes of Israel, and the Ark of the Covenant.

Naturally, Joshua plays an important role in the story. He is the leader of Israel and the prophet with whom YHWH communicates his will. The people duly notice this and follow his orders. Nevertheless, the mode of the miracle gives one pause. Moses' staff is holy because it is Moses' staff. The Ark of the Covenant, on the other hand, is holy in its own right. Furthermore, the priests are not a random group selected *ad hoc* by Joshua to carry the Ark. On the contrary, the priests are an important group with their own independent claims to holiness and importance in Israelite society.

In this sense, the crossing of the Jordan River can be seen as a team effort, with Joshua and the priests each bringing to the process their own unique power and position. This is reminiscent of the position Joshua holds both in the end of

Numbers as well as in the latter half of the book of Joshua; i.e., as Elazar the priest's partner. (Why isn't Elazar mentioned in this account?).[81]

The Ritual of the Stones

As part of the crossing of the river, YHWH tells Joshua to appoint twelve representatives to gather twelve stones and bring them to the Israelite encampment. Joshua does so with an added explanation: he twice tells the people that the stones will be to encourage the next generation to inquire as to their significance, so that they (the parents) can describe the miracle of the crossing of the Jordan.

His two descriptions of what the parents should answer their children differ, however. In his first explanation, he tells the men who gather the stones that they should respond that the river was split before the ark and the stones are meant to be a memorial for this. In his second explanation, Joshua tells the people as a whole that they should respond that the river was dried before them in the same way that the Sea of Reeds had been, and that this was in order to strike fear in the heart of the local population and in order to make the Israelites fear YHWH all their lives.

It is difficult to account for the function of the double explanation given by the text.[82] Nevertheless, some observations about the nature of each are possible. As has been pointed out, the prominence of the Ark of the Covenant in the account of the crossing of the Jordan seems to have a limiting effect on the position of Joshua. In his speech to the twelve representatives, Joshua acknowledges this implicitly by referencing the Ark.

In his speech to the people, however, Joshua conveniently overlooks the Ark, describing the miraculous drying of the riverbed as having been for the people. Rhetorically speaking, this version is both complimentary towards the people as a whole and allows Joshua to take the position of prominence as the leader of the people and orchestrator of the crossing. This subtle shift may be a further indication of Joshua's insecurity before his followers.

Finally, one must again acknowledge the spoken as well as unspoken parallels to Moses. In his second speech, Joshua explicitly compares the two crossings, using the same verb (יבש). Additionally, the very act of creating a memorial

---

81 As will be argued in the next chapter, the similarity between certain sections of Joshua and the end of Numbers is not accidental but represents the position of the priestly authors of the Hexateuch (P).

82 A redaction-critical approach would seem the most intuitive here, focusing on an updating or revamping of an earlier passage that was considered insufficient to a later editor.

as an opportunity for the next generation to inquire about it and as an opening for telling the history of the people, is something Moses does a number of times. There are strong intertextual resonances between Moses' memory rituals and Joshua's.

Joshua 4:6 (or 21)

כִּי יִשְׁאָלוּן בְּנֵיכֶם מָחָר לֵאמֹר...

When your sons ask you tomorrow saying...

Exodus 13:14 (or Deut 6:20)

וְהָיָה כִּי יִשְׁאָלְךָ בִנְךָ מָחָר לֵאמֹר...

When your son asks you tomorrow saying...

Joshua 4:6

מָה הָאֲבָנִים הָאֵלֶּה לָכֶם?

What are these stones to you?

Exodus 12:26

מָה הָעֲבֹדָה הַזֹּאת לָכֶם?

What is this service to you?

Considering the striking similarity between the phrases in Joshua and those in Exodus, it seems likely that Joshua's speech is meant to mimic the language of the Pentateuchal speeches.

Circumcision (Ch. 5)

The first commandment Joshua receives upon crossing into Canaan is the command to circumcise the Israelites. There is no explicit reference to the circumcision of the Israelites in Egypt anywhere in Exodus although Exodus does reference the commandment in chapter 12, describing it as a prerequisite for participation in the Passover ceremony. Nevertheless, Joshua ch. 5 takes for granted that the Israelites in Egypt were circumcised. This creates another parallel between Joshua and Moses. Each presides over a new beginning of the Israelite people, with part of this inauguration being the circumcision of the males.

An especially graphic element of this account is the naming of the implement. The Israelites are to be circumcised by "swords of flint." Although the text probably has something much smaller than a conventional sword in mind, it seems fitting that the sword be Joshua's implement for following YHWH's command here, since the sword will be the main implement through which he carries out the main task entrusted to him by YHWH: the conquest of the Cisjordan. This small detail stands out especially in the LXX, where it is recorded that Joshua is actually buried with the flint swords.

The Paschal Offering (Ch. 5)

Having entered Canaan some time towards the beginning of the first month, the Israelites offer the paschal sacrifice. In a precise parallel to the theoretical structure laid out in Exodus, this occurs immediately after the aforementioned passage regarding circumcision.

This parallels Moses in two ways. First, Moses was the leader who presided over the original paschal offering. Second, Moses is said to have presided over the first commemoration of the paschal sacrifice as well, in a verse with a strong intertextual resonance to the one here in Joshua.

יהושע פרק ה:י Josh 5:10		במדבר ט:ה Num 9:5	
וַיַּחֲנוּ בְנֵי יִשְׂרָאֵל בַּגִּלְגָּל וַיַּעֲשׂוּ אֶת הַפֶּסַח בְּאַרְבָּעָה עָשָׂר יוֹם לַחֹדֶשׁ בָּעֶרֶב בְּעַרְבוֹת יְרִיחוֹ:	And the Children of Israel encamped at Gilgal, <u>and they performed the paschal sacrifice on the fourteenth day of the month</u>, *in the evening, on the plains of Jericho.*	וַיַּעֲשׂוּ אֶת הַפֶּסַח בָּרִאשׁוֹן בְּאַרְבָּעָה עָשָׂר יוֹם לַחֹדֶשׁ בֵּין הָעַרְבַּיִם בְּמִדְבַּר סִינָי...	<u>And they performed the paschal sacrifice during the first month on the fourteenth day of the month,</u> *in the afternoon in the Sinai wilderness...*

Joshua here continues Moses' legacy.

The Day after the Paschal Offering and the Cessation of the Manna (Ch. 5)

The book of Joshua records that on the day after the paschal offering, the Israelites ate from the produce of the land. This imagery appears significant in a number of ways. First, the imagery of the Israelites automatically dominating any place "upon which their feet tread" finds expression in this ability to enjoy a harvest that they did not plant. It is the first act in Joshua which reflects the Deuteronomic ideal expressed in Deuteronomy 6:10 – 11, that the Israelites will inherit a land already fully built and cultivated.[83] Second, the fact that the Israelites first partake of the land's produce "after the paschal sacrifice" is not coincidental. It hearkens back to the rule described in Leviticus 23. The rule appears immediately after the description of the Paschal offering and the Festival of Matzot:

---

83 This ideal is expressed again in the summary of this period found in Neh 9:25.

יהושע ה:יא Josh 5:11

וַיֹּאכְלוּ מֵעֲבוּר הָאָרֶץ <u>And they ate</u> from the
<u>מִמָּחֳרַת הַפֶּסַח מַצּוֹת וְקָלוּי</u> growth of the land—
בְּעֶצֶם הַיּוֹם הַזֶּה. <u>on the day after the paschal sacrifice</u>—un-leavened bread and parched grain, <u>on this very day.</u>

ויקרא כג:י-יד Lev 23:10–14

...כִּי תָבֹאוּ אֶל הָאָרֶץ אֲשֶׁר ...When you arrive in
אֲנִי נֹתֵן לָכֶם וּקְצַרְתֶּם אֶת the land which I am
קְצִירָהּ וַהֲבֵאתֶם אֶת עֹמֶר giving you, and you
רֵאשִׁית קְצִירְכֶם אֶל הַכֹּהֵן. cut the harvest, you
וְהֵנִיף אֶת הָעֹמֶר לִפְנֵי יְהוָה shall bring the first
לִרְצֹנְכֶם <u>מִמָּחֳרַת הַשַּׁבָּת</u> sheaf of your harvest
יְנִיפֶנּוּ הַכֹּהֵן...<u>וְלֶחֶם וְקָלִי</u> to the priest. He shall
<u>וְכַרְמֶל</u> לֹא <u>תֹאכְלוּ עַד עֶצֶם</u> wave the sheaf before
הַיּוֹם הַזֶּה עַד הֲבִיאֲכֶם אֶת YHWH in accordance
קָרְבַּן אֱלֹהֵיכֶם חֻקַּת עוֹלָם with your will, <u>on the</u>
לְדֹרֹתֵיכֶם בְּכֹל מֹשְׁבֹתֵיכֶם. <u>day after the Sabbath</u>
the priest shall wave
it... <u>Bread, parched</u>
<u>grains and fresh</u>
<u>grains you shall not</u>
<u>eat until this very</u>
<u>day,</u> until you bring
the offering of your
God – this is a perma-
nent rule for every
generation wherever
you may dwell.

Although the exact relationship between these two descriptions is difficult to de-termine, there are a number of connections. The Leviticus passage commands the Israelites to perform a ritual in order to eat the new food on the day after the Shabbat some time during or after the Festival of Matzot and the paschal of-fering. This is supposed to be done "upon entering the land." No such ritual is recorded in Joshua, but the new food is eaten on the day after the paschal offer-ing, "on that very day" and not earlier. That this period is the harvest season was already mentioned in 3:15. The list of food differs slightly as well, probably be-cause on this day there would be a requirement to eat *matzah* and not bread.[84]

---

84 Jan Van Goudever suggests that, from a source-critical perspective, the Joshua text may reflect knowledge of a non-priestly version of this law. Perhaps the paschal sacrifice itself, or the eating of *matzah*, once filled the function that the *omer* offering filled for the priests. See: Jan Van Goudoever, *Biblical Calendars* (Leiden: Brill, 1959), 19. See also: Phillipe Guillaume, "Tracing the Origin of the Sabbatical Calendar in the Priestly Narrative (Genesis 1 to Joshua 5)," *JHS* 5 (2005); Louis H. Feldman, *Flavius Josephus: Antiquities of the Jews 1–4* (Leiden: Brill, 2004), 3:250 n. 719. In Israel Knohl's system (*Sanctuary of Silence*), Leviticus 23 is part of the H or HS source, which reworks both priestly as well as non-priestly material. The emphasis on Shabbat instead of Passover reflects priestly ideology.

Third, the discontinuing of the manna on the very day the Israelites partake of their first "native meal" functions as the sign that the wilderness period has truly ended. Again, Joshua functions as an inverse Moses or a completion of Moses. Moses took the Israelites out of settled land and Joshua returns them to settled land. They have come full circle; in Egypt they were slaves, now they are masters.

Revelation outside Jericho (Ch. 5)

Outside Jericho, Joshua encounters an armed man and asks him whether he be friend or foe. Unsurprisingly, Joshua does not try to avoid a possible fight. The potential assailant turns out to be a divine being, the chief of Yhwh's army. Joshua's reaction to hearing this typifies the reaction of heroes in the Bible when learning that they have come face to face with a manifestation of the divine: Joshua falls on his face and requests instruction.

At this point, the angel tells Joshua to remove his shoes since he is standing on holy ground. This instruction is more than just reminiscent of the command to Moses at the burning bush, it is written with the exact same words:

יהושע ה:טו Josh 5:15	שמות ג:ה Exod 3:5
וַיֹּאמֶר שַׂר צְבָא יְהוָה אֶל יְהוֹשֻׁעַ: "שַׁל נַעַלְךָ מֵעַל רַגְלֶךָ כִּי הַמָּקוֹם אֲשֶׁר אַתָּה עֹמֵד עָלָיו קֹדֶשׁ הוּא." The chief of Yhwh's army said to Joshua: "<u>Remove your shoes from your feet, for the place upon which you stand is holy.</u>"	וַיֹּאמֶר[85]: "אַל תִּקְרַב הֲלֹם שַׁל נְעָלֶיךָ מֵעַל רַגְלֶיךָ כִּי הַמָּקוֹם אֲשֶׁר אַתָּה עוֹמֵד עָלָיו אַדְמַת קֹדֶשׁ הוּא." And he said: "Do not come near. <u>Remove your shoes from your feet, for the place upon which you stand is holy</u> ground."

The command to remove shoes and the claim that the ground is holy make the beginning of the revelations to Joshua and Moses parallel.[86] For Moses it is his first revelation; for Joshua it is not.[87]

---

85 Although to the redactor they were all the same being, it is unclear in this verse whether the speaker is supposed to be conceptualized as Yhwh, Elohim or the messenger of Elohim.

86 Ellie Assis argues that the presentation of Joshua as a second Moses in the book of Joshua is actually a crafted literary chiastic—or more accurately mirror-image—presentation in 7 steps (*From Moses to Joshua*, 11–17):

a. Death notice of Moses in both accounts
b. God's encouragement of Joshua/Moses' encouragement of the people,
c. Speech to Transjordanian tribes requiring assistance in conquering the Cisjordan
d. Sending of scouts

Jericho (Ch. 6)

After Joshua complies with the initial instructions, YHWH directs him to take Jericho.[88] The Israelites are to surround Jericho, marching around it in a circle once a day for seven days. Each day, seven priests carrying seven shofars before the ark will lead the procession. On the seventh day, these priests are to blow the shofars, and when the people hear this, they are to scream altogether and, as a result, the walls of Jericho will fall, allowing the Israelites an easy victory.

Joshua relays these instructions to the Israelites, but he modifies them. First, he adds a vanguard and rearguard to the procession—a military formation. The vanguard is supposed to walk before the seven priests and the rearguard behind the ark. It seems that both groups are supposed to be blowing shofars all seven days. Second, Joshua tells the people that they should not cry out until he gives them the word. Joshua wants to maintain control of the exact timeline of even this "miracle-based" military strategy. Joshua's desire to control the timing of the Israelites' scream is reminiscent of his martial reaction to Eldad and Medad.

When the plan finally goes forward, Joshua adds a number of additional commands. First, the city and all that is inside it are to fall under the ban. Anyone who takes anything from it will sully the camp of the Israelites. The people and animals are to be slaughtered while the precious metals are to be placed in YHWH's treasury. The only exception is to be Rahab and her family, because she hid the scouts. The people then carry out the plan as described.

––––––

e. Crossing the Sea of Reeds / Jordan River
f. Paschal sacrifice and circumcision
g. Revelatory moment where shoes must be removed.

See also: Assis, "Divine," 39–42.

87 Perhaps in an older form of a Joshua narrative this was his first experience of revelation.
88 Some see this statement of YHWH as a separate revelation and not part of the communication from the angel, but this would make the revelation of the angel contentless. If one is to see this story as a parallel to the Moses or even the Gideon revelations stories, the reader expects some sort of message or assignment. If this angel is the chief of YHWH's army, a suggestion of war comes as no surprise. The objection that the speaker switches from the chief of YHWH's army to YHWH himself does not pose a serious problem, since this is a standard feature of revelation stories. See James Kugel's essay "The God of Old," published in James L. Kugel, *The God of Old: Inside the Lost World of the Bible* (New York: Free Press, 2003). Cf. Hall (*Conquering*, 79–90), who offers a similar reading.

Joshua does not take an active role in the battle or the ban, but he micromanages the saving of Rahab[89] and he puts a brutal curse on anyone who rebuilds the city of Jericho, stating that doing so would be at the expense of losing one's sons.

The account ends with the name of Joshua becoming known throughout the land. There is a certain irony here. At the end of the description of the crossing of the Jordan the text states that all the Amorites heard how Yнwн dried the riverbed, allowing the Israelites to cross. Here, it is not Yнwн that receives the Amorites' attention, but Joshua. Joshua actually accomplishes very little in this story, however, at least not directly.

The city was conquered through a miracle devised by Yнwн. Joshua did not ask for or suggest this miracle; it was all Yнwн's idea. Furthermore, Joshua did not even carry out the mechanics of the miracle; this was done by the seven priests blowing shofars and by the scream of the people on the seventh day. Finally, Joshua is not even described as having led the "mop-up" operation. One wonders why Joshua's name of all things, as opposed to Yнwн's or Israel's, receives such notoriety at this point.

Most noteworthy is the exceedingly dominant position of the seven priests, the ark and the shofars. As in the account of the crossing of the Jordan, there seems to be some tension between the image of Joshua as the central pillar of Israel and the image of the priesthood and their accoutrements in a similar position. In this sense, Joshua's image here is more like that of "Joshua the administrator" described in the Numbers section. He organizes this event, but he is neither central to the miracle nor to the subsequent military attack.

Ai – Part 1: Israel's Defeat (Ch. 7)

Having successfully conquered Jericho, Joshua begins his next conquest in characteristic fashion, by sending scouts. There are subtle differences, however, between the mission to Jericho and the mission to Ai. First, in chapter 2, Joshua explicitly tells the scouts to go to Jericho, whereas here he leaves the specific destination unstated. Was it up to the scouts to choose the next target? Further, unlike the mission to Jericho, this mission isn't described as being a secret.

---

89 After the initial announcement, he specifically sends the two scouts to find her and bring her out. In yet a third mention of this, Joshua is said to have "kept her alive." It is possible that this extra attention to Rahab may have been a partial inspiration for the Rabbinic midrash that Joshua married Rahab. See chapter 6 for discussion of this midrash.

The end of the scout mission only exaggerates these differences. After their astonishing escape from Jericho, the scouts report confidently to Joshua that YHWH will hand the city over to the Israelites and that the inhabitants are afraid. The scouts in the Ai account also return confident. In their estimation, Ai is not very big and will not be much of a problem to conquer. The first part of their message should jump out to the reader, however. The scouts are not content to tell Joshua what they saw; rather they begin by telling him what to do.

The scouts are so confident that Ai will fall before the Israelite army, that they suggest Joshua send only a fraction of the troops. Even more surprising, Joshua follows this suggestion without comment. The results are disastrous. The people of Ai deal the reduced Israelite army a crushing defeat and the morale of the Israelites plummets. It is now the Israelites whose "hearts have turned to water" instead of the Canaanites.

This literary maneuver, i.e. having the Israelites speak in the language of the people of Jericho, draws the reader's attention to the key distinction between the two accounts. The previous scouts trust in YHWH, trust in Joshua, and report what they found and the state of mind of the people. These scouts trust in the might of the Israelite army and are contemptuous of the natives. YHWH does not readily reward arrogance. Additionally, unbeknownst to Joshua or the scouts, (but known to the reader,) YHWH is already furious with the Israelites, since the ban has been broken.[90]

Upon learning of the defeat, for the first and only time in the book, Joshua reacts with total panic. He puts on sackcloth and ashes and turns to YHWH in prayer. He ends the prayer with a Mosaic trope, claiming that the destruction of the Israelites would sully YHWH's own name. The majority of Joshua's prayer, however, instead of mimicking that of Moses, actually mimics the complaints of the Israelites in the desert, especially the complaints following the report of the ten scouts.

---

90 From a redaction-critical perspective, it appears that the Achan piece was added into the Ai account as an added explanation for their failure.

במדבר פרק יד Num 14:2–3	יהושע פרק ז Josh 7:7
וַיִּלֹּנוּ עַל מֹשֶׁה וְעַל אַהֲרֹן כֹּל And all the Children of	וַיֹּאמֶר יְהוֹשֻׁעַ: "אֲהָהּ אֲדֹנָי Joshua said: "Woe, my
בְּנֵי יִשְׂרָאֵל וַיֹּאמְרוּ אֲלֵהֶם Israel complained	יְהוִֹה לָמָה הַעֲבַרְתָּ הַעֲבִיר Lord YHWH! Why did
כָּל הָעֵדָה: "לוּ מַתְנוּ בְּאֶרֶץ against Moses and	אֶת הָעָם הַזֶּה אֶת הַיַּרְדֵּן you cross this nation
מִצְרַיִם אוֹ בַּמִּדְבָּר הַזֶּה לוּ Aaron, and the entire	לָתֵת אֹתָנוּ בְּיַד הָאֱמֹרִי over the Jordan just
מַתְנוּ! וְלָמָה יְהוָֹה מֵבִיא assembly said to	לְהַאֲבִידֵנוּ וְלוּ הוֹאַלְנוּ וַנֵּשֶׁב to give us into the
אֹתָנוּ אֶל הָאָרֶץ הַזֹּאת לִנְפֹּל them: "If only we had	בְּעֵבֶר הַיַּרְדֵּן." hands of the Amorites
בְּחֶרֶב נָשֵׁינוּ וְטַפֵּנוּ יִהְיוּ died in the Land of	to destroy us? If only
לָבַז? הֲלוֹא טוֹב לָנוּ שׁוּב Egypt or this desert –	we had been content
מִצְרָיְמָה!" if only we had died!	and settled in the
	Why did YHWH take	Transjordan!"
	us to this land so that	
	we fall by the sword	
	and our wives and	
	children be taken as	
	booty? Would it not	
	be better for us to re-	
	turn to Egypt?!"	

In reaction to what they perceive would be a crushing defeat by the inhabitants of the land, the Israelites complain that (a) God brought them to Canaan only to have them slaughtered by the native peoples, (b) that it would have been better if they had already died, and (c) that they should return to Egypt. The opening of Joshua's prayer follows the same outline. He complains that (a) YHWH has brought them to the Cisjordan only to have them killed by the inhabitants and that (c) it would be better if they would just settle in the Transjordan.[91]

This is the irony of all ironies! Joshua, the young scout, who stood up to the panicking Israelites, is now falling into the very same panic. Although the Israelites did actually lose a battle in this case, nevertheless, Joshua has already conquered Jericho and in a fashion that demonstrates YHWH's direct involvement. Joshua seems at a loss to explain what occurred, but this itself is strange. He purposely sent a reduced force into the fray. Moreover, Joshua explicitly states in 6:18 that if any Israelite steals from the ban, he will then be placing the Israelites under the ban, as it were, with terrible consequences. Yet neither possibility crosses Joshua's mind. Instead he jumps to the conclusion that the Israelites are too weak to fight the native Amorites and that YHWH has utterly abandoned them. Joshua's emotional collapse is astounding.

Noting Joshua's fear of the Israelites and his position with them described earlier may help explain this reaction. Joshua seems particularly frightened by what he sees as the inevitable loss of the people's morale. "Now that they

---

91 He skips (b), the claim that it would have been better to have died.

have turned their backs to the enemies," Joshua fears, nothing will persuade them to turn around and fight once again. Joshua sees Israelite morale as precarious at best, requiring constant replenishment in order to remain firm.[92]

YHWH rebukes Joshua (lightly), telling him to get up and asking why he has fallen on his face.[93] Then, YHWH offers Joshua the solution to the problem in a few steps.

First, YHWH says, the people have taken from the ban and YHWH will not be with them until Joshua reclaims the prohibited items. YHWH does not tell Joshua outright who the guilty party is, nor does he require Joshua to investigate and figure it out on his own. Instead YHWH tells Joshua exactly how to find out, by using a certain oracular technique. This Joshua does in a public ceremony. The perpetrator (Achan) is found, and he and his family are stoned to death. Joshua prefaces the execution with a short speech in which he makes a partial pun on Achan's name.[94]

Second, YHWH tells Joshua not to fear, but that he should return to Ai and that YHWH will hand the city over to him as YHWH did with Jericho. This time, however, Joshua should bring the entire army with him; perhaps this is an implied criticism of his previous behavior.

Third, in the MT (not in the LXX), YHWH even tells Joshua what strategy to use; he is to set a trap by placing a hidden force behind the city. This parallels YHWH's previous message. On one hand, YHWH is not actually going to hand over the city the way he did for Jericho, just as he won't hand over Achan in a straightforward manner. On the other hand, YHWH is not leaving Joshua to fend for himself. He tells him what is necessary strategically in order to defeat Ai just as he told Joshua what was necessary in order to catch the perpetrator of the theft from the ban. YHWH may be trying to build up Joshua in his own eyes as well as in the eyes of the people.

---

92 Perhaps we are to imagine that Joshua has been traumatized by his wilderness experience with them?

93 It is possible that this is a play on YHWH's rebuke of Cain "why has your face fallen?" (Gen 4:6). If so, the hint here might be "if you improve, good, but if not, sin is crouching at your door", i.e. the sin of leading the people out of the Promised Land. It may also have intended intertextual resonances with YHWH's rebuke of Moses at the Sea of Reeds (Exod 14:15): "Why are you crying out to me?"

94 Following the LXX's Vorlage and the character's name in Chronicles (Achar) it would be a full pun. Achan's Judahite association may be a polemic against Judah in favor of the northern hero Joshua.

Ai – Part 2: The City is Taken (Ch. 8)

Unlike the previous attack on Ai, Joshua leads this one and plans the battle actively. He begins by sending a force of 30,000 men at night to lie in ambush behind the city. They are to wait until Joshua leads the main army in a sham retreat, at which point they are to enter and take the city. The sign that the city has been taken will be the smoke which will rise from the burning city. Having given these instructions, Joshua joins the people in their camp for the night.

Joshua awakens early the next day and takes the army to Ai. After assigning five thousand soldiers to form an ambush, he feigns an attack on the city.[95] The king of Ai takes the bait and engages the Israelites. As planned, Joshua retreats and the men of Ai give chase. The author describes Joshua's retreat in terms reminiscent of the tenth plague and the attempted retreat of the Egyptians at the Sea of Reeds.

שמות יד:כה	שמות יא:א	יהושע ח:טו
וַיֹּאמֶר מִצְרַיִם אָנוּסָה מִפְּנֵי יִשְׂרָאֵל כִּי יְהוָה נִלְחָם לָהֶם בְּמִצְרָיִם.	וַיֹּאמֶר יְהוָה אֶל מֹשֶׁה עוֹד **נֶגַע אֶחָד** אָבִיא עַל פַּרְעֹה וְעַל מִצְרַיִם.	וַיִּנָּגְעוּ יְהוֹשֻׁעַ וְכָל יִשְׂרָאֵל לִפְנֵיהֶם וַיָּנֻסוּ דֶּרֶךְ הַמִּדְבָּר.
Exod 14:25	Exod 11:1	Josh 8:15
Egypt said: "Let us **flee** from the Israelites for YHWH fights for them in Egypt!"	YHWH said to Moses: "I have one more **strike** to bring against Pharaoh and Egypt…"	Joshua and all of Israel **were struck** before them, and they **fled** by way of the wilderness.

Ironically, unlike the Egyptians, the Israelites have not actually been "struck" and are not really "fleeing."

The army of Ai is also described in terms reminiscent of the Egyptians at the sea:

שמות יד:כח	שמות יד:ח-ט, כג	יהושע ח:טז-יז
וַיָּשֻׁבוּ הַמַּיִם וַיְכַסּוּ אֶת הָרֶכֶב וְאֶת הַפָּרָשִׁים לְכֹל חֵיל פַּרְעֹה הַבָּאִים אַחֲרֵיהֶם בַּיָּם לֹא נִשְׁאַר בָּהֶם עַד *אֶחָד*.	וַיְחַזֵּק יְהוָה אֶת לֵב פַּרְעֹה מֶלֶךְ מִצְרַיִם **וַיִּרְדֹּף אַחֲרֵי בְּנֵי יִשְׂרָאֵל...** **וַיִּרְדְּפוּ מִצְרַיִם אַחֲרֵיהֶם...** **וַיִּרְדְּפוּ מִצְרַיִם וַיָּבֹאוּ אַחֲרֵיהֶם...**	וַיִּזָּעֲקוּ כָּל הָעָם אֲשֶׁר בָּעִי לִרְדֹּף אַחֲרֵיהֶם וַיִּרְדְּפוּ אַחֲרֵי יְהוֹשֻׁעַ וַיִּנָּתְקוּ מִן הָעִיר. וְלֹא *נִשְׁאַר אִישׁ* בָּעִי וּבֵית אֵל אֲשֶׁר לֹא יָצְאוּ אַחֲרֵי יִשְׂרָאֵל וַיַּעַזְבוּ אֶת הָעִיר פְּתוּחָה וַיִּרְדְּפוּ אַחֲרֵי יִשְׂרָאֵל.

---

95 This second setting up of an ambush seems contradictory to the previous section where the ambushing army is sent out in advance the night before. From a redaction-critical perspective, the earlier section appears to be a later addition.

Exod 14:28
The water returned and covered the chariots and horsemen from all of Pharaoh's soldiers that followed after them in the sea. *Not one of them remained.*

Exod 14:8–9, 23
YHWH strengthened the heart of Pharaoh, king of Egypt, and **he chased after the Children of Israel**... and the Egyptians **chased after them**... *Not one man was left* and the Egyptians **gave chase** and came after them...

Josh 8:16–17
The entire people found in the Ai called out **to chase after them, and they chased after** Joshua and left the city behind. *Not one man was left* in the Ai or Bet El who did not leave [to chase] **after Israel.** They left the city open and **chased after** Israel.

Both parallels underscore the fact that the power of Ai is only apparent. Like the pursuing Egyptian troops, the army of Ai is headed for annihilation.[96]

The parallel with the fall of the Egyptian army at the sea is cemented by a revelation to Joshua, which resonates strongly with a similar revelation to Moses.

שמות יד:טו-טז, כא, כו-כז | Exod 14:15–16, 21, 26–27 | יהושע ח:יח | Josh 8:18

וַיֹּאמֶר יְהֹוָה אֶל מֹשֶׁה... "וְאַתָּה הָרֵם אֶת מַטְּךָ וּנְטֵה אֶת יָדְךָ עַל הַיָּם וּבְקָעֵהוּ..." וַיֵּט מֹשֶׁה אֶת יָדוֹ עַל הַיָּם... וַיִּבָּקְעוּ הַמָּיִם... וַיֹּאמֶר יְהֹוָה אֶל מֹשֶׁה: "נְטֵה אֶת יָדְךָ עַל הַיָּם וְיָשֻׁבוּ הַמַּיִם עַל מִצְרַיִם עַל רִכְבּוֹ וְעַל פָּרָשָׁיו." וַיֵּט מֹשֶׁה אֶת יָדוֹ עַל הַיָּם...

YHWH said to Moses: "...And you, raise your staff and spread your arm upon the sea and split it..." Moses raised his arm upon the sea and the water split... YHWH said to Moses: "Spread your arm upon the sea and the water will return upon Egypt, upon its chariots and riders." Moses spread his arms upon the sea...

וַיֹּאמֶר יְהֹוָה אֶל יְהוֹשֻׁעַ: "נְטֵה בַּכִּידוֹן אֲשֶׁר בְּיָדְךָ אֶל הָעַי כִּי בְיָדְךָ אֶתְּנֶנָּה." וַיֵּט יְהוֹשֻׁעַ בַּכִּידוֹן אֲשֶׁר בְּיָדוֹ אֶל הָעִיר...

YHWH said to Joshua: "Spread out your arm, with your spear, towards the Ai, for I have given it into your hands." Joshua spread his arm with the spear towards the city...

Just as Moses controls the splitting and coming together of the waters of the Sea of Reeds with his staff, Joshua controls the burning of the city of Ai with his spear. This is an unexpected twist in the story, since the narrator does not mention that Joshua had prearranged this sign with the ambushing troops, and

---

96 Another possible resonance between the two stories could be the description of the army of Ai surrounded on all sides by the Israelites. This imagery may call to mind the Egyptian army surrounded on all sides by the waters of the sea coming back together.

seems designed specifically to parallel Moses.[97] Joshua's use of a spear instead of a staff highlights the image of Joshua as warrior as opposed to that of elder statesman or prophet.

If this weren't enough of a parallel with Moses, the Joshua-and-his-spear imagery is pushed further, ostensibly in order to bring to the reader's mind to yet another Moses story:

שמות יז:יא-יב	Exod 17:11–12	יהושע ח:כו	Josh 8:26
וְהָיָה כַּאֲשֶׁר יָרִים מֹשֶׁה יָדוֹ וְגָבַר יִשְׂרָאֵל וְכַאֲשֶׁר יָנִיחַ יָדוֹ וְגָבַר עֲמָלֵק... וַיְהִי יָדָיו אֱמוּנָה עַד בֹּא הַשָּׁמֶשׁ.	And it happened that whenever Moses raised his arm Israel would triumph and when he would lower his arm Amalek would triumph... And his arms were an assurance until the sun set.	וִיהוֹשֻׁעַ לֹא הֵשִׁיב יָדוֹ אֲשֶׁר נָטָה בַּכִּידוֹן עַד אֲשֶׁר הֶחֱרִים אֵת כָּל יֹשְׁבֵי הָעָי.	Joshua did not return the arm, which he had stretched out with the spear, [to his side] until all of the inhabitants of the Ai were put to the ban.

Like Moses, Joshua will keep his hand extended until the completion of the battle. The young man who was left on the ground to fight the battle has now become the elder statesman overseeing and controlling the battle from on high – the man who functions as the bridge between YHWH and Israel. At the same time, however, Joshua has not been ordered to climb a mountain and watch the battle; rather he controls it from the ground. Joshua gives the orders as well as providing the miracles. In a certain sense, he is both Moses and Joshua at the same time.

The battle with Ai ends with total victory on the part of Joshua and his army. The city is burned, the people are slaughtered, and the booty is taken. The city is left as a pile of rubble and remains so until the narrator's own day, hence the name of the city, "the Ai," loosely translated as "the rubble heap."[98] As a final act of triumph, the king of Ai is brought alive before Joshua. Joshua hangs his body on a tree but removes it before nightfall.[99] This demonstrates Joshua's compliance with the laws of Moses as recorded in the Pentateuch.[100]

---

97 This is yet another indication that this story has been supplemented with other material. Hall argues that the imagery of the outstretched arm is a sign of a leader doing YHWH's bidding and is meant to parallel Moses and Aaron (Hall, *Conquering*, 133–136).

98 This seems about as clear a sign as possible that the story was written with "the rubble heap" in mind, and that the story-teller does not even know what the ancient ruin's name was.

99 Ostensibly, Joshua killed him first, but this is not recorded.

100 Deut 21:23

He then flings the body onto the ground before the gates of the destroyed city and piles stones upon it, creating a mini-memorial to the king's execution which lasts until the narrator's own day.

From the perspective of Joshua's emotional state and success as a leader, the Ai story is perhaps the most dramatic account in the book. Ai begins with a detached Joshua who makes a thoughtless error and compounds the problem by falling into a panic. He is at a loss as to how to fight Ai's soliders and believes YHWH has abandoned him. The story ends, however, with Joshua taking an active role as a leader, outsmarting the king of Ai and defeating him handily, all the while maintaining direct contact with YHWH and receiving his support. From the low point of mimicking the language of the generation of the desert, he reaches a high point as leader, general, and prophet, perhaps even surpassing Moses.

The Altar and the Ritual of Blessing and Curse (Ch. 8)

Although the placement of this section varies depending on text tradition,[101] its import seems relatively straightforward. Joshua builds an altar on Mount Ebal "as Moses the servant of YHWH commanded the Israelites and as is written in the book of the Torah of Moses." The point could not be more explicit: Joshua fulfills the commands of Moses. He then writes Moses' Torah on stones. Following this, Joshua organizes the ritual of blessing and curse, again "as was written in the Torah of Moses." The section ends by stating that "there was nothing in the commands of Moses that Joshua did not proclaim before the people." In short, Joshua is the inheritor of Moses' Torah.

This image of Joshua as the ultimate performer of Moses' commandments and master teacher of Moses' Torah hearkens back to chapter one, in which Joshua is commanded to study Torah day and night. This section reminds the reader that Joshua is ultimately only a purveyor of the Torah of Moses. He does not really "command" since every command worth following was already commanded by Moses, up to the very rituals that Joshua will perform to consecrate the land.[102]

---

101 For more on the placement of this section, see discussion in Emanuel Tov, "Literary Development of the Book of Joshua as reflected in the MT, LXX and 4QJosh^a," in *The Book of Joshua* (ed. Ed Noort. BETL 250; Proceedings of the Colloquium Biblicum Lovaniense; Leuven: Leuven University Press, 2010), 65–86 [78 ff].

102 The command to perform this ritual was, most likely, added into the Torah late, precisely in order to give Moses some control over the consecration of Israel. As this section seems to have

Treaty with the Gibeonites (Ch. 9)

Following the conquest of Ai, the narrative recounts two different reactions to Joshua and the invading army. Verses 1 and 2 record that all of the Canaanite kings from their various nations and geographic regions heard and gathered together to fight with Joshua and Israel. Verse 3, however, records that the inhabitants of Gibeon also heard, but react differently. They do not want to fight the invading Israelites; they want to join them. Due to "technical difficulties" (i.e., the Israelites' policy of slaughtering all of the native inhabitants), the Gibeonites seek to make a treaty based on the ruse that they are from a faraway land.

There are two major ambiguities in the story that make interpretation complex. First, it is unclear whether the reader is supposed to see this treaty as positive or negative. Are we supposed to be relieved that the ruse works or angered at the perfidious Gibeonites? Second, what role does Joshua play exactly in this process? On one hand, Joshua remains the designated leader of the Israelites. On the other hand, the group of "Israelite Men"/leaders takes an active role in this process.[103] The problem can be seen clearly when attempting to map out the negotiations.

The Gibeonites approach both Joshua and the Israelite representatives and begin to tell their story. The Israelite representatives respond first and accuse the Gibeonites of being locals, and the Gibeonites turn to Joshua and surrender. Joshua then asks them about their story in more detail. The Gibeonites comply with a long account of their (made-up) story, and end their presentation by displaying their worn out clothing and old provisions. The people [of Israel] take from the provisions without asking YHWH. Joshua then makes peace, followed by an oath by the leaders.

After three days, the Israelites learn the truth and are livid with their leaders. The leaders decide that if they cannot destroy the Gibeonites, considering the oath, they will, at least, make them indentured servants to the Israelites. Only after this does Joshua call upon the Gibeonites and rebuke them. The Gibeonites respond that they knew that without subterfuge Joshua would have killed them,

---

been added to the conquest narrative at a rather late stage, it is unclear whether one should assume that the narrative was originally connected with Joshua or with some other Israelite hero.

103 The connection between the two ambiguities is stark when the problem is approached from a source-critical perspective. If the deal is a good thing, then one can argue that Joshua is added to this independent story to give him credit. If it is a bad thing, one can argue that the Israelite council was added to soften the critique of Joshua. Both possibilities have scholarly support, and both perspectives are reflected in the reception history of the text.

since he had been commanded to do so by his god. Joshua accepts this explanation, confirms the status of servitude placed upon them by the leaders, but modifies this to make them servants of Yʜwʜ at the altar.

How is the reader to understand Joshua's place in this narrative? At first, Joshua seems to be the more sensitive party among the Israelites. The Israelite representatives are the ones that first accuse the Gibeonites of being natives and the Gibeonites react by throwing themselves upon the mercy of Joshua. Moreover, Joshua makes the peace treaty with them. On the other hand, Joshua only does so after the people partake of the Gibeonites' bread, something they do without consulting Yʜwʜ.

The blame or responsibility question in the story is fraught and complex. The people seem to blame the leadership entirely. This despite the fact that the leaders only swear to the Gibeonites *after* Joshua has made peace with them. To make matters even more complicated, Joshua only seems to acquiesce to the Gibeonites' overture after the people themselves do. The verse that mentions that Yʜwʜ was not consulted implies a critique of the people, not of Joshua or the leaders.

On the positive side, Joshua seems to be immune to criticism. On the negative side, he seems to be deciding what to do after the fact. This impression gains support from the end of the story. When the Israelites find out that they have been tricked, the leaders curse the Gibeonites, condemning them to be low-level workers in service to the Israelites. Only then does Joshua call over the Gibeonites and curse them himself. Again, Joshua's action seems secondary to that of the Israelite leaders.

Joshua's curse is more than a repetition of the curse of the leaders; it is a reformulation. Joshua wants the Gibeonites to be servants of Yʜwʜ at the altar, not general servants to the Israelites. This move seems less political and more theological than that of the leaders.

In short, Joshua's image in this story can be described as well intentioned and consensus driven, yet not bold or decisive.

The Southern Coalition – Protecting Gibeon (Ch. 10)

The stature of Joshua receives its greatest boost in the story of the defeat of the southern coalition. In this account, Adonizedek, king of Jerusalem, fears the success of Joshua and his entente with the Gibeonites in particular. Adonizedek organizes an alliance of five city-states and attacks Gibeon. The Gibeonites are forced to turn to Joshua and the Israelite army for succor.

This situation puts Israel's oath to the test, since one could imagine that Joshua would respond by allowing the Gibeonites to fall before Adonizedek's army. After all, the treaty was negotiated under false pretenses. The Gibeonites seem aware of this possibility, and their request for aid has a tinge of panic to it. As they did in their previous negotiations, they turn directly to Joshua. They refer to themselves as his slaves, as they did the first time, and ask him to "save" them, a play upon his name.

Joshua demonstrates extreme decisiveness. He leaves Gilgal with his entire army immediately, coming upon the enemy in a surprise attack after an all-night march. As in the Ai story, YHWH assures Joshua before the battle that he (Joshua) has nothing to fear and that he will win. The reassurance seems superfluous, however, since Joshua does not seem to fear losing. Joshua's surprise attack startles the enemy and they beat a retreat. While they are retreating, YHWH rains giant hailstones upon the enemy soldiers.

At this point, Joshua performs the miraculous feat that is, perhaps, the climax of his career. Joshua commands the sun not to set until the Israelites have completely routed their enemies, and the sun complies. The narrator stops to comment that at no point in history had something like this occurred, when YHWH listened to the "command" of a mortal. The narrator (in the MT version) further makes mention that this part of the account comes from a scroll called *The Book of the Righteous*.

This miracle brings up the interesting question of whether the reader is supposed to believe that Joshua at this point has surpassed even Moses. This possibility was alluded to earlier in the battle against Ai, when Joshua both raises his staff (like Moses) and fights the battle. This story seems to follow the same literary strategy, but takes it a step further.

As in earlier stories, Joshua is again painted in Mosaic colors; this is accomplished by the strong use of intertextual resonances to the Sea of Reeds story.

שמות יד:כד–כה Exod 14:24–25		יהושע י:י,יד Josh 10:10, 14	
וַיְהִי בְּאַשְׁמֹרֶת הַבֹּקֶר וַיַּשְׁקֵף	And it happened in	וַיְהֻמֵּם יְהוָה לִפְנֵי יִשְׂרָאֵל	**Yhwh made them**
יְהוָה אֶל מַחֲנֵה מִצְרַיִם	during the morning	וַיַּכֵּם מַכָּה גְדוֹלָה בְּגִבְעוֹן...	**confused** before Isra-
בְּעַמּוּד אֵשׁ וְעָנָן וַיָּהָם אֶת	watch that YHWH	כִּי יְהוָה נִלְחָם לְיִשְׂרָאֵל.	el, and he smote
מַחֲנֵה מִצְרָיִם. וַיָּסַר אֵת אֹפַן	gazed upon the camp		them a great smiting
מַרְכְּבֹתָיו וַיְנַהֲגֵהוּ בִּכְבֵדֻת	of Egypt with a pillar		in Gibeon... for **Yhwh**
וַיֹּאמֶר מִצְרַיִם אָנוּסָה מִפְּנֵי	of fire and cloud **and**		**fought for Israel.**
יִשְׂרָאֵל כִּי יְהוָה נִלְחָם לָהֶם	**he confused** the		
בְּמִצְרָיִם.	camp of Egypt.... And		
	Egypt said: "Let us		
	run from Israel, **for**		
	Yhwh fights for		
	them against Egypt.		

This resonance to the Israelites in Egypt occurs yet again as the soldiers return from their final pursuit of the retreating armies.

שמות יא:ז	Exod 11:7	יהושע י:כא	Josh 10:21
וּלְכֹל בְּנֵי יִשְׂרָאֵל לֹא יֶחֱרַץ	**No** dog **shall snarl at**	וַיָּשֻׁבוּ כָל הָעָם אֶל הַמַּחֲנֶה	And all the people re-
כֶּלֶב לְשֹׁנוֹ לְמֵאִישׁ וְעַד	**any Israelite, from**	אֶל יְהוֹשֻׁעַ מַקֵּדָה בְּשָׁלוֹם	turned to the camp,
בְּהֵמָה לְמַעַן תֵּדְעוּן אֲשֶׁר	**man** to beast, so that	לֹא חָרַץ לִבְנֵי יִשְׂרָאֵל לְאִישׁ	to Joshua at Makeda
יַפְלֶה יְהוָה בֵּין מִצְרַיִם וּבֵין	they know that Yhwh	אֶת לְשֹׁנוֹ.	in peace. **No [one]**
יִשְׂרָאֵל.	distinguishes between		**snarled at a man**
	Egypt and Israel.		**among Israel.**

This parallel implies that the success of Joshua's battle is comparable to the success of Moses in Egypt. In this sense, Joshua has replaced Moses as a successful leader of Israel on behalf of whom Yhwh will fight and whose followers become fearsome to their enemies. One can strengthen this conclusion by pointing to Yhwh's use of hail as a weapon during the battle, hail being one of Yhwh's weapons of choice against the Egyptian people in the plague story.[104]

With his stopping of the sun, however, Joshua performs an unparalleled miraculous act. Even the great Moses needed to listen to Yhwh's commands at all times. It is only Joshua, and only at this one pinnacle moment, who can actually command Yhwh.[105]

The Death of the Five Kings (Ch. 10)

Having won the battle, Joshua encourages the troops to chase down the remaining enemy soldiers.[106] The order demonstrates Joshua's confidence and decisiveness. Even finding the five kings hiding in a cave doesn't distract Joshua from the main objective; he simply has them locked in the cave until the final pursuit is finished.

Eventually, Joshua does turn to the five kings. He has them removed from the cave and tells his generals to place their feet upon the kings' necks.[107] There-

---

104 As will be seen in the chapter on Rabbinic Joshua, the Rabbis pick up on this connection with a midrashic suggestion that it was the same hail stones that were waiting in heaven for years to continue falling after Moses stopped the plague of hail in Egypt.

105 The unique nature of this miracle becomes a point of contention between the early Christian and Rabbinic interpreters.

106 This seems to contradict the previous passage, which states that Joshua destroyed the attacking army utterly.

107 Although the text does not state that the kings were laid upon the ground, this is understood.

upon, in a dramatic recasting of the beginning of the Joshua narrative, Joshua speaks the words of encouragement he had been given numerous times. He tells the people not to fear but be brave and strong.[108] He assures the people that YHWH would do as he had just done to all of their enemies. With this speech Joshua has come full circle; far from needing more encouragement, he now finds himself in the position of encouraging others.

Following the speech, the kings are killed and their bodies hung on trees until nightfall. At nightfall, the bodies are removed from the trees and placed in a cave.[109] As with the execution of Achan, Joshua here follows Mosaic law, which forbids allowing a body to hang overnight. A further parallel to the Achan story is the pile of rocks placed before their graves "until this very day", a strategy Joshua uses in numerous places to leave his mark.

Conquest of the South (Ch. 10)

The conquest of the south is written with systematic repetition. Joshua and his army move from town to town, destroying each and putting each town's inhabitants under the ban. The tedium of the description underscores the ease with which Joshua conquers the south; no serious resistance by the inhabitants seems possible.

Although some of the place names are of unknown import, others are telling. The cities of Hebron and Debir will be conquered (again?) by Caleb and his brother Othniel respectively (Josh 15:13 – 17; Judg 1:10 – 13). These are Judahite heroes, but the narrative informs us that Joshua did it first. Lachish will play an important role as Judah's second strongest city. The defeat of Gezer is an interesting addition, since Pharaoh will later conquer Gezer and give it to Solomon as a gift (1 Kings 9:16). In the book of Judges (1:29), Ephraim is specifically faulted for not conquering Gezer, instead putting it under the ban. This narrative sets the record straight; Joshua did conquer the army of Gezer, and if he didn't finish the job, the Israelites themselves were responsible for doing so.

Jerusalem is conspicuously absent from the list of conquered cities. This is doubly odd since the king of Jerusalem led the attacking coalition in the first

---

108 אַל תִּירְאוּ וְאַל תֵּחָתּוּ חִזְקוּ וְאִמְצוּ

109 From a redaction critical perspective, this story appears to have been expanded to include the execution. Perhaps an early version has Joshua sealing the kings in the cave in which they were hiding while still alive.

place.[110] If this implies some lack of total success on Joshua's part, it is offset by the declaration that Joshua conquered all the Land of Canaan, including the Philistines in Gaza, and even part of the Sinai and maybe more.[111]

This final claim is the ultimate demonstration of YHWH's power and the incomparable greatness of Joshua and the generation of the conquest. The claim about the Philistines stands out when one thinks about why the Israelites took to the wilderness according to Exodus 13:17. YHWH did not take them the way of the Philistines, although it was shorter, for he said, "lest they see war and return to Egypt." In the ultimate irony, Joshua takes them to the war, wins it, and returns to the Philistines to conquer. Specifically mentioned is Kadesh Barnea, the spot where the Israelites waited for 38 years after angering YHWH with the sin of the scouts. Joshua rectifies history.

The Northern Coalition (Ch. 11)

Following the successful conquest of the south, Joshua is faced with yet another attacking army, this time from the north. The organizer of this expedition is Jabin king of Hazor. The northern army is described in frightening terms. Their numbers are like the sands of the beaches, and they have an abundance of horses and chariots.

YHWH encourages Joshua, telling him not to worry. Joshua, YHWH says, will kill Jabin's soldiers, hamstring the horses, and burn the chariots. True to form, Joshua goes on the offensive against the army, appearing suddenly along the waters of Merom. This time, he chases the army north all the way to Sidon and succeeds in wiping them out. Having won the battle, Joshua returns to the chief city, Hazor, and burns it to the ground. Again, as in the southern campaign, Joshua goes on to conquer the rest of the northern towns, although this is not described

---

110 Yarmout is also not mentioned in the list of conquered cities, even though its king was part of the coalition. Since little is known about Yarmout, it is difficult to speculate what the significance of this absence (if any) may be.

111 The text makes the astounding claim that Joshua actually went so far as to conquer Goshen. Since there is a town near Holon mentioned in Josh 15:51 called Goshen, this must have been the area originally intended. In every other place in the Bible, however, Goshen refers to northern Egypt, and the term "Land of Goshen" found only here and in the Joseph and Exodus stories, generally refers to northern Egypt. If the editor of Joshua did not mean to imply northern Egypt, but only the small Israelite town of Goshen, his writing is strange. Perhaps the editor, either purposefully or because he misunderstood the term Goshen, may have intended to claim that Joshua did conquer northern Egypt. Joshua accomplishes this amazing feat after pushing the enemy out of Kadesh Barnea and even Gaza.

in the itemized fashion used for the southern campaign. Joshua does not burn the northern towns, although he does kill all the inhabitants and divide the spoils.

Although the enemy in this account is described as having been the most formidable of all the attacking armies, the story is actually rather schematic. What YHWH says to Joshua and even Joshua's surprise offensive are exact replicas of the southern campaign. The main contributions of this story to Joshua's image are, first, to have him as conqueror of the entire Promised Land and, second, to present him as the tried and true leader of the army. This time no miracles are required, and there is no need for him to prove himself. Joshua has gone from an inexperienced and nervous new leader to the consummate "old rough and ready."[112]

The story ends with a double reference to Joshua's fidelity to the laws of Moses and YHWH. As this allegiance to Torah and Moses has been referenced before, here it simply reinforces Joshua's image as a loyal adherent of Torah. Joshua has been firmly established as the legitimate successor of Moses.

Summary of Conquest (Ch. 11)

After the battle with the northern army, the text offers a short summary of the conquest (vv. 16 – 20), reiterating that Joshua took all the land, in the south going as far as Goshen and in the north going as far as Lebanon. Even Mount Seir is mentioned, implying a conquest of the Transjordan as well. Joshua's battles are described as having been lengthy. Not one city, other than Gibeon, made peace with Joshua. Although this may condemn Joshua to a lifetime of war, this is the will of YHWH; YHWH wants the land cleared of its native inhabitants, who seem to have displeased him–all as Moses foretold.

Removal of Giants (Ch. 11)

Towards the end of the conquest narrative, the text attributes one further "superhuman" feat to Joshua (vv. 21–22). Among the inhabitants of the towns of the Cisjordan are various groups of giants—the very people who struck fear into the hearts of the scouts. Joshua destroys these giants, removing them from He-

---

112 This was the title given to General Zachory Taylor by his soldiers and admirers before he became president.

bron, Debir, Anab, and all of Judah and Israel. The only remaining giants after the conquest are in the Philistine country: Gaza,[113] Gath, and Ashdod. This is another example of Joshua coming "full circle." He said the giants were nothing to fear when he was a young scout in the wilderness, and he demonstrates that this is so as the elder chief of the Israelites.[114]

Conclusion of Narrative (Ch. 11)

Having taken all the land, as Yhwh had promised through Moses, Joshua gives it to the tribes to divide up as inheritance, "and the land became quiet from war" (v. 23). Joshua's long years of fighting pay off, with the ultimate accomplishment being a land and people at peace.[115]

Geographical Addendum (Ch. 12)

Before moving on to the division of the land, the book includes a geographical addendum, summarizing the conquests of Moses on one hand and those of Joshua on the other. The section serves to solidify Joshua's reputation, since the description seems designed to parallel or even surpass Moses' legacy in the Transjordan.[116] Moreover, the list of kings both emphasizes the amazing success of Joshua's campaign as well as fills in the details of the conquest.

The latter is particularly important since the Joshua narrative is in some competition with other narratives and claims about these same cities. For example, whereas Judges 1 grants the conquest of Beit El to the house of Joseph in general, this chapter claims that it was Joshua himself who defeated their

---

113 There is some tension between the description of Gaza remaining full of giants and the verse in chapter 10, which claims that Joshua defeats the southern coalition all the way to Gaza. Although a source critical approach to these texts seems called for here, on the level of the redactor one could posit that Joshua defeats the southern coalition near Gaza but does not take the city. Worth noting is the fact that Gaza does not appear in the list of taken cities but does appear in the list of the "remaining land."

114 Granting this conquest to Joshua may have been meant to neutralize Caleb's image. Even if later on in the book Caleb will be the one to conquer Hebron, and his brother Othniel will conquer Debir, in these verses, the conquest is credited to Joshua. More about the tension between the Joshua and Caleb images will be discussed in the next chapter.

115 The land is at peace because the enemies have been annihilated, but this "ethical quibble" does not seem to bother the narrator, so it will not be a factor in the literary analysis of the story.

116 Moses only conquers 2 kings, although powerful ones, whereas Joshua conquers 31.

king. Similarly, whereas many cities are said to have remained unsubdued by the Israelites, such as Ta'anakh or Megiddo, this list makes the claim that Joshua defeated them. The chapter takes these claims only so far, however, as it limits itself to the claim that Joshua defeated the *kings* of these cities, not that the cities themselves were taken. This strategy has the benefit of making Joshua supreme over the land without flatly contradicting the alternative accounts of the cities' conquests.

The overall project of this chapter makes Joshua into "the founding father" of Cisjordan, in parallel to its view of Moses as "the founding father" of Transjordan. This can be seen not only from the schematic division of the lands in the chapter but especially from the specific transfer of Arad from the list of Moses' conquests (as per Numbers) to the list of Joshua's conquests. According to this chapter's presentation, all cities in the Cisjordan are Joshua's conquests.

The Remaining Land (Ch. 13)

Chapter 13 marks a sudden shift in the position and image of Joshua. Until this point, although not actually young, Joshua functioned as a vibrant leader and military commander. His successes in battle are described as lightening campaigns. One battle follows another rapidly until the Israelites take the entire Cisjordan.

Suddenly, in this passage, the situation seems to have reversed itself. Not only has Joshua become an old man, not a surprising development in and of itself, but he is told by YHWH that he has left a great amount of land unconquered.[117] It is difficult to know what to make of this statement. Is this a criticism or merely a statement of fact? Had Joshua been working consistently towards total conquest but time was not on his side? Or is it that after great initial

---

[117] From a redaction-critical perspective, this section of Joshua (chs. 13–19) is part of the tradition—as with Judges 1—that believes that many Canaanite inhabitants remained after the conquest and became incorporated into Israel during the early monarchic period. This has been the main approach among scholars for more than a century. See, for example, Sigmund Mowinckel, *Zur Frage nach dokumentarischen Quellen in Josua 13–19* (Oslo: I kommisjon hos J. Dybwad, 1946); Rudolph Smend, "Das Gesetz und die Völker: Eine Beitrag zur Deuteronomischen Redaktionsgeschichte," in *Probleme Biblischer Theologie: Festschrift für Gerhard von Rad* (ed. Hans Walter Wolf; München: Kaisar, 1971), 494–509 [497–498, 501]. This is my approach as well. See Koert van Bekkum's recent monograph, however, in which he argues for a literary continuity from chapter 12 into chapters 13–14: Koert van Bekkum, *From Conquest to Coexistence: Ideology and Antiquarian Intent in the Historiography of Israel's Settlement in Canaan* (Culture and History of the Ancient Near East 45; Leiden: Brill, 2011).

success he became remiss in his duties? The text is unclear about this, perhaps intentionally so.[118]

The key element in this chapter, other than the revelation of Joshua's lack of "total success," is his position as divider of land by lot. This hearkens back to the position assigned to him in Numbers. YHWH tells Joshua that it does not matter what has been conquered and what has not, he should divide all the land now among the Cisjordanian tribes. YHWH promises that he will assist with the eventual conquest of the remaining land at some time in the future. In short, at this stage in the narrative, Joshua is both an elder statesman and a failed conqueror.

Oddly enough, instead of beginning to describe the division of the land, the chapter goes off into a long excursus about Moses and the division of the Transjordan. More surprising still, the narrator actually includes a "failure" of Moses; the Israelites under his leadership failed to dispossess the Maachites and the Geshurites. Reading the primary history synchronically, this is a bizarre accusation, since Numbers gives no indication that Moses was supposed to dispossess them. Nevertheless, the claim allows for yet another parallel between Moses and Joshua, since they now share a failing as well: neither fully succeeded in conquering the territory under his charge.

Elazar the Priest (Ch. 14)

Although not mentioned in chapter 13, Elazar the priest is described in chapter 14 as Joshua's partner in the business of land division. This fits with Moses' command in Numbers 32 and makes some intuitive sense, since the decision will be made by lottery. Nevertheless, Joshua's position of associate land-divider seems to be a serious reduction in prestige when compared to the descriptions of him towards the end of the conquest account.

Caleb's Request (Ch. 14)

Forty five years after the debacle with the scouts, the two survivors of this fiasco meet up again. Their positions in life are now very different. Caleb has continued as an important leader in the tribe of Judah and his kinsmen advocate for him here. He does not seem to have risen to a position of national prominence, how-

---

118 There is no clear indication of criticism in YHWH's speech as there will be in Joshua's speech to Israel later in this section.

ever. Joshua, on the other hand, is now the ruler of all Israel, having taken the place of Moses.

Caleb recognizes this reality and, despite a curt reference to "their" unique fate as the only two survivors from that generation, Caleb does not try to establish too much connection between them. Instead he focuses on Moses' promises as well as those of YHWH.[119]

Caleb's request is rather modest. He wants Hebron, the city whose inhabitants caused all the trouble, by striking fear into the hearts of the scouts. Caleb claims that although he is now an old man of 85, he remains strong and will have little problem defeating the inhabitants of Hebron, giants though they be.

Joshua's response is telling. He does not offer to help by sending the army, nor does he relate any of his own exploits against giants. He simply blesses Caleb and grants him the land. In this story, Joshua is no longer the conqueror and warrior, but the elder statesman and man of YHWH.

Caleb – Part 2 (Ch. 15)

Joshua's land grant to Caleb is repeated in chapter 15. There it states that the grant was made by the word of YHWH, something that is not mentioned in chapter 14, which implies that it was Joshua's own executive decision, albeit influenced by the promises of Moses and YHWH. This repetition of the grant to Caleb is the only reference to Joshua in the Judah land grant section. This underscores the presentation of the land grant system in general; i.e., that it required little executive input and ran smoothly on its own.[120]

---

119 From a source critical perspective, this account fits much better with the non-P (or J) account of the scouts, which has Caleb as the hero. Otherwise, it seems odd for Caleb to be bragging to Joshua of all people about his loyalty, since Joshua had been just as loyal as Caleb. It would further seem that this passage is an early gloss on the conquest narrative, since the final words "and the land was quiet from war" function as a resumptive repetition, referring back to the end of chapter 11.

120 From a redaction critical perspective, this may imply that this section was not originally associated with Joshua.

Daughters of Zelophehad (Ch. 17)

The next time Joshua is called upon to use "executive power" appears in the division of Manasseh's territory. As in the case of Caleb's request, the daughters of Zelophehad invoke a specific promise from Moses. Unlike Caleb, however, the daughters turn not only to Joshua but also to Elazar and the heads of the tribes. This, more than even Caleb's request, reflects the limited position of Joshua as "leader of Israel" and in charge of land-division in the minds of the people. Specifically it is worth noting that Elazar's name appears first in the list.[121]

They Did Not Inherit (Chs. 15 – 17)

The accounts of the allotment of land to Judah, Ephraim, and Manasseh each end with a statement of what they did not succeed in conquering. These cities remained Canaanite in ethnicity, joining the Israelite fold when, eventually, the Israelites become strong enough to overtake them. Judah fails to take Jerusalem, Ephraim fails to take Gezer, and Manasseh fails to take a number of cities.

Although this failure does not relate directly to Joshua, it reflects upon his leadership in two ways. First it is a reminder of the incompleteness of the conquest, as the reader learns of even more areas in the Cisjordan which remained Canaanite. Second, each tribe is "faulted" for its lack of success, which reminds the reader that Joshua is, at this point, no longer in the business of leading armies.

Ephraim's Complaint (Ch. 17)

Tucked into the section of the Joseph tribes' land inheritance is, perhaps, the most astonishing conversation Joshua has in the entire book. The Joseph tribes approach Joshua and complain that they have been given an area that it is not big enough considering the size of the Joseph tribes. Joshua first responds by suggesting that they try to take some more land in the area of the Perizzites

---

121 Also odd is that the statement of agreement by the leaders is made in the singular, making one wonder who it was that "confirmed Moses' gift." Apparently, not all leaders are equal. Redaction critically speaking, the singular verb may reflect a stage in the narrative in which there was only one leader (Joshua or Elazar). Alternatively, it could be a mistake.

and the Rephaim.[122] This is a bold suggestion, especially since he does not offer to lead this expedition.

The Joseph tribes balk. They repeat that the mountain area is not enough, and they add that they cannot possibly attack the inhabitants of the valleys, whose armies have iron chariots. At this point, the reader may expect Joshua to react angrily and tell the Joseph tribes to show a little more faith and a lot more courage. Nevertheless, Joshua responds by agreeing with them. He suggests that, instead, they enlarge their holdings in the mountains by going into forested areas and chopping down trees. He ends with the consolation that, in the future, as the tribes grow stronger, they will eventually succeed in conquering the plains. Joshua the commander has permanently retired.

Joshua Rebukes the Seven Tribes (Ch. 18)

Sometime during this process, the Israelites set up the Tent of Meeting in Shiloh. Although this implies the conclusion of the settlement process, the process is not yet complete. Whereas Judah and the Joseph tribes have "inherited" their land with little management from above, the remaining seven tribes have not. Joshua (18:3) rebukes the Israelites, claiming that they have become lazy (מתרפים); a word with strong intertextual resonances to the Egypt story, in which Pharaoh accuses the Hebrews of the same thing (Exod 5:8, 17 – נרפים).

Most important for understanding Joshua's leadership style, in this case he takes the initiative. Afraid to leave the division of the land up to chance at this point, he tells the tribes exactly what to do. Each tribe will appoint three representatives. These representatives will tour the remaining land and divide it into seven plots. Joshua will then take these seven plots and divide them up between the seven tribes in a lottery system he will run in the tabernacle. Joshua's instructions are followed to the letter, and the division of land is carried out successfully.

One element of this story as well as the story of the Joseph tribes is that Elazar is nowhere to be found. Apparently, when real executive decisions are required, it is Joshua who takes charge and not Elazar.[123] Perhaps the conception

---

122 There is a textual problem here, as Joshua seems to be offering contradictory advice. He makes the bizarre statement that they should go to the land of the Perizzites and Rephaim and cut down forest. However one is to understand this, it seems clear from the Joseph tribes' response that he is suggesting a military solution.

123 Most probably, Elazar is added in artificially as a later gloss.

of the biblical authors here is that Elazar really never makes decisions, but that his position is to consult the *Urim ve-Tummim* when necessary.

Timnat Serah/Heres (Ch. 19)

Although Joshua's name does not come up again in the description of the division of the seven territories, he returns to the scene at the very end of this account, this time with a request. Joshua asks for his own plot of land in an area called Timnat Serah.[124]

A number of unusual features are notable. First, this is the first time that this city is mentioned in the book. There is no story about its conquest or its founding, and no reason is given why Joshua wants this city in particular. Second, although the gift is confirmed by YHWH, it is the Israelites as a whole that present the city to Joshua. There is no record of who communicates with YHWH to receive this oracle, and there is no mention of any leadership involved, not even Elazar the priest.

Furthermore, one wonders why an oracle was even necessary. Was it really a question whether the leader and chief conqueror of Israel could have his choice of plots? Most surprising is the fact that Joshua even needed to ask for a plot of land; especially since he gives one to Caleb directly when asked, without going through a lottery or an oracle. However one is to understand this, it is clear that Joshua avoids taking advantage of his leadership position for personal gain, unlike the kings that will eventually rule Israel and Judah. We see here a Joshua who, despite enormous power and influence, remains within the lines of propriety and does not give himself dictatorial powers.

After being granted his request, Joshua builds his town and dwells there. The town never becomes a major center and is mentioned again only twice in the Bible, as a part of Joshua's death and burial notices.

Summary Statement about Land Division (Ch. 19)

After tracing Joshua's behavior throughout the process of land division, the summary statement at the end of chapter 19 rings hollow. It implies that the division

---

124 Different sources spell the name of the town differently. I discuss this issue in, Zev I. Farber, "Timnat Heres and the Origins of the Joshua Tradition," in *The Book of Joshua* (ed. Ed Noort; BETL 250 – Proceedings of the CBL; Leuven: Leuven University Press, 2010), 301–311.

was overseen by Elazar the priest, Joshua, and the heads of the tribes and that it was all organized in Shiloh, the place of the Tent of Meeting. Insofar as the general procedure, this may for the most part be accurate. The plots were given out by lot, which was controlled, ostensibly, by the high priest Elazar in Shiloh. However, the narrative presents Elazar functioning only as the titular head of this process. The impetus for the mapping of borders is Joshua, and Joshua is the man the Joseph tribes and Caleb turn to for executive decisions when problems arise.[125] Elazar and the tribal leaders are active in only one decision, i.e., the land grant to the daughters of Zelophehad – and this is purely perfunctory, as the promise had been made by Moses explicitly. Joshua moves to a position of quiet leadership during this process. Although Elazar is the titular head and the tribal chiefs participate, Joshua continues to lead the Israelites when the necessity arises.

Cities of Refuge (Ch. 20)

The requirement to build cities of refuge appears in Numbers (35) and Deuteronomy (19). Nevertheless, YHWH "re-reveals" the command to Joshua. The opening formula for this revelation is identical to that used for revelations to Moses throughout the Pentateuch. Other than Aaron (Lev 10:8), no other prophet receives legal revelations in this Moses-specific form other than Joshua. Nevertheless, no attempt is made here to cast this in the guise of an original revelation. The very first sentence ends with the words "as I told you by way of Moses," fitting this section in with the theme of Joshua fulfilling Moses' commands.[126]

Worthy of note is the fact that the latter three cities in the Transjordan have already been founded. This is referenced specifically in Deuteronomy 4, and is also acknowledged implicitly in this chapter by use of the perfect verb form. It would be tempting to tie this fact into the analysis of chapters 12 and 13, where it was pointed out that a parallel between Joshua and Moses is being drawn, with Moses as the founder of the Transjordan and Joshua as the founder of the Cisjordan. However, if this were the point here, one would have expected some direct reference to the account in Deuteronomy 4 in which Moses himself

---

125 From a redaction critical perspective, it seems fairly straightforward that Joshua has an earlier place in the division of land narratives, and that Elazar is added in during the final stages of redaction.

126 If anything, the section wants to raise Joshua as high as possible without implying that he is a lawgiver equal to Moses.

founds the cities, instead of the third person plural used here, which implies that the Israelites as a whole founded them.[127]

Levitical Cities (Ch. 21)

The request of the leaders of the Levites for their cities shares a number of similarities with the request of the daughters of Zelophehad. First, as with the request of the daughters of Zelophehad, the request of the Levites is perfunctory, as the granting of these cities to the Levites is already stated clearly by Moses in the Pentateuch. Additionally, like the request of daughters of Zelophehad, the request is submitted to Elazar the priest, Joshua, and the leaders of Israel.

This fits in well with the previous pattern in the land grant section. The formal head of the land division is Elazar, backed up by Joshua and the leaders of the tribes. When the request itself is to be formal as well, it should be submitted to Elazar and his partners. The pure formality of the request becomes even clearer when one notices that the remaining description of the allotment contains no name or statement of any leader. This is clearly not meant to be controversial and requires no real leadership decision-making—hence Joshua's secondary role in the proceedings.

Summary of the Conquest (Ch. 21:41–43)

The most incongruous section in the entire book of Joshua is the summary statement in the last three verses of chapter 21.[128] The text "solves" the jarring tension between chapters 1–12 and 13–19 by suggesting that Joshua has conquered all that he can and that YHWH wants the land divided up before Joshua's immanent death. The reader has almost made peace with the failure of much of the conquest as represented in the accounts of Ephraim, Manasseh and Benjamin. The long list of cities in chapters 20 and 21, when read after chs. 13–19, are not necessarily cities that have been conquered. Some may have been con-

---

127 From a source critical perspective, the simplest answer seems to be that this section has been reworked, and originally it was a straightforward legal revelation to Joshua without reference to Moses.
128 Axel Knauf understands this section as P theology writing in D language ("*P-Theologie in D-Sprache*"). See Ernst Axel Knauf, *Josua* (Zürcher Bibelkommentare AT 6; Zürich: Theologisher Verlag, 2008), 21, 178–179,

quered, but the rest are just divied up by the elderly Joshua and left for others to follow up and conquer.

Then chapter 21 ends with what is almost a description of total success. According to this description, YHWH gives the Israelites all of the land, and no enemy succeeds in even standing up to them. They inherit the entire land and no promised blessing goes unfulfilled. Reading synchronically, one hardly knows what to do with a statement like this when juxtaposed with, for instance, the fear the Israelites express for Canaanite city-states with chariots.

Although there seems no real way to solve this tension—there are limits past which it is very difficult to stretch diachronic readings—one important feature of this summary (for the purposes of this chapter) is that Joshua receives no mention. The notice reads as a direct grant from YHWH to the Israelites. From this perspective, the leader of this sweeping conquest is unimportant; it could have been anybody. This is very different than the almost equivalent summary in chapter 11 that has Joshua as the focal point of Israel's success.

Transjordanian tribes – Release from Vow (Ch. 22)

At this point in the narrative, Joshua has come full circle. The book began with Joshua's timid exhortation of the two and a half tribes to fulfill their promise to Moses and fight alongside their fellow tribes in the conquest of the Cisjordan. At this point, Joshua thanks them for their compliance and sends them home.

Noticeably, Joshua's manner of expression has an air of confidence that it did not have in the first chapter. In his original speech, Joshua refers only to the promise made to Moses and sidesteps the reality that the conquest will be carried out under him (Joshua) and that he would decide whether the Transjordanian tribes lived up to the bargain. As was pointed out earlier, the tribes themselves notice this and promise to listen to Joshua, underscoring the timid nature of Joshua's exhortation.

In this speech, no such timidity haunts Joshua. He refers both to the Transjordanian tribes' promise to Moses and obedience to himself in the same breath. Furthermore, like Moses, he exhorts the tribes in Deuteronomic fashion, to love YHWH, serve him and walk in his ways, at which point he blesses them and sends them home to their families.

Immediately following this account, the text includes two verses summarizing it. The summary of Joshua's speech differs entirely from the speech itself.[129]

---

129 Although from a literary perspective, the speech is meant to have been a "long affair" with

In this version of the speech, Joshua notes the extreme abundance of wealth accumulated by these tribes and "asks" them to spread the wealth among some of the other tribes. How these tribes ended up accumulating more wealth is not stated. The important matter to note is that such "requests" can come only from a leader who takes a broad perspective with regard to the success of all his people as well as from a leader who has strong confidence that such "requests" will be obeyed.

Transjordanian Tribes – Perceived Sacrilege (Ch. 22)

In this story, there is a sacrilege (perceived or real) perpetrated by the Transjordanian tribes – the building of an altar – which so infuriates the Cisjordanian Israelites that war is almost declared. As a final measure before war, Phineas son of Elazar the priest is sent along with ten tribal chieftains in order to rebuke then Transjordanians. The Transjordanians claim that the altar was never meant for worship but only as a monument and memorial, and peace is maintained.

Surprisingly, the chapter never mentions Joshua or even alludes to him once during this entire account. From a literary perspective, this can be explained in one of two ways. Either the account is meant to postdate Joshua's lifetime[130] or Joshua, at this point, is no longer actively leading the Israelites.[131]

In favor of the first possibility is the fact that Elazar is not involved either, but that his son is the leader involved. Additionally, the final speeches of Joshua, which are recorded next, seem to imply that Joshua was still in charge, at least until that point. In favor of the latter interpretation is the placement of the narrative before Joshua's final speeches and immediately after his speech to the Transjordanian tribes, implying that this is when the incident occurred.

Following the former interpretation, this says little if anything about Joshua's character and leadership, since he would have been deceased at the time of the incident. Following the latter interpretation, however, this would be another ex-

---

the narrative and summary description emphasizing different aspects, nevertheless, from a source or redaction critical perspective, it would seem that the narrative section, which is highly deuteronomistic, was added in later to "correct" or "update" this account.

130 I first heard this suggestion from Elie Assis during a round table about this chapter at the CBL.

131 From a source critical perspective, it seems clear that this story originally had nothing to do with Joshua and was placed here by a later editor. During the above-referenced roundtable, I suggested that this story may have originally belonged to a "Phineas cycle" that may have resembled some of the other chieftain cycles, but was split up and spliced into different places. I hope to be able to explore this possibility further in future works.

ample of the teetering power of Joshua in comparison with the priesthood of Elazar and his family in Shilo, during the latter portion of his tenure as leader of Israel.

Joshua's Old Age Exhortation (Ch. 23)

Joshua's old age was already referenced by YHWH in chapter 13, but now it functions as the impetus for a national speech by Joshua. He calls together Israel and all of its leaders to an unspecified location and begins by pointing out his advanced age.

The speech has a dual focus, dealing with both the immediate past and the future. Joshua urges the people to take note of the great success of the conquest and how nothing promised failed to come to pass.[132] Joshua further promises a rosy future, in which the rest of the land that has yet to have been conquered will be taken with ease.

There exists, however, an element of *quid pro quo*: YHWH will only continue to help the Israelites in their conquest, as long as they follow the Torah as commanded by Moses. They must not veer from YHWH or from loyalty to his commandments one iota. Most importantly, they must not mix with the native inhabitants of the land and must never serve their gods. If they do, YHWH will not only discontinue support of the Israelite conquest but will actually kick them out of the land.

This speech functions as a further example of Joshua playing Moses' role. Here Joshua, as an old man, both exhorts the people towards proper adherence to YHWH and his commandments and warns them about the future. This is similar to what Moses (together with Joshua) did at the end of Deuteronomy with the exhortation about Torah and the singing of the *Ha'azinu* song.

Joshua, however, offers a more hopeful message than did Moses. The song in Deuteronomy discusses the definite future rebellion of the Israelites and the harsh punishments that await them. The punishments are described in detail and there seems no realistic hope that they can be escaped. Joshua's speech is more optimistic in that it leaves the punishment as purely in the realm of the

---

132 The language of the speech is so similar to the ending of chapter 21 that it is certain that either one copied the other or they were written by the same hand. See Thomas Römer's discussion of the relationship between chapters 21 and 23: Thomas Römer, "Book-Endings in Joshua and the Question of the So-Called Deuteronomistic History," in *Raising up a Faithful Exegete: Essays in Honor of Richard D. Nelson* (eds. K. L. Noll and Brooks Schramm; Winona Lake: Eisenbrauns, 2010), 87–101.

possible. This may reflect a dichotomy between the images of Moses and Joshua, with the former representing severity and the latter hope.

Joshua's Final Speech (Ch. 24)

Ironically, Joshua's final speech makes no reference to his old age and does not read like the words of a leader contemplating death and the future of his people.[133] Joshua begins his speech with an historical overview going all the way back to the father of the ancestor of the Israelites – Terah, father of Abraham. This odd choice of ancestor (one would have expected Abraham or Jacob) emphasizes the key message of the speech: the Israelites began as worshipers of foreign gods. This point is underlined by the references to Nahor and Esau. They are biologically related to the Israelites, but can hardly be considered YHWH worshipers.

Having established this genealogical overview, Joshua proceeds to offer a summary account of Israel's recent history. He references the plagues and the miraculous escape from Egypt, the wilderness period, the conquest of the Transjordan, the escape from Balaam's curse, the crossing of the Jordan, and the battle with Jericho and the Amorites. The battle, Joshua points out, was not really a battle at all. YHWH sent forth "the wasp," echoing Exodus 23:28 and Deuteronomy 7:20, and the battle was won without the Israelites even lifting a sword. Now, echoing Deuteronomy 6:10 – 11, they are living in houses they did not build and reaping produce they did not grow.

All this was meant as an introduction to Joshua's main point. The Israelites are now settled in the land of the Amorites. Before this they lived in Egypt and even earlier, across the river Euphrates. Now, Joshua claims, the time for a final choice has arrived: what god or gods will the Israelites serve? Will it be YHWH or the gods of the various peoples and places of which the Israelites have been a part? Joshua ends this speech with the dramatic statement that, whatever the Israelites choose, he and his household will serve YHWH.[134]

---

133 From a source critical perspective, I believe that some condensed form of this speech was originally the ending to an account where Joshua "retires" in his prime, like Gideon or Jephthah. By placing it after the speech in chapter 23, the redactor forces the reader to imagine Joshua here as elderly.

134 This is the only reference to Joshua's family in the Bible of which I am aware. This is important to note since the question of whether Joshua had a family becomes a major point of contention between the Rabbis and the Church fathers.

The people respond with a vociferous acceptance of Yhwh as their god, to which Joshua responds with the surprising response that they cannot. Yhwh, he tells them, is a zealous god that will react sternly if abandoned by his followers. The people reiterate that, nevertheless, they will serve Yhwh. Joshua then makes them take a (would-be) oath, calling them witnesses, and they respond that they are witnesses.

This give and take has many unexpected and even astonishing elements. Where did Joshua get the idea that the people have an option whether to choose Yhwh or not? Why once they accept Yhwh does he attempt to talk them out of it? Does Joshua believe that if the Israelites choose not to worship Yhwh at this late stage that Yhwh would not be punitive? He certainly didn't say as much in his previous speech![135]

The key to Joshua's bizarre behavior here seems to be in the "secret knowledge" he possesses: the Israelites have idols. Now that he has gotten them to swear fealty to Yhwh and has warned them that Yhwh will consider any polytheistic behavior to be a form of rebellion, Joshua tells them to remove the idols from their midst. The Israelites agree to this in words reminiscent of their acceptance of Yhwh at Sinai. Joshua then makes a covenant with them, gives them laws, and writes it all down in the Torah of God. He then places a large stone beneath the tree in the Temple of Yhwh, proclaiming that this stone will be a witness to the proceedings. With that, Joshua sends the Israelites home.

The intertextual resonances to other biblical stories in this section are palpable. Specifically, Joshua seems to be playing the role of two other biblical characters, Moses and Jacob. There are a number of parallels to Moses in this account. First, the response of the Israelites to Joshua's command is reminiscent of their words in Exodus 24.

יהושע כד:כד	שמות כד:ג	שמות כד:ז
וַיֹּאמְרוּ הָעָם אֶל יְהוֹשֻׁעַ: "אֶת יְהוָה אֱלֹהֵינוּ נַעֲבֹד וּבְקוֹלוֹ **נִשְׁמָע.**"	וַיָּבֹא מֹשֶׁה וַיְסַפֵּר לָעָם אֵת כָּל דִּבְרֵי יְהוָה וְאֵת כָּל הַמִּשְׁפָּטִים וַיַּעַן כָּל הָעָם קוֹל אֶחָד וַיֹּאמְרוּ: "כָּל הַדְּבָרִים אֲשֶׁר דִּבֶּר יְהוָה נַעֲשֶׂה [וְנִשְׁמָע].[136]"	וַיִּקַּח סֵפֶר הַבְּרִית וַיִּקְרָא בְּאָזְנֵי **הָעָם וַיֹּאמְרוּ:** "כֹּל אֲשֶׁר דִּבֶּר יְהוָה נַעֲשֶׂה **וְנִשְׁמָע.**"

---

135 Again, this discussion is at the level of the redaction and the final product. Most scholars believe that the speeches have their origin in two different sources or at least two different redactional layers. To quote Thomas Römer: "Otherwise one should definitively give up the historical investigation of the Hebrew Bible!" (Römer, *Book-endings*, 91).

136 This term appears in the LXX but not in the MT in this verse. Both versions have this term in verse 7.

Exod 24:7	Exod 24:3	Josh 24:24
He took the book of the covenant and read it before **the people, and they said:** "Everything that Y<small>HWH</small> said we will do and **heed.**"	Moses came and told the people all the words of Y<small>HWH</small> and all the laws, and the **people** responded in one voice **and said:** "All the things Y<small>HWH</small> has said we will do [and **heed**]."	**And the people said** to Joshua: "We will serve Y<small>HWH</small> our god and we will **heed** his voice."

Second, the writing down of an account or a "Torah" is what Moses does a number of times, including in the account of the covenant at Sinai. Third, there is a strong resonance to the Marah story where Moses is said to have given the people of Israel laws.

	Exod 15:25 שמות טו:כה		Josh 24:25 יהושע כד:כה
שָׁם שָׂם לוֹ חֹק וּמִשְׁפָּט	There he placed for him statute and law.	וַיָּשֶׂם לוֹ חֹק וּמִשְׁפָּט בִּשְׁכֶם	And he placed for him statute and law in Shechem.

Fourth, the idea that Joshua is responsible for a covenant seems to belie the Sinai account and Moses' covenant. Is Joshua making an alternative covenant, perhaps one that supersedes the covenant of Moses? Finally, the idea that Joshua wrote an account of these proceedings in the "*Torat Elohim*" strongly implies that this account is part of *the Torah*. In that sense, the final lawgiver and framer of the Torah is actually Joshua and not Moses! Has Joshua now surpassed Moses?

The Jacob parallels are more subtle but hardly less important. The testimony that the rock set up by Joshua is supposed to represent, permanently dividing the Israelites from their former gods across the river, is reminiscent of the account of Jacob and Laban (Gen 31:45 – 54). In that account, a pile of rocks is set up to divide between the place of Laban in Haran and the place of Jacob in Canaan / Transjordan, and each swears in the name of his own god and gives the stone a name in his own language.

Even more striking are the parallels between this speech and the speech Jacob makes after the slaughter of the Shechemites and before his own establishment of the ritual stone in Bet-El.

בראשית לה:ב-ד	Gen 35:2 – 4
וַיֹּאמֶר יַעֲקֹב אֶל בֵּיתוֹ וְאֶל כָּל אֲשֶׁר עִמּוֹ: "**הָסִרוּ אֶת אֱלֹהֵי הַנֵּכָר אֲשֶׁר בְּתֹכְכֶם** וְהִטַּהֲרוּ וְהַחֲלִיפוּ שִׂמְלֹתֵיכֶם. וְנָקוּמָה וְנַעֲלֶה בֵּית אֵל וְאֶעֱשֶׂה שָּׁם מִזְבֵּחַ לָאֵל הָעֹנֶה אֹתִי בְּיוֹם צָרָתִי וַיְהִי עִמָּדִי בַּדֶּרֶךְ אֲשֶׁר הָלָכְתִּי." וַיִּתְּנוּ אֶל יַעֲקֹב אֵת כָּל אֱלֹהֵי הַנֵּכָר אֲשֶׁר בְּיָדָם וְאֶת הַנְּזָמִים אֲשֶׁר בְּאָזְנֵיהֶם וַיִּטְמֹן אֹתָם יַעֲקֹב **תַּחַת הָאֵלָה** אֲשֶׁר עִם שְׁכֶם.	Jacob said to his household, and all that were with him: "**Remove the foreign gods from among you,** purify yourselves, and change your clothing. We will rise and go up to Bet-El, and I will establish an altar there to the god who answers me on the day of my suffering and who was with me on the path that I travelled." Jacob's sons gave him all of the foreign gods that were in their hands, and the rings in their ears, and Jacob buried them **under the oak** which was in Shechem.

יהושע כד:כב-כה	Josh 24:22 – 25
וַיֹּאמֶר יְהוֹשֻׁעַ אֶל הָעָם: "עֵדִים אַתֶּם בָּכֶם כִּי אַתֶּם בְּחַרְתֶּם לָכֶם אֶת יְהוָה לַעֲבֹד אוֹתוֹ." וַיֹּאמְרוּ: "עֵדִים." "וְעַתָּה **הָסִירוּ אֶת אֱלֹהֵי הַנֵּכָר אֲשֶׁר בְּקִרְבְּכֶם** וְהַטּוּ אֶת לְבַבְכֶם אֶל יְהוָה אֱלֹהֵי יִשְׂרָאֵל." וַיֹּאמְרוּ הָעָם אֶל יְהוֹשֻׁעַ: "אֶת יְהוָה אֱלֹהֵינוּ נַעֲבֹד וּבְקוֹלוֹ נִשְׁמָע." וַיִּכְרֹת יְהוֹשֻׁעַ בְּרִית לָעָם בַּיּוֹם הַהוּא וַיָּשֶׂם לוֹ חֹק וּמִשְׁפָּט בִּשְׁכֶם. וַיִּכְתֹּב יְהוֹשֻׁעַ אֶת הַדְּבָרִים הָאֵלֶּה בְּסֵפֶר תּוֹרַת אֱלֹהִים וַיִּקַּח אֶבֶן גְּדוֹלָה וַיְקִימֶהָ שָּׁם **תַּחַת הָאֵלָה** אֲשֶׁר בְּמִקְדַּשׁ יְהוָה.	Joshua said to the people: "You are witnesses that you have chosen YHWH, to serve him." And they said: "We are witnesses." "And now, **remove the foreign gods that are among you** and tilt your hearts to YHWH the God of Israel." The people said to Joshua: "We will serve YHWH our god, and heed his voice." Joshua made a covenant for the nation on that day, and he placed for him statute and law in Shechem. Joshua wrote these words in the scroll of the Torah of God, and took a large stone and set it up there **under the oak** that was in the Temple of YHWH.

Not only does the speech begin with the same exact words, but the final action takes place, ostensibly, under the same exact tree! The stone which will memorialize this final and most binding of covenants will be placed on the same spot under which the idols of the first Israelites were buried. Joshua has not only taken the place of Moses, but he has taken the place of Jacob as well. Joshua ends his career as both lawgiver and patriarch.

Joshua's Death (Ch. 24)

Although Joshua's death is uneventful, the description of it is full of curious and significant details. Joshua dies at the age of 110. This age has a dual significance. First, it is less than Moses' 120 years, a fact which keeps Moses' image as the long-lived father and elder of the nation intact. Second, it is the same age as Joseph was when he died. Joseph is the ancestor of the Ephraim and Manasseh tribes and, therefore, Joshua's ancestor as well.

The connection between Joseph and Joshua is highlighted by the burial notice of Joseph. This notice comes immediately after the death notice of Joshua, although it is hard to believe that the reader is supposed to imagine that they refrained from burying Joseph for the entire tenure of Joshua's leadership. There are a number of reasons the burial notice was postponed until the end of the Joshua account,[137] but one of the effects of this postponement (if not the cause) is to inextricably tie the ancestor Joseph to his eventual successor Joshua.

The burial of Joseph in Shechem, the place where the rift between Jacob and his sons was first opened, is a statement of unity and closure. That this occurred during the golden age of Joshua's unified leadership over the entirety of Israel is only fitting, and underscores Joshua's success. On a more surreal level, David Silber has pointed out that Joshua quite literally fulfills one of Joseph's dreams, since it is to him that the sun and moon eventually "bow."[138]

Joshua is buried in the border of his city, Timnat Serah/Heres, ostensibly by Israel. On one hand, the text describes no large communal mourning as it does for Moses or Jacob. On the other hand, Joshua is granted a different type of legacy in the final verse about him. The reader is told that throughout Joshua's life and the life of the elders that served with Joshua, the people serve YHWH; the covenant was a success, at least during his lifetime and immediately afterwards.

The book ends with two further burials. The first, that of Joseph, was discussed above. The second, and less surprising insofar as placement, is that of Elazar the priest. Although Elazar makes his appearance as Joshua's partner periodically throughout the book of Joshua, his role seems muted.[139] Nevertheless, at times Elazar seems to have sat in the position of seniority, even though at no time is it indicated that he made any actual decisions the way Joshua does. It is,

---

137 Not least as a point of closure with which to end the "Hexateuch."

138 David Silber, *The Joseph Narrative: Reconstruction of a Family* (audio), (New York: Drisha Institute). Silber further argues that if one takes Genesis 15 at its word, the fourth generation (i. e., the generation of Joseph) was supposed to conquer Canaan. With the rift after the defeat of Shechem, this plan was pushed off and the cycle begun again, with Joshua's generation being the next fourth generation.

139 For someone as prominent as he, it is striking that Elazar receives no speaking part in the book, except when issuing a judgment together with Joshua and the elders.

therefore, noteworthy that the death and burial of Elazar, not that of Joshua, ends the book; a nominal leader nominally ends the story.[140]

Postscript (Chs. 1–2:10)

The beginning of Judges can and should be seen as a postscript to the book of Joshua.[141] In this section, various battles led by individual tribes are described, with no mention of a leader. The importance of this narrative structure lies in the fact that without Joshua, the tribes are beginning to fracture and fight as individual units. The golden age of one Israel has ended.[142]

The first and most important tribe in this section is that of Judah. This importance manifests in four ways: they are chosen by YHWH, they fight together with their brother tribe Simeon, they are almost entirely successful in their campaign, and they have two notable leaders, Caleb and Othniel.[143] Additionally, they maintain the treaty with the Kenites, allowing them to conquer the city of Arad for themselves.

Judah's conquests are impressive. Caleb clears the area of giants, and the great city of Bezek with its domineering and torture-obsessed monarch is taken.[144] The great cities of Gaza, Ashkelon, and Ekron are taken, as well as

---

140 The burial notice itself is somewhat odd. He is buried in his son's territory. Since both he and his son are priests, they are not supposed to have territory. Furthermore, if, for some reason, they could have territory, why didn't Elazar get? I suggest that whereas the Phineas traditions may be early, before the solidification of the concept that priest and Levites have no land, the Elazar traditions are late. Phineas may have territory because there is a tradition about the Hill of Phineas, but no such tradition surrounds the later (post-Exilic?) figure of Elazar.

141 I am referring to 1:1aβ-2:10. In my opinion, 1:1aα, is serving in a dual capacity, as it was originally the introduction to the book of Judges proper and was part of verse 2:11.

142 From a source critical perspective, Moshe Weinfeld puts forth a strong argument that this section was originally independent of Joshua and, perhaps, meant as an alternative account to the Joshua conquest tradition. Marc Brettler takes this position in a different and more persuasive direction. He suggests, as I have above, that this section originated as an appendix to Joshua which was later expanded. Eventually, it was moved from being the end of Joshua to the beginning of Judges. He argues that this may have occurred at a time when Joshua and Judges might have been kept on the same scroll. See: Marc Zvi Brettler, "Jud 1,1–2,10: From Appendix to Prologue," *ZAW* 101 (1989): 433–435; Marc Zvi Brettler, *The Book of Judges* (Old Testament Readings; London: Routledge, 2002), ch. 7 "A Conclusion that Became an Introduction," pp. 92–102.

143 This is the same account as that found in Joshua 15.

144 It is virtually impossible that Bezeq was a city of any importance, historically speaking. Thus, it is difficult to ascertain what sparked this tradition. Weinfeld argues that the story must

most of the hill country. The majority of the plains, however, must be left for another time due to the chariots;[145] the same problem the Joseph tribes had even during Joshua's tenure.

The Joseph tribes score a more modest, albeit significant victory as well. They conquer the city of Luz, i.e., Bet El. They do this in a way somewhat reminiscent of Joshua's conquest of Bet El's neighbor, Ai: they employ trickery. They wait for one of the guards to leave the city and force him to reveal the entrance. Having obtained the confession, they go on to conquer the town easily. Despite the token similarity to Joshua's use of trickery at Ai, the story has none of the power of the Ai account, and the Josephite forces pale in comparison to the massive Israelite army once commanded by their fellow tribesman. Splitting into factions has a cost.

Outside of the Judah/Simeon coalition's many successes and the taking of Beit El by the Joseph tribes, the overall picture in this chapter is dismal. The list of failures is long, and no other tribe succeeds in conquering anything. Although there is some overlap with the list of unconquered territory in Joshua, the list here is longer and implicates more tribes.[146]

Judges (parallels)	Joshua (parallels)
פרק א	פרק טו
כא) וְאֶת הַיְבוּסִי יֹשֵׁב יְרוּשָׁלַם לֹא הוֹרִישׁוּ בְּנֵי בֵּנְיָמִן וַיֵּשֶׁב הַיְבוּסִי אֶת בְּנֵי בֵּנְיָמִן בִּירוּשָׁלַם עַד הַיּוֹם הַזֶּה.	סג) וְאֶת הַיְבוּסִי יוֹשְׁבֵי יְרוּשָׁלַם לֹא יָכְלוּ בְּנֵי יְהוּדָה לְהוֹרִישָׁם וַיֵּשֶׁב הַיְבוּסִי אֶת בְּנֵי יְהוּדָה בִּירוּשָׁלַם עַד הַיּוֹם הַזֶּה.
Ch. 1	Ch. 15
[21] But the *Benjaminites* did not drive out the Jebusites who lived in **Jerusalem**; so the Jebusites have lived in Jerusalem among the *Benjaminites* to this day.	[63] But the people of Judah could not drive out the Jebusites, the inhabitants of **Jerusalem**; so the Jebusites live with the people of *Judah* in Jerusalem to this day.
פרק א	פרק טז
כט) וְאֶפְרַיִם לֹא הוֹרִישׁ אֶת הַכְּנַעֲנִי הַיּוֹשֵׁב בְּגָזֶר וַיֵּשֶׁב הַכְּנַעֲנִי בְּקִרְבּוֹ בְּגָזֶר.	י) וְלֹא הוֹרִישׁוּ אֶת הַכְּנַעֲנִי הַיּוֹשֵׁב בְּגָזֶר וַיֵּשֶׁב הַכְּנַעֲנִי בְּקֶרֶב אֶפְרַיִם עַד הַיּוֹם הַזֶּה וַיְהִי לְמַס עֹבֵד.
Ch. 1	Ch. 16
[29] And *Ephraim* did not drive out the Canaanites who lived in **Gezer**; but the Canaanites lived among them in Gezer.	[10] They did not, however, drive out the Canaanites who lived in **Gezer:** so the Canaanites have lived within *Ephraim* to this day but have been made to do forced labor.

---

originally have been about Adoni Tzeddek, king of Jerusalem – a much more prestigious town with a much more formidable monarch.

145 That this claim is totally contradictory to the claim that Judah conquered the Philistine towns is patent; this is the same tension that exists in the book of Joshua proper and represents competing traditions or theological-historical perspectives. The same goes for the numerous contradictory accounts about Jerusalem, a topic too complex to discuss here.

146 The English in the following table is taken from the NRSV.

פרק יז

יא) וַיְהִי לִמְנַשֶּׁה בְּיִשָּׂשכָר וּבְאָשֵׁר בֵּית שְׁאָן וּבְנוֹתֶיהָ וְיִבְלְעָם וּבְנוֹתֶיהָ וְאֶת יֹשְׁבֵי דֹאר וּבְנוֹתֶיהָ וְיֹשְׁבֵי עֵין דֹּר וּבְנוֹתֶיהָ וְיֹשְׁבֵי תַעְנַךְ וּבְנוֹתֶיהָ וְיֹשְׁבֵי מְגִדּוֹ וּבְנוֹתֶיהָ שְׁלֹשֶׁת הַנָּפֶת. יב) וְלֹא יָכְלוּ בְּנֵי מְנַשֶּׁה לְהוֹרִישׁ אֶת הֶעָרִים הָאֵלֶּה וַיּוֹאֶל הַכְּנַעֲנִי לָשֶׁבֶת בָּאָרֶץ הַזֹּאת. יג) וַיְהִי כִּי חָזְקוּ בְּנֵי יִשְׂרָאֵל וַיִּתְּנוּ אֶת הַכְּנַעֲנִי לָמַס וְהוֹרֵשׁ לֹא הוֹרִישׁוֹ.

פרק א

כז) וְלֹא הוֹרִישׁ מְנַשֶּׁה אֶת בֵּית שְׁאָן וְאֶת בְּנוֹתֶיהָ וְאֶת תַּעְנַךְ וְאֶת בְּנֹתֶיהָ וְאֶת יֹשְׁבֵי דוֹר וְאֶת בְּנוֹתֶיהָ וְאֶת יוֹשְׁבֵי יִבְלְעָם וְאֶת בְּנֹתֶיהָ וְאֶת יוֹשְׁבֵי מְגִדּוֹ וְאֶת בְּנוֹתֶיהָ וַיּוֹאֶל הַכְּנַעֲנִי לָשֶׁבֶת בָּאָרֶץ הַזֹּאת. כח) וַיְהִי כִּי חָזַק יִשְׂרָאֵל וַיָּשֶׂם אֶת הַכְּנַעֲנִי לָמַס וְהוֹרֵישׁ לֹא הוֹרִישׁוֹ.

Ch. 1

[27] *Manasseh* did not drive out the inhabitants of **Beth-shean** and its villages, or **Taanach** and its villages, or the inhabitants of **Dor** and its villages,[147] or the inhabitants of **Ibleam** and its villages, or the inhabitants of **Megiddo** and its villages; but the Canaanites continued to live in that land. [28] When Israel grew strong, they put the Canaanites to forced labor, but did not in fact drive them out.

Ch. 17

[11] Within *Issachar* and *Asher*, *Manasseh* had **Beth-shean** and its villages, **Ibleam** and its villages, the inhabitants of **Dor** and its villages, the inhabitants of **En-dor** and its villages, the inhabitants of **Taanach** and its villages, and the inhabitants of **Megiddo** and its villages (the third is Naphath). [12] Yet the *Manassites* could not take possession of those towns; but the Canaanites continued to live in that land. [13] But when the Israelites grew strong, they put the Canaanites to forced labor, but did not utterly drive them out.

שופטים פרק א

ל) וּזְבוּלֻן לֹא הוֹרִישׁ אֶת יוֹשְׁבֵי קִטְרוֹן וְאֶת יוֹשְׁבֵי נַהֲלֹל וַיֵּשֶׁב הַכְּנַעֲנִי בְּקִרְבּוֹ וַיִּהְיוּ לָמַס.

Judges 1 (only)

[30] *Zebulun* did not drive out the inhabitants of **Kitron**, or the inhabitants of **Nahalol**; but the Canaanites lived among them, and became subject to forced labor.

לא) אָשֵׁר לֹא הוֹרִישׁ אֶת יֹשְׁבֵי עַכּוֹ וְאֶת יוֹשְׁבֵי צִידוֹן וְאֶת אַחְלָב וְאֶת אַכְזִיב וְאֶת חֶלְבָּה וְאֶת אֲפִיק וְאֶת רְחֹב. לב) וַיֵּשֶׁב הָאָשֵׁרִי בְּקֶרֶב הַכְּנַעֲנִי יֹשְׁבֵי הָאָרֶץ כִּי לֹא הוֹרִישׁוֹ.

[31] *Asher* did not drive out the inhabitants of **Acco**, or the inhabitants of **Sidon**, or of **Ahlab**, or of **Achzib**, or of **Helbah**, or of **Aphik**, or of **Rehob**; [32] but the Asherites lived among the Canaanites, the inhabitants of the land; for they did not drive them out.

לג) נַפְתָּלִי לֹא הוֹרִישׁ אֶת יֹשְׁבֵי בֵית שֶׁמֶשׁ וְאֶת יֹשְׁבֵי בֵית עֲנָת וַיֵּשֶׁב בְּקֶרֶב הַכְּנַעֲנִי יֹשְׁבֵי הָאָרֶץ וְיֹשְׁבֵי בֵית שֶׁמֶשׁ וּבֵית עֲנָת הָיוּ לָהֶם לָמַס...

[33] *Naphtali* did not drive out the inhabitants of **Beth-shemesh**, or the inhabitants of **Beth-anath**, but lived among the Canaanites, the inhabitants of the land; nevertheless the inhabitants of Beth-shemesh and of Beth-anath became subject to forced labor for them...

---

147 En Dor is missing from this version of the list. The LXX has Balaam (in A) or Balak (in B) here as an added town. I would guess that the former was a corruption/reduplication from Ibleam, and the latter a corruption/adjustment from the former.

^{לה} וַיּוֹאֶל הָאֱמֹרִי לָשֶׁבֶת בְּהַר־חֶרֶס בְּאַיָּלוֹ וּבְשַׁעַלְבִים ‍ ³⁵ The Amorites continued to live in **Har-heres**, וַתִּכְבַּד יַד *בֵּית יוֹסֵף* וַיִּהְיוּ לָמַס. ‍ in **Aijalon**, and in **Shaalbim**, but the hand of the *house of Joseph* rested heavily on them, and they became subject to forced labor.

Following this overall presentation, the reader is left to feel that all of the tribes (other than Judah) are essentially failures when it comes to military conquest. There is no real conquest to speak of after Joshua, except in the south. Even the success of the Joseph tribes in conquering Luz is dampened by the huge list of cities left untouched by Ephraim and Manasseh and the final list of unconquered areas left by the "House of Joseph." The tribes of Zebulun, Asher, Naphtali, and Issachar have no conquests to speak of. The loss of Joshua and the weakness of the divided Israel are palpable.

The final touch of this section, the failure of the house of Joseph in the areas of Heres and Ayalon is the most stunning. The Heres region, probably the area of Joshua's city Timnat Heres,[148] and the place in which his grave resides, is dominated by Canaanites. The Ayalon valley, the very spot over which Joshua stops the sun and moon, is left unmolested by his successors, deemed too powerful to overcome by military force. Truly, the mighty have fallen.

The section ends with a passage that perversely mocks the geography that dominates the latter half of Joshua. The borders of the Amorites are delineated. It is no wonder that the addendum ends with the rebuke of an angel, perhaps the same angel whose revelation to Joshua marks the beginning of the campaign for the Cisjordan.

Tellingly, the angel comes up from Gilgal, Joshua's military center. The angel reminds the people that the deal that YHWH struck with them was that he would support them as long as they, slowly but surely, remove the Canaanites from their midst and destroy their idolatrous centers. However, the Israelites have not done this, but have formed treaties with the natives, violating the terms of their agreement with God. Now, the angel warns, YHWH will no longer remove the Canaanites, but will allow them to become a permanent fixture, constantly testing the Israelites' resolve to worship YHWH exclusively. The legacy of Joshua is now over.

The story ends with the people's response. They weep and call the place Bokhim (crying), and they offer sacrifices to YHWH. This is an appropriate reaction

---

148 Originally suggested by Zechariah Kallai, "The Settlement Tradition of Ephraim: A Historiographical Study," *ZDPV* 102 (1986): 68 – 74. For more details, see: Farber, "Timnat Heres," 301 – 311.

but it has no effect. The Israelites don't have anyone to intercede on their behalf, like Moses or Joshua once did.

Having completed the addendum, the text makes a *Wiederaufnahme* by including Joshua's death notice yet again.[149] Although there are a number of subtle differences between the death account here and that of Joshua 24, there is one that is particularly important for this section.[150] The notice in Joshua 24 ends on a positive note, claiming that throughout his lifetime and even somewhat beyond, the people were loyal to YHWH. Conversely, the notice in Judges ends on a sour note, stating that the next generation, not having seen the great works of Joshua and YHWH, "did not know him."

This is reminiscent of the generation of Egyptians in the beginning of Exodus who "did not know Joseph." It is an ironic ending. The Israelites left Egypt only to be established in the Cisjordan and become themselves just like their former masters. Joshua, like Joseph, was successful in his own time, but within a generation of their deaths, they were no longer known and all was lost.

Other References to Joshua

Judges (Ch. 2:21, 23)

In the primary history, there are only two further references to Joshua. Judges 2 (verses 21 and 23) refers to the Canaanites whom Joshua had not succeeded in conquering before his death. Although this reference is repeated here twice, each has a slightly different nuance.

Verse 21 simply states that since the Israelites have now abandoned YHWH, YHWH will abandon them and no longer assist in their conquest of the nations that Joshua left behind. The implication here is that Joshua just happens to have missed these people. Conquest is a slow business, and age overtakes him before all is complete.

---

149 Rudolf Smend seems to have been the first to point out that this section functions as a resumptive repetition to the end of Joshua. See: Smend, "Das Gesetz," 506.
150 For a full discussion of the many differences between the two accounts and how each fits into the context in which it is found, see Ed Noort, "Josua 24,28 – 31, Richter 2, 6 – 9 und das Josuagrab: Gedanken zu einem Straßenschild," *Biblische Welten: Festschrift für Martin Metzger zu seinem 65. Geburtstag* (ed. Wolfgang Zwickel; OBO 123; Freiburg: Universitätsverlag, 1992), 109 – 130.

Verses 22 and 23, however, offer a different, "behind the scenes" understanding of events.[151] According to these verses, Joshua's lack of success here is actually precipitated by YHWH. YHWH understands that the people's loyalty is ephemeral, so he specifically desires to keep Canaanites in the land in order to test each and every generation and see whether they will worship him exclusively or not. Hence, Joshua, unbeknownst to himself, actually fulfills YHWH's "real plan" correctly.

1 Kings (Ch. 16:34)

In Joshua 6:26, Joshua ends the conquest of Jericho with a curse on any who would rebuild it. In 1 Kings 16:34, the curse comes to fruition. This text tells of the tragic death of Hiel's sons Abiram and Segub, as a result of his rebuilding of Jericho. There is one key difference, however, between the description of the curse and the description of its fulfillment. Joshua 6:26 describes the curse as coming spontaneously from Joshua at the end of the battle. The reader may fairly assume that YHWH "backs the curse," but the text presents it as Joshua's idea. Kings, however, presents the curse as YHWH's, albeit stated by the prophet Joshua. This paints Joshua in the colors of the messenger prophet, a light in which he is never seen anywhere else.[152]

1 Chronicles (Ch. 7:27)

The book of Chronicles begins its narrative with the death of Saul and, as such, it is not surprising that no account of Joshua features in the book. Nevertheless, it is worth noting that the name Moses appears 18 times in the book whereas the name of Joshua appears only once. Moreover, whereas references to Moses are made throughout the narrative sections, Joshua is only referenced in the genealogical section.

1 Chronicles 7:27 mentions Joshua in the Ephraim genealogy as the son of Nun, with nothing whatsoever added to describe his importance in Israelite history. One would have expected at least a note about the character's importance. One wonders what is behind this apparently conscious attempt to, on one hand,

---

151 These two verses seem to be a later gloss on verse 21, perhaps with the explicit intention of exonerating Joshua from any perceived sloppiness or lack of success.
152 The Qumran work, *Apocryphon of Joshua*, will pick up on this image and run with it. See chapter 3 for more discussion of this.

place Joshua in his biological context in Israelite genealogy, but on the other hand, strip him of his mnemohistorical and religious position.

Nehemiah (Ch. 8:17)

Nehemiah 8:17 refers to Joshua as the last leader under whom the people kept the holiday of Sukkot properly. This claim makes an interesting contrast to the parallel claim in Kings about the lack of proper observance of Passover until the time of Josiah. There, the previous proper keeping of Passover was attributed by Kings to "the Judges" and by Chronicles to Samuel (2 Kings 23:22; 2 Chronicles 35:18).

The contrast is particularly noteworthy since the book of Joshua specifically references his observance of Passover, but makes no mention of his observance of Sukkot. This brings up the possibility that either more traditions existed about Joshua than were written in the primary history, or that Joshua and his period were a sort of catch-all for the author of Nehemiah, representing "the good old days" when observance of Torah was done properly. This would be in line with Joshua's image as an exemplar of Torah.[153]

Summary

The biblical texts contain a number of images of Joshua.[154] The first image of Joshua encountered (#1),[155] and the one that persists through much of the

---

153 It is worth noting that in the Damascus Document (5) there is an even more extreme claim of this nature, in which the author states that, from the time of Joshua and Elazar until Zaddok, the Torah itself was not available to be read and that even someone like King David cannot be held responsible for his sins for this reason. This connection was noted by Barthelot, "Joshua in Jewish Sources," 98–99.

154 Literary readers of the Bible debate whether Joshua can be described as a "real" or "complex" literary character. Some consider him to be two-dimensional. Stephen Chapman actually calls him "a cardboard cut-out." See: Stephen B. Chapman, "Joshua Son of Nun: Presentation of a Prophet," in *Thus Says the Lord: Essays on the Former and Latter Prophets in Honor of Robert R. Wilson* (eds. John J. Ahn and Stephen L. Cook; Library of Hebrew Bible/Old Testament Studies 502; New York: T&T Clark, 2009), 13–26 [13]. (See n. 3 for a list of other scholars who think this way.) Elie Assis, at the end of his article on Joshua as a leader, suggests this bold conclusion:

...It is almost impossible to reconstruct Joshua's character, even though he is present in the whole book of Joshua, and in fact, he is the only character portrayed across the entire book.

book of Joshua, is Joshua the warrior. In his younger years he defeats Amalek and in his later career he conquers the Promised Land. The second image encountered (#2) is that of Moses' attendant. This image extends into Joshua's later years, where he becomes the successor of Moses (#4). The text relates these two images, putting them on a continuum. Moses grooms Joshua for leadership in the Pentateuch account, and in the opening of the book of Joshua, he is repeatedly addressed as Moses' replacement and referred to as Moses' attendant. A related image (#3), one that appears only in the Pentateuch, is Joshua the loyal scout. This image combines elements of the first two images, as he is both fearless and faithful.

Joshua is also presented as an administrator (#5), and, when being presented as such, he is often part of a "team" or a partnership of sorts with Elazar the priest and the Elders. Joshua is also presented, implicitly and explicitly, as an elder statesman (#10). Part of this simply has to do with age, since, at a certain point in his career, he is presented as being old and in charge, which makes him an elder statesman. This is especially true in his parting speeches. However, there are other stories that simply paint him as the leader, such as the story of the Joseph tribes requesting aid in settling their territory or of Caleb requesting a land-grant.

The next four images of Joshua, although related to the first five, are somewhat different in character. In the opening of Joshua, YHWH emphasizes in a preliminary communication to him that he must study Torah day and night. This is

---

It seems that the author deliberately did not disclose adequate information regarding his personality, so that the only conclusion the reader may reach regarding his character is his resemblance to Moses (Assis, "Divine", 41).

Bracketing Assis' implied premise, that the author of the Book of Joshua knows the "historical" Joshua personally—a premise I cannot consider valid for many reasons—his analysis of the presentation of Joshua appears too one-sided. Joshua is certainly "Moses-like" but he is not purely Moses-like. Hall also critiques Assis' view and writes:

The numerous divergences between the characters of Moses and Joshua... render the description of Joshua as a "second Moses" insufficient, if not inaccurate. The similarity to Moses is significant but not definitive... Joshua's character is developed with more complexity than Assis allows *(Hall,* Conquering, *198)*.

Hall's conclusion is borne out, I believe, by the analysis in this chapter. For another analysis of Joshua's character in the Bible which understands him as complex and different than Moses, see: Hayyim Angel, "Moonlit Leadership: A Midrashic Reading of Joshua's Success," *JBQ* 37.3 (2009): 144–152.

155 The numbering system here reflects nothing more than the order in which I encountered these images in my analysis and noted them. They are not meant to imply a ranking or anything else.

the image of Joshua as a Torah scholar (#6). This bears some relationship to Joshua as the attendant spending all his days in the Tent of Meeting with YHWH, and should also be seen as related to the periodic assertions throughout the book of Joshua that he follows the laws of Moses properly. Another picture of Joshua is as a miracle worker (#7). Although he presides over miracles at the Jordan River and Jericho, he really comes into his own at the battle of Bet Horon, where the sun and moon stop on his command.

Additionally, Joshua takes on the role of religious leader or figure (#8). Hints of this can already be seen in the images of Joshua as staying in the Tent of Meeting and as a Torah scholar. However, he manifests as a religious leader when he circumcises the people and leads the people in the celebration of Passover. Most obviously, as part of his role as religious leader, he establishes the altar on Mount Ebal and, at the end of his tenure, in a very Mosaic moment, he renews the covenant with Israel, gives laws, writes the Torah, and places a stone before the Temple of YHWH. In addition, in a very brief incident, first referenced as a curse in the book of Joshua but later recast as a prophecy in the Book of Kings, Joshua fulfills the role of classic prophet (#9) by predicting, based on the words of YHWH, the demise of the rebuilder of Jericho.

Finally, there are two images that may be described as personality traits, and contradictory ones at that. The first is Joshua as fearful of being a leader (#11). This is most apparent in the end of Deuteronomy and the beginning of the Book of Joshua, where the refrain "be strong and brave" is often repeated, giving the impression that Joshua was petrified. The image returns after the defeat at the Ai, where Joshua panics and suggests the possibility of everyone living in the Transjordan.

The second is that of Joshua as a confident leader (#12). One can see glimpses of this confidence in his handling of the spies, his quick defense of Gibeon, and his lightening attack on the northern forces, despite their enormous size. The clearest example of this trait is when Joshua stands upon the necks of the enemy kings and repeats the "be strong and brave" refrain to his soldiers. This same confidence is further manifest in his negotiations over the covenant, when he tells the Israelites what he will do regardless of them.

A character with as many roles as Joshua will inevitably have many images, and there is, admittedly, a certain amount of subjectivity in my choice of 12 images, a number that could have been shrunk or expanded, depending upon how broadly or narrowly I chose to understand the term "image." Nevertheless, I offer my analysis and guided reading with a particular goal in mind. The images isolated in this chapter demonstrate a number of discontinuities in Joshua's character. He is both martial and a contemplative tent-dweller. He is both nervous and brave. He is a student of Moses and a leader in his own right. He is the sole commander of the Israelites and part of an administrative team of leaders.

Analyzing the text synchronically, as if presented by one author, the discontinuities in Joshua's character demonstrate that Joshua grows and changes over time and that his character is a complex one. But isolating these discontinuities also facilitates diachronic readings of Joshua, and it does so in two complementary but distinct ways.

First, it isolates real discontinuities in his character that open the door to any understanding of how his character developed. Using tradition-historical as well as source and redaction-critical approaches, these discontinuities will be explored and some suggestions regarding what they imply about the social realities and time and place of their formation will be analyzed and discussed.

Second, these discontinuities were picked up by later interpreters of Joshua and used to facilitate a rereading of his story in ways relevant to their own societies, each with its unique combination of religious or cultural identity needs. These later interpretations of Joshua and their implications about the various societies in which they evolved will be the subject of the last four chapters of this book.

Admittedly, these two projects—exploring the origins of Joshua in the Bible and tracing his later reception—differ in many ways. Yet I hope to demonstrate that the process of character formation in literature and cultural memory that develops over time is best understood linearly, from pre-biblical to post-biblical. The biblical text itself functions as a useful snapshot, orienting the discussion. Nevertheless, the Bible as it exists in its final form is neither a firm beginning nor a firm ending to the study of any character contained in it.

Addendum – Images of Joshua in List Form

1. Warrior
2. Moses' Attendant
3. Loyal Scout
4. Moses' Successor
5. Part of the Elazar-Joshua Administrative Team
6. Torah Scholar
7. Miracle Worker
8. Religious Leader
9. Prophet/Predictor (or Curser) of Future
10. Elder Statesman
11. Fearful Leader
12. Confident Leader

Chapter 2 – Pre-Biblical Joshua(s)

As described in the first chapter, there are a number of discontinuities in the presentation of Joshua, which seem to portray him in different modes. Associating each image with specific interest groups or periods would be methodologically problematic, since this would allow for no natural literary development of the character. Nonetheless, if one takes a step back from the details and looks at the overall picture, certain dominant features of Joshua's presentation in the biblical text stand out as distinct.

First, Joshua is a warrior. This is a persistent image, from his introduction as the general who fights off the Amalekites, to the conquest account that dominates the book of Joshua.

Second, Joshua is the leader of Israel. This is true both when he is conquering the land in the first part of the book and when he is dividing the land in the second part of the book. His elder-statesman status is clearly marked by his two parting speeches to Israel before his death. Although sometimes Joshua is pictured as being part of a team, this appears to be a variation on the theme of Joshua as leader.

Third, Joshua is the student and successor of Moses. This is expressed in a myriad of ways. In the Pentateuch, this is the main image of Joshua, but even in the book of Joshua, this image finds expression, with Joshua's fealty to Torah framed as fealty to the Torah of Moses and the Law of Moses. Additionally, many of Joshua's acts as leader are reminiscent of Moses, such as the sending of spies and the offering of the Paschal sacrifice.

Fourth, Joshua is a miracle worker. Although some of the miracles are reminiscent of Moses', such as the splitting of the Jordon and the rain of hailstones on the enemy, others are uniquely Joshua's, such as Jericho's walls coming down and, most importantly, the stopping of the sun.

Fifth, Joshua is a religious figure. In his youth he stays in the tent of Yhwh. When he takes over leadership, he is told by Yhwh to learn Torah day and night. Even as the conqueror of the Promised Land, Joshua sets up stones and altars all around Israel and finishes his career with a covenant ceremony.

Two further images, Joshua the loyal scout and Joshua the future-predicting prophet, seem to be outliers, as each occurs in one context and in no other place.

Joshua's Place in the Primary History

Although the above-referenced images do not necessarily contradict one another, there are a number of reasons to see some tension in the presentation. First, and most importantly there is the discontinuity of the narrative in the Primary History. Joshua begins out of nowhere as a warrior in Exodus. Immediately afterwards, he becomes a young attendant of Moses. Joshua conquers all of Israel in a lightning campaign but later advises the Joseph tribes to cut down trees to avoid battle with Canaanite chariots. He requests to settle "his city," Timnat Heres, about which the reader knows nothing. Sometimes Joshua is the supreme leader of Israel, and sometimes he is Elazar's partner. In short, the "story" of Joshua appears to be a combination of fragments—or, more probably, one or two major storylines with a number of smaller fragments and supplements added on. These fragments and contradictory storylines would not cohere if the editorial framework didn't attempt to make them cohere by force.[156]

Although one reads the Primary History from beginning to end—from Genesis to Kings—nevertheless, historiography, especially mnemohistoriography, probably flows in the opposite direction. An author knows about his or her own time and is familiar with contemporary local politics and traditions. An author would not necessarily have the same information about traditions or facts from previous eras. Even if one did, there would often have been a number of traditions regarding the past, even among the author's own constituency. Moreover, whether writing about the present or the past, any author or redactor brings in his or her own overall perspective on a given subject as well.

---

[156] I am reminded of the oft repeated mantra of Baruch Schwartz, that the beginning of source criticism lies in the fact that the storyline as presented is virtually unreadable. Unfortunately, as stated in the introduction, it is beyond the scope of this chapter to offer a full attempt to reconstruct the steps with which the book of Joshua was constructed, although I will offer some suggestions when this sheds light on the construction of his image or character. Some works that attempt to trace the development of the Book of Joshua include: Ed Noort, *Das Buch Josua: Forschungsgeschichte und Problemfelder* (Erträge der Forschung 292; Darmstadt: Wissenschaftliche Buchgasellschaft, 1998), 59–113; Klaus Bieberstein, *Josua—Jordan—Jericho: Archäologie, Geschichte und Theologie der Landnahmeerzählungen Josua 1–6* (OBO 143; Freiburg: Universitätsverlag, 1995); Knauf, *Josua*, 16–22; Kratz, *Composition*, 153–221; Römer, "Book-endings," 87–101; Erhard Blum, "Überlegungen zur Kompositionsgeschichte des Josuabuches," in *The Book of Joshua* (ed. Ed Noort; BETL 250 – Proceedings of the CBL; Leuven: Leuven University Press, 2010), 137–157. For a different approach to the question, see Pekka M. A. Pitkänen, *Joshua* (Apollos Old Testament Commentary 6; Nottingham: InterVarsity Press, 2010).

In the case of the primary history, at least the final form of it, the redactor[157] is a Judahite. What he knows is that his own small country has been ravaged by the Babylonians and the Temple of YHWH destroyed. He knows that the kingdom of Israel, his neighbor to the north, suffered a similar fate a century earlier. The work he redacts, containing Genesis/Exodus-Kings, tells the story that leads to this destruction.[158] For the final editor of the Primary History, Israel is a collection of tribes, all of which are the descendants of one man by that name. They were taken out of Egypt by YHWH and brought to the Promised Land. This was accomplished first by Moses, who led them out of Egypt and through the wilderness, and then by Joshua, who led them in the conquest of the land. After Joshua, many local leaders tried to lead Israel but their rule was intermittent; eventually chaos reigned, leading to the establishment of the monarchy. In this schematic, Judah is a part of Israel, and the explanation for the creation of two countries is that the North rebelled at one point against the (legitimate) Judahite King of Israel and established its own rogue country.

The Book of Judges as a Bridge

Looking at this overall picture in an attempt to understand how it was constructed, one element stands out as key: the tension between the Joshua story and the book of Judges. Israel goes from being a unified group under Joshua to a haphazard collection of tribes in the Judges period and back to a unified group again

---

157 I am using the singular here for convenience, although it is likely that there were many redactors.

158 The Primary History, as has been pointed out by many, contains at least two origin stories for Israel-Judah. One story, favored by Exodus, is that the Israelites were slaves in Egypt and YHWH, through his servant Moses, took them out and brought them to the Promised Land. The other story is that of the Patriarchs, who lived in Canaan and were promised that their descendants would eventually inherit it. (Each of these stories has narrative tensions within it and can be reasonably subdivided into earlier traditions that undergird them.) These accounts are in tension with each other, something the final redactor has attempted to smooth over by associating the "ancestors" of Exodus-Deuteronomy with the "patriarchs" of Genesis. For more on this see: Konrad Schmid, *Genesis and the Moses Story: Israel's Dual Origins in the Hebrew Bible* (trans. James Nogalski; Sifrut: Literature and Theology of the Hebrew Bible 3; Winona Lake: Eisenbrauns, 2010); Jan Christian Gertz, "The Literary Connection between the Books of Genesis and Exodus," in *A Farewell to the Yahwist? The Composition of the Pentateuch in Recent European Interpretation* (ed. Thomas B. Dozeman and Konrad Schmid; SBLSymS 34; Atlanta: SBL, 2006), 73–87; Thomas Römer, *Israels Väter: Untersuchungen zur Väterthematik im Deuteronomium und in der Deuteronomistischen Tradition* (OBO 99; Freiberg: Universitätsverlag, 1990); Thomas Römer, "The Exodus in the Book of Genesis," *SEA* 75 (2010): 1–20.

under Samuel, Saul, and David. The editorial framing implies a confederation of the tribes under many of the Judges, but this framing feels artificial and is not reflected in the narrative details of the accounts.

The Book of Judges appears to be based on traditions about a number of charismatic leaders ruling in different areas of the Cisjordan and Transjordan. These leaders were "remembered" among the tribes that confederated—or would eventually confederate—as Israel. A later editor put these traditions together in an attempt to make all the stories cohere.[159] To do so, he made each tribal leader into a leader of all Israel, and ordered the chieftains consecutively.

A desire to connect a constructed mythic past with the vague historiographical recollections of pre-monarchic days drives this revision.[160] The patriarchs and the Exodus represent Israel's mythic past. Israel descends from the patriarch of that name and each tribe, according to this construction, represents one of the patriarch's sons. These Children of Israel end up in Egypt, where YHWH and his servant Moses free them from bondage. YHWH then brings them to the land from

---

159 The idea that the "judges" were once independent local heroes, without reference to any pan-Israelite identity claims or central government in pre-monarchic times, is supported by a number of scholars. What remains controversial is whether any collection of these heroes existed before the Deuteronomistic History which could have served as the core of the book of Judges used by the redactor. (Whether Judges is in fact Deuteronomistic, as Noth originally suggested, or whether it should be seen as a post-Deuteronomistic insertion between Joshua and Samuel, as Knauf argues in his commentary, is beyond the scope of this discussion.) Certain scholars believe that there is an earlier core collection behind the book of Judges. See, for example: Wolfgang Richter, *Traditionsgeschichtliche Untersuchungen zum Richterbuch* (BBB 18; Bonn: Hanstein, 1963), and Alexander Rofé, "Ephraimite versus Deuteronomistic History," in *Reconsidering Israel and Judah: Recent Studies on the Deuteronomistic History* (ed. Gary N. Knoppers and J.G. McConville; Winona Lake: Eisenbrauns, 2000), 462–474. The former argues for a core "Retterbuch" from 3–9, the latter for a much broader Ephraimite History beginning with Josh 24. See also: Thomas Römer, *The So-Called Deuteronomistic History: A Sociological, Historical and Literary Introduction* (London: T&T Clark, 2007), 90–91, and Konrad Schmid, *The Old Testament: A Literary History* (trans. Linda M. Maloney; Minneapolis: Fortress Press, 2012), 78–79. However, following Uwe Becker's monograph, which demonstrated that once the Deuteronomistic redaction is removed, no editorial framework remains, many scholars prefer to see these early hero stories as having been isolated. See: Uwe Becker, *Richterzeit und Königtum: Redactionsgeschichtliche Studien zum Richterbuch* (BZAW 192; Berlin: De Gruyter, 1990). See also: Kratz, *Composition*, 202–210. Scholars in this camp see the creation of the Book of Judges as a way of bridging two separate narrative blocks, that of the Hexateuch and that of Samuel-Kings, by creating a post-conquest pre-monarachic period. Broadly speaking, my overall understanding of the formation of the Book of Judges fits best with this latter model.

160 The accounts of these heroes need not have actually originated in pre-monarchic days. Only the fact the historiographers perceive the accounts as being descriptions of the pre-monrachic reality is significant.

which their ancestors hailed, and they conquer it under the leadership of Joshua. This is the schematic history found in the Hexateuch.

To make an Israelite historiography cohere, an editor wishing to combine the Hexateuch with Samuel-Kings must be able to combine the story of a people that conquered the land as one group with the story of the development of the monarchy from a disconnected and subjugated local population. In order to do that, the historiographer must explain why the period of the monarchy took so long to create. How did such a powerful conquering group become so helpless and disorganized? One can hardly argue that it took a while for Israel as a whole to coalesce if one simultaneously maintains that the nation, born of one man and forged at Sinai, entered the Promised Land in a unified conquest.

This seems to be the purpose of the end of the book of Judges and the beginning of Samuel. The former describes a civil war and uses the refrain "in those days there was no king in Israel and each man would do as he pleased." The latter describes a corrupt priesthood and the partial loss of sovereignty to the Philistines. Each of the above seems to be an explanation for the necessity of kingship; the people fell into anarchy causing both moral and political upheaval that could only be solved by the appointment of a king.

The leaders in the first section of the book of Judges do not create dynasties. For anyone attempting to tell their stories in the framework of Israelite historiography, the "fact" that none of these leaders established dynasties requires explanation. In order to avoid a claim against these revered heroes of the past similar to the claim against the Benjaminites and the sons of Eli,[161] the book of Judges offers a framing to the hero stories that makes each hero a leader of all Israel. However, there is still an overall implication in the book about the military weakness of Israel in this period. In order to explain this weakness, the book includes an introduction in chapter 2, where Israel is described as sinning and the cycle of stories to come is described as due to YHWH's punishing Israel and then sending the various heroic leaders to save them from disaster. The Sin causes YHWH to abandon his people, which makes them militarily weak and in need of saviors—hence the judges. Eventually the military collapse is so great they clamor for a king, and this begins the monarchic period.

---

161 The former are painted as violent rapists (Judg 19–21) and the latter as abusers of power (1 Sam. 3).

Constructing Joshua

The Joshua story forms the end of the "primordial" period of Israelite history, which describes how the ancestors make their way into the land and conquer it. The question is: what were the raw materials from which the Joshua tradition was constructed, and what were the main stages of its development from its earliest form to its full iteration in the Primary History? Unfortunately, in this book I will not be able to offer an exact and full source and redaction critical analysis of Joshua (including the discussion of former research or other hypotheses.) Such a project would require a book-length treatment itself. Instead, I will concentrate on highlighting text fragments and motifs, offer some general speculation on older and younger motifs, and suggest an overall developmental arc. Additionally, I will try to see which motifs play or build off each other, since this inner-biblical phenomenon marks the beginning of Joshua's reception, the theme of this monograph.

To my mind, the oldest Joshua motif is that of a local warrior or leader, similar to the other ancient Israelite chieftains like Gideon or Jephthah.[162] The earliest Joshua traditions, I believe, surround the area of his burial, and, perhaps, an early version of the battle at Bet Horon.[163] From this seed, I see three overall stages of development. First, with the development of a "national" Israelite consciousness, Joshua the Josephite or Ephraimite warrior becomes Joshua the leader of Israel and conqueror of the land. Second, as the Israelite-Judahite mnemo-history consolidates around a Moses and exodus story, the story of Joshua the Israelite conqueror begins to take on a Mosaic hue. The two stories eventually merge, with Joshua cast as Moses' apprentice and successor. Third, as occurred with all stories found in the Primary History, the Joshua story was subject to heavy Deuteronomistic and Priestly revisions; such revisions affect Joshua's image as well as the storyline.

Each of these stages leaves a trace in the biblical records, although sometimes they are apparent only in fragments of text or in editorial layers. In this

---

162 I am certainly not the first to propose this, but a full bibliography of theories of Joshua's development would take pages. My own thinking draws heavily on that of Moshe Weinfeld, who wrote on this subject in a number of venues. His most developed thinking on the subject can be found in his book, *The Promise of the Land: The Inheritance of the Land of Canaan by the Israelites* (Berkeley: University of California Press, 1993). See also Nadav Na'aman's chapter "The 'Conquest of Canaan' in the Book of Joshua and in History," in *From Nomadism to Monarchy: Archaeological and Historical Aspects of Early Israel* (eds. Israel Finkelstein and Nadav Na'aman; Jerusalem: Yad Itzhak ben Zvi, 1994).
163 I make this argument in detail in Farber, "Timnat Heres."

chapter, I will outline the proposed mnemohistorical schematic and highlight the key pieces of evidence for it. The goals of this diachronic study are both to explain the various complexities and inconsistencies in the presentation of Joshua in the biblical text and to draw attention to the various potential "Joshuas" that post-biblical authors had at their disposal with which to work. As will be argued in the conclusion, a study of the reception history of Joshua demonstrates that although the biblical authors attempt to create a tapestry that hangs together, later authors often see the seams and know how to unravel it for their own purposes.

Addendum – Rofé and the Development of Joshua

Before continuing on to offer my own proposed schematic, it seems best to describe an alternative model of development, that of Alexander Rofé, which is popular in current Israeli scholarship and with which my work is in conversation.[164] I will outline his argument here and explain where my schematic differs from his.

Methodologically, much of my work in this chapter is inspired by Rofé and his redaction-critical and tradition-historical methodology, evidenced in his many books and articles, including his programmatic article on Joshua (referenced in the introduction to this book.) Also, I am in agreement with Rofé on some key points. The first part of his article[165] focuses on three different images of Joshua, which Rofé traces to the Deuteronomist, the Priestly school (whether P or H is unimportant for now), and what he calls the Ephraimite History. All of this section I am in agreement with and will reference Rofé's article in the relevant sections of this chapter.

The second part of the Rofé's article is, to my mind, the most important. In this section, Rofé argues that the combination of Joshua and Moses was a secondary development and strongly affected the description of his character in the Bible. Furthermore, Rofé believes that he can trace an independent Exodus tradition that had only Joshua. Although this last point may be too much of a stretch, I will argue in this chapter that Rofé is fundamentally correct about this independent Joshua and the influence of the Moses tradition upon him,

---

164 Rofé, "Joshua," 333–364.
165 I am dividing the article thematically into three main points; the article actually has 8 sections.

which eventually led to the combination of the two characters' stories into one timeline.

However, where I disagree with Rofé is in the third and final part of his article. In this section, Rofé speculates about the earliest layers of the Joshua tradition and argues that Joshua, in fact, begins as a prophetic figure with supernatural powers. To ground this claim, Rofé refers to a number of Joshua's acts which seem to be magical in nature. Joshua curses the rebuilder of Jericho, he tells the sun and moon to stop and they stop, he curses the people of Gibeon, he takes down the walls of Jericho, and he holds out his spear towards Ai during the conquest. All of these acts imply a man with supernatural powers whose words have real effect in the world.

Although I certainly agree with Rofé that these acts imply that Joshua was seen as a man with magical power derived from Yhwh, nevertheless, I remain unconvinced that this represents the earliest stratum of the Joshua tradition. Rather, like Weinfeld, I tend to see the settlement and battle traditions as older and more primary to Joshua.[166]

As stated above, I believe that the earliest Joshua traditions are connected with his place of burial, Timnat Heres,[167] and, therefore, I will begin with this.

Caveat

My goal in this argument is to establish the earliest *tradition* about Joshua. I make no claim about whether there ever was a historical Joshua and if so what he did. My own speculation is that there probably was a local warrior chieftain of this name upon which the larger mnemohistorical narrative has been built, but this is only an educated guess. To quote Levenson, in his discussion of the possibility of a "historical" Abraham:

> ...even if Abraham was a "real" individual, he seems to have left a vastly smaller impression on his contemporaries than the ongoing traditions of the Jews, Christains, and Muslims (including biblical traditions) later imagined (Levenson, *Inheriting Abraham*, 13).

---

166 Some of Joshua's magical acts, like the holding out the spear at the Ai or the splitting of the Jordan River, seem to have been designed to mimic those of Moses.
167 In my article on Timnat Heres, I deal with the problem of the name and argue that the original name is probably Timnat Heres because the region in which the town is situated was called Har Heres. For an alternative view, defending Timnat Serah as the name, see Ed Noort, "Josua 24," 109–130.

This statement applies to Joshua as well.

The Conqueror of the Ḥeres Region

In the final versions of the biblical texts, Joshua is depicted as the leader of all Israel who guides the children of Israel across the Jordan, conquers the entire land of Canaan, and divides up the territory among the tribes.[168] The account of "Joshua's city" is conspicuous for how poorly it fits into this context.

Joshua's Landgrant

In Joshua 19:49–50, the text states:

⁽מט⁾ וַיְכַלּוּ לִנְחֹל אֶת הָאָרֶץ לִגְבוּלֹתֶיהָ;	[49] And they finished settling the land in all its
וַיִּתְּנוּ בְנֵי יִשְׂרָאֵל נַחֲלָה לִיהוֹשֻׁעַ בִּן נוּן בְּתוֹכָם.	boundaries, and the children of Israel gave Joshua bin Nun a settlement among them.
⁽נ⁾ עַל פִּי יְהוָה נָתְנוּ לוֹ אֶת הָעִיר אֲשֶׁר שָׁאָל – אֶת תִּמְנַת	[50] By the word of Yʜwʜ they gave him the city
סֶרַח בְּהַר אֶפְרָיִם. וַיִּבְנֶה אֶת הָעִיר וַיֵּשֶׁב בָּהּ.	which he requested, Timnat Serah, in Mount Ephraim, and he built the city and dwelt there.

According to verse 50, Joshua asks the Israelites for the city of Timnat Serah and is granted his request by oracle. Who receives and communicates said oracle is unspecified. Up until this point, it had been Joshua doing the division of land. Now, all of a sudden, the Israelites "graciously" decide to give Joshua some land so that he can settle among them!

These verses appear to have been added into the tribal inheritance section.[169] Nevertheless, this does *not* mean that the tradition itself is late. In this case, the opposite seems more likely, i.e. that this is an earlier tradition which the redactor has worked into the framework of the tribal inheritance section of Joshua. Moshe Weinfeld has made the case for the early nature of this

---

168 I delivered a version of this section as a paper in the Colloquium Biblicum Lovaniense LIX – The Book of Joshua and the Land of Israel that was subsequently published in the conference volume. See: Farber, "Timnat Heres," 301–311.

169 Auld makes a similar suggestion; see: A. Graeme Auld, *Joshua, Moses and the Land: Tetrateuch-Pentateuch-Hexateuch in a Generation since 1938* (Edinburgh: T&T Clark, 1980), 107.

account.[170] He argues that the use of the terms ויבן (and he built) and וישב (and he settled) are characteristic of the early versions of settlement stories.[171]

In terms of narrative logic, this account fits well into the traditions about Joshua and Caleb, the dual heroes of the (late) priestly version of the scout story.[172] Nevertheless, it reflects an earlier stage of that tradition, one in which Joshua and Caleb are local heroes, unconnected to the wilderness story.[173]

In Numbers 14:30, God promises to give Caleb and Joshua a place to dwell in Canaan. This promise comes at a late stage in the development of the scout story and the Pentateuch, since it solves the problem of how Joshua and Caleb survive the wandering period and make it into Israel. This problem only arises once the two local heroes have been attached to the story of Moses and the wilderness wandering. The two stories were probably earlier independent accouts; Joshua and Caleb were both independent local heros/legends, and the scouts were a nameless and numberless group who speak against the land and are

---

170 Moshe Weinfeld, "Historical Facts behind the Israelite Settlement Plan," *VT* 38.3 (1988): 324–332; "The Pattern of Israelite Settlement in Canaan," in *Congress Volume: Jerusalem 1986* (ed. André Lemaire; VTSup 40, 1988), 270–283.

171 Weinfeld, "Historical," 330; Weinfeld, *Pattern*, 278–279. However, see Ahituv's comments *ad loc.* for an alternative view. Shmuel Ahituv, *Joshua: A Commentary* (*Mikra LeYisrael*; Tel Aviv: Am Oved, 1995), 325 [Hebrew].

172 Richard Hess makes a similar observation, but concentrates on the literary aspect of the placement of the accounts in Joshua itself. Richard Hess, *Joshua: An Introduction & Commentary* (Tyndale Old Testament Commentators; Leicester, England, Inter-Varsity Press, 1996), 276.

173 A discussion of the nature of P and its many layers is far beyond the scope of this chapter. The idea that P is multi-layered has been argued by many. The most obvious example of this layering is the existence of an H edition of P. For more details on this, see Knohl, *Sanctuary*. Additionally, there appears to me to be strong reason to believe that P itself, even before the addition of H, is multilayered. David Frankel believes that an early layer of P may be the oldest source/layer in the Pentateuch. I accept the general contours of David Frankel's reconstruction of the scout story in Numbers (but not all the details, as a number of Frankel's specific interpretations seem overly complex). Frankel argues that there was an early P account that focused on the sin of the scouts and their punishment, and an early D story that focused on the Israelite fear and reluctance to conquer the land. The non-P source (=J) then constructed a version that contained both of these elements, with the scouts frightening the people. A later P editor then combined the non-P story with the P story, and added a number of glosses. On top of this work are at least two or three editorial layers. For the purposes of this chapter, what is important is that if one follows Frankel's reconstruction, Caleb is added to the account *after* the P editor writes his story. The Joshua plus Caleb sections are added even later than that. David Frankel, *The Murmuring Stories of the Priestly School: A Retrieval of Ancient Sacerdotal Lore* (VTSup 89; Leiden: Brill, 2002), 119–201.

punished.[174] Once the overall timeline of exodus-wilderness-conquest was established, since both Caleb and Joshua were known from early settlement traditions, it became necessary to attach both men to the wilderness experience as
well. Attaching them to the wilderness experience, however, begs the question:
How did they survived it?

Caleb is attached first to the J (or non-P) scout story, and then to the P story,
as a loyal scout who opposed his wicked colleagues. This explains why he is not
condemned to die in the wilderness. Joshua is attached to the wilderness experience both by his position as Moses' successor and student (E and D) and sec-
ondarily as Caleb's partner-scout (P) who also condemnes his and Caleb's treacherous colleagues.[175]

All of these steps are derivative of what seem to be the oldest traditions surrounding these characters, the settlement traditions. Thus, the promise of God to
Caleb and Joshua should be understood as the final step in the attempt by the
biblical authors to foreground the earlier tradition in which Caleb inherits Hebron and Joshua Timnat-Serah. It would be instructive to compare this fragment
of the Joshua inheritance tradition with the Caleb inheritance traditions included
in chapters 14 and 15 of Joshua.[176]

In chapter 14, Caleb, together with the Judahites, approaches Joshua. Caleb
reminds him of the promise Moses made and requests Hebron as his inheritance.
Joshua grants the request. A look at the language[177] used in the speech demonstrates that it correlates well with the J or non-P version.

---

174 For a detailed analysis of the origin and development of the Caleb tradition, see Jacob
Wright, *David, King of Israel, and Caleb in Biblical Memory* (Cambridge: Cambridge University
Press, 2014). Unfortunately, Wright's book was published too late for me to engage it in this
section. I hope to be able to do so in the future.

175 As will be discussed later, although I do not accept the documentary hypothesis as such, I
do believe that a number of sources were utilized in putting together the Hexateuch, and when
those sources overlap with a source as understood by the documentary hypothesis I use the
corresponding siglum for simplicity's sake. The main difference between my approach and that
of the documentary hypothesis is that I believe that some sources may be fragmentary, and,
most important, that after the sources were combined, there are still significant layers of redaction on top. In that sense, my work can be categorized loosely as being situated somewhere
between the fragmentary and the supplementary hypotheses.

176 In this section, my thinking has changed from what I wrote in my article on Timnat Heres. I
originally suggested that the explanation for God's allowing Caleb and Joshua to enter the land
was an early stage of P. I now think that it is a later stage of P, since the conquest accounts of
Caleb and Joshua were in no need of an introduction until the idea of the death of the exodus
generation created a problem for these early heroes, and this idea is *not* early P.

177 For example: וְאָנֹכִי מִלֵּאתִי אַחֲרֵי יהוה אֱלֹהָי

Furthermore, Caleb claims to have been the *only* scout who remained loyal to God, a claim that would have been impolitic (to say the least) if this were the conclusion to the P tradition in which Joshua is a loyal scout as well.[178] Nevertheless, this version is instructive. First, it strengthens the idea that the scout traditions were meant to attach to endings. Second, it has a more natural version of the request and granting of land than the request of Joshua for Timnat Ḥeres; it makes perfect sense that Caleb would ask Joshua for land, since Joshua is the leader of Israel in this story.[179]

More instructive is an alternative description of Caleb's land grant in 15:13.

(יג) וּלְכָלֵב בֶּן יְפֻנֶּה נָתַן חֵלֶק בְּתוֹךְ בְּנֵי יְהוּדָה, אֶל פִּי יְהוָה לִיהוֹשֻׁעַ – אֶת קִרְיַת אַרְבַּע אֲבִי הָעֲנָק, הִיא חֶבְרוֹן.	[13] And to Caleb ben Jephuneh he gave a portion among the children of Judah, by word of YHWH to Joshua – The town of Arbah, the father of the Anakites – this is Hebron.
(יד) וַיֹּרֶשׁ מִשָּׁם כָּלֵב אֶת שְׁלוֹשָׁה בְּנֵי הָעֲנָק אֶת שֵׁשַׁי וְאֶת אֲחִימַן וְאֶת תַּלְמַי יְלִידֵי הָעֲנָק.	[14] And Caleb ousted the three children of the Anakites from there – Sheshai, Ahiman and Talmai, the offspring of Anak.

The similarities between this account and the Joshua landgrant account are striking.
- Joshua is given land <u>among</u> the Israelites / Caleb <u>among</u> the Judahites
- In both cases the giver is unspecified (at least at first)[180]
- Both gifts were given "by the mouth of YHWH"

One could postulate that these parallel accounts were the inspiration for the P tradition of the two righteous scouts who were rewarded with a land-grant.

The basic summary of the P story would be that Joshua and Caleb demonstrate their righteousness by maintaining their support for the conquest, and are thereby granted plots of their choosing. With the interspersing of the Joshua and Caleb landgrants into the larger landgrant complex in the book of Joshua,

---

178 Frankel (*Murmuring*, 193) points this out as well.

179 Martin Noth offers a similar hypothesis, although his focus is on teasing out an earlier version of the Caleb/Hebron tradition from before it became attached to the Exodus-Wilderness narrative. Martin Noth, *A History of Pentateuchal Traditions* (trans. B.W. Anderson; Englewood Cliffs: Prentice-Hall, 1972), 130 – 136. Noth does not believe there was a P layer (or even a pre-P layer?) which included an ending to the spy story in the land of Canaan since, in his opinion, the theme of "guidance into the arable land" was of "manifestly no importance" to P (ibid p. 234). I find this last assertion very hard to believe.

180 The phrase, "by word of YHWH to Joshua" seems to be a gloss. The original pointing may have been the passive form *nitan*.

and the separation of the Pentateuch from Joshua, the contiguity of the scout story and the land grants is easily missed.

It seems reasonable to assume that this "two scout" tradition in P is itself a reaction and retelling of the earlier incorporation of the Caleb tradition into the J material. A story with two protagonists from different tribes is awkward, and the combination of a Judahite and an Ephraimite hero implies that the tradition already recognizes a unified Israelite identity for both groups. The inclusion of Joshua in this tradition may have been partially motivated by a need for parity with the south, explaining that the great northern hero Joshua was also brave and righteous and unafraid to fight the natives.[181] Additionally, this tradition postdates the connection between Joshua and the Moses-exodus tradition, hence the need to explain how Joshua was unaffected by God's cursing of the weak-spirited Israelites. Certainly the "scout story" as it exists now is part-and-parcel of the wilderness-wandering and conquest stories.

This observation fits well with another odd feature of this story which implies that this alternative scout story was built upon the back of an even older account which represents an early stage in Joshua's rise to prominence. As pointed out in the beginning of this section, Joshua *requests* land from the Israelites and is *granted* said land through an oracle given, apparently, through somebody else (Elazar is *not* mentioned). This implies that Joshua is not the leader of all of Israel in this account, but rather a righteous and brave warrior, or at most a temporary wartime leader, who was rewarded by God and Israel for exemplary service.[182]

As a schematic overview, I would suggest the following *relative* timeline. Joshua and Caleb begin as local heroes, each from his own respective region. They are remembered as conquerors and settlers of towns, Caleb for Hebron and Joshua for Timnat Serah/Heres. At one point, when the Israelite-Judahite mnemohistorical outline began to coalesce, Caleb was placed in the generation of the wandering and was added to the already existing story of the scouts. In this revised version of the story, his bravery as a young scout is presented as the reason why he was rewarded (by YHWH and Moses) with Hebron. As a parallel maneuver, the (northern) venerators of Joshua, encountering the explanation for Caleb's success in receiving Hebron, create a parallel explanation where Joshua does the same thing as Caleb and receives the same reward. The rewards are the same because they derive from pre-existing parallel sources,

---

181 The idea of the North using Joshua to compensate for a perceived comparative weakness with the South will be explored further in the section on Joshua and Saul.
182 This was noticed by Alexander Rofé as well, see: Rofé, "Joshua", 351.

i.e., the verses in which Joshua and Caleb receive their towns to settle as a gift for helping with or leading the conquest initiative.

This hypothesis accounts for the unusual role Joshua plays in his own land grant tradition. These verses derive from a (lost?) source, unconnected to the wilderness-wandering story, in which Joshua was a powerful warrior and leader among the Israelites. This account would predate the time when his story merged with that of Moses and he became the sole leader of all Israel.[183] The hypothesis also accounts for the literary connection this passage has to the passage about Caleb in chapter 15, since they may have derived from the same early source, in which Joshua and Caleb were heroes on relatively equal footing. Nevertheless, there remains a second aspect to the story which requires explanation, namely, the choice of town.

Mount Heres and the Great Battle of Ayalon

Why does Joshua choose Timnat Heres/Serah? The problem becomes clearer when we compare this account with that of Caleb. In the J Caleb tradition, he and the other scouts are said to have scouted out Hebron and seen giants. When they return to report to their fellow tribesmen, the others create panic about the giants. Caleb tries to calm the people, stating that the giants are conquerable. When the conquest finally takes place, Caleb is rewarded with the very city that caused all the trouble. This is also what Caleb reminds Joshua of in chapter 14. This is the element that is missing in the Joshua land-inheritance tradition. There is no explanation for the choice of Timnat Serah. The town is not mentioned in any of the scout accounts (unlike Hebron), and there is no mention of its having been conquered by Joshua.

In searching for an explanation, I think it would be useful to take a step back and look at the spy accounts from the opposite angle. To explain: if one looks at the traditions from a narrative lens, the essence of the story is that whereas many of the Israelites/Judahites falter, the hero/heroes of the story maintain their faith and confidence. From an etiological perspective, however, the ending of the story is the key. This is clearest when one looks at the Caleb stories. This story has often been interpreted as an etiological tale, that explains how the Calebites came to occupy the great city of Hebron. A tradition grows about the founding

---

183 As will be discussed in this chapter, bits and pieces of this source seem scattered throughout the biblical Joshua account. It is possible that with enough careful work, an entire source could be reconstructed, but this is beyond the scope of my current project.

father of this group, Caleb, who fought bravely against the native giants who once ruled Hebron. Once Caleb enters the story of the wilderness wandering, his future conquest of Hebron is attributed to the merit of his staying calm and loyal when the other scouts panicked.[184]

Is it possible to apply the same logic to the account of Timnat Serah? At first glance it would seem not. There is no discussion of the town of Timnat Serah in the literature other than in connection with Joshua's inheritance of it and his eventual burial there. Nevertheless, following the principle of *Ortsgebundenheit*, and considering the early nature of the Timnat Heres and Joshua connection, it would be useful to explore this question further; to quote Martin Noth: "A grave tradition usually gives the most reliable indication of the original provenance of a particular figure of tradition."[185]

In a 1986 article, Zechariah Kallai offered a key observation about the Timnat Serah/Heres tradition.[186] Kallai took note of the fact that in Judges 1:35, the Amorites are said to have remained on Mount Heres and were eventually dominated by the Josephites. Kallai argues that Timnat Heres must have been an important town in the region of Mount Heres, known especially as the town where the important hero Joshua was buried. Furthermore, Kallai takes note that one of the towns mentioned as being on Mount Heres, Ayalon, is also connected with Joshua.

In the account of the battle against the southern coalition in Joshua 10, Joshua is said to have brought the Israelite army to protect the city of Gibeon. The battle takes a miraculous turn, with Yhwh getting involved in Homeric style, throwing giant hailstones upon the Amorite enemies.[187] At this point in the nar-

---

184 This understanding is even more compelling if one assumes that the oldest traditions about the Calebites understood them to be ethnically Kenizite and not originally Judahite. If this is the case, then the older Caleb as conqueror story would be a further example of a genre which can be called non-Israelite–ally stories. Other examples are the stories of Rahab, the Gibeonites, and the Kenites. How one is supposed to understand the ethnicity of Kenizites is itself complicated. In Genesis 15:19 the Kenizites are listed as people who occupy the land, ostensibly Canaanites, but certainly a people formed before the birth of Esau. However, in Genesis 36, Kenaz is listed as a descendant of Esau, making the Kenizites, in theory, an Edomite clan. It seems that the two references in Genesis reflect different traditions on the matter of Kenizite origins. Alternatively, Jacob Wright argues that the idea of Kenizites being non-Israelite or non-Judahite is actually a later development. He makes a similar argument about the early traditions regarding Gibeonites and Kenites as well. See Wright, *David, King of Israel*, in the section "Was Caleb an Israelite?"
185 Noth, *History*, 169 – 170
186 Kallai, "The Settlement Tradition of Ephraim," 68 – 74.
187 See Weinfeld for a discussion of the resemblance between the stories in Joshua and Greek myth. Weinfeld, *Pattern*, 270 – 284. See also John Brown, who discusses the passage in the Iliad 18:293 in which Hera actually makes the sun go down early in order to make the battle end

rative, the editor brings in a quote from the *Sefer ha-Yashar*,[188] a work that ostensibly contains a poetic rendition of this battle (among other things):

אָז יְדַבֵּר יְהוֹשֻׁעַ לַיהוָה... (יב   12) Then Joshua spoke to YHWH...[189],

וַיֹּאמֶר לְעֵינֵי יִשְׂרָאֵל   he said before the eyes of Israel:

שֶׁמֶשׁ בְּגִבְעוֹן דּוֹם, וְיָרֵחַ בְּעֵמֶק אַיָּלוֹן   "Sun over Gibeon halt, the moon in the valley of Ayalon!"

וַיִּדֹּם הַשֶּׁמֶשׁ, וְיָרֵחַ עָמָד, עַד יִקֹּם גּוֹי אֹיְבָיו... (יג   13) The sun halted and the moon stood still, until a nation[190] was avenged upon its foes...

Kallai connects this account with that of the conquest of the Mount Heres area in Judges, and argues that this conquest tradition is the core of the original Joshua account.

With this in mind, one can suggest a reconstruction of the early development of the Joshua character. Joshua was the famous Josephite conqueror of the Mount Heres region. As the concept of a united Israel began to take over in Ephraimite historiography, Joshua's position as leader of the local Ephraimites or Josephites grew into a position of leader over all Israel.

Joshua as the Josephite Leader of Settlement

There are a number of other stories (or story fragments), in addition to the Timnat Heres grant account, that paint Joshua as a leader in the "Judges" style. By

---

sooner. John P. Brown, "The Templum and the Saeculum: Sacred Space and Time in Israel and Etruria," *ZAW* 98 (1986): 415–433 [426].

188 Auld observes that the reference to the poems title being *Sefer ha-Yashar* is missing from the LXX. He claims that it is a possibility that it was added in the MT based on the reference to *Sefer ha-Yashar* in David's lament over Saul in the book of Samuel (2 Sam 1:18). Because of this, Auld cautions: "Claims that we are dealing here in Joshua 10 with a fragment of an early *Yahweh*-epic and that we know that epic's name must be received with double caution." A. Graeme Auld, *Joshua Retold: Synoptic Perspectives* (OTS; Edinburgh: T&T Clark, 1998), 17. Although Auld's caution is duly noted, and his observation that the title may not be original is well taken, it still seems to be a safe assumption that this poem is a fragment of an older YHWH poem. Even though the title *Sefer ha-Yashar* may be incorrect, I will use it for this essay as a matter of convenience and because it remains a viable option.

189 I assume that the words בְּיוֹם תֵּת יְהוָה אֶת הָאֱמֹרִי לִפְנֵי בְּנֵי יִשְׂרָאֵל are an editorial gloss, since they throw off the parallelism. Whether the gloss is of the editor of Joshua or an editor (?) of the *Sefer ha-Yashar* I cannot say.

190 The LXX reads here אלהים (God) instead of nation. I believe Auld is correct in claiming that this is due to an internal Greek corruption from εθνος to θεος, influenced by the recurring use of θεος by the LXX in this chapter. Auld, *Joshua Retold*, 17.

"Judges" style, I mean that the leader comes from among the people to assist them with a task. Through his assistance he becomes the leader of the group, at least for a time, and dies an important person with a legacy, but *not* with a dynasty. A judge or chieftain is not a patriarch nor is he the founder of the group.

In most biblical texts, Joshua is more than just a judge or chieftain. He comes from the generation of Sinai, he takes over the position of the great law-giver and liberator, Moses, and he leads *the* conquest and settlement of the Promised Land. Once one is familiar with this framework, one automatically reads any account of conquest and settlement attributed to Joshua through this prism. Yet, just as the account of Joshua's land-grant strikes a discordant note with this framing, there are other accounts that do as well.[191] Three primary examples stand out.

Example 1 – The Josephites' Request

The first example is the story in Joshua 17 regarding the land-grant to Joseph.[192]

(יד) וַיְדַבְּרוּ בְּנֵי יוֹסֵף אֶת יְהוֹשֻׁעַ לֵאמֹר: "מַדּוּעַ נָתַתָּה לִּי נַחֲלָה גּוֹרָל אֶחָד וְחֶבֶל אֶחָד וַאֲנִי עַם רָב עַד אֲשֶׁר עַד כֹּה בֵּרְכַנִי יְהוָה."	[14] The Children of Joseph said to Joshua: "Why did you give me one lot and one parcel [of land]? I am a great people having been blessed thus by YHWH."
(טו) וַיֹּאמֶר אֲלֵיהֶם יְהוֹשֻׁעַ: "אִם עַם רַב אַתָּה עֲלֵה לְךָ הַיַּעְרָה וּבֵרֵאתָ לְךָ שָׁם בְּאֶרֶץ הַפְּרִזִּי וְהָרְפָאִים כִּי אָץ לְךָ הַר אֶפְרָיִם."	[15] Joshua said to them: "If you are such a large nation go up to the forest and clear out the area in the land of the Perizzites and Rephaim, for Mount Ephraim is insufficient."
(טז) וַיֹּאמְרוּ בְּנֵי יוֹסֵף: "לֹא יִמָּצֵא לָנוּ הָהָר וְרֶכֶב בַּרְזֶל בְּכָל הַכְּנַעֲנִי הַיֹּשֵׁב בְּאֶרֶץ הָעֵמֶק לַאֲשֶׁר בְּבֵית שְׁאָן וּבְנוֹתֶיהָ וְלַאֲשֶׁר בְּעֵמֶק יִזְרְעֶאל."	[16] The Children of Joseph said: "The mountain is insufficient for us, and chariots can be found among all the Canaanites that dwell in the plains of the land of Bet Shean and its surroundings and in the plains of Jezreel."

---

191 Although, like many scholars, I see the corpus of Josh 13–19 as being multilayered, Olivier Artus argues that it is all of a piece and that the corpus is actually 13–22. He claims that, due to the similarities with Numbers and the emphasis on the high priest and sacerdotal rites ("*la prééminence sacerdotale*") this section should be dated to the Persian/Second Temple period. See: Olivier Artus, "Josué 13–14 et le Livre des Nombres," in *The Book of Joshua* (ed. Ed Noort; BETL 250 – Proceedings of the CBL; Leuven: Leuven University Press, 2010), 233–247.

192 Alt already noted this point, who used this pericope as one of his textual proofs for a slow migration model. See Albrecht Alt, "Die Landnahme der Israeliten in Palästina," *Kleine Schriften zur Geschichte des Volkes Israel* 1 (München: Beck'sche Verlagsbuchhandlung, 1968) 89–125. See also: Martin Noth, *Das Buch Josua* (2nd ed.; HAT; Tübingen: Mohr, 1953), ix-xiii.

(יז יוֹסֵף לְאֶפְרַיִם ¹⁹³[בְּנֵי] (בֵּית) וַיֹּאמֶר יְהוֹשֻׁעַ אֶל
וְלִמְנַשֶּׁה ¹⁹⁴ לֵאמֹר: "עַם רַב אַתָּה וְכֹחַ גָּדוֹל לְךָ לֹא יִהְיֶה
לְךָ גּוֹרָל אֶחָד. (יח כִּי הַר יִהְיֶה לְּךָ כִּי יַעַר הוּא וּבֵרֵאתוֹ
וְהָיָה לְךָ תֹּצְאֹתָיו כִּי תוֹרִישׁ אֶת הַכְּנַעֲנִי כִּי רֶכֶב בַּרְזֶל לוֹ
כִּי (חָזָק הוּא) [תחזק ממנו]."¹⁹⁵

17) Joshua said to the (House) [Children] of Joseph, *to Ephraim and Manasseh:* "You are a big nation and have great power; you will not have only one lot. 18) You will have the mountain, for it is forest and you can clear it, plus you will have the surrounding area when you conquer the Canaanites, *for they have iron chariots for (they are strong) [you will become stronger than them.]*"

Reading this text through the prism of the final redaction, the reader should be stunned. Is Joshua really saying that the Josephites, even with his military leadership, cannot defeat the Canaanites because they have chariots? (Why are Canaanites even still around?) The passage is highly discordant with the narrative framework. This text assumes a very different perspective on the settlement, picturing the Josephites as settling in forested areas and avoiding military confrontation.

There is a further problem with the text. As presented, the dialogue makes little sense. The entire conversation in Rofé's words seems like a "דו-שיח של חרשים" (a conversation where neither is hearing the other.) Joshua tells the Josephites to clear out forest and they say they are afraid of Canaanites on the plains because of their chariots. Joshua then solves this by telling them to clear out forests and conquer the Canaanites. What sense does any of this make? Although one can attempt to force some sense on the discussion, Rofé makes the radical suggestion that the order of the verses has been switched.[196] He proposes reversing the order of Joshua's speeches. Doing so yields a more reasonable conversation.

---

193 The LXX has "sons of Joseph" as opposed to "house of Joseph". The latter is the term used in Judges but not here. It is difficult to say which text is the more authentic as the LXX could be correcting the MT text to make it fit the context.

194 I put this in italics because I believe it to be a gloss to make the concept of "Children of Joseph" fit better with the later biblical usage of this term.

195 The reading in brackets is based on the LXX "σὺ γὰρ ὑπερισχύεις αὐτοῦ" and is preferred by Rofé ("Joshua", 355). Nevertheless, the LXX variant may be an attempt to make sense out of a difficult and incongruous phrase.

196 He is not the only one to suggest that the verses here are out of order. As Rofé himself points out he is resurrecting an older approach, but the specific reorganization is his. For other attempts at reordering the verses, see: K. Budde, *Die Bücher Richter und Samuel, ihre Quellen und ihr Aufbau* (Giessen, 1890), 1–89; Charles Fox Burney, *The Book of Judges with Introduction and Notes* (London: Rivingtons, 1918), 47–52; Volkmar Fritz, *Das Buch Josua* (HAT I/7; Tübingen: Mohr Siebeck, 1994), 176–177.

The Children of Joseph complain that they only received one lot. Joshua responds that this is not true since they have Mount Ephraim, which is forested, and they will have the plains around Mount Ephraim, once they conquer the Canaanites. To this, the Children of Joseph respond that Mount Ephraim is fine, but too small, and they cannot conquer the Canaanites, because they (the Canaanites) have chariots. Joshua then says that if they cannot fight the chariots, they should go to the land of the Perizzites and Rephaim and take their forested areas as their second plot. The odd final phrase may be an attempted gloss added into the text once the order of the verses became garbled.

The location of the land of the Perizzites and Rephaim is unclear, but it certainly is *not* on Mount Ephraim. Noting the references to Perizzites and Rephaim in Genesis 14:5 and Deuteronomy 3:5, 13, Rofé argues that this second plot is in the Bashan area (Fritz notes this correspondence as well). If this identification is correct, then this story may function as an explanation for why the Joseph tribes live on both sides of the Jordan.[197] If true, this represents the reverse of the usual order of conquest in biblical historiography.

Generally, the biblical text presents an Israelite people who are outside the Promised Land, coming in to conquer it by way of the Jordan River, and conquering areas east of the Jordan on the way. This story, in contrast, presents a Josephite people settling the Cisjordan, but unable to conquer all of it and, therefore, spreading out into the Transjordanian Bashan area due to overpopulation. Although it explains the same phenomenon—related tribes on both sides of the river—it works with very different premises. In fact, this section is incongruous with the book of Joshua as a whole, even the landgrant section, and appears to have been added in "to the appropriate place," i.e., the spot in the land-distribution section that deals with Ephraim.[198]

I suggest that this piece represents the story of the Josephites (not the Israelites) and their settlement of Mount Ephraim and the Bashan region. Where the Josephites believed they came from is not recorded here, but this describes the settlement of Joseph in forested land, first in the Cisjordan and then in the Transjordan. The assumption seems to be that in the future, perhaps when the Josephites grew stronger, they would succeed in conquering the plains as well.

---

197 Rofé speculates that the order of the verses may have been switched on purpose to avoid contradicting the other biblical accounts that describe the conquest of the Bashan area differently.

198 Here is where I part company with Rofé, who reads this story as an integral part of the "Joshua as distributer-of-land to all of Israel" section and assumes that the key point is that Joshua is the leader because he has access to the lot, i.e., he is a man of mystical powers.

It is possible that this account connects with the conquest story of the Josephites in Judges 1:22/23 – 26.[199] In this account, the House of Joseph (no mention of Joshua) conquers the city of Bet El. Perhaps there was, at one point, a story of how the Joseph tribes settled and/or conquered the Cisjordan. If so, Joshua may have been associated with some versions of this account as an early (perhaps the earliest) leader of the tribe.

Example 2 – Joshua and his Family

The second example of Joshua as a Judges-like leader comes in what might be the core of the speech in chapter 24. Although one can quibble about certain phrases, the key to retrieving an early version of this speech is removing any reference to the patriarchs, Israel, Amorites, or the Egypt experience. Instead, Joshua speaks to "the nation," whose ancestors came from "across the river." This nation brought the gods of their ancestors with them, but, Joshua tells them, it was YHWH who handed them the land of the Canaanites, without a fight, and they should be grateful for this and loyal to YHWH. The people agree and remove their other gods, which Joshua buries beneath a tree at "The Temple of YHWH" – heretofore an unknown building.

Although this is Joshua's parting speech, he gives no sign of being old here. Instead, Joshua refers to what "he and his household" will do now that the land has been settled. This implies that Joshua was the leading figure in this story of settlement/conquest, but now that the nation has won, he will return to his life as a private citizen the way everyone else will. There is no implication that he will retain his position in some official capacity and no reason to believe that any male descendants from his household will be in a privileged position relative to other members of the nation. This depiction of Joshua works well with the land-grant account. It makes sense that a "first among equals" leader, like Joshua, having led the people in the conquest and/or settlement of the land, requests a landgrant for his troubles before he returns to civilian life.

---

199 Verse 22 is probably a gloss. It is worth noting that there is a shift in terminology in the MT with Joshua using "Sons of Joseph" and Judges "House of Joseph." Although one might consider distinguishing between the sources on this basis, nevertheless, considering the textual problem with the verses in chapter 17 between the LXX and the MT regarding the name, I believe one must be careful not to build too much on the terminology. See: Weinfeld, *Promise*, 105 n. 12.

Example 3 – Joshua the Ephraimite Leader who never Left

The opening sections of the Book of Chronicles contain a number of traditions that are independent of, even contradictory to, other parts of the Bible. The section on Joshua and Ephraim is a prime example (ch. 7).

²⁰וּבְנֵי אֶפְרַיִם שׁוּתָלַח וּבֶרֶד בְּנוֹ וְתַחַת בְּנוֹ וְאֶלְעָדָה בְנוֹ
וְתַחַת בְּנוֹ. ²¹וְזָבָד בְּנוֹ וְשׁוּתֶלַח בְּנוֹ וְעֵזֶר וְאֶלְעָד וַהֲרָגוּם
אַנְשֵׁי־גַת הַנּוֹלָדִים בָּאָרֶץ כִּי יָרְדוּ לָקַחַת אֶת־מִקְנֵיהֶם.
²²וַיִּתְאַבֵּל אֶפְרַיִם אֲבִיהֶם יָמִים רַבִּים וַיָּבֹאוּ אֶחָיו לְנַחֲמוֹ.
²³וַיָּבֹא אֶל־אִשְׁתּוֹ וַתַּהַר וַתֵּלֶד בֵּן וַיִּקְרָא אֶת־שְׁמוֹ בְּרִיעָה כִּי
בְרָעָה הָיְתָה בְּבֵיתוֹ. ²⁴וּבִתּוֹ שֶׁאֱרָה וַתִּבֶן אֶת־בֵּית־חוֹרוֹן
הַתַּחְתּוֹן וְאֶת־הָעֶלְיוֹן וְאֵת אֻזֵּן שֶׁאֱרָה. ²⁵וְרֶפַח בְּנוֹ וְרֶשֶׁף
וְתֶלַח בְּנוֹ וְתַחַן בְּנוֹ. ²⁶לַעְדָּן בְּנוֹ עַמִּיהוּד בְּנוֹ אֱלִישָׁמָע בְּנוֹ.
²⁷נוֹן בְּנוֹ יְהוֹשֻׁעַ בְּנוֹ. ²⁸וַאֲחֻזָּתָם וּמֹשְׁבוֹתָם בֵּית־אֵל וּבְנֹתֶיהָ
וְלַמִּזְרָח נַעֲרָן וְלַמַּעֲרָב גֶּזֶר וּבְנֹתֶיהָ וּשְׁכֶם וּבְנֹתֶיהָ עַד־עַיָּה
וּבְנֹתֶיהָ.

²⁰ The sons of Ephraim: Shuthelah, and Bered his son, Tahath his son, Eleadah his son, Tahath his son, ²¹ Zabad his son, Shuthelah his son, and Ezer and Elead. Now the people of Gath, who were born in the land, killed them, because they came down to raid their cattle. ²² And their father Ephraim mourned many days, and his brothers came to comfort him. ²³ Ephraim went in to his wife, and she conceived and bore a son; and he named him Beriah, because disaster had befallen his house. ²⁴ His daughter was Sheerah, who built both Lower and Upper Beth-horon, and Uzzen-sheerah. ²⁵ Rephah was his son, Resheph his son, Telah his son, Tahan his son, ²⁶ Ladan his son, Ammihud his son, Elishama his son, ²⁷ Nun his son, Joshua his son. ²⁸ Their possessions and settlements were Bethel and its towns, and eastward Naaran, and westward Gezer and its towns, Shechem and its towns, as far as Ayyah and its towns. (NRSV)

In this account, Ephraim's sons are killed by the people of Gath. Whether Gath is meant to refer to the Philistine city of that name, or to the city of Gittim as many scholars believe, the bottom line remains that the Ephraimites must be living in the Cisjordan for this story to make sense. As Sara Japhet points out in her seminal article,

> The story is based on certain historical assumptions and offers some historical data. The primary assumption is that Ephraim is living "in the land".... A comparison of this unit with the established traditions of the Pentateuch immediately reveals the glaring contradictions between them.... According to [the Pentateuchal] tradition Ephraim never was in the land of Israel and could not have been there: he was born in Egypt and died there. The tradition of 1 Chr 7:20 – 24 and that of the Pentateuch are thus mutually exclusive and, understood on their own terms, virtually irreconcilable.... The same independent concept of history, with apparent polemical overtones, is found in the pedigree of Joshua.... The direct line from Ephraim, who is living and functioning in the land, to Joshua ties Joshua to the land as well, and the consequences of that bond cannot be exaggerated. In the major biblical tradition it is Joshua who represents the period and the idea of the conquest.... In 1 Chroni-

cles 7 the historical situation which provides the necessary conditions for Joshua's activity is absent. By his being a descendant of Ephraim who is in the land, the possibility of the accepted tradition is ruled out. Joshua did not conquer the land, he simply was there.[200]

Japhet's suggestion—the passage about Ephraim in 1 Chron. 7 records an alternative tradition that Ephraim was a tribe native to Israel—appears solid. It fits in well with the previous two examples of Joshua as a local leader. Perhaps this tradition fit in with a worldview of an indigenous Israelite, Josephite, or Ephraimite group that fought battles with other indigenous groups for dominance in the area.[201] This would also fit well with academic models that suggest that the core of the patriarchal stories in Genesis may have been associated with a worldview that the patriarchs remained in the land and eventually grew numerous and powerful enough to dominate or expel their rivals in the land.

Summary

Whether the traditions discussed above—the landgrant, the Joseph tribes' request for more land, the final speech, and the Ephraim story and lineage in Chronicles—were all part of one Joshua account or were collected and developed in different times or places is difficult to say. What is relevant for this chapter is that they all point to a stage in Joshua's career where he was the local leader of something less than "the twelve tribes of Israel" and functioned more as a temporary leader than as either a king or a primordial founder/patriarch.

Joshua's City and his Connection to the Sun-Stopping Miracle

As discussed above, Timnat Heres was a town in the district of Har Heres, the same district in which Joshua is said to have fought his battle against the south-

---

200 Sara Japhet, "Conquest and Settlement in Chronicles," *JBL* 98.2 (1979): 205–218 [213–215].
201 See Israel Knohl, *The Bible's Genetic Code* (Israel: Dvir, 2008), 128–129 [Hebrew], for a similar suggestion. For an attempt to make Chronicles work with the Joseph story, see Gershon Galil's commentary on Chronicles (*ad loc.*) in the *Olam HaTanach* series, in which he argues that this was a different Ephraim. This suggestion is difficult to accept since there is no record of this other Ephraim in the geneology. Not surprisingly, the Rabbis attempted to solve this tension as well. They did so by suggesting that the account refers to the tribe of Ephraim, which left Egypt early. See, for example, b. *Sanhedrin* 92b, and discussion in Joseph Heinemann, "The Messiah of Ephraim and the Premature Exodus of the Tribe of Ephraim," *HTR* 68 (1975): 1–15; (previously published in Hebrew, *Tarbiz* 40 (5731): 450–461.)

ern coalition. The word Heres means "sun" and may reflect either the heat of the region or some sort of association with a solar deity. Noort ("Josua 24") observes that the motif most commonly associated with Joshua throughout his *reception history* is the miracle of the stopping of the sun. Although Noort used this observation to argue for the changing of the name from סרח to חרס, I would like to flip this argument on its head.

It is well known that many biblical motifs are based upon midrashic/hermeneutic interpretations of names. Esau is named "Edom" since he asked for "red stuff (adom)" (Gen 25:30); Moab and Ammon are said, based on a pun on their names, to have been born of incestuous unions (Gen 19:37–38), etc. These are examples of derogatory midrash, but the same methodology is used to create accounts of heroic figures as well. Judah "admits" (ו.ד.ה.) his guilt (Gen 38:26, 44:16), Hezekiah "strengthens" (ח.ז.ק.) Jerusalem and the people of Judah (2 Chron. 32:5, 7), Jehoshaphat "judges" (ש.פ.ט.) the people (2 Chron. 19:5–11), etc.

Perhaps, when the early stories of Joshua were developing, some early bards took note of the name of the great hero's town. Although the region was likely named either after the intense heat of the region or after some pre-henotheistic connection to the sun cult, the bards interpreted the name hermeneutically. Joshua's town was the "portion of the sun" because Joshua was connected to the sun in some way.

Tying the sun motif into the battle, the poem from *Sefer ha-Yashar*, which may have begun independently of Joshua, became attached to him.[202] The version that emerged triumphant was that the town was called Timnat Heres because the great hero stopped the sun over this region in order to allow him to defeat his enemies.[203] With that maneuver, the image of Joshua "the-man-who-stopped-the-sun" became firmly planted in Israelite cultural memory.

---

[202] In my Timnat Heres article (op. cit.), I argued that the story may have been inspired by the name of the region. This may be so, but I no longer believe that the story was originally part of the Joshua cycle. Rather I believe it was either originally part of the Saul cycle or, most likely, was an independent poem of unknown origin and context. This point will be clarified in the section on Joshua and Saul.

[203] Another biblical character named Joshua also lives in this region, specifically in Bet Shemesh (1 Sam 6:14, 18). In this story, the Ark of the Covenant is sent off by the Philistines and wanders to the house of Joshua and stays there, prompting an offering on behalf of the Israelites who lived there. It seems possible that both characters may be based on a distant memory or tradition that claims some sort of religious hero associated with the sun that lived roughly in this region.

Joshua as the First Leader of a United Israel

The earlier images of Joshua as a leader of the Joseph tribes or as an early Israelite warrior develops into (or is replaced by) the image of Joshua *the first* leader of all Israel.[204] The core narrative associated with this image was probably the same as that of Joshua the early Israelite warrier, namely the battle of Bet Horon. In attempting to outline the contours of this Joshua account, it will be useful to consider what may have inspired this expansion of Joshua's position in Israelite mnemohistory.

It is my belief that this development was influenced by competition with another figure of Israelite mnemohistory, the early southern hero, King Saul.[205] The period of time most optimal for this northern cultural memory construction was after the fall of the northern kingdom in 720, when Israel was forced to deal with defeat and its own status as a governed Assyrian province while their brethren and neighbors to the south remained an independent polity. Thus, I speculate that the late eighth century or early seventh century is the time when this more expansive Joshua tradition began to take shape.

Scholars have long felt that the collapse of the southern kingdom was one of the main impetuses to the canonization of Judahite lore and historiography in what became the core of the Hebrew Bible. I believe that a similar process occurred in the North.

With Israel's loss of political independence after the Assyrian conquest, and with Judah's independence still intact, there may have been a strong impetus for Israel to open or reopen dialogue with its southern neighbor. This is hardly surprising, since the two groups shared cultural similarities. As Avi Faust has shown, the material cultures of the northern and southern Cisjordanian highlands were identical even before the monarchic period.[206] Furthermore, the groups may have had a feeling of a shared past, whether due to the (real or imagined) period of southern domination under Saul or David and Solomon, or under the period of northern domination attested to in the Book of Kings

---

204 A version of this section was delivered in a paper in the 2012 SBL meeting.

205 Weinfeld also notes the similarities between Joshua and Saul, especially their shared presence in Gilgal. However, he believes that the Joshua tradition became fixed during the time of Saul in the city of Gilgal, which is very different than what I will argue. See Weinfeld, *Patriarchal*, 49–50.

206 See Avraham Faust, *Israel's Ethnogenesis: Settlement, Interaction, Expansion, and Resistance* (Approaches to Anthropological Archaeology; London: Equinox, 2006).

(1 Kings 22), and ostensibly confirmed in the Tel Dan inscription.[207] As one would expect, the once powerful and dominant Israel would not kowtow to the historiography as presented by Judah. Instead, like Joseph and Judah fighting over Benjamin, the tribes of Joseph and Judah fight over the mnemohistorical legacy of the Benjaminite King Saul.

I suggest that the north built up Joshua's position in Israelite historiography at this stage as a counter-weight to Saul, who was already touted in Judahite mnemohistory as the first king of a United Israel. They placed their candidate in a period predating Saul's monarchy but parroting it in a number of ways, although still basing his character loosely on the early Joshua traditions described in the previous sections.

By the time the north promotes Joshua in their historiography to leader of a united Israel it would have been entirely counter to the Judahite historiography, with which the north was now in conversation, to call him *melekh* and count the years of his reign.[208] In fact, the Joshua account has less of a monarchic feel, in certain respects, than the accounts of some of the Judges. Specifically, there is no mention of Joshua having had sons—a curious fact that brought with it much speculation among the early Christian and Rabbinic interpreters.[209] Thomas Dozeman goes so far as to say that the Joshua story, at its core, is anti-monarchic:

> Joshua is portrayed as both an antimonarchical and an antiurban leader who lives in a camp at Gilgal and seeks to destroy all the city-states in Canaan.... At no time in the book is Joshua idealized as a king or even a proto-king. In fact, he represents a virulent

---

[207] In this inscription, the king of Beit-David is killed together with the king of Israel, ostensibly by Hazael, king of Aram-Damascus. Much has been written on this inscription. For a book-length treatment with a full bibliography, see: George Athas, *The Tel Dan Inscription: A Reappraisal and a New Interpretation* (JSOTsup; Sheffield: Sheffield Academic Press, 2003).

[208] The Abimelech account in Judg 9 stands out as a rare exception to this rule of Israelite historiography. Even if one were to argue that the North could have ignored this aspect of Southern historiography—perhaps they did at one stage—there is a further reason for the biblical authors' insistence that Joshua was not a king. Once Joshua is identified as having been the successor of Moses and the completer of the Hexateuchal project of establishing Israel on its land, it would have been of paramount importance to present him as the servant of YHWH not the King of Israel.

[209] This point—i.e. Joshua's lack of offspring or even an official successor—was noted by Christa Schäfer-Lichtenberger as part of her argument that Joshua is not presented as a king. See: Christa Schäfer-Lichtenberger, *Josua und Salamo: Eine Studie zu Autorität und Legitimität des Nachfolgers im Alten Testament* (VTSup 58; Leiden: Brill, 1995), 219–222. As discussed above, it appears that in the version of the Joshua account where he is the leader of the Josephites, he was pictured as having had "a household." Perhaps this version was suppressed as part of the negotiations between the Joshua story and that of Moses or Saul.

form of antiurban and antimonarchical life in the promised land. Joshua kills kings; he does not model them.[210]

Dozeman prefers Doron Mendels' term "territorial hero."[211] Personally, I believe that Dozeman overstates the connection between anti-urbanism and anti-monarchism.[212] Be that as it may, even granting Dozeman's point, the Joshua account does place him in the position of the first *ruler* of Israel in the Cisjordan, and, in that regard, his account bears a direct relationship with that of Saul.

Reasons Why a Joshua-Saul Rivalry May Have Been Overlooked

Although there are a number of signs pointing to a Joshua vs. Saul rivalry, there are three reasons why prior scholarship may have overlooked them.

First, scholars often think of Saul as a northerner, such that they see the Saul/David dichotomy as indicative of the competition between Israel in the north and Judah in the south. Characterizing Saul as a northerner is a misnomer, however. Saul is a Benjaminite, a term that means southerner. The etymology of Ben-Yamin as "son of the south," if it was ever in doubt, was made clear with the discovery of the Mari texts referring to the *banu yamina*. Additionally, as Nadav Na'aman points out, archaeological evidence points to Benjamin—or at least most of it—as having been part of Judah throughout the monarchic period, and most of the stories about Saul take place in the Benjamin and Judah region.[213]

It is true that Na'aman overstates the case when he writes, "the stories of Saul and his house are no less Judahite than those of David." Saul's story *begins* as a southern tale, but at some point in the development of his story, and certainly by the time the biblical account is fully formed, Saul morphs into the repre-

---

210 Thomas B. Dozeman, "Joshua in the Book of Joshua," in *Raising up a Faithful Exegete: Essays in Honor of Richard D. Nelson* (eds. K. L. Noll and Brooks Schramm; Winona Lake: Eisenbrauns, 2010), 103–116 [115].

211 See: Doron Mendels, *The Rise and Fall of Jewish Nationalism: The History of Jewish and Christian Ethnicity in Palestine within the Graeco-Roman Period, 200 BCE to 132 CE* (ABRL; New York: Doubleday, 1992), 99.

212 Attila the Hun was certainly king-like, as was Alaric, even if both could reasonably be described as "anti-urban."

213 See: Nadav Na'aman, "Saul, Benjamin, and the Emergence of Biblical Israel – Part 1," *ZAW* 121 (2009): 211–224; "Saul, Benjamin, and the Emergence of Biblical Israel – Part 2," *ZAW* 121 (2009): 335–349.

sentative of a *united* Israel, north and south, Israel and Judah. Still, Saul is not a northern Israelite figure in the way Gideon, Joshua, or Jeroboam are.

Second, the present shape of the Book of Joshua does not identify its protagonist as a king. Nevertheless, Richard Nelson, among others, points to the many indications of what he calls, "the essentially royal nature of Joshua."[214] Dozeman argues that the originally anti-monarchic Joshua account took on a modified or qualified monarchic position when it was incorporated into the Deuteronomic History.[215] I suggest that the reverse may be the case. If anything, the biblical authors may have inherited a royal Joshua—he could have been seen as ruling a city or a swath of land in the Mount Ephraim region (Timnat Heres? Har Heres?). If they did inherit such a character, the biblical authors downplay this, which makes sense especially once Joshua's story becomes entangled with that of Moses, servant of YHWH, and is then modified even further in the post-exilic period. Even with this downplaying of royalty, the biblical Joshua account does paint him as a *ruler* of sorts.

Third, a significant part of the polemicizing against Saul appears in the Joshua story with its characterization of Joshua. This differs from the Davidic polemicizing against Saul, which makes its appearance felt most strongly in the Saul narrative itself. Although there may be some parts of the Saul account which can be seen as painting Saul less favorably than Joshua, the majority of polemicizing with Saul must be found in the construction of his Ephraimite alter-ego, Joshua.

Joshua's Account Mimicking that of Saul

There are a number of ways that Joshua's career mimics that of Saul's. Both Joshua and Saul are said to have fought in or near Beit Horon. Joshua does so in the battle to save the Gibeonites—an important text that will be explored presently, and Saul does so in the battle against the Philistines, in which Beit Horon is listed as a Philistine encampment (1 Sam. 13:18). The biblical authors have both Joshua and Saul fighting in the area of Ayalon—Joshua in the poem about stopping the sun and Saul at the end of the Philistine campaign (in ch. 14 v. 31). Both Joshua and Saul are described as having fought in the region of Azekah, a Judahite city—Joshua in the battle at Beit Horon and Saul at the opening of the Goliath story (in ch. 17 v. 1). Much of Joshua's military activity takes place in Ben-

---

214 See: Richard D. Nelson, "Josiah in the Book of Joshua," *JBL* 100.4 (1981): 531–540.
215 Dozeman, "Joshua in the Book of Joshua," 116.

jaminite territory, like Jericho and Ai, Gilgal, and Gibeon. Both Joshua and Saul cast lots to determine the guilty party, Joshua in the story of Achan taking from the proscribed booty (Josh 7) and Saul when trying to determine who violated the ban on eating (1 Sam. 14:41–42).[216]

The city of Gilgal plays a significant role in the stories of Joshua and Saul, but it rarely if ever appears in connection with other characters in the primary history (Samuel being an understandable exception). Saul is crowned in Gilgal and often uses the city as a base. Joshua founds the city, erecting the stones that commemorate Israel's crossing over into the land. Saul offers a sacrifice to YHWH at Gilgal, but Joshua offers the first ever Paschal sacrifice in the Holy Land there, something "remembered" in the Book of Joshua as well as in Chronicles. Even the name Gilgal, the Book of Joshua claims, derives from Joshua's having circumcised the Israelite men there. I suggest that Gilgal, as Benjaminite territory, was part of the Saul story, and the biblical account of Joshua in this city is an attempt by the northerners both to paint their hero in Saul's colors as well as to appropriate a site of ritual and mnemohistorical significance to the south and give it to the northern leader and conqueror.[217]

---

216 I thank Richard Nelson for pointing this out during the comments portion of my SBL talk. In fact, Jonathan actually uses the same terminology as Joshua, claiming that his father had sullied (עכר) the land by making the foolish vow against food (1 Sam. 14:29), paralleling Joshua's claim that Achan "sullied us" (עכרתנו) by taking from the proscribed booty (Josh 7:25). The intertextual resonance between these two verses is clear, but it is difficult to know which is playing off which. Once both stories became part of the biblical canon, it is quite possible that slight shifts and expansions could occur to either story in light of the other.

217 As LXX scholars have noted, there are more references to Gilgal in the MT than in the LXX, leading to a debate between scholars about whether the LXX is removing references or the MT adding them. Michaël van der Meer argues that the LXX is removing references in order to make the story line cleaner, with less interruptive returns to base camp. See: Michaël N. van der Meer, *Formation and Reformulation: The Redaction of the Book of Joshua in the Light of the Oldest Textual Witnesses* (VTSup 102; Leiden: Brill, 2004). Kristin de Troyer, on the other hand, argues that the MT is adding the references. See: Kristin de Troyer, *Rewriting the Sacred Text: What the Old Greek Texts Tell Us about the Literary Growth of the Bible* (Text-Critical Studies 4; Atlanta: Society of Biblical Literature, 2003a); "Did Joshua have a Crystal Ball? The Old Greek and the MT of Joshua 10:15, 17, and 23," in *Emanuel: Studies in Hebrew Bible, Septuagint, and Dead Sea Scrolls in Honor of Emanuel Tov* (eds. Shalom M. Paul, Robert A. Kraft, Lawrence H. Schiffman, and Weston W. Fields; VTSup 94; Leiden: Brill, 2003b), 571–590. Although de Troyer's text critical work is strong her theory leaves open the question of why the MT would add references to Gilgal in the Joshua story. If my above assertion is correct, then one possible explanation— assuming one accepts de Troyer's text critical work—would be that there exists some significance to the granting of Gilgal to Joshua, i.e. the appropriation of the southern city by the northern hero, or just the growth of Joshua's image as the founder of important Israelite cult places. Therefore, the more one emphasizes Gilgal the stronger the association would be.

The most explicit example of a Joshua vs. Saul polemic comes with the story of the Gibeonites, specifically the account of the oath and alliance. According to 2 Samuel 21 and Joshua 9, the Israelites made an oath of allegiance to the Gibeonites.[218] The verse in Samuel offers no specifics about who made the oath, but it records that Saul broke it and slaughtered a great number of them. What, if anything, this represents historically is difficult to say, but the presentation fits well with Saul's career as detailed in 1 Samuel. The Book of Samuel depicts Saul as dedicated to fighting off the Philistines and establishing the independence of his kingdom. Fighting to consolidate his power in the southern and northern Cisjordanian highlands, he would have fought pockets of foreign resistance that were not a part of the population element he saw as his constituency. It is certainly possible that he saw these Gibeonites and their four-city alliance as a third wheel at best and a potential enemy at worst. Alternatively, even if one believes that in the earliest traditions the Gibeonites were not foreigners but Israelites, the slaughter of the Gibeonites still resonates well with what is remembered about Saul's career.[219]

However one understands the development of the tradition of Saul's slaughter of the Gibeonites, the David account cashes in on the story by saying that this is the reason David executed Saul's descendants. Whether David did, in fact, execute Saul's descendants and used this as his defense, as Baruch Halpern argues,[220] or whether this story was a later invention, written with the intention of giving David points on the Gibeonite question at Saul's expense, is difficult to say. The latter strategy was employed by the advocates for Joshua and his primacy.

---

218 It is difficult to ascertain from the various accounts of the Gibeonites what their relationship was to their Benjaminite or Israelite neighbors. Were they, in fact, a distinct polity or does that claim stem from later polemic against a group once considered Israelite? With the scant information available to us, it is difficult to answer.

219 Jacob Wright argues in his book on David that the slaughter of the Gibeonites is reminiscent of the account of Saul's slaughter of the entire population of the priestly city of Nob. Wright points out that as the Gibeonites are associated with the priesthood, and the city is said to have been the place of the ark and a cultic site of some importance, this slaughter of the Gibeonite priests is exactly parallel to the slaughter of the Nobite priests. I will add that if one follows the suggestion of some scholars that Nob is a corruption for Gob, itself a short version of the name Gibeon, the slaughter of the Gibeonites and the slaughter of the Nobites would, in fact, be two versions of the *same* account. Finally, it is worth noting that Saul is also said to have slaughtered the Ob diviners; apparently, there is a tradition about his reign, perhaps deriving from some actual tendency of his in the past, that Saul slaughtered cultic functionaries.

220 See: Baruch Halpern, *David's Secret Demons: Messiah, Murderer, Traitor, King* (Grand Rapids, MI: Eerdmans, 2001).

In Joshua 10, the Gibeonites, under attack by a coalition of southern city-states, invoke the oath of protection and request that Joshua save them, *hoshiah lanu* – a request that, quite literally, invokes Joshua's very name, *Yehoshua*. Joshua does save them, and this leads fortuitously to the most glorious of all of Joshua's battles, the battle at the descent of Beit Horon. The polemical value of this claim seems clear. King Saul, the first king, violated the promise made to the Gibeonites and was punished. Joshua, the first leader, kept the promise made to the Gibeonites and was granted a great military victory.[221]

This *"hoshiah lanu"*—save us—opening of the Gibeonite campaign may have another polemical benefit as well. Saul's first act as king was to save the residents of Yabesh-Gilead from the aggression of King Nahash of Ammon. The Yabesh Gileadites search out a *moshiah*, a savior, and Saul succeeds in playing this role, affecting a *t'shua*, a rescue.[222] Whether the Saul story is playing off the Joshua story and his name, or whether the Joshua and Gibeon story is an attempt to claim that Joshua was the first *moshiah* (and not Saul) is difficult to say. Very possibly, both stories are an attempt to adapt an important motif to each respective candidate without any direct borrowing in either direction. Whichever solution one thinks most probable, the parallel highlights the competition between these two characters and their claims on Israelite cultural memory construction.

---

221 Battling near Gibeon may have been a literary trope, or perhaps a relatively common occurrence; the first battle between David's troops and Ish-Boshet's is said to have been fought there as well.

222 In a discussion with Jacob Wright about my chapter on the Samaritan Book of Joshua, he suggested that this work continues the parallel between Saul and Joshua here by giving Joshua a parallel to the end of the Jabesh Gilead-Saul account. In the biblical text, after Saul's death, and the desecration of his body by the Philistines, it was the people of Jabesh Gilead—a Transjordanian town—that entered Beth Shean at night, at great peril, and removed his body from the walls. They then cremated and buried the ashes so that he could not be disturbed (1 Sam 31:11–13). Similarly, in the Samaritan Book of Joshua (chs. 35–36), during Joshua's final battle, he is captured by the enemy and must be rescued by the king of the Transjordan, Nabih, whom Joshua had appointed as king earlier in his career. The theme of "the man who assisted the Transjordanians was then saved by the Transjordanians" may reflect a Transjordanian/Galilean tradition applied both to Saul and, eventually, Joshua. The unique relationship of the Galileans in late antiquity to the character Joshua was explored by Elchanan Reiner and will be discussed in chapter six.

The Sefer ha-Yashar and the Attachment of the Poem to Joshua

Another intriguing similarity between Saul and Joshua is the fact that the only two quoted passages from the *Sefer ha-Yashar* found in the Bible are those that describe: a. Joshua's battle near Gibeon (but only in the MT), and b. Saul's defeat at Mount Gilboa.[223] This may be a coincidence; perhaps the *Sefer ha-Yasher* was a repository of heroic poems about various battles and figures from Israel and Judah's collective past. Nevertheless, I would like to tentatively suggest a different—admittedly highly speculative—possibility.

Following the outline of the story of the battle at Beit Horon, Gibeon is at-tacked and requests aid from Joshua. Joshua and his army appear and rout the enemy, who then take flight. Joshua's army chases the enemy, catching them in the descent of Beit Horon. At this point the biblical text describes Yнwн's intervention (Josh 10:11).

וַיְהִי בְּנֻסָם מִפְּנֵי יִשְׂרָאֵל—הֵם בְּמוֹרַד בֵּית חוֹרֹן[224]—וַיהֹוָה הִשְׁלִיךְ עֲלֵיהֶם אֲבָנִים גְּדֹלוֹת מִן הַשָּׁמַיִם עַד עֲזֵקָה[225] וַיָּמֻתוּ רַבִּים אֲשֶׁר מֵתוּ בְּאַבְנֵי הַבָּרָד מֵאֲשֶׁר הָרְגוּ בְּנֵי יִשְׂרָאֵל בֶּחָרֶב.	And it was as they were running from Israel—they were at the descent of Beit Horon—and Yнwн threw great stones upon them from the heavens *until Azeikah*. More died from the hail-stones than were put to the sword by the Israel-ites.

The battle is won by the miraculous intervention of Yнwн throwing hailstones at the enemy while Joshua's army mops up by putting the surviving enemy soldiers to the sword. And then, suddenly, the second great miracle comes. The text quotes a poem—according to the MT the poem comes from *Sefer ha-Yashar*. The poem has Joshua telling the sun and moon to freeze until Israel defeats its foes. The miracle comes unexpectedly, since, according the story, Israel's foes were already defeated; what was the need for Joshua to stop the sun? Not

---

223 Rofé references a third, following the LXX text in 1 Kings 8:53 "οὐκ ἰδοὺ αὕτη γέγραπται ἐν βιβλίῳ τῆς ᾠδῆς." However, this is more than a little speculative, as Rofé himself admits (n. 80), since it is a reconstruction; the Hebrew Vorlage was clearly "הלא היא כתובה על ספר הַשִּׁיר (Is it not written in the Book of the Poem?)." The possibility that this represents a third quotation from this same work is reasonable, but far from certain. The phrase is similar to that used about the Book of the Just, and to change ישר to שיר requires only a metathesis of one letter.

224 This phrase may be a gloss, as part of the effort to combine the defense of Gibeon story with an older battle at Beit Horon story – but attempting to tease out these details would take the chapter too far afield.

225 This geographical location is almost certainly a gloss. It makes little sense with the story and is probably influenced by the later addition of the southern campaign, as I will argue further on.

only does the narrative arc seem disjointed, but also the text itself, specifically the final line describing this second miracle in v. 14, appears disjointed.

וְלֹא הָיָה כַּיּוֹם הַהוּא לְפָנָיו וְאַחֲרָיו לִשְׁמֹעַ יְהוָה בְּקוֹל אִישׁ And there never was a day like this before or af-
כִּי יְהוָה נִלְחָם לְיִשְׂרָאֵל. terwards, where YHWH hearkened to a man's voice, *for YHWH fought for Israel.*

The final clause does not work well with the rest of the sentence; YHWH had been fighting for Israel even before Joshua's request for the sun to stop.

For these two reasons, i.e., the lack of narrative logic for this miracle and the awkward phrasing of the final verse, I would like to suggest that the insertion from the *Sefer ha-Yashar* is secondary to the story of the battle of Beit Horon and that the awkward final clause of v. 14 was originally the end of v. 11, which would have read:

וַיְהִי בְּנֻסָם מִפְּנֵי יִשְׂרָאֵל—הֵם בְּמוֹרַד בֵּית חוֹרֹן—וַיהוָה And it was as they were running from Israel—
הִשְׁלִיךְ עֲלֵיהֶם אֲבָנִים גְּדֹלוֹת מִן הַשָּׁמַיִם... וַיָּמֻתוּ רַבִּים they were at the descent of Beit Horon[226]—
אֲשֶׁר מֵתוּ בְּאַבְנֵי הַבָּרָד מֵאֲשֶׁר הָרְגוּ בְּנֵי יִשְׂרָאֵל and YHWH threw great stones upon them
בֶּחָרֶב... כִּי יְהוָה נִלְחָם לְיִשְׂרָאֵל. from the heavens... More died from the hail-stones... for YHWH fought for Israel.

This makes much more sense. YHWH's crushing the enemy with hailstones can be fairly described as his fighting for Israel. The phrase also explains well the reason more people died from hailstones than the sword, since YHWH fought for Israel. Thus, I suggest that the sun-stopping account was spliced into the battle of Beit Horon account, and that the older layer of the narrative had only the hailstones as the miraculous intervention.

What may have been the original context of the sun-stopping poem? It describes a miraculous intervention during a battle in the vicinity of Gibeon. Was it an alternative version of Joshua's battle? Conceivably, but I suggest another option. I believe there is reason to suggest that the *Sefer Ha-Yashar*, the probable source of this poem, may have been an epic poem devoted to the heroic rise and tragic fall of *King Saul*. This poem may have highlighted one of the great successes of his career, with the Mount Gilboa ballad serving as the closing of the epic. Thus, the stopping of the sun over Gibeon may have once been part of Saul's battle against the Gibeonites, before it became part of Joshua's battle in

---

226 This phrase also seems like a gloss, which would mean that the earliest text does not identify the spot where this happened, or, at least, did not do so in this verse.

their defence.[227] One may imagine that the supporters of both heroes were in a mnemohistorical tug-of-war about who stopped the sun.

In fact, the myth or motif of the "hero that stopped the sun" probably predates both Joshua and Saul. The poem is more related to the area where it "occurred" than the particular hero involved.[228] Note that, unlike the ballad of Saul's death, the poem about the stopping of the sun and moon mentions no name in its short narrative but only in the framing verse, i.e., "Joshua said."[229]

The Southern Campaign

The sun miracle was not the only addition into the narrative of the battle of Bet Horon. I suggest that an older version of this account jumped immediately from Joshua's success in the battle (due to YHWH's intervention with hailstones) to a version of Josh 11:23.[230]

---

227 Alternatively, if the LXX text is correct, and this poem was not part of *Sefer ha-Yashar*, there would be little if any reason to connect it to Saul. Even so, it seems clear for the reasons stated above that it was added into this narrative later and may not have originally been associated with Joshua at all.

228 The poem, which references both Gibeon and Ayalon, fits well with a battle in this region; the descent of Beit Horon is right in between the two locations. The amount of sun-related place names in this overall area (Har Heres, Timnat Heres, Beit Shemesh) has been noted by many scholars.

229 As noted above, the motif of stopping the sun to effect the timing of a battle is not uniquely Israelite. The idea appears in Homer as well (*Iliad* 18) when, after Achilles finds the body of Patroclus, Hera makes the sun set early in order to end the battle for the day ("And now ox-eyed Queen Hera told the tireless sun, to return, though unwillingly, to Ocean's stream. At last he set, and the noble Achaeans rested from mighty conflict, and war's evils.")

230 The idea of this verse as an ending to an early book of Joshua is supported, in various forms, by Kratz (*Composition*, 192), Römer ("Book-Endings", 87) and Uwe Becker, "End-redaktionelle Kontextvernetzungen des Josua-Buches," in *Die deuteronomistischen Geschichtswerke: Redaktions- und religionsgeschichtliche Perspektiven zur "Deuteronomismus": Diskussion in Tora und Vorderen Propheten* (ed. Markus Witte, Konrad Schmid, Doris Prechel and Jan Christian Gertz; BZAW 365; Berlin: de Gruyter, 2006), 139–161 [151]. Another possibility, suggested by Axel Knauf, is that the account ended with the line "for YHWH fought for Israel." See: Ernst Axel Knauf, "Buchschlüsse im Josuabuch," in *Les dernières rédactions du Pentateuque, de l'Héxateuque et de l'Ennéateuque* (ed. Thomas Römer and Konrad Schmid; BETL 203; Leuven: Peeters, 2007), 217–224; also: Knauf, *Josua*, 17, 109–110.

וַיִּקַּח יְהוֹשֻׁעַ אֶת כָּל הָאָרֶץ [הַזֹּאת]²³¹ כְּכֹל אֲשֶׁר דִּבֶּר יְהוָה Joshua took [this] entire land, *in accordance* אֶל מֹשֶׁה,²³² וַיִּתְּנָהּ יְהוֹשֻׁעַ²³³ לְנַחֲלָה לְיִשְׂרָאֵל כְּמַחְלְקֹתָם *with all that* YHWH *told Moses, and Joshua* לְשִׁבְטֵיהֶם²³⁴ וְהָאָרֶץ שָׁקְטָה מִמִּלְחָמָה. *gave it as an inheritance to Israel, in accordance with their divisions and their tribes, and the land was quiet from war.*

The phrase about the land being quiet from war after the decisive victory of an Israelite military hero is a standard trope in the Book of Judges.²³⁵ The usual phrase describing how many years the land was quiet does not appear here, but this may be because Joshua was not incorporated into the overall structure of the book of Judges and does not participate in the "good years-bad years" cyclical historiography that characterizes this work.

A comparison between this verse and the ending of the story of Caleb's request supports the possibility that this phrase was once the ending of the Joshua account or, at least, a section of it. In chapter 14, Caleb requests Hebron as his city and Joshua grants the request. Caleb then proceeds to conquer the city and rid the area of the *Anaqim*. The section ends with the same words as 11:23, "and the land was quiet from war." When this section was added into the book of Joshua is unknown. Nevertheless, it seems clear from the fact that it ends with a *Wiederaufnahme* to the phrase in 11:23 that the Caleb story was added before Josh 12:1–14:5, and that 11:23 was the final verse of this unit.

To summarize, the older account of Joshua's military conquest probably centered around the battle at Beit Horon and ended with YHWH's intervention. The land is then quiet from war, and Joshua divides it up. At this more advanced stage, Joshua had already moved from being the leader of Joseph to the leader of Israel; however, it is unclear what the borders of "Israel" were meant to be in this account.²³⁶ Most probably, the extreme north and the extreme south were incorporated later in the development of the concept Israel.²³⁷

---

231 The opening phrase of 11:23 is a *Wiederaufnahme* from 11:16, where this word appears. Kratz (*Composition*, 192, 208) connects these two verses as well.

232 This phrase would be a later gloss, once the Joshua and Moses stories were connected.

233 Joshua's name was probably added in later, once the clause referencing Moses was added. Without this clause, reuse of the proper name is unnecessary and reads awkwardly.

234 This phrase is probably a later gloss, emphasizing the complex tribal divisions and the account of the lot for all the tribes that would appear as part of the final editing of Joshua.

235 The syntax is unique here, however, since the phrase is usually in the imperfect (וישקט הארץ).

236 Rachel Havrelock makes a similar observation, but focusing equally on the *ḥerem* (massacre of the locals):

The Addition of the Northern Campaign

The motivation for the addition of the Northern Campaign seems relatively straightforward. As the identity and mnemohistory of the northern tribes became firmly implanted into Israelite historiography, so did their heroes. One hero, Barak ben Abinoam, was known as the man who conquered Jabin king of Hazor and destroyed that city. This account stands in some conflict with the view that Joshua conquered all of Israel. Hence, a Joshua campaign to the extreme north, and focused on the defeat of Jabin, king of Hazor, would have been needed to affirm Joshua's position as the first and preeminent conqueror of all Israel.

This is a classic example of the phenomenon of tradition-cannibalism. (Another example is the account in ch. 11 in which Joshua takes Hebron and vanquishes the giants, a feat attributed to Caleb in the earlier legend recorded in ch. 14.) With this, Joshua joined the ranks of the great legend-cannibalizers, a prestigious group that includes luminaries such as David and Jacob.[238]

Expanding the Southern Campaign

Less obvious than the introduction of the conquest of Hazor and the Northern Campaign in Joshua's story is why the battle at Beit Horon was expanded to include a detailed southern campaign (10:20, 28–42) and an expanded description of the death of the five kings (10:15–18, 22–27). That the campaign was a later addition to the battle story seems clear from a number of factors. A full treatment of this complex and layered section would require a separate study, but the most obvious piece of evidence is, again, the *Wiederaufnahme*.

The Book of Joshua's extreme assertions that Israel exterminated peoples and marched behind an exemplary general intend to obscure the disparate beginnings and affiliations that fall under the term "Israel" (Havrelock, River Jordan, 12).

237 My own belief is that the concept "Israel" begins in the Transjordan, moves into the Cisjordanian Mount Ephraim region, and only then makes its way up and down and into the coast—but arguing this is a project for another time.

238 David appropriates the Goliath story from Elhanan (2 Sam. 21:19). Jacob takes a number of other people's traditions; he is credited with the founding of a number of cities and even, at one point, with the conquest of Shechem. For more details, see: Zev I. Farber, "Jerubaal, Jacob, and the Battle for Shechem: A Tradition History," *JHS* 13 (2013), art. 12.

כִּי יְהוָה נִלְחָם לְיִשְׂרָאֵל. For Yʜᴡʜ fought for Israel. (10:14)

כִּי יְהוָה אֱלֹהֵי יִשְׂרָאֵל נִלְחָם לְיִשְׂרָאֵל. For Yʜᴡʜ, the God of Israel, fought for Israel.
(10:42)

The second use of this term, which was marshaled to explain how Joshua could have conquered the entire south in one campaign, shows a creative use of *Wiederaufnahme*, where the interpolator who added the southern campaign made use of the concept of Yʜᴡʜ fighting for Israel to explain a lightning campaign in the south.

Assuming that the verses between 14 and 42 are later additions, it is useful to subdivide this section of the chapter into two main parts: the execution of the kings at Makedah and the Southern Campaign proper.

The first section, although it has undergone a serious Deuteronomic editing,[239] seems to derive from an etiological tradition about a rock that closes the entrance of a cave in Makedah. This tradition became associated with Joshua at a certain point and was tacked on to this story.[240]

The expanded Southern Campaign account contradicts the rest of the chapter in a number of ways. First, the conquest of Makedah appears after the execution of the kings in Makedah, a timeline of events that makes little sense. Second, the siege and conquest come after the defeat of the armies of these towns in battle. Third, the list of conquered towns does not match the list of aggressors. Most glaring is the absence of Jerusalem from this list—the city which ostensibly leads the campaign and which would have been the most important of all the conquered towns!

Why was the Southern Campaign added and when? A number of scholars have pointed out that the composition of the Southern Campaign bears a striking resemblance to Neo-Assyrian campaign descriptions. The strongest argument

---

239 The Deuteronomistic editing can be seen in the discussion of hanging the bodies, as being in accord with Mosaic law, and the "be strong and brave" language, which frames the Deuteronomistic treatment of Joshua as a whole. In the older account, the kings probably hid in the cave and Joshua simply closed the entrance with a rock and suffocated them. Perhaps the Dtr editor thought this to be an illegitimate form of execution, or simply preferred to expand the story with some rhetorical flourish and classic execution.

240 Many of the traditions about special rock formations in the Cisjordan are attached to Joshua. This reflects the idea that anything ancient in the land marking the conquest must go back to Joshua. The special connection between Joshua and the land was picked up by the Rabbis in some of their discussions about Joshua and the nature of the land and its institutions (see chapter 6).

for this was made by K. Lawson Younger in his work on ancient conquest accounts.[241] After detailing the many parallels, Younger concludes:

> ...[I]t appears that the text of Joshua 9 – 12 is structured on a transmission code similar to that of other ancient Near Eastern royal inscriptions (237).

Not all of Younger's parallels are convincing. Nevertheless, this section stands out. The literary value of the repetitive, almost monotonous repetition of the destruction of cities lies primarily in the effect of painting Joshua in the colors of an Assyrian royal conqueror. Römer understands this stage of the book of Joshua as early Deuteronomistic and dates it to the period of Josiah (*So-Called*, 86 – 90). I believe that this section, which in my reconstruction is more limited than that of Römer,[242] is pre-Deuteronomistic. As such, I suggest that the section was put together towards the end of the Neo-Assyrian period.

At this stage, the North had had a century to settle into their loss of independence and to develop a historiography that would have been in strong conversation with that of the south. Perhaps this explains the odd combination of a conquest of the south by Joshua with an absence of any mention of Jerusalem.[243] On the one hand, it would be polemically useful to have Joshua as the first conqueror of the south, the man who gave the now-more-powerful Judeans their largest cities by conquering them from the Canaanites.[244] On the other hand, perhaps by this stage of the Judahite-Israelite conversation, the tradition of David as conqueror of Jerusalem had become so entrenched so as to make a suggestion that Joshua did this "over-the-top."[245]

In short, the expanded Southern Campaign account reinforces the construction of Joshua as a proto-monarch or founding-leader of Israel and Judah, one depicted in the style of a Mesopotamian monarch.

---

241 K. Lawson Younger, *Ancient Conquest Accounts: A Study in Ancient Near Eastern and Biblical History Writing* (JSOTsup 98; Sheffield: Sheffield Academic Press, 1990). This also seems to be the position of Thomas Römer. See, for example, Thomas Römer, *So-Called*, 83 – 90. See also Earl, *Reading Joshua*, 89 – 93. For a different take, see: John Van Seters, "Joshua's Campaign of Canaan and Near Eastern Historiography," *SJOT* 2 (1990): 1 – 12.

242 Römer includes that the majority of the first 12 chapters in this text; I am only discussing here a possible early version of ch. 10, together with select pieces of some of the earlier accounts, without the Deuteronomic framing. A verse by verse reconstruction of the various layers of Joshua is beyond the scope of this analysis.

243 Interestingly, Gibeah is not mentioned either.

244 It is tempting to ask, historically speaking, on which side of the Sennacherib campaign this Joshua account was written. Is the author picturing the conquest of Sennacherib as he writes?

245 Judg 1:8, in which Judah conquers Jerusalem, is admittedly a very bizarre verse; when could such a verse have been written?

Joshua Meets Moses

As Israelite-Judahite mnemohistory developed, the story of the conquest of the Cisjordan under Joshua met with the story of the Exodus from Egypt and the wandering in the wilderness under Moses. Since virtually all of ritual YHWH-focused practice was being attributed to Moses the law-giver, the Joshua tradition would have had little choice but to fit itself into the rubric of the Moses story.[246] To get a sense of how this may have come to pass, it seems best to begin with how Joshua appears in Moses' book, the Pentateuch.

Joshua in the Pentateuch – Laying out the Contradictions

As was seen in the first chapter, the presentation of Joshua in the Pentateuch is multifaceted and complex. This is no problem *per se*; biblical literature is replete with complex characters. The *problem* stems from the fact that the relationship between these images as presented in the text appears disjointed and often inexplicable.

For instance, Joshua appears out of nowhere in the Amalek account. The reader is not formally introduced to him until his appearance as Moses' attendant. Moreover, the position of personal attendant is very different than that of army general. The former evokes a Joshua who follows his mentor around and spends his time in the Tent of YHWH. The latter is a leader of men, a public persona. The dissonance between these two images is intensified by the description of Joshua as *na'ar*. Although it is true, as a number of private seals demonstrate,[247] that *na'ar* does not *necessarily* refer to a young man, it is not a term one would use of an independent national leader. Oded Lipschits has recently argued that the term, when used in conjuction with royal service, means

---

246 I will not take up here the interesting question of when the Moses story and the patriarch stories began to merge. See Schmid's *Genesis and the Moses Story* for discussion of this question. Albert de Pury argues that, at least during the time of Hoshea, the Jacob and Moses stories were in competition with each other and had not yet been brought into one single timeline. See: Albert de Pury, "The Jacob Story and the Beginning of the Formation of the Pentateuch," in *A Farewell to the Yahwist: The Composition of the Pentateuch in Recent European Scholarship* (eds. Thomas B. Dozeman and Konrad Schmid; SBLSymS 34; Atlanta: SBL, 2006), 51–72.

247 See, for example: Nahman Avigad, "New Light on the Na'ar Seals," in *Magnalia Dei, The Mighty Acts of God: Essays on the Bible and Archaeology in Memory of G. Ernest Wright* (eds. Frank Moore Cross, Werner E. Lemke, and Patrick D. Miller, Jr.; Garden City, NY: Doubleday, 1976), 294–300; Yosef Garfinkel, "The Eliakim Na'ar Yokan Seal Impression: Sixty Years of Confusion in Biblical Archaeology Research," *BA* 53 (1990): 74–79.

something like the king's personal attaché, and is parallel to terms like *'eved ha-melekh* (servant of the king) and *zeroa' la-melekh* (right-hand man of the king).[248] In this sense, the description of Joshua as a *na'ar* of Moses would fit well into this general semantic range. Although I imagine that it is possible to have a general who is also a servant/attendant/lad of the leader, nevertheless, the description fits better with the Joshua who follows Moses around than it does with the Joshua who fights battles.

Similarly, when Joshua is appointed as a scout, the reader is ostensibly already aware of Joshua and his position as Moses' attendant and one of his hand-picked men, not to mention as the military hero who fought the despised Amalekites. Yet none of Joshua's earlier appearances factor into the scout story at all. Somehow, it is not obvious to the other scouts or to the congregation of Israel that Joshua, being so close to Moses and YHWH, was a "company man" of sorts, meaning that he would have no *choice* but to *defend* the conquest plan.

Finally, although it is *possible* that from the very beginning Joshua was meant to be Elazar's equal partner and not the sole leader of Israel, this is hardly obvious from the self-contradictory presentation in Numbers 27. In this text, Joshua is first referred to as YHWH's choice for future leader of Israel only to be instantly demoted to a position subservient to that of Elazar.

The Oldest Pentateuchal Layer

The questions surrounding the redaction of the Pentateuch are highly debated. Since an attempt to offer an overall solution to this question would take this chapter too far afield, I will use what seems to me to be the most useful model for this material – a supplementary approach, but one that assumes the existence of multiple source texts or strands. Furthermore, for the sake of simplicity, when one of the text strands I discuss bears a strong resemblance to one of the classic "documents" in the documentary approach, I will use the standard documentary siglum for the sake of simplicity.

"E" appears to be the oldest Joshua strand in the Pentateuch. In this strand, Joshua begins as a young apprentice to Moses. At a tender age, the great prophet handpicks Joshua to be his personal attendant. He follows Moses up the Mountain of YHWH and spends his days in the Tent of Meeting. During his years of

---

248 This latter term is Lipschits' reading of a disputed term, following Naftali Tur-Sinai's earlier suggestion. For Lipschits' argument as a whole, see: Oded Lipschits, "On 'Servant of YHWH' and 'Servant of the King'," *Shenaton* 13 (2001–2): 157–171 [164; 167–168; Hebrew].

training, Joshua grows into a spiritual person and leader in his own right, and is the natural choice of YHWH for Moses' successor.[249] The story of Joshua as loyal scout comes from either a different source (P) or a later redaction. The image from E is mirrored in D, which introduces Joshua in 1:38 as "standing before Moses." Joshua's position as Moses' understudy allows for a natural progression towards his future as Moses' successor. This same sequence, from understudy to successor, in E and D represents the *earliest* layer of Pentateuchal Joshua... except for one problem.

The Amalek Story

One text not solved by the above reconstruction of the sequence in the E text is the account of Amalek, in which Joshua appears out ot nowhere as a military leader. This account was likely added later. Nevertheless, I do not believe it was woven out of whole cloth by the redactor. To explain, the earliest kernel of the Joshua tradition most probably has its beginning in an Ephraimite or Josephite military figure, with no reference to Moses or the wilderness. This image of Joshua forms the core of the book of Joshua and was probably centered on local stories of battle and conquest.

I would like to propose that the literary core of the battle-with-Amalek story was once part of a Joshua cycle or collection, but was moved to its present location. In other words, I am suggesting that the core story was that Amalek attacked the Israelites *in the Cisjordan*. Joshua, having defeated them, declares eternal war against them. This early layer contained no references to Moses or the wilderness. Rather, the description is of a *local* battle.

Amalekites appear to have been a going concern in Ephraimite history. This can be demonstrated from references to Amalek in the Ephraim region in the Song of Deborah (Judg 5:14) "from Ephraim whose roots are in Amalek," and in the burial notice of Abdon ben Hillel the Pirathonite (Judg 12:15), who was buried in Pirathon in the land of Ephraim *on the Amalekite mountain*.[250]

---

249 Joel Baden makes the intriguing argument that this E source actually includes a scene where Moses turns the leadership over to Joshua, Deuteronomy 31:14–15 & 23. See: Joel S. Baden, *J, E, and the Redaction of the Pentateuch* (FAT 68; Winona Lake: Eisenbrauns, 2009).
250 This reconstruction solves yet another troubling problem in the Pentateuch; namely, if Joshua was the preferred general from the beginning of the Exodus period and will be the military leader of the conquest of Canaan, why is he given no role in the Midianite campaign or in the conquest of the Transjordan? This problem so irked the author of the *Samaritan Book of Joshua*, that he added Joshua into his version of the Midianite campaign. The insertion of the

Why was the Amalek story moved to this spot? I suggest that a later reader, perhaps influenced by the D text, inserted an Amalek story into the Pentateuchal narrative so that this group would be the first enemy Israel encounters, in keeping with the growing image of Amalek as Israel's primordial enemy. This editor placed an account of Joshua's battle with Amalek into the Exodus narrative, and modified it by working Moses into the narrative. The use of the place-name Rephidim would be a redactional insertion, aimed at connecting the Amalek story to the previous one (Exod 17).

ח וַיָּבֹא עֲמָלֵק וַיִּלָּחֶם עִם יִשְׂרָאֵל בִּרְפִידִם.	[8] Then Amalek came and fought with Israel *at Rephidim.*
ט וַיֹּאמֶר מֹשֶׁה אֶל יְהוֹשֻׁעַ בְּחַר לָנוּ אֲנָשִׁים וְצֵא הִלָּחֵם בַּעֲמָלֵק מָחָר אָנֹכִי נִצָּב עַל רֹאשׁ הַגִּבְעָה וּמַטֵּה הָאֱלֹהִים בְּיָדִי.	[9] Moses said to Joshua, "Choose some men for us and go out, fight with Amalek. Tomorrow I will stand on the top of the hill with the staff of God in my hand."
וַיַּעַשׂ יְהוֹשֻׁעַ כַּאֲשֶׁר אָמַר לוֹ מֹשֶׁה לְהִלָּחֵם בַּעֲמָלֵק וּמֹשֶׁה אַהֲרֹן וְחוּר עָלוּ רֹאשׁ הַגִּבְעָה.	[10] So Joshua did as Moses told him, and fought with Amalek, while Moses, Aaron, and Hur went up to the top of the hill.
א וְהָיָה כַּאֲשֶׁר יָרִים מֹשֶׁה יָדוֹ וְגָבַר יִשְׂרָאֵל וְכַאֲשֶׁר יָנִיחַ יָדוֹ וְגָבַר עֲמָלֵק. ב וִידֵי מֹשֶׁה כְּבֵדִים וַיִּקְחוּ אֶבֶן וַיָּשִׂימוּ תַחְתָּיו וַיֵּשֶׁב עָלֶיהָ וְאַהֲרֹן וְחוּר תָּמְכוּ בְיָדָיו מִזֶּה אֶחָד וּמִזֶּה אֶחָד וַיְהִי יָדָיו אֱמוּנָה עַד בֹּא הַשָּׁמֶשׁ.	[11] Whenever Moses held up his hand, Israel prevailed; and whenever he lowered his hand, Amalek prevailed. [12] But Moses' hands grew weary; so they took a stone and put it under him, and he sat on it. Aaron and Hur held up his hands, one on one side, and the other on the other side; so his hands were steady until the sun set.
י וַיַּחֲלֹשׁ יְהוֹשֻׁעַ אֶת עֲמָלֵק וְאֶת עַמּוֹ לְפִי חָרֶב.	[13] And Joshua defeated Amalek and his people with the sword,
יד וַיֹּאמֶר יְהוָה אֶל מֹשֶׁה כְּתֹב זֹאת זִכָּרוֹן בַּסֵּפֶר וְשִׂים בְּאָזְנֵי יְהוֹשֻׁעַ כִּי מָחֹה אֶמְחֶה אֶת זֵכֶר עֲמָלֵק מִתַּחַת הַשָּׁמָיִם.	[14] Then YHWH said to Moses, "Write this as a reminder in a book and recite it in the hearing of Joshua: <u>I will utterly blot out the remembrance of Amalek from under heaven.</u>"[251]
טו וַיִּבֶן מֹשֶׁה מִזְבֵּחַ וַיִּקְרָא שְׁמוֹ יְהוָה נִסִּי.	[15] And Moses built an altar and called it, *YHWH Nissi.*[252]

Amalek story created this problem. Without it, Joshua does not take on military functions until much later in life.

251 This is Deuteronomistic language, taken directly from Deut 25:19.

252 As a piece of extreme speculation, I wonder if this verse wasn't originally part of the Amalek story but was the concluding verse to the previous story, where the Israelites test (נסה) YHWH, and Moses names the place Massa u-Meribah. He then builds an altar, which puns the name, and says YHWH is his banner (נס). However, if, as some commentators suggest, "נסי" is actually a miswriting of "כסי" (my throne)—an emendation that has no textual support that I know of but is still possible—this argument falls apart.

טז וַיֹּאמֶר: "כִּי־יָד עַל־כֵּס יָהּ מִלְחָמָה לַיהוָה בַּעֲמָלֵק מִדֹּר דֹּר." ¹⁶ and he said, "A hand upon the seat of YHWH! YHWH will have war with Amalek from generation to generation."

Removing Moses and the Deuteronomic language, the outline of the story is simple, if schematic. Amalek attacks Israel. Joshua defeats them in the attack and declares the Amalekites to be the eternal enemies of YHWH. In truth, when one thinks about narrative logic, there is little sense in an Amalek attack upon the Israelites in the middle of the Sinai wilderness. What would Amalek have been doing there in the first place? It makes more sense to assume that an older account of a local battle with Amalek was moved, over time, into the wilderness period as part of an attempt to explain the mythopoeic role this enemy assumes in later literature and ideology.

Tracing the Amalek traditions through the Bible, some earlier texts seem to describe Amalek as an actual enemy, while in later texts, they become a symbolic enemy. Joshua, Saul, and David are all said to have battled Amalek, and Balaam's prophecy about Agog (Num 24:7) implies that the poem was written at a time when Israel would have considered Amalek a powerful and live enemy. However, once one gets to the Book of Esther, Agog and his Amalekite descendants are a trope that implies that the person (Haman) is rabidly anti-Jewish.

It appears to me that the Deuteronomic usage of Amalek—and the later Deuteronomy-inspired editing of the Amalek pericope in Exodus—represent a middle stage in this development. Already by the time of these passages, Amalek is a primordial enemy of God, and Moses commands their destruction. They are a wandering desert tribe and no longer the enemy from Mount Ephraim. Looking carefully at the Exodus passage, there is a dissonance between verses 14 and 16 of Exodus 17. According to verse 16, Amalek is an eternal enemy of YHWH but according to verse 14, YHWH vows to wipe Amalek off the earth. These are two very different conceptions. I suggest that the latter verse is original to the old Joshua account and implicitly assumes an existing enemy called Amalek with whom Israel constantly does battle. The Moses recension, however, assumes a reality where Amalek is no more, for YHWH wiped this group off the planet, just like YHWH had promised he would do.

The Joshua versus Amalek tradition also fits well into the argument of the previous section, i.e., that the Joshua traditions and the Saul traditions were in some tension with each other. Although, as previously argued, the legend of Joshua grows at Saul's expense, it would be wrong to believe that Saul's legend did not have its own supporters; the Amalek account is a strong example of this. In 1 Samuel 14:48, there is a verse in which the conquest of Amalek is attributed to Saul. Although a lengthy account of Saul's defeat of Amalek does appear in chapter 15, this version is meant to describe the downfall of Saul, not his triumph. 14:48, however, references it positively.

I suggest that just as Joshua's myth expanded at the expense of Saul's, Saul's myth expanded at the expense of Joshua's, with the final defeat of Amalek being attributed to Saul. In this particular case, a kind of mnemohistorical battle between the two Amalekite-smiters developed. The story of Saul's sparing of Agog in 1 Samuel 15 can be seen as a retaliatory polemic against Saul, and the Benjaminite region he represents: Yes he smote them, this version says, but he ruined it by ignoring the word of God. Similarly, the account of the Benjaminites Mordechai and Esther defeating the Agagite Haman can be seen as a Saulide response to the 1 Samuel 15 account, defending the reputation of Benjaminites by granting the final defeat of King Agag and Amalek to a member of Saul's family and not to Joshua or his family.

Joshua in the Early Priestly Text

Moving on to the "P" text, Joshua ostensibly begins as a loyal scout and is then chosen by Yнwн to be the successor of Moses in ch. 27, when Moses is told that his time to die was approaching. Although at first glance this makes some sense, the timeline actually engenders a number of problems. In the P version of the scout story both Joshua and Caleb are loyal scouts, and yet Joshua is picked and Caleb ignored.

The scout story is not likely an attempt to explain how Joshua was chosen to be leader. Otherwise, one would have to explain why Joshua was chosen and *not* Caleb? Instead, I suggest that the story represents a *reaction* to the J or pre-P scout account. Primarily, the story seems to be yet another example of Joshua's legend cannibalism—albeit an idiosyncratic version, since Caleb is included in the story as well.

As argued in a previous section, the early tradition upon which P is based has Joshua given Timnat Heres by the people in a way parallel to Caleb's receipt of Hebron. As both of these characters become subsumed in the Mosaic wilderness traditions, the explanation for their being granted land shifts from being a prize for their leadership in conquest to a reward for their loyalty as scouts. Furthermore, the scout stories, in the form that we have them, are written with an eye towards explaining why Caleb or Caleb and Joshua, are permitted to enter the Promised Land when the rest of the wilderness generation has been cursed by Yнwн and doomed to die in the wilderness. Hence, even if one deems the scout story to be integral to P, it does not naturally lead to the appointment of Joshua as Moses' successor.

In fact, the appointment of Joshua in the P text poses quite a problem, rhetorically as well as narratively.[253] In Numbers 27:15–23, the choice of Joshua is presented as YHWH's response to Moses' fear that Moses' death will leave the people without proper leadership or guidance. YHWH responds by telling Moses to appoint Joshua as leader and Moses does so. At this point, somehow, Moses accomplishes the incredible and avoids dying for another book and a half. Why doesn't Moses die in Numbers 27?[254]

A possible answer lies in the repetition of YHWH's command to Moses to go up the mountain in Deuteronomy 32. This repetition has the appearance of a classic *Wiederaufnahme*, although admittedly at a serious distance from the passage it is resuming.

דברים פרק לב	במדבר פרק כז
מח) וַיְדַבֵּר יְהוָה אֶל מֹשֶׁה בְּעֶצֶם הַיּוֹם הַזֶּה לֵאמֹר:	יב) וַיֹּאמֶר יְהוָה אֶל מֹשֶׁה:
מט) עֲלֵה אֶל הַר הָעֲבָרִים הַזֶּה הַר נְבוֹ	עֲלֵה אֶל הַר הָעֲבָרִים הַזֶּה
יְרֵחוֹ פְּנֵי עַל אֲשֶׁר מוֹאָב בְּאֶרֶץ אֲשֶׁר	
וּרְאֵה אֶת אֶרֶץ כְּנַעַן	וּרְאֵה אֶת הָאָרֶץ
אֲשֶׁר אֲנִי נֹתֵן לִבְנֵי יִשְׂרָאֵל לַאֲחֻזָּה.	אֲשֶׁר נָתַתִּי לִבְנֵי יִשְׂרָאֵל.
נ) וּמֻת בָּהָר אֲשֶׁר אַתָּה עֹלֶה שָׁמָּה	יג) וְרָאִיתָה אֹתָהּ
וְהֵאָסֵף אֶל עַמֶּיךָ	וְנֶאֱסַפְתָּ אֶל עַמֶּיךָ
כַּאֲשֶׁר מֵת אַהֲרֹן אָחִיךָ בְּהֹר הָהָר וַיֵּאָסֶף אֶל עַמָּיו.	גַּם אַתָּה כַּאֲשֶׁר נֶאֱסַף אַהֲרֹן אָחִיךָ.
נא) עַל אֲשֶׁר מְעַלְתֶּם בִּי בְּתוֹךְ בְּנֵי יִשְׂרָאֵל בְּמֵי מְרִיבַת קָדֵשׁ	יד) כַּאֲשֶׁר מְרִיתֶם פִּי בְּמִדְבַּר צִן בִּמְרִיבַת הָעֵדָה לְהַקְדִּישֵׁנִי
מִדְבַּר צִן עַל אֲשֶׁר לֹא קִדַּשְׁתֶּם אוֹתִי בְּתוֹךְ בְּנֵי יִשְׂרָאֵל.	בַמַּיִם לְעֵינֵיהֶם הֵם מֵי מְרִיבַת קָדֵשׁ מִדְבַּר צִן.
נב) כִּי מִנֶּגֶד תִּרְאֶה אֶת הָאָרֶץ וְשָׁמָּה לֹא תָבוֹא אֶל הָאָרֶץ	
אֲשֶׁר אֲנִי נֹתֵן לִבְנֵי יִשְׂרָאֵל.	

---

253 There is a further problem with seeing Joshua as an integral part of an early or "independent" P. First, the imagery of Joshua being "a man with spirit in him" in Numbers 27 – the P text – is reminiscent of the account of the appointment of the seventy elders in Numbers 11, who have the spirit overflow from Moses onto them – an E text. (To be fair this is not an exact parallel. As Joel Baden pointed out to me in a personal communication, in the E account there is no mention of Joshua receiving this spirit, only the 70 elders.) Second, in the P text of Numbers 27, Moses describes a leader as someone who "goes out and comes in before the people". This is the exact description of leadership Moses uses in Deuteronomy 31 as well – a D text. These two examples of unexpected textual resonances could simply be coincidental. There is no rule against two sources using the same expression fortuitously. Nevertheless, it does seem like a strong coincidence. In fact, the seeming *inability* of P's appointment-of-Joshua narrative to stand alone without knowledge of any non-P texts is what inspired Reinhard Kratz to call it redactional and give it the siglum R^P.

254 To quote Joseph Blenkinsopp: "We may detect in the subsequent narrative in Numbers a note almost of embarrassment that Moses is still alive..." Joseph Blenkinsopp, *The Pentateuch: An Introduction to the First Five Books of the Bible* (ABRL; New York: Doubleday, 1992), 229.

Numbers 27	Deuteronomy 32
[12] And YHWH said to Moses:	[48] And YHWH spoke to Moses on this very day saying:
"Ascend this Mount Ebarim	[49] "Ascend this Mount Ebarim, Mount Nebo, which is in the land of Moab facing Jericho,
and look upon the land which I am giving to the Children of Israel	and look upon the land of Canaan, which I am giving to the Children of Israel as a holding.
[13] And look at it	[50] Die on the mountain which you will ascend,
And be gathered unto your people	and be gathered unto your people,
You also—just like your brother Aaron was gathered.	Just like your brother died on Mount Hor and was gathered unto his people.
[14] When you acted contrary to my word—in the Wilderness of Zin, in the quarrel of the assembly—to sanctify me with water before their eyes. These are the waters of Meribat Qadesh in the Wilderness of Zin.	[51] Since you affronted me among the Children of Israel with the waters of Meribat Qadesh in the Wilderness of Zin, since you did not sanctify me among the Children of Israel.
	[52] For from there you may see the land but you will not go into the land which I am giving to the Children of Israel.

If one thinks of Deuteronomy 32:48 – 52 as a resumptive repetition of the command in Numbers 27, and one understands Deuteronomy 33, Moses' final blessing, as a later addition to the primary text, one is left with the intriguing and rather attractive possibility that in an older version of the P document Moses goes up the mountain to die *immediately* after YHWH tells him to in Numbers 27; a possibility advocated by Konrad Schmid as well.[255]

If this suggestion is correct, then the appointment-of-Joshua story in Numbers 27 is a supplemental addition into the P text; one of many additions into the core text which can be lumped together under the heading of "things Moses did before he died."

This redactional supplement may have been prompted by the redactor's encounter with the E (and D?) narrative strain. Alternatively, this addition may simply reflect a stage at which the stories of the various Israelite leaders, like Joshua and Moses, were being combined into an overarching Israelite-Judahite historiography. The solidification of Israelite/Judahite identity and the construction of their foundational mythologies must have required *some sort* of ordering of leadership from Moses in the wilderness to local Israelite leadership, in this case Joshua.[256] In short, it appears most likely that Joshua did not appear in the original P text as Moses' successor, if he appeared at all.

---

255 Schmid, *Genesis*, 120 n. 439.
256 As will be seen in chapter 3, the narrative technique of using the request for leadership as a way of establishing a tradition-historical continuity was later adopted in *Liber Antiquitatem*

Joshua in Mosaic Colors

It was noted in the first chapter that much of Joshua's character is painted in Mosaic colors. Not only is he Moses' attendant, but in a number of ways he is another Moses. Elie Assis, for example, points to a seven point correlation between Joshua and Moses in the biblical text.[257] Whether one accepts Assis's literary reading or not, it seems indubitable that some parallels between Moses and Joshua are intentional and are meant to make Joshua resemble Moses. The most obvious examples of this phenomenon are the splitting of the Jordan, which parallels the splitting of the Sea of Reeds,[258] the revelatory moment to Joshua outside Jericho, at which his shoes must be removed, the establishing of the cities of refuge, the miracle of hailstones,[259] and the offering of the Paschal sacrifice.[260]

The phenomenon itself is hardly surprising. Once Moses becomes the paradigmatic leader of Israel and Joshua his protégé, it seems a natural development to try and make his successor resemble him as much as possible. It would be both a sign of legitimacy for Joshua as well as a way of strengthening the Mosaic color of the religion of YHWH as a whole. Joshua receives prophecy the way Moses does, he performs similar rituals to those of Moses, and he performs similar miracles to those of Moses. In other words, Joshua is a second Moses but also a secondary or derivative Moses. This relationship is doubly useful as it helps mask the Achilles' heel of the Moses tradition – Moses does not conquer the land; Joshua does.

Biblicarum (ch. 21), where Joshua makes the *exact* same plea for the appointment of a successor, after being informed of his own immanent death.

257 Assis, *From Moses to Joshua*, 11–17 [12]; see chapter 1 for more details.

258 For this miracle, Frank Moore Cross, in his famous essay, "The Song of the Sea and Canaanite Myth," offers the counterargument that Joshua was the original splitter of the waters, and that the story of the splitting of the Sea of Reeds was modeled on that story of the splitting of the Jordan, and not the reverse. See, Frank Moore Cross, *Canaanite Myth and Hebrew Epic: Essays in the History of the Religion of Israel* (Cambridge: Harvard University Press, 1973), 112–144. Without delving into the details of Cross' literary reconstruction, once one accepts that the idea of Joshua as a conqueror from outside the land is a later construct, by definition the splitting of the Jordan River must be a later tradition in the Joshua corpus.

259 These two examples are not on Assis' list. One weakness in Assis' approach is that he offers a literary analysis of Joshua 1–11 only. When comparing Joshua to Moses, this is an artificial divide, and this artificial division seems especially problematic for the literary approach, which is supposed to follow the final form of the text.

260 These comparisons are all on the level of the narrative, on the editorial level there are a number of other correlations and comparisons, which will be looked at in the final section of this chapter.

The above reasons appear to be a sufficient explanation for the parallels between the characters on the narrative level. However, Alexander Rofé suggests a much more radical explanation for some of these parallels. In his understanding, in the early stage of the competition between the Joshua story and the Moses story, Joshua was credited by some Israelites as being the messenger of YHWH who brought Israel out of Egypt and into the land. Rofé notes that in chapter 24, Joshua makes a pact with the people. He argues that this is not a second covenant, but an alternative covenant, from a time when the Joshua story actively competed with the Moses story for prominence.

Rofé makes the same argument about the Paschal sacrifice and the circumcision at Gilgal. This was not originally envisioned as a second sacrifice with a second circumcision, i. e. , as an editorial attempt to put the stories in order. Instead, Rofé argues this is the Joshua version of the first Passover and the origin of circumcision in Gilgal.[261] The term for foreskin in this story is "the humiliation of Egypt," which implies that these people were coming from Egypt in their state of un-circumcision. Presumably, the story had Israel leaving Egypt with Joshua and entering the Promised Land immediately with a miraculous Jordan crossing.

This idea is admittedly bold, creative and attractive. Nevertheless, Rofé does not really offer a textual reconstruction of the Exodus-under-Joshua story. Presumably, this part of the tradition, Rofé would say, has been lost. This could be so, but without this piece, gauging the possibility of a Joshua-as-redeemer-from-Egypt story remains more than a little speculative.

Deuteronomistic and Priestly Redactions

Both the Deuteronomistic editors and the Priestly editors had a hand in updating Joshua's image and crafting his story into the one now familiar from the Bible.

Deuteronomistic Images of Joshua

As part of the (so-called) Deuteronomistic History, the Book of Joshua is infused with the rhetoric, terminology, and world-view of this school of thought.[262] I as-

---

261 It is worth remembering the Rofé is convinced of the primacy of the LXX text that Joshua was buried with the flint-knives he used to circumcise Israel.
262 I use the term "so-called" (taken from Thomas Römer) since there is serious scholarly debate nowadays whether a "Deuteronomistic History" is a reasonable or accurate construct of the Deuteronomy/Joshua through Kings complex. Although there certainly seems to be Deute-

sume that most of the core Joshua stories were already in existence before there was a Deuteronomistic edition of the book of Joshua. Nevertheless, the Deuteronomistic editing had a hand in organizing the information and, more importantly, framing the story as a part of this work's larger narrative.[263]

Ironically, the images of Joshua contributed by this editing are somewhat contradictory to each other. On one hand, the Deuteronomist believes that YHWH commanded the Israelites to annihilate the local population of Canaanites before settling the land. Since Joshua is seen as a heroic figure in the work, and his period is idealized, Joshua is credited with the annihilation of the Canaanites. The first half of the book constantly reiterates Joshua's policy of *ḥerem*, making him appear as a powerful and merciless military commander.

In virtual contradiction to this image of a powerful Joshua, the Deuteronomist paints Joshua as being frightened of leadership. To clarify, with the exception of his reaction to the failure at the Ai, Joshua does not express fear of battle. Rather, he expresses a fear of leadership. The attractiveness of this quality for the Deuteronomist probably derives from the fact that it emphasizes Joshua's secondary role in comparison to Moses. It is Moses, followed by the Israelites, who must calm Joshua's nerves and allow him to feel comfortable with his new position. This image goes hand in hand with the statements peppered throughout the Book of Joshua that Joshua acted in accordance with what YHWH commanded Moses.

Late Deuteronomistic Images of Joshua

As many biblical scholars have argued, there appears to be more than one Deuteronomistic recension. Frank Moore Cross and his student, Richard Nelson, point to at least two major recensions (DTR_1 and DTR_2). The first recension is re-

---

ronomistic editing in these books—especially in Joshua and Kings—I do not want to take a position here on whether there was a Deuteronomistic History proper, in the sense Martin Noth proposed it.

263 Whatever the origins of the first Joshua stories may have been, or their literary context, I suspect that Joshua became part of a Hexateuchal structure before it became part of a Deuteronomistic or Enneateuchal narrative. Ernst Axel Knauf (*Josua*, 17) makes this point incisively:

Eine Geschichte vom "Auszug aus Äegypten" ist   A story of "Exodus from Egypt" is unthinkable
undenkbar ohne iheren Abschluss mit einem   without its ending with "Entry into Canaan."
"Einzug in Kanaan."

I am in full agreement. I further believe that *some* of the Judges narratives began the same way, as appendices to the Book of Joshua (this was suggested to me by Jacob Wright.)

sponsible for the overall story line and was meant as an optimistic description of Israelite-Judahite history, culminating in the reign of King Josiah. The second recension was written post the destruction of the Temple, has a pessimistic flavor, and adds a number of ominous warnings into the book such that the direction of Israelite history changes from the redemption of Judah (and Israel?) under Josiah to the destruction of the Temple by Nebuchadnezzar.[264] Although this thesis has come under attack of late,[265] there does seem to be strong evidence for a negative recension overlaying a more positive core, however one dates this.

The book of Joshua is no exception, and this can be seen most clearly in the double redaction of chapter 23. In his article on bookends in Joshua (pp. 91–95), Thomas Römer points to a redactional layer in Joshua 23—the first of Joshua's final speeches, which warns the Israelites to avoid mingling with the locals in the future.[266] This concern is dissonant with the rest of the speech, which takes a triumphalist tone, describing the panic of the natives and the ease of settlement. Additionally, whereas the earlier layer of the speech is concerned with loyalty to YHWH in the future, the redactional layer discusses obedience to the Torah of Moses and threatens terrible things that the nations will do to Israel if they mix with the natives. The mention of the Torah of Moses and the conception of natives with whom Israel will mix imply a late date to these additions.

This redactional layer is represented in the opening chapter as well. During YHWH's speech to Joshua in the opening verses of the book, YHWH focuses on telling Joshua to be strong and brave in his leadership of Israel and conquest of the land. However, right in the middle of the speech appears a redactional insertion. The insertion begins with a reiteration of the command to be strong and brave, but here it is to be strong and brave in the study of Torah—a bizarre phrase and clear evidence, I believe, of an interpolator's hand. It is in this spot where Joshua is commanded to study Torah night and day. Thus, one of the images of Joshua—that of the Torah scholar—derives from the late and secondary Deuteronomistic redaction of the book. Nevertheless, it is worth noting

---

264 For a full articulation of the theory, see: Richard D. Nelson, *The Double Redaction of the Deuteronomistic History* (JSOTsup 18; Sheffield: Continuum, 1981).

265 See, for example, Philip R. Davies, *The Origin of Biblical Israel* (Library of Hebrew Bible/Old Testament Studies 485; London: T&T Clark, 2007), where—following Martin Noth—he argues for a post-exilic origin of the work as a whole, edited in Mitzpeh during the century after the destruction of Jerusalem.

266 See Römer's article for the exact division of verses. I am in agreement with Römer that chapters 23 and 24 represent two alternative and contradictory endings, and that 23 is the ending of the book of Joshua and 24 is the ending of the Hexateuch. However, as discussed in previous sections, I believe that the core of 24 is much older, whereas 23 is a late editorial creation from beginning to end.

that the seeds for this image existed in the earlier Deuteronomistic work, with the emphasis on Joshua's fealty to the command of YHWH to Moses.[267]

A similar argument can be made for what seems to be one of the latest additions to the book of Joshua, the story of the altar on Mount Ebal. I call this a late addition because it is the one place in the book of Joshua that appears in totally different spots depending on which ancient text one uses. There are, again, multiple references to the Torah of Moses, and the entire pericope seems intent on demonstrating that Joshua did the ritual exactly as Moses had been commanded to do, and as he wrote in his Torah.[268]

Priestly Images of Joshua

There are three major themes in the priest-centered imagery of Joshua, all of which seem to focus on making his role in the leadership of Israel less powerful.

First is Joshua's relationship to the Ark. It is difficult to determine the origin of the Ark of the Covenant tradition, although it was eventually adopted by P and made integral to its religious conception and historiography.[269] The ark is a major feature of two Joshua stories: the crossing of the Jordan River and the conquest of Jericho. Both of these stories (especially the former, where the problems are well known) read like composite tales and have at least one if not two redactional layers.[270] It is the crossing of the Ark, *with the priests*, that splits the river, and it is the circling of the ark, *with the priests*, that causes the walls of Jericho to collapse.

I suggest that one of the reasons for this is that there is an "ark-based" priestly redaction of these two stories aimed at placing YHWH and the ark in center stage and Joshua into a "supporting role." Placing such extreme significance

---

267 For an analysis of Joshua 1–9 and its layers, in an attempt to understand how "Deuteronomistic" it really is, see: Thomas B. Dozeman, "The Beginning of a Book or Literary Bridge?" in *The Book of Joshua* (ed. Ed Noort; BETL 250; Proceedings of the CBL; Leuven: Leuven University Press, 2010), 159–182.

268 The fact that the ritual is not, in fact, done exactly as the Torah prescribes is an interesting problem, which may point to redaction of these sources from two originally unrelated acts made to appear to reference the same thing.

269 Tzemah Yoreh has argued for a separate "ark-tradition" based in Samuel and Kings that is expanded backwards through time into literary units that deal with earlier times. See the introduction to Tzemah L. Yoreh, *The First Book of God* (BZAW 402; Berlin: De Gruyter, 2010).

270 There are three different acts of placing of stones as reminders in this story.

on the cultic object as opposed to the prophetic leader is not Deuteronomistic and is not reminiscent of the Moses stories, but seems priestly in nature.[271]

Second, the most important priestly image of Joshua is that of Joshua as Elazar's partner. In texts where Elazar and Joshua are partners, the image of Joshua becomes that of an administrator. Nevertheless, the man with access to YHWH, through the cultic power of the lot or the *Urim ve-Tummim*, is Elazar the high priest. The addition of Elazar shifts the place of Joshua in the hierarchy. An analysis of the appointment-of-Joshua account in Numbers 27:15 – 23 can demonstrate this most clearly.

Before the revision of the older P text, the story recounts YHWH's choosing of Joshua as Moses' sole successor, and the sole leader of Israel. The later priest-centered revision adjusted this picture, making Joshua Elazar's partner – and even subordinate – in the future administration of Israel. This remains true for the rest of Numbers, although not Deuteronomy, where the character of Elazar is (virtually) non-existent. This secondary revision of Numbers 27 becomes obvious when one looks carefully at the text of the appointment of Joshua scene and the discontinuity between Moses' request and YHWH's response.

---

271 A detailed reconstruction of these layers is a desideratum.

^{טו)} וַיְדַבֵּר מֹשֶׁה אֶל יְהוָה לֵאמֹר:

^{טז)} "יִפְקֹד יְהוָה אֱלֹהֵי הָרוּחֹת לְכָל בָּשָׂר אִישׁ עַל הָעֵדָה:

^{יז)} <u>אֲשֶׁר יֵצֵא לִפְנֵיהֶם וַאֲשֶׁר יָבֹא לִפְנֵיהֶם וַאֲשֶׁר יוֹצִיאֵם</u> <u>וַאֲשֶׁר יְבִיאֵם</u> וְלֹא תִהְיֶה עֲדַת יְהוָה כַּצֹּאן אֲשֶׁר אֵין לָהֶם רֹעֶה."

^{יח)} וַיֹּאמֶר יְהוָה אֶל מֹשֶׁה: "קַח לְךָ אֶת יְהוֹשֻׁעַ בֶּן נוּן אִישׁ אֲשֶׁר רוּחַ בּוֹ וְסָמַכְתָּ אֶת יָדְךָ עָלָיו. ^{יט)} וְהַעֲמַדְתָּ אֹתוֹ *לִפְנֵי אֶלְעָזָר הַכֹּהֵן וְלִפְנֵי* כָּל הָעֵדָה וְצִוִּיתָה אֹתוֹ לְעֵינֵיהֶם.

^{כ)} וְנָתַתָּה מֵהוֹדְךָ עָלָיו לְמַעַן יִשְׁמְעוּ כָּל עֲדַת בְּנֵי יִשְׂרָאֵל.

^{כא)} *וְלִפְנֵי אֶלְעָזָר הַכֹּהֵן יַעֲמֹד וְשָׁאַל לוֹ בְמִשְׁפַּט הָאוּרִים* לִפְנֵי יְהוָה <u>עַל פִּיו יֵצְאוּ וְעַל פִּיו יָבֹאוּ</u> הוּא וְכָל בְּנֵי יִשְׂרָאֵל אִתּוֹ וְכָל הָעֵדָה." ^{כב)} וַיַּעַשׂ מֹשֶׁה כַּאֲשֶׁר צִוָּה יְהוָה אֹתוֹ וַיִּקַּח אֶת יְהוֹשֻׁעַ וַיַּעֲמִדֵהוּ *לִפְנֵי אֶלְעָזָר הַכֹּהֵן* וְלִפְנֵי כָּל הָעֵדָה. ^{כג)} וַיִּסְמֹךְ אֶת יָדָיו עָלָיו וַיְצַוֵּהוּ כַּאֲשֶׁר דִּבֶּר יְהוָה בְּיַד מֹשֶׁה.

¹⁵⁾ Moses spoke to YHWH, saying, ¹⁶⁾ "Let YHWH, the God of the spirits of all flesh, appoint someone over the congregation ¹⁷⁾ <u>who shall go out before them and come in before them, who shall lead them out and bring them in,</u> so that the congregation of YHWH may not be like sheep without a shepherd." ¹⁸⁾ So YHWH said to Moses, "Take Joshua son of Nun, a man in whom is the spirit, and lay your hand upon him; ¹⁹⁾ have him stand before *Elazar the priest and* all the congregation, and commission him in their sight. ²⁰⁾ You shall give him some of your splendor, so that all the congregation of the Israelites may obey. ²¹⁾ *But he shall stand before Elazar the priest, who shall inquire for him by the decision of the Urim before YHWH;* <u>at his word they shall go out, and at his word they shall come in,</u> both he and all the Israelites with him, the whole congregation." ²²⁾ So Moses did as YHWH commanded him. He took Joshua and had him stand before *Elazar the priest and* the whole congregation; ²³⁾ he laid his hands on him and commissioned him—as YHWH had directed through Moses.

Moses requests someone who will "come and go" before the people, i. e. a leader that they will follow. At first, YHWH's response *seems* to give Moses what he wants, by suggesting the appointment of Joshua. The text violates this expectation, however, when it tells the reader that Joshua himself will "come and go" based on Elazar the priest. I suggest that the best solution to this discontinuity is to assume that all references to Elazar the priest in this section are redactional. Once one reads verse 21b as a direct continuation of 20, the problem dissolves. YHWH is telling Moses that that the people will come and go at Joshua's behest, i. e. Joshua will be their leader.

This trend to raise Elazar to the level of Joshua or higher reflects a priest-centered theology where the high priest is the most important figure. A useful example of this phenomenon appears in the *Samaritan Book of Joshua*, where Joshua, although the king of Israel, has to file reports and send them to Elazar the high priest (*imam*). The high priest has played a major role in Samaritan religion from ancient times through medieval times (when Samaritan Joshua was written) and up to the present day; thus, it is not surprising that this image remained popular with them.

Third, there is Joshua's relationship to the Tabernacle. In Joshua 18:1, the Tabernacle is established in Shiloh.[272] Although one can see this as a way of attaching Joshua to cultic places and expanding his importance, I think the reverse occurs here. By having the revered figure, Joshua, place the revered cultic object (the Tabernacle) in Shiloh, the text enhances the importance of Shiloh as a site of great religious significance. What role Shiloh played in early 2nd Temple period history or historiography I cannot say, but the fact that priests trace themselves to this place is clear from the biblical text, so it must have had significance to this group.

It is worth noting that the image of Joshua as an establisher of cultic places is not an image unique to the priestly editors.[273] As argued above, in the late redaction of Dtr, there is a reference to Joshua setting up the altar on Mount Ebal. Additionally, it is possible that Gilgal was meant to have a cultic area around the rock-pillars ostensibly set up by Joshua. Even Joshua's cursing of the Gibeonites could be a way of explaining the low-grade cultic functionaries of the author's period, by tracing their role in Temple service to Joshua. Finally, in Joshua 24 there is a reference to a temple in Shechem.[274] Although it seems that in the oldest layer of this chapter the reference to the temple assumes it to have been in existence *already* when Joshua made his speech, nonetheless, the later editor assumes that Joshua was responsible for its construction. Once Joshua is no longer a local leader of an indigenous people but the leader who brings Israel into the land from the outside, who else could have built it?

Summary

In this chapter, I have offered speculations about the pre-biblical Joshua and how his image developed into the composite character found in the biblical text today. I argue that the earliest image of Joshua we possess is that of a local warrior-chief in the Mount Heres region of the Ephraimite hill country

---

272 Knauf believes this verse to be the original ending of a P redaction of the Hexateuch (Knauf, *Josua*, 17, 20, 154–155). He argues that this verse forms an inclusio with the creation story, giving the impression that with the placing of YHWH's Tabernacle in Shilo, creation has finally been completed. (He calls this, *"Die Vollendung der Schöpfungsordnung."*)

273 As will be seen in the next chapter, this image is integral to *L.A.B.*'s understanding of Joshua.

274 For a suggestion that this section, along with a handful of others, reflects very late editing well into the Greek period, see: Ernst Axel Knauf, "Die Adressatenkreise von Josua," in *The Book of Joshua* (ed. Ed Noort; BETL 250; Proceedings of the CBL; Leuven: Leuven University Press, 2010), 183–210.

who was rewarded with the town of Timnat Heres for his valor. As his reputation expanded over time, his battles took on a "miraculous" quality, and he became known as the "father" of the Josephite tribes and the one who established their covenant with YHWH. This Joshua was a military leader but also a statesman who understood when not to fight, as his advice to the Josephites to deforest an area to avoid engaging chariotry demonstrates.

With the consolidation of Israelite identity in the north, Joshua's position expands to leader of Israel in primordial times. This Joshua is responsible for the covenant with YHWH that takes place in the temple of Shechem and the abandonment of other gods once worshipped by the Israelites' ancestors. Eventually, as the North began to consolidate their historiography in conversation with that of the south, Joshua became the first leader of Israel and the conqueror of the whole land; eventually a campaign account was written in the Neo-Assyrian style.

Once Israel-Judah began to combine the Moses story with the conquest account, to create a timeline of their pre-monarchic past, the Joshua story began to merge into the dominant Moses story. Whether there was ever a Joshua-redeems-Israel-from-Egypt story as suggested by Rofé, I am unsure, but once the two characters' stories merged, the Joshua as-student-of-Moses-and-successor-to-Moses account was born. This was probably the point where an old Hexateuch was created.

The Deuteronomist took parts of this account, specifically the seeds of the battle of Beit Horon and possibly older versions of other battle accounts, and put together the Joshua 1–11(12), 23 account more or less as it exists now. He created the image of a Joshua who annihilated the Canaanite population of the country and was fiercely loyal to YHWH and his commandments to Moses. This edition also features the Joshua who is frightened of leadership and needs reassurance. A later Dtr redaction added a note of pessimism about the future and, most importantly, the explicit statement that Joshua studied the Torah of Moses day and night and followed the Torah to the letter.

At this point, later editors expanded the book in two ways. First, various pieces of the older Joshua account that were left out of the Deuteronimistic Joshua work were included (like ch. 17 and ch. 24 for example), and some priestly additions were written and included as well. The former additions brought about a number of contradictions in the text, since the older Joshua accounts did not picture him annihilating Israel's enemies.[275] The latter additions added

---

275 The older Joshua won some fights but avoided many others, while assisting his followers in

a number of priestly elements into the story, including Shiloh, the Ark of the Covenant, and most importantly, Elazar the high priest and Joshua's partnership—and sometimes even subservience—to him.

Although the biblical text in its final forms attempt to smooth over Joshua's historiography, the various images isolated in this chapter and the previous one were never fully reconciled with each other. This is important since, as will be seen in the next four chapters, different images resonated with different groups of readers who received the texts. These readers make use of the fissures in Joshua's personality, emphasizing some and deemphasizing others, in order to create very different reframings of Joshua—new Joshuas that would speak to identities and values in the religious cultures that would continue to venerate him, each in its own way.

---

settling the land. The Deuteronomist, who believed in *ḥerem*, assumed that no Canaanites—other than the Gibeonites—survived.

Chapter 3 – Hellenistic and Second Temple Joshua(s)

The Judaisms of the Hellenistic period varied from each other considerably, as do their works. Some works participate in already familiar genres of biblical literature such as wisdom literature or narrative. Others participate in Greek genres, such as philosophical or historical writing. There are works which reflect the thinking and writing of the Qumran community, with their emphasis on prophesy fulfillment. Some works participate in more than one genre. Not surprisingly, the Joshuas found in Hellenistic Jewish literature are equally as varied, as each community reinvents the hero with images that would resonate as meaningful and familiar to them.

Ben Sira

The book of Ben Sira (or Sirach) is part of the genre of wisdom literature, and in many ways mimics the book of Proverbs. The greater part of the book (chs. 1–43) is dedicated to encouraging the reader to pursue wisdom in study and in practice. There is much advice about good parenting, the proper choice of spouse, the nature of friendship, and ethical treatment of workers. The book concludes (ch. 51) with a prayer.

Before the book reaches its conclusion, however, the author offers a long hymn in praise of the great men of Israel's past. The hymn has a number of unusual features. First, it does not appear to be in keeping with the theme of the rest of the book, as there is no particular emphasis on wisdom. Second, the hymn itself seems to consist of at least two distinct parts. The first part (chs. 44–45) praises Enoch, Noah, the three Patriarchs, Moses, Aaron, Phineas, and David. The lion's share of the praise goes to Aaron, and the entire section ends, after a brief mention of Phineas and David, with a blessing that God grant wisdom to the listeners (or the readers?) to judge Israel righteously.

The second part of the hymn (chs. 46–50) begins abruptly with a historical survey of Israelite leaders, beginning with Joshua. Not only is the opening abrupt, but the theme of this section differs significantly from that of the first.[276] The first part of the hymn, at least from Abraham and on, praises God

---

276 Unfortunately, a redaction-critical or source-critical analysis of this section is beyond the

for the gifts he gave the figures mentioned in the poem. The second part of the hymn details the accomplishments of its leaders and even their failures. It is hard to understand what the basis for selection was in this latter section, but it ends with a very complimentary encomium to Simon the Righteous, a Hellenistic Period figure.[277]

Joshua in Ben Sira

The second section of the hymn leads off with Joshua (46:1), opening with a common epithet "mighty warrior" (גבור בן חיל).[278] Immediately after using this term, Ben Sira references yet another of Joshua's images – that of prophet – referring to Joshua as Moses' successor in this regard (משרת[279] משה בנבואה).

Despite this apparent attempt at parity when treating Joshua's role, general and prophet, the rest of the passage deals almost exclusively with Joshua's role as conqueror, emphasizing his military persona.[280] Naturally, the miracles are referenced, but these are portrayed less as examples of Joshua's prophetic ability than as signs that God was supportive of Joshua in his capacity as leader and general of the Israelite forces.

---

scope of this work. It seems plausible that Ben Sira incorporated pieces of older hymns in his creation of this section.

277 Jeremy Corley suggests that since the focus of this poem is the military defense of Judah with which Simon the Righteous was involved, discussing the figures of Joshua and David as a lead in makes some sense. See: Jeremy Corley, "Joshua as Warrior in Ben Sira 46:1–10," in *Visions of Peace and Tales of War* (ed. Jan Liesen and Pancratius C. Beentjes; Deuterocanonical and Cognate Literature Yearbook; Berlin: De Gruyter, 2010), 207–248 [211]. See also: Elßner, *Josua*, 22–56.

278 When available, the Hebrew MS B of Ben Sira will be used, and when partially available, I will use the Hebrew text with the suggested lacuna in brackets. For the Hebrew, I used Pancratius C. Beentjes, *The Book of Ben Sira in Hebrew: A Text Edition of All Extant Hebrew Manuscripts and a Synopsis of All Parallel Hebrew Ben Sira Texts* (VTsup 68; Leiden: Brill, 1997). When there is virtually no Hebrew text extant, I used the Greek LXX text.

279 Jeremy Corley (218), based on the LXX text (διάδοχος Μωυσῆ ἐν προφητείαις), suggests that the Hebrew text we have is actually a correction from an original משנת, which would be the *lectio difficilior*.

280 Corley points out that as much as the modern reader would like to imagine that a "wise sage" such as Ben Sira would not emphasize Joshua's military side but look to his more religious or appealing (to the modern reader) characteristics, one must admit that Ben Sira appears to be interested in Joshua primarily as a warrior. As will be seen, in this sense, Ben Sira resonates much more with Josephus than it does with the *Apocryphon of Joshua* or the *L.A.B.* Corley admits that, although Ben Sira cannot be considered a "warmonger" (Corley's term), he expresses only pride and satisfaction in Joshua's military achievements (Corley, "Joshua", 209–211).

In introducing Joshua's main accomplishment, Ben Sira begins with a play on his name (46:1). Joshua, whose name carries in it the root for "saving," affects a saving (תשועה). The Greek translator, who cannot make use of a similar play on words in the Greek, takes the unusual expedient of actually pointing out the word play in the Greek, writing "like his name states (κατὰ τὸ ὄνομα αὐτοῦ)." This use of a pun, implicit in the Hebrew and explicit in the Greek, is reminiscent of the statement of Abigail (1 Sam 25:25) that her brute of a husband Nabal was "like his name" or Naomi's claim that she can no longer be called by her name, "pleasant", since her life was so bitter (Ruth 1:21). The idea that a person's name has meaning and relates to an essential quality or characteristic of his or her life is ubiquitous in biblical literature.

From this perspective, Ben Sira's comment is more than just a clever pun, but represents an attempt to capture the essence of this biblical character, Joshua. Furthermore, this is not just a late midrashic play. Ben Sira is drawing out a meaning of the name that is implicit in the biblical authors' minds as well. Joshua is, in fact, a savior.[281]

Joshua the Conqueror

The survey of Joshua's accomplishments is full of intertextual references to the book of Joshua. Ben Sira begins with a general description; Joshua takes vengeance on God's enemies and gives Israel the land as an inheritance. Both of these phrases have very specific intertexts in the Bible.

The concept of Joshua being the one to avenge God's enemies is reminiscent of Joshua 10:13. During the defeat of the southern coalition, the author quotes from the *Book of the Just* that on that day the sun stood and the moon was still "until a nation took vengeance upon its foes" (עַד יִקֹּם גּוֹי אֹיְבָיו).

The concept of Joshua giving Israel the land as inheritance appears in a number of places in the Bible.

אֵלֶּה שְׁמוֹת הָאֲנָשִׁים אֲשֶׁר יִנְחֲלוּ לָכֶם אֶת הָאָרֶץ אֶלְעָזָר These are the names of the men who will **give** הַכֹּהֵן וִיהוֹשֻׁעַ בֶּן נוּן. you the land as **inheritance:** Elazar the Priest and Joshua son of Nun. (Num 34:17)

---

281 There is an ironic play on this name in the book of Joshua where he is the "savior" of the Gibeonites (Josh 10:6).

יְהוֹשֻׁעַ בֶּן נוּן הָעֹמֵד לְפָנֶיךָ הוּא יָבֹא שָׁמָּה אֹתוֹ חַזֵּק כִּי הוּא יַנְחִלֶנָּה אֶת יִשְׂרָאֵל.

Joshua son of Nun is standing before you – he will bring you there, strengthen him since he will **give** Israel the land as **inheritance.** (Deut 1:38)

וַיִּקְרָא מֹשֶׁה לִיהוֹשֻׁעַ וַיֹּאמֶר אֵלָיו לְעֵינֵי כָל יִשְׂרָאֵל חֲזַק וֶאֱמָץ כִּי אַתָּה תָּבוֹא אֶת הָעָם הַזֶּה אֶל הָאָרֶץ אֲשֶׁר נִשְׁבַּע יְהוָה לַאֲבֹתָם לָתֵת לָהֶם וְאַתָּה תַּנְחִילֶנָּה אוֹתָם.

Moses called Joshua and said to him before all of Israel: "Be strong and brave, since you will bring this nation into the land that Yнwн promised their fathers to give them, and you will **give** them the land as **inheritance.** (Deut 31:7)

חֲזַק וֶאֱמָץ כִּי אַתָּה תַּנְחִיל אֶת הָעָם הַזֶּה אֶת הָאָרֶץ אֲשֶׁר נִשְׁבַּעְתִּי לַאֲבוֹתָם לָתֵת לָהֶם.

Be strong and brave, since you will **give** as an **inheritance** to this nation the land that I promised their fathers to give them. (Josh 1:6)

These two images, vanquisher of enemies and granter of land, are the two main images of Joshua in the book of Joshua, with the former representing the first half of the book and the latter the lion's share of the second half.

Having established these two core images, both intimately related to conquest, Ben Sira goes on to describe Joshua in battle (46:2).

מה נהדר בנטותו יד

בהניפו כידון על עיר.

How praiseworthy when he extended his arm, when he brandished his spear against the city.

Although Joshua certainly "brandished his spear" against many cities, there is a strong resonance in imagery with a scene during the second battle of Ai (Josh 8:18).

וַיֹּאמֶר יְהוָה אֶל יְהוֹשֻׁעַ: "נְטֵה בַּכִּידוֹן אֲשֶׁר בְּיָדְךָ אֶל הָעַי כִּי בְיָדְךָ אֶתְּנֶנָּה." וַיֵּט יְהוֹשֻׁעַ בַּכִּידוֹן אֲשֶׁר בְּיָדוֹ אֶל הָעִיר.

And Yнwн said to Joshua: "Extend [your arm] with the spear in your grasp towards Ai, since I will give it into your hands." So Joshua, extended [his arm] with the spear in his hand, towards the city.

In both cases, Joshua is described as stretching out his arm with a weapon against a city.

Ben Sira next compares Joshua to other warriors (46:3), claiming that none of them had the staying power he had: "Who before him has stood thus (מי הוא לפניו יתיצב)?" This imagery brings up Yнwн's promise to Joshua at the beginning of the biblical book (Josh 1:5):

לֹא יִתְיַצֵּב אִישׁ לְפָנֶיךָ כֹּל יְמֵי חַיֶּיךָ...

No one will **stand** before you all the days of your life...

Ben Sira finishes this verse (46:3) with, "for the wars of Yнwн he fought (כי
[נלחם] מלחמות יי)." Although this can be described fairly as an accurate portrayal
of Joshua's activity in the first half of the biblical book, it has an additional resonance with the description of Moses' conquest of the Transjordan. In this account, the Book of Numbers (Num 21:14) references an older collection of the
Transjordanian wars, in which a fuller account could be read, and refers to
this work as "the Book of the Wars of the Lord." Perhaps this is a subtle way
for Ben Sira to compare Joshua to Moses, something he did in the opening
verse of this pericope as well.

Ben Sira next describes Joshua's core miracle (46:4):

הלא בידו עמד השמש Was it not through his hands that the sun was

יום אחד [כשנים היה]?[282] fettered, and one day was turned to two?

This is the same battle hinted at by Ben Sira earlier – when referencing vengeance upon God's enemies – and will be the subject of the next verse as well. Ben
Sira here emphasizes that it is Joshua who stops the sun, without mentioning the
involvement of God,[283] certainly a powerful image.

Ben Sira's description of the next miracle differs, however (46:5):

כי קרא אל אל עליון He called out to the Most High God,

כאכפה ל[ו אויביו מסביב] as his enemies pressed in on him from all

ויענהו אל עליון sides, and the Most High God responded to

באבני [ברד] [וא]ל[גביש]. with stones of hail and ice.

Here Ben Sira emphasizes the extraordinary support Joshua receives from God
during his battles. When surrounded by enemies, Joshua need only call out to
God and God will respond with powerful force, in this case hail, to scatter Joshua's foes. The element of Joshua's calling out to God is added by Ben Sira, perhaps in order to paint a picture of control. Joshua invites God into the battle, or,
at least, requests God's assistance.[284]

Ben Sira begins the next verse with a simple couplet emphasizing the overwhelming nature of Joshua's victory (46:6):

---

282 The two words are missing from the Hebrew manuscript but are retroverted from the Greek
(ἐγενήθη πρὸς δύο) and from context.

283 This is in keeping with the poem in Joshua 10, but not with the editorial comment, which
ties Yнwн in.

284 Ben Sira makes an adjustment here. In the biblical story, Yнwн involves himself in the
battle without being asked. This stands in tension to Ben Sira's claim that the enemies were
surrounding Joshua at this point. In the biblical account, there is no indication that Joshua was
in danger of losing without Yнwн's intervention.

κατέρραξεν ἐπ' ἔθνος πόλεμον καὶ ἐν καταβάσει He fell headlong upon the enemies in battle,
ἀπώλεσεν ἀνθεστηκότας. and on the slopes he destroyed the opposition.

The reference to the "slopes" brings to mind the slopes mentioned in Josh 10:11, the place where YHWH began throwing down the hailstones. The couplet itself seems like a general summary of Joshua's success in battle; he falls upon them confidently and routes them soundly.

The second half of the couplet takes a differenttwist (46:6):

למַ[ען] [דע]ת כֹּל גוי חרם In order for all enemies to know destruction,[285]
כי צופ ה י[הוה] מלחמתם. for YHWH was watching their wars.

This couplet is difficult to unpack. The first half seems to be related to the common biblical theme of "the nations knowing the Lord." This theme comes up in the Exodus story a number of times, and there is even a description in Joshua of the nations' having heard of YHWH's power and being frightened (Josh 2:9 and 5:1).

The second part of the couplet, however, surprises the reader with the assertion that the enemies are being crushed because they made war with God. From the biblical account, one would have stated something different; namely, that the enemies are being crushed because of their sins and God's promise to the Patriarchs—it would be for these reasons God makes war upon them. This inversion of aggressor and besieged may be a way for Ben Sira to soften what could appear to readers as an overly aggressive story of invasion and conquest on the part of Israel by describing the native Canaanites as aggressors against God.[286]

Joshua and Caleb

Although the previous verse ends the section devoted to Joshua, there is a transition section as well (46:7–8), which discusses Joshua and Caleb as a lead-in to discussing Caleb.

---

285 The Greek has "his armor (πανοπλίαν αὐτοῦ)," which seems rather inexplicable. Moshe Tzvi Segal, in his translation and commentary on Ben Sira, assumes that the term πανοπλίαν is a scribal error, and that the verse meant to say πάντα ἀπωλείας, i.e., total destruction, like in the extant Hebrew text.

286 From the biblical perspective, it is true that they are fighting God, but what choice did they have? Even if one suggests that they could have surrendered, the Book of Joshua explicitly states that they were unable to surrender since God forced their minds towards war in order to destroy them (Josh 11:19–20).

וגם] כי מלא אחרי אל   For he followed after God,

וּבימי משה עשה חסד.   and in days of Moses he dealt kindly,

הוּא וכלב בן יפנה   He and Caleb son of Jephuneh,

להתיצב בפרע קהל   to stand before the wild assembly

להשיב חרון מעדה   to prevent wrath from people

ולהשבית דבה רעה.   to cease their wicked grumbling.

לכם גם הם בשנים נאלצו   And these two were brought safely through,

מששׁ מאות אלף רגלי   out of the six hundred thousand foot-soldiers,

להביאם אל נחלתם   to lead them to their inheritance,

ארץ זבת חלב ודבש.   to a land flowing with milk and honey.

Ben Sira jumps back to an earlier time in Joshua's life, when he was a young scout together with Caleb. Ben Sira praises Joshua for two good qualities: loyalty and kindness. Joshua is loyal to God—and kind to Moses—by sticking with the divine plan.[287]

Joshua's (and Caleb's) kindness (חסד), according to Ben Sira, is manifested in the attempt to stop the people from disobeying God, sinning, and behaving wickedly. Joshua and Caleb do not succeed in this attempt, as recorded in the biblical text, but are rewarded with the merit of being the only two adults from the wilderness generation to be permitted to enter the Promised Land. Even more than this, they are granted the position of leadership such that they will lead the Israelites into the new land themselves.

One quality that Ben Sira does not mention, surprisingly, is bravery. Considering the fact that he specifically writes that they "stood up" to the Israelites, one would imagine that this could function as an excellent opening to describe their courage, a characteristic that fits well with the picture Ben Sira has already painted of Joshua, that of military hero.[288]

Although this jumping back to the scout days primarily serves as a bridge to the Caleb encomium, it also rounds out the presentation of Joshua by touching upon an aspect of his history mentioned at the beginning, namely Joshua as successor of Moses. Joshua succeeds Moses because Joshua was loyal to God and kind to Moses when no one else was.[289]

---

287 Nevertheless, the very term "loyalty" is lifted straight out of the biblical text. For example, in the spy account, God praises Caleb in a speech to Moses, saying that he was "loyal to me" (וימלא אחרי), and this assertion is repeated in Deut 1:36, and Joshua 14:14. Joshua, together with Caleb, is also referred to in Numbers31:12 as being loyal to God during his tenure as a scout.
288 It is also worth noting that Ben Sira has already played with this term earlier, claiming that no one ever "stood" in the way that Joshua did.
289 Other than Caleb, but he was also appointed as a leader of sorts according to Ben Sira.

Summary

The overall picture of Joshua in Ben Sira is as God's warrior. The imagery is most-ly taken from the battle defending Gibeon but does have some imagery from the battle of Ai.[290] Joshua's role as Moses' successor is mentioned, but Ben Sira does not really try to paint Joshua in Mosaic colors. Although there are some similar-ities in the imagery, as God does make Moses fearsome to his enemies and glo-rifies him publicly, nevertheless, Ben Sira mainly describes Moses as one who receives commandments, hears God's voice, and sees God's glory. None of these latter descriptions apply to Joshua.

Oddly enough, despite the great compliments to Moses, his section covers only five verses. It is slightly shorter than Joshua's (six or eight verses), and is much shorter than Aaron's (seventeen verses). In fact, if one looks at Ben Sira's section on Moses, one gets the impression that the great prophet is being downplayed in comparison with the character of most interest in this hymn, that of Aaron. The huge break between the encomium to Moses and the encomium to Joshua, twenty one verses, has the effect of severing the narrative connection between the two leaders. When Ben Sira references their connection, it only reestablishes this perfunctorily.

Ben Sira's praises for Joshua are actually somewhat surprising when one considers the overall program of the book. Ben Sira would have had ample prec-edent to describe Joshua as a wise Torah scholar, a religious leader and prophet, or an establisher of holy places, as the author of *L.A.B.* does. Even if Ben Sira wished, for some reason, to focus on Joshua's military prowess he could have emphasized strategy, intelligence and calm in the face of battle, two wisdom characteristics for which Josephus praises Joshua extravagantly. This question could be asked in various ways about a number of the characters chosen for this hymn. In fact, considering the dissonance between the values expressed in the hymn and the values expressed in the rest of the book, there exists a seri-ous question about the relationship of the hymn to the rest of Ben Sira.

---

290 The lack of reference to the battle of Jericho and the miracle of the walls falling is sur-prising. So is the lack of reference to the crossing of the Jordan, although less so since it is not a battle proper.

1 Maccabees

In the first Book of Maccabees, Joshua is referenced once explicitly, but there are also a number of tacit uses of Joshua imagery.[291]

Joshua the Judge in the Speech of Mattathias

Joshua is invoked explicitly by Mattathias during his death-bed speech to his sons. Part of this speech consists of Mattathias's invocation of previous heroic leaders that persevered and won; specifically, Abraham, Joseph, Phineas, Joshua, Caleb, David, Elijah, Hananiah, Mishael, Azariah, and Daniel.

Although it is hardly surprising that Mattathias would reference Joshua, what he actually says is unexpected (2:55).

Ἰησοῦς ἐν τῷ πληρῶσαι λόγον ἐγένετο κριτὴς ἐν Ισραηλ.	Joshua, in his fulfillment of the word [of God] became a judge in Israel.

There is nothing here about Joshua fighting an overwhelmingly large force and defeating them, as stated in Josh 11:4, for instance. This would have been a perfect model for Mattathias to use. (Perhaps the prayer is not original to 1 Maccabees but was brought in by the editor and imperfectly placed into the mouth of Mattathias? Moreover, the reference to Joshua as a judge is highly unusual, since Joshua is never referred to by this term anywhere in the Hebrew Bible.

Tacit Joshua Imagery

Attempting to find implied imagery is always a speculative enterprise. Nevertheless, there seem to be multiple examples of this phenomenon in 1 Maccabees.

The clearest example appears in Mattathias's response to the Greek official's request for him to participate in the pagan sacrifice. Mattathias responds to this request by stating that it matters nothing to him if all the other people in the empire serve other gods. He and his family will not (2:19–22).

---

291 For an analysis of how 1 and 2 Maccabees make use of Joshua, see Johannes Schnocks, "Rezeption des Josuabuches in den Makkabäerbüchern," in *The Book of Joshua* (ed. Ed Noort; BETL 250 – Proceedings of the CBL; Leuven: Leuven University Press, 2010), 511–521. See also, Elßner, *Josua*, 56–70.

εἰ πάντα τὰ ἔθνη τὰ ἐν οἴκῳ τῆς βασιλείας τοῦ βασιλέως ἀκούουσιν αὐτοῦ ἀποστῆναι ἕκαστος ἀπὸ λατρείας πατέρων αὐτοῦ καὶ ᾑρετίσαντο ἐν ταῖς ἐντολαῖς αὐτοῦ. κἀγὼ καὶ οἱ υἱοί μου καὶ οἱ ἀδελφοί μου πορευσόμεθα ἐν διαθήκῃ πατέρων ἡμῶν. ἵλεως ἡμῖν καταλιπεῖν νόμον καὶ δικαιώματα. τῶν λόγων τοῦ βασιλέως οὐκ ἀκουσόμεθα παρελθεῖν τὴν λατρείαν ἡμῶν δεξ- ιὰν ἢ ἀριστεράν.

If all the nations under the auspices of the kingdom listen to him, abandoning each one the divine service of their fathers, and choosing his laws. Even so, I and my sons and my broth- ers will proceed to follow the covenant of our fathers. God forbid that we should leave [our] laws and statutes! To the words of the king we will not listen, to veer from the divine serv- ice to the right or to the left.

Although this speech is framed in a narrative context foreign to the book of Josh- ua, i.e., that of a subjected nation standing up to foreign conquerors, the speech strikes a strong chord with a part of Joshua's final speech (24:15).

אִם רַע בְּעֵינֵיכֶם לַעֲבֹד אֶת יְהוָה בַּחֲרוּ לָכֶם הַיּוֹם אֶת מִי תַעֲבֹדוּן אִם אֶת אֱלֹהִים אֲשֶׁר עָבְדוּ אֲבוֹתֵיכֶם אֲשֶׁר [מֵ]עֵבֶר הַנָּהָר וְאִם אֶת אֱלֹהֵי הָאֱמֹרִי אֲשֶׁר אַתֶּם יֹשְׁבִים בְּאַרְצָם וְאָנֹכִי וּבֵיתִי נַעֲבֹד אֶת יְהוָה.

If it is evil in your eyes to serve YHWH, chose for yourselves today whom you will serve, if it is the gods that your fathers served from the other side of the river or if it is the gods of the Amorites in whose land you are dwelling – However, I and my household will serve YHWH.

In Joshua's speech, there is nothing about Israelites being forced to worship other gods, but the rhetoric is similar to Mattathias'. Joshua and his family will serve YHWH no matter what anyone else chooses to do. This is exactly Mat- tathias' point as well. Additionally, Mattathias makes this speech out loud, cer- tainly as an attempt to influence his Jewish listeners with this steadfast commit- ment to God, exactly as the great Joshua did centuries earlier.

There are a few other examples as well, although less certain. The Israelites are described as having made themselves "strong and resolved" (ἐκραταιώθησαν καὶ ὠχυρώθησαν) not to eat non-kosher food (1:62). This phrase is certainly a translation of the Hebrew חזקו ואמצו, which would have brought up Joshua to any reader familiar with the biblical books.

Additionally, one of the battles which Judah fights ends with a chase down the slopes of Beit Horon (3:24), just like Joshua's most famous battle (10:10), which ended with the stopping of the sun and the hailstones from heaven. One can argue that if Judah did in fact chase the Greeks down these slopes, how can one call this a literary allusion. Nevertheless, it is hard to imagine an author writing about Jews chasing their enemies down the slopes of Beit Horon without invoking the image of Joshua for himself and his readers.[292]

---

292 One very tenuous example is the mention of Jews undoing their circumcision (1:15), which

Summary

The use of Joshua imagery in 1 Maccabees should be tied in with the mission of the heroes of the book. As Mattathias and Judah were attempting to re-conquer their homeland from the Greeks, the image of Joshua, the first conqueror of the land, was one that they held in high regard as a model. On the other hand, Joshua was far from being the only model for the Hasmonean warriors, with others like Phineas being equally if not more important.

Short References (2 Maccabees and 4 Ezra)

2 Maccabees

Joshua is referenced in 2 *Maccabees* 12:15 as well, but only in passing.

οἱ δὲ περὶ τὸν Ιουδαν ἐπικαλεσάμενοι τὸν μέγαν τοῦ κόσμου δυνάστην τὸν ἄτερ κριῶν καὶ μηχανῶν ὀργανικῶν κατακρημνίσαντα τὴν Ιεριχω κατὰ τοὺς Ἰησοῦ χρόνους ἐνέσεισαν θηριωδῶς τῷ τείχει.	But those who were with Judah—calling against the great Sovereign of the world, who without battering-rams or siege engines cast down [the walls of] Jericho in the time of Joshua—drove furiously into the walls.

This passage does not focus on Joshua but on God. Joshua happens to be the leader in whose days God miraculously destroyed the walls of Jericho without the use of battering-rams. This event is being spoken of by Judah's soldiers to bolster their courage to confront the enemy they were currently facing, with confidence that if God could overthrow walls without weapons, he could grant Judah's (well-armed) soldiers the power to win the battle against this walled city (Caspin), whose residents had been taunting Judah's army and trying to dispirit them.

Not surprisingly, the speech has its effect; the attack is successful and the enemy slaughtered. Although this verse tells us little about Joshua's character per se, it is evidence that his story was remembered as a military story and that recounting of the tale of Joshua could inspire one to fight hard and win a battle. Furthermore, Joshua is remembered as one whom God supports in battle

---

could bring up reverse Joshua imagery, since he circumcised the Israelites after they crossed the Jordan.

so that emulating him or invoking him could be seen as a way of making a claim on God and ensuring that God would assist in fighting one's own battles.[293]

4 Ezra (2 Esdras)

A reference to Joshua is found in the late Second Temple period apocalyptic work, 4th Ezra. The work is not preserved in the original Hebrew, but only in a Latin translation of an older Greek translation. Additionally, it has a number of later Christian additions and reworkings. Nevertheless, the verse in questions appears to come from the older, Jewish section.

The book is organized around a number of visions that Ezra receives, many of which disturb him.[294] In the section in which Joshua is referenced, Ezra has just learned that in the time of judgment, loved ones and family members will not pray for each other, but will be concerned only with themselves. Ezra is horrified at this knowledge and begins to protest (7:106–108).

et respondi et dixi: "et quomodo invenimus modo , quoniam rogavit primus Abraham propter Sodomitas , et Moyses pro patribus qui in deserto peccaverunt, et Iesus qui post eum pro Israhel in diebus Achar, et Samuhel in diebus Saul, et David pro confractione..."	I answered and said: "How then do we find that first Abraham prayed for the people of Sodom, and Moses for our ancestors who sinned in the desert, and Joshua after him for Israel in the days of Achan, and Samuel in the days of Saul, and David for the plague..."

Ezra's point is that the great leaders of the past prayed for the people when they exhibited weakness, so why shouldn't the righteous pray for the "frail" in the time of judgment? Ezra's plea fails. Nevertheless, what is important for our purpose is how Ezra views Joshua. Unlike 2 Maccabees, Joshua is being invoked not for his military record but for his behavior as a prophet-like figure who intercedes on behalf of the people. In this sense, Joshua is in the company of the famous intercessors of the past, such as Abraham, Moses, Samuel and David.[295]

---

293 Schnocks ("Rezeption", 519–520) suggests a resonance with the story of Timotheos running away from the Judean army, which then lays siege to the city, breaks down its walls, and burns it to the ground (2 Macc 10:32–38). However, I am uncertain there is any real resonance to the Joshua stories other than the fact that, like Joshua's conquest of the Ai or Hazor, the story is a boiler-plate siege and conquest account.
294 Scholars note that the book seems to be written in the wake of a crisis, perhaps the destruction of the Temple by Titus.
295 The passage continues with Solomon, Elijah, and Hezekiah.

Of all the stories about Joshua, 4 Ezra invokes Joshua's reaction to Achan's stealing from the booty of Jericho which had been dedicated to God. Most surprising about this reference is that Joshua doesn't ever do this in the biblical story. According to the biblical account, after the defeat at the Ai, Joshua falls into a panic and tells God that if Israel is to lose, God will be embarrassed. God then informs him that someone has taken from the sacred booty. Joshua then finds this person, and orders him (and his family) stoned to death to rid Israel of the curse. Then he attacks the Ai again. At no time does he, like Abraham, Moses, and David, use the argument that God should forgive the people or that they should not have to pay for Achan's sin. It seems that Ezra imagines that since Joshua was such a great leader, he must have offered this argument, even if it is not recorded. A clearer case of "rewriting scripture" could hardly be wished for. The account says much more about what 4 Ezra is looking for in a leader than it does about Joshua, who in the older story acts in line with what might be expected from a military figure.

Philo

Opening Caveat

Philo is more a philosopher than an exegete. In order to appreciate how a given biblical text or character really fits into Philo's thinking, one must take into account his philosophical-allegorical system. A chapter like this is not the place for such an analysis. For this reason, I wish to clarify that the following is simply a *schematic* look at how the character of Joshua is used in Philo and an overview of the academic literature that deals with Joshua in Philo. The reader will notice that the treatment of Philo here is exceedingly thin, compared with some of the other subsections in this chapter. Undoubtedly, there is much more to say, and I hope that, in the future, my overview and contextualization will be helpful for those who wish to explore the subject in more depth.

Joshua in Philo

Philo has little if any interest in Joshua. Whereas Philo spends much time discussing characters like Moses, Abraham, and even Aaron, Joshua is rarely mentioned.[296] In some ways, Philo's lack of interest is not surprising. Philo really comments only on the Pentateuch, in which Joshua's role is minor. His main role comes in the book of Joshua, a work with which Philo does not deal.

Nevertheless, even in the Pentateuch, Joshua does play a role. Furthermore, Joshua is appointed to be Moses' successor in the Book of Numbers, and to be the leader who will bring the Israelites into the Promised Land. It would be reasonable to imagine that this should play some role in Philo's allegorical taxonomy of biblical characters, but this is not how Philo uses him.

Louis Feldman believes that Philo was so focused on increasing the esteem of Moses that he saw any compliment to Joshua as a threat.[297] Feldman writes: "[I]n his overwhelming concern to aggrandize the role of Moses as a leader comparable to the great leaders produced by the Greeks, Philo downgrades the role of Joshua..." (p. 167). Pointing out how Philo shifts the focus of the scout story onto Caleb, and even more so onto Moses, Feldman argues that elevating Joshua and Caleb to the status of heroes would be "to the detriment of Moses."

Katell Barthelot, although agreeing to the broad outlines of Feldman's view, challenges the extent of the reduction of Joshua, and argues that although it is true that Philo tends to expand Moses' role, this does result in any negative description of Joshua.[298] The descriptions of Joshua in Philo, she argues, are uniformly positive. Philo's minimizing of Joshua should instead be seen as reflecting his great love for the character of Moses. To understand this debate, it is worthwhile to survey the few passages in which Philo references Joshua—in my research, I found only five—and evaluate the tenor of his description.[299]

De Virtutibus (1:55 – 56)

In his work "On the Virtues," Philo describes the virtue of "humanity" (φιλαν-θρωπίαν), which he defines as love for one's fellow human. As is usual for

---

296 If one follows Goodenough's interpretation of Philo, one could say that Joshua, unlike Aaron and Moses, does not have his own "mystery." Erwin R. Goodenough, *By Light, Light: The Mystic Gospel of Hellenistic Judaism* (New Haven: Yale University Press, 1935).

297 Louis H. Feldman, "Philo's Interpretation of Joshua," *JSP* 12.2 (2001): 165–168. See also: Elßner, *Josua*, 105–112.

298 Barthelot, "Joshua," 105–106. Barthelot exaggerates Feldman's view. He never actually says that Philo describes Joshua negatively, only that he shrinks his role as much as possible.

299 As this is only meant as a schematic overview, and I am not a Philo scholar, I decided not to translate the sources myself. The English translation I used is the standard translation of Charles Yongue.

Philo, he chooses Moses as one of his primary examples of a person exemplifying this trait.

⁵⁵ πίστις δὲ σαφεστάτη τοῦ δηλουμένου γένοιτ᾽ ἂν ἥδε. φίλος ἦν αὐτῷ καὶ γνώριμος σχεδὸν ἐκ πρώτης ἡλικίας γενόμενος, Ἰησοῦς ὄνομα, οὗ τὴν φιλίαν προὐξένησεν οὐδὲν τῶν παρὰ τοῖς ἄλλοις εἰωθότων, ἀλλ᾽ ἔρως ὁ οὐράνιος καὶ ἀκήρατος καὶ θεῖος ὄντως, ἐξ οὗ πᾶσαν ἀρετὴν φύεσθαι συμβέβηκεν· οὗτος ὁμωρόφιος καὶ ὁμοδίαιτος ἦν αὐτῷ, πλὴν ὁπότε ἐπιθειάσαντι καὶ χρησμῳδουμένῳ προσταχθείη μόνωσις· ὑπηρέτει μέντοι καὶ τὰς ἄλλας ὑπηρεσίας ἀεὶ διαφερόντως τῷ πλήθει, μόνον οὐχ ὕπαρχος ὢν καὶ τὰ τῆς ἡγεμονίας συνδιοικῶν.

⁵⁵ II. And the clearest proof of what I have said may be afforded by the following consideration. He (Moses) had a friend and pupil, one who had been so almost from his very earliest youth, Joshua by name, whose friendship he had won, not by any of the arts which are commonly in use among other men, but by that heavenly and unmixed love from which all virtue is derived. This man lived under the same roof, and shared the same table with him, except when solitude was enjoined to him on occasions when he was inspired and instructed in divine oracles. He also performed other services for him in which he was distinguished from the multitude, being almost his lieutenant, and regulating in conjunction with him the matters relating to his supreme authority.

⁵⁶ ἀλλὰ καίτοι βάσανον ἀκριβῆ λαβὼν ἐκ μακρῶν χρόνων τῆς ἔν τε λόγοις καὶ ἔργοις καλοκἀγαθίας αὐτοῦ καὶ τὸ ἀναγκαιότατον εὐνοίας τῆς πρὸς τὸ ἔθνος, οὐδὲ τοῦτον ᾤήθη χρῆναι καταλιπεῖν διάδοχον, δεδιὼς μή ποτε ψευδοδοξῇ νομίζων ἀγαθὸν τὸν οὐκ ὄντα πρὸς ἀλήθειαν, ἐπειδὴ τὰ κριτήρια τῆς ἀνθρωπίνης γνώμης ἀμυδρὰ καὶ ἀβέβαιά πως εἶναι πέφυκεν.

⁵⁶ But yet, though Moses had thus an accurate knowledge of him from his experience of him for a long time, and though he knew his excellence both in word and deed, and the greatness of his good will towards his nation, yet he did not think fit to leave him as his successor himself, fearing lest he might perchance be deceived in looking on that man as good who in reality was not so, since the tests by which one can judge of human nature are in a great degree indistinct and unstable.

In this text, Philo describes Joshua as someone whom Moses has known since he (Joshua) was a child. Joshua essentially grows up in Moses' house, and serves Moses when necessary. The two men love each other based upon their shared love of virtue. And yet, Philo writes, when it comes time for Moses to choose a successor, he does not automatically choose Joshua, since he worried that perhaps his love of Joshua could cloud his judgment. Moses wishes to rely on God, the objective judge, to ensure that the Israelites receive the best possible leader. Moses' concern for the people outweighs his love for his friend and student, although, luckily, Joshua turns out to be God's choice anyway.

For our purposes, the importance of this text is that even though Philo describes Joshua in positive terms, this text is not about Joshua. It is about

Moses' great attachment to the welfare of the Israelites. Joshua and his good qualities are brought in only to demonstrate this point.

De Virtutibus (1:66 – 69)

Joshua is mentioned one more time in this work, in a longer piece, also part of the section dealing with "humanity."

⁶⁶ τοῦτο μὲν δὴ πρῶτον ἐναργέστατον δεῖγμα τῆς πρὸς ἅπαν τὸ ὁμόφυλον αὐτοῦ φιλανθρωπίας καὶ πίστεως· ἕτερον δὲ τοῦ λεχθέντος οὐκ ἀποδέον. ἐπειδὴ γὰρ ἀριστίνδην ὁ φοιτητὴς αὐτοῦ καὶ μιμητὴς τῶν ἀξιεράστων ἠθῶν Ἰησοῦς ἄρχων ἐδοκιμάσθη κριτηρίοις θείοις, οὐχ ὥσπερ ἂν ἕτερος ἐπὶ τῷ μὴ τοὺς υἱοὺς ἢ τοὺς ἀδελφιδοῦς αἱρεθῆναι κατήφησεν,

⁶⁷ ἀλλὰ ὑποπλησθεὶς ἀλέκτου χαρᾶς, ὅτι μελλήσοι τὸ ἔθνος ἐπιτρόπῳ χρῆσθαι τὰ πάντα ἀρίστῳ καλὸν γὰρ κἀγαθὸν ἐξ ἀνάγκης ᾔδει τὸν εὐάρεστον θεῷ, λαβόμενος τῆς τούτου δεξιᾶς καὶ παραγαγὼν αὐτὸν εἰς ἠθροισμένον τὸ πλῆθος, μηδὲν περὶ τῆς αὐτοῦ τελευτῆς εὐλαβηθείς, ἀλλὰ ταῖς ἀρχαίαις εὐφροσύναις νέας ἑτέρας προσειληφὼς οὐ μόνον διὰ μνήμην τῶν πρότερον εὐπαθειῶν, αἷς κατακόρως διὰ παντὸς εἴδους ἀρετῆς ἐνετρύφησεν, ἀλλὰ καὶ διὰ τὴν ἐλπίδα τοῦ μέλλειν ἀθανατίζεσθαι μεταβαλὼν ἐκ φθαρτοῦ βίου εἰς ἄφθαρτον, ἱλαραῖς ὄψεσιν ἐκ τῆς κατὰ ψυχὴν εὐθυμίας φαιδρὸς καὶ γεγηθὼς φησιν·

⁶⁶ This, now, is the first and most conspicuous proof of his (=Moses) great humanity and good faith towards and affection for all those of his own people, and there is also another which is not inferior to that which I have already mentioned. For when Joshua, being his most excellent pupil and the imitator of his amiable and excellent disposition, had been approved of as the ruler of the people by the judgment of God, Moses was in no respect downcast as some other men might have been at the fact of its not having been his own sons or nephews who were appointed;

⁶⁷ but he was filled with unrestrained joy because there was secured to the nation a governor who was in all respects excellent (for he was sure that the man who was pleasing to God must be virtuous and pious); and accordingly, taking him by the right hand, he led him forth to the assembled multitude, not being at all alarmed at the idea of his own impending death, but feeling that he had received a new cause of joy in addition to his former reasons for cheerfulness, not only from the recollection of his former happiness, in which he had passed his life abundantly in every species of virtue, but from the hope also that he was now about to become immortal, changing from this corruptible to an incorruptible life; and accordingly, with a cheerful look proceeding from the joy which he felt in his soul, he spoke to them with joy and exultation in the following manner, and said:

⁶⁸ "ἐμοὶ μὲν ἀπαλλάττεσθαι καιρὸς ἤδη τῆς ἐν σώματι ζωῆς· ὁ δὲ τῆς ὑμετέρας ἐπιτροπῆς διάδοχος οὗτός ἐστιν αἱρεθεὶς ὑπὸ θεοῦ"· καὶ τὰ χρησθέντα λόγια τῆς δοκιμασίας εὐθὺς ἐπεῖπεν, οἷς ἐπίστευσαν.

⁶⁸ "It is time for me now to be released from the life in the body; and my successor in the government of your nation is this man, having been appointed thereto by God." And then he proceeded to detail to them the oracular words of God which he had received as the proofs of this his successor's appointment by God; and the people believed them.

⁶⁹ καὶ πρὸς τὸν Ἰησοῦν ἀποβλέψας ἀνδραγαθίζεσθαι παραινεῖ καὶ σφόδρα ἰσχύειν ἐν ταῖς εὐβουλίαις, ἀγαθὰς μὲν γνώμας εἰσηγούμενον, ἀνενδότοις δὲ καὶ ἐρρωμένοις λογισμοῖς τὰ γνωσθέντα καλῶς τελειοῦντα. καὶ ταῦτ' ἔλεγεν ἴσως οὐ δεομένῳ παραινέσεως, ἀλλὰ τὸ φιλάλληλον καὶ φιλοεθνὲς πάθος οὐ στέγων, ὑφ' οὗ τρόπον τινὰ κεντριζόμενος ἃ συνοίσειν ἐνόμιζεν ἀπεγύμνου.

⁶⁹ And then, looking upon Joshua, he exhorted him to approve himself a valiant man, and to be very strong in good and wise counsel, and to show himself the interpreter of his counsels, and to accomplish all his purposes with unyielding and vigorous decision. And he said this much to him though he was not perhaps in need of any recommendation, but because he would not conceal their mutual affection for one another and for the whole people, by which he was spurred on as it were to lay bare before him what he thought would be advantageous.

The terms describing Joshua in this section are glowing. He is the most excellent (ἀριστίνδην) pupil of Moses, and the imitator (μιμητής) of Moses' great qualities. Even though Moses exhorts Joshua to be valiant and strong and wise in counsel, Joshua was already all these things;³⁰⁰ Moses only gave this speech to demonstrate to the Israelites how much he loved Joshua. But again, the greatness of Joshua is just the background for Philo. His point is that even though Joshua was chosen, as opposed to either of Moses' two sons, Moses was perfectly happy. This demonstrates that Moses' concern for the Israelites and their future was so great that even love for his own sons could not cause him to feel any disappointment, since clearly if they were being overlooked it was for good reason.

De Ebrietate (1:96–98)

In his work "On Drunkenness," Philo describes the interaction between Joshua and Moses on the mountain, when Joshua hears the celebration of the people before the golden calf and assumes that it is the sound of an outbreak of war.

---

300 Philo does not seem to interpret these exhortations as signs that either Joshua needed this encouragement or, at least, Moses (and God) believed that he did.

Philo's analysis of this interchange, which he interprets as philosophical allegory, is rather long. I will quote only the beginning part relating to Joshua's words to give a flavor for how Philo approaches this passage.

[96] λέγεται γὰρ ὅτι ἀκούσας Ἰησοῦς τῆς φωνῆς τοῦ λαοῦ κεκραγότων εἶπε πρὸς Μωυσῆν· φωνὴ πολέμου ἐν τῇ παρεμβολῇ. καὶ λέγει... ἃ δὲ διὰ τούτων αἰνίττεται, παραστήσωμεν, ὡς ἂν οἷοί τε ὦμεν·

[96] For it is said, that when Joshua heard the people crying out he said to Moses, "There is the sound of war in the camp. And he (Moses) said... And the enigmatical meaning, which is concealed under these figurative expressions, we will explain to the best of our ability.

[97] τὰ περὶ ἡμᾶς τοτὲ μὲν ἠρεμεῖ, τοτὲ δὲ ὁρμαῖς καὶ ἐκβοήσεσιν ἀκαίροις ὡσανεὶ χρῆται· καὶ ἔστιν ἡ μὲν ἡσυχία τούτων εἰρήνη βαθεῖα, τὰ δὲ ἐναντία πόλεμος ἄσπονδος.

[97] XXV. Our own affairs are at one time in a state of tranquility, and at another they behave as it were with unseasonable impetuosity and loud cries; and their tranquility is profound peace, and their condition, when in an opposite state, is interminable war;

[98] μάρτυς δ᾽ ὁ πεπονθὼς ἀψευδέστατος· ἀκούσας γὰρ τῆς φωνῆς τοῦ λαοῦ κεκραγότων λέγει πρὸς τὸν σκεπτικὸν καὶ ἐπίσκοπον τῶν πραγμάτων· "φωνὴ πολέμου ἐν τῇ παρεμβολῇ." ἕως μὲν γὰρ οὐκ ἐκινοῦντο καὶ ἐκεκράγεσαν ἐν ἡμῖν αἱ ἄλογοι ὁρμαί, σταθερώτερον ὁ νοῦς ἵδρυτο· ἐπειδὴ δὲ ἤρξαντο πολύφωνον καὶ πολύηχον ἀπεργάζεσθαι τὸ ψυχῆς χωρίον τὰ πάθη συγκαλοῦσαι καὶ ἀνεγείρουσαι, στάσιν ἐμφύλιον ἐγέννησαν...

[98] and the witness to this fact is one who has experienced its truth, and who cannot lie; for having heard the voice of the people crying out, he says to the manager and superintendent of the affairs, "There is a sound of war in the tent;" for as long as the irrational impulses were not stirred up, and had not raised any outcry in us, our minds were established with some firmness; but when they began to fill the place of the soul with all sorts of voices and sounds, calling together and awakening the passions, they created a civil sedition and war in the camp...

As he does for many passages, Philo assumes that the simple words of the speakers are allegories for complex philosophical discourse. In this section, in which Joshua interprets the noise in the camp as an outbreak of war, Philo explains that Joshua was making a philosophical observation to Moses about the internal struggle of reason versus irrational impulses. Joshua's point is that when these impulses are stirred up in a person, the ensuing struggle fills the person's soul with a cacophony of voices and noise, resembling the sound of war. Although, as in the biblical passage, Moses will respond with an interpretation of the noise in the camp that will "trump" that of Joshua, nevertheless, this passage clearly demonstrates that Philo sees Joshua as a fellow philosopher, the philosophical conversation partner of the greatest philosopher in history, the lawgiver, Moses.

De Mutatione Nominum (XXI; 121–122)

In his "On the Change of Names," Philo brings up the changing of Hoshea's name to Joshua, referenced in the Book of numbers as part of the scout story.

ταῦτα καὶ περὶ τούτων. ἀλλὰ καὶ τὸν Ὡσηὲ μετονομάζει Μωυσῆς εἰς τὸν Ἰησοῦν, τὸν ποιὸν εἰς ἕξιν μεταχαράττων. Ὡσηὲ μὲν γὰρ ἑρμηνεύεται ποιὸς οὗτος, Ἰησοῦς δὲ σωτηρία κυρίου, ἕξεως ὄνομα τῆς ἀρίστης. ἕξεις γὰρ τῶν κατ᾽ αὐτὰς ποιῶν ἀμείνους, ὡς μουσικὴ μουσικοῦ καὶ ἰατρικὴ ἰατροῦ καὶ παντὸς τεχνίτου τέχνη ποιά, καὶ ἀιδιότητι καὶ δυνάμει καὶ τῇ περὶ τὰ θεωρήματα ἀπταίστῳ ἀκρότητι. ἡ μὲν γὰρ ἕξις ἀίδιον ἐνεργοῦν, τέλειον, ὁ δὲ ποιὸς θνητόν, πάσχον, ἀτελές· κρεῖττον δὲ θνητοῦ μὲν τὸ ἄφθαρτον, πάσχοντος δὲ τὸ δρῶν αἴτιον, τὸ δὲ τέλειον ἀτελοῦς. οὕτω μεταχαράχθη καὶ τὸ τοῦ λεχθέντος νόμισμα πρὸς ἰδέαν βελτίονα...

Thus much we have thought fit to say on this subject. But, moreover, Moses also changes the name of Hosea into that of Joshua; displaying by his new name the distinctive qualities of his character; for the name Hosea is interpreted, "what sort of a person is this?" but Joshua means, "the salvation of the Lord," being the name of the most excellent possible character; for the habits are better with respect to those persons who are of such and such qualities from being influenced by them: as, for instance, music is better in a musician, physic in a physician, and each art of a distinctive quality in each artist, regarded both in its perpetuity, and in its power, and in its unerring perfection with regard to the objects of its speculation. For a habit is something everlasting, energising, and perfect; but a man of such and such a quality is mortal, the object of action, and imperfect. And what is imperishable is superior to what is mortal, the efficient cause is better than that which is the object of action; and what is perfect is preferable to what is imperfect. In this way the coinage of the above mentioned description was changed and received the stamp of a better kind of appearance...

Although Philo's idiosyncratic interpretation of the name Hoshea bears no resemblance to its meaning in Hebrew, his interpretation of the name Joshua as "salvation of the Lord" does. More importantly, the reason for the name change, in Philo's understanding, is that since Joshua is such an excellent person, it would be more fitting for him to receive this "most excellent of names" (ὄνομα τῆς ἀρίστης). Philo certainly believes Joshua to have been a great person.

De Vita Mosis (216)

Finally, in his "Life of Moses," Philo discusses Joshua's role in the battle with Amalek.

Μωυσῆς δὲ παρὰ τῶν σκοπῶν γνοὺς οὐ μακρὰν διεστηκότα τὸν ἐχθρὸν στρατόν, καταλέξας τοὺς ἡβῶντας καὶ στρατηγὸν ἑλόμενος ἕνα τῶν ὑπάρχων Ἰησοῦν, πρὸς τὴν μείζονα συμμαχίαν αὐτὸς ἠπείγετο· περιρρανάμενος γὰρ τοῖς εἰωθόσι καθαρμοῖς ἐπὶ κολωνὸν τὸν πλησίον μετὰ σπουδῆς ἀναδραμὼν ἱκέτευε τὸν θεὸν ὑπερασπίσαι καὶ νίκην καὶ κράτος περιποιῆσαι τοῖς Ἑβραίοις, οὓς ἐκ χαλεπωτέρων πολέμων καὶ κακῶν ἄλλων ἐρρύσατο μὴ μόνον τὰς ἐξ ἀνθρώπων ἐπικρεμασθείσας συμφορὰς ἀποσκεδάσας, ἀλλὰ καὶ ὅσας ὅ τε τῶν στοιχείων νεωτερισμὸς ἐκαινούργησε κατ' Αἴγυπτον καὶ ὁ ἐν ταῖς ὁδοιπορίαις ἀνήνυτος λιμός.	But when Moses had learnt from his scouts that the army of the enemy was marshaled at no great distance, he chose out those men who were in the flower of their youth, and appointed one of his subordinate officers, named Joshua, to be their general, while he himself went to procure a more powerful alliance; for, having purified himself with the customary purification, he rode up with speed to a neighboring hill, and there he besought God to hold his shield over the Hebrews and to give them the victory and the mastery, as he had delivered them before from more formidable dangers and from other evils, not only dissipating the calamities with which they were threatened at the hands of men, but also all those which the transformation of the elements so wonderfully caused in the land of Egypt, and from those which the long scarcity inflicted upon them in their travels.

Joshua is referenced here simply as one of Moses' subordinate officers (ἕνα τῶν ὑπάρχων) and who is in charge of the young fighters. However, the victory is not Joshua's but rather Moses'. Philo makes this clear by saying that Moses went to form "a more powerful alliance" (μείζονα συμμαχίαν). Furthermore, whereas the biblical story ends with God telling Moses to place the scroll into the hands (ears) of Joshua, implying that Joshua/Israel will continue the war against Amalek, Philo does not mention this, or even the name of Joshua, again in this account.

However, before we can interpret this as Philo pushing Joshua down, it is worth noting that this is in line with the biblical description which says that Israel only won when Moses raised his arms, but lost when Moses put them down. In fact, if one accepts the argument that the Amalek account was originally only Joshua's but was added into the Exodus account later and put under Moses, Philo is simply taking the biblical editor's work to its logical conclusion.

Conclusion

From all of the above, it would seem that Barthelot's description of Philo's relationship with Joshua is the most accurate. It is true that Philo is not overly interested in the character of Joshua and that he often uses him as an opening to discuss Moses. This is true even when Philo says exceedingly nice things about Joshua. Nevertheless, it is clear that Philo sees Joshua as a positive character and is in no way attempting to denigrate him. But in comparison with Moses, Philo just isn't all that interested in Joshua. The reason for this may be because Joshua's life is filled with battles and not laws or philosophy, or it may be only that Joshua does not appear all that much in the Pentateuch, which is the only biblical work of great interest to Philo.

Assumptio Mosis

The available manuscript of *Assumptio Mosis*, an apocalyptic work from the first or second century CE, is incomplete and in Latin, although the work was most probably written originally in Greek.[301] The book is framed as a final speech from Moses to Joshua describing events that would occur in the distant future; a standard apocalyptic theme.[302]

Although Joshua is referenced only in the beginning and end of the book as we have it, and he takes an active role only at the end, nevertheless, in order to understand the significance of his character's function and position in *Assumptio Mosis*, it is necessary to offer a schematic overview of the basic "plot" of the apocalypse.

---

[301] Some have argued for a Hebrew original; I follow here the argument of Johannes Tromp: Johannes Tromp, *The Assumption of Moses: A Critical Edition with Commentary* (Studia in Veteris Testamenti Pseudepigrapha 10; Leiden: Brill, 1993), 116–118. Insofar as the dating of the composition, as I will argue in a forthcoming article, I am in agreement with Solomon Zeitlin that the work should be dated to the post-Bar Kokhba Hadrianic persecutions. Solomon Zeitlin, "The Assumption of Moses and the Revolt of Bar Kokba: Studies in the Apocalyptic Literature," *JQR* 38 (1948): 1–45. My reasoning for the dating is rather different than that of Zeitlin, and I do not endorse his other conclusions in the article, only the dating.

[302] Unfortunately, the manuscript is cut off in the middle of chapter 12, and we do not know how the book is supposed to end. However, it is worth noting that Jude 1:9 refers to the archangel Michael fighting with the devil over Moses' body, so we seem to, at least, have some idea what is missing. (This is assuming, as many do, that Jude is referencing *Assumptio Mosis*.)

Overview of the Text

The text opens by explaining its origins – it is the text of prophecy referred to in Deuteronomy that Moses gave to Joshua when transferring leadership.[303] Moses offers a preamble to the prophecy as well.

Moses tells Joshua that the contents of the prophecy are a secret. This refers not only to the details of the prophecy, but to its overall message. The message is that the world was created for Israel. The gentiles are not supposed to know about this so that they will – unwittingly – disgrace themselves in their treatment of Israel. In order to keep the secret, Joshua is to take the scroll of prophecy, embalm it, and bury it in jars at a spot preordained by God during creation to protect the scrolls until the proper time to reveal them arrives.

After some encouraging words to Joshua, which we will look at in a later section, Moses begins to describe the future ages. He begins by describing the sin of the ten tribes and their breaking off from the two southern tribes, only to be followed, eventually, by the conquest of all twelve by a king from the east, who will bring them into exile. However, God will have mercy on the people and allow some of them to return to their homeland, due to the righteous prayer of someone greater than them (*unus qui supra eos*).[304]

The people will sin again, and the altar will be serviced by fake priests and the people will be ruled by bribe-taking officials.[305] Eventually, these "priests" will claim the high priesthood and even the throne.[306] Finally, as if this weren't enough, a "petulant king" (*rex petulans*) will arise from among them, and he will be "wicked and cruel" (*homo temarius et improbus*). He will rule with malice for 34 years, killing indiscriminately. His sons will follow him.[307] During the reign of this family, a king from the west (Rome) will take dominion over Israel/Judea.

At this point, the most immoral of people will begin to rule Judea, although they will proclaim themselves righteous. This is the lowest point to which the people of Israel will sink, and God will respond in kind. A (Gentile) king of kings will come to reign over Israel. He will crucify the circumcised Jews, torture

---

303 Johannes Tromp suggests that this may be a midrashic reading of Deuteronomy 31:14, since God states there that he will address Joshua, but the contents of that address are never given (Tromp, *Assumption*, 136). This is an attractive suggestion although one problem is that *Assumptio Mosis* has Moses addressing Joshua, not God, as it is in the LXX. See later for more discussion of this.
304 Taking into account the gross schematization, this is meant as a summary of the First Temple period.
305 This probably refers to the period of Antiochus IV
306 This probably refers to the early Hasmoneans
307 This is clearly a reference to Herod and his sons.

the ones who deny their circumcision, and force all Jewish men to replace their foreskin. He will take their wives and force them to worship idols.[308]

This is the pivot point of human history. (It is also, perhaps, the moment in time in which the author was living, or, at least, his perception of where things were headed.) At this point a great man from the tribe of Levi named Taxo will arise together with his seven sons. However, unlike Mattathias and his sons, Taxo will not lead a rebellion. Rather, he and his family will lock themselves in a cave and starve themselves to death.

This pitiable act will be the one that brings the final salvation and the kingdom of God. The "One from Heaven" (*Caelestis*) will leave his throne and pounce upon the hated enemies of Israel on earth. The world will shake, the sun and moon will go dark and turn to blood, the stars will scatter, the sea will fall into the abyss, etc. In short, creation will be undone. Having punished the hated gentiles, God wil bring Israel to heaven "on eagle's wings," to live with the Creator as it was always intended they should.[309]

Other than the virulent anti-gentile tone and the cyclical nature of Jewish history as presented, what stands out most about this prediction/retelling of history is the passivity of the Israelites as a whole and the hero-figure Taxo in particular. The job of the good amongst the Israelites is to wait for God's help, and the job of Taxo is to get God's attention by an act of self-sacrifice. In fact, as Moses points out to Joshua at the beginning, this entire cycle is pre-ordained. The purpose of the revelation/scroll of *Assumptio Mosis* is simply to give testimony at the end of days, when the scroll will ostensibly be re-revealed, to the fact that this has all been part of the plan since creation. It is against this theological/ eschatological background that the description of Joshua in the book must be assessed.

Introduction – Joshua the Righteous

Joshua is first introduced as a man approved by God (*hominem probatum Domino*) to succeed Moses as leader of the people, the tabernacle, and the "testimony" and to lead the people into the land of their fathers (1:6–8).

---

308 I believe this is a reference to the Hadrianic persecution, the event which serves, in my estimation, as the catalyst for the apocalypse included in this work. I hope to write more about this in a different venue.

309 For an analysis of the meaning of the eschatological vision and the messianic figure Taxo, see my article in *Relegere*, "*Assumptio Mosis* and the Eschatology of Despair."

Moses gives Joshua a job description. Ironically, the first item is that he is to embalm and bury the scroll of *Assumptio Mosis*. Other than that, Joshua is to go into the land with the people, bless them (*benedicis*), give that (2:1-2), Joshua shares, found a kingdom (*regnum*), and arrange local rule (*magisteria locarum*);[310] after this follows the above-summarized eschatological prediction. Ostensibly, Joshua is to understand that his efforts will be for naught, as Israel will quickly throw off the shackles of God's law, and the cycles of punishment in Jewish history will begin.

The job of Joshua as described by Moses is rather schematic. There is no mention of conquest or any of the challenges of leadership. It would seem that all Joshua needs is his piety and a very basic competence. To Moses, the piety is the key. Joshua must promise to keep God's law diligently (*promitte secus industriam tuam Omnia quae mandata sunt*; 1:10). Furthermore, Moses repeats the requirement that Joshua maintain his fealty to the revelation set out in *Assumptio Mosis* both in the introduction to the Apocalypse (*<custodi> verbum hoc*; 1:9) as well as in its conclusion (*custodi verba haec*; 10:11).

Only at the very end of the apocalypse is the familiar encouragement of Joshua to "be strong" (*firma <te>*) heard (10:15). Moses then caps his speech with a final reminder to Joshua that he (Joshua) was chosen by God (*te elegit deus*) to succeed him (Moses). The speech does not seem to have the effect that Moses intended.

Joshua the Panic-Stricken

Joshua takes the revelation of Moses' imminent death and his own position as successor rather badly. First, Joshua collapses at Moses' feet and tears his clothes (11:1). Initially, Moses takes this as a simple sign of mourning for the Jewish people of the future, and joins in Joshua's weeping (11:2).

Far from being comforted, however, Joshua begins a complaint-filled and fear-driven rant that continues on for thirteen verses. He claims that Moses has terrified him (*me terres*), and that he wants to hide himself (*celabor*) from Moses' terrible words (11:4). What is particularly surprising, however, is not the fact of Joshua's fear, but what it is he fears.

Joshua makes no mention of any fear or sadness about the future plight of the Israelites as detailed in Moses' prophecy. Rather, Joshua is afraid of Moses' immanent death and the burden of leadership this will place on himself. He fears this despite the fact that Moses has not predicted that anything terrible

---

310 This last task has a very "Roman" flavor to it.

or gloomy will happen during Joshua's tenure. It is almost as if Joshua wasn't really listening to the speech at all. To paraphrase a modern idiom, Joshua effectively says to Moses: "you lost me at immanent death."

This extreme focus on Moses' death is underlined by the first section of Joshua's response, the most peculiar section of the entire speech. Although Joshua will eventually enumerate the various aspects of his new responsibilities that frighten him, he begins by stating his fear that no one will succeed in burying Moses. Joshua gives two reasons for this surprising assertion. First, he claims that no mortal would have the courage to move Moses' body. Second, he claims that since Moses' impact and importance is over the entire world, no specific burial spot can ever do him justice (11:5 – 8).[311]

Having begun with this unconventional fear, Joshua continues on to list his more conventional concerns about life without Moses (11:9 – 11). Essentially, he lists three fears. How will he get the Israelites ample food and drink? Who will pray to God on their behalf for mercy? Who will defend them against the Amorites when the Amorites inevitably attack after hearing that Moses has died.[312]

The first fear is, perhaps, the most understandable. Joshua may not feel as if he has control over miracles the way Moses had. If the manna stops falling, what is he to do? The second fear is rather ephemeral, and connects to Joshua's perception that Moses has an intimacy with God that Joshua will never have. Joshua fears that he may end up inadequate to the task, if his responsibilities are really to mimic those of Moses. In that sense, his first two fears are related.

It is the third fear that stands out: since when is Joshua the general afraid of a fight? Furthermore, why should Joshua be afraid that the Amorites will attack when he is planning on attacking them anyway?! A close look at Joshua's description of his fear sheds some light on this problem. He claims that when the enemies hear that Moses is gone, they will say to themselves (11:16 – 17):

---

311 It is interesting to note that based on the little we know of the end of the book from external sources, with angels burying Moses, it would seem that Joshua's assertion has merit.

312 Joshua has other extremely poetic statements that are not clearly related to any particular fear. For example, Joshua asks (11:12), "How can I <protect> this people, like a father his only son, or like a mistress her daughter – a virgin who is being prepared to be surrendered to a man – who is in dread, protecting her [daughter's] body from the sun and her unshod feet from running over the ground." I do not think there is any place in the Bible where Joshua speaks with such poetic and rhetorical flourish.

Eamus ad eus. Si inimici impie fecerunt semel adhuc in Dominum suum, non est defensor illis qui ferat pro eis praeces Domino quomodo Monse erat magnus nuntius, qui singilus horis, diebus et noctibus, habebat genua sua infixa in terra orans...	Let us go up unto them. If the enemies commit an impiety once more against their God, there is no one to defend them who will bring on their behalf supplications before the Lord, in the way of Moses who was the great messenger, who every single hour, day and night, would bend his knees to the earth praying...

From this comment it seems clear that Joshua believes that wars are won by greater piety. Hence, this comment fits into the rubric of the other two comments as well. Joshua believes that since he is less pious than Moses, he will fail as a leader. This model fits well into the overall theology set out in the apocalyptic section. The fate of the world is directed by God, and hence the actions of humans are of little consequence other than how they affect the divine governance of the world.

Moses' Response

Despite Joshua's extreme panic, Moses' response can hardly be considered comforting. Moses starts kindly enough. He warns Joshua not to belittle himself (*te ne contemnas*), and to show himself secure (*praebe te securum*; 12:3). Moses then reminds Joshua that God is the creator of the world and that he foresees all and overlooks nothing (12:4).

One may have expected Moses to continue in this vein and state that, therefore, since God wills Joshua's success, it is assured to happen, but this is not what Moses says. Instead, Moses tells Joshua that it is true that God listens to Moses' prayers, but this is because God appointed Moses specifically for this purpose (12:6). Additionally, Moses claims that this was not because of his (Moses') own virtue or steadfastness (*et enim propter meam virtutem aut in firmitatem*), but because of God's mercy and patience (12:7).

These two claims are somewhat contradictory. The first claim implies that Moses succeeded because he was chosen by God; the second implies that he succeeded because God is merciful. Although Moses' meaning here is hard to determine, it may be that this hearkens back to a claim Moses makes at the beginning of the book.

In 1:10 – 15, Moses begins his long speech with a reference to God as creator and the key role Israel plays in God's overall plan (1:12 – 13). Moses then discusses his own role (1:14):

Itaque excogitavit et invenit me qui ab initio orbis terrarium praeparitus sum ut sim arbiter testamenti illius.	Therefore, [God] contrived and designed me, who from the beginning of the world has been prepared so that I may be the overseer of his covenant.

It would seem that the author of *Assumptio Mosis* sees a core difference between Moses and Joshua and their respective missions. Moses is a part of God's plan the way Israel is. He was created and designed for the purpose of receiving and transmitting God's plan to Israel. In this sense, he is actually not replicable.

Joshua's job is both to lead the people of Israel and to (physically) carry Moses' message on a scroll, burying it until the proper time in the future for it to be revealed will arrive. Although it is true that Joshua was chosen by God to do these things and succeed Moses, neither Joshua nor Moses believes that Joshua can really fill his (Moses') shoes.[313] What Moses is trying to tell Joshua is that Joshua should not feel bad about his inferiority to Moses, since Moses was designed to be superior and that the key factor in God listening to a leader's supplications is not the leader's piety but God's own mercy, which will remain the same.

Additionally, Moses reminds Joshua of the importance of the people's obedience to God's law. Those who follow God's word will succeed, and those who do not will perish. Nevertheless, Moses ends by stating that no matter what the people do, they will not be destroyed. This is because God ordained from the creation of the world that this will not occur, so Joshua can rest assured that it will not. The manuscript ends on this note, which appears to be the end of Moses' speech. As stated above, the end of the story, with Moses' death and burial, is lost, other than a few fragments.

Literary Analysis

Although the official descriptions of Joshua offered in the book are complimentary, the rhetorical strategy of the work seems to focus on magnifying the character of Moses in contrast to that of Joshua and any subsequent leader. Joshua recognizes the difference between himself and his teacher viscerally and explicitly, and makes this clear in his speech. Nothing in Moses' "polite" response really succeeds in altering this impression. Moses remains the visionary while Joshua simply records the vision; he will not be having one of his own.

---

313 With this analysis, I disagree with the interpretation offered by Tromp (265) that Moses is attempting to make Joshua feel like his equal.

Additionally, Joshua's military persona as well as his impetuousness and his leadership qualities – all essential qualities of his in the biblical books – are not factors in this work. His righteousness, his closeness to God, and even his observance of mitzvot are mentioned only perfunctorily. The only real character-traits Joshua demonstrates in this work are panic and feelings of inadequacy.

Although there is basis for Joshua panicking in the Bible – i.e., his reaction to the failure of the first attack on Ai in Joshua (7:6–9) – this account stands out in the Bible as unusual. There is a somewhat stronger basis for Joshua's feelings of inadequacy, as it is implied by the constant repetition in the beginning of Joshua and the end of Deuteronomy of the exhortation to "be strong and stead-fast." Nevertheless, Joshua bears his feelings stoically in these books, as opposed to the verbose poetic style of *Assumptio Mosis*.

One is tempted to suggest that Joshua's image here has been intentionally designed as a foil to Moses. Instead of the author fawning on Moses in the third person, or worse, having Moses fawn over himself, he places the sycophantic language in the mouth of Moses' student and successor. This would make the point clear to the reader, since if the great Joshua felt this inadequate around Moses, how much lower should the average person feel in comparison to the great law-giver!

Redaction-Critical Analysis

The above conclusion about Joshua's function may shed some light on a previously mentioned problem. Joshua's response to Moses' speech reads like a non-sequitur. Moses offers an overview of the future until the eschatological age and Joshua brings up only concerns about Moses' immanent death. Why is "the great Joshua" so unconcerned and uninterested in Israel's future?

Additionally, the reason offered in *Assumptio Mosis* for Moses offering Joshua his eschatological revelation appears forced. If Joshua's role is simply to bury the document and not to teach it, why frame the work as a speech from Moses to Joshua? It would seem more in keeping with the theme to hear it as a revelation from God to Moses. For this reason I suggest that the work may be a composite document and that the narrative frame may derive from a combination of old midrashic readings of the final days of Moses.

Joshua's Insecurity

There are two sticky points in the narrative that the midrash behind *Assumptio Mosis* may be detecting. The first is Moses' commanding of Joshua. Throughout the process of Joshua's appointment, he is constantly encouraged to be brave and steadfast. In Deut 3, for instance, Moses tells him not to fear the natives. This is followed by Yʜwʜ telling Moses that he must encourage Joshua more. In Deuteronomy 31 Moses encourages Joshua again, as does God in Joshua 1. The careful reader may ask: Why all this encouragement? Is Joshua afraid of something?

For an ancient commentator interested in the genre of rewritten bible, this offers a perfect opportunity to explore the question of what Joshua feared. The simple answer appears to be that he was afraid of being the leader. However, following the exhortations of Moses, it is possible to "divine" even more specifically what Joshua was afraid of.

First, Moses tells him not to fear the nations of the land (Deut 3:21), hence it would appear that he was afraid of losing the battle. This theme is expanded upon by the author of *Assumptio Mosis* by using a well-known midrashic reading of the Arad story as a template.

In Num 21, immediately after the description of Aaron's death, it is related that the king of Arad heard that Israel was coming and attacked them. The beginning of this sequence is repeated in Num 33:39–40. According to an ancient midrash, there is a connection between the death of Aaron and the war with Arad. For example, in the Tosefta (*Soṭ.* 11:1), it states:

כל זמן שהייתה מרים קיימת היתה באר מספקת את	As long as Miriam was alive the well gave water
ישראל משמתה מרים מהו או' ותמת שם מרים ולא היה	to Israel. When she died, what does it say?
מים לעדה שנסתלקה הבאר כל זמן שהיה אהרן קיים	"Miriam died there, and there was no water
עמוד ענן מנהיג את ישראל משמת אהרן מהו או' וישמע	for the people to drink" The well was gone.
הכנעני מלך ערד יושב הנגב וגו' נעשו ידים לאותו רשע	As long as Aaron was alive the pillar of cloud
ובא ונלחם את ישראל אמרו איה הלך התייר שלהן	stood and led the Israelites. When Aaron
המכבש להם את הארץ.	died, what does it say? "The Canaanite, king of Arad who dwelt in the Negev heard..." This became an opening for that wicked man, and he came to fight with Israel. They (the Canaanites) said: "Where has their guide gone, who was going to conquer the land on their behalf?!"

Joshua's fear in *Assumptio Mosis* is described in these same terms. He fears that once the king of the Amorites hears about the death of Moses, the Amorites will attack with full force.

Joshua's description of the Amorites "hearing" may also be inspired by the emphasis on their hearing in the book of Joshua. Rahab (Josh 2:10) talks about the Amorites having "heard" about the splitting of the Sea of Reeds, claiming that they feel afraid. After the splitting of the Jordan, the Amorites "hear" about it (5:1) and are afraid of Joshua. The introductions to the treaty with the Gibeonites, the battle against the southern coalition and the battle against the northern coalition all begin with the Canaanites and/or the kings "hearing" about Joshua's conquests.

Insofar as the substance of Joshua's fear, the author makes use of another midrashic theme. Joshua believes that the Amorites will know that God only protects the Israelites when they do not sin. This theme is seen in the midrashic treatment of Balaam. In the main Balaam story, Num 22–24, Balaam learns that YHWH loves Israel and will not condone cursing them. He crafts his words accordingly and blesses Israel. Despite this, he is killed by the Israelites in their battle against Midian (Num 31:8).

Lest one think this was an accident, or that the Israelites didn't know who he was, Moses references "Balaam's act" as the *casus belli* and the reason the Israelites should kill the Midianite women (Num 31:16). What was this infamous act of Balaam? An ancient homiletical interpretation is recorded in the *Sifrei Numbers* (*"Maṭṭot"* 157):

מה היה דבר בלעם אמר להם אפילו אתם מכניסים כל המונות שבעולם אין אתם יכולים להם. שמא מרובים אתם מן המצריים... אלא בואו ואני נותן לכם עצה מה תעשו אלהיהם של אלו שונא זימה הוא העמידו להם נשיכם ובנותיכם לזימה והם שטופים בזימה ואלהיהם שולט בהם שזה כל כל שכל זמן שישראל עושים רצונו הוא נלחם להם ... ובזמן שאין עושים רצונו כביכול הוא נלחם בם...	What was the act of Balaam? He said to them (the Moabites and Midianites): "Even if you bring in all the hordes in the world, you could not defeat [the Israelites]. Are you perchance more numerous than the Egyptians... Rather, come and I will give you advice. What can you do? Their god hates licentiousness. Send your wives and daughters to seduce them and they will become steeped in licentiousness; then their own god will overcome them. For this is the general rule, as long as they do his will, he fights for them... but when they do not do his will, it is as if he fights against them...

This midrash explains Moses' hatred of Balaam and his obscure reference to Balaam's act, but with an eye towards the main Balaam narrative. Of course Balaam understood that God loves Israel; this is why he towed the line when necessary. But Balaam also understood that God could be made to punish Israel, and this is what he taught the Moabites and Midianites. This explanation also draws upon the fact that the story of the Moabite/Midianite women immediately follows the story of Balaam; this is what Balaam did next, it was his idea.

It appears that this same motif is at work in Joshua's fear of the Amorites. Not only will the Amorites know that Moses is dead, but they will know that Moses was an intercessor to protect the Israelites when they sin. Knowing this, they will reason that it is only a matter of time before the next sin, and then the Israelites will be where the Amorites want them. Implicit in this claim is the assumption that Joshua will not be a successful intercessor, which is exactly what Joshua assumes here.

An additional fear Joshua mentions is that he will not be able to feed the people. This is also a natural fear that a careful reader could tease out from other biblical narratives. Moses himself was able to provide the Israelites with food only because God made water miraculously flow from rocks, blew quail in with the wind, and rained manna from the heavens. How could Joshua be sure that he would have that power?

In fact, even Moses isn't sure until it happened. When the people ask Moses for meat he responds with total panic (Num 11:11–14).

וַיֹּאמֶר מֹשֶׁה אֶל יְהוָה לָמָה הֲרֵעֹתָ לְעַבְדֶּךָ וְלָמָּה לֹא מָצָתִי חֵן בְּעֵינֶיךָ לָשׂוּם אֶת מַשָּׂא כָּל הָעָם הַזֶּה עָלָי. הֶאָנֹכִי הָרִיתִי אֵת כָּל הָעָם הַזֶּה אִם אָנֹכִי יְלִדְתִּיהוּ כִּי תֹאמַר אֵלַי שָׂאֵהוּ בְחֵיקֶךָ כַּאֲשֶׁר יִשָּׂא הָאֹמֵן אֶת הַיֹּנֵק עַל הָאֲדָמָה אֲשֶׁר נִשְׁבַּעְתָּ לַאֲבֹתָיו. מֵאַיִן לִי בָּשָׂר לָתֵת לְכָל הָעָם הַזֶּה כִּי יִבְכּוּ עָלַי לֵאמֹר תְּנָה לָּנוּ בָשָׂר וְנֹאכֵלָה. לֹא אוּכַל אָנֹכִי לְבַדִּי לָשֵׂאת אֶת כָּל הָעָם הַזֶּה כִּי כָבֵד מִמֶּנִּי. וְאִם כָּכָה אַתְּ עֹשֶׂה לִּי הָרְגֵנִי נָא הָרֹג אִם מָצָאתִי חֵן בְּעֵינֶיךָ וְאַל אֶרְאֶה בְּרָעָתִי.

Moses said to YHWH: "Why have you hurt your servant and why have I not found favor in your eyes, that you place the burden of this people upon me? Did I conceive this nation or did I give birth to it that you tell me to carry it in my bosom like a wet-nurse on the land you promised to its ancestors? From where can I get meat to feed all these people, such that they cry to me saying give us meat and we shall eat of it? I cannot bear the burden of this people myself, as it is too heavy for me. If you treat me thus, you should certainly kill me, if I have found favor in your eyes, so that I need not see my bitter end.

When God tries to calm his nerves, Moses responds with the most "blasphemous" complaint of his career (v. 21–22)

וַיֹּאמֶר מֹשֶׁה שֵׁשׁ מֵאוֹת אֶלֶף רַגְלִי הָעָם אֲשֶׁר אָנֹכִי בְּקִרְבּוֹ וְאַתָּה אָמַרְתָּ בָּשָׂר אֶתֵּן לָהֶם וְאָכְלוּ חֹדֶשׁ יָמִים. הֲצֹאן וּבָקָר יִשָּׁחֵט לָהֶם וּמָצָא לָהֶם אִם אֶת כָּל דְּגֵי הַיָּם יֵאָסֵף לָהֶם וּמָצָא לָהֶם.

Moses said: "600,000 men are in this nation in whose midst I am, and you say: 'I will give them meat and they will eat for a month'?! If the livestock and cattle were slaughtered would that be enough for them? If all the fish of the sea were gathered would that be enough form them?

God actually has to remind Moses that it is to the Creator he is talking.
Joshua's speech in *Assumptio Mosis* is reminiscent of this (11:12–14):

Quomodo ergo potero <...> plebem hanc tam- How can I <protect> this people, like a father
quam pater unicum filium, aut tamquam filiam his only son, or like a mistress her daughter –
domina[m], virginem quae paratur t<r>adi a virgin who is being prepared to be surren-
viro, quae timebat, corpus custodiens ejus a dered to a man – who is in dread, protecting
sole et ne scalciati pedes ejus ad currendum her [daughter's] body from the sun and her un-
supra terram? <Aut un>de voluntatem eorum shod feet from running over the ground. And
praestabo illis ciborum et potui secus volunta- whence will I fulfill their desire to take food
tem voluntatis eorum?[314] *...enim illorum erant* and drink which they fervently desire? For
C milia. Nam isti in tantum qui creverunt in their <number> was a hundred thousand, but
tuis orationibus, domine Monse. now they have grown into this great multitude
here, due to your supplications, Master
Moses.[315]

Like Moses before him, Joshua is afraid that he cannot lead the people on his
own, specifically that he cannot even feed them.

Another possible inspiration for this fear is the passage in Joshua about the
manna. In Joshua 5:11–12, the Israelites eat from the land's produce the day after
the Paschal offering. Only then does the manna stop. One can imagine that Joshua would worry that the manna would not last until the Israelites crossed over
into the Promised Land, but would stop immediately upon Moses' death, condemning the people to starvation before they even had a chance to begin the
conquest.

There seems to be support for this idea (that the manna should stop after the
death of Moses) in a different ancient Jewish work, the *Liber Antiquitatum Biblicarum*. There it states (20:8):

Et postquam defunctus est Moyses, desiit After Moses died, the manna stopped descend-
manna descendere filiis Israel, et tunc ceperunt ing for the Children of Israel, and then they
manducare de fructibus terre. Et hec sunt tria began to eat from the fruits of the land. And
que dedit populo suo Deus propter tres homines, these are the three [things] that God gave his
id est, puteum aque mirre pro Maria et colum- people because of three individuals: They are:
nam nubis pro Aaron et manna pro Moyse. Et the well of water of Marah for Miriam and the
finitis his tribus ablata sunt hec tria ab illis. pillar of cloud for Aaron and the manna for
Moses. And with the end of these three [peo-
ple], these three [things] were taken away
from them.

This is related to the same tradition from the Tosefta discussed earlier, and
seems to have been an inspiration for the author of *Assumptio Mosis*.

---

314 The syntax here and in the above phrase is very awkward. The basic meaning, however, is
clear.
315 In his commentary, Tromp also notes the probable use of the Numbers passage as a
template for Joshua's speech here. Tromp, *Assumption*, 248, 250.

The Burial of Moses

As noted earlier, Joshua's most bizarre fear is his first one. Joshua is afraid that no one can bury Moses. The author may have been inspired here by the question of why YHWH himself buries Moses.[316] This quasi-miraculous act, with YHWH alone burying Moses, stands out against the backdrop of the death and burial of Aaron, where Moses together with Aaron's son and successor Elazar go up with him to the mountain where he is to die. The careful reader may ask: Why didn't Joshua accompany Moses up the mountain and bury his master himself?

The author of *Assumptio Mosis*' answer to this question may be derived from Joshua's comment: It is humanly impossible to bury Moses, and even if it weren't, there is no way to do so appropriately. Surprisingly, this suggestion of Joshua's turns out to be correct, since it is God who will bury Moses. Furthermore, the lost ending of the book, as referenced in the Epistle of Jude 1:9, seems to have dealt with just this issue; angels are involved in the proper disposal of Moses' body. A similar attitude, albeit to Moses' death as opposed to his burial, can be seen in the *Midrash Peṭirat Moshe* (Eisenstein, *Otzar ha-Midrashim*, 367):

כיון שהשלים נפשו למות, אמר הקדוש ברוך הוא למיכאל וגבריאל צאו והביאו לי נשמתו של משה, אמר גבריאל מי שקול כנגד ששים רבוא היאך אני יכול ליטול נשמתו ולהיות חצוף לפניו. אח"כ אמר למיכאל כך ובכה מיכאל אמר לו לזנגזיאל כך, אמר לפניו רבש"ע אני הייתי רבו והוא תלמידי איך אטול נשמתו?	Once Moses made his peace with dying, the Holy One said to Michael and Gabriel: "Go and bring me Moses' soul." Gabriel said: "How can I take the soul of a man who is equal to 600,000 men, and be found wanton in his eyes?" Afterwards he said this to Michael, and Michael cried. He said this to Zanga-ziel, and he said: "Master of the universe, I was his teacher and he was my student, how can I take his soul?"

This *aggada* seems to be a version of the theme addressed in Joshua's fear. Again, the scriptural source or midrashic hook for this extreme unease at burying Moses (or taking his soul) may be the fact that YHWH buries Moses himself. Additionally, the fear emphasizes the unique nature of Moses and his prophecy, an idea that is central to Judaisms that are focused on Torah observance and the unique status of the Pentateuch.

---

316 Although it would be possible to read the unpointed biblical text as a niphal and translate "Moses was buried", this is not how the MT, the LXX or the ancient interpreters read the verse. Also, it would contradict a literal read of "nobody knows where he is buried." If someone buried him, then somebody knew.

Moses' Lost Speech

There is a third sticky point as well, and one that yet again relates to Moses' speech to Joshua. Following the narrative structure of the Pentateuch as a whole, Moses seems to command Joshua at least twice. The first time is when Moses places his hands upon Joshua in Num 27:23, which states that Moses "commands" Joshua, but does not relate what he said.

Next, in Deuteronomy 31:7–8, Moses speaks to Joshua in the presence of all of Israel, telling him not to fear, that he (Joshua) will bring the people into the land and that YHWH will be with him. As if this were not enough, YHWH tells Moses in verse 14 to bring Joshua to the tent of meeting so that he (YHWH) can command him. Moses then brings Joshua to the tent, and in verse 23 Joshua is given the command to be strong and take the people into Israel. Again he is told that YHWH will be with him.

One glaring problem is the repetitive nature of these commands to Joshua. One can imagine a careful reader in the Second Temple Period asking himself or herself, "Why all the commands to Joshua? Are Moses and YHWH really just telling Joshua the same thing over and over again?"[317] For someone looking to add a speech into Moses' repertoire, this problem provides an excellent opening: If Moses really did give Joshua another message, why is it not recorded? Perhaps, the ancient reader speculates, it was a secret message, not meant for the masses.

---

317 Additionally, there is a textual problem with Deut 31:23. The MT and the SP are not necessarily in agreement with the LXX about who commands Joshua here.

וַיְצַו אֶת יְהוֹשֻׁעַ בֶּן נוּן וַיֹּאמֶר חֲזַק וֶאֱמָץ כִּי אַתָּה תָּבִיא אֶת בְּנֵי יִשְׂרָאֵל אֶל הָאָרֶץ אֲשֶׁר נִשְׁבַּעְתִּי לָהֶם וְאָנֹכִי אֶהְיֶה עִמָּךְ.	He commanded Joshua bin Nun and said: "Be strong and brave, for you will bring the Children of Israel in to the land that I promised them, and I will be with you."
καὶ ἐνετείλατο Μωυσῆς Ἰησοῖ καὶ εἶπεν αὐτῷ Ἀνδρίζου καὶ ἴσχυε· σὺ γὰρ εἰσάξεις τοὺς υἱοὺς Ισραηλ εἰς τὴν γῆν, ἣν ὤμοσεν κύριος αὐτοῖς, καὶ αὐτὸς ἔσται μετὰ σοῦ.	And Moses commanded Joshua and said to him: "Be brave and strong, for you will bring the children of Israel into the land which the Lord swore to them, and he will be with you."

This is more than just a slip of the pen, but two contradictory claims about who it was that commanded Joshua. For the LXX, it would seem that God's promised command to Joshua comes only after Moses' death, i.e. God's speech in Joshua 1; an understanding at some tension with the simple reading of 31:14. The command in Deut 31:23 would then be, according to the LXX, Moses' third command to Joshua!

Summary

In short, I suggest that *Assumptio Mosis* is made up of three discrete midrashim. First, there is the writing of Joshua's response to Moses' message to him that he (Moses) was going to die and Joshua would be the leader. No response is recorded in the Pentateuch, and it may have seemed to an ancient author like a speech that was "begging to be written." The speech would reflect Joshua's fears, since that is what Moses' message seems to imply about Joshua's state of mind.

Second there is the discussion of Moses' miraculous burial. This was probably an independent tradition originally, and, as was pointed out above, different versions of it exist in ancient Jewish literature. This account may have been combined with Joshua's speech by adding into Joshua's list of fears the fear that he cannot bury Moses. This addition would have the added benefit of putting the explanation for why Joshua did not bury Moses himself into Joshua's own mouth.

Finally, an ancient author with an eschatological message decided to utilize this framework for his own purposes. Perhaps inspired by the problem of Moses' "missing" speech in the Pentateuch, he adds the eschatological prediction into the above posited text, creating the final edition of what we call *Assumptio Mosis*. I suggest that this final reworking of the book occurred significantly later than the first two parts, probably during the Hadrianic persecution.

At the core of Joshua's image in *Assumptio Mosis* are fear and feelings of inadequacy. Joshua does not feel up to the task. As suggested above, it would seem that this was inspired by the many encouragements Joshua receives in the Pentateuch and the book of Joshua.

When read in context with the death of Moses sequence and the question of burial, Joshua's image is shrunk even more. There is no real comparison between Moses and any other human or even angel, Joshua included. Joshua is a successor only in name, but nobody can really succeed Moses.

Finally, when read together with the apocalypse, Joshua's image is reduced yet again. Although he is told the eschatological prediction, this turns out to be unimportant, since Joshua's job is to bury the scroll in the appointed spot, nothing more. Although Joshua will be successful as a leader, this was preordained and will have limited future impact. Other than Moses, the hero of the apocalypse is Taxo, a character almost totally opposite to that of biblical Joshua. Taxo does not fight the enemy, but starves himself and his family to death in a cave, thereby awakening God's mercy.

According to *Assumptio Mosis*, the world functions based on predestination, tempered only by God's mercy. There is no place in this world for initiative-taking and battle-hardened leaders like Joshua. This may be why, in the retelling of *As-*

sumptio Mosis, all that remains of Joshua's positive image is a throw-away line about his piety. Joshua's leadership and military prowess are simply uninteresting to this author, and those who follow his worldview.

Liber Antiquitatum Biblicarum

The *Liber Antiquitatum Biblicarum* (*L.A.B.*), also known as Pseudo-Philo, retells biblical history from creation to the death of Saul.[318] Although we have the work only in Latin, it is believed to be a translation from Greek, which was itself most probably translated from a Hebrew original. *L.A.B.* is a very truncated version of biblical history starting with Genesis and continuing into the reign of Saul. However, it does include a number of expansions, both in genealogies as well as in narrative.[319]

Structure of the Joshua Narrative

The Joshua narrative is structured around a series of speeches delivered by Joshua, with an overall skeletal narrative frame. The frame, although reminiscent of the book of Joshua, differs greatly in its emphases.

Although the narrative recounts the fact of Joshua's conquest of Canaan, no battle scenes are described; other than Jericho, no specific battles are even referenced. There is one half-verse (20:9a) that states that Joshua conquered the 39 kings of the Amorites. Other than one further reference to enemies (23:1), that is

---

318 It is called Pseudo-Philo because some early manuscripts included this work together with some of Philo's works, not because the author was attempting to write as if he were Philo. The work is not at all reminiscent of Philo. For an edition of the work, including an introduction, the original Latin plus translation, and commentary, see: Howard Jacobson, *A Commentary on Pseudo-Philo's Liber Antiquitatum Biblicarum, with Latin text and English translation* (2 vols.; Leiden: Brill, 1996.) The Latin quotes in this chapter are all from this edition.

319 For an overview of *L.A.B.*'s work and analysis of how it rewrites the Bible in general, see: Frederick J. Murphy, *Pseudo-Philo: Rewriting the Bible.* New York: Oxford University Press, 1993. For a discussion of how L.A.B. creates its characters, see: George W.E. Nickelsburg, "Good and Bad Leaders in Pseudo-Philo's Liber Antiquitatum Biblicarum," in *Ideal Figures in Ancient Judaism: Profiles and Paradigms* (eds. John J. Collins and George W.E. Nickelsburg; Society of Biblical Literature: Septuagint and Cognate Studies 12; Chico: Scholars Press, 1980), 49 – 66. For an analysis of how *L.A.B.* rewrites the Joshua account, see Christopher Begg, "Josephus' and Pseudo-Philo's rewritings of the Book of Joshua," in *The Book of Joshua* (ed. Ed Noort; BETL 250 – Proceedings of the CBL; Leuven: Leuven University Press, 2010), 555 – 588 [565 ff].

the entirety of the description of Joshua as warrior. Additionally, the seven or so full chapters dedicated in the biblical book of Joshua to his division of the land among the tribes are summarized in one half-verse in *L.A.B.* (20:9b).

On the other hand, Joshua's building of the altar and founding of a place of worship in Shiloh are given entire chapters of their own in *L.A.B.* Joshua is also given a major role in the story of the altar in Transjordan, a story in which he is not mentioned even once in the biblical narrative. In short, *L.A.B.* presents Joshua as "a different person" than the biblical Joshua, or, at least, as a "reframing" of biblical Joshua.[320]

Mourning for Joshua: A Second Moses?

When Joshua dies at the end of chapter 24, the people offer a poetic eulogy:

Plangite super pinnam aquile huius levis quoniam evolavit a nobis, et plangite super virtutem catuli leonis quoniam absconsus est a nobis.

Beat in lamentation over the wing of this lithe eagle, for he has escaped from us; beat in lamentation over the courage of the lion's whelp, for he has been concealed from us.

Et quis iens renuntiet iusto Moysi quoniam habuimus quadraginta annis ducem similem ei.

And who, going, will report to the just Moses that we have had a leader resembling him for forty years?

A number of things stand out about this eulogy. First is the poetry. The people compare Joshua to an eagle and a lion's cub, both powerful images, often reserved for warriors. Both are also very positive images, reflecting the admiration of the people for Joshua and their feelings of loss at his death.

Second, and even more striking, is the comparison of Joshua to Moses. According to the people, Joshua was a leader who resembled Moses, leading them for 40 years, as Moses did. Clearly, the author would like to draw a parallel between the leadership of Joshua and the leadership of Moses.

Finally, the very fact of the eulogy is striking. Moses himself does not get one in *L.A.B.* The death of Moses is recorded in chapter 19, but only Joshua, in the beginning of chapter 20, is described as mourning. There is no record of him or anyone else delivering a eulogy, let alone singing a dirge.

---

320 It stands to reason that the author of *L.A.B.* assumes that his readership is familiar with the biblical texts, although this is not certain, as it is possible that he only assumes that the Pentateuch is well known.

Joshua's Appointment

The description in *L.A.B.* of the process of Joshua's appointment as leader of Israel presents a number of interpretive difficulties. The usual scene, so prominent in the biblical account as well as in *Assumptio Mosis*, where Moses appoints Joshua in full view of all of Israel, never occurs in this work. Furthermore, when Joshua is appointed, it is directly by God and appears to come out of nowhere.

God establishes his covenant (*disposuit Deus testamentum suum*) with Joshua after Moses' death. This is only the second time he (Joshua) is mentioned in *L.A.B.* The first mention of Joshua is in the scout story (ch. 15), where it records his lineage and the fact that he and Caleb were alone among the scouts in opposing the negative message.[321]

If one were to read the *L.A.B.* independently, without reference to biblical texts, the choice of Joshua is unexpected, or, at the very least, was only one of a number of options the reader could have imagined. It is even unclear from the opening in chapter 20 that Joshua himself was supposed to have been expecting this appointment.

However, in two different "flashback scenes," the reader learns that Joshua has been the expected successor of Moses after all. First, in God's opening speech to Joshua, where he chides Joshua for stalling, he asks Joshua rhetorically (20:2):

Nonne pro te locutus sum Moysi servo meo dicens: Iste ducet populum meum post te et in manum eius tradam reges Amorreorum?!	Was it not about you that I spoke with Moses my servant saying: "This one will lead my people after you and in his hands will I place the kings of the Amorites"?!

Second, a prophecy to this effect is referenced by the Israelite people in the middle of the chapter. After Joshua delivers his opening speech to the Israelites, the people offer him their heartfelt approval and say that now they understand why

---

321 Unlike in the biblical account, in *L.A.B.* the punishments given to the scouts and the people are not spelled out clearly. In the biblical version, there is a long description of the punishment of the people, that no one from the wilderness generation (other than Joshua and Caleb) would be permitted to enter the land. This is, at most, hinted at in God's speech to Moses in *L.A.B.* when God says that the bodies of the people (i.e., the wilderness generation) would be cast into the wilderness (*corpora eorum deiciam in heremo*) as they feared (15:6).

Moses rejoiced (*gavisus est*) when Eldad and Medad prophesied that Joshua would be the next leader (20:5). [322]

Despite the above, from the way God communicates with Joshua in the opening of chapter 20, it appears that Joshua was not ready to take over at the time of Moses' death. God begins by taking Joshua to task for taking up his role as leader without sufficient gusto. Specifically, he accuses Joshua of stalling in the vane hope that Moses may still be alive and retake the reins (20:2):

Ut quid luges et ut quid speras in vanum cogitans quod Moyses adhuc vivet? Et ideo superflue sustines, quoniam defunctus est Moyses.	For what are you bewailing and for what are you hoping in vain, imagining that Moses yet lives? You are sustaining a false idea, seeing as Moses is gone.

God accuses Joshua of not wanting to be the leader, preferring instead to cling to the unreasonable fantasy that Moses will lead forever.

Why Joshua might want this can be, perhaps, deduced from God's next commands to him (20:2).

Accipe vestimenta sapientie eius et indue te, et zona scientie ipsius precinge lumbos tuos, et immutaberis et eris in virum alium.	Take his (Moses') clothing of wisdom and put them on, and with his belt of knowledge gird your loins, and you will change and you will be a different man.

Since God is specifically suggesting that Joshua should become a different man, one may deduce from this that Joshua was afraid that he could not live up to the high standards Moses set for leadership. God seems to accept this fear and suggests that Joshua can become a second Moses if he puts on Moses' clothes.

Although the idea that Joshua receives the spirit of Moses by taking his clothing does not appear in other sources, nevertheless, this method of transmission of the spirit of the master prophet to that of the student has a strong resonance with the account of Elisha's assuming the mantle—literally—from his master Elijah (2 Kings 2:12–15).[323]

---

322 This technique of referring back to stories that are actually not recorded in the *L.A.B.* is one the author uses a lot. It would be interesting to try to determine whether this is a literary technique or a consequence of his assumption that the reader was already familiar with the biblical texts.

323 I thank Luke Timothy Johnson for pointing this out to me.

יב וֶאֱלִישָׁע רֹאֶה וְהוּא מְצַעֵק אָבִי אָבִי רֶכֶב יִשְׂרָאֵל וּפָרָשָׁיו וְלֹא רָאָהוּ עוֹד וַיַּחֲזֵק בִּבְגָדָיו וַיִּקְרָעֵם לִשְׁנַיִם קְרָעִים. יג וַיָּרֶם אֶת אַדֶּרֶת אֵלִיָּהוּ אֲשֶׁר נָפְלָה מֵעָלָיו וַיָּשָׁב וַיַּעֲמֹד עַל שְׂפַת הַיַּרְדֵּן. יד וַיִּקַּח אֶת אַדֶּרֶת אֵלִיָּהוּ אֲשֶׁר נָפְלָה מֵעָלָיו וַיַּכֶּה אֶת הַמַּיִם וַיֹּאמַר אַיֵּה יְקֹוָק אֱלֹהֵי אֵלִיָּהוּ אַף הוּא וַיַּכֶּה אֶת הַמַּיִם וַיֵּחָצוּ הֵנָּה וָהֵנָּה וַיַּעֲבֹר אֱלִישָׁע. טו וַיִּרְאֻהוּ בְנֵי הַנְּבִיאִים אֲשֶׁר בִּירִיחוֹ מִנֶּגֶד וַיֹּאמְרוּ נָחָה רוּחַ אֵלִיָּהוּ עַל אֱלִישָׁע וַיָּבֹאוּ לִקְרָאתוֹ וַיִּשְׁתַּחֲווּ לוֹ אָרְצָה.

[12] Elisha kept watching and crying out, "Father, father! The chariots of Israel and its horsemen!" But when he could no longer see him, he grasped his own clothes and tore them in two pieces. [13] He picked up the mantle of Elijah that had fallen from him, and went back and stood on the bank of the Jordan. [14] He took the mantle of Elijah that had fallen from him, and struck the water, saying, "Where is YHWH, the God of Elijah?" When he had struck the water, the water was parted to the one side and to the other, and Elisha went over. [15] When the company of prophets who were at Jericho saw him at a distance, they declared, "The spirit of Elijah rests on Elisha." They came to meet him and bowed to the ground before him.[324]

In this account, Elisha gains some of Elijah's power when he picks up the master's mantle. Onlookers recognize this and declare that Elisha has the spirit of Elijah within him. *L.A.B.*, possibly inspired by this account, imagines a similar method of transmission from Moses to Joshua. What stands out about the usage of this imagery here is that the biblical text already contains a description of Moses passing his spirit onto Joshua during his lifetime through the ritual of laying his heads upon the head of his protégé (Deut 34:9). One wonders what made *L.A.B.* choose the Elijah-Elisha model over the explicit alternative already featured in the Moses-Joshua account.

One element worth noting about the *L.A.B.* passage is the phrase "*virum alium*" *(20:2)*. This idea that Joshua will turn into a different man has strong resonance with the speech of Samuel to Saul in 1 Sam. 10. In that account, Samuel meets the lad Saul, who is searching for his father's donkeys. Samuel unexpectedly anoints Saul king, yet Saul does not feel kingly. To ease him into the role, Samuel gives Saul a series of tasks and signs. At a certain point, Saul will meet up with a band of prophets. As they are prophesying, some of the divine spirit will leave them and enter Saul, and he "will become another man" (ונהפכת לאיש אחר).[325] It is possible that the author of this story is using the imagery of the young Saul, who feels unworthy or unprepared for the task, as a way of expanding upon the hesitation of Joshua, a hesitation implied in the biblical texts by the multiple admonitions to "be strong."

---

324 The English is based on the NRSV with slight modifications.
325 The Vulgate translates this phrase as, "*et mutaberis in virum alium.*"

Joshua the Speech Maker

Although there is certainly biblical precedent for Joshua making speeches, *L.A.B.* turns this activity into a key organizing principle around which Joshua's years as leader are described.

Joshua's public career begins with a speech in the one account in which Joshua is mentioned in *L.A.B.* before he assumes the leadership of Israel. Together with Caleb, the young Joshua calls out to the people poetic words of encouragement to counteract the discouraging words of the scouts (15:2):

Sicut possunt ferra dura superare astra, aut sicut vincunt arma coruscations, aut extinguuntur tonitrua a volatilibus hominum, sic poterunt isti repugnare Domino.	Just like sturdy iron can overcome stars, or just like weapons can vanquish flashes of lightening, or just as the will of man can extinguish thunder, thus can this [people] oppose God.

As an opening quote for Joshua, the comment is striking for its poetic form as well as its sarcastic wit. In the Bible, Joshua never speaks this way. Furthermore, Joshua's first appearance in the biblical account is as a warrior, defending the people against Amalek at the command of Moses. In fact, Joshua does not speak at all during the biblical Amalek account in Exodus.

Joshua's Opening Speech

The differences between the biblical portrayal of Joshua and his portrayal in *L.A.B.* are clear from his first speech as leader as well. Whereas Joshua begins his career in the biblical book of Joshua with a command to his subordinates to prepare the people to march, he begins his career in *L.A.B.* with an elegant exhortation to the people. It seems that the biblical military leader is being recast in *L.A.B.* as a pious statesman.[326]

Joshua's *first* speech as leader focuses on the necessity for the people to heed God's voice and not to walk in the ways of the previous generation. He warns them that if they do not follow God's commands he will cast them off. In a surprising rhetorical move, Joshua undoes the assumption that Moses uses in the Bible to make God forgive the people. In Exodus 32:11–13, Moses talks Yhwh out of destroying the people of Israel for the sin of the golden calf:

---

326 This is not to say that Joshua *never* plays this role in the Bible, only that it is not his primary image.

וַיְחַל מֹשֶׁה אֶת פְּנֵי יְהוָה אֱלֹהָיו וַיֹּאמֶר: "לָמָה יְהוָה יֶחֱרֶה
אַפְּךָ בְּעַמֶּךָ אֲשֶׁר הוֹצֵאתָ מֵאֶרֶץ מִצְרַיִם בְּכֹחַ גָּדוֹל וּבְיָד
חֲזָקָה? לָמָּה יֹאמְרוּ מִצְרַיִם לֵאמֹר בְּרָעָה הוֹצִיאָם לַהֲרֹג
אֹתָם בֶּהָרִים וּלְכַלֹּתָם מֵעַל פְּנֵי הָאֲדָמָה? שׁוּב מֵחֲרוֹן אַפֶּךָ
וְהִנָּחֵם עַל הָרָעָה לְעַמֶּךָ! זְכֹר לְאַבְרָהָם לְיִצְחָק וּלְיִשְׂרָאֵל
עֲבָדֶיךָ אֲשֶׁר נִשְׁבַּעְתָּ לָהֶם בָּךְ וַתְּדַבֵּר אֲלֵהֶם אַרְבֶּה אֶת
זַרְעֲכֶם כְּכוֹכְבֵי הַשָּׁמָיִם וְכָל הָאָרֶץ הַזֹּאת אֲשֶׁר אָמַרְתִּי אֶתֵּן
לְזַרְעֲכֶם וְנָחֲלוּ לְעֹלָם."

Moses petitioned the face of YHWH his god and said: "Why, YHWH, should your anger be kindled against your people, whom you took out of the land of Egypt with great power and a strong arm? Why should the Egyptians say: 'He took them out with evil intent to kill them in the mountains and to wipe them out from the face of the earth'? Turn away from your wrath and rethink the evil [you intend] towards your people! Remember Abraham Isaac and Israel your servants, to whom you promised in your own name saying to them: "I will increase your offspring like the stars of the sky and all this land which I spoke of I will give to your offspring and they shall inherit it forever'."

In his argument with YHWH, Moses makes two major points. First, the Egyptians will get the wrong idea and think that YHWH had it in for the people of Israel the whole time. Second, destroying the Israelites would be, in essence, reneging on his promise to the patriarchs. Joshua undoes both of these premises in his first speech to the Israelites (20:4).

Si autem non obuadieritis voci eius et similes fueritis patribus vestris, corrumpentur opera vestra, et vos ipsi confringemini, et periet de terra nomen vestrum. Et ubi erunt verba que locutus est Deus patribus vestris ? Nam etsi dixerunt gentes : "Forsitan defecit Deus, quoniam non liberavit populum suum," agnoscentes tamen quod non elegerit sibi plebes alia faciens cum eis mirabilia magna, tunc intelligent quoniam personam non accepit Fortissimus, sed quia peccastis per extollentiam, ideo abstulit virtuten suam a vobis et subiecit vos.

However, if you do not listen to his voice, and you become similar to your fathers, your works will be ruined and you yourselves will be shattered, and your name will pass away from the earth. And where will be the words which God spoke to your fathers? For although the nations will say: "Perhaps God has failed, inasmuch as he has not freed his people," nevertheless, acknowledging that he has not selected for himself another people, doing with them great miracles, thereupon they will know that the Almighty is no respecter of persons, rather, because you sinned through pride, for that reason he took his power from you and cast you out.

Joshua's two main points are in direct contradiction to those of Moses. Moses says that God should not destroy Israel, because the Egyptians, i.e., the gentiles will say that this was malicious on God's part, since he would not or could not give his people the land that he promised. Joshua says that it doesn't matter what the nations will say, especially since they will eventually understand that it was because Israel sinned against God, not out of any lack of power or malicious intent on God's part. A colleague, Ryan Wood,[327] suggested that perhaps *L.A.B.* uses the term *Fortissimus* (Almighty) to underline the absurdity of the claim that God would not be powerful enough to deliver on his promise. Even the gentiles, in Joshua's opinion, will soon realize the error of this approach and understand the truth, that Israel was abandoned due to its iniquity.

Attempting to change God's mind, Moses reminds him of his promise to the patriarchs. Joshua, on the other hand, sadly expresses his belief to the Israelites that if they defy God and are destroyed, the age-old promise to the patriarchs will be undone. Nonetheless, this will not stop God from destroying them, rather it will be another example of the unfortunate consequences of Israel's wicked behavior.

The author of *L.A.B.* has given Joshua a rather severe theology. In this speech at least, Joshua does not seem to have an idea of God having mercy, or God favoring Israel despite their sins. He sees things in the more black and white terms of justice and fairness. This is not the way Moses sees things, even in *L.A.B.* Although *L.A.B.* does not use the two arguments of Moses in Exodus, even when describing Moses' defense of Israel after the Golden Calf episode, *L.A.B.* still gives Moses an alternative argument to make in Israel's defense.

Moses assumes that God would like Israel to survive and reminds God that if God abandons Israel, they will not survive. Later on in the text, Moses is told that God will, in fact, not abandon Israel in the long term. This information is just one part of a larger series of revelations from God to Moses about the overall plan of the world and the part Moses and Israel will play in this. Joshua gets no such revelations. The importance of this fact lies in its illustration of a key difference between the character of Moses and the character of Joshua in *L.A.B.* Joshua is the great leader. The people will adore him and follow him and he will establish Israel on the right foot. Moses, on the other hand, is a friend of God; more an angel than a man. This may also be why Joshua is given a eulogy and a human mourning-ritual and Moses is not; instead Moses is buried and mourned by the angels – humanity has no real claim on him.

Joshua's *second* major speech to the people occurs during the crisis of the almost civil war between the Transjordanian tribes and the Cisjordanian tribes. The speech is not aimed at the entire people, but is aimed at the Transjordanian tribes who built an altar in their territory. Having been generally rebuked for this, the people explained that they felt that this sin was necessary in order to keep their children loyal to God. Joshua responds to this with strong words (22:5–6).

---

327 Personal communication.

The opening of Joshua's speech has resonance with certain prophetic passages; in particular with Samuel's rebuke to Saul in 1 Samuel 15:22.

Nonne fortiori est rex Dominus super milia sacrificia?	Is not the LORD King stronger than thousands of offerings ?
הַחֵפֶץ לַיהוָה בְּעֹלוֹת וּזְבָחִים כִּשְׁמֹעַ בְּקוֹל יְהוָה?	Does YHWH prefer burnt offerings and sacrifices to obeying the voice of YHWH?

Like Samuel, Joshua sets up a contrast between following God's commands and offering God sacrifices. Although the two behaviors are obviously not meant to be mutually exclusive, Joshua (like Samuel) is faced with the predicament of "unauthorized" or "unacceptable" sacrifices. The people must make a choice – follow God's law or offer unauthorized sacrifices.

There is an added nuance to Joshua's rebuke. He accuses the Transjordanian tribes of promoting ignorance of Torah. God's laws are in the Torah, Joshua reminds them. If they would teach their children Torah, they would know that building an altar in the Transjordan is forbidden. Furthermore, if the children would study Torah, they would be building a direct relationship with God anyway, and would have no need of sacrifices. This idea is highly redolent of what will develop as the rabbinic post-destruction Talmud-Torah theology. However, the idea surely has its origins in the book of Deuteronomy and even in the book of Joshua itself.

The idea that it is incumbent upon fathers to teach their sons about God and Torah, and that the children should actively speak about Torah, is explicit in the book of Deuteronomy (6:7, 20). However, the idea of constant learning of Torah as a primary religious experience actually finds its most powerful articulation in the book of Joshua. During God's first speech to Joshua as leader, God tells him that he should study Torah day and night. This is exactly what Joshua tells the Transjordanian tribes that their children should be doing (22:6; *docete legem filios vestros et erunt meditantes eam die ac nocte*). This perspective on Israelite continuity places Joshua firmly in the Torah-study-as-Jewish-future camp.

Joshua ends his speech by commanding the Transjordanian tribes to destroy the altar and warning them that this will only save them if they have been honest to Joshua about their pure intentions. God will know the truth, he tells them, and will act accordingly. The speech has a spectacular effect. The people accept Joshua's command. Additionally, they fast and pray to God asking for mercy. The objective of this story seems to be to paint Joshua in the light of a religious leader, one who successfully handles internal crises.

The power of Joshua's leadership comes from his strong sense of Torah, God, and proper ritual. Joshua does not mention military enforcement of the law to the Transjordanian tribes, although one may assume this was implied. The importance of this point becomes evident when this account is compared to other accounts of this story. In the biblical account, Joshua plays no role at all; Phineas negotiates the truce, and the military threat from the Cisjordanian tribes was more than just implied. Alternatively, in Josephus's version of the account, Joshua is again at the head of the rebuke, but this time military action is explicitly threatened, as one would expect from a general like Joshua. Hence, in dialogue with the other versions of this narrative, it becomes evident that *L.A.B.* is attempting to craft a Joshua who is a successful leader, but more because of his powerful religious leadership than for his military abilities.

Joshua's third speech is by far the longest and most intricate. The importance of the speech is framed by two facts: Joshua was close to death and enemies of Israel remained in the land.[328] The date of the speech may also have significance: the 16th day of the third month, i.e., sectarian Pentecost. However, this dating is not so simple. Louis Feldman, followed by Jacobson, suggest an emendation to 6th day of the month, i.e. Pharisaic Pentecost.[329] The speech is framed by Joshua as his final speech (although it is not) and is delivered at Shiloh before the ark.

There is a preamble to the speech delivered the evening before "the big event." It begins with the extremely significant opening of "Hear, oh Israel," clearly meant to mimic Deuteronomic language, and perhaps even invoke the important passage known by that name, which had already become part of the liturgy by the time of *L.A.B.*'s writing.[330] The Deuteronomic language of this preamble continues (23:2):

---

328 Oddly enough, in the opening of this chapter (23:1), Joshua is referred to as a mighty warrior (*potens in virtute*), apparently a direct translation of the Hebrew גבור החיל. The phrase is oddly placed, since in this chapter, Joshua is already elderly. A redaction critical approach to this work might be instructive.

329 Louis H. Feldman, "Prolegemenon," in *The Biblical Antiquities of Philo* (trans. by M.R. James; reprint; Translations of Early Documents 1; New York: Ktav, 1971), ix-clxix [cxiii-cix]; Jacobson, *Commentary*, 711. (It is worth noting that Jacobson uses the amended text for the English but the un-amended text for the Latin, without noting this in the Latin. Without reading the commentary—which is in a separate volume—it is quite confusing.) There are a number of elements in *L.A.B.* that make one think that the book may have come from the Pharisaic/Proto-Rabbinic group, but a discussion of that is beyond the scope of this chapter. For an attempt to maintain the 16th as the date and an analysis of the complex and contradictory implications of *L.A.B.*'s holiday calendar, see chapter 14, "The Calendar in Pseudo-Philo's Biblical Antiquities," in Van Goudoever, *Biblical Calendars*, 116–123.

330 See: Moshe Weinfeld, *The Decalogue and the Recitation of "Shema": The Development of the Confessions* (Tel Aviv: Hakibbutz Hameuchad, 2001), 124–162 [Hebrew].

Ecce ego dispono ad vos testamentum legis huius, quam disposuit Dominus patribus nostris in Oreb.	Behold, I place before you the covenant of this law which the Lord placed before your fathers in Horeb.

One can hear the echoes of Deuteronomy 5:2–3 in this opening.

...וַיִּקְרָא מֹשֶׁה אֶל כָּל יִשְׂרָאֵל וַיֹּאמֶר אֲלֵהֶם שְׁמַע יִשְׂרָאֵל. יְהוָה אֱלֹהֵינוּ כָּרַת עִמָּנוּ בְּרִית בְּחֹרֵב. לֹא אֶת אֲבֹתֵינוּ כָּרַת יְהוָה אֶת הַבְּרִית הַזֹּאת כִּי אִתָּנוּ אֲנַחְנוּ אֵלֶּה פֹה הַיּוֹם כֻּלָּנוּ חַיִּים.	Moses called together all of Israel and said to them: "Hear Israel... YHWH, our god, established a covenant with us at Horeb. Not with our fathers did YHWH establish this covenant, but with us all who are here today and living.

These are the introductory words of Moses' main speech in Deuteronomy; a book that is framed as Moses' final message to the Israelites. Insofar as the law is concerned, Joshua continues Moses' legacy, with this significant difference: Moses delivered his message at in intermediate point in Israel's move towards the Promised Land. Joshua, however, speaks at the holy site of Shiloh, a site in the center of the Promised Land that he himself establishes at God's command. Joshua's speech functions as the consummation of Moses' mission.

Joshua's main speech, which follows on the next day, is presented as a transcription of God's message to Joshua the night before. Joshua presents an overview of Israel's past, present and future. Particularly remarkable about the speech is what receives the most emphasis and what receives very little.

The speech begins by introducing Abraham in extraordinarily poetic style. Four long verses are spent discussing Abraham's piety and God's promise to him of progeny. Isaac and Jacob/Esau each receive half a verse in a schematic form similar to that used for them in the biblical version of Joshua's speech in Joshua 24. Egyptian persecution and Moses' saving of Israel each get one quarter of a verse. The Exodus, the Sea of Reeds and the cloud each get a passing reference followed by an extremely long, detailed and poetic treatment of the Sinai experience.

Having offered an overview of the past, Joshua dedicates one short verse to the entrance of Israel into Canaan (23:11). There is no mention of conquest or battle, only the cities "which you did not build." He next (23:12) lays out the general contours of the covenant; if Israel follows God's law, things will go well for them, the rain will fall, etc. The speech ends in an unusual manner. Joshua informs the people that after they die they will be granted eternal life with God until such time as all are resurrected and placed back on Earth.[331] The speech is received warmly, with the Israelites accepting God and agreeing to serve him exclusively.

---

331 A similar motif was present in *Assumptio Mosis*, but there it was part of the secret know-

When comparing this speech to the biblical speech at Shechem in Joshua 24, a completely different set of emphases is apparent. First, insofar as the historical survey element, the biblical speech deals with all of the forefathers – including Abraham – schematically. The two main foci of the biblical speech are the destruction of the Egyptian army at the Sea of Reeds and the conquest of Canaan on both sides of the Jordan. Second, insofar as the point of Joshua's speech, it is framed as an explanation for why the Israelites worship other gods (since their ancestors from the Trans-Euphrates did) and how they must stop doing so if YHWH is to continue to support them. Finally, there is no future element to the biblical speech, and certainly nothing about afterlife and resurrection.

Whether in the Bible or the *L.A.B.*, Joshua is being painted as the completer of the divine mission. Hence, one cannot help but assume that each speech was crafted to present the mission in a way commensurate with Joshua's persona in their respective accounts. For the Bible, Joshua is the conqueror (or at least inheritor) of Canaan. Hence, the lion's share of the historical description is about conquest and war. God destroys the Egyptians, overturns Balaam and Balak, and removes the pagan inhabitants of Canaan. This military expedition begins with Moses and Aaron and ends with Joshua.

In *L.A.B.*, military conquest is secondary. Primarily, Joshua is a Torah personality. He represents proper worship of God and observance of divine laws. Hence, the emphases are on Abraham, the "founding father" of monotheistic worship and on the Sinai experience, the foundation of Jewish law. Additionally, the acceptance of the covenant is not only about keeping the land which YHWH gave them, the focus of the biblical covenant, but on the future benefits to the loyal worshiper's soul in the afterlife and beyond. In this sense, Joshua's message takes on a much more classically "religious" even otherworldly character in *L.A.B.* than the more land-focused and national focused message of the biblical Joshua.

Joshua delivers his *fourth and final* speech abruptly and with significantly less eloquence than one has come to expect from his character in *L.A.B.* There is a suspicious and threatening quality to it. Like in the biblical speech, Joshua wants the people to officially decide whether they will follow God exclusively or not, and tells the people that he and his family will do so, no matter what the people decide to do themselves. Despite this overall similarity to the biblical speech, the style of the two is very different, as is the context.

---

ledge Moses passed on to Joshua. Here Joshua tells the people in clear and unambiguous language. This may reflect the differences between the religious groups at which each of these books was aimed.

Insofar as context, the biblical final speech is actually the end of the long final speech of Joshua 24. This speech is broken into two parts in *L.A.B.*; the former being an overall positive speech and the latter reflecting some suspicion or hesitation.

With regard to style, in *L.A.B.* Joshua begins by calling the heaven and earth as witness to the covenant. This use of celestial witnesses recalls the song of Moses in Deuteronomy 32, where the same witnesses are invoked. Although the nature of the speech is a standard formulation of the reward and punishment speech, the actual content is rather benign when compared with other versions of this message. For example, the very song suggested by the witness invocation predicts doom and disaster with graphic descriptions of gory punishments. Joshua's "threat" here has a much gentler cadence (24:1); he simply says that if the Israelites will not worship God exclusively, they should leave (*proficiscimini*).

The people, always inspired by Joshua, pick up on his more pessimistic tone and begin to cry. They will take their chances with God, they say, better to die before God then live outside of the Promised Land. Joshua accepts their response, blesses them with the hope that God will send an angel to protect them, and reminds them to keep the covenant after his (Joshua's) passing.[332]

Supporter of the Cult and Cultic Sites

Joshua's image as Torah personality is strongly bound in *L.A.B.* to the cult and cultic places. Immediately after he ends his conversation with God about his upcoming death and the needs of the future generations, Joshua begins to fulfill his religious and cultic responsibilities in a whirlwind of activity.[333]

Joshua first heads to Gilgal and erects a stone altar. Next, he goes to Mount Ebal and sets up a number of stones upon which he plasters the words of the Torah. Having done this, he gathers the people and reads them the Torah.

---

332 The element that stands out most in this speech is Joshua's request that the people remember him and Moses. The concern for his and his master's legacy seems uncharacteristic of biblical characters in general, and may be an unconscious reflection of the author of *L.A.B.*'s values or the values of his contemporaries. I do not know how this fits in with Joshua's overall image in *L.A.B.* In fact, it strikes a discordant note.

333 It is unclear whether the fact that this activity comes so late in Joshua's career is intentional, or whether it is an accident of the redactive style of this work, i.e., working with a biblical frame and plugging in pieces and rewrites where appropriate. In a number of places one gets the feeling that the latter is at play, and that the frame's timeline and the placement of certain descriptions and accounts are in some tension.

Then, together with the people, he offers peace-offerings,[334] sings songs of praise and dances with the ark; all classically Levitical and priestly activities. Only after this does Joshua turn the ceremony over to the Levites and priests, who place the ark before the altar and sing a song together with the people. Following this song, Joshua blesses the people and the ceremony ends. Similar to Moses' position in the Pentateuch as the inaugurator of the service in the Tabernacle, Joshua is seen here as the inaugurator of the cult in Ebal and Gilgal.

This imagery is more than reinforced in chapter 22 of *L.A.B.* when Joshua sets up a semi-permanent cult site in Shiloh.[335] Having narrowly avoided a civil war over an improper cult site, Joshua takes the Tabernacle from Gilgal and establishes a semi-permanent central cult site in Shiloh. The site is meant to function as the centralized cult site until the building of the Temple in Jerusalem. Joshua installs Elazar as the priest in charge of this area and puts him in charge of the Urim and Tummim. The text summarizes Joshua's work in Shiloh (22:8):

In sacrario autem novo quod erat in Galgalis constituit Ihesis usque in hodiernum diem que offerebantur a filiis Israel holocaustomata per singulos annos.	However, in the new shrine which had been in Gilgal,[336] Joshua established continuously, throughout the ages, a day for offering sacrifices by the Children of Israel once a year.

It is possible that this account of a yearly holiday is meant to explain the origins of the celebration described in Judges 21:19. The point is that, like Moses, Joshua sets up the sacrificial worship which is then carried out by the Levites and Priests. It is also worth noting in this context that Joshua's final deathbed talk is with Elazar and Phineas, of all people, and his final act is to kiss them and bless them.

---

334 "On what altar?" one may ask. This inconsistency may be a result of a polemical attempt to erase Shechem as a possible worship site to undermine the Samaritan claims of authenticity. As can be seen in the Samaritan book of Joshua, the Samaritans respond in kind with regard to Shiloh.

335 The fact that the people are already in Shiloh at the beginning of chapter 22 seems to be yet another example of the editorial frame being in tension with the narrative details.

336 This is a difficult phrase and a number of interpretations have been offered. Jacobson believes that this is simply a "slip of the pen" and should read "which was in Shiloh." Feldman thinks that Joshua actually is supposed to have set up a holiday in Gilgal. See Jacobson (708–9) for discussion. Whatever the interpretation, for the purposes of this chapter, what is important is that Joshua sets up a sacrificial holiday, not where he set it up.

The Lord's Confidante

Like Moses, Joshua converses freely with God throughout his tenure. Joshua's eloquent defense of Israel before God (ch. 21) epitomizes this relationship in a scene very reminiscent of Moses and his mediations on behalf of the Israelites.

In this account, whose beginning parallels Joshua 13, God warns Joshua that although there is plenty of undivided land still remaining, Joshua is too old to finish the job. Unlike in Joshua 13 however, God adds that after Joshua's death the Israelites will "mingle" (*commisciatur*) with the inhabitants of the land and go after false gods (21:1). Joshua responds to this with an elegant 5-verse-long plea.

To defend the Israelites, Joshua begins by using imagery offered by God in Job 38 and turning it on its head. He "reminds" God that only God has great wisdom, having moved the sea and ordered the stars. Perhaps if God would only share some of that wisdom with Israel they would not sin (21:2).[337]

Joshua next recalls an event described in the biblical narrative as part of the Jericho and Ai accounts, but not actually appearing in *L.A.B.* in the conquest section.[338] Joshua relates his own reaction to the failure of the Israelites (in battle) after Achan stole from the ban (21:3). Joshua's choice of this event is telling, as it remains the one place in the biblical book of Joshua where Joshua actually panics.[339] Oddly enough, the panic Joshua describes in this *L.A.B.* flashback appears much more severe than the biblical version. Joshua claims to have said that it would have been better had the Israelites drowned in the Sea of Reeds or died in the wilderness than to be killed in battle by the native Amorites.

This seems like an absurd claim to make before God. Would it really have been that much better to die in Egypt or the wilderness than to die in Canaan? Are those really the only options Joshua can envision after one defeat? The fantastic nature of this complaint stands out when comparing it to the tamer quasi-panic recorded in Joshua's name in the biblical account. There, in addition to his request that God spare the Israelites, if only for the sake of God's own name, he

---

337 The irony here is that Joshua only really begins his career as leader in *L.A.B.* when he inherits Moses' wisdom by donning his cloak and belt.

338 As noted earlier, it is a common characteristic of *L.A.B.* that references to previous occurrences are made even when the occurrences do not actually occur in *L.A.B.* but only in the Bible. It is not always possible to tell whether this represents an intentional stylistic choice or the accident of the author abridging the biblical tradition but assuming his reader knows the original.

339 This is discussed at length in the first chapter.

says that it would have been better for the Israelites to settle in the Transjordan than to be killed in battle over the Cisjordan. This, at least, makes some sense.

Why does *L.A.B.* use such an extreme version of Joshua's panic, especially in a flashback scene where Joshua reminds God of the past – is this really a past worth remembering? The complaint seems especially problematic since it recalls for the reader the sarcastic complaints offered by the Israelites at the Sea of Reeds and in the wilderness. My only explanation for this peculiar stratagem on Joshua's part is that, perhaps, he has become so comfortable in his discussions with God that he even allows his own rhetoric to get the best of him.

Next, Joshua returns to his main theme (21:4). He claims that really he (Joshua) knows that God will not allow Israel to be destroyed, even if they are sinful in the future. Being eternal, God sees with broad, long-range vision, and will find a way to keep his world (21:5).

Having established this, Joshua requests that God appoint a successor to lead the people after Joshua's death, ostensibly to stop them from going astray (21:5). This is reminiscent of Moses' reaction in Numbers when he is told to ascend Mount Abarim and die. Joshua reminds God that he (God) promised to allow for a consistent succession, and quotes the verse in Genesis where Jacob promises Judah the staff forever.[340] Joshua then concludes the main thrust of his response with the familiar trope that God's keeping his faith with Israel will give him "an honest reputation" with the rest of the world.

Having, apparently, concluded his speech, Joshua adds a poetic afterthought (21:6). In the distant future Israel will be like a dove who laid eggs; i. e. they will stand firm and stay close to their obligations like a dove does for her offspring. It is only a matter of time before Israel will turn from its evil ways and merit salvation. The eloquence, boldness, and intimacy of Joshua's talk with God sends the message to the reader that Joshua is in fact an intimate of God's just as Moses was.

Moses is not the only prophet in whose mold Joshua is being cast. In the short preamble to Joshua's long speech in *L.A.B.* (ch. 23) he ends with this final message (23:2):

Et ideo sustinete hic ista nocte, et videte quid lo-quatur ad me pro vobis Deus.	And therefore, wait here this night and you will see what God says to me concerning you.

This description of prophecy, where the prophet will sleep and receive information from God, which he will then share with those who need or have requested

---

340 As this verse seems to be a promise to Judah specifically and not Israel in general, I am not sure how *L.A.B.* is reading it such that he applies it to this context.

the information, may be drawn from the account of Balaam's dreams in Numbers (22:8). The resonance between these two accounts is strong:

וַיֹּאמֶר אֲלֵיהֶם: "לִינוּ פֹה הַלַּיְלָה וַהֲשִׁבֹתִי אֶתְכֶם דָּבָר כַּאֲשֶׁר יְדַבֵּר יְהוָה אֵלָי."	He (Balaam) said to them (Balak's messengers): "Stay here tonight and I will bring you the matter as YHWH will tell me."[341]

L.A.B. casts Joshua here as a prophet like Balaam, who can receive messages from God at will and deliver them accurately to people.

Joshua the Miracle Worker

Despite what seems like a desire to make Joshua into a more prophetic figure than he appears to be in the Bible, especially the push to make him closer to God, the trend in *L.A.B.* with regard to miracles seems to move in the opposite direction. In the short section dedicated to the conquest of the Amorites, there is a long verse (20:8) that interrupts the account. *L.A.B.* informs the reader that upon the death of the three great religious figures, Moses, Aaron and Miriam, three miraculous interventions by God, manna, cloud and well, came to an end.

What makes this interruption so conspicuous is that it is out of place. All three of these characters died before the conquest of Jericho, whereas this verse is placed after the conquest. Even more problematic, no miraculous interventions on behalf of Joshua are recorded as having occurred during the conquest in *L.A.B.*'s Joshua pericope. It appears that *L.A.B.* wants the reader to compare Joshua unfavorably to the previous generation of leaders insofar as it concerns his access to miracles.

Stranger still, Joshua's greatest miracle in the Bible, the stopping of the sun, does, in fact, receive mention in *L.A.B.*, but not in the section about Joshua. Later in the narrative, in chapter 30, Deborah reprimands the people in a speech. As a part of this speech, she surveys God's support of Israel in the past, as well as the solid leadership of the previous generations. She mentions specifically that God stopped the luminaries on Israel's behalf (*propter vos precept luminaribus et steterunt in locis iussis*) as her example (30:5). She then lists the great leaders from before her time, Moses, Joshua, Cenaz, and Zebul (30:5). However, she never explicitly ties Joshua into the miracle of the stopping of the sun. It seems that the

---

341 This exact message is repeated by Balaam when the next set of messengers arrives.

author of *L.A.B.* was willing to grant Joshua many things, but miracle working was not one of them.

Joshua as Commander

Although this image functions in the Bible as his primary persona, it gets little play in *L.A.B.*; the entire conquest is treated in only four verses (20:6 – 7, 9 – 10). Having received the encouragement of the people after his successful first speech, Joshua appoints two scouts to go to Jericho: Cenaz and Naam the two sons of Caleb. He tells them the story of his own scouting mission from the wilderness period and how he and their father were the only two scouts that remained loyal to God. This connection with Caleb through his sons will be reinforced at the end of this section when Caleb essentially makes the same speech back to Joshua, reminding him of their past, and requesting a landgrant for his son Cenaz.[342]

Joshua's choice of scouts demonstrates both his intelligence as well as his prescience. Considering Caleb's own legacy as the loyal scout, choosing his sons would seem prudent. Joshua knows firsthand how risky it is to send scouts with a questionable sense of loyalty to God and his mission. The choice appears prescient, since Cenaz will be the next leader of Israel after Joshua's death. This parallels Moses' choice of Joshua, his own successor, as one of the scouts.

Other than the account of the scouts, where Joshua speaks, the rest of the conquest is told in a rather schematic fashion. Jericho is taken and burnt, thirty nine kings of the Amorites are killed, and their land is taken and distributed among the Israelites. One gets the impression that the absolute minimum is being described here.

Death and Legacy

Joshua's final words are not in a public speech but in a private deathbed communication to Phineas, referred to as "the son of Elazar the priest" in this sec-

---

342 Naam is left out of this request. From a narrative logic perspective this is inexplicable, as there is no reference to any sinning on Naam's part. However, since *L.A.B.* is clearly written off of a biblical template, verse ten should be understood as a combination of Caleb's request for Hebron in Joshua 14 and Akhsa's request on behalf of Caleb's brother Othniel ben Qenaz in Josh 15 and Judg 1. This latter character is certainly the "inspiration" for the much more developed character of Cenaz in *L.A.B.*

tion. Joshua can only die after turning over the spiritual leadership of the people to his spiritual heir, apparently Phineas.

Joshua kisses Phineas, Phineas's sons, and his father Elazar and blesses them with a hope for their prosperity and the prosperity of Israel. However, oddly enough, before doing this he turns to Phineas and says (24:4):

Ecce iam video oculis meis transgressionem populi huius in quo incipient prevaricari...	Behold, now I see with my eyes the sin of this people with which they will begin to violate...

After Joshua's resoundingly optimistic principal speech, he ends his career with the fear that Israel will not keep the covenant. Only on his deathbed can he see clearly what will occur. His immediate comment to Phineas after having this vision strikes a similarly ominous chord. Joshua offers Phineas the hope that he will be strong enough to keep the people in line during his own lifetime. All that can be hoped for is the short-term delay of the inevitable.

In this sense, *L.A.B.*'s Joshua presents a sharp contrast, even a diametrical opposition to his master Moses, at least on his death bed. Moses constantly expresses concern at the knowledge that the Israelites will inevitably sin, but he consistently begs God to promise to be merciful to Israel. Contrariwise, Joshua constantly attempts to enforce the idea that Israel can keep the covenant and remain loyal to God. The other option Joshua suggests is failure and the abandonment of Israel by God. Although it is true that he offers a strong poetic defense early on, Joshua seems to have either kept that attitude private, between him and God, or abandoned it altogether as a strategy.

The one thing that seems to have remained consistent in Joshua's thinking is the possibility of Israel staying on course, which is why he originally asks God to name a successor to keep Israel on the straight path. This is also the message of his optimistic speech: stay on the straight path. Only on his deathbed does the inevitable reality, which is, ostensibly, the proximate cause of Joshua's final speech, actually fully register in Joshua's consciousness; Israel will not stay on the right path.

Considering this realization, the oddity of his choice for companionship during his last moments seems striking and somewhat disconsonant with Joshua's goals as a whole. As noted earlier: Phineas will not be Joshua's successor. Phineas will be his father Elazar's successor as priest in Shiloh, but Joshua's successor will be Cenaz. Surprisingly, especially considering his request in chapter 21, Joshua does not seem to know this.

This reality points to one of the conspicuous features of *L.A.B.*'s presentation as a whole. The political leadership is chosen by God directly up through Cenaz, and then by the people starting with Zebul. There is no "passing on the mantle" from one leader to the next as there is in the biblical account. Discontinuity between generations becomes a salient feature of early Israel in *L.A.B.*

Summary and Conclusion

The overall theme of the Joshua pericope in *L.A.B.* is centered on the need for loyalty to God and the unfortunate recognition that, over time, this required fealty will not be sustainable. Joshua swims against the tide, delivering speeches and setting up ritual sites to attempt to ensure this future, but to no avail. Joshua's dominant image in this work is as a spiritual and religious leader, with a close connection to God and a gift for dramatic oratory. Although the work implies he is a competent militarily leader, this aspect of his person is treated tersely and with understatement.

Finally, the under-emphasis of Joshua's "historical" role as conqueror of the Cisjordan can be felt in another idiosyncrasy in *L.A.B.*. The Joshua account is actually shorter than the Cenaz account. The pivotal historical character in *L.A.B.* is not the conqueror of Israel, but his successor, the last truly successful leader before Israel begins to sin, Cenaz.[343] The land is not the key; fealty to God is the key. It is difficult to know why this position was given to Cenaz as opposed to Joshua himself, but perhaps for this very reason; in the end Joshua will always represent the conquest of the land in the imagination of the Jewish audience of *L.A.B.*'s readership; this despite the author's vigorous efforts to paint a different portrait. In the end, the author of *L.A.B.* may have needed to invent his own character to truly make his voice heard.

The Apocryphon of Joshua

The Apocryphon of Joshua is the name given to the (hypothetical) work represented by the fragments 4Q378, 4Q379, and 4Q522; 5Q9 and MS. Mas 11 may be fragments of this same work as well. The first two fragments (4Q378 and 4Q379) were first published by Carol Newsom as *Psalms of Joshua*, the title originally given the work by John Strugnell. The third fragment (4Q522) was published by Emile Puech as *A Hebrew Manuscript from Cave 4*.[344] Robert H. Eisenman and

---

343 Zebul was also successful, according to *L.A.B.*, but his story is extremely short and schematic.
344 Carol Newsom, "The 'Psalms of Joshua' from Qumran Cave 4," *JJS* 39 (1988): 56–73; Carol Newsom "4Q378 and 4Q379: An Apocryphon of Joshua," in *Qumranstudien* (ed. H.J. Fabry, A.

Michael Wise were the first to suggest that 4Q522 was related in some way to the *Psalms of Joshua*; Elisha Qimron made the same suggestion independently, arguing that all three were part of "Joshua cycles."[345] Emanuel Tov went a step further and argued that they were actually all part of the same work, which Newsom had previously renamed *The Apocryphon of Joshua*.[346] This identification has become the consensus position among many scholars.[347]

Devorah Dimant characterizes the work as consisting of "a narrative framework, interspersed with speeches, blessings and prayers, mostly pronounced by Joshua."[348] Unfortunately, the work as we have it is very fragmentary and extremely hard to parse. Even the connection between the various fragments cannot be assumed as a certainty, although F. Garcia Martinez writes that what does seem certain is that 4Q378 and 4Q379 were part of one work, and 4Q522 and 5Q9 were part of one work.[349] Whether these were all part of the same work or are two distinct revisions of the Book of Joshua is uncertain, but I will analyze the fragments will together as part of the *Apocryphon of Joshua* for the sake of convenience.[350]

Lange, and H. Lichtenberger; Göttingen: Vandenhoeck & Ruprecht, 1996), 35–85; Carol Newsom, "Apocryphon of Joshua," *DJD* 22: *Qumran Cave 4 17: Parabiblical Texts Part 3* (Oxford: Clarendon Press, 1996), 237–288; Emile Puech, "Fragments du Psaulme 122 dans un manuscrit hébreu de la grotte IV," *RevQ* 9 (1978): 547–554; Emile Puech, "La pierre de Sion et l'autel des holocaustes d'après un manuscrit hébreu de la grotte 4 (4Q522)," *RB* 99 (1992): 676–696; Emile Puech, "4Q522, 4QProphétie de Josué (4QapocrJosué^c?)" DJD 25 – *Qumrângrotte 4. XVIII: Textes hébreux (4Q521–4Q528, 4Q576–4Q579)*, (Oxford: Clarendon Press, 1998), 39–74.

345 Robert H. Eisenman and Michael Wise, *The Dead Sea Scrolls Uncovered* (Shaftesbury, Dorset: Element, 1992), 89–93; Elisha Qimron, "Concerning 'Joshua Cycles' from Qumran (4Q522)," *Tarbiz* 63 (1994): 503–508 [Hebrew].

346 Emanuel Tov, "The Rewritten Book of Joshua as Found at Qumran and Masada," in *Hebrew Bible, Greek Bible and Qumran: Collected Essays* (Texts and Studies in Ancient Judaism 121; Tübingen: Mohr Siebeck, 2008), 71–91.

347 For more details and bibliography, see: Devorah Dimant, "*The Apocryphon of Joshua*-4Q522 9 ii: A Reappraisal," in *Emanuel: Studies in Hebrew Bible, Septuagint and Dead Sea Scrolls in Honor of Emanuel Tov*, (ed. Shalom M. Paul, Robert A. Kraft, Lawrence H. Schiffman, and Weston W. Fields; Supplements to Vetus Testamentum 94; Leiden: Brill, 2003), 179–182.

348 Dimant, *Apocryphon*, 181

349 See: Florentino Garcia Martinez, "The Dead Sea Scrolls and the Book of Joshua," in *Qumran and the Bible: Studying the Jewish and Christian Scriptures in Light of the Dead Sea Scrolls* (ed. Nora David and Armin Lange; Leuven: Peeters, 2010), 97–110 [103–105].

350 This position is also the simplest in an Occam's razor sense since, "[b]y arguing against the identification of 4Q522 as a copy of the *Apocryphon of Joshua* Puech resorts to an even less likely hypothesis, namely, the presence at Qumran of two different, but very similar, works on the same topic" (Dimant, "Apocryphon," 180 n. 5).

Joshua as Presented in the Apocryphon

Since the *Apocryphon of Joshua* is so fragmentary, it is impossible to describe either the scope of the work or even its overall structure.[351] At times, it is difficult even to know who the speaker is in a given narrative; sometimes it seems as though Joshua is making a speech, and sometimes it sounds as though a third person is the narrator. For this reason, I will analyze Joshua's character in this book sparingly, and attempt to draw out only what appears to be particularly distinctive about Joshua in this work, trying as far as possible to rely on passages that seem relatively clear.

First, the fact that the work reaches back into the period before Moses' death (4Q378 frag. 14) appears significant. Whether this section is part of the narrative or part of a speech reflecting on the past (like Deuteronomy) is difficult to say. Either way, describing the death of Moses and Moses' speech to Joshua in an *Apocryphon of Joshua* underlines the fact that Joshua's story as portrayed in the final form(s) of biblical literature cannot really be told without reference to some of the Pentateuchal stories and specifically those about Moses. This framing of the story is not only familiar from expansive works such as *L.A.B.* or Josephus, but can be seen in works with a more limited scope such as the Samaritan Book of Joshua and *Assumptio Mosis*. With regard to the latter work, there are other important similarities as well. Two such similarities were pointed out by Emanuel Tov: the long farewell speech delivered by Moses to Joshua and the frequent references to the covenant with the patriarchs.[352]

From what may be gleaned from the extant fragments of the *Apocryphon*, Joshua is cast in two of his usual roles; first as the student of Moses par excellence, receiving Moses' final speech and presiding over the weeping people during the mourning period for Moses, second as the leader of Israel, bringing the people across the Jordan River and into the Promised Land.[353] Additionally, Josh-

---

351 As Katell Barthelot points out ("Joshua," 100), it is certainly possible that in other parts of the work, Joshua is presented as a military hero or a teacher of Torah.

352 Tov, "The Rewritten Book of Joshua," 71–72.

353 Another Qumran work that references Joshua is Pseudo-Jubilees. In 4Q266 (frag. 4), Joshua is said to be the person who will replace Moses and lead the people across the river; the theme seems to be continued in frag. 6. I follow the edition of Atar Livneh (and I thank her for making me aware of this fragment and sending me a copy of her dissertation). See: Atar Livneh, *The Composition Pseudo-Jubilees from Qumran (4Q225; 4Q226; 4Q227): A New Edition, Introduction and Commentary* (Ph.D. diss., University of Haifa, 2010 [Hebrew]). 4Q266 is dealt with in chapter 3 of Livneh's dissertation. The reference to Joshua in fragment 4 (Livneh, pp. 126–127) seems to be a direct quote from Deuteronomy 31:3, as Livneh points out. Since quoting Deuteronomy and discussing Joshua's position as the leader of the Israelites in the crossing of the Jordan would be

ua fulfills certain classically religious functions, such as praising God in song (4Q379 frag. 22), something that is highly reminiscent of his role in *L.A.B.*, in which he sings a number of religious hymns.[354]

However, the most striking element of Joshua's image in *The Apocryphon of Joshua* is his role as prophet, particularly when he predicts the distant future. This imagery of Joshua as a prophet describing the future is another tie to the *Assumptio Mosis*, in which Moses does this in a private talk with Joshua. However, whereas Moses describes the messianic future, Joshua describes matters that occur in the biblical text, which would have already been fulfilled by the time the *Apocyphon* was first read. For this reason, the work appears to be more similar to the Qumran-style, "prophecy-fulfilled" genre than it is to Apocalyptic works like *Assumptio Mosis* or Revelation.[355] Since the work also makes use of the Jubilee system for dating events (4Q379 frag. 12), it seems likely that the *Apocryphon of Joshua* had its origin in the Qumran or proto-Qumran group.[356]

Two examples of this are relatively clear in the text. The first is the *Apocryphon*'s shifting of the curse against anyone who will build up Jericho into a prediction or prophecy that this will happen and a description of the unfortunate consequences of doing so.[357] Turning the curse into a prophecy fits with the overall Qumran approach to prophets and prophecy as seen in the *pesharim*.[358] This

---

expected in any rewritten bible dealing with this period, and since there is really no clear context within which to place the Joshua reference due to the exceedingly fragmentary nature of the manuscript, Pseudo-Jubilees has little if anything to add to Joshua's image in reception history.

354 This is the reason for Strugnell's original title for the work.

355 Martinez writes: "*4QApocryphon of Joshua* is a composition which does not contain any sectarian expressions but shares a series of ideas with sectarian texts or with texts associated with the Qumran community." See Florentino Garcia Martinez, "Light on the Joshua Books from the Dead Sea Scrolls," in *After Qumran: Old and Modern Editions of the Biblical Texts – The Historical Books* (ed. H. Ausloos, B. Lemmelijn and J. Trebolle Barrera; BETL 246; Leuven: Peeters, 2011), 145–159 [158]. For more on the *Apocryphon of Joshua* as pertains to its genre and its place among the various Second Temple Jewish sects, see: Devorah Dimant, "Between Sectarian and Non-Sectarian: The Case of the *Apocryphon of Joshua*," in *Reworking the Bible: Apocryphal and Related Texts at Qumran*, (ed. Esther G. Chazon, Devorah Dimant and R.A. Clements; STDJ 58; Leiden: Brill, 2005), 105–134.

356 One could also call this group Essene or proto-Essene if one is inclined to identify this group with the Essenes. The relationship between these two groups is a matter of contention in modern scholarship, and any discussion is beyond the bounds of this work.

357 For more on this passage, see Hanan Eshel, "The Historical Background of the Pesher Interpreting Joshua's Curse on the Builders of Jericho," *RevQ* 15 (1991/1992): 409–420.

358 As Dimant notes ("Between," 124–125), the first line of this *pesher* is quoted in 4QTestimonia (4Q175).

eschatologically minded community seems to have had a strong appreciation for the importance of very specific prophesies that get fulfilled exactly. Demonstrating an example of this phenomenon with Joshua would serve to buttress the possibility and significance of the phenomenon of specific prophecies fulfilled, which would support the Qumran community's overall hermeneutic project. In Devora Dimant's words: "Although lacking the formal terminology and structure known from the Qumran pesharim, the exposition of the biblical curse makes use of pesher exegetical techniques."[359]

The second example of Joshua offering a specific prophecy is the overall theme in the extant fragment of 4Q522. In this fragment, Joshua actually prophesies the birth of David and the conquest of Jerusalem. The context of this prophecy is apparently a speech Joshua makes to Elazar about his failure to consult with him and the *Urim ve-Tummim* when approached by the Gibeonites.[360] For their trickery, Joshua says, he made them servants at the altar of the Tent of Meeting. The connection between the prophecy and this discussion is that Joshua predicts that eventually they will serve in Zion, where the Tent of Meeting will rest and where the Temple will eventually be built as desired by David.

As a prophecy, this is extremely specific. Joshua names David's father and describes the building of the Temple, or at least the preparation of the materials to do so, by David, in a way reminiscent of Chronicles. The prophecy fills a significant lacuna in the biblical text. Joshua 9:27 says that the Gibeonites will serve at God's altar in the place where he shall choose, but it never says where that is and whether the Gibeonites actually end up doing this. In fact, the record of a high place in Gibeon (Jer 28:1; 1 Chron 15:39, 21:29) where even King Solomon makes an offering (1 Kings 3:4; 2 Chron 1:3, 13) may be understood as calling into question the interpretation of the verse as referring to Jerusalem into.[361]

---

359 Dimant, "Between Sectarian and Non-Sectarian," 130; Dimant believes that the *Apocryphon of Joshua*, like Jubilees and The Temple Scroll, should be seen as occupying a middle category, participating in many of the ideas of the sectarian community but not as narrow in scope or intended audience.

360 It is not explicit that the passage is a speech by Joshua to Elazar, however, since the speaker claims that the Gibeonites tricked him (החטיוני) and the listener is the one who holds the *Urim ve-Tummim*, it seems to be a safe guess. At some point later in the passage, the third person narrator takes over, with both Joshua and Elazar being referred to in the third person.

361 In Samaritan interpretation, and in the SP, the chosen place would be Mount Gerizim. However, since the Samaritans do not have the Book of Joshua, at least not in their canon and not in this form, and the verb here is in the imperfect and not the perfect, reflecting the MT's text in Deuteronomy where this term is introduced, one can safely discount Gerizim as the referent in the biblical text.

The significance of having Joshua prophecy about David and Jerusalem may be twofold. First, it puts Joshua in a privileged position with regard to two of the most significant developments in Israelite history, the Temple and the monarchy. Although Joshua founded neither, he may be said to have predicted them, which would give him some tie to these institutions.[362] Second, since Joshua is a sort of primordial character in the formation of Israel, having the most significant developments foretold in advance would go far towards presenting a picture of a world directly controlled by God. This would be a comforting view for a group that wished for other prophesies about the future to come true as well.

Josephus

Josephus' image of Joshua, as described in his *Antiquities of the Jews*, stands out as something unique, although sharing some aspects (broadly speaking) with Joshua's image in Ben Sira.[363] Josephus takes the opposite approach to that of *L.A.B.*, emphasizing Joshua's military acumen and his overall competence as a clear-headed and confident Israelite statesman.[364] Joshua's religiosity is acknowledged but is painted in the colors of the philosophical religion of Greek piety as much as possible.[365]

---

362 Worth noting here is the opposite interpretation suggested by Ed Noort and Devorah Dimant, and followed by Katell Barthelot. They argue that Joshua's reference to his sin should be seen as an attempt by the author to diminish his character and his prophesying of David and Solomon should be seen as Joshua admitting that these are the successful leaders of Israel, and not he. See: Noort, "Joshua," 214, Dimant, "Apocryphon," 202, Barthelot, "Joshua," 102.

363 For an analysis of Josephus' method of interpreting the Bible, see: Louis H. Feldman, *Studies in Josephus' Rewritten Bible* (JSJsupp 58; Leiden: Brill, 1998a) and Louis H. Feldman, *Josephus's Interpretation of the Bible* (Hellenistic Culture and Society 27; Berkeley: University of California Press, 1998b).

364 For an analysis of Joshua's portrayal in Josephus's Antiquities, see: Louis H. Feldman, "Josephus's Portrait of Joshua," *HTR* 82.4 (1989): 351–376.

365 In this sense, Josephus bears some resemblance to Philo, although, as stated above, Philo has little interest in Joshua. Even the miracles appear to be softened somewhat, although never denied. However, it should be noted that Michael Avioz disputes the idea that Josephus softens the miraculous or divine in his *Antiquities*. See: Michael Avioz, *Josephus' Interpretation of the Books of Samuel* (The Library of Second Temple Studies 86; London: Bloomsbury T&T Clark, 2015).

Early Training (Pentateuch)

As in the Bible, Joshua is first introduced in the account of Israel's wilderness battle with Amalek. Unlike Exodus, however, which introduces Joshua abruptly, with no explanation for Moses' choice of him as general, Josephus gives Joshua a lengthy introduction (*Ant*. 3:49).

ὁ δὲ τῆς πληθύος ἀποκρίνας πᾶν τὸ μάχιμον Ἰη-σοῦν ἐφίστησιν αὐτῷ Ναυήκου μὲν υἱὸν φυλῆς τῆς Ἐφραιμίτιδος, ἀνδρειότατον δὲ καὶ πόνους ὑποστῆναι γενναῖον καὶ νοῆσαί τε καὶ εἰπεῖν ἱκανώτατον καὶ θρησκεύοντα τὸν θεὸν ἐκπρε-πῶς καὶ Μωυσῆν διδάσκαλον τῆς πρὸς αὐτὸν εὐσεβείας πεποιημένον τιμώμενόν τε παρὰ τοῖς Ἑβραίοις.	And he (Moses), having separated out all the war-ready men from the multitude, appointed Iesous (Joshua), son of Naukos, born of the tribe of Ephraim, most brave and strain-enduring by birth, in mind and speech sufficient, and in worship of God most distinguished. And he (Joshua) made Moses a teacher of piety to him, who was respected before the Hebrews.

Josephus is clear about why Joshua was chosen. Joshua was already Moses' student; one with intelligence and piety as well as good pedigree. Knowing all this, Joshua seems like an obvious choice for the job.

Joshua's military skill also receives an explanation in Josephus; he learned this from Moses. The reader has already learned of Moses' military prowess. From his earlier life as an active member of the Egyptian royal family, Moses had ample opportunity to prove himself in battle, which he did especially in the Nubian campaign (*Ant*. 2:243–253).[366] In fact, throughout the Moses narrative, Josephus refers to him often as στρατηγός, the general.

Considering this, Josephus' description of Moses spending the night organizing the camp, repairing the weapons and briefing the generals offers no surprise. After Moses accomplishes all this, he spends the rest of the evening discussing military tactics and strategy with his protégé Joshua. At daybreak, Moses gives Joshua some words of encouragement, telling him that this will be the time for him to make his reputation as a military leader. Moses then delivers words of encouragement to the people, mentioning certain individuals by name. Only then does he go up the mountain.

Although Joshua is the "commanding general," there is no mention of him or any actions or commands coming from him during the entire battle. Josephus

---

366 According to Josephus, Moses put down a rebellion in Nubia when he was prince. This incident caused tremendous jealousy in the court, as well as fear of Moses on Pharaoh's behalf, which was the precipitant cause of Moses running in fear from Egypt. A somewhat different version of this Nubian campaign is recorded in rabbinic midrash as well.

describes the courage and eagerness of the Israelite army as well as the effect of Moses' raised arms and how he succeeded in keeping them up for the entire day of battle. Following this, Josephus describes the tremendous booty obtained, the electric effect of the success on the Israelite camp, and the disastrous psychological effect it had on Israel's other enemies.

On the day after the battle, Joshua is mentioned again. He is praised by Moses for doing a fine job, especially since the Israelite army suffered no casualties. Moses then builds an altar and prophecies the future annihilation of Amalek in retribution for their having attacked Israel in the wilderness. Unlike in the biblical text, there is no mention that a convenant is being made about this or that this covenant needs to be entrusted to Joshua of all people.

For Josephus, this story functions as the introduction to a young Joshua.[367] He is a man with potential, who will be trained by Moses as both a leader and a military tactician. Although Joshua leads the battle, the real force behind the battle, according to Josephus, was Moses. Most importantly, Josephus does not present Moses' decisive involvement in the battle as a consequence only of his arms and the implication of divine assistance. For Josephus, Moses is the general who designs the strategy that the young Joshua executes. Ironically, one could make the claim that instead of painting Joshua in Mosaic colors, Josephus paints Moses in Joshua's colors.

The next time Joshua receives mention is in the scout account.[368] As Josephus never lists the names of the scouts, the reader is, at first, unaware of the fact that Moses' protégé was one of them.[369] Additionally, throughout the first encounter between the scouts and the people, we never hear of Joshua, nor do we hear about any opposition to their message of despair. Not until the next morning, when the people assemble to stone Moses and Aaron and return to Egypt, does Josephus relate opposition to this rebellion (3:308–310).

---

367 Not so young actually; as will be seen later, according to Josephus, Joshua was 45 at the time of the Exodus.

368 The Golden Calf episode, the Eldad and Medad episode and the description of Joshua as frequenting the tent of meeting receive no mention in Josephus.

369 Whether one thinks that Josephus assumed his readers knew this depends upon whom one believes Josephus's audience was supposed to be. Since it seems clear that he was at least partly if not primarily writing to gentiles, one can argue that this was really meant to be unknown to the reader until revealed by Josephus. This is one of the ways that Josephus's writing style differs from that of *L.A.B.*, which was most probably written for a Hebrew-speaking Jewish audience that was familiar with the biblical characters and their stories. For a general comparison of the style of the two works, see: Louis H. Feldman, "Josephus's *Jewish Antiquities* and Pseudo-Philo's *Biblical Antiquities*," in *Josephus, the Bible and History* (eds. Louis H. Feldman and Gohei Hata; Detroit: Wayne State University Press, 1989), 59–80.

Joshua, together with Caleb, attempts to restrain the masses of people (τὸ πλῆθος κατεῖχον), telling them to be brave, to ignore the false words of the scouts, and to trust in those who really have their best interests at heart. At this point, Joshua and Caleb wax poetic (*Ant.* 3:309):

οὔτε γὰρ τῶν ὁρῶν τὸ μέγεθος οὔτε τῶν ποτα- μῶν τὸ βάθος τοῖς ἀρετὴν ἠσκηκόσιν ἐμποδὼν στήσεσθαι πρὸς τὰ ἔργα καὶ ταῦτα τοῦ θεοῦ συμπροθυμουμένου καὶ ὑπερμαχοῦντος αὐτῶν.	For not the height of the mountains or the depth of the seas should stand as a fetter – for those who practice virtue – against their works; those in which God shows equal desire and on behalf of which he fights.

They end their speech with the advice that the people should simply obey God and their leader, Moses, unquestioningly, following them into battle and taking the Promised Land.

Despite the eloquent speech, Josephus refers to it as an "attempt" (ἐπιχει- ρεω) to calm the people. The attempt is a failure, unfortunately, prompting Moses and Aaron to fall on the ground and pray for the forgiveness of the rebels. The rebellion only ends with appearance of God in the cloud descending into the camp.

Joshua seems to be the initiator of the defense; he gets first mention as well as a patronymic, implying his greater importance. The intervention shows Joshua's loyalty as well as his aspirations for leadership. Nevertheless, his powers of persuasion are clearly not up for the task at this point in his career.

Appointment as Moses' Successor

Moses' appointing of Joshua as his successor comes abruptly after the account of the war with Midian (4:165).

Μωυσῆς δὲ γηραιὸς ἤδη τυγχάνων διάδοχον ἑαυτοῦ Ἰησοῦν καθίστησιν ἐπι τε ταῖς προφη- τείαις καὶ στρατηγὸν εἴ που δεήσειε γενησόμε- νον, κελεύσαντος καὶ τοῦ θεοῦ τούτῳ τὴν προστασίαν ἐπιτρέψαι τῶν πραγμάτων. Ὁ δὲ Ἰησοῦς πᾶσαν ἐπεπαίδευτο τὴν περι τοὺς νόμ- ους παιδείαν καὶ τὸ θεῖον Μωυσέος ἐκδιδάξαν- τος.	Moses, who happened to be old already, ap- pointed Iesous to succeed him, with regard to prophecy and the generalship – if somewhere this became necessary – having been urged by God to entrust the leadership over [Israel's] affairs to this person. Iesous had been fully educated; Moses having instructed him with legal training as well as matters divine.

Although the mention of Joshua's choice as the next leader is abrupt, the choice is hardly surprising. From the first mention of Joshua, the reader is aware of his many good qualities, his loyalty to Moses, and the fact that Moses has, ostensibly, been training him from his youth.

The one surprising element in this paragraph is the mention of prophecy. Does this mean that Joshua has already received prophecies or does this mean that he will do so? The statement is ambiguous. Some clarification of this appears in a later passage (4:311). At the very end of his parting speech to the people, Moses offers advice on how best to sacrifice to God and how to use the auger stones (*Urim ve-Tummim*). Josephus then, almost as an afterthought, throws in a command that Joshua prophesied in Moses' presence.

After a few more comments, Moses encourages Joshua to get his army ready to invade Canaan (4:315) and offers his final words to the people. He then walks off to die. At first, he is followed by Joshua, Elazar, and the elders, but when he reaches Mt. Abarim, he sends off the elders. Joshua and Elazar remain with him until the end, which comes when a cloud descends upon Moses and he disappears forever (4:324–326).

This "equal status" between Joshua and Elazar is not new to this section but was foreshadowed in two previous references to Joshua. After Moses agrees to the request of the tribes of Reuben, Gad, and half-Manasseh that they be permitted to remain in the Transjordan on the condition that the males cross over the Jordan and fight on behalf of their brethren–he summons Joshua and Elazar as well as other authorities in order to witness the deal. Ostensibly, this is because it will be these authorities who will be charged with seeing the conditions of the agreement through (4:171). Additionally, and even more explicitly, as Moses begins his final long address to the people, he tells them that Joshua, Elazar, the elders, and the tribal chiefs will be in charge of governing Israel (4:186).

Josephus never explicitly states that Elazar and Joshua will have equal power, but neither does he delineate exactly what the difference in power between the two will be. Joshua is a prophet and general whereas Elazar is a priest; it is often unclear in the biblical books which of the two leaders is senior. Josephus will make the hierarchy very clear in the section on Joshua's rule in the first part of the fifth book.

Preparing for War

The Israelites mourn Moses' death with the customary rites, after which Joshua begins the preparations for crossing the Jordan and making war on Jericho. Unlike in the biblical account, or the accounts of *L.A.B.* and *Assumptio Mosis*, Josephus' Joshua has no need for encouragement by God or the people.[370] He waits for the end of Moses' mourning period not out of any paralysis on his part, but because granting his former mentor the customary mourning-rites would only be proper. Nevertheless, one gets the impression that Joshua was waiting for this period to end and stood ready for action from the moment the leadership fell upon his shoulders.

Joshua's first move is to send scouts to Jericho to ascertain its defenses (5:2). Then he begins to organize the troops for a crossing. Additionally, he speaks with the tribes of Gad, Reuben, and half-Manasseh to remind them of their responsibilities as well as their promise to Moses. He adds a drop of rhetorical flourish to this reminder, describing Moses as someone who worked tirelessly on Israel's behalf until his dying day such that he deserves prompt fulfillment of his instructions, even after his death (5:4). Unlike in the biblical account, Josephus does not record the response of the Transjordanian tribes, implying that Joshua was not requesting their compliance but demanding it. He is a confident leader and need not wait for an answer.

The action of the scouts as related by Josephus reflects well upon Joshua. In the biblical story, the scouts appear only in Rahab's home and they obtain information only with regard to the psychological state of the inhabitants. Josephus, on the other hand, relates that they succeeded in scouting out the entire city, inspecting the walls and the gates, and recording their strengths and weaknesses. Only then did they go to Rahab's tavern.[371]

When the scouts return to the camp, Josephus is somewhat ambiguous about whom they report to. Although he records that the scouts reported to their fellows (οἰκείους), Josephus then writes that Joshua reported their pact with Rahab to Elazar and the elders, who approved of it (5:15); "fellows" here must refer to Joshua and the army. It would seem that Joshua, who has been preparing for the war and the crossing on his own, has taken firm control of the leadership of Israel, and Elazar receives his information from Joshua.

The crossing of the Jordan, although still described as a miraculous event, has a rather subdued quality to it in comparison with the biblical account. The issue here is purely pragmatic; the Israelites need to cross. Josephus does

---

370 For a comparison of Joshua as he appears in Josephus and *L.A.B.* see: Begg, "Josephus' and Pseudo-Philo's Rewritings," 555–588.
371 Josephus prefers the translation "tavern-keeper" to "harlot" for Rahab's profession. This understanding of the term זונה is reflected in certain rabbinic interpretations as well (see, for example, R. Eliezer's position as recorded in *Sifrei Numbers* 78), but this is not the translation of the LXX, which has πορνης.

not use this as an opportunity to magnify Joshua's image by comparison with Moses or to discuss the panic of the natives.

The people are understandably nervous. Joshua handles this well by first sending in the priests with the ark, followed by the Levites with the tabernacle and other paraphernalia, and finally by the people as a whole. The people walk with the women and children in the center because they are nervous about the water current. The miracle, according to Josephus is not the actual drying of the land but the lowering of the water level together with the calming of the sea.[372]

The crossing having been accomplished without a hitch, Joshua pitches camp near Jericho. Taking the twelve stones he had requested that the various tribes take from the river bed, he builds an altar as a memorial to the crossing and offers a sacrifice upon it. He then celebrates the Passover. With that, the Israelites begin to plunder the countryside and harvest the Canaanites' ripe grain.

Joshua's first act as leader, the bringing of the Israelites into Cisjordan, is a success. This officially ends the wilderness period and the manna ceases to fall. Unlike in *L.A.B.*, this is not tied to the death of Moses, but only to the crossing over into Canaan.

The Conquest

Whereas the author of *L.A.B.* shrinks the description of Joshua's conquest down to half a verse, Josephus maintains the five-part structure of the biblical conquest

---

372 Although this motif of a deity calming the sea for the protagonist's army to cross is not typical in Jewish literature, an interesting parallel is found in Hindu literature, in which Varuna, god of the sea, calms the sea on behalf of Rama, so that Nala can build a causeway over which Rama and his army of Vanaras (talking apes) can cross over into Lanka and battle the ten-headed demon king Ravana and take back Sita, Rama's kidnapped wife. There may be other ties between the Hindu account and the biblical version of the crossing story. First, both stories have an etiological element. The book of Joshua has the 12 stones in the Jordan river, which were apparently still there during the author's day and the Ramayana has what is now referred to as Adam's bridge, a causeway from Pamban Island to Mannar Island (near Sri Lanka) that was apparently submerged in a storm around 1480 CE. The remnants of the causeway can still be seen by aerial photography. Second, both stories explain and justify a past genocide (real or imagined) in such a way as to make the victims deserving of their fate. The Book of Joshua makes the Canaanites wicked and enemies of God, the Ramayana claims that all the inhabitants of Lanka were demons (*rakshasa*) and, moreover, were responsible for the kidnapping of Rama's wife, thereby bringing their punishment on their own heads. This latter point makes the Ramayana an excellent parallel to the Iliad as well.

account. This is hardly surprising since the dominant image of Joshua in Josephus' *Antiquities* is that of general.

As the Canaanites of Jericho hide in their fortified city, Joshua decides on a siege (5:22). The siege begins on the first day of the festival (ostensibly, the festival of *matzot*). The siege begins in an unorthodox manner, with a number of priests carrying the ark around Jericho, with seven others walking before them and blowing shofars. This is done for six days.

On the seventh day Joshua tells the people that God will miraculously make the walls collapse and the city will be theirs. He commands the army to kill every single inhabitant of the city, not to tire, and not to have pity. Also, they should take nothing for themselves, but destroy everything and deposit the gold and silver into God's treasury. Joshua having given the speech, the entire army, along with the ark and the shofar-blowers, go around the walls seven times, and the walls collapse. Jericho is then sacked, all the inhabitants killed, and the city burned to the ground – the only exceptions being Rahab and her family because of the oath.

Although there are spots in *Antiquities* where Josephus softens the narrative to protect the image of the Israelites, this story is not one of them. If anything, Josephus adds a touch of gore to the story by specifically mentioning the killing of women and children and describing the city as being full of corpses (νεκρῶν ἡ πόλις ἦν ἀνάπλεω; 5:29). Josephus also adds a touch of gallantry, with Joshua specifically telling Rahab that Israel's repayment to her would in no way be inferior to her kind treatment of the scouts, then granting her land and honor. The city of Jericho is demolished, and the story ends with Joshua laying a curse on anyone who would dare to rebuild it. All in all, Joshua presents a competent figure, tough but honorable, and supported by the deity.

As in the biblical account, the first attack on Ai is a failure, with Joshua losing 36 men in the attack out of an army of 3,000 (5:35). Also, as in the biblical account, Joshua does not know that this was because of the infidelity of Akhar, who violated the ban. However, unlike in the biblical account, there does not seem to be an implied criticism with regard to the inadequate size of the force that Joshua sent.

The most striking feature of Josephus's account of this setback is Joshua's calm leadership during the crisis. The people, having believed until this point that no harm would befall their army at all during the conquest, are dismayed. They spend the day crying, mourning, and fasting. Seeing this, Joshua speaks "frankly" (παρρησία) with God. He reminds God that the invasion of Canaan was not brought about by Israelite presumption (αὐθαδείας), but was directly commanded by Moses (5:38–41). Furthermore, God himself had promised to support the conquest. Now, however, the Israelites have lost a battle and are distraught. They are beginning to mistrust Moses' prophecies and are losing hope in the future. Since God is the only one who can remedy the situation, remedy it God must.

This forceful speech stands out as something altogether different than the versions of the speech found in the Bible and *L.A.B.* In the Bible, Joshua himself appears to give up hope and states that it would have been better had all of Israel settled the Transjordan and left the Cisjordan alone. His speech in *L.A.B.* is even worse. Although described as part of a flashback, hence lacking the natural tension of the biblical and Josephan narratives, nevertheless, Joshua's panic in *L.A.B.* is so extreme that he claims it would have been better had all the Israelites died in Egypt rather than invade Canaan and die there. In comparison with these accounts, Joshua's rebuke to God in Josephus is an example of a leader who does not panic under pressure but keeps his cool and makes his case calmly and forcefully to the deity.[373]

The speech has the desired effect, and God tells Joshua the reason for the defeat, i. e., the violation of the ban. It is at this point in the narrative that Joshua again calls upon Elazar the priest. Joshua is in need of someone to divine the culprit. Elazar does this, and Joshua then puts Akhar to death and buries him.

In these last two details, Josephus appears to be cleaning up Joshua's behavior. First, as opposed to the biblical account in which Joshua kills Akhan's entire family, Josephus mentions the execution of only the culprit. Second, Joshua buries Akhar, as required by Mosaic Law. Joshua may be harsh, but he is law-abiding.

Having removed the stain from the Israelite army, Joshua resumes the siege of Ai. Joshua takes the city with a ruse. He sets up an ambush, then attacks the city and pretends to retreat. The army of Ai follows Joshua's retreating army, allowing the soldiers hiding in ambush to raid the city and destroy it. Joshua then starts fighting seriously and the army of Ai retreats towards the city only to find that it has already been taken. The morale of the soldiers of Ai collapses, and the day is won. Israel takes booty and prisoners, and Joshua divides it all between the troops.

A number of elements in this story are worth noting. First, the ambush is Joshua's idea and not God's. This increases Joshua's image as a military tactician. Second, Joshua turns the Ai army back towards their city in retreat before they know that the city has been taken. Again, this points to Joshua's ability to lead an army in battle. Third, Joshua's division of the spoils points to his pater-

---

373 Of course, Joshua realizes that it is up to God, and Josephus has no desire to make Joshua appear sacrilegious, so Joshua does end the speech with a prostration.

nalistic concern for the troops as opposed to the self-interest exhibited by poor leaders and generals.

Turning to the Gibeonite story, Christopher Begg sums up Josephus' version best: "In his version of Joshua 9, harmony prevails."[374] Although the Gibeonite account follows the biblical account in many respects (5:49–57), the apparent discord between the Israelite leadership on one hand and Joshua on the other, found in the biblical account, is erased.

From the beginning of the story, it is clear to the Gibeonites that the person they need to talk to is Joshua. This assumption on their part proves to be correct, as Joshua functions as the primary mover and decision maker throughout the account. As part of Josephus's explanation for the ruse, he describes the perception of Joshua among the Gibeonites. They believe that it would be pointless to negotiate with him honestly, since he appears bent on exterminating the Canaanite inhabitants. This observation would appear to be correct as well.

Joshua negotiates with the Gibeonite ambassadors, albeit under false pretenses, and accepts their offer of treaty. Unlike in the biblical text, Joshua does not suspect deceit on their part, nor is there any attempt on Josephus' part to place the blame for his naiveté upon the Israelite leadership as a whole. Elazar and the elders simply follow suit after Joshua's decision, confirming the treaty with an oath.

When Joshua, during the course of a battle near the Jerusalem area, finds out the truth about the Gibeonites, it is he that summons their leadership for a dressing down. Having heard their explanation for the deceit, Joshua turns over the decision of what to do with them to Elazar and the elders. Although it will be Elazar and the elders who decide to accept the Gibeonites into Israel as low-grade servants, they have the power to make this decision only because Joshua delegated it to them. This is the second time Joshua delegates work to Elazar, and both examples may be connected to the possible ritual/religious overtones to the decision.[375] Finally, after Elazar and the elders come to their decision, Joshua enforces it.

Next, the king of the Hierosolumites organizes a coalition to lay siege to Gibeon (5:58). The Gibeonites naturally call upon their new ally (σύμμαχον), Joshua. As in the biblical version, Joshua comes immediately, after a forced march of his troops through the night. He attacks at daybreak and the enemy is routed. Joshua then pursues the enemy, pressing his advantage like a good general.

374 Christopher T. Begg, *Judean Antiquities, Books 5–7: Translation and Commentary* (Flavius Josephus: Translation and Commentary 4; Leiden: Brill, 2005) book 5, n. 158.
375 In the case of Akhar, it is the lottery; in the case of the Gibeonites, it is the existence of an oath.

At this point in the narrative, Josephus records two miracles, demonstrating what he calls divine cooperation (συνεργία). First, he describes divine assistance through thunderstorm. Lightning strikes the battlefield as does a "greater than usual" (μείζονος τῆς συνήθους) barrage of hail. Although Begg (ad loc.) is correct that Josephus adds some drama by discussing thunder and lightning where the biblical text only has hail, nevertheless, what seems more striking is Josephus's softening of the hail miracle by stating that what is odd about the storm is that the hail was greater than usual. The softened nature of this miracle becomes clear when one compares this to the biblical description, where YHWH is described as literally throwing giant hail stones onto the enemy, killing more people in this fashion than Joshua does in battle.

Josephus has a tougher time softening the next miracle (5:61).

ἔτι γε μὴν καὶ τὴν ἡμέραν αὐξηθῆναι πλέον, ὡς ἂν μὴ καταλαβοῦσα νὺξ ἐπίσχῃ τὸ τῶν Ἑβραίων πρόθυμον... ὅτι δὲ τὸ μῆκος τῆς ἡμέρας ἐπέδωκε τότε καὶ τοῦ συνήθους ἐπλεόνασε, δηλοῦται διὰ τῶν ἀνακειμένων ἐν τῷ ἱερῷ γραμμάτων.	And, verily, the daytime was further augmented, such that nighttime could not take hold, to restrain the Hebrew's eagerness... That the length of the day was increased, and went past the usual, was disclosed through the writings sitting in the Temple.

Although it is difficult to soften the miraculous nature of stopping the sun, Josephus does so through a circumlocution, stating that the day was augmented and the nighttime unable to take hold. Even so, he apparently remains bothered by the fantastic nature of the claim, so he defends it by stating that the miracle was documented and existed in the "files" of the Temple in Jerusalem.[376]

By both mentioning the miracles but softening them, Josephus produces a double win for Joshua. On one hand, God shows his approval for Joshua by his direct involvement in the battle. On the other hand, God's involvement is really secondary, and the win is accomplished handily by Joshua.[377]

It is in the final campaign that Josephus places the greatest emphasis. The northern Canaanites join together with the Philistines and attack Joshua with a tremendous force: 300,000 troops, 10,000 horsemen and 20,000 chariots. For the first time during the campaign, Joshua and the Israelites express fear (5:64).

---

376 By the time of the writing of *Antiquities*, the Temple had already been destroyed; nevertheless, the claim still has the *sound* of authenticity, which may have been sufficient for Josephus' purposes.

377 This differs, for example, from Josephus' treatment of Gideon (5:215–217), which emphasizes the opposite: Gideon wins purely by God's might, and his army of 300 is made up of only worthless rabble.

καταπλήττειδὲ τὸ πλῆθος τῶν πολεμίων αὐτόν τε Ἰησοῦν καὶ τοὺς Ἰσραηλίτας καὶ πρὸς τὴν ἐλπίδα τοῦ κρείττονος εὐλαβεστέρως εἶχον δι' ὑπερβολὴν τοῦ δέους.

The numerousness of the enemy terrified both Joshua and the Israelites, and their hope for greater strength was overtaken by an overwhelming feeling of fear.

Luckily, God intervenes and rebukes them for their fear.[378] He promises them victory and orders them to burn the chariots and hamstring the horses. Joshua does not need to be told twice and, feeling the return of his "daring" (θαρσαλέος), attacks the enemy. Josephus relates that five days later, Joshua engages the enemy at battle, and the Canaanite army suffers a defeat and a slaughter that was "beyond belief" (κρείττων πίστευς). Having destroyed the enemy army and all of the kings, Joshua ransacks the countryside, laying siege to towns and killing all the inhabitants.[379]

Again, although this account is very similar to that of the biblical story in Joshua 11, Josephus makes a number of small adjustments that make the story more plausible and paint Joshua in a better light. Although afraid at first, once Joshua is inspired by God's promise, he fights the war on his own. The success is Joshua's, not God's. Second, Josephus includes numbers for the enemy forces instead of the biblical "numerous as the sands of the sea." He also throws in the phrase "for those who have heard of it" when describing the unbelievable carnage, implying that some sort of firsthand knowledge or tradition existed in Israel with regard to this battle, to which Josephus was privy.

The overall picture one gets of Joshua in this section is of an exceptionally competent leader and military officer. Joshua is beloved by God, and generally keeps a cool head during crisis. He knows how to inspire his troops, has a good head for tactics and strategy, and leads his army successfully through battle after battle, no matter the odds. Although God does support Joshua throughout this process, the miracles are presented as secondary to Joshua's talented leadership.

---

378 The Greek is ἐξονειδίσαντος, literally "casting in his teeth," a colorful expression.
379 There is no mention in Josephus' account of Hazor or the burning of that city. Perhaps this has less to do with Joshua and more to do with Josephus' attempt to solve the doublet problem; Hazor will feature prominently in the Deborah and Barak account.

The Establishment of the Country

Having defeated the natives in a five-year campaign, Joshua ends the war. He leaves a small number of survivors hiding in well-fortified towns that he, apparently, decides are not worth laying siege to.

With the war at its end, Joshua moves his center from Gilgal to Shiloh, where he plans on setting up a worship site. Joshua then takes the people to Shechem to perform the blessing and curse ritual on Mt. Gerizim and Mt. Ebal, and to set up the altar, as commanded by Moses. The Israelites perform the ritual, sacrifices are offered, and the blessings and curses are written upon the altar. With that, Joshua and the people return to Shiloh.

As one of Joshua's major moments as a religious figure, the description appears quite subdued. Josephus is no stranger to writing impressive speeches, but he skips over this opportunity, reporting only the bare-bones fact that Joshua did exactly what Moses commanded him to do. One could reasonably explain this subdued tone by claiming that Josephus has little interest in Joshua as religious guru. However, there may be another factor at work. A number of scholars have suggested that Josephus has an anti-Samaritan bias.[380] Since Mount Gerizim is the holiest spot for the Samaritans, perhaps Josephus' downplaying of this event has less to do with Joshua and more to do with location.[381]

Joshua then calls an assembly at Shiloh (5:72). At the assembly, he makes a closing speech as commander of the army. He begins by praising the army for its excellent showing in battle. Joshua reminds them of the 31 kings that they vanquished as well as of the enormous army of Canaanites they annihilated. Additionally, he speaks to them of their fidelity to God and their proper observance of God's laws throughout the campaign.

Joshua then informs them of his observations about the current situation; observations that Josephus already recorded for the reader immediately before the description of the assembly but which he will have Joshua repeat in the speech. The remaining Canaanites are hiding behind fortifications that are too massive for the Israelites to successfully attack. Considering this Joshua states it would be best to end the campaign at this point and begin to divide up the conquered land among the remaining tribes. In addition to this observation, there seems to be another factor at play, one with which Josephus opens this sec-

---

380 See Magnar Kartveit, *The Origin of the Samaritans* (Leiden: Brill, 2009), for discussion and bibliography.

381 One could support this argument with the observation that Josephus, breaking with the order of events in the biblical account, has Joshua founding Shiloh before he goes to Shechem.

tion: Joshua is now old, and he would like to ensure that the division of land is carried out properly before he is too old to supervise it.

In this short section, Josephus has actually tackled the key problem in the Book of Joshua, namely the contradiction between the claim that Joshua took everything and the claim that much of the land remained in Canaanite hands. Josephus strikes a compromise position by claiming that Joshua won every battle and conquered every city except for a few heavily fortified cities that were not worth taking. This compromise also saves Joshua from the implication found in the biblical book (in chapter 13) that he was not fully successful during his long campaign. In the biblical text, this can be read as a criticism of Joshua. However, for Josephus, it was a tactical decision not to continue the attack. Furthermore, Josephus does not record any rebuke of Joshua by God for this decision, implying that it was acceptable to God, at least for the time being.

Josephus actually returns to this theme after his description of the division of the land; this time, however, a little more "bite" can be detected in Josephus' tone. He begins by listing a number of places that were not divided among the Israelites, ostensibly because they had not been conquered (5:89).[382] He then goes on to say that Joshua addressed the people directly, reminding them to purge their territories of Canaanites, since if they did not, the natives would eventually lead them to sin against God. Josephus adds that the reason he aimed this statement at the people and not the chiefs was that the chiefs who were overseeing matters already in Joshua's old age had shown themselves to be careless guardians of the common good (παραλαβόντων ἀμελῶς προστάντων τοῦ κοινῇ συμφέροντος; 5:90).

Joshua plans to begin by sending one man from each tribe to measure the land "in good faith" (πιστῶς; 5:75). As a prudent administrator, Joshua shows himself to be aware of the potential abuses of land surveying. The people understand Joshua's concern and decide to send professional surveyors along with the tribal representatives to make sure that no false information is included in the report.

Additionally, Joshua sets out the overall policy for the survey. The parceling of land will not only be based on size but must also factor in quality. Joshua mandates that the overall "value" for various parcels of land should be set on the basis of these dual factors, size and quality (5:78). Having set these parameters, Joshua then consults with Elazar and the elders as to of which tribe will get

---

382 This differs from the biblical picture of the allotment, in which areas are granted to tribes even if they remain in the hands of the Canaanites. It is hardly surprising that Josephus would modify this highly impractical picture of land division.

which plots. As this decision will be determined by the casting of lots, this process will be led by Elazar and the priests. Yet again Joshua keeps the executive decisions as his own prerogative and involves Elazar and the elders only at later stages and for ritual functions that may require the high priest.

The division of the land goes smoothly, Joshua having preempted any possible subterfuge or inequity with his foresight. The section ends with a summary statement that Joshua divided up the Canaanite lands among the nine and a half tribes just as Moses divided up the Amorite lands among the two and a half tribes. Josephus' point seems to be that Joshua was Moses' successor not only as a general but also as a competent administrator.

Joshua then establishes the Levitical cities, including the designation of three cities of refuge, again as Moses did in the Transjordan. Finally, he divides up the booty. The emphasis in this section is on Joshua's fair and prudent leadership. Joshua delegates when necessary and when desirable but always maintains a firm control of any important process, like Moses did.

The Transjordanian Tribes

Josephus uses the occasion of the dismissal of the Transjordanian tribes as an opportunity to write the longest speech he will give Joshua. Josephus uses a "thinking out loud" style of speech, in which Joshua lays bare the motivations for his actions.

The speech begins with Joshua reminding the audience that the land was given to them by God (5:93). He continues by thanking the Transjordanian tribes for their willing cooperation (συνεργίας). It would only be just (δίκαιον), therefore, now that the conquest was over, to dismiss the Transjordanian army and allow them to return to their families. He adds that it would be not only just but even prudent, as a rested army is more likely to be of help in the next campaign, whereas an overtaxed one (καμοῦσαν) will be sluggish (βραδυτέρον) in response.

This opening has a syllogistic style to it, i.e., *since* God promised us the land, and *since* you have voluntarily assisted us to conquer it, *therefore* you deserve to be granted the boon of a return to your families for an indefinite time. One subtle premise of this speech is that the promise to Moses actually applies in perpetuity. If the Cisjordanian tribes have need of military assistance in the future, the Transjordanian tribes must come and assist them. Although it may be possible to interpret the oath of the Transjordanian tribes in this way, the more likely interpretation would be that since all the tribes assisted the two and a half in their conquest of the Transjordan, it would only be fair for these tribes to, in turn, help the other tribes conquer their territory in the Cisjordan, at which point the tribes would be even. Joshua's speech surreptitiously discounts this possibility by his reference to their future eagerness (προθυμίας) to pick up where they left off.

Having underlined this important expectation, Joshua, like any good leader, turns to the quid pro quo (5:95). He states that "we," ostensibly the Cisjordanians, "will do well to remember our friends" (ὄντες ἀγαθοὶ μεμνῆσθαι τῶν φίλων), implying that the military aid pact is two directional. In making this argument, Josephus makes use of the classic Greek topos of *philia* (φιλία), friendship.[383] The rhetorical use of *philia*, as well as the ethical responsibilities people in a relationship of *philia* have towards each other, was explored by many ancient Greek writers, including Aristotle, and generally refers to a virtuous, dispassionate, but affectionate regard or love (in contrast to eros, for example, which describes a passionate love or longing). Joshua's point here is that the Cisjordanians and Transjordanians should relate to each other as allies or family members would, with each striving to help the other succeed to the greatest extent possible.

To further emphasize the mutually beneficial bond between the Cisjordanians and the Transjordanians that exists in fact, Joshua describes the great wealth and plunder that the Transjordanians have already shared in and will be allowed to bring back with them into their own lands. He makes the point here that even though assisting their Cisjordanian brethren was a selfless act, it turned out to be worthwhile materially as well.

Having made these points Joshua, continues in a different direction. Despite the fact that the two groups live on opposite sides of the Jordan River, this should not cause them to feel as though they are two different peoples. They are all Hebrews, all descendants of Abraham, and they all worship the one God. This last line leads Joshua into his warning. The Transjordanians must worship God and maintain fealty to his system of living (πολιτείας). If they do, God will remain with them as their ally (σύμμαχον),[384] but if not, God will abandon them.

One can see how far afield Josephus has gone with this speech when one compares it to the biblical account. Although Josephus follows the basic outline of the biblical Joshua's speech, he adds a number of details and nuances which change the basic emphasis. In the biblical speech, Joshua simply acknowledges the fact that the Transjordanian tribes fulfilled their promise to Moses and that

---

383 I thank Luke Johnson for pointing this out during my defense.
384 Interestingly, this is the same term Josephus used for Joshua's relationship with the Gibeonites.

now that God has given victory to the Israelite army, the Transjordanians should feel free to return home. It ends with an upbeat reminder in Deuteronomic style to keep the Torah and love God.

Joshua's speech in Josephus, on the other hand, demonstrates the subtleties of a concerned leader. Throughout the speech, one gets the feeling that Joshua is concerned about a possible break between the two groups. He fears that the Transjordanians may resent their years of assistance to their brothers and that once they return to their own land they will break off ties with the Cisjordanians. Furthermore, Joshua seems to fear that they will abandon the worship of God and his Torah altogether in the Transjordan, perhaps imagining that they are now their own people and free to find their own god.

Hence, Joshua smoothly attempts to undo this possibility. He reminds them of God's promises to the people and his beneficence to them. He reminds them of the future relevance of their oath and of the material benefits that accrued to them from keeping this oath. Finally, he reminds them that they are all brothers and all are God's people and need to behave in this manner. In short, Josephus' Joshua is a shrewd political leader who attempts to use oratory to adjust what he sees will be potential problems in the future.

Although it is impossible to say why Josephus takes this opportunity to give Joshua this role, two possibilities present themselves. First, unlike in the biblical account, which records no link between Joshua and the story of the Transjordanian altar, Josephus, like *L.A.B.*, will tie him into this story. The speech functions as a strong tie between these two parts of the biblical chapter, with Joshua demonstrating the perspicacity of a leader who predicts the next crisis. Second, throughout his account of Joshua, Josephus has emphasized Joshua's wise leadership. The ability to predict a crisis and use shrewd oratory to combat it goes hand in hand with this type of leadership.

With the close of the speech, Joshua comes down from the pulpit, as it were, to shake hands with his generals and say goodbye to the troops (5:99). At this point the Cisjordanians walk the Transjordanian troops out and say goodbye, with everyone shedding tears; apparently Joshua's speech has the desired effect.

The Incident with the Altar

One of the major interpretive difficulties in the biblical account of the altar incident is divining the intent of the Transjordanian tribes in building it. Josephus takes the opposite strategy to that taken by *L.A.B.* in solving this problem, and assumes that the Transjordanian tribes never intended to use the altar for worship, but only as a symbol of their connection to God and their brothers in the

Cisjordan. This intention of theirs, although introduced to the reader at the very beginning, is unknown to the people living in the Cisjordan.

The Cisjordanian tribes react immediately and aggressively. Without first consulting with Joshua they take up arms (ὅπλοις), preparing to attack the Transjordanians (5:101). Luckily, Joshua, Elazar and the elders learn of the plan and calm the people down. Counseling them with words (λόγοις βουλεύοντες), they advise the people to parley first and find out what the intention behind the Transjordanian altar really is (5:103). The people accept the advice and appoint Phineas, together with a number of other tribal representatives, with the task of travelling to the Transjordan and ascertaining the truth of the matter.

At this point, the story follows Phineas, who delivers a long and intricate speech to the Transjordanians, followed by their explanation of the altar. Phineas accepts their explanation and returns home to report to Joshua.[385] Joshua expresses elation (χαίρων) at this turn of events, relieved that there will be no need for a civil war. He then offers sacrifices of thanksgiving (χαριστηρίους) to God and dismisses the people, sending them back to their homes while he remains in Shechem.[386]

The picture Josephus paints here is of a people gathered around their leader, waiting for the outcome of a very tense negotiation. Joshua may be too old to travel and negotiate himself, and at first the people pass over obtaining his counsel altogether. However, once he asserts himself, the people naturally fall into their pattern of trust in his leadership and he keeps them in check long enough to determine that no armed conflict would actually be necessary. This ability to avoid internal strife is an important sign of good leadership, as Josephus will point out later in the book when comparing Gideon to Jephthah (5:230, 267–9).

Josephus' treatment of Joshua in this account contrasts sharply with that of *L.A.B.* The author of *L.A.B.* gives Joshua a long speech, filled with biblical allusion and fire and brimstone. It is Joshua that expresses anger and threatens civil war and it is only the contrition of the Transjordanian tribes that avoids the conflict. Of course, in the *L.A.B.*'s version of the events, the anger was justified, since the Transjordanians did in fact use the altar for sacrifice according to this account. That said, the two versions of the story paint very different pictures of Joshua.

In *L.A.B.* Joshua is the indignant religious leader ready to defend God and God's Torah from any possible breach. In Josephus, he is the wise and seasoned

---

385 It is worth noting here that he specifically reports to Joshua, not to Elazar and the elders as well. This stands out especially since Elazar is Phineas's own father.
386 Josephus does not explain why Joshua is in Shechem and not Shiloh.

leader, able to keep his young followers from acting rashly and bringing about an unnecessary civil war. Even the sacrifice at the end of the story has less of the official ritual feel that one finds in *L.A.B.*'s description of sacrificial rites and more the feel of a spontaneous expression of joy and relief.

Joshua's Death

The final scene occurs twenty years later, when Joshua is extremely old (ὑπέργη-ρως).[387] He calls together the most prominent men (ἀξιώματος μάλιστα) of the cities, the leaders, the elders, and any of the average citizens who are available. He reminds them that they are enjoying God's benefits, ostensibly since they represent the ruling class.

He then takes this opportunity to exhort them on the importance of maintaining their piety (τῇ εὐσεβείᾳ), for it is only through pious behavior that they can maintain God's goodwill and allegiance to them. Josephus adds in a parenthetical comment to the effect that it was fitting for Joshua to admonish them, as that is the proper behavior on a death bed. Finally Joshua asks the people to remember this exhortation. With that Joshua dies, at age 110.

It would be difficult to overstate the enormous difference between this minuscule parting address and the grand final speech of Joshua 24. In Josephus, Joshua spends his post-war years in semi-retirement, and there is no time for big speeches. Joshua says a modest goodbye and offers an optimistic exhortation. This is the opposite approach to that taken by *L:A.B.*, who has Joshua end his life with a number of long "final" speeches, and also allows Joshua the opportunity to prophecy the doom that he so long fought against.

Additionally, the death bed scenes in *L.A.B.* and Josephus differ. The deathbed scene in *L.A.B.* has an exceedingly personal touch, with Joshua kissing Elazar, Phineas, and Phineas' sons and blessing them. When Joshua dies in *L.A.B.*, his own sons close his eyes. None of this type of personal detail appears in Josephus.

Unlike the biblical account, in which the reader does not know how long Joshua's leadership of Israel lasted, was said to have lasted, Josephus breaks the numbers down specifically. Joshua trained forty years under Moses, fought the conquest campaign over five years, and ruled in semi-retirement for another

---

387 See Christopher Begg's analysis comparing this death account with that of the Bible, *L.A.B.* and Sam. Chron. II: Christopher T. Begg, "The Demise of Joshua according to Josephus," *HTS* 63 (2007): 129 – 145. http://www.ajol.info/index.php/hts/article/viewFile/41188/8576

twenty years. One can even deduce from all this that Joshua was forty-five years old when Israel escaped from Egypt, hardly a lad.

Joshua is buried in Thamna. Although Josephus tells the reader that this is in Ephraim, he does not tell the reader anything about this city (5:119). After recording Joshua's burial, Josephus immediately jumps to the death and burial of Elazar, which he tells us happened around the same time. This leaves Phineas with the shoes of both to fill, as he will eventually be both priest and leader. In fact, Phineas' first act will be to prophecy which tribe should lead the next battle.

Josephus' choice of Phineas as next leader and successor to Joshua is a surprising one. The next named leader in the bible is either Caleb or, more properly, Othniel ben Kenaz, Caleb's younger brother. *L.A.B.* chooses Cenaz as the next leader, and the Samaritan Book of Joshua chooses Abil, Caleb's son; both characters are apparently based upon the biblical Othniel. One would have thought that this character would have fit Josephus's mold well, as he was a military leader, not a priest or a prophet.

It is possible that Phineas was chosen more for chronological reasons than for some preference for him over Othniel, who will appear as leader later on (5:182). Perhaps Josephus is simply looking for an ephemeral leader who can be said to be working behind the scenes while the battles recorded in Judg chs. 1–2, 17–19 occur. Since Phineas is named explicitly in Judg 20, he may be the best choice, especially since he is more priest than military leader.

Unlike *L.A.B.*, in which a powerful and poetic eulogy is sung for Joshua, Josephus records no eulogy for him. However, Josephus eulogizes Joshua himself (5:118).

ἀνὴρ [δὲ] μήτε συνέσεως ὢν ἐνδεὴς μήτε τοῦ τὰ νοηθέντα πρὸς τοὺς πολλοὺς σαφῶς ἐξενεγκεῖν ἄπειρος, ἀλλ᾽ ἐν ἀμφοτέροις ἄκρος, πρός τε τὰ ἔργα καὶ τοὺς κινδύνους εὔψυχος καὶ μεγαλότολμος, πρυτανεῦσαί τε τὰ κατὰτὴν εἰρήνην δεξιώτατος καὶ πρὸς ἅπαντα καιρὸν τὴν ἀρετὴν ἡρμοσμένος.	He was a man not falling short in sagacity, nor unacquainted with setting out his thoughts clearly to the masses, rather [he was] topmost in both of these. In both works and hazards he was of stout heart and greatly adventurous. He held sway with great skill over matters of peace, at all times adapting himself to the good.

Josephus's eulogy for Joshua sums up well the character as he is portrayed in this work. Joshua is a successful statesman: talented in war, organized in peace, brave when necessary but calm when the people need a steady hand. One can easily imagine how an image like this would appeal to the Hellenistic philosophical culture. Although there is no doubt that Josephus wants the reader to believe that Joshua was a religious figure who worshiped God in the Jewish way and kept Torah, the terminology Josephus uses focuses most on general piety, good character, and judgment. This is Josephus' unique image of Joshua.

Summary

In the Hellenistic and Early Roman periods a number of different images of Joshua held sway. Ben Sira, the earliest of the texts, holds a model of Joshua most similar to his depiction in the biblical text. Joshua was a warrior of YHWH, a miracle worker and the loyal scout. Ben Sira, as a work, is the most continuous with biblical literature, so it is hardly surprising that his account fits best with the biblical presentation of Joshua. Furthermore, since the encomium to the ancient heroes was a prelude to his encomium to or defense of Simon the Just, who was himself a defender, militarily speaking, of Judah, this Joshua imagery, followed by David imagery, was par for the course.

The First Book of Maccabees, also relatively early, although referring to him curiously as a judge, uses tacit Joshua imagery to buttress the positions of Mattathias and Judah. Since the project of the Maccabees was military in nature, with the goal being the reclamation and independence of Judea, one can easily see the significance of Joshua as a model. The same is true of Second Maccabees. All three of these works see Joshua through the lens of his historiographical role as conqueror of the Promised Land, and find this useful in their world of *realpolitik*.

Josephus, also a man with heavy involvement in *realpolitik*, found the basic contours of the Joshua story to be inspiring. However, Josephus did not participate in the Maccabean desire for a Judean renaissance, but was writing from a highly Hellenized and Romanized perspective, after the destruction of the Temple. Josephus' project seems to have been to make Judean history and culture accessible and admirable to his Greek and Roman readers. To this end, Josephus takes the conqueror Joshua, an image and persona Romans could respect, but tweaks his story by adding an emphasis on tactics and, more importantly, calm and reasoned leadership. Thus, Josephus takes Joshua, the warrior of God into Joshua, the Judean general and statesman.

Philo, on the other hand, sees Joshua through the lens of philosophy, as he sees everything and everyone else. Joshua is a great philosopher who modeled himself after Moses. The love of these two men for each other in Philo's understanding (perhaps modeled on the love of David and Jonathan) is the paradigm example of the mutual love of philosophers and great thinkers.

Coming at Joshua from a totally different angle was the author of the *Apocryphon of Joshua*. As opposed to Josephus' goal of making Joshua accessible to the larger world, the *Apocryphon of Joshua* is in conversation only with fellow Jews, and primarily with those associated with the proto-Qumran sectarian community. To this end, the *Apocryphon of Joshua* sees its story's hero through the lens of what makes heroes significant to the sectarian community, having the gift of prophecy. Like other great prophetic leaders of the past, Joshua, in this work, describes the future specifically and accurately, revealing to the Israelites (and his future Judean readers) that important developments such as the Temple and the Davidic monarchy, both institutions that will reappear in messianic times, were foreordained. This image of Joshua as one who predicts events that came true strengthened the sectarian belief that other prophecies, as understood by the authors of the *pesharim*, were also foreordained and would also come true. Most similar to the *Apocryphon's* Joshua is that of *4 Ezra*, who describes Joshua as a prophetic intercessor on behalf of the people, like Abraham and Moses.

The final editor of *Assumptio Mosis* shared the sectarian hope in a better future. The eschatological prediction found in this work was written during a major persecution (in my estimation the Hadrianic persecution) and hope for the future was probably a psychological necessity, not to mention an ontological one for those Jews who were remaining loyal to their tradition at significant risk and cost. However, this author did not give Joshua the prophecy which would predict the coming of Taxo's martyrdom and the ushering in of the final days, but gave it to Moses. As such, the author of the eschatological prediction wrote this prophecy into a preexisting literary framework which dealt with the transfer of power to Joshua and the death of Moses. In this midrashic frame-text, which could be more than a century or two older than the eschatological prediction, Joshua is a passive and stupefied student whereas Moses is a man beyond this world whose life must be taken by God and whose body would be buried by angels. This midrashic framework functioned well for the author of the eschatological prediction. Moses is godlike in his oracular powers and Joshua is Taxo-like in his passivity. The political message is that all one can do is wait and watch, while the terror eventually turns on the aggressors and God shows God's true love for the chosen people.

Finally, *L.A.B.* shows great interest in Joshua but very little interest in politics. The work emphasizes Joshua's role as a religious figure, one who sings praises to God, edifies the people with Torah and divine wisdom, and establishes the places of worship throughout the Holy Land. The author of this work uses Joshua as a model of piety and religious leadership, perhaps with the intent of making him a heuristic model for his own generation. In this sense, *L.A.B.* shows the greatest continuity with what will be seen in the chapter on Joshua in Rabbinic literature.

All in all, this overview of Joshua in Hellenistic and early Roman period Jewish literature demonstrates the ability of various Jewish communities to maintain their veneration of the Ancient Israelite hero, Joshua, thereby solidifying their identities as heirs to the Ancient Israelites, while recasting him in such a way that he would function as relevant and even inspiring to their coreligionists, whose concerns—depending on the group—were quite different than those of ancient Israelites as presented in the biblical texts.

Chapter 4 –Samaritan Joshua(s)

Although the Samaritans do not have a canonical book of Joshua akin to the biblical book, Joshua is an integral part of their historical consciousness. The most significant work the Samaritans have related to Joshua is the Arabic book of Joshua,[388] which will be the focus of this chapter.[389]

The *Samaritan Book of Joshua* (*S.J.*) was originally introduced to Western scholars in 1584 by Joseph J. Scaliger, who had purchased a copy of the book from a Samaritan community in Cairo. The manuscript (as well as the text itself) is a composite work; the oldest piece of the *manuscript* dates to 1362 and the later piece to 1513.[390] The manuscript was stored in the University Library of Leiden and remained only partially published until the 19th century.[391]

In 1848, T. W. J. Juynboll published an accurate and complete edition of the Leiden manuscript together with a translation and commentary in Latin.[392] This remains the standard edition for scholars interested in the work.[393] It was the basis for the Hebrew summary and paraphrase of the work, published by Ra-

---

[388] There are two Samaritan Hebrew versions of Joshua as well, one of which has been dealt with extensively in a recent German monograph: Friedrich Niessen, *Eine Samaritanische Version des Buches Yehošua und die Šobak-Erzählung* (Texte und Studen zur Orientalistik 12; Hildesheim: Georg Olms Verlag, 2000). The other was published (in a non-scholarly edition) by two young members of the Samaritan community. See: *Sefer Yehushua ha-Shomroni* (ed. Baruch Marhiv and Shahar Yehoshua; Holon: Betzel-El, 1976). I will not be focusing on these works since they were apparently written in the late 19th century, probably, with the intention of selling them to overzealous academics looking for "old Samaritan traditions." Nevertheless, some of the traditions incorporated in the works may have been genuine Samaritan religious traditions. I thank Binyamim Tsedaka for clarifying some of these issues with me and for giving me an advanced copy of his chapter on Samaritan Joshua traditions from his forthcoming book on Samaritan history.

[389] The other significant work that overlaps the Arabic book of Joshua is the *Kitab al-Tarikh*, or *Chronicles of Abu 'l-Fath*; a Samaritan work, also written in Arabic and dating from circa 1355. The *Kitab al-Tarikh* draws heavily from the Arabic Book of Joshua, although the author does not use this work exclusively in his retelling of the Joshua narrative. Since Abu 'l-Fath used the Arabic book of Joshua as his main source, there seems little need to devote much time to his chronicle, but the *Kitab al-Tarikh* will be critical in one section, in which 'l-Fath seems to be supplementing his version with a story missing from *S.J.* but part of the biblical text.

[390] In the 19th century, other manuscripts of the work were purchased from the Samaritans and published, but the Leiden manuscript remains the oldest.

[391] Johann Heinrich Hottinger did publish some excerpts of the book in the 17th century.

[392] See: Robert Anderson and Terry Giles, *Tradition Kept: The Literature of the Samaritans* (Peabody: Hendrickson, 2005), 49–50.

[393] Personal correspondence with Anderson and Giles; it is worth noting that in addition to this translation, Juynboll published a history of the Samaritans (also in Latin) in 1846.

phael Kirchheim in 1851 as a part of his book on the Samaritans called *Karmei Shomron*.[394] Additionally, Juynboll's edition was the basis for Oliver Crane's English translation of the book in its entirety. Crane's translation remains the standard English translation, although it has been modernized and updated in the newer edition of Anderson and Giles.[395]

Although the book focuses on Joshua, even a cursory reading demonstrates that the work cannot be understood as a unified whole. The simplest way to understand the work is to divide it into a number of sections.[396]

a. Chapter 1 is a scribal or editorial note, explaining the nature of the work and comparing it to the Torah.
b. Chapters 2–8 seem to rewrite the end of Numbers, and are tacked on to the original work as a sort of introduction to Joshua and the conquest narrative.
c. Chapters 9–25 are a loose rewrite of most of the book of Joshua.
d. Chapters 26–37 tell the Nabih and Shaubak story.
e. Chapters 38–44 record the death of Joshua and Elazar and describe the rule of their successors.
f. Chapter 45 discusses Persian-period conflicts regarding Jerusalem and Mount Gerizim.
g. Chapter 46 discusses Alexander the Great.
h. Chapters 47–50 tell the Hadrian vs. Aqbun account, in the middle of which the manuscript is cut off.

That chapters 45–50 are later additions seems obvious and, I think, not in serious dispute. The various pieces after chapter 44 have no smooth transition into each other and jump from epoch to epoch. Additionally, there is no direct connection narratively or historiographically between the "Judges period" described in chapter 44 and the Persian period conflicts in chapter 46. As none of these sections have any bearing on the character of Joshua, they will not be dealt with here.

---

394 Raphael Kirchheim, *Karmei Shomron* (Frankfurt: Isaac Kaufman, 1851), 55–91. I thank Binyamim Tsedaka for making me aware of this source.
395 Oliver Turnbull Crane, *The Samaritan Chronicle, or The Book of Joshua Son of Nun* (New York: John B. Alden, 1890). "The English translation found in this chapter is Crane's. The authors have modernized the language, corrected typographical errors, leveled the spelling of names, and provided explanatory footnotes." (Anderson and Giles, *Tradition*, 50.) I note one small criticism of Anderson and Giles' update: they do not include translations of the original chapter headings, which Crane does, as does Kirchheim, albeit often in summary form.
396 This analysis is my own. For a slightly different division of the material, see Anderson and Giles, *Tradition*, 50–52.

That chapters 2–8 are a later addition is clear both from the nature of the work, which is a rewrite of Numbers, and from the chapter heading in chapter 9:

إبتدى سفر يوشع بن نون تلميذ السيد موسى النبى عم   The beginning of the book of Joshua son of Nun, student of the master Moses, peace be upon him

This heading clearly assumes that the book begins in chapter 9. It would seem that chapters 2–8 were added, perhaps to give context to the conquest narrative and to place Joshua into the thick of the conquest of the Transjordan. Chapter 1 could have been added to chapters 2–8 as a general introduction, although this is not necessarily the only option.

The overall redactional question that is most difficult to solve is the relationship between the rewritten Joshua account, the Nabih account, and the account of Joshua and Elazar's successors. The most likely possibility is that the core of this work was made up of chapters 9–25 with some version of the death notices in 38 and 40 rounding off a classic "rewritten Bible." To this was added the Nabih account, between the Joshua story and the death notices. Then the book was reframed from a positive Joshua account to a negative account of "the fall of Israel" by adding most of chapters 38–44 and the introduction. Finally, the last six chapters were tacked on in successive "editions."

The above is a macro-redactional analysis of the text and is sufficient for the purpose of this chapter. However, to quote Anderson and Giles: "These major sections can be subdivided, and recognizable units of material can be observed throughout" (p. 51 n7). These "subsections" will be noted when relevant.

Joshua's Images in the Book

Moses' Successor

Joshua is first mentioned at the very beginning of the introduction (ch. 1).

هذا كتاب سير اخبار بني اسرائيل من وقت ان قلد سيدنا موسى ابن عمرم النبي عليه السلام يوشع ابن نون خلافة على قومه[397]	This book (narrates) the course of events of the children of Israel from the time when as ruler – Master Moses son of Amram, the prophet, may peace be upon him – Joshua son of Nun succeeded him over the people.

This opening sets the stage for Joshua's image in the book as the leader of Israel after Moses. The comparison between Moses and Joshua and the idea of Joshua taking up Moses' legacy receives greater emphasis in chapter two, which offers three consecutive pictures of Joshua's assumption of leadership.

The chapter begins with a description of the spiritual or esoteric knowledge Moses will impart to Joshua.

عند تمام ماية وتسعة عشر سنة فى اول يوم من الشهر الحادى عشر من عمر سيدنا موسى النبي – عليه السلام – اوحا الله اليه فى بقاع ماب ان يسند يده الى راس يوشع ابن نون الروحانى.	At the end of one hundred and nineteen years, on the first day of the eleventh month of the life of Moses the prophet – may peace be upon him – God revealed to him in the valley of Moab to lean his hand upon the head of Joshua son of Nun, the spiritual one.[398]
يعنى بذلك, ان يقضى اليه من سر الاسرار ويكشف له الحلم من حلمه وعلم العلوم ما يستطيع حمله ما يقوى به قلبه, ويكمل به روحه, ويرفع به نفسه, ويهون عليه امر المخلوقين.	Meaning by this, that he (Moses) should grant to him (Joshua) the secret of secrets, and to lay bare before him the vision of his visions, and the knowledge of science – whatever he could bear, with which his heart would be strengthened, and his spirit perfected, and his soul elevated, and ease his authority over the creatures.[399]
ويعرفه بالاسم الذى يهزم به العساكر وتتشوش به الامه التى لا يسعها بلد ولا ياتى عليها عدد.	And he should make known to him the name with which he will defeat the soldiers and muddle with it a nation that the land cannot contain and whose number cannot be counted.

In this first section of chapter 2, Moses receives the command to make known to Joshua the many esoteric secrets to which only Moses has been privy. These secrets are not even divulged to the reader; only references to visions, science, and a hidden name of God are made, ostensibly to give the reader a taste of the mystery surrounding the esoteric knowledge Joshua will receive.

---

397 See Quran 7:142.
398 Clearly a reference to Num 27:18, where Joshua is described as איש אשר רוח בו "a man with spirit in him."
399 Ostensibly a reference to the Israelites.

The text divides the secrets into two categories. The first category is aimed at making Joshua, already a spiritual person, into one that is stronger and more perfect, thereby making his rule over the Israelites that much easier. This fits in with the "be strong and bold" theme prevalent in the biblical account of Joshua and his assumption of leadership. The second category comprises the learning of the secret name and is tied to Joshua's future success as a military leader. Proper use of the knowledge of the secret name will allow Joshua to vanquish his enemies by magical means, ensuring his success during the conquest period.[400]

After commanding Moses to transfer the secret wisdom to Joshua, God further commands him to organize Joshua's inauguration as king and ruler of Israel.

ورسم له ان يوقفه بين يدى العزر الامام – عليه السلام –
ويجمع له اهل العلم والمعرفة والنباهة والرياسة ويعقد له
العقد ويجدد له العهد ويقلده الملك ويجعل له الحكم على
ساير بنى اسراييل.

And He commanded him (Moses) to stand (Joshua) before Elazar the imam – may peace be upon him – and to gather unto him people of knowledge and learning, as well as the notables and chiefs, and to make a pact with him, and to renew the covenant with him, and to confirm his rule as king, and to appoint him as ruler of the children of Israel.

ثم جعل النبى لالعزر الامام – عليه السلام – الامر عليه
بالنظر فى الكمال والزهر وان لا يدخل فى امر ولا
يخرج ان حال الا بعد ما يطالعه.

Then, the prophet gave Elazar the imam – may peace be upon him – the command, subject to his authority, with fullness and radiance, and [Moses commanded him] not to enter into a [different] commission, and not to deviate in any way except after he accomplishes [this].

وعند فراغه من تقليده ضربت الكهنه بالابواق ونادت
المناديين لعلمه وانتشرت الاعلام والبنود لملكه.

When the conferral was finished, the priests sounded the trumpets, and the heralds announced his flag, and the flag and banner for his kingship were spread.

Joshua's inauguration will be presided over by Elazar the priest, and all the notables of Israel will be there. This differs from the biblical description in a number of ways. First, although Moses will stand Joshua before Elazar according to Numbers and Deuteronomy as well, Moses is the only character given a "speaking part" in these texts; Elazar is simply there. Hence, there would seem to be no place in the biblical picture for the command to Elazar, found in Samaritan Josh-

---

400 That this section is a late addition becomes obvious when one notices that Joshua never actually uses the divine name in battle, even when he is losing and invokes other miracles for support.

ua, to make sure to hold the inauguration immediately. In the Pentateuch, Moses will hold the inauguration and he will assuredly do so in the proper timeframe.

Second, the audience for the inauguration in Samaritan Joshua has shrunk. In the Pentateuch (Deut 31:7) the inauguration is held before all of Israel; however, in the Samaritan Joshua version, the invitees to the ceremony seem to be people of prominence: scholars, nobles, and priests.

Third, in the Bible, Joshua is appointed leader, not king. However, in Samaritan Joshua, Joshua is most definitely a king. This point is clearly expressed throughout the book, with the royal imagery utilized already here in the inauguration scene. In this scene Joshua not only receives the title king (*malik*), but also enjoys a royal inauguration ceremony, replete with the blowing of trumpets and the raising of his flags ('*alam, a'lām*) and banners (*band, bunūd*). This theme will continue throughout the book, in which more royal paraphernalia will be referenced, such as Joshua's crown, purple robe, and throne.

Following the inauguration, Moses immediately turns to battle with the Midianites, except, unlike in the biblical story, Moses has Joshua on his mind.

رأى سيدنا النبي موسى – عليه السلام – ان يخرج فى اول الملاحم فى ايامه ليكون على تجربة من بيان مما عرفه ونظره.	Our master, the prophet Moses – may peace be upon him – perceived that [Joshua wished] to go out in the first battles, in his own (Moses') days, in order to gain experience through explication of what he understood and observed.

According to this account, Moses notices that Joshua wants to gain more experience at battle while Moses is still alive. Joshua's desire is not just an example of Joshua's military proclivities or his powerful yearning to get into the thick of the battle, but rather a calculated maneuver to get practical experience under Moses' master tutelage. What appears striking in this presentation is the idea of Moses as a military expert. In theory, one could make the argument that Moses has had ample practical experience in battle, since he has already fought Sihon, Og and the city of Arad. Nevertheless, one cannot help but notice the strong resonance this idea of Moses as military master has with the picture of Moses in Josephus.

As discussed in the section on Joshua in Josephus, Josephus considers Moses to be primarily a general, calling him στρατηγός throughout the work.[401] Additionally, in the section describing the battle with Amalek, Josephus details how Joshua and Moses stayed up all night discussing tactics (*Ant.* 3:47–50). Hence, Samaritan Joshua's idea that Joshua wants to take yet another opportu-

---

[401] See, for example, *Ant.* 2:243–253.

nity to learn at the feet of the great military master is not surprising if one assumes that the author of Samaritan Joshua had access to Josephus, as many scholars of Samaritan studies assume.

Finally, it should be noted that Samaritan Joshua solves a story-line problem that plagues the book of Numbers; Joshua does not seem to participate in any of the military actions in the Pentateuch other than the Amalek battle. This is especially problematic in the account of the battle with Midian since there are many details of this battle given, and even the participation of Elazar is described. Samaritan Joshua solves this problem by placing Joshua into the battle in its narrative retelling of the Midianite campaign.[402]

In describing the transition between Moses and Joshua, *S.J.* gives Joshua three distinct images. Like Moses, he is to be a bearer of secret and divine wisdom; like Moses he is to be a cunning and powerful military commander; however, unlike Moses, it would seem, he is to be crowned king of Israel, with all the relevant royal paraphernalia. These three images, or, at least, variations of them, will appear consistently throughout this work. However, before continuing on to describe Joshua's career as king as presented by *S.J.*, first it is worth concentrating on the other aspect of Joshua's career touched upon in *S.J.* – Joshua as Moses' loyal servant.

Joshua as Loyal Servant of Moses

After a digression explaining the reason for the battle with Midian, the book picks up with a resumptive repetition in chapter 5, reminding the reader that Joshua was put in charge of the battle. As Balaam and his plot to seduce Israelite men into idolatry was the cause of the war, Joshua intends on taking Balaam alive as a prisoner to Moses. Nevertheless, the troops from the tribe of Simon have other plans.

وعمل يوشع ابن نون علي ان يبقيه ليشاهده سيدنا موسى — سلام الله اليه — فلم يستطيع من شاهده من سبط شمعون حتى صاحوا عليه بالتوراة فقتلوه.	Joshua son of Nun worked to try to keep him (Balaam) alive, so that the Master Moses – peace of God upon him – could see him. But he could not avoid the tribe of Simon seeing him. They shouted at him the Torah and killed him.

---

402 For a general discussion of Samaritan biblical interpretation, see: S. Lowy, *The Principles of Samaritan Bible Exegesis* (Studia Post-Biblica; Leiden: Brill, 1977).

فقال يوشع: "من قتله؟ لم فعلت هذا وقد ذممنا له؟" Joshua said: "Who killed him? Why did you do this, since we had already taken him in custody?"

The story continues with the Simonites explaining their action. Ostensibly, the tribe of Simon disobeys Joshua's orders as a sort of over-reaction to the fact that it was their leader that brought the Midianite princess before Moses and the elders at the tent of meeting. Nevertheless, they explain to Joshua that their killing Balaam was both religiously justified, as he is an infidel (*kāfar*), as well as a preventative measure. Balaam is a wizard (*sāḥar*), and would be a danger to the Israelites alive. The Simonites speak respectfully to Joshua throughout, calling him "master" and complimenting his benevolence and broad-mindedness. Joshua accepts their answer and no punishment of the Simonites ensues.

The development of Joshua's character in this short narrative is telling. Joshua begins by simply wanting to capture the enemy and bring him to Moses for judgment. This reflects Joshua's overall view of himself as Moses' understudy. However, once confronted by the decision of the Simonites to kill Balaam on the spot, Joshua decides *on his own* whether their action was justified or not. There is no mention of bringing the Simonites before Moses for judgment. Joshua's taking of responsibility for compliance or non-compliance with his orders reflects his growing comfort with what will soon be his position of authority, Moses' death being immanent.

Chapter 6 picks up again with Moses' death and the transition of authority to Joshua. Although this chapter rewrites Deuteronomy 32–34, a number of colorful details have been added. Between Moses investing Joshua publicly at the beginning of the chapter and his death at the end of the chapter, Moses invites whoever wants to see him one last time to come visit him near the tabernacle. He then offers an incense offering and makes a speech to the people, something that will be consciously paralleled in Joshua's own death scene in ch. 39.

One of the elements of Moses' speech is the future of the tribes, based upon Deut 33, but he also gives them esoteric knowledge about the future apocalypse as well as informing them of the time when he will return. This latter concept seems highly reminiscent of the Elijah and/or Jesus mythology, while the former echoes *Assumptio Mosis*.

As Moses goes up the mountain to die, he is accompanied by Joshua, Elazar, and the elders. In fact, according to *S.J.*, these followers never actually leave Moses' side. Instead, a pillar of fire descends towards evening; when it is gone, so is Moses.

That this account is taken straight out of Josephus' *Antiquities* (4:324 – 326), but with one important change. As in Josephus, it is striking here that no hierarchical differentiation between Joshua and Elazar is made. Following a leader to his death can be seen as a symbolic act of authority transference, as seems to be the case with Elijah-Elisha and Aaron-Elazar. The equality of Joshua and Elazar is a sign that there is some ambiguity as to the transference of authority. This is true in Numbers, true in Josephus, and is made glaringly obvious in *S.J.*

However, unlike in Josephus, the elders also remain with Moses until the very end, whereas Josephus has Moses dismissing the elders earlier on. The fact that Joshua, Elazar, and the elders *all* follow Moses up the mountain, may reflect an interpretation of the latter half of the book of Numbers, specifically 32:38, and 34:17ff, in which it seems that all three are sharing authority. Alternatively, it may simply be an incomplete retelling of the Josephus account, with insufficient attention or concern for detail.

Another sign of loyalty has to do with Joshua's emotional reaction upon Moses' death, an image one can call "the crying Joshua." After Moses' death, Joshua breaks into tears and recites an enormous lament in honor of Moses.[403] It takes God's direct rebuke of Joshua to return him to his senses and begin the process of organizing the army for the invasion. God's command is phrased harshly, and he even accuses Joshua of breaking God's commandment by stalling.

That Joshua breaks down at the thought or experience of Moses' death is a theme found both in *L.A.B.* and *Assumptio Mosis*. As described in the section on *Assumptio Mosis*, Joshua is more of an anti-hero in this work, and his crying borders on panic over his feelings of insufficiency and fears of his inability to successfully lead the Israelites and defeat their enemies. Additionally, Joshua breaks down before Moses actually dies. He cries and complains to Moses himself, almost begging him not to die.

The narrative parallels are much stronger with *L.A.B.* As in *S.J.*, in *L.A.B.* God takes Joshua to task for spending too much time crying and, thereby, stalling the process of his taking authority. There are two major differences between the two accounts, however.

First, in *S.J.*, Joshua recites a long dirge to Moses; *L.A.B.* contains no such hymn. The dirge Joshua writes is structured in two parts. The first part is a series of rhetorical questions aimed at expressing the irreplaceability of Moses. In this sense, it is reminiscent of Joshua's rant in *Assumptio Mosis*, including the emphasis on the miraculous nature of Moses' burial. The second section is made

---

403 The lament takes up most of chapter 7.

up of statements of praise for Moses. The dirge ends with an over-the-top complaint by Joshua, highly reminiscent of his defeatist attitude in *Assumptio Mosis*.

يا سيدنا ومولاى! كيف اكون ويكون قومك بعدك؟! Oh our lord and master! How can I continue and your people continue without you?!

Intend this could be seen as Joshua taking some exaggerated "poetic license," the fact following this dirge comes a scene of excessive weeping that ends only with God scolding Joshua leads the reader to assume that Joshua is, in fact, in danger of paralyzing himself with grief.

The second major difference between *S.J.* and *L.A.B.* In *L.A.B.* the problem of Joshua's fear of continuing without Moses is solved by Joshua's donning Moses' garments and becoming a new man; in *S.J.*, Joshua simply calms himself and moves on, albeit after receiving a scolding by God.

Another connection between *S.J.* and *Assumptio Mosis* appears in chapter 8 – the final section of the introduction. In this chapter, Joshua leads the 30-day morning period for Moses. During this period, "the nations" hear about the death of Moses and decide that it is time to strike Israel. This reaction by the nations is, quite literally, *exactly* what Joshua fears will happen in *Assumptio Mosis*. Additionally, this reaction of the nations will appear in ch. 39 as a reaction to the death of Joshua.

To calm the people's spirits, God promises Joshua and the people that as long as they are loyal to God, God will remain with them, just as he was in the past under Moses' leadership. This response is clearly based on the biblical passages that state this explicitly, such as Deut 31:8, 23 and Josh 1:5, 3:7.

The Conquest Narrative

God's Call to Joshua

With the ninth chapter, *S.J.* begins its rewriting of the biblical book of Joshua. This section opens with a divine call to Joshua which is exceedingly similar to the structure of the revelation in Joshua 1. The revelation has two major parts. The first section promises Joshua a successful conquest and the second exhorts him to keep the Torah. There are three slight differences between *S.J.*'s account and the biblical account which color the speech, however, and by doing so paint the reader's perception of Joshua in a slightly different hue.

First, the standard biblical encouragement of "be brave and strong" is not given. The reader has no reason to think, at this point, that God felt that Joshua might not express these two traits of bravery and strength adequately on his own. Second, instead of saying that no man (איש/*ish*) will stand before Joshua, as it does in the biblical text, this text reads no enemy (عدو/'*adūw*) shall stand before him.[404] The biblical text is ambiguous, and can be interpreted as God promising Joshua that no Israelite would stand against his leadership. However, the Arabic text in *S.J.* does not lend itself to this possibility.

Finally, the ending of God's speech includes strikingly bellicose imagery, concluding with the promise that if Joshua serves God faithfully, he (Joshua) will succeed in treading upon the necks of the enemies – something that actually occurs towards the end of the biblical account of the southern campaign (Josh 10:24) as well as in the parallel account in *S.J.* (ch. 20). These three factors combine to paint a Joshua more sure of himself and ready for battle than the parallel biblical account with its implications of Joshua's lack of self-assurance.

King Joshua and Elazar the Imam

Having received final instruction by God to take command of Israel, the opening scene (ch. 10) of Joshua's kingship is telling.[405]

عمد سماع يوشع ما أوحا الله اليه اجتمع العزر الامام – عم. وهو جالس على كرسى قدسه ويوشع على كرسى ملكه.	After Joshua heard that which God revealed to him, he united with Elazar the imam – may peace be upon him. And he (Elazar) sat upon his holy chair and Joshua sat upon his royal chair (i. e., throne).

The parity between the two characters is emphasized by the description of the chairs. Each one of the leaders has a special chair. This stands out when thinking about Elazar, since although there is a clear expectation that a king sits upon a throne, there is no equally obvious "special chair" for the high priest. More subtly than this implied comparison between the characters is the fact that Joshua unites with Elazar, i.e., he literally goes to Elazar.[405]

---

404 It is worth noting that the Arabic Van Dyke (AVD) Bible translation of Josh 1:5 reads إنْسَان (*insān*) "man", like the Hebrew.

405 The Arabic verb is a reflexive form (with a tav infix) of the root j-m-' – literally Joshua gathers himself.

Once the two leaders are seated on their respective thrones, an assembly is convened with all of the Israelites in attendance. Joshua then delivers a speech that is described in the title of the chapter as renewing the covenant (وتجديده العهد). The speech is highly reminiscent of two different sections of the Hebrew Bible. First, the idea that Joshua makes a new or renewed covenant with the people appears to be based upon Josh 24. Whereas in the Bible, Joshua does this at the end of his career, in *S.J.* he does this at the very beginning.[406] Insofar as the wording of the speech, there is a strong resonance to pieces of Moses' final speeches in Deuteronomy, especially with the covenantal speech of Deut 29.

Casting the speech in this way reinforces the image of Joshua as Moses' successor. It isn't just that Joshua makes a covenant with Israel, as Moses did, but that the very wording and rhetoric of the covenant sounds like that of Moses. Joshua ends the speech by specifically calling on the people to add this "second covenant" (العهد الثني) to that of Moses.

The speech is a resounding success. The people burst into tears and, "casting their souls into his hands" (طارحين ارواحهم بين يديه), they swear to keep the covenant. They promise to listen to and obey whatever they are commanded – a phrase highly reminiscent of the acceptance formula of the covenant in Exod 24:7 (נעשה ונשמע). In referencing whom they will obey, the reader gets a quick schematic look at how the Israelites view their leadership. Moses is the prophet, Joshua the king, and Elazar the imam, and then there are sages; the list is in order of rank.

This ranking, again, underlines the ambiguity of the power relationship between Joshua and Elazar. Joshua is certainly the face of power. He delivers the speech, and the people list him before Elazar. However, Joshua himself seems to express some deference towards Elazar when he "gathers himself unto" Elazar to call this meeting. Other examples of this deference occur periodically throughout *S.J.*

This division of Joshua's leadership persona as publicly greater than Elazar's but privately equal and somewhat deferential may be a reflection of the author's interpretation of God's message in Num 27. In this section, God says that the people should follow Joshua, but that Joshua should consult with Elazar and the *Urim ve-Tummim*. This command, reflected only occasionally in the biblical book of Joshua, seems to be operant on and off in *S.J.* as well.

The speech being a smashing success, Joshua compliments the people, renews the covenant with them, and offers sacrifices on their behalf. This is odd, as one would have expected Elazar to do this. Perhaps, again, there is an

---

406 There is no great final speech at the end of Joshua's life in *S.J.*

attempt to align Joshua with the biblical Moses, who offers the sacrifices himself at the inauguration of the Tent of Meeting in Exodus 29/Leviticus 8, as well as being the sprinkler of the blood in the covenant ceremony in Exodus 24. Following Joshua's performance, Elazar the imam blesses them.

At this point, Joshua is going to command a census; this is not a surprising move considering that the impending invasion of Canaan will require a full organization of the Israelite military. Before Joshua gives this command, there is yet another description of Joshua on his throne seated next to Elazar. Here the parity between them is even clearer, since it states that each sat upon his respective "elevated seat" (مرتبته/*martaba*). With the completion of the census, the leaders with the enrollment numbers appear specifically before Joshua, and he greets them with the blessing that each person will grow to be a thousand people. Again it would appear that from the public's perspective, Joshua was the sole or primary leader, regardless of what occurs behind the scenes.

Joshua the Übermensch

Joshua sends out two spies to bring him back information about the land (ch. 13). However, this is not actually what the spies do. Instead, they dress up as if they had been on a long journey, and pretend to be allies to the Canaanites.[407] They claim that they heard rumors of the overwhelming power of the Israelites and came to investigate, fearing for themselves as well as their comrades the Canaanites. At first, they say, they found the camp of the Israelite army in disarray, with the Israelite god angry at his people. However, when they met the new leader of Israel, their worst nightmares were confirmed.

They tell the Canaanite natives that on their way back to their compatriots, they were stopped by three or four Israelite men and brought back to the Israelite camp.

...فتسلم كل واحد منهم واحد منا واوقفنا بين يدى الملك الجديد, الذى تقلد الملك خلافه عن موسى النبى – عايه افضل السلام.	...and each one of them delivered one of us, taking us with them to the new king, he that rules in the place of the previous king, Moses the prophet – may the greatest peace be upon him.[408]

---

407 This is clearly inspired by the biblical story of the Gibeonites.
408 Obviously this phrase is to be understood as an editorial comment, required for religious reasons of respect to Moses; otherwise, such respect would be a dead giveaway to the Canaanites.

ولقد كان صاحبه رجوم (رووف)[409] لا يوفع طرفة الى
احد – وهذا رجل جبار, حديثه (وكسر)[410] النفوس,
وكلامه يفطر القلوب, وانتهاره يذهل العقول.

فما هو ان وقفنا بين يديه حتى عرف اسمانا وانسابنا
وبلادنا ومتى خرجنا والمواضع الذى نزلناها فصدق فى
كل ما ذكره لنا.

Now, his associate[411] was merciful and kind, not lifting his gaze towards anybody; but this man was a colossus.[412] His speech shatters [people's] spirits, and his words cleave hearts, and his reprimand stunned the intelligent.

No sooner had we stood before him when he announced our names and our lineage and our country, as well as when we began our journey and the spots where we went – and he was correct about everything he said to us.

Although this image of Joshua as both a giant and a wizard is clearly meant to scare Israel's opponents, and is not meant by the author of *S.J.* as a serious image of Joshua, it is telling for what it attempts to portray about Joshua to the Canaanites. Joshua wishes to be seen both as physically frightening and as possessing inexplicable powers, like being able to know other people's secrets. Considering the earlier mention in *S.J.* of the enemies of Israel feeling empowered by the death of Moses to organize an attack on Israel, this picture of Joshua seems designed specifically to undo this newfound confidence.[413]

The speech they put in Joshua's mouth is designed to cause panic and perhaps a general retreat and abandonment of the land by the natives. The spies claim that Joshua informs them point blank that they must abandon the land, because he will soon be crossing over to take it. The crossing, Joshua warns them will be miraculous, as will the conquest, with fortresses collapsing after a seven-fold circuit around each is made.[414]

---

409 I assume this is supposed to say something like "ورءوف", which is what my translation reflects above. Otherwise, I have no explanation for this term.

410 I do not understand the opening "waw" and assume the form should be يكسر (3rd per. sg. m. impf.) analogous to the form of the other two verbs in this section of the verse.

411 i.e. Elazar

412 The reader will be informed later in chapter 29 that Joshua is, in fact, 8 feet tall.

413 Equally interesting is the incredibly benign image of Elazar thrown in to the description of the spies. It is not clear what strategic benefit the spies imagine they will get from painting the picture of a kind holy man sharing the helm with Joshua. Perhaps they believe this will make the Canaanites respect Israel more? Conversely, it may just be that the author would have considered it offensive to paint the holy imam in such a pugnacious light, even as part of a ruse.

414 It is unclear to the reader how the spies know this is going to happen, since, in the narrative itself, Joshua has not yet announced this to the people, nor, as far as the reader knows, has God announced it to Joshua. This seems to be an example of an author getting a little "carried away" since he knows what is coming, as would any reader familiar with either the biblical account or Josephus.

The spies are unquestionably painting a frightening picture here and proceed to back up the claim with two points. First, the spies end with a return
to their description of this "new king" by telling the Canaanites exactly who
he is and what he has accomplished thus far (ch. 13).

وعرفنا ان اسمه يوشع بن نون, وانه الهازم للعملق[415]	And we know that his name is Joshua son of
والقاتل لسيحون والمهلك لعوج والمتلف لملوك مدين	Nun, and that he put to flight the Amalekites,
وماب.	and is the killer of Sihon, and the destroyer of Og, and the annihilator of the kings of Midian and Moab.

The denouement of introducing the new king, apparently, is the revelation of his
name. This name should cause fear in the hearts of the natives, at least in the
estimation of the spies. This reputation grows out of Joshua's previous military
experience. He is apparently known, or believed to be, not only the general
who defeated Amalek but also the general behind the campaigns against
Sihon and Og as well as the kings of Midian and Moab (no battle with Moab
is recorded in the Torah and the reference is probably an embellishment of
the Midianite war). This description fits well into the general outline of Joshua's
career presented in *S.J.*; Joshua begins as a military leader and continues in this
vein for the rest of his career.

The spies end their speech with a concomitant description of the Israelite
army; a group of people, as they put it, worthy of such a monster for a leader.
"Woe to us" they moan, and "woe to you" – their real message. The Israelites
have no mercy at all. They leave no survivors and accept no peace treaties.
They consider all gentiles to be infidels and treat them as such. The only suggestion the spies can offer is that everyone take their loved ones by the hand and
run.

This picture of a monstrous Joshua commanding an army of fanatical cut-
throats has a particular poignancy, for this is exactly the rhetoric one would expect from groups who read the book of Joshua with disdain. A Samaritan author
putting this very claim in the mouth of two Israelite "counter-intelligence officers" reframes this moral critique of Joshua's behavior as an ironic statement.
In *S.J.*, this work, this controversial claim functions almost satirically, a useful
piece of rhetoric painting the historiographical account of Joshua's conquest
in a terrible way in order to inspire fear in the enemy. Ostensibly, the careful
read is giggling along with the spies.

---

415 I am not sure why the double *lamed*.

This Joshua imagery, i.e., Joshua as giant and cruel wizard, is unique as far as I know, at least in works sympathetic to the character.

Joshua Crosses the Jordan

Joshua's deportment during *S.J.*'s crossing of the Jordan account (chs. 14 – 15) can only be described as confident and decisive. Having heard the spies' account, he orders the people to be ready to cross. The account is largely parallel to the biblical story in chapters 1 and 3 – 4 with a handful of exceptions. The main difference in Joshua's deportment is the use of the "pep-talk" motif.

In the biblical text, the "be strong and brave" (חזק ואמץ) refrain is used in speeches to Joshua, first by God and then by the army of the Transjordanian tribes. The use of the refrain in the biblical text implies that Joshua is the one who is worried and needs to be strong and brave, and that this was noticed both by God and the army. However, in *S.J.*, Joshua begins his speech with a pep talk reminiscent of the one Moses gives the people (and Joshua) in Deuteronomy 31:6, 8. Joshua tells the people not to fear or worry (لا تخافوا و لا تجزعوا), parallel to the biblical "אַל תִּירְאוּ וְאַל תַּעֲרְצוּ."

Joshua tells the people about the upcoming miracle, emphasizing the importance of the ark and the very special quality of the tablets, which, he claims, are made from divine substance. He assures them that the ark standing in the middle will be sufficient to hold back the water and that the people will cross over perfectly dry.

Having established the overall parameters of the miracle, Joshua begins to command specifics. The people need to remain 2,000 cubits away from the ark. The twelve chiefs each need to take a stone from underneath the priests and write their names upon them as a sign for the future generations. At this point the Levites sing out in praise of God. Conspicuously absent from this priest and Levite focused project is Elazar the imam.

During the actual crossing, Joshua does not take a particularly active role. Instead, the cloud lifts itself up from the camp and the priests follow it towards the Jordan, with the people trailing behind as commanded. Upon reaching the Jordan, the Levites shout praises to God, and the people join them. The miracle is then performed and the crossing goes as planned. The only mention of Joshua in this chapter is actually in one detail that contains a change from the biblical text. According to *S.J.*, Joshua himself, along with the tribal leaders, takes a stone from underneath the feet of the priests. It is not clear to me why this detail was added. Perhaps it was important to the author to remind the reader that Israel was ruled not by twelve chiefs but by one king.

The ending of this account paints a dramatic picture. As in the biblical text, the reader is told that the nations were in a panic after hearing of this miracle. However, *S.J.* adds that during the miracle, the waters of the Jordan and the wind that held the waters at bayv destroyed many settlements along the banks, adding a practical basis for the fears of the natives, since they would now have already begun to suffer at the hands of the Israelite god.

The crossing having been successfully accomplished, Joshua is returned to center stage. In a scene highly reminiscent of Exodus 15, Joshua accompanied by the people sing the Song of the Sea, Moses' prayer, adding extra praises of God at the end. This scene is more than just an implicit comparison of Joshua to Moses, or even just a construction of Joshua in Moses' image. *S.J.* makes the point explicitly after recording the additions to the hymn that the Israelites sung (ch. 16).

في هذا اليوم عظم يوشع بن نون عند بنى اسراييل	On that day, Joshua son of Nun became great in
وتخوفوا منه مثل خوفهم من موسى النبى—عم—وعلموا ان	the view of the children of Israel, and they
الله معهم.	feared him the way they feared the prophet
	Moses – may peace be upon him – and they
	understood that God was with them.

With the exception of the final phrase, this is an exact translation of Josh 4:14. The difference is in the placement of the verse. In the biblical text, this statement comes immediately after the completion of the crossing, before the mention of the fear of the nations, and without an accompanying song. The line implies something more potent in *S.J.*, since the miracle has already frightened the nations and Joshua has just sang the song of Moses. In *S.J.*, the fear of the Israelites is being compared to the fear of the nations, and Joshua takes on the mantle of Moses in more ways than one.

The statement of the people's awe of Joshua leads into the erection of the twelve stones and the founding of Gilgal. Inexplicably, no mention is made of the thirteenth stone taken by Joshua himself.[416] At this point, the fear of the gentiles is referenced with even more rhetorical flourish. The kings of Syria (ملوك الشام) hear about the crossing, and they fall into such a panic that they put on funeral garb, and some of them literally drop dead. With that, God tells Joshua that his reputation has been made internationally, and all fear him. Joshua names the place Gilgal – which remains its name "until this very day." By

---

416 On the other hand, the significant problems in the biblical account with regard to the tripling of the stone ceremony are smoothed over in *S.J.* – as would be expected from the Rewritten Bible-genre.

ending the crossing account on this note, with the panic of the Syrian kings and the naming of Gilgal, Joshua takes his position at the center of Israel's image among the nations and its history on the land.

As in the biblical account, the end of the wilderness period is rounded out at this point. Upon arriving at Jericho on the 14th day of the first month, the people keep the Passover and make their unleavened bread from the local crops.[417] With this, the manna stops falling and the wilderness period is over. Although not explicitly stated, this solidifies the relationship between Joshua and Moses, since the wilderness period begins with Moses' leadership and ends with Joshua's.

Jericho – the Conquest Begins

The outline of the Jericho story and Joshua's participation in it parallels that of the biblical account in most ways. The account begins with Joshua encountering a "man" holding a sword. When Joshua challenges the man to identify himself as friend or foe, the man does neither but identifies himself as an angel. Upon hearing this, Joshua falls prostrate on the ground and asks what the angel commands. The angel tells him to remove his shoes, as he is standing upon holy ground.

Despite the overall similarity in the outlines of the story, there are a number of differences relevant to Joshua's image and his behavior. First, unlike in the biblical text, the angel always addresses Joshua with a vocative reference. Upon first calling out to him, the angel calls him by his name, Joshua. This has the effect both of personalizing the correspondence and, more importantly, of casting it in the image of other famous revelation stories, like those of Abraham, Jacob, or Moses, whose names were called as well.

When commanding him to remove his shoes, the angel actually calls him king. This term of respect softens the apparent disrespect of telling Joshua to remove his shoes. This increase in respect for the leader can also be seen in the fact that between Joshua's falling prostrate and asking for the angel's command, Joshua stands up of his own accord. In truth, this could have been added by *S.J.* simply to solve an interpretive problem, i.e., Joshua is described as "standing" on holy ground but he is actually lying prostrate on the ground. Nevertheless,

---

417 In the biblical account, the Passover is celebrated in Gilgal. I do not know why *S.J.* felt the need to adjust the timeline. As I see no connection between this issue and the image of Joshua, it will not be dealt with in this analysis.

whatever its motivation, the change has the effect of making Joshua appear as having more confidence and pluck.

The angel then informs Joshua how the city will be conquered.[418] There will be a week of circuits around the city walls and then a final blowing of the trumpets that will miraculously bring the walls "tumbling down."[419] Joshua explains to the people what they need to do, and it is done. The absence of Elazar from any part of this story is again conspicuous.

During Joshua's explanation of what to do, he adds the rule of the ban, warning the people to leave no one but Rahab and her family alive and not to take anything from the city. Upon the city's destruction, Joshua invokes his famous curse upon anyone who would dare rebuild the city. *S.J.* describes Joshua making this curse "at the top of his voice" (باعلا صوته).

The story ends with yet another statement about the fear of Joshua falling upon the nations of the earth (ch. 17).

> ...Due to this act, the name of Joshua reached ... وبلغ اسم يوشع بفعله هذا الى اقطار الارض.
> [all] the regions of the earth.

One can see clearly here the trend to magnify the effect of the miracles upon Joshua's reputation. First, *S.J.* reported that the local nations were scared. After the splitting of the Jordan, even the kings of Syria were scared. Now, after the miraculous collapse of Jericho, the entire earth is frightened of Joshua.

---

418 This is another example of *S.J.*'s smoothing of the narrative bumps in the Bible. Since the command to take of his shoes and the explanation of the conquest strategy are separated in biblical Joshua by verse 6:1, and the former is commanded by an angel and the latter by YHWH, it is unclear if this is supposed to be understood as a continuation of the conversation between the same two characters or as a new scene. *S.J.* fixes this by making it clear that this was all one conversation between Joshua and the angel.

419 *S.J.* does change a number of details, such as switching ram's horns for trumpets, and shrinking the number of key priests from seven to two. Particularly interesting is the command for the people to recite praises of God the entire time and the prohibition for them to speak about anything else. In the biblical text they are simply to remain silent until the time for blowing the ram's horns and screaming arrives. This underlines *S.J.*'s love of psalms, as does the fact that the people are commanded in *S.J.* not just to scream but to say "God is almighty in wars; God is his name" (الله جبار فى الحروب, الله اسمه) three times as their cry – a quote from the Song of the Sea (Exod 15:3). This is a favorite quote of *S.J.*'s and will come up again in other scenes.

Violation of the Ban

Despite Joshua's explicit command that no one take any object from Jericho, the ban is violated by a man from the tribe of Judah. This act angers God, although what form this anger takes and how Joshua finds out about it is not described.[420] In order to find the culprit, Joshua commands representatives from the various tribes to come before Elazar the imam while he (Elazar) is wearing the breastplate (ch. 18). The jewel with the name Judah upon it blackens when the name of this tribe is called. The culprit is found by successively dividing up the guilty tribe of Judah into families and subunits until Zarah is identified.[421]

Having found the culprit, Joshua takes over the lead role. His questioning of the man is significantly harsher than the parallel account in the Bible. He tells the criminal to look up into the heavens towards the king of kings, reminding him that God was all-knowing and hence, there would be little point in trying to hide his crimes. Joshua points out that all of Israel is suffering due to his sin. The man accepts the rebuke, apologizes for his sin, and confesses all. King Joshua sends men to investigate the claim and it is demonstrated to be true. This done, Joshua sends the man, along with his entire family and possessions, to be burned in the valley. Stones are then piled upon the grave and Joshua names the place Emeq Akhor (the valley of dirtiness) in remembrance of the man and his deeds. With this, God's trust is regained.

Unlike in certain retellings and commentaries, there is no attempt in *S.J.* to retell the story in such a way that Joshua does not actually execute the man's children. This was, apparently, not particularly troubling in the eyes of the author of *S.J.* or his readers. On the other hand, the story of Ai and Joshua's many problematic behaviors in the story are skipped over entirely.

The Expurgation of the Huta (Ai) Story – Comparison with Kitab al-Tarikh

The lack of an Ai account may be the most conspicuous of all plot changes in this section of *S.J.* It is nearly impossible to believe that this was not done purposefully, since the story of the violation of the ban is intrinsically linked to this account, both in the biblical text as well as in the Arabic *Kitab al-Tarikh*. In fact, by removing the Ai story, the *S.J.* leaves a gaping hole, since the reader does not know in what way God has shown his displeasure, and how Joshua and Elazar

---

420 This problem, i.e. the lack of an Ai story, will be dealt with in the next subsection.
421 In the biblical account, it is Achan son of Zabdi from the family of Zarah.

know about it. In the biblical account, Joshua and the Israelites deduce that God is angry from Israel's loss to the army of Ai during its first assault on the city.

Considering *S.J.*'s strong interest in promoting Joshua's image, it is possible that the Ai account was left out due to the way it tarnishes Joshua's record. As discussed in other chapters, there are at least two critiques of Joshua in the Ai story. First, Joshua sends a reduced-in-size army to Ai, which implies overconfidence. Second, after losing the battle, Joshua falls into an extreme panic, requiring God's intervention to snap out of it and handle the situation. On top of this, the story records a loss on the part of the Israelite army and a number of Israelite deaths, two very unpleasant spots on Joshua's record.

Interestingly enough, despite the fact that Abu 'l-Fatḥ uses *S.J.* as his main source for his Joshua narrative, he includes an Ai story (ch.3; in his text, the city is called Huta). We do not know if he had a version of *S.J.* with the story, or whether he used the biblical text or some third text as his basis.[422] However, one can see clearly the "offending passages" in his work. For example, the *Kitab al-Tarikh* (*K.T.*) records that upon Israel's attack on Huta: "36 men came out from Huta, and these drove off the sons of Israel and killed all of them except for a very small number who were left."[423] Upon hearing this, Joshua "fell prostrate upon his face, imploring Almighty God and humbling himself – esteeming himself as nothing."

One can see from the above what might be some reasons to leave out the Ai account. Nevertheless, something of Joshua's image is lost by leaving out the account, specifically his strategic acumen upon his second attack on the city, and his masterful handling of the complicated battle strategy. Again, we can see something of the power of Joshua's imagery in the *K.T.* version of the city's capture: "Joshua and his company thereupon turned round, shrieked at them, and went on killing them until there wasn't one of them left. They captured the king of Huta and brought him before Joshua." Nevertheless, as will be seen in a later section, *S.J.* makes up for this to a certain degree by including some strategy in a subsequent battle.

---

422 It is very improbable that he was using a version of *S.J.*, since the names of the perpetrators are different (in *K.T.* it is Aiden son of Zabdi) and the order of the stories in *K.T.* follow the MT not *S.J.* here (the next story in *S.J.* is the Gibeonite pact, the next story in *K.T.* and MT is the building of the altar in Shechem.) Also, the manuscript of *S.J.* is very old, so we probably have the same version 'l-Fatḥ had for this section.

423 This translation is from Paul Stenhouse's edition; I do not have access to an Arabic text of this work.

King Joshua and the Gibeonite Covenant

The outline of the Gibeonite covenant account in *S.J.* (ch. 19) is almost identical to that of the biblical account. The main difference is that the biblical account seems to involve two different "leadership bodies" in the negotiation. The biblical text has "איש ישראל" (some sort of Israelite governing body) conducting part of the negotiations and has the chiefs of the group (נשיאי העדה) taking an oath.

In *S.J.*, not only do the Gibeonites come directly to Joshua (as they do in the biblical account as well), but it is Joshua, once he has accepted their story, who *tells* certain of his people (من قومه) to make a pact with them. This makes the dividing line between the king and his subjects clearer, as the other governing force has disappeared. Furthermore, it will be Joshua who makes the covenant and takes the oath of peace (وعهادهم وقسموا لهم), not the chieftains as in the biblical account.

Finally, there is a hint of criticism in the biblical text, aimed perhaps at Joshua or at the Israelite leadership, or both. Josh 9:14 states that the people accepted the story of the Gibeonites and did not consult with YHWH. This detail or criticism is skipped over entirely in *S.J.* Leaving out this criticism fits in well with the overall project of *S.J.*, which leaves out anything negative about Joshua that might impinge his positive image.

Finally, it is worth noting that *S.J.* here is taking the exact opposite approach to the one Josephus took in solving the Gibeonite problem (*Ant.* 5:49–57). In Josephus' account of the Gibeonite episode, Joshua is not even mentioned and the entire affair is said to have been conducted by Elazar and the elders. Ironically, both Josephus and *S.J.* may have the same goal: to protect Joshua's reputation.

The Defense of Gibeon

With the fall of Jericho, the nations decide that they have no choice but to attack Israel, starting with their newfound allies, the Gibeonites. Again, the outline of *S.J.*'s version of this account is similar to that of the biblical account. As in the biblical account, Joshua is given a revelation from God saying that he will win the battle, although *S.J.* adds the requirement to annihilate the enemy. Also, as in the biblical account, Joshua surprises the enemy by attacking them at Gibeon after an all-night march from Gilgal.[424] This all-night march will come up again as a criticism against Joshua from his enemy Shaubak in a later chapter.

Oddly, the miracle of the sun standing still is mentioned but downplayed, with no poem and no statement about how amazing it was for God to listen to the command of a mortal, as in the biblical text. It would appear that even though this phrase is useful in promoting the image of Joshua, it may have been considered problematic in its lowering of the deity by the author of *S.J.* In addition, although mention is made of unspecified miraculous intervention by God and his angels, no mention is made of the hailstones described in the biblical text.[425]

The battle itself is described tersely, with no mention of the southern campaign, which, in *S.J.*, will be discussed in the next chapter. The main focus of this section, insofar as Joshua is concerned, is the fulfillment of the promise God made to him in chapter 9. There, God promised Joshua that he would tread upon the necks of his enemies. In this story, Joshua fulfills this promise literally, by removing the captured kings from the cave in Makkedah, and ordering his army chiefs to stand upon their necks while he delivers a pep talk. Although this action is described in nearly identical terms in the biblical text, the main difference lies in the fact that in *S.J.*, this act fulfills God's oracle to Joshua given earlier in the book, while in the biblical text it is an act of spontaneous belligerence.

The battle ends with an account of the execution of the kings. The bodies of the kings are left hanging until sunset and then thrown into a cave with the wood used to hang them. Joshua has boulders placed before the mouth of the cave, so that people will know the story for all time.[426] With that, the people rejoice and assemble together for the campaign of conquest.

---

424 *S.J.* adds here that the soldiers were given a "slogan" (شعار), the same as they used during the siege of Jericho: "God is almighty in wars; God is his name" (الله جبار فى الحروب, الله اسمه), i. e., Exod 15:3.

425 Again *S.J.* has done the opposite of Josephus, who skips the sun standing still but includes the hailstones. The "other half" of these miracles will be described in the account of the next battle (ch. 21). As will be discussed, *S.J.* splits what is one campaign in the biblical text into two.

426 One small difference is that the verb used in the Arabic (وصلبهم) means "crucify" as opposed to the Hebrew, which means "hang" (ויתלם). I do not know if this is significant since, clearly, crucifixion was not the manner of execution but purely the manner of display.

The Battle for Canaan – Joshua the Military Strategist

Having won the first round, Joshua prepares the army for the main assault. It is in this account that the reader is introduced to Joshua as a military tactician. Although the story reads like a continuation of the previous battle, the date seems to belie this. Joshua begins the campaign in the eighth month, which is "the time of the marching of this army" (وقت مسير هذا العسكر). This unusual description is highly reminiscent of ancient Near Eastern chronicles of a king's campaigns; this is, perhaps, the impression the author of *S.J.* is attempting to make, since it reinforces the image of Joshua as king.[427]

The king divides the army into four groups, three of which he sends on different routes, with his group as a fourth front. This idea of dividing up the army and surprising the enemy is a common theme in biblical war stories.[428] Most importantly, this kind of surprise tactic is the basis for Joshua's conquest of Ai in the biblical text. One is tempted to speculate that the author of *S.J.*, having jettisoned the Ai story for the reasons suggested above, wants to keep the image of Joshua as the shrewd tactician. Hence, he incorporates this aspect of the Ai story into his account of the conquest of Canaan, modifying it, of course, to fit the story into which it is being incorporated.

Joshua approaches the enemy with his small band and attacks them. The enemy is caught off-guard and while they fight Joshua's small band, they are fighting from all sides by the remaining three sets of troops and roundly defeated. Although the battle was well planned, the reader is rightly impressed not only by the strategy but by the bravery of Joshua in leading the first assault. This feint was clearly the most dangerous aspect of the battle, and Joshua's choosing to lead it himself demonstrates his lack of fear as well as trust in both himself and God.

God's place in this battle emerges very clearly in several ways. First, the army seems to have a new slogan: "God is our Lord who fights for us" (الله ربنا المحارب عنا!).[429] Most importantly, the Israelites are granted a whole slew of miracles. Retreating enemies are burned up from the sky. Horses

---

427 I am not saying that the author of *S.J.* had access to Ancient Near Eastern battle accounts, only that, perhaps, elements of that genre remained attractive even after any memory of these works had long since vanished.

428 Abimelech does it when he attacks Shechem (Judg 9:43), the Philistines do it when they attack Saul (1 Sam 13:17), the Israelites do it when attacking the city of Gib'ah (Judg 20:37) and, of course, Joshua does it during the attack on Ai (Josh 8).

429 Like the previous slogan, this one is reminiscent of Moses' words before crossing the Sea of Reeds (Exod 14:14) as well as the response of the frightened Egyptian army (Exod 14:25).

(الخيل) are confused by a "specter" (الخيال) and run wild to escape, killing the riders.[430] Finally the day is prolonged so the Israelites can finish off their enemies.

Other than the specter miracle, the other two miracles are more than a little reminiscent of the previous battle and, more to the point, the description of this battle in the biblical text. Fire, although not appearing in the biblical account, is paired with hail stones in Exodus 9:24, a feature of the battle for Canaan in Joshua 10:11. More importantly, the idea that the day lasted longer is intimately connected with the miracle of stopping the sun (this is how the day lasted longer), which is explicitly mentioned in the previous chapter of *S.J.* The artificial splitting of the miracle into two halves leaves both inexplicable, and seems to leave the two battle accounts with some artificial loose ends. Again this may be a product of *S.J.*'s attempt to carve an extra battle scene into its version of Joshua 10 to make up for the loss of the Ai story.

The Homing Pigeon

Upon completion of the battle, Joshua does something rather unusual. He writes a letter to Elazar explaining the success and detailing the miracles. He then attaches this letter to the leg of a bird (طير) and sends it to Elazar. The relative positions of Joshua and Elazar are difficult to characterize. Elazar is not a factor in the crossing of the Jordon, the siege of Jericho, or in the battles of Gibeon and Canaan. Additionally, he is not even a factor in the negotiations with the Gibeonites. His only appearance since sitting down on his throne was in the story of the violation of the ban, in which the services of his divinatory vestments are needed.

Here, after winning the battle, Joshua feels an urgent need to report to Elazar. It is unclear what the reader is supposed to make of this. Is Joshua simply exuberant upon winning the battle? Does he need Elazar to sing a hymn of praise immediately, lest God change his mind? Or does he feel the need to report on progress to Elazar? These questions are difficult to answer, which is why the exact position of Elazar in relation to Joshua remains so difficult to pin down.

---

430 The horse/specter account may be a midrashic play on words, which sound similar in Arabic.

Canaanite Campaign

Having essentially won the war, Joshua commences a "mopping up" operation, in which he will assert the dominance of Israel and its army over all of Canaan. Although this operation parallels the description of the southern campaign in the biblical book, its character is very different in *S.J.* Here, it is not a number of southern city-states being conquered, but the cities of the seven nations, i.e., the entirety of Canaan. This Joshua accomplishes in a matter of months such that he is able to return from war after only a year of fighting.[431]

The Purification Ritual

With the war finally over, Joshua and his army are in need of purification. Instead of some pedestrian solution being devised, another miracle occurs. Water begins to flow from the "blessed mountain" (*Har-Gerizim*), and in its purifying waters dunk Joshua and other soldiers. Having done this, Elazar is invited to offer sacrifices on behalf of the people, and the Israelites feast. Elazar's involvement here is reminiscent of Aaron's in Lev 9, in which the latter performs the final sacrifices that consecrate the Tabernacle. This is, of course, what one would expect of a high priest.

Dividing the Land – Joshua as Administrator

Having conquered the land, Joshua now needs to divide it between the nine and a half Cisjordanian tribes (ch. 22). To accomplish this fairly and accurately, he enlists the services of engineers (المهندسة) and surveyors (مساح) and other such experts. The idea that Joshua hired professionals appears to be taken from Josephus (*Ant.* 5:76), who writes that Joshua hired knowledgeable surveyors (γεωμετρίας ἐπιστήμονας) to oversee the mapping and division of the land. However, the overall framing of the section in *S.J.* remains very different from that of Josephus or the biblical book.

The division of the land in the biblical book of Joshua follows upon God's statement to Joshua that much of the land remains to be conquered. This ar-

---

431 This great success and lightening campaign obviates the need for a description of a northern campaign such as is found in Joshua 11. However, as will be seen later, an alternative and highly modified version of this campaign appears in a later section of *S.J.*

rangement is difficult to reconcile with the first half of the biblical book, which says that Joshua conquered all the land. Josephus solves this dissonance by claiming that Joshua had not conquered all, and that the work was simply too much for one man to do in one lifetime. Hence, Joshua divides up all the territory, even the unconquered territory, and the appropriate Israelites will eventually settle it when the territory is conquered. *S.J.* solves the problem in the opposite way, stating explicitly that Joshua conquered all the land. This division will be followed immediately by the occupation, since no land is left unconquered by Joshua in the opening campaign.

Also emphasized in this account is that all of Joshua's commands are in line with what Moses had previously commanded regarding the land. Joshua quotes and explains the former leader's geographical pronouncements to the Israelites, including the future borders of Israel and the need for 48 Levitical cities and six refuge cities. Finally, as in Josephus, and unlike in the biblical account, Elazar is conspicuously absent from this process. This seems odd since division of land is exactly the sort of "lot-throwing" divinatory exercise over which one would expect Elazar to preside.

Joshua and Elazar Dismiss the Transjordanian Army

Although Elazar is conspicuously absent from the land division account, he is conspicuously present at the dismissal of the army.[432] I call his presence "conspicuous" since Elazar does not appear in this story either in Josephus or in the biblical account, and he serves no obvious narrative purpose. However, the explanation for Elazar's appearance may not be a narrative one; rather, it may be exegetical. According to Num 32:28, the Transjordanian tribes are supposed to submit to the authority of Joshua *and Elazar* and return to their homes only once these two leaders have determined that they have fulfilled Moses' requirements. Perhaps the author of *S.J.* simply wants to emphasize that the Transjordanian tribes fulfilled this requirement properly.

However one understands Elazar's role in this story, the effect is to remind the reader of the Joshua and Elazar partnership. The tribes are told by the king to line up before Elazar and the other leaders. "They" – probably Joshua

---

[432] In this case, *S.J.* has followed the biblical order of Joshua dismissing the two and a half tribes after surveying the land, as opposed to Josephus order, in which this is done before the survey.

and Elazar and perhaps the leaders as well – thank the tribes for their work and deliver a short complimentary speech in their honor.

At this point, the work of the two leaders is divided. Joshua gives the leadership of the Transjordanian tribes gifts (robes and the like), checks the rosters to see if any soldiers are missing (none are), and holds a covenant-renewing feast in which the two sides that swear they will defend each other without hesitation. Elazar then offers sacrifices on their behalf.

Joshua and Nabih – The King and his Vassal

The account of the dismissal of the Transjordanian tribes ends with the introduction of a very important new character (ch. 23). At the end of Num 32,[433] three Manassite leaders are mentioned who conquer areas of land in the northern Transjordan/Golan region. Machir conquers the Gilad region, Yair conquers the area of *Havot*, calling it Havot Yair, and Novah conquers a city named Kenat, which he renames Nobah after himself. The city is referred to once more in the Bible as Nobah (Judg 8:11). As opposed to Yair and Machir, Nobah will not be mentioned again in Deuteronomy 3:14–15, where the conquest of these areas is repeated.

Nevertheless, and quite unexpectedly, Nabih (the Arabic form of Nobah) is given the ultimate honor in *S.J.* Joshua chooses him of all people to be the sovereign king of the Transjordan, although he will remain a vassal to the king of the Cisjordan, i.e., Joshua. The crowning of Nabih is, in fact, doubly surprising. Not only is it odd that such an obscure figure was chosen with virtually no introduction, but the very fact that there would be one leader of the Transjordanian tribes and that this leader would be a king seems to come out of the blue. Since when is Israel – Cisjordan and Transjordan – not one country with one leader?

But there is no escaping the fact that in *S.J.*, Nabih is a king. He gets a royal robe (خلعة الملك) and a crown (تاجا), one of Joshua's chosen horses, and a herald that proclaims before him that he (Nabih) is the king of the two and a half tribes.[434] The Transjordanians are warned that they must obey Nabih in all things and whoever does not obey him forfeits his life. Additionally, if there is anything too difficult for Nabih to decide, he should feel free to approach the high priest Elazar. In this sense, Nabih is like Joshua and not like a subject of Joshua, since

---

433 The text here is basically the same in MT and SP.
434 The possible influence of Esther ch. 6 is hard to overlook; Mordechai rides on the king's horse with a herald running before him calling out that this is what is done to people the king wishes to honor.

he gets direct access to the high priest who lives in Cisjordan and does not need to first consult with the king of the Cisjordan.[435]

Joshua continues the process of appointing Nabih with an act that strongly parallels the appointment of Joshua earlier on in the book (ch. 23).

ثم سلم اليه نسخة كتاب سيدنا موسى بن عمران النبى – عم – وتقدم اليه بقراته ليل ونهار .	Thereupon he (Joshua) handed him (Nabih) a copy of the Book of our master Moses son of Amram – may peace be upon him – and directed him to read it night and day.
وعرفه ان فيه اشارة عجيبة مظهرة لبقا الحياة فى العجل والاجل, وان فى قراته حفظ من الارواح والاعين السو[ء] والمناحس والسحر وكفاية العدو .	And he informed him that in it are wondrous signs supporting the preservation of life now and in the future, and how reading it protects one from spirits, and the evil eye, and ominous events, and witchcraft, and the skill of enemies.

Joshua gives Nabih a Torah and tells him to study it day and night. This parallels God's message to Joshua upon his taking the mantle from Moses (ch. 9). Additionally, Joshua explains to Nabih about the esoteric knowledge one can glean from the Torah, something Moses explained to Joshua earlier in *S.J.* (ch. 2). This message becomes important later on in *S.J.*'s narrative, since Nabih becomes a greater warrior than even Joshua and ends up rescuing his mentor and former teacher.

One very peculiar detail of this appointment is the statement that Joshua gives Nabih twelve tribes (اثنا عشر سبطا). Since Nabih remains, throughout the work, the king of the Transjordan, it would seem that this reference means to say that Joshua redistributed the Transjordan into twelve polities. If this interpretation is correct, this act would be an example of heavy micromanagement on the part of the overlord king. This management, or micromanagement, continues with Joshua selecting administrators to work with Nabih and giving him access to 2,000 Levites to live in the Transjordanian Levitical cities, collect their tithes, and perform necessary ritual rites on behalf of the Transjordanians.

With the conclusion of Joshua's establishment of the Transjordanian administration, Joshua and Nabih climb upon their horses and ride off together to the sound of trumpets and the unfurling of banners. With that, the Transjordanians take their leave of Cisjordan.

---

435 The phrase about Elazar here is difficult to parse. I am following Kirchheim's rendering of this passage, as I find Crane's interpretation (followed by Anderson and Giles) hard to understand.

The image of Joshua in this interchange is that of a supportive and extremely active mentor. Joshua sets up Nabih's government and grants the vassal king very public and conspicuous honors. Whether this is intended to establish loyalty or not, Nabih will have little reason in the future to be disloyal to Joshua, a fact that will be clearly demonstrated in the Shaubak account.

The Return of the Surveyors

Upon the return of the surveyors, Joshua and the 12 chiefs involve themselves in dividing up the land into ten parcels equivalent in value.[436] The issue of who exactly is in charge concerns the author. This is because of the ambiguity in Num 34:17–29. In this section, Moses commands Joshua, Elazar and ten representatives from the Cisjordanian tribes to divide up the land. How is authority to be determined in this group? *S.J.* solves this problem by devising a clear division of responsibility.

Elazar's job will be to take the ten portions and determine by lot which tribe gets which portion. Joshua and the twelve representatives will determine the size and nature of each portion. Although the representatives have input, *S.J.* tells the reader that Moses restricted them from arguing with Joshua or putting up any substantial opposition to his decisions. They are, apparently, an advisory group, but Joshua has the final say.

After Elazar divides up the plots to the various tribes, the tribal leaders, in turn, divide the land up into family plots for each of their tribal constituencies. When this is done, Joshua enjoins the leaders to be in constant touch with Elazar the imam, informing him of what occurs in their areas. It is unclear why Joshua gives them this command. Doesn't he, as king, need to be informed of what occurs in the various tribal allotments in his kingdom? There again seems to be some confusion regarding who will be "in charge" on a day-to-day basis.

Mount Gerizim as Joshua's and Caleb's Allotment

Joshua himself is allotted the choicest of plots. He is given the "favored mountain" (الجبل المفضل), meaning Mount Gerizim.[437] This stands out for two reasons.

---

436 This issue of value equivalence and how one determines this is a key aspect of Josephus telling of this story.
437 This is the Arabic term; *S.J.* sometimes uses the Aramaic term טור בריך, blessed mountain, although spelled out in Arabic (طور بريك).

First, in the biblical text, Joshua is awarded the much more obscure town of Timnat Heres. Second, there is no comparable tradition in the Jewish tradition granting Joshua Jerusalem. *S.J.* further writes that Joshua built a synagogue on the top of Mount Gerizim, and kept the Tabernacle in it. After his death, the site would be taken over by priests and Levites – Joshua being the only non-Levite ever to control the holy area. With this, Joshua becomes not only Israel's first king, but the founder and builder of its holiest site.

Another very odd feature of Joshua's land grant is that his companion Caleb is also assigned "the favored mountain," and the two comrades live together the rest of their lives in Shechem. This detail is most peculiar. First, Caleb is granted Hebron in the biblical text, not Shechem. Of course, Joshua isn't granted Shechem in the biblical text either, so the divergence from biblical tradition is, at least, consistent. Odder is how two different men from two different tribes can be granted one territory. After all, Caleb is the leader of the tribe of Judah, a tribe whose possession is far south of Shechem. (Joshua's tribe of Ephraim is also a bit south of Shechem, which is located in the Manasseh region.)

I would venture to guess that making Caleb an aide-de-camp to Joshua breaks this hero's ties with Judah in all but name. This may have been desirable since Judah is a tribe probably associated in the mind of the Samaritan community with Jews. It would be worthwhile for Samaritan tradition to sever the bonds between Jews and the hero Caleb and place him firmly in the camp and the land of the Samaritans.[438] This may also explain the very odd locution about Caleb in this chapter, which describes him as "leader of the whole tribe" (مقدم على جماعة السبط) without the name of any tribe being mentioned.[439]

Perhaps the most striking claim in this section is that in addition to his holdings on Mount Gerizim, Joshua goes a little north and builds a fortress called Samaria (شمرون). According to this, Joshua is not only the first king of Israel and the establisher of the holy site of Gerizim, but even the founder of the future capital city from which the Samaritans derive their name. Joshua's record of accomplishments in *S.J.* is truly astounding.

Joshua's Daily Routine

At the end of chapter 24, *S.J.* describes Joshua's daily routine as king.

---

438 This is similar to how the Bible severs the ties between the Samaritans and the Northern Tribes, by including the famous story about Cuthians and lions in 2 Kings 17.
439 Although to be fair, his tribe will be mentioned in chapter 39, when his nephew Abil is chosen as the next king.

وكان يجتمع مع العزر فى كل جمعة يوما واحد, ومع اهل And he would get together with Elazar one day
الرياضة يوما لمذاكرتهم, ومع الروسا يوما لتفقد احوالهم, every week, and with people of training one
وفى شغله هو يوما والنظر فى اموره, وثلث ايام لا يفارق day, in order to deliberate with them, and
كتاب الله ليل ونهر. with the chiefs one day, in order to inspect
their strength, and one day for his own job
and consideration of his affairs, and for three
days he would not leave the book of God
night and day.

وهذه كانت سيرته فى ملكه ان لم يخرج الى ملحمة ولا And this was his procedure as king, if war did
يتوجه الى حال منهم. not break out against them, and when not deal-
ing with their affairs.

The presentation of Joshua in this section attempts to strike a perfect balance. Joshua is primarily a Torah scholar, spending three days each week studying Torah day and night. He is also cognizant of the importance of Elazar the priest, visiting him weekly. He takes care of his own needs and business, albeit minimally. He is also a smart administrator, spending one day a week checking with the leaders about what is occurring and one day a week consulting with learned advisors. Finally, as any good leader, Joshua is flexible with his time, such that if war or some necessity were to occur, he would abandon his routine and take command. A better king would be hard to imagine.

Peace

Chapter 25 ends the first part of the book and was possibly the original ending to an older form of *S.J.* In this chapter, a situation of total peace is described, one that lasts for twenty years. Joshua and his army rest throughout this period and form cordial relationships with their neighbors. All of Israel keeps in touch daily, and Joshua hears only good things throughout this period.

Originally, this chapter probably served to round out Joshua's rule with an idyllic final portrait. However, in the current version of *S.J.*, this forms merely a peaceful interlude leading up to the greatest battle Joshua would fight – the battle against Shaubak, the Persian sorcerer.

The Battle with Shaubak

Before analyzing the portrayal of Joshua in the Saubak account, it is worth pointing to some outstanding features of this story. In one sense, the story seems to come out of nowhere; in fact, as I argued previously, it seems to be a later supplement. At this point in the story, Joshua and Israel are at peace with their neighbors and have utterly vanquished the local opposition, which is why the introduction of the Shaubak story is so jarring.

Additionally, the identity of the enemies in this account is surprising. Shaubak is the son of Ḥamam[440] the king of Persia, who was killed by Joshua in battle.[441] The reader can be forgiven for an initial question, of "since when did Joshua conquer Persia?"

Another surprising character is the son of Japheth the giant. Japheth is the son of Noah and would have lived more than a thousand years before Joshua. Nevertheless, considering the fact that rabbinic midrash makes Og into an antediluvian figure, it is possible that conventional wisdom in the past was that giants can live for an extremely long time. Since the biblical book of Joshua explicitly has Joshua killing giants, this character may be less surprising than he would at first appear to be.

Although the war with Shaubak does seem to come out of nowhere, if one compares the storyline in *S.J.* to that in biblical Joshua, there is one major battle (other than Ai) missing from *S.J.*'s story, the battle with the north. It is possible that this "lost battle" was reworked or combined with an independent story about Nabih and Shaubak to create the Joshua, Nabih, and Shaubak account in *S.J.* There are some elements of the battle that suggest this, especially the place of the battle, which occurs in the north.

The Threat of Battle – Shaubak's Image of Joshua

Shaubak and his allies, seeking revenge for Joshua's conquest and slaughter of fellow kings (including Shaubak's own father), decide to send a spy to get a sense of Joshua's forces. They do this by sending the man officially as a messenger, as messengers are protected. The message they send to Joshua is designed to frighten him and the Israelites. The threatening rhetoric is clear from the way the letter is addressed (ch. 27).

---

440 Ḥamam may possibly be meant to parallel biblical Haman, although the spelling is very different (Arabic = حمام; Hebrew = המן). If true, there would be an extreme mixing of stories and time periods, since according to the biblical chronology the conquest and the Purim story are separated by a thousand years. Also, in the biblical story, the hero is Mordechai, not Joshua, and Haman is not the king of Persia but the king's vizier.
441 It is possible that Shaubak may be loosely based on Shobak, the general of King Hadadezer of Aram defeated by David in 2 Sam 10:15 – 18.

ابتدا الكتاب: من جملعة الجبابرة, المتضافرة, المعروفة, المشهورة, المويدة, المنصورة, الشديدة الباس, العصيمة اللباس, المقدمين عاى ساير الناس الى يوشع بن نون والى قومه الراعى منا اليك السلام.

The letter began: From the assembly of giants, the confederated, the well-known, the re-nowned, victorious, the triumphant, coura-geous, *protected of dress* (=wearing armor?), foremost of humans – to Joshua son of Nun, shepherd of his people, peace from us to you.

The self-description of Shaubak and his followers is meant to frighten the ad-dressee of the letter and his people. The enemies describe themselves as giants, well-known, dressed for battle and more powerful than other humans. Joshua is not called king here, but by his full name and with the epithet "shepherd of his people." This epithet does not bring to mind a threatening military conqueror, but an elderly congenial statesman.

Joshua suffers in comparison to the army of triumphant and courageous giants. Additionally, part of the rhetoric might be an implication that Joshua should not oppose these enemies, who are all-powerful, if he is really interested in what is "best for his flock." Finally, it is difficult to know if the greeting of peace is meant ironically or is just a meaningless convention like the modern "dear" or "sincerely."[442] Either way, the irony is palpable, since the letter will begin by addressing Joshua as "the murdering wolf" (الذيب القاتول).

The first part of the letter is the most relevant to this study (ch. 27).

عرفلنا, الذيب القاتول, ما فعلته فى مدن اصحابنا وانك اهلكت جماعة من وجوههم بالقتل وانزلتهم الى قرار الاسفل...

We know, oh murdering wolf, what you have done in the cities of our comrades, and you wiped out the league of their prominent [lead-ers] with murder, and sent them to the bottom-most depths...

ولم تحتشم من شيخ كبير ولم ترحم طفل ضغير ولم تسمع لهم حرمة ولم تترك لصلاحك مكان ولا بقيت للخير اوان.

And you were not diffident to very elderly, and you had no pity on the young infant, and you did not pay attention to their inviolability, and you left no place for those requesting peace of you. And you left no time to decide [on their best options].

The difficult irony of this claim against Joshua is that it is true. The policy of the Israelite war was to annihilate the Canaanite inhabitants, which they did. Fur-thermore, Joshua, as a shrewd tactician, did use surprise attacks and all-night marches, making it difficult for the enemy to organize themselves for defense. Peace was not really an option.

---

442 The letter ends with a declaration of peace as well, but certainly is not meant in earnest.

Nevertheless, one must not fall into the trap of anachronism. The author of *S. J.* presents Joshua's behavior as having been commanded by God. One cannot fault Joshua for carrying out God's commands successfully; this is what he was supposed to do. That said, *S.J.* does give us a fascinating glimpse of Joshua from the perspective of the enemy: Joshua the cruel barbarian.

Having taunted Joshua with his savagery, Shaubak's letter explains why things are about to change. Joshua's success in the previous campaign was due to disharmony among the Canaanites, which led to their being picked off one by one. Now, however, Shaubak is putting together an organized campaign. They have numerous troops, including giants and wizards, and implements of war inherited from Noah himself.[443]

Shaubak warns Joshua that in thirty days his army will show up before the Blessed Mountain (جبل البركة)[444] and destroy the Israelites and their holy place. He taunts Joshua by pointing out that, unlike Joshua, Shaubak is not afraid to announce the campaign beforehand and promises to come in the daytime, not at night as Joshua did. This is meant as a sign of Shaubak's supreme confidence; he believes that nothing can defeat them.

Joshua Receives the Letter

As part of the messenger's job was to get an impression of Joshua and the Israelites, *S.J.* carefully describes the scene in which Joshua first receives the letter from the messenger. The reader is told that the day the messenger arrived was the day before Pentecost.[445] The messenger hands Joshua the letter while the Israelite leader is sitting on his throne (وهو جالس على كرسى ملكه).

Joshua at first ignores the messenger since the day before Pentecost is a busy day for judging. Joshua is described as sitting all that day judging cases. This image has a number of rhetorical functions. First, it reminds the reader of Moses in Exodus 18. Joshua, like Moses, is the chief judge of the people, the *sine qua non* of the wise leader. Second, from the messenger's perspective, it puts Joshua into the center of the picture. He is truly in charge of Israel in more ways than one. Finally, the nature of the cases should put a chill into the messenger (ch. 28).

---

443 The most interesting piece of magic is the weapon of Japheth's son. He has a thunderbolt of steel that kills either 1000 or 500 men at every shot, depending on his aim.

444 Yet a third term for this place, parallel to the Aramaic term used previously. I do not know why three separate synonymous terms are used by *S.J.* for Mount Gerizim.

445 Literally "the Day of Reading, which is the Festival of Weeks" (يوم المقرى وهو حج السوابيع).

منهم من قد وجب عليه القتل, ومنهم من قد وجب عليه الحريق, ومنهم من قد وجب عليه الرجم, ومنهم من قد وجب عليه الحبس, لان الاحكام الكبار كانت ترتفع اليه فى الاعياد.

Upon some of them he imposed death, and upon some of them he imposed burning, upon some of them he imposed stoning and upon some of them he imposed prison, for difficult cases were brought up to him during the festival.

Clearly, Joshua is a strict judge. The image here is of a tough but just leader. He puts to death his own when they deserve it as well. The justice of Joshua's decisions is certified in a somewhat enigmatic passage.

فمضى الحكم فيها بنور الله وامر وليه.

And the justice of [his decisions] was supported by a fire from God and the instruction of his saint.

Again, the position of Elazar here is unclear. Joshua makes the decisions, but it seems that Elazar functions to confirm the divine approval of Joshua's work. Whether this was meant to have been done on case-by-case basis or an overall basis is unclear.

S.J.'s presentation of this scene focuses on Joshua's self-control. He doesn't even look at the messenger until he is done judging. Furthermore, after he gets the letter, he doesn't read it until he gets home, presumably so that no one can see his initial emotional reaction and ask what the letter said before he is ready to tell anyone. Finally, Joshua keeps the information to himself for all of Pentecost.

ولم يعلم به احد الى ان جاز عيده وكانوا الناس فارحين بعيدهم وهو مشغول القلب.

And not one person learned of it until the festival passed. And the people were able to enjoy their festival but he was apprehensive in his heart.

The power of Joshua's personality will be shown through how he handles a situation that he clearly feels is difficult and dangerous.

Locking the messenger away where he will not overhear deliberations, Joshua calls a meeting, inviting all his generals and his assembly. He reads them the letter and comments honestly that despite his sixty years as a warrior, he has never heard the like. The people are naturally disturbed, as was he when he first read it, but they respond with confidence. They have never heard the like either, but they trust Joshua and God and are ready to fight Shaubak's army if that is what Joshua thinks is best.

Joshua then adds a finishing touch. He has already written a response, assuming that this would be the reaction of the people and he reads this response to them. In a final nudge towards confident modesty, he says that this is only a tentative response that he has drafted, but if his trusted advisors disagree, he will scrap it. This was probably meant as a gesture, but it is a nice touch.

Joshua's Response

Joshua's letter to Shaubak (ch. 29) is a masterpiece of bellicose rhetoric. He more than gives back in kind to Shaubak's original threatening letter. Joshua's response has three major foci. His first major point is to emphasize the greatness of the Israelite God in comparison to the speciousness of Shaubak's idols and false gods. In praise of the Israelite God, Joshua uses frightening imagery such as "destroyer of infidels" (المتلف الكافرين) and "annihilator of tyrants" (المهلك للمتجبرين). In comparison with a God like this, Joshua states, the enemies with their false gods have no chance.

To further emphasize the power of his God, Joshua makes use of the genre of historical retelling, listing the many miracles that God wrought on behalf of Israel and the mighty enemies that have been vanquished by him. This makes up the lion's share of the response.

More important for the purposes of this chapter is the imagery of Joshua one can derive from this letter. Joshua's pious confidence in God is clear. His self-assured and strident tone, however, is not just a natural consequence of this piety, but is strategic, aimed at winning over the Israelite listeners and frightening the enemy. This is clear since *S.J.* already informed the reader that Joshua was actually afraid in his heart.

Joshua's skill as a political strategist can be seen even more clearly by how he turns the threat back on the enemy. The enemy stated that they will come and attack Joshua in his holy city in thirty days. Joshua informs Shaubak that he will not have the chance to do so, because Joshua's army will, in fact, be attacking Shaubak in seven days. Joshua even names the place – el-Qaimun.[446] This is the name of one of the cities in Shaubak's alliance.

The importance of Joshua stating that he will attack this city is two-fold. First, it demonstrates extreme confidence which will buttress his troops. Second, it is very strategic. It puts the battle ground on the enemy's territory and off of Joshua's, and it gives the enemy less time to prepare than they desired.

---

446 It is unclear where this place is supposed to be. Anderson and Giles suggest Yokneam.

The most intriguing piece of the letter for the purposes of outlining Joshua's image is the ending. After reminding Shaubak that, with God's help, Joshua stopped the sun and will do so again in the upcoming battle, Joshua concludes the letter with a physical description of himself (ch. 29).

ليس افتخر اننى جبار ولا تلميد جبار ولا ولد جبار.	I do not boast to be a giant, or the disciple of a giant, or the child of a giant.[447]
انا افتخر انتى تلميد كليم الله النسوتى الاهوتى وولد خليل الله اساس الانبيا[ء] وفرع الازكيا[ء]. انا افتخر بربوات القدس السايرة حول عسكرى	I boast that I am a disciple of the Speaker of God (Moses), physically and spiritually, and the child of the Friend of God (Abraham), foundation of the prophets and the pure branch. I boast in the myriads of the holy who march with my army.
ليس انا جبار بل رب الجبابرة معى وطولى من الارض خمس اذرع ملكى.	I am no giant, but the master of giants is with me, and my height from the ground is five royal cubits.
ليس بلباس الدروع ايضا والجواش والخوذ بل لباس غلايل الاسمانجون والارجوان والقرمز الملون وتاج الملك على راسى واسم ربى مكتوب على التاج, راكب مهر ابيض جله من الارجوان وسرجه من الذهب الخالص.	There is no armor in my dress, likewise for mail and helmets; rather my dress is a gown colored of azure and purple and scarlet, and a royal crown is upon my head, and the name of my Lord is written upon the crown; riding a white colt, whose cloth is purple and whose saddle is of pure gold.
هذا اوصافى وفخرتى!	These are my distinguishing marks and my boasts.

Joshua attempts to counter the description of the enemy in Shaubak's letter with a description of himself. Unlike the son of Japheth and some others of Shaubak's confederation, Joshua is not a giant and has no giants on his side or in his lineage. Who he does have in his lineage are the people of God, and specifically God's two favorite people, Moses and Abraham.

Joshua could have stopped with this religious message, a message he began with and that he will return to in the final lines of the letter. However, he continues on to physically describe himself. He is not a giant, but he is about eight and a half feet tall. He wears no armor, but he does dress as a king, with a multicolored royal robe (including the royal purple), and even his foal wears purple – on top of his saddle of pure gold that is. In other words, Joshua is rich, powerful, fearless, supported by God and God's people, and pretty big. These features would be well-known to Shaubak (at least after his messenger re-

---

447 The tone here is reminiscent of Amos 7:14: "I am not a prophet or the son of a prophet."

turns) and to the Israelites hearing the letter, but underline Joshua's self-confidence and his belief in his own power and God's support.

The letter has an electric effect on the Israelite audience (ch. 30). They fall to the ground in praise of God and tell Joshua that they are consoled. They are ready to go to the ends of the earth for Joshua and fight the enemy with faith that God will give them triumph. They begin to gather the army and within the hour amass 300,000 skilled troops. When the Israelite leaders begin to worry that this is not enough, Joshua calms them by saying that if God can defeat Shaubak with 600,000 he can do so with 300,000 as well.

The extremely positive reaction of the people and Joshua's handling of the situation demonstrates the full development of this seasoned and powerful leader. Despite the fact that the reader is aware that Joshua has some personal apprehensions, the people are presented with a confident, eloquent, and powerful charismatic figure. He is decisive but not authoritarian, modest but not self-effacing, and even his confidence is tinged with some realism and much faith. In the story in which Joshua will be supremely tested, he shows himself to be supremely ready for it.

The Reaction of the Messenger and of Shaubak and his People

Although Joshua had been careful to keep the messenger out of ear- or eye-shot during the sensitive discussions, the messenger/spy had already begun to make observations from the moment of his arrival in Joshua's court. Beginning in chapter 28, *S.J.* describes the messenger's perception of the court.

وشاهد الرسول من كثرة العسكر وحسنه واحوال الملك	And the messenger observed the size of the
وضبطه وامور البرئ وقدرته, ونزول عمود النار	army, and its proper state, and the authority
وعظمته ونظر ولى الله وهوله ما لم يشاهد مثله ولم يسمع	of the king and his discipline, and the power
بمثله فى الدهور السالقة.	of the Creator and his decree, and the descend-
	ing pillar of fire and its exaltedness, and the
	peerless saint of God, and he had never seen
	the like of him, and had never heard the like
	in ages past.

The messenger notices a number of things that make an impression on him. Two of them are in the realm of the natural – the size and state of the army and the authority and discipline of its commander, Joshua. "Perhaps Shaubak was underestimating the opposing force?" the spy thinks to himself. This potential fear is strengthened by a number of otherworldly matters the messenger notes.

He notes the power of Joshua's God and the pillar of fire that descends on Joshua's behalf. Additionally, Elazar makes a great impression on him; the messenger believes that he has never heard of such a person in all of history.

Although *S.J.* does not explain what about Elazar stood out to the messenger, it seems that the impression was that Elazar is otherworldly. It cannot be that he was physically intimidating since the messenger is coming from an army of giants and Joshua himself was almost nine feet tall. The difference between the Elazar imagery and the Joshua imagery was already made clear in an earlier chapter, albeit with an opposite valence. In the spy account, the spies attempt to scare the natives with stories of Joshua's size and ferocity, while almost dismissing Elazar as a nonthreatening, benevolent figure. The messenger of Shaubak has the opposite feeling; the benevolent priest is so otherworldly that he frightens the messenger more than the colossus, Joshua. As Shaubak made clear, the opposing army has no shortage of colossi.

After Joshua points out the size of the army to him (ch. 30) – 300,000 strong – noting that he gathered them in only one hour. Then Joshua reads the response to the messenger. Noting again the discipline and size of the army and having heard the strident tone of the response, the messenger is crushed and returns to his people with downcast eyes and a heavy heart (ch. 31). When he arrives in el-Qaimun and sees the army of his people assembled, he begins to cry.

During the rant of the messenger, the overwhelming success of Joshua's psychological warfare tactics becomes evident. The messenger blubbers about how he could not possibly describe Joshua and the Israelites sufficiently to make clear how serious the problem Shaubak and his army have gotten themselves into is. The messenger proceeds to read the letter, including a section that the reader has not yet seen: the address.[448]

Joshua's address to Shaubak attempts a parallel to what Shaubak wrote to him (ch. 32).

الى جماعة الملاغين, العاصيين, الفاسقين, الكافرين, اهل البهتان, والعصيان, والنجس, والخذلان الانجاس الارجاس, الذى قد دنا هلاكهم وقرب تلافهم.	To the assembly of nonsense speakers, the insubordinate, the evil-doers, the heretics, the people of slander and insurrection, the unclean and forsaken, the filthiest of the filthy, those whose destruction has already been stipulated and whose annihilation is near.

---

448 Holding the address back until this point is a piece of literary mastery that makes the account of the messenger that much more powerful.

Joshua's rhetoric differs from Shaubak in that it is full of contempt. Shaubak accuses Joshua of being bloodthirsty and a coward, due to his strategy of sneak attacks. Joshua's response to Shaubak also employs name-calling, referring to Shaubak as foolish and heretical, even dirty. However, the sting is that Joshua is totally contemptuous of Shaubak and his "giants," claiming loudly that he (Joshua) has no doubt that Shaubak's army waits on the eve of its own destruction. Unsurprisingly, Joshua complements the disdainful characterization of Shaubak's army with a positive description of his own, mostly emphasizing his people's reliance on God, as he does in the body of the letter.

Just the address itself has a devastating effect on Shaubak and his people.

فبكوا عند قراة هذا العنوان حتى سالت عيونهم الدما[ع].449	The enemy cried at the reading of this address until their eyes shed tears.

The letter itself has an even stronger effect.

ثم فتحوا لاكتاب فقراه رجل حنون الصوت, فاخذوا يلطمون وجوههم ينوجوا على نفوسهم فى كل فضل حتى فرغوا من قراته.	Then they opened the letter and a man read it with a tender voice, and they started striking their faces whispering to themselves with every section, until they finished the reading.
فما تم الكتاب حتى انحلت [اوساطهم]450 وتنكست روسهم وانكسرت قلوبهم واستهلت دموعهم وذهلت عقولهم ولم يقدروا على النهوض من مواضعهم ولا القرار فيه قد اخذهم الخبال والوبال.	And the letter was not even finished when their middles shrunk, and their heads bent, and their hearts shattered, and their tears poured, and their minds were stupefied; and they were unable to rise from their places, nor to rest in them, since confusion and curse had overtaken them.
ثم صرخوا باكيين وقالوا: "الويل لنا ولاولادنا! اهلكنا نفوسنا وهتكنا حريمنا [انبهنا]451 اللبوة النايمة ثورنا الاسد الرابض خلينا الفيل المربوط هيجنا الثور المشكول."	Then they cried out weeping and said: "Woe to us and to our children! We have destroyed ourselves and we have disgraced our women. We have wakened the sleeping lioness! We have stirred the crouching lion! We have released the bound elephant! We have agitated the fettered bull!"

---

449 The emendation is that of Juynboll and is (apparently) followed by Kirchheim; the manuscript has الدما (blood) – this is the text preferred by Crane and followed by Anderson and Giles.

450 The emendation is that of Juynboll; the manuscript has اوصاطهم.

451 The emendation is that of Juynboll; the manuscript has انبهن نا.

و[خطلت]⁴⁵² السنتهم فى افواههم مختبطة جدا معتقلة
لايفهم ما يقولوا ولا ما يقال لهم. قد انطرشوا وانبكوا
وحاروا وتحيروا ونفشوا رووسهم وخرقوا ثيابهم.

And their tongues spoke nonsense in their mouths, its struggling of no avail as if imprisoned. They could not understand what they were saying or what was said to them. Already they became deaf, and were dumbfounded, they were confused and they were helpless, and [the hair on] their heads bristled, and they tore their clothes.

Joshua has now proven himself to be the absolute master of rhetoric. What was once a bustling and confident army has been reduced to blithering idiocy and bawling lamentation. Instead of thinking about their giants and magical weaponry, they compare Joshua and/or the Israelite army to a lioness, a lion, an elephant, and a bull.

Luckily (or unluckily) for Shaubak's army, the chief sorcerer (شيخ من اهل السحر) and Shaubak's sorceress-mother, show up to calm their spirits. They tell the army to pull themselves together, that they are giving up before the fight has even taken place, a sure way to turn a possible loss into a definite loss.⁴⁵³ Instead, they call over the messenger and ask for his report. The reader can't help but smile at this command, since *S.J.* has already described some of the messenger's impressions of Joshua and the army.

Having been called over to report, the messenger speaks as predicted. He begins to describe Joshua and the army and gets carried away. He predicts the doom of Shaubak's army and states that no magic can fight Israel. This latter statement seems to be based on *S.J.*'s interpretation of Balaam's prophecy (Num 23:23) "for there is no sorcery in Jacob." Perhaps inspired by this, the messenger compares the impending fate of the army to that of Balaam.⁴⁵⁴ Most important for our purose, the messenger describes Joshua to the listeners (ch. 32).

فاحضروا الرسول فاخذ يصف الملك والهيبة التي حملها
منه...

And they called over the messenger, and he began to describe the king and the prestige conveyed by him...

---

452 The emendation is that of Juynboll; the manuscript has حصلت.

453 Ironically, it will be Shaubak's mother that collapses in fear at the sight of Nabih and his army.

454 Interestingly enough, in *S.J.*, as described above, Joshua actually attempts to save Balaam and capture him alive to bring to Moses, but his troops (the Simonites) kill Balaam anyway. Like Balaam, Shaubak will not be killed by Joshua but by Joshua's vassal, Nabih.

انه امر جليل ليس بدون ولا قليل... He is a commander not without majesty and not insignificant...[455]

The panic and warning have little emotional effect on the sorcerers, including Shaubak's mother.[456] Instead, they begin to plan how to defeat Joshua by making him "bewildered" (تحييره) and causing him to break off his attack. They, divine, correctly in this case, that magic can impact Joshua negatively, despite the messenger's claim to the contrary.

Joshua Parts from Elazar (Ch. 33)

The scene before the battle shows the parting of Joshua and Elazar. The scene only adds to the complexity already described with regard to the relationship of these two characters and their relative powers.

لما اراد يوشع الملك المسير اجتمع مع ولى الله العزر الامام–عم. When Joshua the king wanted to depart, he met with the Saint of God, Elazar the Imam – may peace be upon him.

ثم قال له: "اخرج ادعوا لقومك وباركهم واذا سرنا فعاود ولا تزل قايما مبتهلا بين يدى ربك الى ان تسمع باحبارنا." Then, he said to him: "Go out and summon your people and bless them. And then we will depart. Keep doing this and do not stop standing in supplication between the hands of your Lord unless you hear our tidings."

On the one hand, Joshua is clearly in power. It is Joshua who decides when the army will march and when Elazar will bless the people. Furthermore, Joshua, in effect, commands Elazar to continue with his supplications of God until such time as he (Elazar) hears that the battle has been determined one way or the other. Elazar's response is simply to do what Joshua commands him.

On the other hand, Elazar is clearly a revered person. As usual, Joshua goes to meet him, Elazar is not "summoned." Additionally, from the fact that Joshua requires Elazar to bless the people and to consistently beseech God, it is clear that Joshua believes Elazar has a unique relationship to God, one of more signif-

---

455 This is a difficult phrase to parse; Juynboll translates: "Dux nimirum ille ilustrius non est contemnendus, nec parvi aestimandus!" Crane (as well as Anderson and Giles) follows suit, "For verily he is a magnificent commander, he is not to be held as contemptible or insignificant." I admit that I am unsure why they translate this way.

456 This character may have been meant to resemble Sisra's mother from the Song of Deborah.

icance than even Joshua's. The holiness of this character is underscored by how he is introduced – the Saint of God – and the inclusion of the honorific "may his memory be blessed." The remainder of this short chapter consists of ritual performances by Elazar and Phineas, underlining the special nature of the priests and their position, and quoting biblical verses and injunctions to illustrate this.

One final point worth noting; from Joshua's request for constant supplication, it is clear that he remains uncertain about the outcome of the battle and is still nervous. Joshua has shared this feeling with no one up until this point; Elazar is the only person with whom Joshua shares it. Moreover, the image of Elazar standing in supplication before God throughout the battle evokes the behavior of Moses during the battle with the Amalekites (Exod 17:11–12), Joshua's first battle when he was a young man.

Joshua Trapped by Wizardry (Ch. 34)

Considering the excellence of Joshua's rhetoric and military preparation, the fear it inspires in the enemy, and the faith he demonstrates in God – what occurs at the opening of the campaign is a complete shock. Joshua and the entire army of 300,000 strong are captured by the magical artifices of the guild of sorcerers.

Most of chapter 34 is dedicated to attempting to explain why this was allowed to occur. *S.J.* is clear that God wanted this to happen, that it was all part of the divine plan. Some of the reasons are practical (to avoid a retreat and make the giants over-confident) and some are theological, intended to heighten the miraculous effect of the win. One reason in particular stands out.

وتمت حيلة السحرة فيهم لتمام امر الله—تعالى—من ارتفاع ذكر نبيح ملك [السبطين]⁴⁵⁷ ونصف الذى حلف الاردن وما تمم من هذا الفعل شى الا للافتخار بذكر نبيح واشهار اسمه.	And the matter of the sorcerers was fulfilled with regard to them to fulfill the word of God – may he be exalted – in order to raise the reputation of Nabih, king of the two and half tribes who are across the Jordan. None of what was done or fulfilled occured except to make excellent the reputation of Nabih and to make his name public.

The reader may be forgiven if it is not obvious why it is necessary to make Nabih's name great, especially at the expense of Joshua. One possible explanation for this may derive from a line later in the chapter.

---

457 The emendation is that of Juynboll; the manuscript has الصبطين.

هذا الحرب اخر حرب شاهده يوشع الملك اذا كان قد قرب This war was the last war Joshua the king saw,
وفاته. since his end was already close.

One could argue that God did not want the enemies giving Joshua all the credit, especially since it was almost time for him to die. However, the weakness of this explanation is that Nabih will not be Joshua's successor; Nabih will remain as king of the Transjordan. Joshua's successor will be a man named Abil, Caleb's nephew.

I would venture to guess that no synchronic explanation will be satisfactory for explaining the importance of Nabih here. Rather, the likeliest explanation is that an older and independent Nabih vs. Shaubak story has been incorporated into the Joshua cycle, and that it was necessary to remove Joshua as an active participant in order to tell the Nabih story properly.

Joshua Entreats Nabih for Help (Chs. 35 – 36)

Having been trapped by the sorcerers, Joshua is scared but does not panic. He has an idea of how he can be saved (ch. 35).

لما شاهد يوشع ما صار اليه بقى فى حيرة عظيمة ومخافة شديدة, When Joshua saw what was designed upon him, he remained in a great confusion and intense fear.

واخذ يتمنى على ربه حمام يحط عليه من حمام نبيح ابن[458] عمه. And he began to desire of his Lord to set down on him one of the doves of Nabih his cousin.

فلم يفرغ من تمنية حتى حطت الحمامة فى حجرة, فحمد الله – عز وجل. And he had barely finished wishing when a dove descended into his cell, and he praised God – powerful and mighty.

ثم شاهدها وتيقن بالفرج. Then he looked at it and was certain of deliverance.

The use of bird-communication was mentioned previously, when Joshua sends word to Elazar the Imam of the victory of the Israelites in battle (ch. 21). Here Joshua is desperate and needs to find Nabih, but he requires God's help. Apparently Joshua either did not bring any of his own homing pigeons or, more likely, he specifically needs one of Nabih's; otherwise the dove would go to the wrong

---

458 The emendation is that of Juynboll; the manuscript has بن.

place. Again, Joshua does not imagine that Elazar could put together an army with the remaining 300,000 men and rescue him, although he believes that Nabih can rescue him, despite his smaller forces. God heeds Joshua's prayer and sends the appropriate messenger-dove.

The opening of Joshua's letter strikes a rather pathetic tone, very different from his confident letter to Shaubak (ch. 36).

كاتبتك][459 يا [ابن]460 عمى حفظك الله ورعاك وانا كايب القلب ضعيف القوة باكى العين صغير النفس مشرف على الهلاك وثلث ماية الف رجل معى.	I write to you, oh cousin – may God preserve you and protect you – pained of heart, languid in strength, weepy of eye, humble of spirit, on the brink of destruction, and three hundred thousand men with me.

Joshua informs Nabih about the sorcerers and their successful trap of seven walls surrounding the Israelite army. He describes the joy in the enemy camp and the despair in the Israelite camp. Joshua guesses – correctly – that this is all part of God's plan and that part of this plan is for Nabih to demonstrate his own greatness. He then tells Nabih, in a very strident tone, to hurry as fast as he can to the battlefield. This is again done with rather poetic imagery (ch. 36).

فانهض لوقتك ولا تنيم, وان كنت نايم انتبه, وان كنت منتبه فاجلس, وان كنت جالس فقوم, وان كنت قايم فامشى وان كنت ماشى فاجرى...	And get up right now, do not sleep! And if you are sleeping – awake, and if you are awake – sit up, and if you are sitting – stand, and if you are standing – walk, and if you are walking – hurry![461]...
فلا يلحقك فتور ولا قرار ولا تضجيع ولا توقف واسبق الرياح الهابة...	And let not overtake you listlessness or sedentariness. Do not slumber, and do not hesitate, and precede the blowing winds...

Joshua may have begun his letter with pathos and he may be in a weak position, but he is ever the commander and inspiring orator. Nevertheless, even with this inspiring tone, the image of Joshua as trapped and requesting to be saved— and, as Ed Noort points out, by the tribes of the Transjordan no less—represents an unparalleled and unique contribution to Joshua imagery.[462]

---

459 The emendation is that of Juynboll; the manuscript has كاتبت.
460 The emendation is that of Juynboll; the manuscript has بن.
461 Anderson-Giles only translate an abridged version of this list, I am not sure why; perhaps they felt the phrasing to be awkward and repetitive, or perhaps it was simply an oversight.
462 Noort sums up the significance of this story nicely:

Nabih

Although the battle of Nabih and Shaubak is not particularly relevant to the concerns of this chapter, the physical description of Nabih and how this relates to the physical description of Joshua is telling (ch. 37).

فلم يشهر نبيح وهو جالس على كرسى حكمه, مشدود
الوسط عليه لباس عخضر وعمامة خضرى وهو فى نظر
احكام حتى طرحت الحمامة الورقة فى حجرة ففتحها
وقراها, وتغرغرت عيناه بالدموع وصاح صيحة عظيمة
اضطرب المجلس لها...

And Nabih was unaware,[463] and he was sitting on his judgment seat, wrapped about his waist in a green robe and a green turban, and he was handling judicial matters when the dove threw the paper into the room, and he opened it and read it. And his eyes were bathed in tears, and he cried out a great cry and his court became unsettled...

Like Joshua, Nabih is sitting in judgment when the message arrives. Unlike Joshua, he is not described as sitting on a throne, but on a "judgment seat." Also, he does not wear purple, but green. *S.J.*'s description of Nabih impresses the reader with his importance, but still gives the impression of someone lower than Joshua. Also, unlike Joshua, who takes the whole day before he even looks at the message, Nabih reads the message immediately and reacts publicly, frightening his people. This is not a criticism of Nabih, as he was supposed to react immediately. It is rather a sign that Nabih has someone who outranks him that can send him messages that require immediate attention.

————

Es ist diese Geschichte, die teils mit Ablehnung, teils mit Argwohn und teils mit unaufgebbarer Verwandtschaft annotiert worden ist, die der samaritanischen Darstellung, die Josua als einen Geretteten durch das Eingreifen der ostjordanischen Stämme porträtiert, eine besondere Stellung einräumt.

It is this story, which has been glossed with some disapproval, some suspicion, but with some affinity towards it as "unrelinquishable," that gives the Samaritan image of Joshua— portrayed as having been rescued by the intervention of the Transjordanian tribes—a special place (Noort, "Reißende Wolf," 173).

The fact that this imagery really does not jibe (not "jive") well with the rest of the book supports the above suggestion that the Shaubak and Nabih story was artificially grafted onto the Joshua account at some later point.

463 This phrase is not translated either by Crane or Anderson-Giles and it is unclear why; it is translated by Juynboll and Kirchheim.

Nabih gathers an impressive army, colorfully described by *S.J.*, and begins his march. As part of the description of the army, *S.J.* adds one more physical description of Nabih (ch. 37).

وخرج نبيح راكب مهر منمر مشهر يجرى مع الرياح
وبسكره خلفه وهو يقول: "النار النار! لا هدو ولا قرار!"

And Nabih went out riding a well-known spotted colt that ran like the wind, and his army was behind him and he called out: "Fire! Fire! Do not be tranquil and do not be sedentary!"

As was done for Joshua, Nabih's mount is described. Joshua's mount is white and wears purple with a golden saddle. Nabih's is spotted like a leopard, and very fast. When compared, the different presentations of their steeds may hint to youth and vigor for Nabih but status and power for Joshua. Additionally, Nabih is pictured in full compliance with Joshua's request not to rest but to hurry.

The battle of Nabih and Shaubak does not have real relevance to Joshua's image. In short, with Nabih's approach, Shaubak's mother panics and Shaubak kills her. Shaubak then challenges Nabih to a duel and loses. At this point, God finally communicates to Joshua how to get out of the trap (something the reader already knows). The priests are to blow two trumpets, which they do and the walls collapse.

If the collapse of the walls by trumpet blast is reminiscent of Jericho, then the rest of the battle is reminiscent of Joshua's major campaign. Joshua again stops the sun, but this time he calls upon the winds as well. The wind-power is key; with it Joshua can blow the thunderbolts of Japheth's son back on him as well as any of the thrown arrows or spears from the other giants. With this advantage on Shaubak's side lost, Joshua and his army quickly clean up.

Having won a great victory, Joshua proceeds to praise God. Specifically, he uses some of Moses' most famous lines. He recites a part of the Song of the Sea, "God is the overcomer of enemies in war, God is his name (الله المتجبر عنا فى الحرب الله اسمه)[464]" and "Who is like you perfect in holiness (من كمثلك متناهى فى القدس)[465]?" etc. In case this fact is lost on the reader, the author of *S. J.* specifically says that these lines are those Moses sang from the Song of the Sea. This parallel between Joshua and Moses is clearly a crucial point for the author.

---

464 Exod 15:3
465 Exod 15:11

Additionally, Joshua says: "God shall fight and you shall hold your peace (الله يحارب عنكم وانتم تصمتون)،"[466] also a Moses line from before the crossing. The fact that this line fits so poorly in this context, since the army does fight, underscores just how important it is for *S.J.* to paint this final battle of Joshua's in Mosaic colors. Additionally, one is struck by the total disappearance of Nabih and his army from the story once Shaubak has been killed.[467] The story ends on the note of Joshua the powerful general and Moses-like leader of Israel.

Characterizing and Concluding Joshua's Reign

Joshua having won all his battles, his end is described as peaceful. In fact, from chapter 38, one receives an idyllic picture of Israel under Joshua's authority, a period actually called "the period of divine favor" in the title of the chapter. The chapter begins with an overall positive description of the period (ch. 38).

و[مبلغ]468 ذلك مايتى و[ستين]469 سنة وكان ترتيب ايام [الرضى]470 فى ايام يوشع الملك ومن بعده الى تمام المدة471 على ما انا ذاكره وواضعه	And the amount of this [period] was two hundred and sixty years, and the days of [divine] favor were arrayed in the time of Joshua the king, and from then until the end of that period, as I will describe and set forth.

The rest of the chapter describes an ideal society in terms of observance of covenantal law. The poor are taken care of, sacrifices are brought properly, sinners are caught and punished, the priests and Levites do their jobs well. All in all, Joshua's years were all good ones.

Joshua's Farewell

Unlike in the biblical accounts and other versions, Joshua does not end with any speeches of great consequence (ch. 39).

---

466 Exod 14:14

467 This again seems to be evidence that the Shaubak vs. Nabih story as not integral to the Joshua war history but was fit into Joshua's final battle creating a combined account.

468 Juynboll's emendation; the manuscript reads ملع.

469 Juynboll's emendation; the manuscript reads ستون.

470 Juynboll's emendation; the manuscript reads الرصا.

471 In the manuscript there is a gloss: بعد دخولهم الارض ("after entering the land").

ملك يوشع بن نون خمسة واربعون سنة فعند قرب وفاته | Joshua son of Nun reigned 45 years,[472] and
جمع بنى اسرايل وعاهدهم واكد عليهم يحفظوا ما دونه | when his death approached, he gathered the
النبى موسى – عم. | Children of Israel and made a covenant with
them and emphasized to them that they should
observe what was set out by the prophet Moses
– may peace be upon him.[473]

وقرب عنه وعنهم القرابين وودعهم وعمل قريب ما عمله | And he brought on his own behalf and on their
سيدنا موسى النبى – عم – فى التوديع. | behalf sacrifices, and he bid farewell, for he
followed closely what was done by our master
Moses the prophet – may peace be upon him –
in his farewell.

As in the biblical book of Joshua, there is a final speech and re-establishment of
the covenant. However, the speech is not recorded but summarized in half a sentence. What is emphasized is that Joshua reaffirmed the laws of Moses and that
he conducted himself in his farewell just like Moses did at the beginning of *S.J.*

Joshua's Successors

At this point, Joshua turns to appointing a successor. He chooses twelve representatives from the Cisjordanian tribes, tests them for knowledge and aptitude
(امتحنهم بالعلم والعمل,) and casts lots. The combination of Joshua's use of intelligent criteria and divination is typical of *S.J.* Joshua is both a talented leader
and a man of God with access to divine wisdom. Why it is Joshua that casts
the lot and not Elazar the imam goes unexplained.

The lot being cast, the leader chosen is Abil, the nephew of Caleb and a Judahite. Abil is, ostensibly identical to the biblical Othniel son of Kenaz (*L.A.B.*'s
Cenaz). Abil having been chosen, Joshua holds a coronation ceremony (ch. 39).

فقلده الماك والحكم والبسه التاج ونادى فى الجماعة ان | And he gave him the kingship and jurisdiction,
يطيعوا امره. | and placed the crown upon him, and pro-
claimed to the assembly to follow his orders.

---

472 Josephus has 25 years (*Ant.* 5:1.29).
473 Anderson-Giles have a haplography here; they jump from the Moses in this sentence to the
Moses in the next sentence, yielding gibberish. The original Crane translation has it correct, as
do Kircheim and Juynboll.

وأمره ان يطيع ولى الله واطالعه بكل احواله ولا And he commanded him to obey the Saint of
[يمضى]474 امر الى ما يعلمه به. God involving him in all matters, and not to
pursue any policy until he knows of it.

What stands out in this coronation is the position of the new king relative to the
Saint of God, now Elazar but soon to be Phineas. Again the separation of powers
is complex: Abil will be king and everyone must follow him, however, Abil himself must agree to consult with Elazar and even to obey him. Yet, like Joshua,
Abil is to be active. It will be Abil's policies, but he has to bring them to the
imam for approval. Ostensibly this is because the imam has access to divine wisdom and information.

Joshua Dies

Having appointed his successor, Joshua dies and is buried in the village of Ghuweirah (كفر غويرة), a word that means jealousy or zealotry. Immediately following this it is recorded that Caleb dies and is buried next to Joshua.

Exactly as happened after Moses' death, the nations hear of the loss of the
great leader and attack. This time, the enemy nation is Moab. Happily, Abil mus-
ters his troops and handily defeats the enemy. The chapter ends with a quick
overview of the remaining leaders through to the end of the period of divine
favor inaugurated by Joshua and ends with Samson.

Elazar Dies

In chapter 40, Elazar the imam dies. His farewell mimics that of Joshua – the author says so explicitly – reminding the people of the covenant, bidding them a
farewell and serving God, ostensibly through sacrifice.

As he leaves the assembly, he strips off his holy garments that still smell of
incense and gives them to his son Phineas, who will be the new imam. Elazar
then dies and is also buried in the village of Ghuweirah, along with Joshua
and Caleb. The people mourn Elazar. Thus passes the generation of the conquest.
The remainder of this section of the book discusses the imams that follow, similar to the end of the previous chapter, ending with Uzi, the last of the imams
during the period of divine favor.

---

474 Juynboll's emendation; the manuscript reads يمطى.

Summary

As described in *S.J.*, Joshua is the perfect leader—as close to Moses as humanly possible.[475] He is confident, strategic, and intelligent. He is close to God, respectful of the imam, and kind to his subordinate kings. He annihilates the enemy and inaugurates a period of divine grace. Most importantly, Joshua is the first king of Israel, the establisher of the holy Temple on Mount Gerizim, and the founder of the capital city of Samaria. Most if not all of Joshua's more unpleasant characteristics are almost totally expurgated from the narrative of *S.J.*

The only case of Joshua's weakness appears in the Nabih and Shaubak story, which is the exception that proves the rule. Even in this story, Joshua maintains his calm, gives orders, and lives to sing the victory hymn. Even though *S.J.* is a late work and non-canonical—there is no canonical book of Joshua in Samaritan tradition—it seems that the image of Joshua in Samaritan tradition did not suffer from neglect or disapproval, as many other biblical Israelite heroes did. This could be because Joshua, unlike Samuel for instance, appears in the Pentateuch as Moses' successor, and demands the believer's respect. However, even if this is true, there may be another, deeper reason. Unlike the Jewish and Christian traditions, which will be explored next, the Samaritan Joshua story expands by adding elements of magic and military prowess to Joshua's battles. In other words, the contours of the Joshua story remain the same overall. Joshua is the military commander and leader of the Israelites who conquers the Holy Land with the help of God.

I would argue that it is hardly just happenstance that it is the Samaritan community that maintains strong continuity with this same land. While the power centers of Judaism and Christianity move away from the biblical land, the Samaritans remain entrenched there, with an unbroken tradition of high priests and worship on Mount Gerizim. It is no coincidence that the more traditional image of Joshua, conqueror and settler of the land, retains its appeal and resonance in this community.[476]

---

475 Samaritan tradition holds Moses in such high regard that the practice developed not to pronounce his name, replacing it with "Marqah" (the *reish* and the *qof* added together produce the number 300, the numerical equivalent to *shin*.) Hence the title of the Samaritan midrash collection "*Tibat Marqah*" (The Word of Moses). Moses' name is placed on par with the Hebrew names of God, which are not to be pronounced outside of ritual contexts. In this sense, there is no way any leader, even Joshua, could really be "like Moses."

476 As referenced in the introduction, this same phenomenon can be seen in the renewed interest in this image of Joshua among Zionist writers and thinkers.

Chapter 5 – Early Christian Joshua(s)

Joshua and Jesus had the same name. Although it took some time before "Christian"[477] exegetes determined how to make use of this coincidence, eventually a robust Joshua-Jesus typology was created, in which Joshua becomes a prefigurement of Jesus. The typology has its beginning in polemical writing, peaks in the *Homilies* of Origen, and then tapers off. Later exegetes show markedly less interest in Joshua.[478]

In this chapter, I will survey the creation of the typology, its peak moments and then how it played out in the writings of some later church fathers. I will also draw attention to a number of Church Fathers who made no use of the typology as part of their discussion of Joshua, or else saw nothing special in the name identity other than its attractive rhetorical value.[479]

Joshua in the New Testament

A cursory look at the Gospels (and the New Testament in general) leads one to the conclusion that these authors took little or no interest in Joshua.[480] Certain biblical characters, such as Elisha and Elijah, play important roles in the shaping of the description of the main characters in the New Testament, such as Jesus

---

477 I am aware that the term is anachronistic for the early period, but "Jesus-believing" feels rather cumbersome.

478 For a survey of early Christian interpretations of Joshua in general, see: John R. Franke, *Joshua, Judges, Ruth, 1–2 Samuel* (Ancient Christian Commentaries on Scripture, Old Testament 4; Downers Grove: Inter-Varsity Press, 2005). For an analysis of early Christian interpretation of Bible in general, see: Frances Margaret Young, *Biblical Interpretation and the Formation of Christian Culture* (Cambridge: Cambridge University Press, 1997).

479 An earlier survey of this typology—and one which was the starting point for my own research—was put forth by Jean Daniélou. See: Jean Daniélou, *From Shadows to Reality: Studies in the Biblical Typology of the Fathers* (trans. Dom Wulston Hibberd; Great Britain: Burns and Oates Ltd, 1960), 229–243. Much of what is put forth here is in agreement with the basic outline of Daniélou, although I have added much material. Where my conclusions differ from his will be discussed in the notes at the appropriate points.

480 This point was noted as well by Cornelis de Vos. See: J. Cornelis de Vos, "Josua und Jesus im Neuen Testament," in *The Book of Joshua* (ed. Ed Noort; BETL 250 – Proceedings of the CBL; Leuven: Leuven University Press, 2010), 523–540.

and John the Baptist. However, such resonances are almost entirely lacking for Joshua.[481]

Acts of the Apostles

Joshua is mentioned twice in the New Testament, both times in passing. First he is mentioned in Acts 7:45. The context is Stephen's speech before the Sanhedrin, where he offers a synopsis of Israelite history. Referring to the Tabernacle, Stephen states:

ἣν καὶ εἰσήγαγον διαδεξάμενοι οἱ πατέρες ἡμῶν μετὰ Ἰησοῦ ἐν τῇ κατασχέσει τῶν ἐθνῶν, ὧν ἐξῶσεν ὁ θεὸς ἀπὸ προσώπου τῶν πατέρων ἡμῶν...	Our fathers, in turn, brought (the Tabernacle) in when, under Iesu (Joshua), they dispossessed the nations that God expelled from the face of our fathers...

As a part of his retelling of Israelite history, Stephen mentions that the Tabernacle was built in the wilderness, was brought into the Holy Land by Joshua, and was used (until the time of David.) There is no sense in this passage that there is anything special or unique about Joshua any more than the other leaders mentioned, and it certainly makes no implicit or explicit connection with Jesus. This should be contrasted to the usage of Joseph and Moses, whose "ministries" fol-

---

481 Although this statement represents the consensus view, there is a strong dissenting voice in the South African University of Pretoria, in the person of Andries van Aarde. See, for example: Andries van Aarde, "Jesus as Joshua: Moses en Dawidiese Messias in Matteus," (*Scriptura* 84:3, 2003), 453–467. Unfortunately, most of van Aarde's research was published in Afrikaans, which I cannot read and so cannot fairly evaluate. From secondary descriptions of his work, and from the few references to this idea in his English scholarly contributions, it seems that Van Aarde's main argument is that the Gospel of Matthew uses Joshua as the paradigm for Jesus, implicitly understanding that Jesus is the second Joshua (See in this chapter the sub-section on Cyril of Jerusalem for a possible precursor to Van Aarde's thinking). For example, van Aarde writes: "Matthew presented his writing as a story that re-tells the 'history' (biblos) of how God sent Joshua from Egypt as Moses' successor to save Israel;" Andries van Aarde, "Jesus' Mission to All of Israel Emplotted in Matthew's Story," SBL 2005, Philadelphia, http://www.sbl-site.org/assets/pdfs/aarde_jesus.pdf. Personally, other than the crossing/dipping in the Jordan River connection, I see little evidence for such a claim, but I look forward to more of van Aarde's work being translated into English so that the larger world of New Testament scholars can engage it properly. For a positive evaluation of this work in English, see Jurie H. le Roux, "Andries van Aarde's Matthew Interpretation," *Hervormde Teleogiese Studies* 67.1 (2011): #1013 (10 pgs.).

low the Jesus-like pattern of being sent to the people and rejected, returning with signs and wonders, and being rejected again.[482]

One element used in Stephen's speech that eventually becomes one of the many hooks for the Joshua-Jesus typology is his invocation of Deut 18:15, in which Moses states:

προφήτην ἐκ τῶν ἀδελφῶν σου ὡς ἐμὲ ἀναστήσει σοι κύριος ὁ θεός σου αὐτοῦ ἀκούσεσθε.	נָבִיא מִקִּרְבְּךָ מֵאַחֶיךָ כָּמֹנִי יָקִים לְךָ יְהוָה אֱלֹהֶיךָ אֵלָיו תִּשְׁמָעוּן.	A prophet from among your brethren like me YHWH your God will establish for you; hearken unto him.

Stephen quotes this verse in his speech (Acts 7:37) but does not connect the dots to Jesus. However, from the perspective of the author of Luke-Acts, Stephen hardly needed to, since Peter had already drawn this connection (Acts 3:20 – 22). This same connection between Moses' statement about a future prophet like him and Jesus is made in the Gospel of John (1:21– 27) as well. In that passage, John the Baptist is asked whether he is "the prophet," ostensibly the prophet referenced by Moses in Deut 18:15. John says that he is not but that the prophet is coming, whom he identifies as Jesus the next day (v. 29).

Although in neither of these texts is Joshua referenced as the prophet that God raises up like Moses, this possibility will be picked up by later exegetes (Clement of Alexandria, for example) once the Joshua-Jesus typology begins to appear in the exegesis of the church fathers.

Epistle to the Hebrews

The other reference to Joshua in the New Testament is even clearer about Joshua's non-identification with Jesus.[483] This reference is found in the Epistle to the Hebrews (4:8). Although refered to as "Paul's Epistle to the Hebrews," the work is really more of a sermon than a letter, and most if not all academic scholars of the New Testament believe Paul not to have been the author. The work makes a sustained argument for the incomparable greatness of Jesus, and successively argues that he was/is greater than the angels, greater than Moses, greater than

---

482 For more details on this pattern and how it is used in Acts, and specifically in Stephen's speech, see: Luke Timothy Johnson, *The Acts of the Apostles* (ed. Daniel J. Harrington; Sacra Pagina 5; Collegeville, MN: Liturgical Press, 1992), 80.
483 Elßner (*Josua*, 82– 105) takes up the Acts reference as well as the two passages in Hebrews. Additionally, since his lens is war and ethics, not the image of Joshua, he also takes up the reference to Rahab in the Epistle of James (2:25), which will not be discussed here.

Abraham or any high priest in Israel's history. The last two points come from what is the underlying rhetorical project of the book, which is to offer a reading of Psalms 110, in which Jesus is identified with the character of the "priest from the order of Melchizedek." The work ends with an encomium to faith and faith-fulness, surveying acts of faith by biblical characters in Israelite history.

In the section of Hebrews in which Joshua is referenced, the author attempts to demonstrate that until Jesus, there was no time in which the people actually achieved "rest" (κατέπαυσεν), which in the biblical text refers to the inheritance of the land, but which the author of Hebrews uses in a more general sense of paradise. To prove that real rest only came after the ministry of Jesus, the author uses a hermeneutical approach to Psalm 95 (94 in the LXX) to demonstrate that the generations of Moses and Joshua were unsuccessful at this. The significance of these two characters failing is that although Moses gave Israel the Torah and Joshua gave them the Promised Land, still this is considered a failure, which "proves" that God's intention when describing "rest" is something altogether different that that which the Jews/Hebrews imagine it to be.[484]

Starting from the final two verses, the author shows that the generation of the wilderness did not succeed in achieving rest, since the lack of rest was specifically a punishment for their stubborn intransigence and rebellion. Hence, as the psalm states, God swore that they would never achieve rest. The author of Hebrews equates this threat with the account of God's punishment of the generation of the wilderness after their failure during the scout story in Numbers 14.

However, a simple understanding of this story brings to mind the equation of rest or blessing with receiving the land of Israel. The implication of Numbers 14 is that the generation of the wilderness would not receive the promise but their children would. Furthermore, the book of Joshua, in fact, narrates the taking of the Promised Land, strongly implying that this is the reception of the divine promise.

In order to prove that wrong, the author of Hebrews references the middle of the Psalm (95:7–8):

σήμερον ἐὰν τῆς φωνῆς αὐτοῦ ἀκούσητε, μὴ   If today you listen to His voice, do not harden
σκληρύνητε τὰς καρδίας ὑμῶν.   your hearts.

Since this Psalm was ostensibly written by David, it is striking, argues the author of Hebrews, that he refers to hearing God's voice "today" and compares this to the requirement in the wilderness period and the failure of that generation to

---

484 Ostensibly, the reason the work is titled "To the Hebrews" is that it appears to have a Jewish —or, at least, a Jewish-Christian—audience in mind.

achieve rest. Was not rest already achieved in the time of Joshua? Apparently not; he argues (Heb 4:8):

εἰ γὰρ αὐτοὺς Ἰησοῦς κατέπαυσεν, οὐκ ἂν περὶ ἄλλης ἐλάλει μετὰ ταῦτα ἡμέρας.	For if Iesu (Joshua) had given them rest, [God] would not have spoken after this about another day.[485]

Although this rhetorical question functions as the hermeneutic hook upon which the author will place his idea of a different rest, it also fits into the overall earthly/heavenly contrast which forms the backbone of Hebrews. The physical successes of Israel's past leaders are merely shadows of the future spiritual or heavenly successes of Jesus. The settling of the Promised Land, although a great achievement, was merely the forerunner of the real "Promised Land," the kingdom of heaven heralded by the coming of Jesus. So too, the Temple with its high priests was merely a (crude) foreshadowing of the future ministry of the true high priest, Jesus, and the sacrifices offered in the Temple bear only a symbolic resemblance to the true sacrifice, that of Jesus when he appeared in human form on earth.

For the purposes of our analysis, what stands out is that there appears to be no insinuation at all that there is some important connection between Joshua and Jesus. If anything, Joshua, like Moses, fails to give the people rest, leaving the job of giving the people rest for another leader (Jesus) in another time.

The author's lack of interest in drawing a parallel between Joshua and Jesus stands in strong contrast to the treatment of characters like Melchizedek and Aaron in the very next section of the letter. Following his treatment of the "rest" topic, the author of Hebrews expounds upon Jesus' role as a high priest (ἀρχιερεύς). In this section, the author compares Jesus' priesthood to that of two characters: Aaron and Melchizedek.

The idea of Jesus as a high priest is inspired by the author of Hebrews' interpretation of Psalm 110 (109 in the LXX), which is understood to refer to Jesus. In this psalm, God is understood to be telling Jesus that he will be a priest like Melchizedek (Ps 110:4).

ὤμοσεν κύριος καὶ οὐ μεταμεληθήσεται σὺ εἶ ἱερεὺς εἰς τὸν αἰῶνα κατὰ τὴν τάξιν Μελχισε-δεκ.	The Lord has sworn and will not repent: "You will be a priest forever just like Melchizedek."

---

485 This passage will be picked up by later commentaters, such as Tertullian and Aphrahat, as will be seen further on.

The statement in Psalms itself is unusual, since the model for the priesthood is generally considered to be Moses' brother, Aaron, the first Israelite high priest. In fact, the author of Hebrews states that Jesus will function like another Aaron (5:4).

καὶ οὐχ ἑαυτῷ τις λαμβάνει τὴν τιμὴν ἀλλὰ καλούμενος ὑπὸ τοῦ θεοῦ καθώσπερ καὶ Ἀαρών.	And one does not take this honor himself; rather one is called by God like Aaron.

The author of Hebrews notes that what Aaron and Melchizedek have in common is that neither was born into the priesthood but was chosen due to merit. So too was Jesus chosen due to merit, despite having been born a Judahite and not a Levite. For the purposes of this analysis, the stark contrast between the author of Hebrews' use of Aaron and Melchizedek as comparative models for Jesus and his total silence with regard to Joshua as a model should demonstrate that such an idea would have been foreign to him.

Perhaps the clearest demonstration of the author's lack of interest in Joshua as a comparative model comes towards the end of the epistle, where the author discusses past figures that were successful due to their faith or faithfulness (πίστις) in chapter 11. The author lists various ancient heroes and describes their acts of faithfulness: Abel, Enoch, Noah, Abraham, Isaac, Jacob, Joseph, the Israelites (crossing the Red Sea), and Rahab. He then stops and asks rhetorically if he really needs to go on and list other heroes and describe their deeds, heroes such as Gideon, Barak, Samson, David, Jephthah, Samuel, and the prophets. The author of Hebrews then finishes the chapter by describing the plight of the faithful ancestors in general.

The name of Joshua is not just absent from this list, but conspicuously so. First, he isn't even mentioned alongside the minor judges, even though he plays a much more central role in the biblical account. Second, Rahab is mentioned for her faith; as she is a character in the Joshua narrative, this would call Joshua to mind for the reader, thereby calling attention to his absence.[486] Finally, verse 30, which sits between the description of the people's faith at the Red Sea and the faith of Rahab, appears almost inexplicable without a reference to Joshua.

---

486 This point can be seen even more clearly we examine a similar passage in 1 Clement 12. In this passage, the author of 1 Clement also discusses the faith of Rahab but sees no need to skip over the name of Joshua in telling the story.

Πίστει τὰ τείχη Ἰεριχὼ ἔπεσαν κυκλωθέντα ἐπὶ   By faith the walls of Jericho fell, having been
ἑπτὰ ἡμέρας.   circled for seven days.

One is tempted to ask: By whose faith? Of course, one can answer that it is by the
faith of the Israelite people who circled the city, just as the faith of the Israelites
was emphasized in the previous verse about crossing the Sea. However, this just
poses the question: Why is the author of Hebrews going out of his way to avoid
referencing Joshua in this context?

Looking at the progression of characters, Hebrews goes from Moses to the
people of Israel under Moses, to the people of Israel under Joshua (without saying so), to Rahab and to Gideon. Although I do not have an answer for why Joshua was specifically avoided here, it seems clear that the character troubles the
author of Hebrews enough such that he does not want to mention Joshua in a
list of great people of the past that demonstrated faith. This combined with
the fact that the only explicit mention of Joshua in Hebrews describes him negatively, as someone who did not succeed in facilitating Israel's "rest," suggests
that Joshua is a problematic figure in the eyes of this author.

Contrary to the above argument, Bryan Whitfield makes the case in his dissertation that Hebrews uses Joshua as a typology for Jesus (pp. 287–302).[487] He
bases much of this argument on two main points. First, he notes the role of Numbers 13–14 in the discourse of Hebrews. It is difficult to imagine, Whitfield argues, that Hebrews would make extensive use of the scout account in Numbers
without assuming the reader will know/remember that it was Joshua, together
with Caleb, who makes the case for faith in God and following God's command
to enter the land. Second, he points to the use of the term ἀρχηγός in Hebrews
2:10 to describe Jesus. Quoting Harold Attridge,[488] Whitfield points out that this
term, meaning leader or pioneer, calls Joshua to mind. However, unlike Attridge,
Whitfield believes that this was intentional, and notes the many possible caden-
ces of the term and the connections it could draw in the reader's mind to Joshua.

Here I must disagree with Whitfield and side with Attridge. As tempting as it
is to connect the dots between Joshua and Jesus, a hermeneutic maneuver of
which the reception history of this and other texts is full, nevertheless, there
seems strong reason to argue that Hebrew is specifically not doing this. First, Hebrews never actually connects these dots; even if doing so seems obvious from
hindsight, this is no proof that the author of Hebrews thought of it. Second, de-

---

487 See: Bryan Whitfield, *Joshua Traditions and the Argument of Hebrews 3 and 4* (Ph.D. diss.,
Emory University, 2007).
488 Harold W. Attridge, *The Epistle to the Hebrews* (Hermeneia; Philadelphia: Fortress Press,
1989), 130.

spite all the positive attributes of Joshua exhibited in the scout account, the only actual reference to Joshua in Hebrews is *negative*. A negative comment is hardly solid ground upon which to build a Joshua-Jesus typology. Third, Joshua is specifically skipped in the list of the faithful in Hebrews 11.[489]

Whitfield notes this last objection and, after surveying a number of explanations for why Joshua is skipped, concludes in favor of the suggestion by C. P. M. Jones that Joshua is too good of a model and is being saved for the end (pp. 301–302).[490] Jones (and Whitfield) seem to believe that Joshua son of Nun is the model upon which the climactic description of Jesus in Hebrews 12 is built. This seems more than a little speculative, since Joshua is not referenced in the chapter at all. For these reasons, it seems that the better understanding of Hebrews here is that the author has a skeptical attitude towards Joshua and avoids referencing him positively.

Whitfield makes a more plausible argument in the next (and final) section of his dissertation, in which he argues that the author of Hebrews uses Joshua the high priest as a model for Jesus (pp. 302–321). Since Hebrews is saturated with priestly imagery, including a lengthy quote from and discussion of the character of Joshua the high priest as presented in Zechariah 3, it seems possible that this discussion was intended to suggest a Joshua (the high priest)-Jesus typology. Whitfield suggest that this Joshua-Jesus typology should be understood as based upon a merging of both biblical Joshuas. Daniélou suggests something similar: "[T]he author is perhaps thinking of a fusion between Joshua the successor of Moses and Joshua the High Priest of Zechariah" (231).

In an article based on his dissertation, Whitfield adjusts his argument:

Although the author of Hebrews uses the Joshua of Numbers and the Joshua of Zechariah, his task is not a mere narration of their faithful deeds. Just as he is concerned with a better priesthood and a better covenant, he is ultimately interested in "a better Joshua." This third Joshua (Jesus) combines the characteristics of the precursors whose name he bears, but he surpasses them in importance. He invests the name he has inherited with new significance and glory.[491]

---

489 De Vos makes this point very well in his conclusion (539):

Im Hebräerbrief erscheint Josua direkt, jedoch negativ, und da, wo er positiv hätte erscheinen müssen, wird er nicht genannt. In the Epistle to the Hebrews, Joshua appears explicitly albeit negatively; and where he should appear positively, he is not mentioned.

490 C.P.M. Jones, "The Epistle to the Hebrews and the Lucan Writings," in *Studies in the Gospels: Essays in Memory of R. H. Lightfoot* (ed. Dennis E. Nineham; Oxford: Blackwell, 1955), 113–143.
491 Bryan J. Whitfield, "The Three Joshuas of Hebrews 3 and 4," *Perspectives in Religious Studies* 37 (2010): 21–35 [35].

This is a more attractive suggestion, since it builds upon the negative image of Joshua, which is the only explicit image referenced in Hebrews. Furthermore, it fits in with the fact that Joshua is skipped over in Hebrews 11. De Vos ("Josus," 528–529) also affirms Whitfield's argument here, since it fits in with his overall thesis, with which I concur, that the New Testament in general, and Hebrews in particular, is not interested in, or is even antagonistic to, Joshua.

It is important to note that the version of Whitfield's argument that appears in the article is a rather thin basis for a Joshua-Jesus typology. There is no explicit reference to the name similarity and no explicit explanation of the typological or allegorical connection between these two characters. Nevertheless, there is no question that once the Joshua-Jesus typology begins to circulate among early Christian exegetes, Hebrews 3–4 will be one of the primary sources used to solidify and expand upon it.

Why is the Joshua-Jesus Typology Missing from the New Testament?

J. Cornelis De Vos writes that even though arguments from silence should generally be avoided, in this case the silence of the New Testament is so glaring that it must be considered meaningful. He suggests eight possible reasons for the lack of a Joshua-Jesus typology in the New Testament.[492]

---

[492] In the same volume as de Vos' essay, Stefan Koch has an article arguing for a limited appearance of the Joshua-Jesus typology in the New Testament itself. See: Stefan Koch, "Mose sagt zu 'Jesus'—Zur Wahrnehmung von Josua im Neuen Testament," in *The Book of Joshua* (ed. Ed Noort; BETL 250 – Proceedings of the CBL; Leuven: Leuven University Press, 2010), 541–554. Much of Koch's argument is based on what he calls the "extent of the indirect referencing" (*der breite der indirekten bezugnahme*) of the book of Joshua in New Testament passages. Koch admits that nowhere in the New Testament—even in the birth stories—are the names of Joshua and Jesus explicitly linked. Nevertheless, he states that since the names of the two individuals are identical (at least in Greek), one cannot categorically exclude the possibility that Joshua was being used as a model (548). Therefore, Koch argues, since the book of Joshua is referenced a number of times in the New Testament, implicitly and explicitly, and since early Christian texts, like Barnabas, see the identical nature of the two men's names as significant, it is reasonable to assume that the New Testament authors were already using Joshua as a model. To me, this argument seems methodologically problematic. Rather, as argued above, it seems significant that New Testament texts that reference the book of Joshua avoid discussion of him, or even discuss him negatively. This argues for the probability that the New Testament authors noticed the name similarities (they would have had to) and chose to avoid mentioning Joshua so as *not* to call this comparison to the readers' minds. The fact that once the typology was hammered out by Barnabas and Justin, it became widely known and used in Christian circles argues against Koch's thesis, not for it. The New Testament authors certainly would have buttressed Jesus' claim

De Vos' eight reasons are as follows: First, the name may have been so common among Galilean Jews that the similarity was "lost in the noise." Second, emphasis on the Pentateuch, Psalms, and Isaiah made the authors of the New Testament fail to notice Joshua. Third, Joshua is intimately associated with the land, and is best avoided to avoid bringing up that subject, which has no resonance with gentile Christianity. Fourth, Joshua is a character of violence, something at odds with the image of Jesus portrayed in the New Testament. Fifth, Jesus is associated with Isaiah and not Joshua. Sixth, Jesus is a new Moses and keeping Joshua in the picture obscures this. Seventh, Jesus is the successor of Moses, and keeping Joshua in the picture obscures this. Finally, Jesus is identified with Elijah and not Joshua.[493]

Most of these answers are forced and unpersuasive, and De Vos recognizes this for the first two. In his conclusion, De Vos combines the last six reasons into two main categories and states that the New Testament avoided Joshua for two main reasons: first, because he was a character associated with the land and with violence, two matters that did not resonate with the authors of the New Testament; second, because Joshua was already associated with other characters (Moses, Isaiah, and Elijah), especially Moses, and bringing in Joshua (Moses' attendant) would complicate this. Although I find this latter reason unpersuasive, the former reason, I think, may very well be why the New Testament authors avoid him.

Joshua, as he is presented in the Bible, didn't resonate with them—worse, his legacy actually contradicted the message of the New Testament. This is why the invention of the Joshua-Jesus typology was so useful. The typology redeems Joshua for use in Christian hermeneutics and even gives the Christian interpreter ammunition with which to debate or critique their "unbelieving" Jewish counterparts.

---

with references to Joshua as the successor of Moses and redeemer of Israel if they had thought of it. Instead, because they pictured Joshua as militant and tied to the land of Israel, they avoided him as problematic for their new version of the biblical religion.

493 This is surprising, as I would have suggested that Jesus is identified with Elisha; John the Baptist is identified with Elijah.

Creating the Joshua-Jesus Typlogy

Antecedents: The Epistle of Barnabas

The earliest reference to Joshua as a prefiguration of Jesus, based on the similarity of their names, is found in chapter 12 of the Epistle of Barnabas.[494] This epistle, whose author is unknown, (the attribution to Barnabas, the Jew from Cyprus who was a friend of Paul, is almost universally understood as pseudonymous,) was written at some point in the late 1st or early 2nd century, probably in Alexandria. The work offers a strong polemic against the "Jewish" interpretation of scripture, and offers an allegorical reading of many of the stories and commandments in scripture, ironically in a style very similar to that of Philo. The work, although not part of the contempory Christian canon, seems to have been part of some early "canonical" collections, such as the Codex Sinaiticus.

Barnabas makes an analogy between Joshua and Jesus as part of his interpretation of the Amalek story in Exodus. As this story will be one of the key texts for establishing the Joshua-Jesus hermeneutic, it is worth looking in detail at how Barnabas uses it. Barnabas begins with his interpretation of God's command to Moses:

2. Λέγει δὲ πάλιν τῷ Μωϋσῇ πολεμουμένου τοῦ Ἰσραὴλ ὑπὸ τῶν ἀλλοφύλων καὶ ἵνα ὑπομνήσῃ αὐτοὺς πολεμουμένους ὅτι διὰ τὰς ἁμαρτίας αὐτῶν παρεδόθησαν εἰς θάνατον λέγει εἰς τὴν καρδίαν Μωϋσέως τὸ πνεῦμα ἵνα ποιήσῃ τύπον σταυροῦ καὶ τοῦ μέλλοντος πάσχειν ὅτι ἐὰν μὴ φησίν ἐλπίσωσιν ἐπ' αὐτῷ εἰς τὸν αἰῶνα πολεμηθήσονται.

² And he says to Moses, as Israel is under attack by outsiders – and in order to remind those under attack that due to their sins they have been given over to death – the Spirit says to the heart of Moses that he should make the form of a cross and of him who is destined to suffer, saying that unless they place their hope in him they will be under attack forever.

Τίθησιν οὖν Μωϋσῆς ἓν ἐφ' ἓν ὅπλον ἐν μέσῳ τῆς πυγμῆς καὶ σταθεὶς ὑψηλότερος πάντων ἐξέτεινεν τὰς χεῖρας καὶ οὕτως πάλιν ἐνίκα ὁ Ἰσραήλ.

And so, Moses places one shield on top of the other, in the midst of the battle, and standing high above everyone, he extends his arms and thus, again, Israel prevailed.

Εἶτα ὁπόταν καθεῖλεν πάλιν ἐθανατοῦντο.

Then, when he would put them down, they would again be subject to death.

---

494 Cf. Elßner, *Josua*, 202–211. For background on the Epistle of Barnabas in general, see: James Carleton Paget, *The Epistle of Barnabas: Outlook and Background* (Wissenschaftliche Untersuchungen zum Neuen Testament 64; Tübingen: Mohr Siebeck, 1994); Reidar Hvalvik, *The Struggle for Scripture and Covenant: The Purpose of the Epistle of Barnabas and Jewish-Christian Competition in the Second Century* (Wissenschaftliche Untersuchungen zum Neuen Testament 82; Tübingen: Mohr Siebeck, 1996).

³· Πρὸς τί; ἵνα γνῶσιν ὅτι οὐ δύνανται σωθῆναι ³ Why so? So that they know that they cannot
ἐὰν μὴ ἐπ᾽ αὐτῷ ἐλπίσωσιν.   be saved unless they place their hope in him.

Although the details of the story differ somewhat from the biblical text, the basic contours are recognizable.[495] Israel is attacked by enemies and Moses saves them with a miracle. The miracle consists of him holding his arms extended.[496] This receives a symbolic interpretation from the author of Barnabas, namely, that Moses was making the sign of the cross, hinting at the future position of Jesus, who died on the cross, as the real savior of the Israelites.

If the imagery was not explicit enough in these verses, the author of Barnabas makes the point even more explicitly in the beginning of verse 5.

⁵ Πάλιν Μωϋσῆς ποιεῖ τύπον τοῦ Ἰησοῦ ὅτι δεῖ ⁵ Again, Moses made a type of Iesu – [indicat-
αὐτὸν παθεῖν καὶ αὐτὸς ζωοποιήσει ὃν δόξου- ing] that he (Iesu) must suffer and that he
σιν ἀπολωλεκέναι ἐν σημείῳ πίπτοντος τοῦ would again give life – he whom they will be-
Ἰσραήλ.   lieve to have been killed. [This type came] in a
                                                sign given when Israel would fall.

In short, the author of Barnabas interprets the miraculous element of the story of the defeat of Amalek by making Christological imagery the source of Moses' miraculous power. This is a standard hermeneutical approach for early Christian authors, and just one of many examples in the Epistle of Barnabas itself. For our purposes, the importance of this interpretation lies in the connection it establishes with a different interpretation that appears further on in the same chapter (12).

⁸ Τί λέγει πάλιν Μωϋσῆς Ἰησοῦ υἱῷ Ναυή ἐπι- ⁸ Again, what does Moses say to Iesu son of
θεὶς αὐτῷ τοῦτο τὸ ὄνομα ὄντι προφήτῃ ἵνα Nau when he gave him this name? – being a
μόνον ἀκούσῃ πᾶς ὁ λαὸς ὅτι πάντα ὁ πατὴρ prophet, only in order for all the nation to
φανεροῖ περὶ τοῦ υἱοῦ Ἰησοῦ.   hear that the Father was making all known re-
                                               garding his son Iesu –

---

495 I do not know how to explain the origin of Barnabas' image of Moses standing upon a pile of shields as opposed to a mountain. It is further worth noting the absence of Aaron and Hur in this retelling.
496 The biblical text (Exod 17:11) in Hebrew (ה.ו.מ) and Greek (ἐπείρω) actually says that Moses' arms were lifted, giving the reader the impression that his hands pointed up and not out. Nevertheless, the temptation to picture Moses' action as forming the sign of the cross is easy to understand.

⁹ Λέγει οὖν Μωϋσῆς Ἰησοῦ υἱῷ Ναυή ἐπιθεὶς αὐτῷ τοῦτο τὸ ὄνομα ὁπότε ἔπεμψεν αὐτὸν κατάσκοπον τῆς γῆς· "Λάβε βιβλίον εἰς τὰς χεῖράς σου καὶ γράψον ἃ λέγει κύριος ὅτι ἐκκόψει ἐκ ῥιζῶν πάντα τὸν οἶκον τοῦ Ἀμαλὴκ ὁ υἱὸς τοῦ θεοῦ ἐπ᾽ ἐσχάτων τῶν ἡμερῶν."
¹⁰ Ἴδε πάλιν Ἰησοῦς οὐχὶ υἱὸς ἀνθρώπου ἀλλὰ υἱὸς τοῦ θεοῦ τύπῳ δὲ ἐν σαρκὶ φανερωθείς.

⁹ And so Moses said to Iesu son of Nau, when he gave him this name, when he sent him to scout out the land: "Take a book in your hands and write that which the Lord says, that the son of God will uproot the whole house of Amalek at the end of days."
¹⁰ See, again, not Iesu the son of man but the son of God, made known in the flesh by a symbol.

The exposition in Barnabas is confusing for a number of reasons. The most problematic element is the conflation of two different biblical Joshua stories into one. In the book of Exodus (17:14), after the defeat of Amalek, Moses is told by God to place a book in the ears of Joshua, which says that God will erase Amalek from under the heavens. In the book of Numbers (13:16), Joshua is chosen as one of the scouts and sent on a mission to scout out the land of Canaan. As a part of this story, the reader is told that Joshua's given name was actually Hoshea, but that Moses changed it to Joshua.

Barnabas has combined these two stories. In his telling, Joshua is given the book about Amalek when he is appointed as a scout and right after Moses has renamed him. Joshua is then told that he is to take this book with him as he scouts out the land. This is an odd request, since Joshua is not being sent to attack Amalek or even to scout out Amalek, but to scout out all of Canaan in preparation for the attack.

The reason Joshua is to carry this book, according to Barnabas, is symbolic. With his new name, Joshua himself becomes a symbol for Jesus, the future redeemer. Furthermore, the book itself states that the future redeemer, the son of God, will be the one to uproot Amalek.[497] Although he does not say so explicitly, Barnabas appears to understand this future Amalek symbolically, as representing sin. To ensure that the reader does not mistake his intention, the author of Barnabas clarifies that it will be Iesu the son of God (Jesus), *not* Iesu the son of man (Joshua), that will finally destroy Amalek.

In short, the author of the Epistle of Barnabas makes use of the biblical account of the war with Amalek to introduce Christological imagery to explain Israel's success in the wilderness as well as Israel's future success against Amalek.[498] The wilderness success is attributed to faith in Jesus by interpreting

---

497 According to the biblical account, the book says no such thing, but again, Barnabas seems to take a certain amount of license in retelling the biblical stories.
498 Luke Johnson, in his notes on this chapter, commenting on this point as presented in the dissertation, suggests that this allegorical reading of Amalek as sin, and their smiting at the

Moses' outstretched arms as symbolizing the cross. Israel's future success against Amalek is symbolized by Joshua's scouting out the land, after receiving the special name Joshua, and holding a book predicting the coming of his name-sake, the son of God, and his future involvement in the uprooting of Amalek.

Interestingly enough, Barnabas stops short of attributing the original victory against Amalek to Joshua's being a symbolic incarnation of Jesus. These dots will be connected by one of the earliest church fathers, Justin Martyr.

The Typology: Justin Martyr

Although Barnabas references the symbolic connection between Joshua and Jesus based upon the similarity of their names, the paradigm of Joshua prefigur-ing Jesus was developed much more extensively by Justin Martyr.[499] Justin, one of the earliest church fathers (103 – 165), was born into a pagan family in Neop-olis (Shechem), a predominantly Samaritan town. After trying out a number of different philosophical schools, he became a Christian. Eventually, he moved to Rome and taught the gospel, for which he was denounced and executed.

Whether Justin was aware of Barnabas is unclear, but Justin was certainly aware of the interpretation found in Barnabas for Moses' renaming of Hoshea to Joshua and the defeat of the Amalekites at Joshua's hands.

Justin makes use of the Joshua-Jesus typology in a number of places in the *Dialogue with Trypho*, a polemical work that records (or more likely, invents) a debate between Justin and a Jew named Trypho. The importance of the typology is its contribution to the overall project of Justin in this work, which is to con-vince Trypho the Jew (and any biblically interested readers) that "Jewish" scrip-ture proves the authenticity of Jesus as the savior and son of God.[500]

Like the author of Barnabas, Justin takes note of the fact that Joshua was not the given name of the son of Nun/Nau, but that his given name was Hoshea/

---

hands of Joshua-Jesus, is a theme that runs through the church fathers. This theme connects the interpretation of Barnabas with that of Justin (discussed in the next section) and comes to fruition in the work of Origen.

499 Cf. Elßner, *Josua*, 211–225.

500 There is a serious debate among Justin scholars whether the intended audience of the *Dialogue* is a Jewish/Jewish sympathetic audience, to convince them of Jesus, or a Marcionite/Gnostic-sympathetic audience, to convince them that the "Jewish" scriptures are, in fact, im-portant works for Christians. For a discussion of this question, see the second chapter of: David Rokeah, *Justin Martyr and the Jews* (Jewish and Christian Perspectives Series 5; Leiden: Brill, 2002).

Ausei. It is Moses that gives Hoshea the name of Joshua. Justin reminds Trypho of this more than once.

The first reference to the name change appears in section 75.[501]

2. τίς οὖν εἰς τὴν γῆν εἰσήγαγε τοὺς πατέρας ὑμῶν; ἤδη ποτὲ νοήσατε ὅτι ὁ ἐν τῷ ὀνόματι τούτῳ ἐπονομασθεὶς Ἰησοῦς, πρότερον Αὐσῆς καλούμενος. εἰ γὰρ τοῦτο νοήσετε, καὶ ὅτι τὸ ὄνομα αὐτοῦ <τοῦ> εἰπόντος τῷ Μωυσεῖ· τὸ γὰρ ὄνομά μου ἐστὶν ἐπ' αὐτῷ. Ἰησοῦς ἦν, ἐπιγνώσεσθε...	2. And so, who led your fathers into the land? Now, at last, you know that he whose name was changed to Iesu (Joshua), beforehand being called Ausai (Hoshea). If you know this, you will learn, then, that the name of he that spoke to Moses saying (Exod 23:21) "For my name is upon him," was Iesu...
3. ...καὶ ὅτι προφήτης ἰσχυρὸς καὶ μέγας γέγονεν ὁ ἐπονομασθεὶς τῷ Ἰησοῦ ὀνόματι, φανερὸν πᾶσίν ἐστιν.	3. ...and that as a strong and great prophet did the one who was renamed with the name of Iesu become visible to all.

According to Justin, it was Jesus – in an earlier, pre-incarnation form – that appeared in the past to rename the various patriarchs. Even Joshua (Iesu) receives a name change from this pre-incarnation Jesus (Iesu). Justin then points out how great a prophet Joshua became.

One matter worth emphasizing is that, according to Justin's reading of Exodus 23, Jesus seems to be both the speaker, i.e., in the place of God, and the angel or messenger the speaker is sending. The latter point is implied—since the messenger must be Joshua for Justin's point to make any sense—although he does not spend time explaining it. This is probably due to the fact that Justin's emphasis throughout the *Dialogue* is on Jesus as the incarnation of God that *speaks* with the prophets. However, Tertullian in his *Adversus Iudaeos* (ch. 9) will make strong use of the latter point (as will be seen in the next sub-section), and spends more than a couple of lines proving that the angel sent was, in fact, Joshua.

Larry W. Hurtado sums up Justin's point nicely:

In short, Justin's exegetical logic is as follows: (1) God promised a figure who would lead Israel into Canaan and who would bear God's name; (2) in the biblical record the figure who led Israel into Canaan is Joshua; and (3) this figure had been given this name by

---

501 Greek taken from: Miroslav Marcovich, *Iustini Martyris: Apologiae Pro Christianis* (Patrische Texte und Studien 38; Berlin: Walter de Gruyter, 2005 [or. 1994]). The English is my own, but as a basis for comparison I used: Thomas B. Falls, *St. Justin Martyr: Dialogue with Trypho* (revised by Thomas P. Halton; ed. Michael Slusser; Selections from the Fathers of the Church 3; Washington D.C.: Catholic University of America Press, 2003). Any substantial difference between my translation and that of Falls and Halton will be noted.

Moses; therefore, (4) "Joshua/Ιησους" must be God's name, given to Hoshea to prefigure his greater namesake, Jesus.[502]

Justin's point about the name is reiterated in section 106.

3. σημαντικὸν ἦν τοῦ αὐτὸν ἐκεῖνον εἶναι, δι' ο<ὗ> καὶ τὸ ἐπώνυμον <τῷ> Ἰακὼβ τῷ Ἰσραὴλ ἐπικληθέντι, ἐδόθη, καὶ τῷ Αὐσῆ ὄνομα Ἰησοῦς ἐπεκλήθη, δι' οὗ ὀνόματος καὶ εἰσήχθη εἰς τὴν ἐπηγγελμένην τοῖς πατριάρχαις γῆν ὁ περιλειφθεὶς ἀπὸ τῶν ἀπ' Αἰγύπτου ἐξελθόντων λαός.	3. It is significant that it is from that same one (i.e., Jesus), through whom [in addition] to the surname of Jacob the additional name Israel was given, and to Hosea the additional name Iesu, through which name he led into the land promised to the patriarchs the survivors of the people of the Exodus from Egypt.

Here Justin adds something to the previous argument. Justin claims that it was "through the name" (δι' οὗ ὀνόματος) of Iesu (Jesus/Joshua) that Joshua accomplishes the settlement of the Promised Land. Although the point seems mysterious and obscure, later in the dialogue (113) Justin expands on this point and clarifies what is at stake.

1. Ὃ δὲ λέγω τοιοῦτόν ἐστιν. Ἰησοῦν, ὡς προέφην πολλάκις, Αὐσῆν καλούμενον, ἐκεῖνον τὸν μετὰ τοῦ Χαλὲβ κατάσκοπον εἰς τὴν Χαναὰν [ἐπὶ τὴν] γῆν ἀποσταλέντα, Ἰησοῦν Μωυσῆς <ἐπ>εκάλεσε. Τοῦτο σὺ οὐ ζητεῖς δι' ἣν αἰτίαν ἐποίησεν, οὐκ ἀπορεῖς, οὐδὲ φιλοπευστεῖς· τοιγαροῦν λέληθέ σε ὁ Χριστός, καὶ ἀναγινώσκων οὐ συνίης, οὐδὲ νῦν, ἀκούων ὅτι Ἰησοῦς ἐστιν ὁ Χριστὸς ἡμῶν, συλλογίζῃ οὐκ ἀργῶς οὐδ' ὡς ἔτυχεν ἐκείνῳ τεθεῖσθαι τοὔνομα.	1. What I am saying is this: Iesu (Joshua), as I have said many times, was called Ausei (Hoshea); when with Caleb he was sent to scout out the land of Canaan, Moses renamed him Iesu. You (Jews) do not search out for the reason he did this, nor are you fond of inquiring. Accordingly, Christ has escaped your notice, and when reading you do not perceive, and not even now, hearing that Iesu is our Christ, you do nothing to discover that he was given this name purposefully, not accidentally.

---

502 See Larry W. Hurtado, "'Jesus as God's Name, and Jesus as God's Embodied Name in Justin Martyr," in *Justin Martyr and his Worlds* (ed. Sara Parvis and Paul Foster; Minneaopolis: Fortress Press, 2007), 128–136 [130]. Hurtado's analysis of the use of Joshua's name in Justin is thorough and well argued; however, his overall contention, that the use of the name of Joshua as a divine name based on a pre-Pauline Jewish-Christian hermeneutic, appears to me to be overly speculative. As will be seen, if anything, the use of the Joshua-Jesus typology expands over time and is actually fueled by polemic *against* the character of Moses and his law-giving, as argued by Daniélou.

2. ἀλλὰ διὰ τί μὲν ἓν ἄλφα πρώτῳ προσετέθη τοῦ Ἀβραὰμ ὀνόματι, θεολογεῖς, καὶ διὰ τί ἓν ῥῶ τῷ Σάρρας ὀνόματι, ὁμοίως κομπολογεῖς· διὰ τί δὲ τὸ πατρόθεν ὄνομα τῷ Αὐσῇ, τῷ υἱῷ Ναυῆ, ὅλον μετωνόμασται τῷ Ἰησοῦ, οὐ ζητεῖς ὁμοίως.

2. Rather, you theologize about why one *alpha* was added into Abraham's name, and you speak boldly about why one *rho* was added into Sarah's name,[503] but you do not search out in a like fashion why from the name of Ausai, the son of Nau, given by his father, the entire thing was changed to Iesu.[504]

---

503 Whether there was a Hellenistic Jewish interpretation of Abraham's and Sarah's name changes along the lines Justin suggests I do not know; however, Justin does demonstrate in this passage a lack of knowledge of the Hebrew text of the Pentateuch; as Rokeah argues (*Justin*), there are a number of signs in the *Dialogue* that Justin does not know Hebrew at all, despite his having grown up in Neopolis (Shechem) among Samaritans. According to the Hebrew text, Abraham did indeed gain a letter – *hey* – but so did Joshua – *yod*. It is Sarah's name that goes through the greatest transition, as it both gains a letter – *hey* – and loses one – *yod*; thus prompting the rabbinic interpretation that the *yod* of Joshua is actually the lost *yod* from Sarai (*Gen Rab. Lekh Lekha* 47; also *Lev. Rab. Metzora* 19:2):

[ולא תקרא את שמה שרי כי שרה שמה] – אמר ר' יהושע בן קרחה יוד שנטל הקדוש ברוך הוא משרי היה טס ופורח לפני הקדוש ברוך הוא, אמר לפניו רבן כל העולמים בשביל שאני קטן מכל האותיות הוצאתני משם הצדקת, אמר לו הקדוש ברוך הוא לשעבר הייתה בשמה שלנקבה ובסוף האותיות, עכשיו אני נותנך בשם זכר ובראש האותיות ויקרא משה להושע בן נן יהושע (במדבר יג טז).

'Her name will no longer be Sarai, but Sarah is her name' (Gen 17:15) – R. Yehoshua ben Qorḥa said: "The *yod* that the Holy One, bb"h, took from Sarai was flying and floating before the Holy One, bb"h. [The yod] stated before Him: "Master of the worlds, is it because I am the smallest of all letters that you took me out of the righteous woman's name?" The Holy One, bb"h, replied: "In the past you were in a woman's name and the last letter, now I will place you in a man's name and the first letter." – "And Moses called Hoshea son of Nun, Yehoshua."

One can appreciate the irony that the source of this *derasha* is a man named Joshua. This entire midrash may be a polemical response to Justin. It is difficult to say.

504 Halton's translation seems to have missed the point here. He translates: "But why do you never inquire why the name of Hosea, the son of Nun, which his father gave him, was changed to Jesus?" Justin's point seems to be that the change of Ausai to Iesu is much more extensive than merely adding a letter, as was done to Abraham and Sarah, and still the Jews notice only these two but not Joshua.

3. ἐπεὶ δὲ οὐ μόνον μετωνομάσθη αὐτοῦ τὸ ὄνομα, ἀλλὰ καὶ διάδοχος γενόμενος Μωυσέως <ἐνεπλήσθη τοῦ πνεύνατος αὐτοῦ,>[505] μόνος τῶν ἀπ' Αἰγύπτου ἐξελθόντων ἐν ἡλικίᾳ τοιαύτῃ ὄντων εἰσήγαγεν εἰς τὴν ἁγίαν γῆν τὸν περιλειφθέντα λαόν·

καὶ ὃν τρόπον ἐκεῖνος εἰσήγαγεν εἰς τὴν ἁγίαν γῆν τὸν λαόν, οὐχὶ Μωυσῆς, καὶ ὡς ἐκεῖνος ἐν κλήρῳ διένειμεν αὐτὴν τοῖς εἰσελθοῦσι μετ' αὐτοῦ, οὕτως καὶ Ἰησοῦς ὁ Χριστὸς τὴν διασπορὰν τοῦ λαοῦ ἐπιστρέψει, καὶ διαμεριεῖ τὴν ἀγαθὴν γῆν ἑκάστῳ, οὐκέτι δὲ κατὰ ταὐτά.

4. ὁ μὲν γὰρ πρόσκαιρον ἔδωκεν αὐτοῖς τὴν κληρονομίαν, ἅτε οὐ Χριστὸς ὁ θεὸς ὢν οὐδὲ υἱὸς θεοῦ, ὁ δὲ μετὰ τὴν ἁγίαν ἀνάστασιν αἰώνιον ἡμῖν τὴν κατάσχεσιν δώσει.

3. Since not only was his name itself changed, but having become the successor of Moses <having been filled with his spirit>, he alone of those who left Egypt, being of that generation, led the remaining people into the Holy Land.

And in the same way that this one led the people into the Holy Land – not Moses, and thusly this person with a lottery divided it up among those who entered with him, so too Jesus the Christ will gather up the people in the diaspora, and distribute the good land to each, but not in accordance with these [same methods.]

4. However, for (only) a limited time did he (Joshua) give them the inheritance,[506] for he was not Christ the God nor the son of God, but after the holy resurrection, [Jesus] will give us an eternal possession.

Justin chides Trypho for not paying attention to the important mystery surrounding Joshua's name. The importance, according to Justin, is that by renaming Hosea "Iesu," Joshua was given symbolic significance as a prefiguring of Jesus as well as special powers derived from the new name.

If one understands that Joshua is a prefiguring of Jesus, Justin argues, it then makes sense why only Joshua – not Moses – could lead the people into the Promised Land. In this understanding, Moses represents the Jews and the first covenant with God. Joshua represents the believers in Jesus, whether Jews or gentiles, and the new covenant with God. The inheritance of the Promised Land is symbolic of the arrival of the new kingdom of God with the second coming of Christ.

This allegorical interpretation of the first settlement of the Holy Land is not unique to Justin. As described above, Hebrews makes the same argument about Joshua and the incompleteness of his conquest. What is new in Justin's presentation is the idea that, due to the special name of Joshua/Jesus, his conquest was designed to prefigure the coming of the real Joshua/Jesus, that for this reason his

---

505 This is a suggested emendation by Marcovich to a spot he marks in the text as "*lacunam indicavi.*" He bases this reconstruction on the text in 49.6 earlier in the Dialogue. I am unsure why he feels this reconstruction is necessary, but as it is immaterial to the argument in the chapter, I simply follow Marcovich's suggestion.

506 The language here is reminiscent of 1 Peter 1:4, which references the future incorruptible inheritance (κληρονομίαν ἄφθαρτον) that awaits those who accept Jesus.

name was changed to Joshua/Jesus, and that is why it had to be him and no other to conquer the land.

The import of the renaming is not merely symbolic. Joshua receives actual powers from his new name. It is from these powers that he draws the strength to conquer the land of Canaan and even to stop the sun. The former example seems to have been the intent in 106.3 (quoted above), in which Justin states that it was the name that gave Joshua the power to take the Promised Land. The latter example is proffered by Justin immediately following the above-quoted passage (113.4).

τὸν ἥλιον ἔστησεν ἐκεῖνος, μετονομασθεὶς That one (Joshua) stopped the sun, having
πρότερον τῷ Ἰησοῦ ὀνόματι καὶ λαβὼν ἀπὸ been renamed with the name of Iesu, and pos-
τοῦ πνεύματος αὐτοῦ ἰσχύν. sessing the strength of his spirit.

Justin repeats the connection between Joshua's name and the miracle of the sun towards the end of the dialogue as well (132.1). The context of the statement is Justin's criticism of the Israelites building the Golden Calf after having witnessed God's miraculous interventions on their behalf.

...καὶ [μετὰ] ταῦτα πάλιν τῆς γῆς ὑμῖν παραδο- ...and again after this, your land was delivered
θείσης μετὰ δυνάμεως τοσαύτης, ὡς καὶ τὸν to you with miracles so great, that you wit-
ἥλιον θεάσασθαι ὑμᾶς προστάξει τοῦ ἀνδρὸς nessed – at the command of that man who
ἐκείνου τοῦ ἐπονομασθέντος τῷ Ἰησοῦ ὀνόματι was renamed with the name of Iesu – the sun
σταθέντα ἐν τῷ οὐρανῷ καὶ μὴ δύναντα μέχρις standing in the sky without power for as long
ὡρῶν τριάκοντα ἕξ... as 36 hours.

Although he does not say so explicitly in this text, Justin strongly implies that such great power was wielded by Joshua because he was renamed with the name of Jesus. The awesome nature of the miracle of the sun is a comparatively minor point in the *Dialogue with Trypho*, but it will receive great attention by Origen, as I will discuss below.

What seems to be of more consequence to Justin is the defeat of Amalek at the hands of Joshua. In an analysis strongly reminiscent of that found in the Epistle of Barnabas, Justin writes (90.4–5):

4. Ότε ὁ λαός, φημί, ἐπολέμει τῷ Ἀμαλὴκ καὶ ὁ τοῦ Ναυῆ υἱός, ὁ ἐπονομασθεὶς τῷ Ἰησοῦ ὀνόματι, τῆς μάχης ἦρχεν, αὐτὸς Μωυσῆς ηὔχετο τῷ θεῷ τὰς χεῖρας ἑκατέρωσ<ε> ἐκπετάσας, Ὢρ507 δὲ καὶ Ἀαρὼν ὑπεβάσταζον αὐτὰς πανῆμαρ, ἵνα μὴ κοπωθέντος αὐτοῦ χαλασθῶσιν. εἰ γὰρ ἐνεδεδώκει τι τοῦ σχήματος τούτου, τοῦ τὸν σταυρὸν μιμουμένου, ὡς γέγραπται ἐν ταῖς Μωυσέως γραφαῖς· ὁ λαὸς ἡττᾶτο· εἰ δὲ ἐν τῇ τάξει ἔμενε ταύτῃ, Ἀμαλὴκ ἐνικᾶτο τοσοῦτον, καὶ ἰσχύων <ὁ λαὸς> διὰ τοῦ σταυροῦ ἴσχυεν.

4. When the people, I say (to Trypho), fought with Amalek, and the son of Nau, who was renamed with the name of Iesu, led the battle, Moses himself prayed to God for help with hands extended. Hur together with Aaron bore them from underneath all day, lest from his weariness they be slackened. For if he were to yield from that figure, which mimicked that of the cross – as written in Moses' scripture – the people would lose. But when he remained in this arrangement, Amalek was defeated, and the people were strengthened through the cross.

5. οὐ γάρ, ὅτι οὕτως ηὔχετο Μωυσῆς, διὰ τοῦτο κρείσσων ὁ λαὸς ἐγίνετο, ἀλλ' ὅτι, ἐν ἀρχῇ τῆς μάχης τοῦ ὀνόματος τοῦ Ἰησοῦ ὄντος, αὐτὸς τὸ σημεῖον τοῦ σταυροῦ ἐποίει...

5. Really it was not because Moses prayed that the people were made stronger, rather because at the battlefront was the name of Iesu while he [Moses] made the sign of the cross...

According to Justin the defeat of Amalek is to be explained by the double invocation of Jesus symbolism. Up on the mountain, Moses makes the sign of the cross with his hands, symbolizing Jesus. Down on the battlefield, Joshua, bearing the name of Jesus, defeats the Amalekites in battle. As in Barnabas, it would appear that Amalek represents something more than just the physical enemy. Justin will make this point clearer in a different passage.

Justin reiterates this point in the context of his discussion of the power of Jesus symbolism. After noting certain symbolic references to the cross in the blessing of Joseph, Justin notes how the same symbol is a curse for unbelievers (91.3):

τοῖς δὲ ἀπίστοις τὸ αὐτὸ σχῆμα εἰς κατάλυσιν καὶ καταδίκην δηλοῦται· ὃν τρόπον ἐν τῷ ἀπ' Αἰγύπτου ἐξελθόντι λαῷ διά τε τοῦ τύπου τῆς ἐκτάσεως τῶν χειρῶν τοῦ Μωυσέως καὶ τῆς τοῦ Ναυῆ υἱοῦ ἐπικλήσεως τοῦ ὀνόματος Ἰησοῦ ὁ Ἀμαλὴκ μὲν ἡττᾶτο, Ἰσραὴλ δὲ ἐνίκα.

But for the unbelievers, the same symbol manifests destruction and condemnation. As at the time when the people left Egypt and by the form of the outstretched hands of Moses and the son of Nau being called by the name of Iesu, the Amalekites were conquered and Israel was victorious.

Justin appears to be drawing on the biblical precedent of 1 Cor 1:18:

---

507 This is the spelling in Marcovich; the text on TLG has Ὢρ.

Ὁ λόγος γὰρ ὁ τοῦ σταυροῦ τοῖς μὲν ἀπολλυ- μένοις μωρία ἐστίν, τοῖς δὲ σῳζομένοις ἡμῖν δύναμις θεοῦ ἐστιν.

For the word about the cross is foolishness to those who would perish but it is the power of God to those who would be saved.[508]

Paul seems to be using this concept metaphorically, in the sense that those who reject Jesus laugh at the idea that this demi-god was crucified, thereby increasing their sinfulness and punishment, whereas believers, who see this as an example of the power of God, increase their merit by believing it. Justin, however, seems to use this idea in a different way, pointing to the fact that the granting of the Savior's name to Joshua gave him power to help the Israelites and to destroy the Amalekites.

Finally, in a later section, Justin greatly expands on this point (131.4–5):

4. καὶ σημεῖον <δε ὑμῖν> τοῦ σταυροῦσθαι μέλ- λοντος καὶ ἐπὶ τῶν ὄφεων τῶν δακόντων ὑμᾶς, ὡς προεῖπον, γεγένηται (πάντα προλαμβάνον- τος πρὸ τῶν ἰδίων καιρῶν τὰ μυστήρια χαρίζε- σθαι ὑμῖν τοῦ θεοῦ, πρὸς ὃν ἀχάριστοι ἐλέγχε- σθε ἀεὶ γεγενημένοι) καὶ διὰ τοῦ τύπου τῆς ἐκτάσεως τῶν χειρῶν Μωυσέως, καὶ [ὡς] τοῦ ἐπονομασθέντος Ἰησοῦ πολεμούντων τὸν Ἀμα- λήκ. περὶ οὗ εἶπεν ὁ θεὸς ἀναγραφῆναι τὸ γεγε- νημένον, φήσας καὶ εἰς τὰς ὑμῶν ἀκοὰς Ἰησοῦ παραθέσθαι τὸ ὄνομα, εἰπὼν ὅτι οὗτός ἐστιν ὁ μέλλων ἐξαλείφειν ἀπὸ τῆς ὑπὸ τὸν οὐρανὸν τὸ μνημόσυνον τοῦ Ἀμαλήκ.

4. And to you a sign was given of he who was destined to be crucified, both with regard to the serpents that bit you, as I stated previously[509] (all the mysteries were presented to you, before their time, by the grace of God, before whom you have always been possessed by ingrati- tude), as well as through the arms of Moses making the form of the cross, and through the renaming of Iesu during the war with Ama- lek, about which God said: "Write down what happened," and said to keep in mind the report of the name of Iesu stating that this is the one coming to erase from underneath the heavens the memory of Amalek.

---

508 It seems possible that Paul himself is drawing on scripture for this idea, specifically the final verse in Hosea (14:9/10):

τίς σοφὸς καὶ συνήσει ταῦτα ἢ συνετὸς καὶ ἐπιγνώσεται αὐτά; διότι εὐθεῖαι αἱ ὁδοὶ τοῦ κυρίου καὶ δίκαιοι πορεύσονται ἐν αὐταῖς οἱ δὲ ἀσεβεῖς ἀσθενήσουσιν ἐν αὐταῖς.

מִי חָכָם וְיָבֵן אֵלֶּה נָבוֹן וְיֵדָעֵם כִּי־יְשָׁרִים דַּרְכֵי יְהוָה וְצַדִּקִים יֵלְכוּ בָם וּפֹשְׁעִים יִכָּשְׁלוּ בָם.

Who is wise to discern these things, and discerning to know them? That the ways of Yнwн are straight; the righteous walk upon them but the sinners stumble upon them.

509 Justin believes that the bronze serpant was also a symbol of the cross, no doubt basing himself upon John 3:14–15.

5. καὶ ὅτι τὸ μνημόσυνον τοῦ Ἀμαλὴκ καὶ μετὰ τὸν τοῦ Ναυῆ υἱὸν μένει, φαίνεται· διὰ δὲ τοῦ Ἰησοῦ τοῦ σταυρωθέντος, οὗ καὶ τὰ σύμβολα ἐκεῖνα προκηρύγματα ἦν τῶν κατ' αὐτὸν ἁπάντων, ὅτι μέλλει ἐξολοθρευθήσεσθαι τὰ δαιμόνια καὶ δεδιέναι τὸ ὄνομα αὐτοῦ, καὶ πάσας τὰς ἀρχὰς καὶ τὰς βασιλείας ὁμοίως ὑφορᾶσθαι αὐτόν, καὶ ἐκ παντὸς γένους ἀνθρώπων θεοσεβεῖς καὶ εἰρηνικοὺς δείκνυσθαι εἶναι τοὺς εἰς αὐτὸν πιστεύοντας, <καὶ ἡ γραφὴ> φανερὸν ποιεῖ, καὶ τὰ προανιστορημένα ὑπ' ἐμοῦ, Τρύφων, σημαίνουσι.

5. Now it is well-known that the memory of Amalek remains after the time of the son of Nau. But through the Iesu that was crucified, of whom those signs were a proclamation of what would happen to him, the demons were destined to be destroyed by him and to be afraid at his name, and all of the chiefs and kings together would tremble on his account, and from all the races of mankind the righteous and peaceful would prove themselves, those who believe in him. And the Scripture makes manifest, Trypho, and my demonstrations indicate this.

Again Justin points to the dual signs regarding Jesus: Moses extending his arms like a cross and Joshua receiving the name of Iesu. However, in this restatement of the point, Justin adds a key interpretive crux: the meaning of Amalek.[510] Justin tells Trypho that it is undeniable that the memory of Amalek was not wiped out by Iesu the son of Nau. Hence, it must be to the crucified Iesu that the verse actually refers.

Justin explains this by stating that the true purpose of the reference was to say that after the incarnation and crucifixion of Iesu, people of all nations around the world began to show their true goodness due to their faith in him. Apparently, this is the way Amalek (evil?) will be wiped out from the world. Again, Iesu son of Nau is meant to be understood as functioning symbolically on behalf of his namesake, Iesu Christ. Amalek is also functioning allegorically, apparently referring to the demons (δαιμόνια) that Jesus will eventually destroy.

Justin extends here the interpretive paradigm already existent in Hebrews, that since after Joshua there is failure, whether this is expressed as lack of rest (Hebrews) or the continued existence of Amalek (Justin), the biblical verses promising these things must be referring to something in the future: the coming of Jesus.

Justin makes this point in the clearest and most unambiguous way when discussing the circumcision of the Israelites after entering the land of Canaan (113).[511]

---

510 This element is implied in Barnabas but not explicitly expressed.
511 Justin actually makes an obscure reference to this very early in the dialogue (24.2), but this line would have been virtually impossible to understand if the reader did not already know the analysis Justin proffers later (113.6).

6. ἐκεῖνος λέγεται δευτέραν περιτομὴν μαχαίραις πετρίναις τὸν λαὸν περιτετμηκέναι (ὅπερ
κήρυγμα ἦν τῆς περιτομῆς ταύτης ἧς περιέτεμεν ἡμᾶς αὐτὸς Ἰησοῦς Χριστὸς ἀπὸ τῶν
λίθων καὶ τῶν ἄλλων εἰδώλων) καὶ θημωνιὰν
ποιῆσαι τῶν ἀπὸ ἀκροβυστίας (τουτέστιν ἀπὸ
τῆς πλάνης τοῦ κόσμου) ἐν παντὶ τόπῳ περιτμηθέντων πετρίναις μαχαίραις, (<τουτέστι>
τοῖς Ἰησοῦ τοῦ κυρίου ἡμῶν λόγοις). ὅτι γὰρ
λίθος καὶ πέτρα ἐν παραβολαῖς ὁ Χριστὸς διὰ
τῶν προφητῶν ἐκηρύσσετο, ἀποδέδεικταί μοι.

6. This one (Joshua) was said to circumcise the people of foreskins a second time with swords of stone (thus it was a sign of that circumcision with which Jesus Christ would circumcise us – from stones and other idols) and to make a gathering from all of the uncircumcised (that is from the deception of the world) in every place circumcising them with stone swords (namely with the words of Jesus our Lord.)[512] For rock and stone are allegories for Christ through the proclamation of the prophets, as has been demonstrated by me.

7. Καὶ τὰς μαχαίρος οὖν τὰς πετρίνας τοὺς λόγους αὐτοῦ ἀκουσόμεθα, δι᾽ ὧν οἱ ἀπὸ τῆς ἀκροβυστίας πλανώμενοι τοσοῦτοι καρδίας περιτομὴν περιετμήθησαν ἣν περιτνηθῆναι καὶ τοὺς
ἔχοντες τὴν ἀπὸ τοῦ Ἀβραὰμ ἀρχὴν λαβοῦσαν
περιτομὴν ὁ θεὸς διὰ τοῦ Ἰησοῦ προύτρεπεν
ἔκτοτε, [καὶ] τοὺς εἰσελθόντας εἰς τὴν γῆν ἐκεί-
νην τὴν ἁγίαν δευτέραν περιτομὴν πετρίναις
μαχαίραις εἰπὼν τὸν Ἰησοῦν περιτετμηκέναι
αὐτούς.

7. And so, by the stone swords the meaning of his words we hear [properly], by which those who were wandering were circumcised from their uncircumcision with the circumcision of the heart.[513] God exhorted through Jesus that thereafter they who had circumcision and were in possession of this from as early as Abraham should receive [the new] circumcision, for upon those who entered into the Holy Land it is said that Iesu (Joshua) performed a second circumcision with stone swords.

Picking up on the unusual description of Joshua circumcising the Israelites for a second time—how can a man be circumcised twice?—Justin argues that the significance of this event is entirely symbolic.[514] Joshua's act foreshadows the eventual spiritual circumcision that the world will undergo after the coming of Jesus

---

512 Although the "stone sword" alludes to Josh 5:2, the concept also has resonance with Eph 6:17:

καὶ τὴν περικεφαλαίαν τοῦ σωτηρίου δέξασθε καὶ Take the helmet of salvation and the sword
τὴν μάχαιραν τοῦ πνεύματος, ὅ ἐστιν ῥῆμα θεοῦ. of the spirit, which is the word of God.

513 See Rom 2:29, in which Paul states that (*true*) circumcision is of the heart (περιτομὴ καρδίας.)

514 The theme of spiritual circumcision is a dominant one in Christian exegesis, especially that of the polemical variety. See, for example, Col 2:11:

Ἐν ᾧ καὶ περιετμήθητε περιτομῇ ἀχειροποιήτῳ In him also you were circumcised with a spi-
ἐν τῇ ἀπεκδύσει τοῦ σώματος τῆς σαρκός, ἐν τῇ ritual circumcision, by putting off the body of
περιτομῇ τοῦ Χριστοῦ. the flesh in the circumcision of Christ.

For a discussion of spiritual circumcision, see: Everett Ferguson, "Spiritual Circumcision in Early Christianity," *SJT* 41 (1988): 485–497.

(once more following the interpretive program of Hebrews). The Jesus symbolism is doubled in this case as well. Joshua (Iesu) carries the name of Jesus and the stone implements are reminiscent of Jesus, since he – in Justin's exegesis – is often referred to by the prophets as "rock."[515]

Justin is focused on the name of Joshua and not his character. This can be seen by the fact that he uses a similar argument about yet another Iesu: Joshua the Beit Shemshite, referenced in 1 Samuel 6 (vv. 14 and 18).[516] In that story, the Philistines have been plagued by Υηωη after taking the Ark the Covenant. They decide to return the ark to Israel on the back of a cart and let the oxen go where they may. The oxen end up on the property of Joshua of Beit Shemesh. At that point, a sacrifice is offered on a large rock on his property, and the Philistines eventually dedicate five golden mice to adorn this area. Discussing this story (132), Justin describes the miraculous coincidence of the oxen ending up on the field of someone named Joshua.[517]

3. καὶ πραξάντων <αὐτῶν> τοῦτο αἱ δαμάλεις, ὑπὸ μηδενὸς ὁδηγούμεναι ἀνθρώπων, οὐκ ἦλθον μὲν εἰς τὸν τόπον ὁπόθεν εἴληπτο ἡ σκηνή, ἀλλ' εἰς χωρίον τινὸς ἀνδρὸς καλουμένου Αὐσῆ, ὁμωνύμου ἐκείνου τοῦ μετονομασθέντος τῷ Ἰησοῦ ὀνόματι, ὡς προελέλεκτο, ὃς καὶ εἰσήγαγε τὸν λαὸν εἰς τὴν γῆν καὶ κατεκληροδότησεν αὐτοῖς αὐτήν·	3. Carrying this out, the heifers, without any human guidance, did not go to the place from where the tabernacle was taken, rather to the field of a certain man named Ausei (Hoshea),[518] the same name as that of him whose name was changed to Iesu (Joshua), as I stated above, who led the people into the land and divided it among them.

---

515 See the imagery in 1 Cor 10:4, interpreting the biblical stories about the Israelites drinking from the rock with the same allegorical understanding:

... ἔπινον γὰρ ἐκ πνευματικῆς ἀκολουθούσης πέτρας, ἡ πέτρα δὲ ἦν ὁ Χριστός.	...for they drank from the spiritual rock that followed them, for the rock was Christ.

As will be seen in a later section, Origen references this verse explicitly in his interpretation of the stone knives.

516 Although a number of exegetes apply the paradigm to Joshua the high priest, Justin is the only one who foregoes this opportunity, applying it instead to Joshua of Beit Shemesh.

517 One odd fact about Justin's rendition that must be noted is that instead of the ark being taken and returned, as in the MT (ארון) and LXX (κιβωτός) texts, Justin has the story referencing the tabernacle/tent of meeting (σκηνή). I do not know whether this stems from a different biblical text in Justin's possession or if it is just a mistake on his part. Either way, it makes little difference whether one imagines the ark or the tabernacle being returned for the purposes of analyzing the significance of a character named Joshua in the narrative.

518 Halton translates this name as Joshua and the latter as Jesus. This is misleading, as Jesus and Joshua have the same spelling in Greek, whereas Hoshea is spelled differently.

εἰς ὃ χωρίον ἐλθοῦσαι μεμενήκασι, δεικνυ-
μένου ὑμῖν καὶ διὰ τούτων, ὅτι τῷ τῆς δυνάμεως ὀνόματι ὡδηγήθησαν, ὡς πρότερον ὁ
περιλειφθεὶς λαὸς ἀπὸ τῶν ἀπ' Αἰγύπτου ἐξελθόντων διὰ τοῦ λαβόντος τὸ Ἰησοῦ ὄνομα,
Αὐσῆ πρότερον καλουμένου, εἰς τὴν γῆν
ὡδηγήθη.

Having arrived at this field, they stopped, demonstrating to you through this that they were
led by a powerful name, just like earlier the
surviving people who left Egypt were led into
the land through the leadership of the one
called Iesu (Joshua) who was formerly called
Ausei (Hoshea).

Justin argues that it was the name of Iesu that brought the oxen carrying the tabernacle to the field in Beit Shemesh. Since, in Justin's text, the name of the man
was Hoshea and not Joshua, Justin is required to make a tortuous argument.[519]
He states that since Hoshea is the same name that Joshua had before he was renamed, this ties Hoshea the Beit Shimshite to Hoshea the leader of Israel, who in
turn is tied to Jesus (Iesu) through the changing of his name to Joshua (Iesu) by
Moses.[520]

From this example, Justin makes clear that it is the name of Iesu, and not
some characteristic of Joshua as a leader or prophet, that gives Joshua such
power and importance. The fact that Joshua the Beit Shimshite–someone
about whom almost nothing is known–has the power to "call" the oxen carrying
the tabernacle over to his property, demonstrates that the power of the name
works on its own.[521]

Although Joshua son of Nun was a much more important personage, having
led the descendants of the Israelites who survived Egypt into the Promised Land,
the reason for this is that God chose him at the time to do so. God has Moses give
Hoshea the special name of Joshua so that he would have the power to accomplish his important task. The bottom line is that both Joshuas and the incidents
that befell them were meant to function, in addition to their historical importance, as symbols for the coming of Jesus and his power in the world.

The significance of this argument about Joshua's name in Justin's program
can be seen by the fact that – on this particular point – Trypho acquiesces. In
section 89, Trypho is attempting to explain why he and the Jews find it so difficult to believe in a messiah that was crucified, considering the humiliation associated with this kind of a death.

---

519 The MT has the man's name as Joshua, not Hoshea, but that does not mean that Justin did.
In fact, the LXX reads Ωσηε, an alternative spelling of Hoshea.
520 Ironically, if Justin had known Hebrew and had been familiar with the MT, in which the
character's name is, in fact, Joshua, his argument would have been much simpler.
521 Justin does reference Joshua the high priest (79.4) but makes no attempt to draw a parallel
comparison between him and Jesus.

1. Καὶ ὁ Τρύφων· Εὖ ἴσθι, ἔφη, ὅτι καὶ πᾶν τὸ γένος ἡμῶν τὸν Χριστὸν ἐκδέχεται, καὶ ὅτι πᾶσαι αἱ γραφαί, ἃς ἔφης, εἰς αὐτὸν εἴρηνται, ὁμολογοῦμεν· καὶ ὅτι τὸ Ἰησοῦς ὄνομα δεδυσώπηκέ με, <τὸ> τῷ τοῦ Ναυῆ υἱῷ ἐπικληθέν, ἐκδότ<ικ>ως ἔχειν καὶ πρὸς τοῦτο<ν>, καὶ τοῦτό φημι.

1. And Trypho said: You know well that all of our tribe await the messiah, and we agree that all of the scriptures that you stated proclaim him. Also, that the name Iesu (Joshua), which was given to the son of Nau, has prompted me to hold an inclination towards this, and that [much] I will say.

The first part of Trypho's admission is not surprising. The fact that Jews believed in the messiah and understood a number of scriptural verses to be referring to his coming is well-known. What is surprising is Trypho's second admission, that the fact that "the son of Nau" was given the name Iesu inclines him to believe in the messiah, perhaps even in the messianic aspirations of Jesus or someone named Jesus. This is a strange admission, since Trypho's very next words are that he has trouble believing that Jesus was the messiah since he was crucified. Is Trypho saying here that he believes that the Messiah will be named Joshua (Iesu) only that it wasn't the Joshua (Jesus) in whom Justin believes? This does seem to be the case—though it would be a strange position for a Jew to take. Even though the name of the messiah is a comparatively minor point, giving in on this would bring a "non-believing" Jew halfway to belief in Jesus.

Justin believes that the analogy between Joshua and Jesus is a critical one for interpreting scripture and convincing Jews of the truth of the Gospel's assertion. Joshua, in taking over for Moses, leading the people into the land, fighting Amalek, and circumcising the Israelites, symbolizes the future spiritual accomplishments of his namesake, Jesus.

Justin does not completely allegorize the character of Joshua. Although Justin picks up on a number of significant themes regarding Joshua to be parallel to Jesus, this does not stop him from understanding Joshua as someone other than Jesus as well, and he discusses Joshua as Joshua in a number of other places in the dialogue.

In 49.6, Justin compares Joshua receiving Moses' spirit to John the Baptist received Elijah's spirit, without also stating that Joshua received Jesus' spirit. Similarly, in 61.1 and 62.4–5, Justin discusses the scene in which God (or the angel of God) appears to Joshua outside Jericho. As part of this discussion, Justin makes no attempt to understand Joshua as Jesus or to explain why it is that an incarnation of Jesus would be unfamiliar with God the father the way Joshua seems to be in the scene. Origen will be the exegete who creates a complete typological interpretation for all of the Joshua stories as a foreshadowing of Jesus.

The Typology Goes Latin: Tertullian

The usefulness of the Joshua as Jesus typology for polemics between Jews and Christians can be seen by the way it is used by Tertullian in his *Adversus Iudaeos*.[522] Quintus Septimius Florens Tertullianus (c.160 – 225) lived in Carthage and was one of the first of the Church Fathers to write in Latin. He was a prolific writer, and many of his works have survived. His works are characterized by strong language and a solid knowledge of Latin and Greek style rhetorical conventions.[523]

In putting together his *Adversus Iudaeos*, it is clear that Tertullian had access to Justin's *Dialogue with Trypho* and that this work served both as an inspiration for this genre and as a source for a number of the specific arguments Tertullian made use of in his own polemics.[524] However, even though Tertullian does begin his treatise with a description of a debate between a Jew and a Christian that turned sour, he does not cast his work in the form of a debate, but rather in the form of an essay; Geoffrey Dunn calls it a "position paper" or a "pamphlet."[525]

The overall project of *Adversus Iudaeos* is to prove that the Old Testament both foreshadows the salvation of Christians and that the Christian claim actual-

---

522 Although there is some debate about whether this particular tract was written by Tertullian, Geoffrey Dunn makes a strong case for this work being an unpolished draft which Tertullian never completely edited or published. Pieces of this work were later incorporated into the third book of Tertullian's much more famous (and completed) work *Adversus Marcionem*. For a survey of the scholarly debate about Tertullian's authorship, see the first chapter of Geoffrey D. Dunn, *Tertullian's Aduersus Iudaeos: A Rhetorical Analysis* (North American Patristics Society: Patristic Monograph Series 19; Washington D.C.: Catholic University of America Press, 2008), 5 – 30, and the bibliography cited therein. For our purposes it does not make much difference whether one sees Tertullian as the author or not, as the important point is that the Joshua-Jesus typology was seen as useful by the author of *Adversus Iudaeos* in proving his point about Jesus' replacement of Moses and the Torah. To paraphrase a glib saying: If it was not written by Tertullian, then it was written by some other second-third century North African Church Father named Tertullian.
523 For an analysis of how rhetoric is used by Tertullian in a number of his works, see: Robert Dick Sider, *Ancient Rhetoric and the Art of Tertullian* (Oxford: Oxford University Press, 1971). Dunn (among others) argues that Tertullian's style may be best understood as a sort of "protest" to the style most popular among readers and rhetoricians during his period of time, known as the Second Sophistic. Whereas the main concern of popular (pagan) writers at the time was to entertain eruditely, Tertullian used his rhetoric for what he considered to be more serious purposes (Dunn, *Tertullian's*, 32 – 36). Nevertheless, Luke Timothy Johnson (personal communication) believes that the notion of "opposing rhetoric" has been overdone.
524 "His dependence on St Justin is obvious" (Daniélou, *From Shadows*, 238).
525 Dunn, *Tertullian's*, 44.

ly supersedes that of the Jews. In other words, not only is it true that gentiles (and Jews) who accept Jesus are granted salvation according to the Bible, but once Jesus was resurrected, belief in him is now the only way to receive salvation, with the Jewish adherence to Torah outdated and no longer effective. In order to prove this point, Tertullian must make the argument directly from the Old Testament; otherwise the argument would not be effective against Jews in future polemics and would not inoculate Christians against Jewish attacks on Christianity as biblically inauthentic. It is within this context that Tertullian makes use of the Joshua-Jesus typology.

Tertullian's most extensive discussion of Joshua comes towards the end of chapter 9.[526]

[20] *Sed Christus, inquiunt, qui venturus creditur, non et Iesus dicitur. Quare igitur is qui venit, Iesus Christus appellatur?*	[20] "But if Christ", they say, "who is believed to be coming is not called Iesu, why, therefore, was he that has come called Iesu Christ?"[527]

---

526 The translation is mine, but I used Geoffrey Dunn's translation as a baseline reference; Geoffrey D. Dunn, *Tertullian* (The Early Church Fathers; London: Routledge, 2004), 63–104.

527 This seems like an odd way of phrasing the point for a Jew, as one would expect more distancing from any belief in Jesus being the messiah or Jesus having come. In fact, Tertullian does this in a number of places, most egregiously at the beginning of chapter 9, in which he has the Jew state "Christo qui iam venit" (the Messiah who has already come). Dunn takes note of this tendency:

> Even though put onto the lips of the opponent, it reveals the thinking of Tertullian. In other words, I think that here we find a degree of slackness in Tertullian's writing, in that he did not present a Jewish opponent's position accurately enough. Given his rhetorical objective, which was to persuade his readers that he, not his opponents, was right, it is not surprising to see this. One gets the sense that a real opponent, or a more careful and less rhetorical Tertullian, would have written "the so-called Christ" or "the Christ which you (Christians) believe to have come" (Dunn, Tertullian's, 123).

The phenomenon of imprecise or rhetorical writing of an opponent's view is even starker, in my opinion, in Justin's *Dialogue with Trypho*, in which Trypho proffers many surprising, even inexplicable, admissions to Justin. However, for an attempt to argue that the dialogue represents an actual Jew's debate with Justin, see Timothy J. Horner, *Listening to Trypho: Justin Martyr's Dialogue Reconsidered* (Contributions to Biblical Exegesis and Theology 28; Leuven: Peeters, 2001).

²¹ Constabit autem utrumque nomen in Christo dei, in quo invenitur etiam Iesus appellatus. Disce et erroris tui morem: dum Moysi successor destinaretur Auses filius Naue, transfertur certe de pristino nomine et incipit vocari Iesus. "Certe", inquis. Hanc prius dicimus figuram futuri fuisse.

²¹ However, each name will stand together in the Christ of God, in whom is found also the name Iesu. Learn the nature of your errors: As the successor to Moses is determined to be Ausi (Hosea) son of Nau, certainly his original name is transposed and he begins to be called Iesu (Joshua). "Certainly," you say. This first [Iesu] we declare to have been a figure of the future [Iesu].

²² Nam quia Iesus Christus secundum populum, quod sumus nos nationes in saeculi deserto commorantes ante, introducturus esset in terram repromissionis melle et lacte manantem, id est in vitae aeternae possessionem qua nihil dulcius,
idque non per Moysen id est non per legis disciplinam, sed per Iesum id est per novae legis gratiam provenire habebat circumcisis nobis petrina acie id est Christi praeceptis – petra enim Christus multis modis et figuris praedicatus est.

²² For since Iesu Christ was to introduce the second people – for our nations were a race lingering previously in the desert – into the Promised Land, flowing with milk and honey; that is to say in possession of eternal life, than which nothing is sweeter.[528]
And it originates not through Moses, that is to say not through the discipline of law, but through Iesu, that is to say through the grace of the new law, having our circumcision through the sharp rock, that is to say the precepts of Christ, for Christ is a rock in many ways and was predicted in this form.[529]

Ideo is vir qui in huius sacramenti imagines parabatrur etiam nominis dominici inauguratus est figura, ut Iesus nominaretur. Nam qui ad Moysen loquebatur, ipse erat dei filius qui et semper videbatur; deum enim patrem nemo umquam vidit et vixit.

For that reason, that man who was being prepared in the likeness of this sacrament was likewise installed with the form of the name of the Lord, and Iesu was his name. For he that spoke to Moses was himself the son of God; and he was always the one who was seen. Indeed, no one could ever see God the father and live.

²³ Et ideo constat ipsum dei filium Moyseo esse locutum et dixisse ad populum: "Ecce ego mitto angelum meum ante faciem tuam, id est populi, qui te custodiat in itinere et introducat te in terram quam praeparavi tibi. Intendite illi et audite eum et ne inobaudiens fueris ei; non enim celabit te, quoniam nomen meum super illum est." Populum enim introducturus erat Iesus in terram repromissionis, non Moyses.

²³ And therefore, it has been agreed upon that it was the son of God that spoke to Moses and said to the people: "Behold, I send my angel before your face, in order to protect you on your way and bring you into the land which I have prepared for you. Pay attention to him and listen to him and do not be disobedient to him, for he will not conceal you, since my name is upon him" (Exod 23:20–21). For Iesu (Joshua) was to bring the people into the Promised Land, not Moses.

---

528 Like Justin, Tertullian is influenced by the thinking of Heb 3–4.
529 Like Justin, Tertullian is using the Christ as rock imagery in 1 Cor 10:4.

Angelum quidem dixit eum ob magnitudinem virtutum quas erat editurus[530] *– quas virtutes fecisset Iesus Naue, et ipsi legistis – et ob offici-um prophetae nuntiantis scilicet divinam volun-tatem. Sicuti et praecursorem Christi Iohannem futurum angelum appellat per prophetam spiri-tus dicens ex persona patris: "Ecce ego mitto angelum meum ante faciem tuam, id est Chris-ti, qui praeparabit viam tuam ante te." Nec novum est spiritui sancto angelos appellare eos quos ministros suae virtutis deus praeficit...*

Indeed, he (God) called him an angel because of the magnitude of the deeds which he was to perform—which deeds Iesu son of Nau per-formed, and you have read so yourselves— also through the duty of the prophet announc-ing, of course, the divine will. This is just like what the spirit, speaking as the person of the father says about the precursor of Christ, John, calling him a future angel: "Behold I am sending my angel before your (i.e. Christ's) face,[531] who will prepare your way before you." Nor is it novel for the Holy Spirit to call those whom God has chosen for his ministry "angels."[532]

[25] *Sic et Iesum <autem> ob nominis sui futurum sacramentum. Id enim nomen suum confirmavit quod ipse ei indiderat, quia non [angelum nec] Ausen sed Iesum eum iusserat exinde vocari. Sic igitur utrumque nomen competit Christo dei, ut et Iesus [et Christus] appellaretur.*

[25] Thus, was Iesu <also> through his name a fu-ture sacrament. For that name he (the son of God) confirmed to him because it itself would be given him, because neither [angel nor] Ausi but Iesu he was commanded to be called thereafter. Thus, consequently, each name fits the Christ of God, such that he should be called both Iesu and Christ.

In this lengthy passage, Tertullian argues that there is precedent for the name Jesus, i.e., that there is a specific prophetically based reason for the messiah to have been named Jesus. This is an important claim since the Jewish counter-claim—based on Isaiah 7:14—was that if Jesus really is the person being referred to by Isaiah, then his name should have been Emmanuel. This claim is parried by Tertullian by asserting that it was the meaning of the name Emmanuel—God

---

530 Dunn translates this as "courage which he was to produce" (Dunn, *Tertullian*, 88); ANF translates "deeds he was to achieve." My translation follows the latter reading, since I think this is a reference to the miracles wrought by Joshua, especially the stopping of the sun. This would place Tertullian in the same interpretive path as Justin and Origen.

531 This "verse" is referenced in Mark 1:2, which is attributed to Isaiah in certain manuscripts and in Matt 11:10. There is no such verse in the Hebrew Bible. This appears to be a composite verse beginning with Exod 23:20 and ending with Mal 3:1.

532 Interestingly, Heb 1–2 has a long description of angels and their position in the world, and how they differ both from human messengers and from Jesus, which seems to be out of con-sonance with Tertullian's statement here. Nevertheless, Tertullian's description finds some res-onance in one verse from this passage, Heb 1:14:

οὐχὶ πάντες εἰσὶν λειτουργικὰ πνεύματα εἰς διακονίαν ἀποστελλόμενα διὰ τοὺς μέλλοντας κληρονομεῖν σωτηρίαν;

Are not all angels spirits in the divine service, sent to serve for the sake of those who are to inherit salvation?

is with us—that is the important message of the verse. Still, the best defense being a good offense, Tertullian replies that a proper reading of scripture would lead one to understand that the name of the messiah is *supposed* to be Joshua.

Like Barnabas and Justin, Tertullian notes that the name Joshua must be significant, seeing that Moses specifically changed the son of Nun's name from Hoshea to Joshua. The significance Tertullian finds in this relates to Joshua's position as Moses' successor, and, more importantly, as the one who will bring Israel into the Promised Land. For Tertullian, the fact that it would be Joshua and not Moses is critical.

Tertullian's main argument hinges upon an allegorical understanding of Moses, Joshua, and the entry into the land. Tertullian interprets Moses as the Torah law, Joshua as Jesus and the law of grace, and the entry into the Promised Land as possession of eternal life (Heb 3 – 4 again); hence it is Jesus and the law of grace, not the Torah Law of Moses, which will lead Israel to eternal life. Tertullian buttresses this reading by pointing out that it was, in fact, the second generation—not the exodus generation—that entered the Promised Land. He interprets this second generation as an allegory for gentiles, since they wandered the spiritual desert before they found Christ.

Turning to another biblical account, Tertullian comments on the re-circumcision of the Israelites by Joshua. The verse has Joshua circumcising this second generation of Israelites with a sharp rock. The sharp rock is an allegory for Jesus, who was compared to a rock by the prophets, and the circumcision is the spiritual circumcision, bringing the community of faith into the grace of God.

Adding to this picture, Tertullian notes that the book of Exodus refers to an angel that will bring Israel into the Promised Land. Tertullian understands this as a reference to Joshua himself, and claims that it is proper to call him an angel, meaning an agent of God, considering the impressive miracles that he wrought. This brings Tertullian to a long excursus on how John the Baptist was also called an angel.

Tertullian then ends with a summary statement that the perceptive reader of scripture should already understand that Joshua is a prefigurement of Jesus and that the messiah would certainly share this name. This is also why Tertullian emphasizes Joshua as a messenger or angel, since this is what John/Elijah was called as well, fitting Joshua into the typology of future-savior-foreshadowed-by-Israelite-hero, already established with John the Baptist.

Tertullian uses Justin's *Dialogue with Trypho* as a template for many of his arguments. There are a number of specific correspondences between Tertullian's reading of scripture and that of Justin. Both emphasize the importance of the name change of Joshua by Moses. Like Tertullian, Justin (75) makes use of the verse in Exodus about the messenger of God bringing the Israelites into the Promised Land, and assumes that the messenger/angel is Joshua himself, since "God's name (=Jesus's name) is upon him."[533] Other similarities include the understanding that Joshua bringing the people into the Promised Land prefigures Jesus' bringing the gentiles into eternal life (*Dialogue* 113), the idea of the circumcision by stone knives is an allegory for the circumcision of the heart that will be effected by Jesus (*ibid*), and the notion that Joshua's name is what gives him his special powers (*Dialogue* 113.4, 132.1).

Nevertheless, the focus of the overall argument in the two works is different. Tertullian's main objective in this passage is to prove that Iesu is the correct and expected name of the messiah. He needs this to counteract the Jewish claim against using Isaiah 7:14 as a proof for Jesus, i.e., that Jesus' name was Iesu and not Emmanuel. His scriptural readings all fit under this rubric. The son of Nun was given the name Iesu, and the powers that come with it, since it would have sent the wrong message to let Moses give the Israelites the Promised Land. This important act, which foreshadows the eventual gift of eternal life by Christ, had to be done by someone with Christ's name, namely Joshua, and not by someone who represented the old covenant, that is, Moses.

Justin, on the other hand, makes more sporadic and less systematic use of the Joshua-Jesus typology. Justin wants Trypho to notice that the Jews have missed yet another foreshadowing of the messiah by not taking note of the import of Moses changing Hoshea's name to Iesu. If they had taken note of this, Justin argues, they would have noticed the awesome power Joshua wielded and the significance of Joshua having been the one to give the Promised Land to the Israelites. The argument is almost identical to that of Tertullian except that it is not being made in service of the proof from Isaiah 7:14, and Justin does not go so far as to say that the messiah's name—or Joshua's name—*needed* to be Jesus. Additionally, Justin has Trypho admitting to this point, as if the Jews had always assumed the messiah's name would be Jesus. For Tertullian, this is exactly the point the Jews will not give in on, which is why he spends so much time and energy attempting to prove it.[534]

---

533 Both Tertullian and Justin prefer the Exodus verse implying Joshua's future leadership to the Deuteronomy verse employed by Clement of Alexandria (see further on).

534 Dunn (*Tertullian's*, 127) writes:

> He (Tertullian) wished to demonstrate that the Christ was prophesied in the Hebrew Scriptures to bear the name Jesus, for when the Son of God spoke to Joshua, son of Nun and assistant to Moses (for God could not be seen or heard directly), what is recorded is the fact that the Son's name was upon Joshua (Exod 23:20–21), hence the Son's name must be Jesus

In other words, for Justin, the son's name happens to be Iesu. Hence, whenever this name is used by others, it brings these characters power and allegorical significance. For Tertullian, Hoshea's name had to be changed to Joshua since he was going to bring the Israelites into the Promised Land, which could be done only by someone who foreshadowed the messiah; otherwise, it would send the wrong message. In this sense, Tertullian's use of the Joshua-Jesus typology functions as a useful bridge between Justin and Origen, whose ideas about the allegorical interpretation of history are the most systematic and developed.

In his discussion of the Exodus story of the defeat of Amalek, Tertullian follows the path trod by Barnabas and Justin (10:10).

Iam vero Moyses quid utique tunc tantum, cum Iesus adversus Amelech proeliabatur, expansis manibus orabat residens, quando in rebus tam attonitis magis utique genibus positis et manibus caedentibus pectus et facie humi volutante orationem commendare debuisset, nisi quia illic, ubi nomen domini Iesu dicebat dimicaturi quandoque adversus diabolum, crucis habitus quoque erat necessarius, per quam Iesus victoriam esset relaturus?	Now, in truth, why did Moses, in any case, only just then, with Iesu fighting against Amalek, with outstretched arms, pray sitting down, when during circumstances so critical, at any rate, he would have been bound to offer prayer with bent knees and arms beating his heart, and with face turning over in the dirt, if not because in that circumstance, when he that fought—as he would against the devil—was called by the name of the Lord Iesu, the sign of the cross was necessary, so that through this, Iesu would carry back a victory?

Again, although it seems clear that Tertullian is aware of Justin's use of this argument,[535] he has modified it slightly to fit his own understanding of the Joshua-Jesus typology. For Justin, the cross and the name of Iesu were a type of revelation, both to the wilderness generation and to the later readers of scripture, that there will be a messianic figure name Iesu that will be crucified, and that he will be the one to rid the world of the wicked Amalek, understood metaphorically as the power of evil.

For Tertullian, the point of the cross symbolism is that Joshua is really merely a partial Jesus, since he was not crucified but only shares the messianic name,

---

(although Tertullian allowed his readers to draw this conclusion for themselves) (9:22–23).
Hence, Joshua "figuram future fuisse." This same argument can be found in Justin.
Although I agree with this analysis for the most part, as I said above, Justin appears to me, at least, to be saying something a little different than Tertullian.
535 As in the *Dialogue with Trypho*, the stories of Amalek and of the bronze snake are put together, since they both have Moses doing something inexplicable that is interpreted as, in reality, forming a mystical sign of the cross.

and therefore, had insufficient mystical power to defeat Amalek. In order for Joshua to gain sufficient power, Moses needed to mimic the cross, thereby completing Joshua's Jesus imagery and allowing him to conquer Amalek, understood here historically, not allegorically.

Also like Justin, Tertulian believes that Joshua son of Nun is not the only Joshua that prefigures Jesus. Whereas Justin uses the paradigm in relation to Joshua of Beit Shemesh who housed the ark (or Tabernacle), Tertullian applies the paradigm to Joshua son of Jehozadak, the high priest. Specifically, Tertullian interprets one of Zechariah's prophecies about Joshua the high priest to really have been about Jesus (14.7–8).

Sic et apud Zachariam [ait] in persona Iesu, immo et in ipsius nominis sacramento verissimus sacerdos patris Christus ipsius duplici habitu in duos adventus deliniatur: primo sordibus indutus id est carnis passibilis et mortalis indignitate... dehinc spoliatus pristinas sordes, exornatus podere et mitra et cidari munda id est secundi adventus, quoniam gloriam et honorem adeptus demonstratur.

And thus also in Zechariah, in the person of Iesu, and by all means in the secret of his own name, the truest priest of the father, Christ himself, by way of two garments is delimited for two comings: First, putting on dirty [ones] – it is the flesh capable of suffering and the indignity of death... Afterwards, he was stripped of his earlier dirty clothes, and equipped with a long garment, a turban, and a pure crown – it is the second coming, signifying that he 'obtains glory and honor' (Heb 2:9).

Nec poteritis eum Iosedech filium dicere qui nulla omnino veste sordida sed semper sacerdotali fuit exornatus nec umquam sacerdotali munere privatus, sed Iesus iste Christus dei patris summi sacerdos qui primo adventu suo humanae formae et passibilis venit in humilitate usque ad passionem, ipse effectus etiam hostia per omnia pro omnibus nobis, qui post resurrectionem suam indutus podere sacerdos in aeternum dei patris nuncupatur.

Neither will you be able to say that this is the son of Jehozadak, who never wore dirty garments but always priestly ones, having never been deprived of priestly office. However, Iesu that is the Christ, high priest of God the father, whose first coming was in human form and he came in pain and humiliation, even before the passion, he also became the victim of all, for us all, who after his resurrection wears the robe, and is named priest of God the father for eternity.

Tertullian is making use of the imagery of Jesus as high priest in Hebrews (perhaps even Barnabas.) However, like Justin, he makes an implicit connection between the two characters of Iesu the high priest and Iesu the Christ explicit, by calling attention to their similarities in name.[536] It is not just that Jesus is a high priest as Joshua son of Jehozadak was, but that the imagery Zechariah uses to describe Joshua the high priest is really a thinly veiled reference to Jesus himself.

---

536 But see Whitfield (Ph.D. thesis, 302ff), who argues that this connection based on names was actually assumed already in Hebrews.

This text should be seen as a testimony to the efficacy and versatility of the name-equivalency hermeneutic.

Finally, like Justin, Tertullian does not make consistent use of the Joshua-Jesus typology. This can be seen in his demonstration of why the Sabbath cannot be considered essentially holy. Among his proofs is the fact that certain Israelite leaders violated the Sabbath. The leaders he references are the Maccabees, who fought the Syrian-Greeks on the Sabbath, and Joshua (4.8–9), who laid siege to Jericho on the Sabbath.

Denique adeo non in vacatione septimi diei haec sollemnitas celebranda est, ut Iesus Naue eo tempore quo Hiericho civitatem debellabat praeceptum sibi a deo diceret, uti populo mandaret, ut sacerdotes arcam testamend dei septem diebus circumferrent in circuitu civitatis, atque ita septimi diei circuitu peracto sponte ruerent muri civitatis.	In fact, to such a degree is this festival not to be celebrated through rest on the seventh day, that Iesu son of Nau, at the time he was subduing the city of Jericho, said that [he received] a command to him from the deity to require the people that the priests should go around in circuits with the ark of the testimony for seven days; as soon as the circuit of the seventh day would be accomplished, the walls of the city would immediately collapse.

In this text, Joshua is just Joshua and not an instantiation of Jesus.[537]

Excursus: The Joshua-Jesus Typology in Early Jewish-Christianity

Joshua-Jesus in the *Sibylline Oracles*

There is an allusion to a morphed Joshua and Jesus in what seems to be early Jewish-Christian literature, but both the passage and the work itself are enigmatic. The passage comes from the fifth oracle. Like their pagan neighbors, Jews and Christians collected oracles from "sibyls"—women who had the power to see glimpses of the future, or, more likely, wrote works in the genre of sybilline oracles. Although the collection found in the Pseudepigrapha seems to have sections derived from Jewish as well as Christian sources, there seems to be little doubt that the passage below is from a Christian source (5:256–259).[538]

---

537 Joshua's violation of the Sabbath will be used by Aphrahat as well.

538 This is Ed Noort's argument in his discussion of the oracle in "Joshua: Reception and Hermeneutics," 213–214. This was also the claim of John Collins, who believes that the fifth oracle is actually Jewish, but that this passage was a Christian interpolation. See: John J. Collins, *"Sibylline Oracles,"* in *The Old Testament Pseudepigrapha* 1 (ed. James H. Charlesworth; Garden

εἷς δέ τις ἔσσεται αὖτις ἀπ᾽ αἰθέρος ἔξοχος ἀνήρ, ὃς παλάμας ἤπλωσεν ἐπὶ ξύλου πολυκάρπου, Ἑβραίων ὁ ἄριστος, ὃς ἡέλιόν ποτε στήσει φωνήσας ῥήσει τε καλῇ καὶ χείλεσιν ἁγνοῖς.	Then there will come from the sky an exalted man, whose hands they nailed upon fruitful wood, the noblest of the Hebrews, who once caused the sun to stand still, when crying with fair speech and pure lips.

As both Noort and Barthelot (p. 103, n. 30) point out, there seems little question that the man who caused the sun to stand still is a reference to Joshua. Additionally, as Noort writes, there is little question that the man whose hands were nailed upon fruitful wood is Jesus. Therefore, despite the enigmatic nature of the oracle, it seems clear that the characters of Joshua and Jesus are being conflated in this text into one individual who both stopped the sun and was nailed to wood. The crying out is probably a reference to Jesus' recitation of the verse from Psalm 22, "My God my God, why have you forsaken me?"[539]

The meaning of the oracle seems to be that at some point in the future, Joshua-Jesus will return to earth from the heavens. Interestingly, this very literal identification of these two characters is reminiscent of the rabbinic trend to declare that two different characters in the Bible—such as Elijah and Phineas or Shem and Melchizedek—were actually one and the same person.[540]

The Jesus-Fish

The imagery of the Jesus fish, still common today, dates back at least to the second century. However, the symbol is as enigmatic as it is old. Tertullian appears to be the earliest invocation of the image in writing (*De Baptismo* 1) we have. (The earliest epigraphic evidence for the image comes from the Inscription of Abercius, dated 216 C.E.). The context of the quote in Tertullian is his attempt to combat the "Cainite heresy," in part by strengthening the place of the ritual of baptism for believers.

City: Doubleday, 1983–1985), 317–472 [354, 390]. However, J.C. O'Neil makes the argument that this passage could have derived from Jewish sources. See: J.C. O'Neil, "The Man from Heaven: SibOr 5.256–259," *JSP* 9 (1991): 87–102. I agree with Noort that it is virtually impossible to imagine that a description of the savior being nailed on wood could be anything but Christian.
539 Matt 27:45–46 and Mark 15:34.
540 *Midrash Ha-Gadol*, Numbers, Pinḥas 28:12, s.v. "*lakhen amar*"; *Midrash Tehillim*, 76:3

Sed nos pisciculi secundum ichthun nostrum But we, little fishes, after the example of our
iesum christum in aqua nascimur, nec aliter fish Jesus Christ, are born in water, nor have
quam in aqua permanendo salui sumus. Itaque we safety in any other way than by permanent-
illa monstrosissima cui nec integre quidem do- ly abiding in water; and so that most mon-
cendi ius erat optime norat necare pisciculos strous creature (a leader of the Cainite sect),
de aqua auferens. who had no right to teach even sound doctrine,
knew full well how to kill the little fishes, by
taking them away from the water![541]

Augustine, in *Civitate Dei* (18:23), points to a passage in the *Sibylline Oracles* (8:150–217 in the Greek; 284–330 in the English) which has an acrostic of Ἰησοῦς Χριστὸς Θεοῦ Ὑιος Σωτήρ, meaning "Jesus Christ, son of God, savior," which can be referenced in shorthand as ΙΧΘΥΣ (fish). Augustine explains the reasoning:

horum autem graecorum quinque verborum, But if you join the initial letters of these five
quae sunt iêsous chreistos theou huios sôtêr, Greek words, Ἰησοῦς Χριστος Θεοῦ υἱὸς
quod est latine iesus christus dei filius saluator, σωτήρ, which mean, "Jesus Christ the Son of
si primas litteras iungas, erit ichthus, id est pis- God, the Saviour," they will make the word
cis, in quo nomine mystice intellegitur christus, ἰχθύς, that is, "fish," in which word Christ is
eo quod in huius mortalitatis abysso uelut in mystically understood, because He was able
aquarum profunditate uiuus, hoc est sine pecca- to live, that is, to exist, without sin in the
to, esse potuerit. abyss of this mortality as in the depth of wa-
ters.

Although it is possible that the above explanations are correct, i.e., that the image originates as an acrostic and/or it represents Jesus's life of sinlessness, they feel forced, and a number of scholars agree that the acronym should be seen as a result of the symbol and not the cause of the symbol.[542] Gedaliahu Stroumsa suggests an alternative origin for the image.[543]

---

541 It is fascinating that the very same analogy was made in the Talmud (b. *Berakhot* 61b) in the name of Rabbi Akiva, who, in a parable, accuses the Romans (foxes) of trying to destroy Jews (fish) by taking them out of the water of Torah.
542 See, for example, Isidor Scheftelowitz, "Das Fisch-Symbol im Judentum und Christentum," *Archiv für Religionswissenschaft* 14 (1911): 1–54, 321–392; Franz Cumont, "ΙΧΘΥΣ," in *Pauly-Wissowa Encyclopädie der klassischen Altertumswissenschaft* IX.2 (1916), 844–850; and Franz Dölger, *Der Heilige Fisch in den antiken Religionen und im Christentum* (Münster: Aschendorff, 1922).
543 Gedaliahu G. Stroumsa, "The Early Christian Fish Symbol Reconsidered," in *Messiah and Christos: Studies in the Jewish Origins of Christianity – Presented to David Flusser on the Occasion of his Seventy-Fifth Birthday* (eds. Ithamar Gruenwald, Shaul Shaked, and Gedaliahu G. Stroumsa; Texte und Studien zum Antiken Judentum 32; Tübingen: Mohr Siebeck, 1992), 199–205.

Stroumsa points out that early on in "Christian" tradition (as has been demonstrated in this chapter) the idea that Joshua was a manifestation of Jesus, or even an early incarnation of Jesus, was gaining traction. As such, a reference to one could bring up the other in the mind of the speaker or listener. The biblical Joshua was generally referred to with his patronymic "bin Nun" or in Aramaic "bar Nun." Although the Aramaic really means "son of Nun," it can also be translated as "son of the fish."[544]

To demonstrate that the association of Joshua's father's name with its meaning of "fish" was not foreign to Aramaic-speaking Jews, Stroumsa references a midrash found in *Genesis Rabba* (Theodor-Albeck; "*Va-Yeḥi*" 98), which offers an explanation of the phrase, "and they will multiply (*yidgu*) greatly in the land" in the blessing of Ephraim and Manasseh (Gen 48:16).

מי ששמו כשם הדג בנו מכניסן לארץ נון בנו יהושע בנו.   He whose name is that of "fish" (*dag*), his son will bring [Israel] into the land (1 Chron 7:27): "Fish (*Nun*), his son, Joshua, his son,"

Stroumsa even references a late midrash that gives the reason for Joshua being called "son of the fish.". According to the story, Joshua was thrown into the Nile by the Egyptians as all the Hebrew boys were, but he was swallowed by a fish. The fish was caught, and when it was cut open, the living baby boy Joshua appeared, so they called him "Joshua son of the fish."[545] Thus, the connection between Joshua and fish was clear to the Aramaic-speaking Jews.

For this reason, Stroumsa argues that the fish imagery might be a result of Jesus being associated with Joshua, who already was known as "the fish." If this is correct, then it points to the possibility that the Jewish Christians saw a strong connection between the two Yeshuas and saw them as interchangeable referents. This would fit well with the passage from the Sibylline Oracles quoted above.

---

544 Stroumsa references Robert Eisler as the first to point this out. See, Robert Eisler, *Orpheus the Fisher: Comparative Studies in Orphic and Early Christian Cult Symbolism* (London: Watkins, 1921), 171 n.1, 253 n.1.

545 There seem to be a number of versions of this legend; in some it is Joshua's father that is swallowed by a fish and not him. See Louis Ginzberg, *Legends of the Jews* (7 vols.; Philadelphia: Jewish Publication Society, 1909–1938), pp. 841–842, and here: http://btjerusalem.com/b/b044.htm for more references.

The Full Typology: Origen's Homilies on Joshua

The most complete version of the Joshua-Jesus typology is found in Origen's *Homilies on Joshua*.[546] Origen (born circa 185) was educated in Alexandria, where he spent much of his life, but eventually moved to Caesarea in 231 and remained there as an ordained preacher until his arrest and torture led to his death during the persecution of Decius in 250 CE.[547] As with many of his works, the original Greek for the *Homilies on Joshua* has been lost,[548] and one must use the Latin translation of Rufinus.

Origen's allegorization of Joshua functions, in many ways, as the logical next step in the development of the typology in Justin Martyr and Tertullian. It is not surprising that Origen would be the one to develop the allegory into its fullest form, since this was the essence of Origen's method of interpretation for all of the works of the Old Testament. Having found the typology already extant, Origen used it as a key to understanding the entire book of Joshua. The *Homilies on Joshua* consists of 26 homilies, covering almost the entirety of the book of Joshua and thought to have been delivered towards the end of Origen's life.

Much of what Origen does has more to do with allegorical interpretation of the story line in Joshua, rather than with the figure of Joshua himself,[549] so the majority of the work is not relevant to this chapter. However, he does advance and extend the typology in his allegorical understanding of the person of Joshua. Most of these developments are laid out in the first homily.

The Name of Jesus

Origen begins his very first homily with an emphasis on the importance of Jesus' name (1:1).

---

546 Cf. Elßner, *Josua*, 226–254.

547 The background information has been taken from Barbara Bruce's introduction to her English translation of the work: Barbara J. Bruce, *Origen: Homilies on Joshua* (ed. Cynthia White; The Fathers of the Church 105; Washington D.C.: The Catholic University of America Press, 2002).

548 There are some original language quotes in the *Philocalia* (an anthology of Origen's texts, probably put together by Basil the Great and Gregory Nazianzen) as well as in Procopius of Gaza's *Catena on Joshua*.

549 For example, Origen interprets the defeat of the southern coalition of five kings as an allegory for the dominance faith in Jesus should have over a person's five senses.

Donavit Deus nomen, quod est super omne nomen, Domino et Salvatori nostro Iesu Christo. Est autem nomen, quod est super omne nomen, Iesus. Et quia est istud nomen super omne nomen, idcirco in nomine Iesu omne genu flectitur coelestium et terrestrium et infernorum. Et quia est hoc nomen super omne nomen idcirco multis generationibus a nullo cognominatum est.

God gave the name which is above all names to our Lord and Savior Iesu Christ. Moreover, the name which is above all names is Iesu. And because this is the name above all names, on that account in the name of Iesu every knee will bend – in heaven, on earth, and in the netherworld. And because this name is greater than all names, on that account for many generations none were called by it.

Quoting from the end of the "Christ hymn" in Philippians 2, Origen opens here with a "midrashic" reading of the passage.[550] The hymn begins with a description of Jesus' divinity on the one hand and his humility on the other. It then continues with a description of how believers should respond to him.

⁹ διὸ καὶ ὁ θεὸς αὐτὸν ὑπερύψωσεν καὶ ἐχαρίσατο αὐτῷ τὸ ὄνομα τὸ ὑπὲρ πᾶν ὄνομα,
¹⁰ ἵνα ἐν τῷ ὀνόματι Ἰησοῦ πᾶν γόνυ κάμψῃ ἐπουρανίων καὶ ἐπιγείων καὶ καταχθονίων

⁹ Wherefore, God also exalted him, and gave him freely the name which is above all names,
¹⁰ So that in the name of Iesu all knees should bend, in the heavens, and on the earth, and in the netherworld.

The simple meaning of the text in Philippians seems to be that since Jesus was so unique, being both divine and exceedingly humble and submissive, God rewards him with "a name above all names." The name referred to here is either Christ or Lord (see v. 11), and to him (Christ Jesus the Lord) everyone must bow.[551] Before Barnabas and Justin, the idea that the name Joshua/Jesus was inherently significant was not a major part of proto-Christian rhetoric, and doesn't appear in Paul's letters at all.[552] However, once this paradigm is established, certain authors like Tertullian and Origen take this paradigm to be implicit in earlier works.

---

550 This section of the Christ Hymn is itself a midrashic reading or reinterpretation of Isa 45:23, but this is not germane to the analysis of Origen's use of the passage in Philippians.
551 I thank my colleagues Justin Schedtler and Meghan Henning for their assistance in digesting the Philippians passage and helping me organize my thoughts.
552 The idea does appear in Matt 1:21, which offers a midrashic reading of the name Joshua as part of the angel's speech to Joseph.

τέξεται δὲ υἱόν, καὶ καλέσεις τὸ ὄνομα αὐτοῦ Ἰησοῦν· αὐτὸς γὰρ σώσει τὸν λαὸν αὐτοῦ ἀπὸ τῶν ἁμαρτιῶν αὐτῶν.

She (Mary) will give birth to a son, and you will call his name Iesu, for he will save the people from their sins.

What the Greek reader was to make of this, I do not know, but it seems clear that the origins of this concept must have been in the Hebrew/Aramaic-speaking Jewish community, since the play off the name יהושע as the מושיע makes sense only in the context of the Semitic root י.ש.ע/.

Although Origen and Tertullian both emphasize the significance of Jesus's name, they do so in different ways. Tertullian sees the special gift of the name Iesu to Hoshea as an early revelation to Israel that the savior will have the name Iesu. In this scheme, it is the actions of the original Iesu (Joshua) in bringing Israel into the Promised Land and replacing Moses that facilitate the proper understanding of this revelation. Origen, however, seems to believe that the name itself has some essential properties. Given that, God is naturally going to be selective about who is allowed to carry that name.

Working with the special-name paradigm, Origen notes that it is no coincidence that the name is so rare. It never appears in Genesis, he points out, and this brings him to focus on the first appearance of the name in the Bible, in the story of Amalek.

Amalek

After pointing out the rareness and specialness of the name Iesu, Origen writes (1:1):

Sed Iesu nomen primo invenio in Exodo et volo intueri primum nomen Iesu cognominatur.	However, the name Iesu I find first in Exodus, and I would like to consider when the name Iesu was first used.

As was seen earlier, it is the Amalek story that formed the core or inspiration for the typology to begin with, especially when combined with the scout account and Moses' changing Hoshea's name to Joshua. Origen's use of the story is somewhat different (1:1).

"Venit" inquit, "Amalec, et expugnabat Istra-hel,[553] et dixit Moyses ad Iesum in Raphidim." Haec est prima appellatio nominis Iesu.	"Amalek came," it says, "and fought with Israel, and Moses spoke to Iesu in Raphidim." This is the first mention of the name Iesu.

---

553 I do not know why Rufinus transcribes the name Israel this way (*Istrahel* – with the "t" and the "h"). Perhaps the "t" was added as a prosthetic consonant by some speakers to ease pronunciation a phenomenon called "epenthesis of a consonant" or "excrescence." For example, the Hebrew name Mamre (מַמְרֵא) is transcribed in the LXX as Mambre (Μαμβρη); the beta seems to be introduced to ease pronunciation. The same is true for the name Samson (Judg 13:24), for which the Hebrew is Shimshon (שִׁמְשׁוֹן) and the Greek is Sampson (Σαμψων), with the "p" being an example of excrescence. Insofar as the "h" is concerned, this seems to be a common consonantal interchange, with a glottal stop being replaced with a pharyngeal fricative, and is found in the Vulgate as well (Israhel, Samuhel.) As both are pronounced with the same part of the mouth, it is a common occurance. (I thank Joel LeMon for discussing this with me.)

"Elige," inquit, "tibi viros potentes ex omnibus filiis Istrahel, et egredere, et conflige cum Amalec crastino." Moyses confitetur non posse se exercitum ducere, confitetur se non posse obtinere, quamvis eum "de terra Aegypti eduxerit."...

"Choose for yourself," it says, "powerful men from among all the sons of Israel, and go out and fight with Amalek tomorrow." Moses confesses that he cannot lead the army; he confesses that he cannot gather it, even though he "led them out of the land of Egypt."...

In hoc primo nomen discimus Iesu, ubi eum videmus ducem exercitus: non cui Moyses iniunxerite principatum, sed cui cesserit primatum. "Tu," inquit, "elige tibi viros potentes ex omnibus filiis Istrahel." Hic ergo ubi primum disco nomen Iesu, ibi continuo etiam mysterii video sacramentum; ducit enim exercitum Iesus.

In this we first learn the name Iesu, whom we see him as leader of the army, not as one who joins Moses in primacy, but one who is granted primacy. "You," he says, "choose for yourself powerful men from among all the sons of Israel." This, therefore, is where I first learn the name Iesu; there I also persist in seeing a sign of mystery; indeed Iesu leads the army.

Unlike the allegory established by Barnabas and Justin, Origen does not focus on the defeat of Amalek or on the use of Jesus symbolism such as Joshua's name or Moses making the sign of the cross. What interests Origen is that he sees in Moses' appointing of Joshua as general and subsequent retirement up the mountain, a sign that Moses felt that this task was beyond his abilities. Only Joshua could gather the troops and succeed in the war with Amalek.

Since Moses succeeded in freeing Israel from Egyptian bondage, Origen understands that this account must be understood allegorically as a sort of mystery. The reader is being told that Joshua is greater than Moses in some way; and that this is related to Joshua being "general of the army"—a concept Origen will expand upon greatly in his homilies.

Joshua as Greater than Moses

The idea of Joshua as greater than Moses should be seen as the main thrust of Origen's project. This is because, to Origen, Joshua is Jesus and Moses is the law—allegorically speaking. In this light, he continues his comparison between the two characters in the homily.

3. Quo igitur nobis haec cuncta prospiciunt? Nempe eo quod liber hic non tam gesta nobis filii Nave indicet quam Iesu mei Domini nobis sacramenta depingat. Ipse est qui ducit exercitum et confligit adversus Amalec...

3. What, then, do all these things discern for us? Certainly this: That this book does not indicate to us so much the acts of the son of Nau as much as it depicts for us the secrets of Iesu my Lord. It is he that led the army and fought against Amalek...

Defunctus est ergo Moyses famulus Dei; defuncta est enim lex et legalia praecepta iam cessant...
4. Iesus igitur Dominus et Salvator meus suscepit principatum.

Therefore, "Moses the attendant of God is dead" (Deut 34:5); indeed the law is dead, and the legal precepts are now defunct...
4. Therefore, Iesu, my Lord and Savior took up the headship.

Here Origen clarifies his radical position on the historical character of Joshua. The stories of Joshua in the Pentateuch and the book of Joshua are not there to tell us about the historical figure of Joshua (assuming there was one—which I believe Origen does), but only about Jesus. The entire recorded life of Joshua bin Nun must be seen as designed to teach the careful reader truths about Jesus.

Since Joshua's primary roles were to take over the leadership of Israel from Moses and to conquer the land of Canaan for the Israelites, these two concepts, understood in their proper allegorical sense, must be the key element to understanding the purpose of the Joshua narratives.

Origen's focus in the above passage is to clarify the meaning of Joshua's taking the reigns of leadership from Moses. This transfer of authority is an allegory for nothing less than the transfer of authority from the Torah to Jesus. To show that the narrative of Joshua is consistent with this interpretation, Origen continues in this homily with a comparison of Moses to Joshua.

...si videtur, conferamus gesta Moysei cum principatu Iesu.

If it seems right, let us compare the works of Moses with the leadership of Iesu.

Some of the comparisons Origen makes are rather forced. For example, Origen compares Moses' splitting of the Red Sea with Joshua's splitting of the Jordan River. Any simple comparison would point to the splitting of the Red Sea as the greater miracle; nevertheless, Origen makes the opposite claim.

Cum Moyses educeret populum de terra Aegypti, nullus ordo in populis, nulla in sacerdotibus observantia. Transeunt aquam maris, aquam salsam nec quicquam in se dulcedinis continentem... Haec Moyseo duce gesta cognoscimus.

When Moses led the people out of the Land of Egypt, there was no order in the population, no reverance among the priests. They crossed the sea water—salt water that contained no sweetness... These, we know, were the deeds of Moses when he was leader.

Cum vero Dominus meus ducit exercitum, quae sunt, quae iam tunc adumbrabantur, videamus. "Sacerdotes praecedunt, arca Testamenti portatur in humeris sacerdotum," nusquam iam mare, nusquam salsus fluctus occurit, sed duce Domino meo Iesu venio ad Iordanen et venio non perturbation fugae neque perterritus metu sed venio cum sacerdotibus arcam Testamenti Domini, in qua Dei lex et divinae litterae servantur, cervicibus suis humerisqe portantibus. Ingredior Iordanen non cum furtive silentiom, sed in tubarum cantibus mysticum quiddam divinumque canentibus, ut ad praedicationem tubae coelestis incedam.	Truly, when my Lord leads the army, let us see what was then foreshadowed. "The priests will be first, and the Ark of the Testimony is carried on the shoulders of the priests." Nowhere, now, is the sea. Nowhere does the salty wave charge. But with my Lord Iesu as leader I come to the Jordan, and I come not in the commotion of flight nor frightened with anxiety, but I come with the priests who carry upon their necks and shoulders the Ark of the Testimony of the Lord, in which the law and divine words of God are kept. I go into the Jordan, not in furtive silence, but with the sounding of the trumpets—blaring something mystical and divine, so that I may advance to the proclamation of the heavenly trumpet.

In order to make Joshua's crossing appear more impressive then that of Moses, Origen makes use of some of the secondary details of the story. The crossing of the Red Sea was part of the Exodus from Egypt, and, as such, was done as part of a retreat from the Egyptian army. The Israelites were runaway slaves, afraid of the Egyptian cavalry, not yet organized into military formation, and still lacking a priestly class or holy accoutrements.

Joshua, on the other hand, led the Israelites towards conquest. The people were already organized along military lines, and the priestly class—with divine accoutrements—was well established. Hence Joshua could lead a disciplined army, led by the priests and the Ark of the Covenant, into the Jordan River in a quiet and orderly fashion. Moses could only lead a panicking group of escaped slaves into the Red Sea, allowing them to "run for their lives" until they reached the other side. In this sense, Origen argues, one must observe that Joshua's leadership represents the more advanced state than did that of Moses, just as the period of Jesus's leadership represents the more advanced state of religion in comparison with the Age of the Law.

Although the previous example is a stretch, Origen knows (1.5) that he has at his disposal one example in which the biblical text itself is clear about the impressive nature of Joshua's miracle: Joshua's stopping of the sun in the battle over Gibeon.

Moyses non dixit: "Stet sol" nec maximis imper- Moses did not say: "Stop, sun," nor did he
avit elementis, sicut Iesus fecit. "Stet," inquit, command the greatest elements as Iesu did.
"sol super Gabaon et luna super vallem "Stop, sun," he said, "over Gibeon, and moon
Aelom." Et praeterea addit Scriptura et dicit over the valley of Ayalon." Moreover, Scripture
quia: "Numquam sic audivit Deus hominem." adds to this, and says that, "Never did God
thus listen to a human."

Here Origen has his strongest example. Not only is the stopping of the sun and
moon in the sky a miracle that demonstrates great power, but scripture itself at-
tests to the fact that God intervened here in a way that God never did before or
since. Justin already made mention of the awesome power of this miracle (*Trypho* 113.4), but Origen picks up on the polemical potential of the scriptural attes-
tation regarding the uniqueness of the event.[554] Here, scripture (the Old Testament) is in effect admitting that Joshua was greater than Moses (at least, that
is how Origen reads this verse.)

Conquest of the Land

Having established the primacy of Joshua over Moses, Origen begins to lay out
what is at stake in his analysis and what Joshua's tenure represents. As was already argued by Justin, it is Joshua—not Moses—who brings the Israelites into
the Promised Land, granting them their final rest. Moses' tenure is marked by
wilderness wanderings, not the finality of settlement.

Origen lays out the symbolic significance of Joshua as conqueror.

---

554 This is why the rabbis feel the need to give Moses this miracle as well, as I will argue in the
chapter on Rabbinic traditions. Aphrahat also makes mention of the stopping of the sun,
comparing it to an account of Jesus making the day end early. However, since Aphrahat compares almost everything Joshua did with Jesus in an almost rote form, it is difficult to know if he
picked up on the unique polemical potential here.

⁷ Sub Moyseo non est dictum hoc quod sub Iesu dicitur quia: "Cessavit terra a proeliis." Certum est quod et terra nostra haec, in qua agones habemus et certamina sustinemus, solius Iesu Domini virtute cessare poterit a poeliis. Intra nos etenim sunt omnes gentes istae vitiorum, quae animam iugiter et indesinenter oppugnant. Intra nos sunt Chananaei, intra nos sunt Pherezaei, hic sunt Iebusaei. Qualiter nobis laborandum est, qualiter vigilandum vel quanto tempore perseverandum, ut omnibus istis de nobis vitiorum gentibus effugatis tandem "terra nostra cesset a bellis"?

⁷ Regarding Moses' time, it does not say that which it says regarding Iesu's time that: "The land ceased from strife." It is certain that this, our land, as well, in which we have had struggles and endured contests, only by the strength of the Lord Iesu, will be able to cease from strife. Within us, in fact, are all those kinds of vices, which perpetually and incessantly besiege the spirit. Within us are the Canaanites; within us are the Perizzites; here are the Jebusites. In what way must we labor? In what way must we be vigilant, at least, for how long must we persevere so that all these kinds of vices of ours flee, so that finally "our land will cease from wars."

Origen makes his point in two steps. First, he notes that it is not Moses who takes the Promised Land and gives it to Israel as their reward. Joshua fights the battles and, more importantly, passes out the ultimate spoil: rest from strife.[555] Part of this argument implicitly reiterates the previous point: Joshua accomplishes more than Moses; his tenure is more successful, and he is the better leader.

However, Origen is also making a second point here, and it is the introduction to the main theme of all of the homilies. Joshua's work as battler for the Promised Land on Israel's behalf should be taken as a heuristic model for believing Christians. Joshua's enemies—Jesus' enemies—are internal to all people of faith. The Canaanites are simply an allegory for wicked personality traits that push believers off the proper path. One can see the beginnings of this type of interpretation in Barnabas and Justin, who see Amalek as representative of sin and demons (including internal demons?), respectively. What we need to do, Origen preaches, is fight our internal battles, as Joshua/Jesus fought the Canaanites. If this is done successfully, then each and every believer can achieve peace in his or her own "Promised Land."

With this interpretive key, Origen continues in his homilies to interpret the entire book of Joshua along the lines of this allegory, with Joshua the conquerer battling various forces of evil and the world of the senses in order to finally grant peace to his followers. Joshua's wars are understood as Jesus' conquest of the worldly (Jericho), the instincts (Ai), the senses (southern coalition), and even

---

555 Ironically, this is the opposite claim as that made by Hebrews, that Joshua did not succeed in giving the people rest.

the devil himself (Jabin king of Hazor). Joshua also succeeds in eradicating false philosophical doctrine (Achan).

There is a difference between Origen the preacher and Justin (or Tertullian) the polemicist. Of course, Origen takes shots at his religious adverseries and competitors, the Jews. However, unlike the goal in the *Dialogue with Trypho* or *Adversus Iudaeos*, this is not the main purpose of his *Homilies on Joshua*. Instead, Origen's main focus is on his congregants, the people who will be hearing his sermons and, hopefully, adjusting their lives accordingly.

Second Circumcision

Considering the focus in earlier examples of the Joshua-Jesus typology on the second circumcision, I do not find it surprising that Origen ends his first homily with attention to this passage. The point comes up again in other homilies, and is made most starkly in the fifth homily (5.5).

5 *Post haec iubetur filius Nave "facere cultros ex petra et sedens*[556] *circumcidere filios Istrahel secundo."*

Velim ego in hoc loco percontari a Iudaeis, quomodo potest quis secundo circumcidi circumcisione carnali. Semel enim circumcisus quis ultra non habet, quod secundo possit auferri. A nobis vero, quibus dicitur quia "lex spiritalis est", vide quam digne et convenienter ista solventur.

5 After this (the crossing of the Jordan), the son of Nun is commanded "to make knives from stone and, sitting down, circumcise the sons of Israel a second time" (Josh 5:2).

I may wish, in this place, to inquire of the Jews, in what way it would be possible for anyone to be circumcised with a circumcision of the flesh a second time. Indeed, once a person is circumcised, he has nothing more that can be removed a second time. By us, in truth, to whom it is said that "the law is spiritual" (Rom 7:14), see how this is solved fittingly and conveniently.

---

556 This strange part of the command clearly comes from the LXX's text: "καθίσας." This text in turn seems to assume a Hebrew original of שֵׁב (sit) as opposed to the MT's שׁוּב (return).

Dicimus enim quia ille, qui in lege eruditus est et per Moysen edoctus, abiecit idolatriae errors, simulacrorum superstitionem cultumque deposuit. Haec est circumcisio prima per legem. Si vero is veniat a lege et prophetis ad evangelicam fidem, tunc accipit etiam secundam circumcisionem per "petram, qui est Christus," et completur hoc, quod dixit Dominus ad Iesum: "Hodie abstuli opprobrium Aegypti a filiis Istrahel."	Indeed, we say that he who is instructed in the law and is taught by Moses throws off the errors of idolatry, and sets aside the belief in and service of likenesses. This is the original circumcision of the law. If he comes from the law and the prophets to the gospel faith, then he receives still a second circumcision by "the rock, who is Christ" (1 Cor. 10:4), and that which the Lord said to Iesu is accomplished: "Today the disgrace of Egypt has been cast away from the children of Israel" (Josh 5:9).
Sicut autem dixit Apostolus: "bibebant autem de spiritali sequenti petra; petra vero erat Christus," ita etiam nos in hoc loco competenter possumus dicere: circumcise sunt autem "de spiritali sequenti petra; petra vero erat Christus." Nisi enim quis fuerit per evangelium secunda circumcision pergatus, not potest opprobrium Aegypti, id est illecebras corporalium deponere vitiorum.	Therefore, just as the Apostle said (1 Cor. 10:4): "They, therefore, drank from the spiritual rock following them; really the rock was Christ," thus, indeed, we are able to say aptly in this place that they were circumcised "in the spiritual rock following them; really that rock was Christ." For if anyone has not been cleansed through the gospel by a second circumcision, he is unable to cast aside the disgrace of Egypt, that is, the lures of the vices of the flesh.

Here is an excellent example of how Origen takes inherited polemical themes and blends them with the religious or spiritual message he wishes to impart to his congregants. As was seen in Justin (and to a lesser extent Tertullian,) Origen uses the odd phrase "circumcise for a second time" to prove that the text is hiding an allegory. Also, like Justin and Tertullian, Origen interprets the rock as a reference to Jesus. However, he does not stop there but continues on to the moral lesson.

To Origen, even the original, physical circumcision is important not in and of itself but only for its symbolic import. The original circumcision of the Torah/ Moses was the first step towards cleansing humanity of idolatry. Judaism, even according to Origen, is not idolatrous. However, the next step was accomplished by Jesus. The Gospels, Origen claims, purge a person of his (or her) fleshly desires. In other words, Torah is not idolatrous, but it is base. The Gospels, on the other hand, are sublimity itself. This is what the message from God to Joshua in the book of Joshua is meant to imply. Origen is inviting his parishioners to join him in fulfilling this important second circumcision by casting away their own desires of the flesh and leading a life of the spirit.

Summary

The Joshua-Jesus typology reaches its most advanced form in Origen's homilies. Here the typology serves to prove to Jews (or Judeo-sympathisers) not only that Jesus was foretold in the Old Testament through the character of Joshua, but that the deepest ideals behind the Jesus narrative can be found hinted at in the book of Joshua. The paradigm, therefore, moves here from its birth as a critique of Judaism and defense of Christianity to something uniquely Christian.

Tracing the Typology: Moderate Usage

The previous sections outlined the development of the typology and highlighted the key stages in its growth and articulation. However, from Justin on, the typology was known to many Christian exegetes and was used to a greater or lesser extent in their own works. This section will survey the writings of some of the Church Fathers who used the typology moderately, taking it seriously as an important piece of exegesis.

Clement of Alexandria

Titus Flavius Clemens (c.150 – 215), known as Clement of Alexandria, shares with Justin the belief that Joshua's name was meant to prefigure Jesus. Clement, however, bases his claim on a different passage in the Hebrew Bible. The context of Clement's comment is his *Paedagogus* (1:7.60 – 61). In this section, Clement is demonstrating for his reader who "the Teacher" is. The passage about Joshua comes towards the end of this section.

Αὐτίκα γοῦν ὁ Μωσῆς, τῷ τελείῳ προφητικῶς παραχωρῶν παιδαγωγῷ τῷ λόγῳ, καὶ τὸ ὄνομα καὶ τὴν παιδαγωγίαν προθεσπίζει καὶ τῷ λαῷ παρατίθεται τὸν παιδαγωγόν, ἐντολὰς ὑπακοῆς ἐγχειρίσας·	Therefore, forthwith Moses, prophetically, yielding to the perfect Teacher of the Word, foresees both the name and the instructorship, and sets the Teacher before the people, undertaking a command [to the people] of obedience.

"προφήτην ὑμῖν ἀναστήσει", φησίν, "ὁ θεὸς ὡς ἐμὲ ἐκ τῶν ἀδελφῶν ὑμῶν", τὸν Ἰησοῦν τὸν τοῦ Ναυῆ αἰνιττόμενος τὸν Ἰησοῦν τὸν τοῦ θεοῦ υἱόν· σκιαγραφία γὰρ ἦν τοῦ κυρίου τὸ ὄνομα τὸ Ἰησοῦ προκηρυσσόμενον ἐν νόμῳ. Ἐπιφέρει γοῦν, τὸ λυσιτελὲς τῷ λαῷ συμβουλεύων, "αὐτοῦ ἀκούσεσθε" λέγων, "καὶ ὁ ἄνθρωπος, ὃς ἂν μὴ ἀκούσῃ" τοῦ προφήτου τούτου, τούτῳ ἀπειλεῖ. Τοιοῦτον ἡμῖν ὄνομα σωτηρίου προφητεύει παιδαγωγοῦ.

"God will raise a prophet for you," he says, "like me from among your brethren" (Deut 18:15). Speaking in riddles of Iesu son of God [while overtly referring to] Iesu son of Nau; for the name Iesu predicted in the Law was a painting in shadows of the Lord. And so, he adds, considering the advantage to the people: "Listen to him," saying, "and the person who does not listen" (Deut 18:19) to that prophet, him [Moses] threatens. He predicts for us such a name (Iesu) for the Teacher of salvation.

Instead of the Amalek account, the scout story, or the second circumcision, Clement turns to a passage in which Moses describes his successor. As noted above, this passage was already used by Luke-Acts and John as an allusion to Jesus as the prophet like Moses.

One difficulty with the passage Clement chooses is that Moses does not actually refer to Joshua explicitly at all in this passage; he simply speaks about the future in a general way.[557] Israel will have another prophet (or prophets) like Moses, to whom the people are required to listen. Clement assumes that this statement is a reference to Joshua. Since the New Testament already identified Jesus as the prophet like Moses, by saying that the simple meaning of Moses was as an allusion to Joshua, Clement places this text into the rubric of the Joshua-Jesus typology in which Old Testament passages concerning Joshua are automatically assumed to foreshadow Jesus. Wheras Joshua was the "historical" successor of Moses, Jesus is the *true* successor of Moses.

---

557 This makes Clement's point weaker than that made by Justin (*Trypho* 75) based on the verse in Exodus (23:21) in which God says that His name is attached to the messenger who will bring Israel into the Promised Land. Since the person who brings Israel into the Promised Land is Joshua, Justin can then argue backwards that the speaker must also be named Joshua and hence the speaker is Jesus. Clement has no such hook. On the other hand, Clement has the explicit statement of Peter in Acts that Jesus is the prophet being alluded to by Moses, and since Moses must have had some "historical" referent as well, Joshua seems the obvious choice for referent, especially if one assumes that Clement was already familiar with the Joshua-Jesus typology in some way.

Irenaeus

Irenaeus (d. 202 C.E.), who served as bishop of Lyon, also made use of the Joshua-Jesus typology. Although it does not appear in his main work *Adversus Haereses*—which is surprising considering the genre—the typology appears in a fragment from a lost work, as well as in his *On the Apostolic Preaching*.

In *On the Apostolic Preaching* (27), Irenaeus takes note of the name change from Hoshea to Joshua, which he explains as relevant to the special nature of the name Joshua/Jesus.

> And when they were near to the land which God had promised to Abraham and his seed, Moses, choosing one from each tribe, sent [them] to spy out the land and the cities in it and the inhabitants of the cities. Then God revealed to him the Name, which alone is able to save those who believe in it; and Moses, renaming Osee, the son of Nave, one of the envoys, called him Jesus; and thus sent [him] with the power of the Name, believing that he would receive them back safe because of the guidance of the Name—as indeed came to pass.[558]

The renaming of Hoshea as Joshua was part of the Joshua-Jesus typology from its earliest appearance in Barnabas. However, Irenaeus seems to understand the significance of the renaming differently. In Barnabas and Justin, the renaming is connected both to the defeat of Amalek as well as to Joshua's future conquest of the Promised Land and its symbolic import. Irenaeus, however, sees the renaming of Joshua as a way of Moses protecting him and assisting in the mission of the scouts; with one of the scouts carrying the powerful name Iesu with him, there would be no question that they would return to the camp safely from their dangerous mission.

The other extant example of Irenaeus's usage of this paradigm comes from a fragment (19) that was most likely part of his *Miscellaneous Dissertations*.[559] In this passage, Irenaeus makes use of the more common—and more significant —argument that Joshua taking over for Moses and conquering the Promised Land should be understood as symbolic of Jesus taking over for the Law.

---

[558] Irenaeus, *On the Apostolic Preaching* (trans. from the Armenian by John Behr; Popular Patristics Series 17; Crestwood, NY: St. Vladimir's Seminary Press, 1997).
[559] The fragment was found in three manuscripts in the Imperial Collection at Paris on the Pentateuch, Joshua, Judges, and Ruth; see: *Ante-Nicene Fathers* 1:571–572, *PG* 7b 1240–1241.

"Λάβε πρὸς σεατὸν τὸν Ἰησοῦν υἱὸν Ναυῆ". "Take unto you Iesu son of Nau" (Num 27:18)
Ἔδει γὰρ ἐξ Αἰγύπτου Μωϋσῆν τὸν λαὸν ἐξαγα- – for it was necessary that Moses lead the peo-
γεῖν, τὸν δὲ Ἰησοῦν εἰς τὴν κληροδοσίαν εἰσα- ple out of Egypt but that Iesu lead them into
γαγεῖν. καὶ τὸν μὲν Μωϋσῆν ὡς νομον ἀνάπαυ- the Promised Land. Also that Moses, as the
λαν λαμβάνειν, Ἰησοῦν δὲ ὡς Λόγον, καὶ τοῦ Law, should take a rest, but Iesu, as the Word
ἐνυποστάτου Λόγου τύπον ἀψευδῆ, τῷ λαῷ —and not a false type of the Word made flesh
δημηγορεῖν. καὶ τὸν μὲν Μωϋσῆν τὸ μάννα —should preach to the people. Also, that
τοῖς πατράσι τροφὴν διδόναι τὸν δὲ Ἰησοῦν Moses should give manna to the fathers as
τὸν σῖτον, ἄρτι τὴν ἀπαρχὴν τῆς ζωῆς, τύπον nourishment, but Joshua wheat, just like the
τοῦ σώματος τοῦ Χριστοῦ, καθὰ φησὶ καὶ ἡ first-fruits of life, a type of the body of Christ,
Γραφὴ, ὅτι τότε ἐπαύσατο τὸ μάννα Κυρίου as Scripture states that the manna of the Lord
μετὰ τὸ φαγεῖν τὸν σῖτον λαὸν ἀπο τῆς γῆς. ceased when the people ate wheat from the
land.

In this short passage, Irenaeus puts forth the basic elements of the Joshua-is-su-
perior-to-Moses argument. Since Moses is the law, his tenure had to be short-
lived and could not end in complete success. Even the food Moses gave the Israelites was temporary. Only through Joshua-Jesus could the true mission of divine
salvation be fulfilled. This argument—already put forward by Justin—was taken
to its logical conclusion shortly after Irenaeus, by Origen, as was seen in the previous section.

Eusebius of Caesarea

Eusebius (263–339), bishop of Caesarea, was a prolific Christian writer, covering
subjects such as history, biblical exegesis, and polemic. As a theologian highly
influenced by Origen, Eusebius's use of this typology is hardly unexpected. However, unlike Origen, Eusebius has little interest in using the typology to interpret
large swaths of biblical texts. In fact, if anything, Eusebius expresses hyper-in-
terest in the name itself, and little if any interest in things Joshua actually does.

Eusebius references the typology in great detail in a number of places. In the
Historia Ecclesiastica (1:3) he describes Moses' prophetic knowledge of the two
names of the Savior, Iesu and Christ, and how he made use of these names
for the two leaders which he appointed.

[1] Ὅτι δὲ καὶ αὐτὸ τοὔνομα τοῦ τε Ἰησοῦ καὶ [1] At this point, it is time to demonstrate that
δὴ καὶ τοῦ Χριστοῦ παρ' αὐτοῖς τοῖς πάλαι both the very name Iesu and also Christ
θεοφιλέσιν προφήταις τετίμητο, ἤδη καιρὸς along with it were honored by the prophets of
ἀποδεικνύναι. old, beloved of God.

² σεπτὸν ὡς ἔνι μάλιστα καὶ ἔνδοξον τὸ Χριστοῦ ὄνομα πρῶτος αὐτὸς γνωρίσας Μωυσῆς τύπους οὐρανίων καὶ σύμβολα μυστηριώδεις τε εἰκόνας ἀκολούθως χρησμῷ φήσαντι αὐτῷ "ὅρα, ποιήσεις πάντα κατὰ τὸν τύπον τὸν δειχθέντα σοι ἐν τῷ ὄρει" παραδούς, ἀρχιερέα θεοῦ, ὡς ἐνῆν μάλιστα δυνατὸν ἄνθρωπον, ἐπιφημίσας, τοῦτον Χριστὸν ἀναγορεύει, καὶ ταύτῃ γε τῇ κατὰ τὴν ἀρχιερωσύνην ἀξίᾳ, πᾶσαν ὑπερβαλλούσῃ παρ' αὐτῷ τὴν ἐν ἀνθρώποις προεδρίαν, ἐπὶ τιμῇ καὶ δόξῃ τὸ τοῦ Χριστοῦ περιτίθησιν ὄνομα οὕτως ἄρα τὸν Χριστόν. θεῖόν τι χρῆμα ἠπίστατο.

³ ὁ δ' αὐτὸς καὶ τὴν τοῦ Ἰησοῦ προσηγορίαν εὖ μάλα πνεύματι θείῳ προϊδών, πάλιν τινὸς ἐξαιρέτου προνομίας καὶ ταύτην ἀξιοῖ. οὔποτε γοῦν πρότερον ἐκφωνηθὲν εἰς ἀνθρώπους, πρὶν ἢ Μωυσεῖ γνωσθῆναι, τὸ τοῦ Ἰησοῦ πρόσρημα τούτῳ Μωυσῆς πρώτῳ καὶ μόνῳ περιτίθησιν, ὃν κατὰ τύπον αὖθις καὶ σύμβολον ἔγνω μετὰ τὴν αὐτοῦ τελευτὴν διαδεξόμενον τὴν κατὰ πάντων ἀρχήν.

⁴ οὐ πρότερον γοῦν τὸν αὐτοῦ διάδοχον, τῇ τοῦ Ἰησοῦ κεχρημένον προσηγορίᾳ, ὀνόματι δὲ ἑτέρῳ τῷ Αὐσῆ, ὅπερ οἱ γεννήσαντες αὐτῷ τέθεινται, καλούμενον, Ἰησοῦν αὐτὸς ἀναγορεύει, γέρας ὥσπερ τίμιον, παντὸς πολὺ μεῖζον βασιλικοῦ διαδήματος, τοὔνομα αὐτῷ δωρούμενος, ὅτι δὴ καὶ αὐτὸς ὁ τοῦ Ναυῆ Ἰησοῦς τοῦ σωτῆρος ἡμῶν τὴν εἰκόνα ἔφερεν, τοῦ μόνου μετὰ Μωυσέα καὶ τὸ συμπέρασμα τῆς δι' ἐκείνου παραδοθείσης συμβολικῆς λατρείας, τῆς ἀληθοῦς καὶ καθαρωτάτης εὐσεβείας τὴν ἀρχὴν διαδεξαμένου

⁵ καὶ Μωυσῆς μὲν ταύτῃ πῃ δυσὶ τοῖς κατ' αὐτὸν ἀρετῇ καὶ δόξῃ παρὰ πάντα τὸν λαὸν προφέρουσιν ἀνθρώποις, τῷ μὲν ἀρχιερεῖ, τῷ δὲ μετ' αὐτὸν ἡγησομένῳ, τὴν τοῦ σωτῆρος ἡμῶν Ἰησοῦ.

² August and held in very high esteem, the name of Christ was first known by Moses as a type of the heavens and a symbol of the mysterious images, in accordance with the oracle that said to him (Exod 25:40): "Look, make everything according to the form shown to you on the mountain." He chose as high-priest of God a man—as best he could, and in affirmation, called him Christ. And thus, to this value of the high-priesthood, he placed above all of the other privileges among men, for the sake of the honor and glory, he gave thus the name of Christ; he knew it was a divine matter.

³ And this same person, foreseeing especially well through divine spirit the appelation Iesu, gave it, in turn, distinguished privilege and a certain value. The name of Iesu, at all events, had never been uttered among people before it was learned by Moses. And Moses gave it, as a type and symbol, first and only to him whom he knew would, after his death, receive command over all.

⁴ His successor, at any rate, had not been furnished with the name Iesu previously, having been called by another name, Ausei, which his parents had given him. He (Moses) proclaimed him Iesu, bestowing the name upon him as a gift of honor and even respect, much greater than any kingly crown. And indeed, Iesu son of Nau himself bore the image of our Savior; he alone, after Moses and the conclusion of the symbolic service offered him by that person, he received the leadership of the true and pure religion.

⁵ Thus Moses, in this way, bestowed [the name] of our Savior Iesu upon the two men who, after him, surpassed all of the people in goodness and judgment; the high priest and the leader who would succeed him.

The only matter discussed here is Moses' divining of the special names of the savior, and his usage of them to crown Aaron and Joshua in respect and glory. Although it is true that Eusebius adds a new verse to the repertoire of the paradigm, arguing the the image Moses sees on the mountain was that of Jesus, complete with his two sacred names, Eusebius has little of substance to say about the typology.[560] He does not even deal with most of the classical loci of the paradigm, whether it be the Amalek account or the second circumcision.

The impression of Eusebius' verbiage and repetitiveness is exacerbated by his even lengthier (and more repetitive) presentation of this same point in *Demonstratio Evangelica* 4.7 (*PG* 22, 325–328).[561] Eusebius begins by discussing the amazing powers of Moses' prophecy.

[1] Πρῶτος πάλιν Μωσῆς πρὸς τὸν αὐτοῦ διάδοχον ἑτέρᾳ χρώμενος προσωνυμίᾳ Ἰησοῦν μετωνόμασεν. γέγραπται γάρ· "ταῦτα τὰ ὀνόματα τῶν ἀνδρῶν, οὓς ἀπέστειλεν Μωσῆς κατασκέψασθαι τὴν γῆν, καὶ ἐπωνόμασεν Μωσῆς τὸν Ναυσὴν υἱὸν Ναυὴ Ἰησοῦν, καὶ ἀπέστειλεν αὐτούς".

[2] ὅρα δὴ οὖν τίνα τρόπον οὐ μικρὰ νοήσας περὶ φύσεως ὀνομάτων ὁ προφήτης, ἀλλὰ καὶ πλεῖστα ὅσα περὶ τῶν παρ' αὐτῷ μετονομαζομένων θείων ἀνδρῶν καὶ ὧν ἕνεκα μετονομάζονται φιλοσοφήσας,

εἰσάγει τὸν Ἀβρὰμ ἔπαθλον ἐπ' ἀρετῇ ἀπολαμβάνοντα πρὸς τοῦ θεοῦ τὴν πατρὸς Ἀβραὰμ ἐντελῆ προσηγορίαν, ὅπερ τί ποτε δηλοῖ οὐ νῦν διασαφεῖν καιρός.

[3] οὕτω δὲ καὶ τὴν Σάραν Σάρραν ἐπονομάσας, καὶ Γέλωτα τὸν Ἰσαὰκ πρὸ γενέσεως ἐπικεκλημένον, καὶ τὸν Ἰακὼβ τῆς πάλης τὸ βραβεῖον διὰ τῆς τοῦ Ἰσραὴλ ἐπωνυμίας ἀναδούμενον, μυρία τε ἄλλα περὶ ὀνομάτων δυνάμεώς τε καὶ φύσεως θειότερα ἢ κατ' ἄνθρωπον ἐνθέῳ σοφίᾳ καὶ ἐπιστήμῃ διαλαβών,

[1] The first [to use the name] was Moses, who renamed his successor—who was called by a different name—Iesu. For it is written (Num 13:16–17): "These are the names of the men, whom Moses sent to scout out the land, and Moses named Nausei[562] the son of Nau, Iesu, and he sent them."

[2] And so, look, the prophet understood more than a little about the origin of names, rather he pursued these matters a great deal – [exploring] the divine changing of men's names and on what account the names were changed. He discussed Abram, who received the full name Abraam, a reward from God the Father, on account of his virtue, the reason for which it is not now the time to clarify.

[3] And thus he named Sara Sarra, and Isaac he called "The Laugh" before his birth,[563] and Jacob on account of his wrestling, he was given the name of Israel. And in many other cases regarding the power and divine origin of names he (Moses) exhibited inspired wisdom and knowledge beyond human.

---

560 There may be added polemical benefit in making Moses learn about Jesus on Mount Sinai, of all places, the spot where the Old Testament has him receive the Ten Commandments and the Rabbis believe he received the entire Torah, oral and written. If one sees this in conversation with the rabbis, then the claim is that in addition to the two tablets Moses received not the two Torahs, but the two names of Christ.

561 The same basic presentation, albeit in a different order, appears as well in Eusebius' earlier work *Eclogae Propheticae* 1:11 (*PG* 22: 1055–1058). As these passages are virtually identical, I will discuss only *Demonstratio Evangelica* above.

562 Every other Greek source—including Eusebius's own *Historica Ecclesiastica* and *Eclogae Propheticae*—transliterates the name Hoshea as Ausei, not Nausei; it is tempting to assume that this is a mistake.

563 Eusebius knows what the name Isaac means, but whether this is from some rudimentary knowledge of Hebrew (unlike Justin) or whether he got it from Philo (*Leg.* 3:219. *Det.* 124), I cannot say.

μηδενὸς τῶν πρὸ αὐτοῦ τῶν ἐξ αἰῶνος τῷ τοῦ Ἰησοῦ κεχρημένου ὀνόματι, πρῶτος αὐτὸς θείῳ πνεύματι θεοφορηθεὶς τὸν μέλλοντα αὐτοῦ διάδοχον τῆς ἀρχῆς τοῦ λαοῦ καταστήσεσθαι, ἑτέρῳ πρότερον ὀνόματι κεχρημένον, μεταβαλὼν Ἰησοῦν καλεῖ,

οὐκ ἀρκεῖν ἡγούμενος τὴν ἐκ προγόνων ἐπικληθεῖσαν αὐτῷ γεννωμένῳ προσηγούμενος τὴν ἐκ προγόνων ἐπικληθεῖσαν αὐτῷ γεννωμένῳ προσηγορίαν· Ναυσῆν γὰρ αὐτὸν ἐφώνουν οἱ γεννήσαντες.

⁴ ἀλλ᾽ ὅ γε προφήτης τοῦ θεοῦ τὸ ἐκ γενετῆς ἀμείψας ὄνομα Ἰησοῦν τὸν ἄνδρα κατὰ τὸ θεῖον νεῦμα καλεῖ· οὐκ ἄλλως αὐτὸν καθηγεῖσθαι τοῦ παντὸς λαοῦ μετὰ τὴν ἑαυτοῦ τελευτήν, τῆς <δὲ> πρὸς αὐτοῦ τεθείσης νομοθεσίας μεταστησομένης ποτὲ καὶ τέλος ἰσχούσης καὶ αὐτῷ γε ὁμοίως Μωσεῖ τρόπον τινὰ τελευτώσης, μηδένα ἕτερον ἢ μόνον Ἰησοῦν τὸν Χριστὸν τοῦ θεοῦ πολιτείας ἑτέρας ἡγήσεσθαι κρείττονος ἢ κατὰ τὴν προτέραν.

⁵ οὕτω μὲν δὴ Μωσῆς ὁ πάντων προφητῶν θαυμασιώτατος, ἀμφοτέρας τοῦ σωτῆρος ἡμῶν Ἰησοῦ Χριστοῦ θείῳ πνεύματι διαγνοὺς τὰς ἐπωνυμίας, ταύταις ὡς ἂν βασιλικοῖς διαδήμασιν τοὺς παρ᾽ αὐτὸν πάντων τῶν ἀρχόντων ἐκκρίτους ἐτίμησεν, δυσὶν ἄρχουσιν καὶ ἡγεμόσιν τοῦ λαοῦ, τῷ τε ἀρχιερεῖ καὶ τῷ οἰκείῳ διαδόχῳ, τὸν Χριστὸν καὶ τὸν Ἰησοῦν ἐπιφημίσας κατ᾽ ἀξίαν, τῷ μὲν Ἀαρὼν τὸν Χριστόν, τῷ δὲ Ναυσῆ ὡς ἂν τὴν αὐτοῦ τελευτὴν διαδεξομένῳ τὸν Ἰησοῦν ἀπονείμας.

⁶ τοῦτον μὲν οὖν τὸν τρόπον ἡ αὐτοῦ Μωσέως γραφὴ ταῖς τοῦ σωτῆρος ἡμῶν Ἰησοῦ Χριστοῦ κεκόσμητο προσηγορίαις.

– No one before him had ever called someone by the name Iesu, he was the first, inspired by the Holy Spirit, he called him who was about to be established as (Moses') successor as the leader of the people Iesu, changing the other name he had been called originally.

He did not hold that which he was named at birth by his parents to be sufficient, for his parents had named him, calling him at his birth by the name Nausei.

⁴ Rather the prophet of God changed the name of Iesu from his birth-name, and named the man in accordance with the will of God. He could not, otherwise, guide the entire nation after his own death, with the law he (Moses) gave being changed and having an end, just like Moses himself comes to an end; only with none other than Iesu the Christ of God leading that other polity in a manner even better than the first one (Joshua).

⁵ Thus, Moses, the most wonderful of all prophets, having discerned through the Spirit of God, both names of our Savior, Iesu Christ, honored the most select out of all the leaders with these [names], like kingly crowns, properly naming the two rulers and leaders of the people—the high priest and his own successor—Christ and Iesu. He called Aaron, Christ, and Nausei, who would succeed him in the end, Iesu.

⁶ And so, in this manner, the writings of Moses himself have been adorned with the names of our Savior, Iesu Christ.

It is true that Eusebius adds some small points that were not in his presentation of the paradigm in *Historia Ecclesiastica*. He makes reference to the verse in Numbers at the opening of the scout account as evidence that it was Moses that gave Joshua his name. However, this treatment of the scout story pales in comparison with the treatments by earlier Church Fathers, who describe the giving of the name as a way of symbolically demonstrating Jesus' coming (Barnabas and Justin) or protecting Joshua during his scouting mission and guaranteeing its success (Irenaeus).

Somewhat more substantially, Eusebius adds that the reason Moses did not take the name Joshua's parents gave him as definitive, and felt it necessary to change it, was that he saw the opportunity to hint to the Israelites that his (Moses') Torah would die, just as he would, and that a leader would then come and fulfill God's true promise for the world, and that leader would be called Iesu, just as Moses' successor was called Iesu.[564]

That said, it is hard not to notice how *extremely* repetitive the above section sounds. The point that Moses was a great prophet and the first to learn the name Iesu is made numerous times with great verbosity. Even more repetitive is Eusebius' treatment of the fact that Joshua was not originally called Joshua, but that his parents had named him something else; he repeats this relentlessly, as if this were a matter of great subtlety or enormous theological import. Why he does this —unless this is simply his style—I cannot guess.

The above, however, is not the end of Eusebius's treatment of the Joshua-Jesus typology. Having established the correlation between Joshua and Jesus to his satisfaction, Eusebius turns to a number of passages from scripture in order to demonstrate his point that Moses was aware of the import of the name Iesu (*Demonstratio Evangelica*, 4.17).

Ἀπὸ τῆς Ἐξόδου.
"Ἰδοὺ ἀποστέλλω τὸν ἄγγελόν μου πρὸ προσώπου σου, ἵνα φυλάσσῃ σε ἐν τῇ ὁδῷ, ὅπως εἰσαγάγῃ σε εἰς τὴν γῆν, ἣν ἡτοίμασά σοι. πρόσεχε σεαυτῷ καὶ εἰσάκουε αὐτοῦ, μὴ ἀπείθει αὐτῷ· οὐ γὰρ μὴ ὑποστείληταί σε· τὸ γὰρ ὄνομά μού ἐστιν ἐπ' αὐτῷ."
[7] ἐμοῦ, φησὶν αὐτὸς ὁ κύριος, τοῦ σοι ταῦτα χρηματίζοντος τοὔνομα ἐπιγέγραπται ὁ μέλλων εἰσάξειν τὸν λαὸν εἰς τὴν γῆν τῆς ἐπαγγελίας· εἰ δ' αὐτὸς ἦν ὁ Ἰησοῦς, οὐκ ἄλλος, πρόδηλον ὡς τοὔνομα τὸ αὐτοῦ φησιν ἐπιτεθεῖσθαι αὐτῷ.

– From Exodus (23:20):
"Behold, I am sending my angel before you in order to guard you on the way, in order to bring you into the land which I prepared for you. Attend to him and listen to him, do not provoke him, for he will not dissemble for you, for my name is upon him."
[7] "He, who teaches you these things, is inscribed with my name," says the Lord himself, "he who is to lead the people into the Promised Land." If this was Iesu and no other, it is clear why He says that *His* name was set upon him.

---

564 "Joshua symbolized Jesus as the true heir of Moses and the Law, who would lead mankind to the Promised Land," Aryeh Kofsky, *Eusebius of Caesarea against Paganism* (Jewish and Christian Perspectives Series 3; Leiden: Brill, 2000), 55.

⁸ οὐ θαυμαστὸν οὖν εἰ καὶ ἄγγελον αὐτὸν ἀπο- καλεῖ, ὅτε καὶ περὶ Ἰωάννου ἀνθρώπου γεγο- νότος λέλεκται τὸ "ἰδοὺ ἀποστέλλω τὸν ἄγγε- λόν μου πρὸ προσώπου σου, ὃς κατασκευάσει τὴν ὁδόν σου ἔμπροσθέν σου".

⁸ Therefore, it is not surprising that he calls him an angel, since this is stated regarding John as well, who was human: "Look, I will send an angel before you, who will scout out your way before you."[565]

In this subsection, one can see the influence of the more expansive uses of the typology on Eusebius. The first verse about God's/Jesus's name being upon the "angel" who brings the Israelites into Israel was the cornerstone of Justin's exegesis (75), and, thus was part of the Joshua-Jesus typology from its inception.

More outstanding is the analogy to John being called "angel," and the use of the passage from Mark to prove this. As was seen above, Tertullian makes this exact argument in his *Adversus Iudaeos*. Although it is possible that Eusebius was familiar with Tertullion's work (either the *Adversus Iudaeos* or the *Adversus Marcionem*,) it seems more likely that the Joshua-Jesus typology was sufficiently well-known and diffuse by Eusebius' time that the use of this verse could have been a literary topos or an obvious enough application of the typology such that both exegetes could have come to it independently.[566]

Finally, considering the importance Eusebius attaches to the name Iesu, I do not find it surprising that he takes the opportunity in the next section to make similar comments about Joshua son of Jehozadak, the high priest, although, to be sure, this is a secondary use of the name in comparison with the significance of Joshua son of Nun.

Eusebius begins by quoting a number of verses from Zechariah chapters 3 and 6, about Joshua the high priest. Then he ties the high priest's name in with his Joshua-Jesus typology 4.17.12.

Καὶ ὁ ἐν τῷ παρόντι προφήτῃ μέγας ἱερεὺς ἀναγορευόμενος Ἰησοῦς λευκοτάτην εἰκόνα καὶ σύμβολον ἐναργὲς δοκεῖ μοι σῴζειν τοῦ σωτῆρος ἡμῶν Ἰησοῦ τοῦ Χριστοῦ, τῇ τε αὐτοῦ προσηγορίᾳ τιμηθεὶς καὶ τῆς ἐπανόδου τῆς ἀπὸ Βαβυλῶνος αἰχμαλωσίας τοῦ λαοῦ καθηγησάμενος,...

Also in this passage from the prophet, the high priest called Iesu presents a clear image and palpable symbol, in my estimation, of our Savior Iesu Christ, being honored with his name and given the leadership over the people returning from the captivity in Babylon...

---

565 As was stated in the section on Tertullian, there is no such verse in the Old Testament. This "verse" is referenced in Mark 1:2, where it is attributed to Isaiah in certain manuscripts, and in Mathew 11:10. It appears to be a composite verse beginning with Exod 23:20 and ending with Mal 3:1. John is identified with Elijah in Christian hermeneutics.

566 It is also possible that Eusebius adapted the argument from Origen's *Homilies on Joshua* (3.3), but this would be a stretch, since Origen is making a different point (he is speaking of the spies who were sent to Jericho, not to Joshua).

ἔχεις τοιγαροῦν ἤδη δύο μεγάλους ἀρχιερεῖς, τὸν μὲν παρὰ Μωσεῖ Χριστόν, τὸν δὲ μετὰ χεῖρας Ἰησοῦν, τὰ σύμβολα τῆς περὶ τὸν σωτῆρα καὶ κύριον ἡμῶν Ἰησοῦν Χριστὸν ἀληθείας δι' ἑαυτῶν ἐπενηνεγμένους.	You have, then, two high priests, the one made Christ by Moses and the Iesu just discussed, truly bearing in themselves the symbols of our Savior and Lord, Iesu Christ.

Eusebius is hardly the first or only Church Father to apply the Joshua-Jesus typology to Joshua the high priest. This was done just as extensively by Tertullian as well, and can be understand as having been inspired by the text in Hebrews 3–4.[567] For Eusebius and Tertullian, including Joshua the high priest only solidifies the paradigm, but does not take away from it.[568]

In summary, it would seem that Eusebius is not simply giving lip-service to a popular hermeneutic correlation; he takes the truth of it seriously. Knowing that Moses predicted the name Iesu and that he attempted to prepare the Israelites for Iesu's future coming was important to Eusebius. He even goes so far as to claim that Moses predicted the abrogation of the Sinaitic covenant and its replacement with Iesu's death and the consequent divine grace and that by naming his successor Iesu, he was attempting to help the Israelites come to terms with this future reality.

Lactantius

Lucius Caecilius Firmianus Lactantius (c.250–c.325), served as the appointed Chief of Rhetoric under Emperor Diocletion, until his conversion to Christianity in 317 C.E., when he resigned the post to become the tutor of Emperor Constantine's son Crispus.[569] In his book, *Divine Institutes*, in a section titled: "Of the Superstitions of the Jews and their Hatred against Jesus" (4:17), Lactantius makes

---

567 See, again, the section on Whitfield's dissertation. Interestingly, as was noted above, Justin does not suggest such a correlation, although he applies the typology to Joshua of Beit Shemesh from Samuel.

568 This contrasts with the work of Gregory of Nyssa (as will be seen), who uses Joshua bin Nun and Joshua the high priest in almost the same way, seeing little significance in the typology.His terse statements about both Joshuas—as if the typologies were exactly the same for each—underline this fact.

569 Lactantius's training in rhetoric can be seen in his direct and forceful style of writing, earning him the title "Christian Cicero" (earlychurch.org.uk; Catholic Encyclopedia.) For a discussion of the importance of Lactantius' activity to the formation of the Church in Rome, and particularly with Constantine, see: Elizabeth DePalma Digeser, *The Making of a Christian Empire: Lactantius and Rome* (Ithaca: Cornel University Press, 2000.)

use of the Joshua-Jesus typology as part of his presentation on the issue of circumcision.

Item Moyses ipse: in novissimis diebus circumcidet deus cor tuum ad dominum deum tuum amandum.	Likewise, Moses himself (Deut 30:6): "In the last days, God will circumcise your hearts to love the Lord your God."
Item Iesus Naue successor eius: et dixit dominus ad Iesum: fac tibi cultellos petrinos nimis acutos et sede[570] *et circumcide secundo filios Israhel.*	Likewise, Iesu son of Nau his successor (Josh 5:2): "And the Lord said to Iesu: "Make for yourself exceedingly sharp, stone knives and sit and circumcise the sons of Israel a second time."
Secundam circumcisionem futuram esse dixit non carnis, sicut fuit prima, qua etiam nunc Iudaei utuntur, sed cordis ac spiritus, quam tradidit Christus, qui verus Iesus fuit.	The second circumcision of the future would not be, he said, of the flesh—as was the original one, which the Jews even now still employ—but of the heart and spirit, which was bequeathed by Christ, who was the true Iesu.
Non enim propheta sic ait "et dixit dominus ad me", sed "ad Iesum", ut ostenderet quod non de se loqueretur, sed de Christo, ad quem tum deus loquebatur. Christi enim figuram gerebat ille Iesus.	For the prophet did not say thus "and the Lord said to me," but "to Iesu," in order to demonstrate that it was not about him that [God] spoke but about Christ, to whom God was then speaking; for that Iesu bore the figure of Christ.
Qui cum primum Auses vocaretur, Moyses futura praesentiens iussit eum Iesum vocari, ut quoniam dux militiae delectus esset adversus Amalech, qui obpugnabat filios Israhel, et adversarium debellaret per nominis figuram et populum in terram promissionis induceret.	Originally he was called Aussi. Moses, predicting the future, commanded him to be called Iesu, since he had been chosen as leader of the army against Amalek, who fought the children of Israel, and so that he subdue the adversary with the figure of the name and lead the people into the Promised Land.
et idcirco etiam Moysi successit, ut ostenderetur novam legem per Christum Iesum datam veteri legi successuram, quae data per Moysen fuit.	And for this reason, he succeeded Moses, in order to show that the new law given by Christ Iesu was to succeed the old law, which was given by Moses.
Nam illa carnis circumcisio caret utique ratione, quia si deus id vellet, sic a principio formasset hominem, ut praeputium non haberet...	For the circumcision of the flesh is, assuredly, without reason. Because, if God had wished it, he would have formed man this way from the beginning, so that he wouldn't have had any foreskin...

---

570 Although the Latin here differs significantly from that of Rufinus' translation of Origen, nevertheless, one can see that Lactantius uses a text similar to that of the LXX's ("sit" as opposed to "return.") Since Lactantius writes in Latin, perhaps this was the Old Latin translation as well.

Lactantius uses the above as an opening for his spiritual interpretation of circumcision, namely that the removal of the foreskin from the glans is meant as an allegory for laying one's heart bare, i.e., the institution of confessing one's sins to a Christian priest.

Although this particular take on the meaning of circumcision is not evidenced in the earlier discussions, much of what Lactantius writes is clearly based on the classic uses of the Joshua-Jesus model, such as are found in Justin, Tertullian, and Origen. However, for Lactantius, Joshua is not an early instantiation of Jesus. Rather, the naming of Joshua was consciously done in order to imply to the Israelites the coming of Jesus in the future.

Since Joshua had been chosen to lead the people against the Amalekites and into the Promised Land, it was only fitting that he should be given the special name Iesu. This renaming would communicate to the people that, in the future, another Iesu (the true Iesu) would defeat the Adversary and lead them to the Promised Land.

Although Lactantius does not spell out the symbolic meaning of Amalek or the Promised Land as Justin and Origen do, he does do this with the symbolic meaning of the second circumcision. Again, Lactantius does not claim that Joshua was, in fact, told to circumcise the people's hearts by instituting confession of sin; rather, Joshua wanted it recorded that this is what God commanded the true Iesu—not him—to institute in the future. Joshua would continue with the humdrum and irrational practice of physical circumcision, as is done "even now" by Jews.

In summary, Lactantius makes use of the typology, but in a limited way. There is no Origen-like expansion to reread Joshua as a sort of precursor to the Gospels; one could even fairly characterize Lactantius' understanding of the relationship between Joshua and Jesus as less than Justin and Tertullian themselves envisioned it to be.[571]

Zeno of Verona

Zeno of Verona (c.300 – c.380), like Lactantius, makes use of the typology in his exegesis regarding Joshua and the second circumcision. The quote appears in the first of his *Sermons*, in the chapter about circumcision (13). The tone, like that of

---

571 Daniélou (*From Shadows*, 242), in a footnote, compares Lactantius's use of the typology to that of Eusebius. This does not seem to me to be correct, as Eusebius appears much more in line with Origen's expansive model than Lactantius does.

many Christian writings that focus on the question of circumcision but even more so, is extremely polemical and aggressive.

The passage about Joshua comes as part of Zeno's attempt to prove that circumcision is allegorical. To do this, he quotes Deut 30:6 (as did Lactantius above,) where it states that God will, in the future, circumcise the hearts of the Israelites. Using this as a jumping off point, Zeno begins his taunt (Sermon 1.13).

Hinc nunc vobis iterum dicam: 'Pharisaee, responde, ubi cor habeas constitutum. Si in regione pectoris, quid deformi vulnere inferna metiris? Si, quod quidem recte aestimas, in infernis, procul dubio omnes sacrilegos antecedis, qui Moysi reprobans dictum per hanc iniuriosam corporis stipem deo placere te posse praesumis.'

Now I say to you again: 'Pharisee, answer! Where is your heart? If it is in the area of your chest, why do you mete out loathsome wounds to your lower regions? If, however, as you seem to think is correct, [it is] in the lower regions, then you doubtless greatly surpass all sacreligious people, [you,] who, rejecting the word of Moses, presume to be pleasing to God with this noxious compression of your bodies'.[572]

Iam completa est, inquit, in me per Iesum Naue domino iubente secunda, quam Moyses annuntiaverat, circumcisio. Scriptum est enim: et dixit Deus ad Iesum: 'Fac tibi cultellos petrinos nimis acutos et adside[573] et circumcide secundo filios israel.'

At present, he says, I am fulfilling the command of the Lord to Iesu son of Nau, about the second circumcision, which Moses [originally] announced. For it is written: "And God said to Iesu: 'Take for yourself stone knives, exceedingly sharp, and sit and circumcise the sons of Israel a second time.'"

Videamus nunc ergo, fratres carissimi, secunda illa circumcisio ab Iesu Naue quo genere celebrata sit petrinis illis cultris: cor an praeputium circumciderit.

Let us see, now, therefore, my dearest brothers, this second circumcision of Iesu son of Nau, in what manner was it solemnized with these stone daggers – did he circumcise the heart or the foreskin?

Etenim si secundum ipsos nos quoque carnaliter sentiamus, ambo prophetae tenebuntur in crimine, ut aut moyses fallax sit, si circumcisio recircumciditur rursum, ut hoc idem faciat aut ut quod non habet perdat; aut certe Iesu Naue parricida sit, si cultris corda hominum desecat.

Truly, if we were to think carnally, as these [Jews] do, we would be insisting on the criminal nature of the prophets! Either Moses was mistaken: since a circumcision being recircumcised is impossible, as it was already done there is nothing to remove. Alternatively, Iesu is certainly a murderer if he cut the heart of a person with a dagger.

Sed absit, fratres, ut spiritales viros ullo tangamus errore, maxime cum prophetia ad sui dicti iam pervenerit veritatem.

But it is wrong, brothers, for us to attach any error to these spiritual men, especially since that which the prophecy states has now come true.

---

572 Zeno is nothing if not colorful.

573 This is a different Latin word than used by Lactantius (*sede*), but with the same meaning (sit).

Iesus enim Naue Christi imaginem praeferebat, qui verus omnium salvator esse cognoscitur et factis et nomine.	In reality, Iesu son of Nau—in deed and name—represented a type of Christ, who is known to be the true savior of all.
Hic enim, quia ipse dictus est etiam petra, recte cultellos petrinos fecit (unde non sine ratione et simoni, super quem aedificavit ecclesiam, petrus nomen imposuit), id est sua doctrina formatos, spiritus sancti lima acuminatos constituit viros apostolos omnes que discipulos.	In truth, he who himself was also called rock, correctly made knives of rock, (whence not without reason he gave the name "rock" [Peter] to Simon, upon whom he built the church), that is, his apostles and all his disciples, formed by his doctrine, he made sharp with the file of the Holy Spirit.
Quorum salutaria monita canentibus linguis, quasi quibusdam spiritalibus cultris, credentium populorum secundum Moysi dictum non in damnum hominis praeputium carnis, sed in augmentum hominis praeputium facinorosi cordis incidit.	Their tongues recited healthy admonitions, as if with spiritual daggers, that the word of Moses was not, like the people believed, to damage a person through the foreskin of flesh, but to bless a person by cutting away the foreskin of villainy from his heart.

Zeno appears to be following in the well trodden path of Justin, Tertullian, Origen, and Lactantius. It is not only that he interprets the second circumcision as an allegory for circumcision of the heart; this is the standard Christian interpretation and is hardly linked in any unique way to the Joshua-Jesus typology. The important aspect of Zeno's hermeneutic, from the perspective of this chapter, is that he uses the typology as one of the ways in which he proves his point "to the Jews."[574]

Zeno wants to prove that the circumcision discussed in the Law is not physical but spiritual. His first approach is to use the verse in Deuteronomy about the circumcision of the heart as a lens with which to view any discussion of circumcision in Jewish texts. However, although Zeno does not actually admit this, this approach is a dead end. It is clear from the early stories and the description of circumcision in the Old Testament that actual physical circumcision is meant.

This is, probably, why Zeno moves on to a different track. He points to the odd verse in Joshua about a second circumcision. Having taunted his (imaginary) Jewish interlocuters about how absurd it would be for Moses or Joshua to attempt to circumcise a circumcised man (what would they cut?), he moves the reader to the crucial interpretive crux. Joshua, who is told to circumcise the Israelites a second time, is really a stand-in for Jesus. As we all know, Zeno writes, Jesus has actually succeeded in circumcising the hearts of the entire world (or large swaths of it at any rate.) It is Jesus and his apostles who have removed

---

574 Whether Zeno actually knew any Jews or was actively trying to convince them of Christian dogma is hard to say, but even if he was not, the polemic would be useful to bolster the confidence of his Christian readers in the correctness of their religion.

the criminal baseness from the pagan nations, and have tried, albeit unsuccessfully, to stop the Jews from practicing their outdated and barbaric practice of circumcision now that they know, or should know, what the Lord's command really intended.

Finally, it is worth noting that Zeno includes an ecclesiastical element in the usual "Christ is the rock" element of the interpretation of the stone knives, by mentioning that Jesus gave Simon the name Peter, which means rock, and Peter established the church.

In short, although Zeno does not offer a robust use of the typology, covering multiple Joshua stories with an overall hermeneutic Joshua-Jesus lens, he does use the typology as an interpretive key to understand at least one, if not more, of the Joshua stories.[575]

Hilary of Poitiers

Another church father who makes use of the correlation in name between Jesus and Joshua was Hilary (Hilarius) of Poitiers (France; c.300 – 368). Hilary is best known for the strong stand he took against Arianism as Bishop of Poitiers. In his *Tractatus Mysteriorum*, in the section discussing the statement of the prophet Hoshea about marrying a harlot (book 2), Hilary dedicates a number of pages to understanding his imagery, specifically in light of the story of Rahab in the book of Joshua. As part of the lead in to his analysis of the Rahab story, Hilary writes (Tractatus Mysteriorum, book 2).

---

575 On the other hand, it should come as no surprise that, for Zeno, sometimes Joshua is just Joshua. For example, in the middle of this same treatise (36), Zeno waxes poetic about miracles and writes.

Haec Moysi in mari rubro terram vitream fecit: haec, ut cursus soliti contempta mensura Iesu Naue desiderio pareretur, soli lunae que suos frenos induxit; haec de armato Golia David inermi triumphos attulit;	Thus Moses made verdant land in the Red Sea. Thus, through necessity, Iesu son of Nau brought it about that the course of the sun be held in light esteem, and he led the sun and moon with his bridle. Thus, defenseless, David brought forth triumph against the armed Goliath.

In this passage, Joshua functions in the same way as Moses and David; he is a great leader of Israel who, with the help of God, accomplishes the miraculous.

In Iesu enim cognominato absoluta futuri sacramenti ratio monstrata est: namque post multum Dei ad Moysen sermonem, cum dictum ei esset, ut omnia secundum speciem, quam in monte vidisset, faceret in terra, Iesum, qui Auses antea vocabatur, cognominavit ducem populo ad terram repromissionis pergenti futurum; ad speciem coelestis visionis iussus Moyses universa disponere, illud duci futuro nomen adlegit quod erat aeterno duci iam in coelestibus praeparatum.

For in the name "Iesu" is shown the absolute meaning of the sacrament of things to come: for after there was much conversation of God with Moses, when it was said to him (Moses) that he should do on earth according to the image which he saw on the mountain, he gave the name Iesu to him who earlier was called Ause (Hoshea), to be the one to lead the people to the land of future promise. In order to orient all to the image of the heavenly vision, the just Moses chose for the future leader that name which was already prepared in heaven for the eternal leader.[576]

Taken on its own, the passage is rather enigmatic. Nonetheless, Hilary seems to echo the thinking of those church fathers before him who saw great significance in the name Iesu. Like Justin, Origen, Tertullian, and Eusebius, Hilary sees Moses' act of renaming Hoshea Joshua as something more than just a sign for the future. Rather, it was necessary that the person who would prefigure Jesus by leading the people into the Promised Land and—in Hilary's understanding —redeem the prefigured church (Rahab) to have the name foretold by God.

According to Hilary, Moses learned this on the mountain and followed God's instructions by renaming his future successor Jesus-Joshua and placing him on his destined path to lead the people to the Promised Land and redeem the harlot Rahab, who prefigures the church. As was seen above, the idea that Moses learned of the great mystery of the name Jesus through some sort of image or vision on Mount Sinai was already used by Eusebius, although he emphasizes the name Christ as well.

Cyril of Jerusalem

Cyril of Jerusalem (c.313–386) sees significance in the identical names of Joshua and Jesus and ties this into a number of parallel actions. What is unique about Cyril's use of the typology is that, other than referencing the name change, he does not go down the trodden path of Amalek and circumcision, but finds a number of different parallels.

The context for Cyril's use of the Joshua-Jesus typology is in his *Catecheses*, a collection of doctrinal essays meant for upcoming converts to Christianity. The

---

576 My thanks to Adam Ployde for helping me translate this text.

tenth catechesis, whose theme is, "The only-begotten Son of God who was born of the father as true God before all ages through whom all things were made," attempts to prove that if one believes in the Father one should believe in the Son as well. As part of this argument (10:11) Cyril claims that Moses himself foresaw the coming of Jesus Christ, and for this reason he renamed Hoshea, Joshua.

Ἰησοῦς δὲ Χριστὸς καλεῖται διώνυμος· Ἰησοῦς διὰ τὸ σῴζειν, Χριστὸς διὰ τὸ ἱερατεύειν. Καὶ τοῦτο γινώσκων ὁ θεσπέσιος τῶν προφητῶν Μωϋσῆς, ἀνδράσι δυσὶ τοῖς πάντων ἐγκρίτοις τὰς δύο ταύτας προσηγορίας ἐχαρίσατο· τὸν μὲν οἰκεῖον τῆς ἀρχῆς διάδοχον Αὐσὴν, Ἰησοῦν μετονομάσας· τὸν δὲ οἰκεῖον ἀδελφὸν τὸν Ἀαρών, ἐπονομάσας Χριστόν, ἵνα διὰ δύο ἀνθρώπων ἐγκρίτων, τὸ ἀρχιερατικὸν ἅμα καὶ βασιλικὸν τοῦ μέλλοντος ἑνὸς Ἰησοῦ Χριστοῦ παραστήσῃ.

Ἀρχιερεὺς μὲν γάρ ἐστιν ὁ Χριστὸς κατὰ τὸν Ἀαρών· ἐπειδὴ οὐχ ἑαυτὸν ἐδόξασε γενέσθαι ἀρχιερέα, ἀλλ᾽ ὁ λαλήσας πρὸς αὐτόν· "Σὺ εἶ ἱερεὺς εἰς τὸν αἰῶνα κατὰ τὴν τάξιν Μελχισεδέκ".

Iesu Christ is called by two names: Iesu because he saves;[577] Christ because he is a priest. Knowing this, that most marvelous of prophets, Moses, called two men, accepted by all, by these two appelations. He that was to be his own successor in leadership, Ause, he renamed Iesu; he that was his own brother, Aaron, he gave the name Christ, so that through these two select people he could establish the high-priesthood together with the kingship of the future coming one, Iesu Christ.

For Christ is a high priest like Aaron, since he did not request to be high-priest, rather it was told to him: "You will be a priest for eternity according to the order of Melchizedek" (Ps 109[110]:4 as understood by Heb 5:5 – 6).

---

577 Referencing Matt 1:21.

Τύπον δὲ ἔφερεν αὐτοῦ ὁ τοῦ Ναυῆ Ἰησοῦς κατὰ πολλά. Ἀρξάμενος γὰρ ἄρχειν τοῦ λαοῦ, ἤρξατο ἀπὸ τοῦ Ἰορδάνου· ὅθεν καὶ ὁ Χριστὸς βαπτισθεὶς ἤρξατο εὐαγγελίζεσθαι. Δώδεκα δὲ διαιροῦντας τὴν κληρονομίαν καθίστησιν ὁ τοῦ Ναυῆ υἱός· καὶ δώδεκα τοὺς ἀποστόλους, κήρυκας τῆς ἀληθείας, εἰς πᾶσαν τὴν οἰκου-μένην ἀποστέλλει ὁ Ἰησοῦς. Πιστεύσασαν Ῥαὰβ τὴν πόρνην ἔσωσεν ὁ τυπικός· ὁ δὲ ἀλη-θής φησιν· "Ἰδοὺ οἱ τελῶναι καὶ αἱ πόρναι προ-άγουσιν ὑμᾶς εἰς τὴν βασιλείαν τοῦ Θεοῦ". Ἀλαλαγμῷ μόνον ἐπὶ τοῦ τυπικοῦ κατέπεσε τὰ τείχη τῆς Ἰεριχώ· καὶ διὰ τὸ εἰπεῖν τὸν Ἰησοῦν, "Οὐ μὴ ἀφεθῇ ὧδε λίθος ἐπὶ λίθον", πέπτωκεν ὁ ἀντικρὺς ἡμῶν τῶν Ἰουδαίων ναός· οὐχ ὅτι ἡ ἀπόφασις τοῦ πεσεῖν αἰτία, ἀλλ' ὅτι ἡ ἁμαρτία τῶν παρανόμων γέγονε τοῦ πεσεῖν αἰτία.

Iesu son of Nau exhibited a type of him in many ways. For the beginning of his rule over the people began near the Jordan, and there, the Christ, having been baptized, began to preach the good news. Twelve [people] to di-vide the inheritance were appointed by the son of Nau, and twelve apostles, heralds of truth, Iesu sent throughout the inhabited [world]. Rahab the harlot, as a believer,[578] he that is a type [of Christ] saved; the true one says: "Look, the tax collectors and harlots will precede you in entering the Kingdom of God" (Matt 21:31). With a loud noise alone, from him that is a type [of Christ], the walls of Jericho fell; and through the speech of Iesu (Matt 24:2; Mark 13:2; Luke 19:44), "There will not even be left one stone upon another," down fell the temple of the Jews opposite us. It is not that this negative statement caused it to fall; rather it was the sins of the unlawful that were responsible for the fall.

Cyril lists here four parallel actions between Joshua and Jesus.

a. Joshua begins by crossing the Jordan, and Jesus begins by being baptized in the Jordan and preaching.
b. Joshua appointed twelve people to divide the Promised Land, and Jesus ap-pointed twelve apostles to spread the good news.
c. Joshua saved Rahab the harlot, and Jesus offered salvation to tax-collectors and harlots.
d. Joshua, with a sound, made the walls of Jericho fall, and Jesus, in a speech, predicted the fall of the Temple.

These are not the usual parallels.

Regarding this unusual passage, Daniélou writes:

> In St. Cyril of Jerusalem we find a different interpretation, for the author represents the ty-pology of St. Matthew. He sets out to show that that Joshua was the type of the historical events in the life of Jesus (Daniélou, *From Shadow*, 242).

Daniélou's observation, that Cyril's interpretation fits particularly well with the Gospel of Matthew is interesting, and brings up the question of whether Cyril

---

578 See James 2:25, in which Rahab is said to have been saved by works and not faith alone.

the Jerusalemite preferred this Gospel over others (a question that is beyond the scope of this chapter and outside my expertise).[579] I would further observe that there is a difference in approach between Justin and Cyril. Justin chooses events in Joshua's life and parallels them to Jesus. Cyril does this (with Rahab for instance) but also chooses events in Jesus's life and finds parallels for them in Joshua's. However one understands Cyril's method, this sort of paralleling of the lives of the two characters is done by a number of patristic authors, and, as will be seen, in great detail by Aphrahat.

Tracing the Typology: Light Usage

Although the Joshua-Jesus typology was well known after Justin, not all authors familiar with it necessarily saw it as important or useful. In this section I will survey authors who reference (or seem to reference) the typology but do not make much use of it.

Cyprian

Thascius Caecilius Cyprianus (d. 248) was the bishop of Carthage. He makes a quick reference to the paradigm in his *Testimonia* (2:21),[580] a work which is dedicated to refuting the Jews.

Hoc signo crucis et Amalech victus est ab Jesu per Moysen. By this sign of the cross was Amalek also overcome by Iesu through Moses.

The remainder of the section is simply a literal quoting of the account of the defeat of Amalek in Exodus 17. This is an example of the classic use of the paradigm as it appears already in Barnabas. It is the combination of Moses making the sign of the cross and the leader of the assault being Iesu that affects the defeat of the Amalekites in battle.

Cyprian makes use of the typology, and this is hardly surprising since his work was modeled on that of Tertullian (the earlier, celebrated Carthiginian

---

579 Daniélou's observation about Cyril can be supported by the work of Andries van Aarde (referenced above) who believes that Matthew himself was already making use of a Joshua-Jesus typology.

580 *PL* 4:744 (*ANF* 5:525); the title given to this chapter is: "That in the passion and the sign of the cross is all virtue and power" (*Quod in passione crucis et signo virtus omnis sit et potestas*).

Church Father.) Nevertheless, Cyprian's one line and subsequent direct quote from Exodus can hardly be characterized as a significant usage of this typology. It would seem that although Cyprian took the idea seriously, he did not find it particularly useful as a focal point of his polemic against the Jews. In this way, he differs from his model, Tertullian, who gave much more attention and rhetorical/polemical value to the correlation between Joshua and Jesus.

Gregory of Nyssa

Gregory, bishop of Nyssa (c.335–c.395), makes an ambiguous reference to the importance of Joshua in his *Baptism of Christ*.[581] The reference comes as part of a historical survey; Joshua appears between Moses and Elijah.

Πολλὰ γὰρ παθών, ὡς ἐδιδάχθημεν, ὁ τῶν Ἑβραίων λαός, καὶ τὴν μοχθηρὰν διανύσας τῆς ἐρήμου περίοδον, οὐ πρότερον τὴν γῆν τῆς ἐπαγγελίας ἀπέλαβε, πρὶν ὁδηγοῦντος Ἰησοῦ, καὶ τὴν ζωὴν αὐτοῦ κυβερνῶντος, εἰς τὸν Ἰορδάνην ἐπεραιώθη. Ἰησοῦς δὲ καὶ τοὺς δώδεκα λίθους ἀποθέμενος ἐν τῷ ῥεύματι, πρόδηλόν ἐστιν, ὅτι τοὺς δώδεκα μαθητὰς, τοὺς ὑπηρέτας τοῦ βαπτίσματος, προηυτρέπιζεν.

For the people of the Hebrews, having suffered much—as we have learned—and having achieved their laborious way in the desert, did not earlier receive the Promised Land until under the guidance of Iesu, the steersman of their lives, the Jordan was crossed. Additionally, it is obvious that Iesu placed twelve stones in the stream, in order to anticipate the twelve disciples, the servants of baptism.

Although Gregory does not say this explicitly, one could understand his complimentary attitude towards Joshua, especially his implication that it needed to be Joshua that brought the Hebrews to the Promised Land, as evidence of his acceptance of the Joshua-Jesus typology. As was seen in our discussion of the earlier exegetes, the reason offered by a number of Church Fathers for this necessity is that Joshua prefigures Jesus. However, this is a rather thin usage of the correlation.[582]

Gregory adds another element to Joshua's significance. He argues that, like many other prophets, Joshua foresaw the coming of Christ and his ministry. This is why, Gregory writes, he placed twelve stones in the Jordan – to teach the peo-

---

581 It is subtitled "A Sermon for the Day of Lights." The Greek Text can be found in *PG* 46:592; an English translation (not the one above, which is my own) can be found in *NPNF* 5:522.

582 Daniélou (*From Shadow*, 233) references Gregory of Nyssa as having been influenced by Justin in his understanding of Joshua. Unfortunately, Daniélou does not reference a passage so I do not know if the above is what he was referring to (which is all I was able to find, but does not mean that this is all there is) or something else. If it is the above, Gregory seems hardly interested in this idea compared to other Church Fathers.

ple that in the future twelve apostles of the Christ will come, and they will begin to baptize the world.[583] Although this certainly emphasizes Joshua's prophetic position, it does not necessarily stem from the Joshua-Jesus typology; all the Israelite prophets, according to the Church Fathers, foresaw Jesus, but none of them (except Joshua) shared his name.

Even if one accepts that Gregory does see some significance in the identical names of Joshua and Jesus, the importance of this diminishes when looking at Gregory's treatment of Zechariah and his vision of the high priest ("A Sermon for the Day of Lights," PG 46:593):

Ἐναργέστατα δὲ καὶ Ζαχαρίας τόν τε Ἰησοῦν προφητεύει τὸν ἐνδεδυμένον τὸ ῥυπαρὸν ἱμάτιον, τὴν δουλικὴν καὶ ἡματέραν σάρκα, ἐκδύων δὲ αὐτὸν τῆς σκυθρωπῆς ἐσθῆτος, κοσμεῖ τῇ καθαρᾷ καὶ λαμπούσῃ στολῇ. διδάσκων ἡμᾶς διὰ τοῦ εἰκονικοῦ ὑποδείγματος, ὅτι δὴ ἐν τῷ βαπτίσματι τοῦ Ἰησοῦ πάντες ἡμεῖς ἐκδυόμενοι τὰς ἁμαρτίας ὡς χιτῶνα πτωχικόν τε καὶ πολυκόλλητον, τὸν ἱερὸν καὶ κάλλιστον τὸν τῆς παλιγγενεσίας μετενδυόμεθα (*PG* 46:593).

And most palpably, Zechariah (Zech. 3:3) prophecied about Iesu being clothed in filthy garments—the flesh of a slave, even ours— and stripping him of his pathetic garments, adorns him with clean and lustrous dress. This teaches us, by way of illustrative example, that indeed in the baptism of Iesu we are all stripped of sins like beggarly and patched garments, and we are clothed in the finest garment of regeneration.

Gregory again seems to notice the identical nature of the names of Jesus and the high priest Joshua ben Jehozadak, and he uses this to sharpen the allegory he sees in Zechariah's words; this is the same method he used when discussing Joshua son of Nun. The most one can say about Gregory's usage of the correlation between Joshua and Jesus is that he believed this typology to be "icing on the cake" when dealing with the Joshuas of the Old Testament and what they teach about Jesus. However, he does not seem to attach great significance to the matter.[584]

Prudentius

Aurelius Prudentius Clemens (347–c.413) was a Latin poet, who wrote a number of Christian hymns. In the twelfth hymn of the *Cathemerinon Liber* (lns. 169–

---

583 As will be seen, Prudentius also interprets the meaning of the twelve stones in this manner.
584 Tertullian himself used the paradigm for Joshua the high priest, as did Eusebius. Nevertheless, it is clear that, to Tertullian and Eusebius, Joshua the high priest was a secondary figure; the lion's share of time was spent on Joshua son of Nun and the significance of his prefiguring of Jesus.

180), Prudentius makes reference to Moses and Joshua in a survey style section of the poem.[585]

Hic praeliante exercitu,	And he, remote on peaceful height,
pansis in altum brachiis,	Amalek's banded hosts did smite:
sublimis Amalech premit,	He prayed with arms stretched out above,
crucis quod instar tunc fuit.	Foreshadowing the Cross of Love.
Hic nempe Iesus verior,	Yet truer Iesu surely he,
qui longa post dispendia	Who after many a victory
victor suis tribulibus	And labours long the tribes' renown
promissa solvit iugera.	With promised heritage did crown;
Qui ter quaternas denique	Who when the waters rose on high
refluentis amnis alveo	And now the Jordan's bed was dry,
fundavit et fixit petras,	Set up twelve stones of memory,
apostolorum stemmata.	Types of apostles yet to be.

Prudentius makes reference to the cross in the Amalek account. He alludes to the similarity in names by called Joshua "Iesus verior" – truer Jesus. His point seems to be that although Moses made the sign of the cross with his arms, making him Christ-like, Joshua is more a typos of Jesus because of his name. Additionally, like Gregory of Nyssa, Prudentius sees the setting up twelve stones by Joshua to represent Jesus' appointing of the twelve apostles.

Nevertheless, Prudentius does not seem to put too much of an emphasis on the typology. When he speaks about the conquest and the crossing of the Jordan, he does so in the simple way one would expect about any heroic character, irrespective of their name or relationship to Jesus. When he notes the correlations, he makes note of the name in passing, but doesn't seem to place the same theological or polemical significance in this correlation as did Justin and Tertullian.

Jerome

Jerome (Eusebius Sophronius Hieronymus, c. 337–420) was a Latin Church Father, and is famous for his translation of the Bible into Latin, known as the Vulgate. In a letter to Paulinus, Bishop of Nola (*Epistles* 53; dated 393),[586] he urges the bishop to take Bible study more seriously. To this end, Jerome offers a survey of some of the salient points a solid reader of the Bible could glean. He does this

---

585 Since the passage is poetic, I do not offer my own translation here, but use that of R. Martin Pope, http://www.gutenberg.org/files/14959/14959-h/14959-h.htm.
586 He is believed to be the inspiration for Augustine's writing his *Confessions*; this Paulinus is not to be confused with Paulinus, bishop of Antioch, the man who ordained Jerome.

in order, book after book in quick succession. His thoughts on Joshua appear between Job and Judges.[587]

Veniam ad Iesum Naue, typum domini non solum in gestis, verum et in nomine: transit Iordanem, hostium regna subvertit, dividit terram victori populo et per singulas urbes, viculos, montes, flumina, torrentes atque confinia ecclesiae caelestis que Hierusalem spiritalia regna discribit.	I come to Iesu son of Naue, a type of the Lord not only in deed but actually in name. He crossed the Jordan, subdued hostile kingdoms, divided the land among the victorious people; and in all of the cities, villages, mountains, rivers, torrents and even the frontiers, he marked out the spiritual realms of the heavenly Jerusalem,[588] [that is] of the church.
In Iudicum libro quot principes populi, tot figurae sunt.	In the book of Judges, there are as many figures [of Christ] as there are popular leaders.

On one hand, in this quick survey, Jerome covers a number of Joshua's activities, and argues that they are meant to prefigure the activities of Christ. These include crossing the Jordan, conquering the enemies of Israel, and dividing up the land. Jerome points out that Joshua prefigures Jesus not only in deed but also in name.

Nevertheless, despite the fact that the identical names are unique to Joshua, Jerome does not seem to see this as something extraordinarily important. In the very next sentence—one almost flippant in tone—he claims that every single judge in the book of Judges prefigures Jesus in some way.[589] Hence, it would appear that the Joshua-Jesus typology functions only minimally in Jerome's thinking.

Augustine

Augustine of Hippo (354–430) is the most celebrated of the Church Fathers, or, at least, of the Latin Church Fathers. In his work, *Contra Faustum* (12:31), he makes (exceedingly moderate) use of the typology. The context is Augustine's attempt to refute Faustus' claims that the Old Testament makes no prediction of Jesus and that this idea is a false invention of Christian exegetes. In response, Augustine offers a long list of what he understands to be predictions or allusions

---

587 This is the order of the biblical books in the Syriac Peshitta (Jerome was ordained in Antioch), and probably reflects the Jewish/midrashic understanding that Moses was the author of Job. (This is not the order in the MT, but the rabbis do accept the Mosaic authorship of Job.)
588 This reference calls to mind Gal 4:26, with its "Jerusalem from above" (admittedly, "*sursum*" in the Latin, not "*caelestis*"), as well as Heb 12 (*Hierusalem caelestem*).
589 This is the approach of Aphrahat, as will be seen in the upcoming section.

to Christ in the Old Testament. The Joshua reference appears where one would expect it: after Moses and before the Judges.

Videat Iesum introducentem populum in terram promissionis. Neque enim hoc temere ab initio vocabatur, sed ex ipsa dispensatione nomine mutato Iesus appellatus est.	He will see Iesu bringing the people into the Promised Land. For not by chance or at first was he thus called, but his name was changed to Iesu on account of this same stewardship.

Augustine's use of the typology here appears generic. Joshua leads Israel into the Promised Land and, therefore, receives the name of the savior, Iesu.[590] Augustine makes no mention of the Amalek story or the re-circumcision of Israel. More surpising still is the fact that Augustine continues on in the Joshua story, writing a paragraph more than twice as long as the above about the collapse of the walls of Jericho, and without so much as a mention of Joshua or his special name.

Augustine does not appear to see the typology as significant or worthy of emphasis. Perhaps the reason he makes use of it at all is due to the nature of this chapter of Contra Faustum. The chapter, being an attempt to make a long and impressive list of hints and prophecies about Jesus in the Old Testament, has a certain "everything-but-the-kitchen-sink" feel to it. It seems reasonable that Augustine, although not a lover of this particular hermeneutic, considered it good enough to throw in a short reference to it as a part of constructing an impressive list of prophecies to combat Faustus' challenge.

Theodoret of Cyrrhus

Theodoret (393–457), was born in Antioch, and spent much of his life as Bishop of Cyrrhus. Although he writes in Greek, Theodoret is from an area populated by Syriac speakers, which may go far in explaining his attitude towards the Joshua-Jesus correlation.[591]

In his *Questions on the Octateuch* (Exod #34), Theodoret takes up the story of the battle with Amalek.[592]

---

590 Not surprisingly, this piece is reminiscent of Lactantius.

591 As will be seen in the final two sections, the Syriac speakers either saw the parallel of Joshua to Jesus as one of many parallels between Old Testament characters and Jesus (Aphrahat) or ignored it completely (Ephrem and Pseudo-Macarius).

592 Theodoret of Cyrus. *The Questions on the Octateuch* (rev. John F. Petruccione; trans. and annot. Robert C. Hill; Library of Early Christianity 1, 2; Washington, D.C.: Catholic University of America Press, 2007).

Διὰ τί τῶν Μωϋσέως χειρῶν ἐκτεταμένων ἐνίκα Ἰσραήλ, καθιεμένων δὲ ἡττᾶτο;	Why is it that when Moses stretched out his hands, Israel would win, but when he laid them down, they would be defeated?
Τοῦ σταυρωθέντος ὑπὲρ ἡμῶν ἐπλήρου τὸν τύπον ἐκτείνων τὰς χεῖρας. ἐδείχθη τοίνυν καὶ ἐν τῷ τύπῳ τῆς ἀληθείας ἡ δύναμις· ὥσπερ γὰρ τοῦ θεράποντος τὰς χεῖρας ἐκτείνοντος ἔπεσεν Ἀμαλήκ, οὕτως τοῦ δεσπότου τὰς χεῖρας ἐκτείναντος, κατελύθη τοῦ διαβόλου τὸ στῖφος,	Stretching out his hands was a fulfillment of a form of him that was crucified on our behalf. Accordingly, the power was manifest even in a form of the true one. For as the arms of the servant were stretched out Amalek fell, just like when the arms of the master stretched out, the masses of the devil were put down.
καὶ ἐν ἐκείνῳ δὲ τῷ πολέμῳ ὁ τοῦ σωτῆρος ἡμῶν ὁμώνυμος τὸ τρόπαιον ἔστησε τότε ταύτην τὴν προσηγορίαν λαβών, καὶ τοῖς λογάσι χρησάμενος συνεργοῖς, ὡς ὁ δεσπότης Χριστὸς ὑπουργοῖς τοῖς ἱεροῖς ἀποστόλοις.	And in that same battle, he whose name is that of our savior set up a monument [of the enemy's defeat], taking that name at that time, and making use of picked men to assist, just like the master, Christ, [made] the holy apostles [his] assistants.

Theodoret is well aware of the fact that Joshua and Jesus share the same name. He makes reference to this specifically, calling Joshua "he whose name is that of our savior (ὁ τοῦ σωτῆρος ἡμῶν ὁμώνυμος)." He also draws attention to a parallel in the actions of Joshua and the actions of Jesus; Joshua makes use of picked men for battle just like Jesus made use of picked apostles. Theodoret even argues that Joshua took this name at this time specifically to emphasize this parallel.[593]

However, Theodoret only makes quick mention of this correlation between Joshua and Jesus, and puts it as part of an overall argument showing the parallels between biblical chapters in general and Jesus. In this sense, Theodoret uses the typology perfunctorily, not granting it the sort of outstanding theological or polemical weight as Justin and Tertullian give it.

Typology-Mania: the Method of Aphrahat the Persian

One exegete who made extensive use of the typology was the Syriac church-father and apologist, Aphrahat (Adiabene c.270 – 345). His work offers a unique

---

593 Theodoret does not explain here how Joshua could take the name now if Moses was to give him the name in Numbers. This is one difference between how the issue was approached in Barnabas, Justin, and Tertullian and how it is approached by Theodoret. The problem lies not in the exegesis but in the biblical text itself; the name of Joshua does appear "too early" in the narrative, with Exodus and Numbers seeming to contradict. See the chapter on pre-biblical Joshua for a redaction-critical approach to this problem.

blend of methodologies in his approach to Joshua. On one hand, he is aware of the identical nature of the names of Joshua and Jesus (how could he not be?) and makes repeated allusion to it in a number of his essays. On the other hand, he does not seem to think that this had either theological significance or polemical significance the way Justin, Tertullian, Origen, and Eusebius did. Joshua was Jesus-like the way any other biblical character who acted in such a way parallel to Jesus was Jesus-like; the name correlation is just an added benefit.

Circumcision

Aphrahat's *Demonstrations* is a collection of essays aimed at solidifying the viewpoint of Christians, often over and against the expressed viewpoint of the Jews, who seem to be his main adversaries.[594] His first and most explicit use of the typology occurs in the eleventh demonstration, in which Aphrahat attacks the Jewish practice of physical circumcision, comparing it unfavorably to the spiritual circumcision advocated by the Christians. In this context ("On Circumcision" 11.12), the reference to the circumcision of the Israelites a second time by Joshua, in Josh 5:2–9, leads Aphrahat into a general comparison between Yeshua son of Nun (Joshua) and Yeshua the savior (Jesus).

ܝܫܘܥ ܒܪ ܢܘܢ ܓܙܪ ܠܥܡܐ ܒܣܦܣܪܐ ܕܛܪܢܐ ܬܢܝܢܘܬ ܟܕ ܥܒܪ ܝܘܪܕܢܢ ܗܘ ܘܥܡܗ. ܘܝܫܘܥ ܦܪܘܩܢ ܓܙܪ ܠܥܡܡܐ ܕܗܝܡܢܘ ܒܗ ܒܬܢܝܢܘܬ ܒܓܙܘܪܬܐ ܕܠܒܐ ܘܥܡܕܘ ܒܡܥܡܘܕܝܬܐ ܘܓܙܪܘ ܒܣܦܣܪܐ ܕܐܝܬܝܗ ܡܠܬܗ ܕܚܪܝܦܐ ܗܝ ܡܢ ܚܪܒܐ ܕܬܪܬܝܢ ܦܘܡܝ̈ܗ.	Yeshua son of Nun circumcised the people with a flint knife a second time when he and his people crossed the Jordan. And Yeshua our savior circumcised the people that believed in him a second time with a circumcision of the heart, and they dipped in baptism and circumcised with a knife of his word, which is sharper than a two-edged sword.[595]
ܝܫܘܥ ܒܪ ܢܘܢ ܐܥܒܪ ܠܥܡܐ ܠܐܪܥܐ ܕܡܘܠܟܢܐ. ܘܝܫܘܥ ܦܪܘܩܢ ܡܠܟ ܐܪܥܐ ܕܚܝܐ ܠܟܠ ܕܥܒܪ ܒܝܘܪܕܢܢ ܕܫܪܪܐ ܘܗܝܡܢܘ ܘܓܙܪ ܥܘܪܠܘܬ ܠܒܗܘܢ.	Yeshua son of Nun crossed his people over to the Promised Land. And Yeshua, our savior, promised the land of life to all that crossed the true Jordan, who believed and circumcised the foreskin of his heart.

594 For more on Aphrahat, including a translation of the main demonstrations aimed at debating the Jews, see Jacob Neusner, *Aphrahat and Judaism: The Christian-Jewish Argument in Fourth-Century Iran* (South Florida Studies in the History of Judaism 205; Atlanta: Scholars Press, 1999 [Brill, 1971]). The use of the Joshua-Jesus correlation in polemical writing fits in with that of Barnabas, Justin, and Tertullian, who also made use of their version of the typology in their polemical writings against Judaism.

595 Aphrahat is evoking imagery from Heb 4:12 and, to a lesser extent, Eph 6:17.

ܝܫܘܥ ܒܪ ܢܘܢ ܐܩܝܡ ܟܐܦܐ ܠܣܗܕܘܬܐ ܒܐܝܣܪܝܠ. ܘܝܫܘܥ ܦܪܘܩܢ ܠܫܡܥܘܢ ܩܪܝܗ ܟܐܦܐ ܫܪܝܪܬܐ ܘܐܩܝܡܗ ܣܗܕܐ ܡܗܝܡܢܐ ܒܝܬ ܥܡܡܐ.	Yeshua son of Nun erected rocks as testimony in Israel. And Yeshua, our savior, called Simon the true rock, and established him as a faithful testimony among the peoples.[596]
ܝܫܘܥ ܒܪ ܢܘܢ ܥܒܕ ܦܨܚܐ ܒܦܩܥܬܐ ܕܐܝܪܝܚܘ ܒܐܪܥܐ ܠܝܛܬܐ ܘܐܟܠ ܥܡܐ ܡܢ ܠܚܡܐ ܕܐܪܥܐ. ܘܝܫܘܥ ܦܪܘܩܢ ܥܒܕ ܦܨܚܐ ܥܡ ܬܠܡܝܕܘܗܝ ܒܐܘܪܫܠܡ ܩܪܝܬܐ ܕܠܛܗ̇ ܕܠܐ ܬܬܩܘܡ ܒܗ ܟܐܦ ܥܠ ܟܐܦ. ܘܝܗܒ ܬܡܢ ܐܪܙܐ ܒܠܚܡܐ ܕܚܝܐ.	Yeshua son of Nun made a Paschal offering in the valley of Jericho, in a cursed land, and the people ate from the bread of the land. And Yeshua, our savior, made a Paschal sacrifice with his students in Jerusalem, the city which he cursed that no stone should remain upon stone, and he gave them there the sacrament with the bread of life.
ܝܫܘܥ ܒܪ ܢܘܢ ܚܝܒ ܠܥܟܪ ܡܚܒܐ ܕܓܢܒ ܘܛܫܝ. ܘܝܫܘܥ ܦܪܘܩܢ ܚܝܒ ܠܝܗܘܕܐ ܡܚܒܐ ܕܓܢܒ ܘܛܫܝ ܟܣܦܐ ܡܢ ܓܠܘܣܩܡܐ ܕܐܚܝܕ ܗܘܐ.	Yeshua son of Nun condemned the greedy Akhar who stole and hid. And Yeshua, our savior, condemned the greedy Yehudah, who stole and hid silver from the money box he was holding.
ܝܫܘܥ ܒܪ ܢܘܢ ܚܪܒ ܥܡܡܐ ܛܢܦܐ. ܘܝܫܘܥ ܦܪܘܩܢ ܣܚܦ ܠܣܛܢܐ ܘܠܚܝܠܗ.	Yeshua son of Nun destroyed unclean nations. And Yeshua, our savior, cast out Satan and his army.
ܝܫܘܥ ܒܪ ܢܘܢ ܐܩܝܡ ܫܡܫܐ ܒܫܡܝܐ. ܘܝܫܘܥ ܦܪܘܩܢ ܐܥܪܒ ܫܡܫܐ ܒܛܗܪܐ ܟܕ ܙܩܝܦܘܗܝ.	Yeshua son of Nun caused the sun to stand still in the sky. And Yeshua, our savior, brought the sunset at noon when he was crucified.
ܝܫܘܥ ܒܪ ܢܘܢ ܦܪܘܩܐ ܕܥܡܐ. ܘܝܫܘܥ ܐܬܩܪܝ ܦܪܘܩܐ ܕܥܡܡܐ.	Yeshua son of Nun redeemed his people. And Yeshua was called redeemer of the peoples.

The comparisons between Joshua and Jesus are built around events in the Joshua narrative. Each event in the Joshua narrative is then connected to an event in Jesus' narrative in order to establish a link between the two characters. Circumcision of the body is linked to circumcision of the heart; the gift of the Promised Land is linked to the gift of the land of the living, i.e., eternal life; Joshua stopped the sun, Jesus made the sun set. Some of the parallels are somewhat banal (Joshua held a Passover sacrifice and Jesus held a Passover sacrifice), and some are forced (like Joshua erected rocks, and Jesus had a disciple he called "rock").

Joshua and Jesus vs. Moses and Jesus

Although the trope Aphrahat is using makes good use of the identical names of the two characters—Yeshua son of Nun and Yeshua our savior—he never actually

596 This interpretation was offered by Lactantius as well; see above.

states that the former was an early instantiation of the latter or that there is some sort of theological significance to the fact that Moses' successor was named Yeshua. In this sense, Aphrahat's approach differs from that of Justin, Tertullian, or Origen, who emphasize these ideas and find polemical and theological significance in the name correlation. To illustrate this, if one compares the above litany of similarities between Joshua and Jesus with the litany of similarities between Moses and Jesus in the twelfth demonstration ("On the Paschal Sacrifice" 12.8), one hardly notices anything distinct about the Joshua-Jesus typology.

ܠܘ ܗܘܐ ܠܗܘܢ ܡܘܫܐ ܡܕܒܪܢܐ ܘܠܢ	For them Moses was their leader, for us Yeshua
ܗܘܐ ܠܢ ܝܫܘܥ ܡܕܒܪܢܐ ܘܦܪܘܩܐ.	is our guide and savior.
ܠܗܘܢ ܦܠܓ ܡܘܫܐ ܝܡܐ ܘܐܥܒܪ ܐܢܘܢ	For them Moses split the sea and brought them
ܘܦܪܘܩܢ ܦܠܓ ܠܫܝܘܠ ܘܬܒܪ ܬܪܥܝܗ ܒܕ	through, our savior split Sheol and broke its
ܥܠ ܒܗ ܘܦܬܚ ܐܢܘܢ ܘܒܥܐ ܐܘܪܚܐ	gates, when he went into it and opened them,
ܘܩܕܡ ܠܟܠ ܐܝܠܝܢ ܕܗܝܡܢܘ ܒܗ.	and sought a path [to open] before all those who believed in him.
ܠܗܘܢ ܐܬܝܗܒ ܡܢܢܐ ܠܡܐܟܠܬܐ: ܘܠܢ ܡܪܢ	To them was given manna to eat, but to us our
ܝܗܒ ܦܓܪܗ ܠܡܐܟܠ.	Lord gave his body to eat.
ܠܗܘܢ ܡܝܐ ܡܢ ܟܐܦܐ ܐܬܢܓܕ: ܘܠܢ ܐܘܪ,	For them water was drawn from a stone, for us
ܦܪܘܩܢ ܡܝܐ ܚܝܐ ܡܢ ܟܪܣܗ.	our savior brought down living waters from his belly.
ܠܗܘܢ ܡܠܟ ܐܪܥܐ ܕܟܢܥܢ ܠܝܪܬܘܬܐ: ܘܠܢ	To them he promised the land of Canaan as an
ܡܠܟ ܐܪܥܐ ܕܚܝܐ ܠܡܘܪܬܢܐ.	inheritance, to us he promised the land of the living as our inheritance.
ܠܗܘܢ ܐܩܝܡ ܡܘܫܐ ܚܘܝܐ ܕܢܚܫܐ ܕܟܠ ܡܢ	For them Moses raised a bronze serpent, so
ܕܚܐܪ ܒܗ ܢܚܐ ܡܢ ܡܚܘܬܐ ܕܚܘܝܐ: ܘܠܢ ܐܩܝܡ	that anyone that looked at it could survive
ܝܫܘܥ ܢܦܫܗ ܕܐܡܬܝ ܕܢܚܘܪ ܠܘܬܗ ܢܬܐܣܐ ܡܢ	the bite of the serpent, for us Yeshua raised
ܡܚܘܬܗ ܕܚܘܝܐ ܕܐܝܬܘܗܝ, ܣܛܢܐ.	himself, so that when we gaze towards him, we will be healed from the bite of the serpent, who is the Satan.
ܠܗܘܢ ܥܒܕ ܡܘܫܐ ܡܫܟܢܐ ܕܙܒܢܐ ܕܢܩܪܒ ܒܗ	For them Moses made the temporary taberna-
ܕܒܚܐ ܘܩܘܪܒܢܐ ܕܢܚܣܘܢ ܒܗ ܚܛܗܝܗܘܢ:	cle to offer sacrifices and offerings upon, so
ܘܐܩܝܡ ܝܫܘܥ ܡܫܟܢܗ ܕܕܘܝܕ ܕܢܦܠ ܩܡ.	that they could atone for their sins, and Yeshua established the tabernacle of David which fell but has now risen.

The basic method here is similar. A number of events in the Moses narrative are compared to ostensibly similar events in the Jesus narrative. Moses split the sea while Jesus split Sheol; Moses gave his followers manna and Jesus gave his followers his body. Aphrahat even makes use of the same Promised Land vs. land of the living comparison as he did with Joshua.

An important thing to notice, however, is that the tone of the two pieces is different. Whereas the comparison between Joshua and Jesus has a more neutral sounding tone, the comparison with Moses is polemical, with Moses' gifts to the Jews consistently painted as *less* good that Jesus' gifts to the world. Nevertheless, this difference is really more one of style than substance, as it is clear that Aphrahat believes Joshua's gifts to the Jews to be inferior to Jesus' gifts to the world as well.

The Litany of Biblical Characters

Aphrahat also makes use of the typology as part of larger sections which compare Jesus with a list of biblical characters. In the seventeenth demonstration ("On the Messiah" 17.11), for instance, after describing God's sacrifice of his son in order to redeem the world, Aphrahat waxes poetic in thanking God, and Jesus, for this sacrifice.

ܣܓܕ ܚܢܢ ܠܗܠܝܢ ܪ̈ܚܡܐ ܘܟܘ̈ܦܝܢ ܐܢܚܢ ܒܘܪ̈ܟܐ	We worship these mercies and we bend the
ܩܕܡ ܪܒܘܬܐ ܕܐܒܘܗܝ܂ ܕܐܦܢܝ ܣܓܕܬܢ	knees before the greatness of his father who
ܠܘܬܗ܂ ܘܩܪܝܢܝܗܝ܂ ܐܠܗܐ ܐܝܟ ܡܘܫܐ܂	turned our worship towards him. We call him
ܘܒܘܟܪܐ ܘܒܪܐ ܐܝܟ ܐܝܣܪܐܝܠ܂ ܘܝܫܘܥ	"god" like Moses, "firstborn" and "son" like Is-
ܐܝܟ ܝܫܘܥ ܒܪ ܢܘܢ܂ ܘܟܗܢܐ ܐܝܟ ܐܗܪܘܢ܂	rael, "Yeshua" like Yeshua son of Nun, "priest"
ܘܡܠܟܐ ܐܝܟ ܕܘܝܕ܂ ܘܢܒܝܐ ܪܒܐ ܐܝܟ	like Aaron, "king" like David, "great prophet"
ܟܠܗܘܢ ܢܒ̈ܝܐ܂ ܘܪܥܝܐ ܐܝܟ ܪ̈ܥܘܬܐ ܕܪܥܘ	like all the prophets, and "shepherd" like the
ܘܕܒܪܘ ܠܐܝܣܪܐܝܠ܂	shepherds that herded and led the Israelites.

Here again, although it is clear that Aphrahat is making use of the identical names of Joshua and Jesus (Yeshua), there is no indication that this proves anything about Jesus and Joshua in a way different than the correlations with the other biblical characters.

Virginity of Joshua and other Israelite Heroes

The same is true for Aphrahat's use of Joshua in comparison with Jesus in the eighteenth demonstration ("Against the Jews and on Virginity and Sanctity" 18.7), in which Aphrahat lists Israelite heroes that he believes loved virginity and sanctity.

ܟܡܐܝ ܪ‍‍‍‍‍‍‍‍‍‍‍‍‍‍‍‍‍‍‍‍‍‍‍‍‍‍‍‍‍ Moses cherished holiness and was cherished by the Holy one, and showed him His glory.

Yeshua son of Nun loved virginity and dwelt in the tent, a place where the Holy One was served.

Eliyah abounded in virginity and dwelt in the desert, on mountains, and in caves. And the Holy One brought him up to a holy place, a place where those who love licentiousness[597] have no authority.

Elisha remained alone and became chaste. And astounding works he performed by the hand of God.

Furthermore, Jeremiah said that "the birthday of a person he does not desire" (Jer. 17:16). Additionally the Lord even commanded him and told him: "Do not marry a wife, and do not have sons and daughters" (Jer. 16:2).

Aphrahat then discusses the Jewish retort to the quote from Jeremiah. They claim, says Aphrahat, that the command was only not to have children in a particular place; however, they argue that, of course, Jeremiah—all the prophets in fact—were married and had children. Aphrahat responds to this with sharply sarcastic rhetoric (18.7):

But show me, oh master, regarding Yeshua son of Nun, that he took a wife and had children. And persuade me also about Elijah and Elisha his student in what house was their subsistence in this world. For in the wilderness and in the mountains and in caves they dwelt, in need and in persecution. And neither of them had a wife but they were served by their students.

Again, although Joshua is compared to Jesus here insofar as his virginity (in Aphrahat's estimation at least), there is no indication that Joshua's name makes him aligned with Jesus or prefigures Jesus in a way different than Elijah, Elisha, or Jeremiah.

---

597 Neusner translates "filth," but "licentiousness" seems to fit the context better and is the translation of the term in the Payne-Smith dictionary.

The Persecuted Joshua and the Persecuted Jesus

The twenty-first demonstration is probably the most important insofar as Aphrahat's comparisons of Jesus with biblical characters. In this section ("On Persecution" 21.9 – 20) Aphrahat lists all the biblical figures that he believes were persecuted, as Jesus was: Jacob, Joseph, Moses, Joshua, Jephthah, David, Elijah, Elisha, Hezekiah, Josiah, Daniel, Hananiah, Mishael, Azariah, and Mordechai.[598] Each character gets a rather long list of parallels. The Joshua section (21.11) strongly resembles the first set of parallels in the eleventh demonstration described earlier.

ܘܐܪܐ ܝܫܘܥ ܒܪ ܢܘܢ ܐܬܪܕܦ ܡܢ ܢܨ̈ܝܐ ܘܝܫܘܥ ܦܪܘܩܢ.	Similarly, Yeshua son of Nun was persecuted and Yeshua our savior was persecuted.
ܝܫܘܥ ܒܪ ܢܘܢ ܐܬܪܕܦ ܡܢ ܥܡ̈ܡܐ ܛܡ̈ܐܐ ܘܝܫܘܥ ܦܪܘܩܢ ܐܬܪܕܦ ܡܢ ܥܡܐ ܣܟܠܐ.	Yeshua son of Nun was persecuted by unclean nations. Yeshua our savior was persecuted by a foolish nation.
ܝܫܘܥ ܒܪ ܢܘܢ ܢܣܒ ܝܪܬܘܬܐ ܡܢ ܪ̈ܕܘܦܘܗܝ ܘܝܗܒܗ ܠܥܡܗ ܘܝܫܘܥ ܦܪܘܩܢ ܢܣܒ ܝܪܬܘܬܐ ܡܢ ܪ̈ܕܘܦܘܗܝ ܘܝܗܒܗ ܠܥܡ̈ܡܐ ܢܘܟܪ̈ܝܐ.	Yeshua son of Nun took the inheritance from those who were persecuting him and gave it to his nation. Yeshua our savior took the inheritance from those who were persecuting him and gave it to foreign nations.
ܝܫܘܥ ܒܪ ܢܘܢ ܐܩܝܡ ܫܡܫܐ ܒܫܡܝܐ ܘܢܩܡ ܬܒܥܬܐ ܡܢ ܥܡ̈ܡܐ ܪ̈ܕܘܦܘܗܝ ܘܝܫܘܥ ܦܪܘܩܢ ܐܥܪܒ ܫܡܫܐ ܒܦܠܓܗ ܕܝܘܡܐ ܕܢܒܗܬ ܠܥܡܐ ܪܕܘܦܐ ܕܙܩܦܗ.	Yeshua son of Nun stood the sun still in the heavens and took vengeance upon the nations persecuting him. Yeshua our savior made the sun set in the middle of the day to shame the persecuting nation that crucified him.
ܝܫܘܥ ܒܪ ܢܘܢ ܦܠܓ ܝܪܬܘܬܐ ܠܥܡܗ ܘܝܫܘܥ ܦܪܘܩܢ ܡܠܟ ܕܢܬܠ ܠܥܡ̈ܡܐ ܐܪܥܐ ܕܚ̈ܝܐ.	Yeshua son of Nun divided the inheritance among his nation. Yeshua our savior promised to give the nations the land of the living.
ܝܫܘܥ ܒܪ ܢܘܢ ܐܚܝ ܠܪܚܒ ܙܢܝܬܐ ܘܝܫܘܥ ܦܪܘܩܢ ܟܢܫ ܘܐܚܝ ܠܥܕܬܐ ܙܢܝܬܐ.	Yeshua son of Nun kept Rahab the harlot alive. Yeshua our savior gathered and kept alive the harlot church.
ܝܫܘܥ ܒܪ ܢܘܢ ܠܝܘܡܐ ܫܒܝܥܐ ܙܟܐ ܘܐܪܡܝ ܫܘܪ̈ܐ ܕܐܝܪܝܚܘ ܘܝܫܘܥ ܦܪܘܩܢ ܒܝܘܡܐ ܫܒܝܥܐ ܕܢܝܚܬܐ ܕܐܠܗܐ ܥܠܡܐ ܗܢܐ ܢܫܬܪܐ ܘܢܦܠ.	Yeshua son of Nun on the seventh day overcame and threw down the walls of Jericho. Yeshua our savior on the seventh day, on the Sabbath of the rest of God, this world will dissolve and fall.

---

598 In the next section (21.22), Apharahat throws in Abel, Samson, Barak, Gideon, Jeremiah, Esther, Judah Maccabee, and Eliezer.

ܥܟܢ ܒܪ ܢܘܢ ... | Yeshua son of Nun stoned Akhar who stole
ܘܫܩܠ ܝܘܫܥ ... | from the consecrated. Yeshua our savior re-
ܫܘܒܚ ... | moved Judas from among his student-compan-
| ions since he stole from the silver of the poor.
ܝܫܘܥ ܒܪ ܢܘܢ ... | Yeshua son of Nun, when he died, set up a tes-
| timony for his people. Yeshua our savior, when
| he went up, set up a testimony with his apos-
| tles.

As in the demonstration on circumcision, Aphrahat runs through events in the Joshua narrative and aligns them with aspects of the Jesus narrative. Some of them are the same, such as the parallel between Akhar and Judas, or Joshua stopping the sun and Jesus making the sun set early. Other parallels are unique to this section, such as the parallel between saving Rahab and saving the church or violating the Sabbath and eliminating the Sabbath.

However, as in the previous sections, despite the use of the name similarity for literary affect, there is no implication by Aphrahat that the fact that these figures had the same name means that they were in some essential way the same person.[599] This is reinforced by Aphrahat's summary statement in the next section (21.22).

---

599 The fact that Aphrahat sees the Joshua-Jesus correlation as being essentially the same as the other correlations can be seen by looking at his treatement of another character for comparison. Again, I will choose Moses (20.10).

ܐܦ ... | Moses was persecuted and Yeshua was perse-
| cuted.
| Moses, when he was born, they hid him so that
| he not be killed by the Egyptians; Yeshua,
| when he was born, was taken to Egypt so that
| Herod, his persecutor, could not kill him.
| In the days of Moses, when he was born, little
| boys were drowned in the river; at the birth of
| Yeshua little boys from Bethlehem and its
| surroundings were killed.
| God said to Moses: "All those people who were
| trying to kill you have died." An angel said to
| Joseph in Egypt: "Get up and take the child and
| go to the land of Israel because all those who
| were trying to take the life of the child have
| died."

Moses took his people out of the bondage of Pharaoh. Yeshua saved all the nations from their bondage to Satan.

Moses grew up in the house of Pharaoh. Yeshua grew up in Egypt after Joseph fled there.

Miriam stood upon the banks of the river when Moses floated on the water. Miriam (Mary) gave birth to Yeshua after the angel Gabriel announced [the news] to her.

Moses, when he slaughtered the sheep, the first-born sons of the Egyptians were killed. Yeshua, the true sheep, when they crucified him, the nation that killed him died.

Moses brought manna down on the nation. Yeshua gave his body to the nations.

Moses cleansed the bitter waters with wood. Yeshua cleansed our bitterness with his crucifixion and the wood of his cross.

Moses brought the law down to his nation. Yeshua gave testaments to the nations.

Moses defeated Amalek by spreading his arms. Yeshua defeated Satan with the sign of the cross.

Moses drew water out of a rock for his nation. Yeshua sent Simon the Rock to bring his teaching to the home of the nations.

Moses removed the veil from his face and God spoke with him. Yeshua removed the veil from the faces of the nations, so they would hear and accept his teachings.

Moses placed his hands upon his agent and they accepted the priesthood. Yeshua placed his hands upon his apostles, and they received the holy spirit.

Moses went up the mountain and died there. Yeshua went up to heaven and sat on the right-hand side of his father.

The correlations between between Moses and Jesus offered here have the same character as the correltions between Joshua and Jesus. One correlation (the rock) was even transferred from Joshua (Dem. 11) to Moses. The name similarity between Jesus and Joshua seems to function only as rhetorical flourish for Aphrahat.

ܫܡܥ ܚܒܝܒܝ ܠܗܢ ܫܡܗܐ ܕܣܗܕܐ Listen, my cherished [friend], to these names of
ܘܡܘܕܝܢܐ ܘܪܕܝܦܐ. witnesses, martyrs, and persecuted ones.

ܗܒܝܠ ܐܬܩܛܠ ܘܓܥܐ ܕܡܗ ܡܢ ܐܪܥܐ. Abel was killed and his blood moaned from the
ܘܝܥܩܘܒ ܐܬܪܕܦ ܘܗܘܐ ܐܟܣܢܝܐ. ground. Jacob was persecuted and ran away
ܘܝܘܣܦ ܐܬܪܕܦ ܘܐܙܕܒܢ ܘܢܦܠ ܒܓܘܒܐ. and became a refugee. Joseph was persecuted
ܘܡܘܫܐ ܐܬܪܕܦ ܘܥܪܩ ܠܡܕܝܢ. ܘܝܫܘܥ and was sold and fell into the pit. Moses was
ܒܪ ܢܘܢ ܐܬܪܕܦ ܘܩܪܒ ܩܪܒܐ. ܘܢܦܬܚ persecuted and ran away to Midian. Yeshua
ܘܫܡܫܘܢ ܘܓܕܥܘܢ ܘܒܪܩ ܘܗܠܝܢ son of Nun was persecuted and made war.
ܐܬܪܕܦܘ. Jephtah, Samson, Gideon, and Barak – these
were also persecuted.

ܗܠܝܢ ܕܥܠܝܗܘܢ ܐܡܪ ܫܠܝܚܐ ܛܘܒܢܐ Regarding these said the blessed apostle (Heb
ܗܘ ܕܠ ܣܦܩ ܠܝ ܙܒܢܐ ܕܐܫܬܥܐ ܢܨܚܢ̈ܝܗܘܢ. 11:32): "Time is too short for me to relate
these triumphs."[600]

Joshua's story is made to correlate with that of Jesus, but not in any way reflecting any significance to his name. It is true that Joshua is the only one with a patronymic listed, but this is in order to distinguish him from Jesus; Aphrahat does not indicate in any way that this gives his parallels to Jesus any different significance or nuance than those of the other Israelite heroes of the past.

Looking carefully at the above examples of comparisons, one can't help but notice that many are extremely forced. It is true that Joseph and Jephthah were persecuted (or at least rejected,) but Joshua and Barak can hardly be seen as persecuted figures. Aphrahat's strategy in creating parallels between biblical figures and Jesus is an example of creating a typology around Jesus' life (persecution, virginity, etc.) and forcing a host of biblical characters into it. In that sense, the most one can say about Aphrahat's comparison of Joshua with Jesus is that their identical names gives added rhetorical force, but nothing more.

It would seem that either Aphrahat was unaware of (or uninterested in) the motif of using Joshua's name as a proof that the messiah would be named Jesus or that Joshua succeeding Moses proved that Jesus would succeed the Torah. His ignorance or indifference to this motif explains one further unique feature of Aphrahat's presentation of the Joshua-Jesus correlations: Aphrahat never uses the standard or core examples of the phenomenon which are the bread and butter of Church Fathers like Justin, Tertullian, and Origen (except for circumcision). Aphrahat never brings up the name change from Hoshea to Joshua, and when discussing the Amalek account, he notices Moses making the sign of the cross but makes no mention at all of Joshua as Jesus' name incarnate on the battlefield.

---

600 The catalogue as a whole strongly resembles Heb 11.

Joshua as Joshua

Finally, like other Church Fathers, who do use the typology, Aphrahat does discuss Joshua on his own terms as well. In fact, he uses the same example as Tertullian, i.e., Joshua's purported violation of the Sabbath ("On the Sabbath" 13.12).

ܟܬܒܐ ܘܐܝܟ ܐܢܫ ܠܐ ܒܢܘܗܝ ܓܝܪ ܝܫܘܥ	Indeed, Yeshua son of Nun did not let them rest on the Sabbath when he was making war on Jericho, as the renowned apostle said (Heb 4:8–9): "For if Yeshua son of Nun had allowed them to rest, there would not have been talk again about the Sabbath day. Rather, from that time on, the Sabbath of God existed."

Aphrahat here makes essentially the same argument that Tertullian did, and both are inspired by the same passage in Hebrews. Resting on the Sabbath cannot be that important since Joshua himself did not allow the Israelites to rest on the Sabbath during the siege and conquest of Jericho. As described above in the section on Hebrews, the "rest" referred to in the text seems to be the receipt of God's promise of rest in the land, not resting on the seventh day of the week. Hebrews argues that this cannot really be the rest promised by God since later in the biblical text (Ps 95) God will say that the Israelites will not take part in his rest. Therefore, Hebrews argues, the "rest" referred to in God's promise is the future rest that will come with the kingdom of Christ.

Aphrahat (and Tertullian) apply the argument of Hebrews to the Sabbath, stating that God could not have really meant that Israelites should rest on the Sabbath—again because of Psalm 95—but must have meant the future rest of Christ's kingdom. Once that switch is made, Aphrahat (again like Tertullian) marshals the Jericho story to prove the point, since Joshua at the command of God must have violated the Sabbath during this siege.

---

601 In the Greek text (BGT) it reads that the Sabbath was of the people of God "τῷ λαῷ τοῦ θεοῦ," as does the Peshitta (ܫܒܬܐ ܕܥܡܐ), which would imply something rather different, more akin to the simple meaning namely, that the people will receive a real Sabbath rest in the future. Aphrahat's text is enigmatic.

Rejection or Non-Implementation of the Typology

Hippolytus of Rome

Although Justin's and Tertullian's use of the Joshua-Jesus typology made it popular and widely known, its use was not ubiquitous. For example, Hippolytus of Rome (170 – 235)[602] makes reference to Joshua's desire for and attachment to the *Logos* in his commentary on the Song of Songs, without implying that Joshua and the *Logos* were one.

> In expectation of having become desirous of it (i.e., the *Logos*), blessed Joshua the son of Nun became the helper of Moses. Now, behold, O people, the commendation of all the righteous, how they became desirous of it, in this fragrant anointing oil. O blessed Joshua [son] of Nun, he who pointed to the new thing from a stone,[603] that he might reveal the anointing! When he desired it, blessed Joshua once again began circumcising the sons of Israel with stones.[604]

Other than the fact that Joshua "desires the Logos," as did all the other important Israelite leaders referenced by Hippolytus in this section, there is nothing that stands out as uniquely Jesus-like in Joshua's behavior. In fact, Yancy Warren Smith (*Hipplytus* 241) assumes that Hipplytus was actually influenced by Jewish sources in writing this complimentary nod towards circumcision.

Gregory Nazianzen

Gregory Nazianzen (329 – 389/390), also known as Gregory the Theologan, was the Archbishop of Constantinople. In his *Orations* ("In Defense of his Flight to Pontus" 2:88) he makes reference to Moses making the sign of the cross, but does not mention of Joshua as the instantiation of Jesus' name on the battlefield.[605]

---

602 He was a controversial character, called by some the first "anti-pope" for his schismatic activities.

603 The meaning of this phrase is unclear.

604 Translated from Georgian by Yancy Warren Smith, *Hippolytus' Commentary on Song of Songs in Social and Critical Light* (Ph.D. diss., Brite Divinity School, 2009), 279.

605 This comment is referenced by Joseph T. Lienard in his commentary on Exod 17:11. I thank Luke Johnson for helping me locate this source.

Πρὸς δὲ τὸν ἐμὸν πόλεμον οὐκ ἔχω τίς γένω- | For my own warfare, however, I am at a loss
μαι, τίνα συμμαχίαν ἐξεύρω, τίνα λόγον | what course to pursue, what alliance, what
σοφίας, τίχάρισμα, ποίᾳ πανοπλίᾳ πρὸς τὰς | word of wisdom, what grace to devise, with
τοῦ πονηροῦ μεθοδείας ὁπλίσομαι. Τίς νικήσει | what panoply to arm myself against the wiles
τοῦτον Μωϋσῆς ἐκτείνας τὰς χεῖρας ἐπὶ τοῦ | of the wicked one. What Moses is to conquer
ὄρους, ἵν' ὁ σταυρὸς ἰσχύσῃ τυπούμενος καὶ | him by stretching out his hands upon the
προμηνυόμενος; Τίς Ἰησοῦς μετὰ τοῦτον, τῷ | mound, in order that the cross thus typified
ἀρχιστρατήγῳ τῶν θείων παρατάξεων συμπα- | and prefigured, may prevail? What Joshua, as
ραταττόμενος; Τίς Δαβὶδ, ἢ ψάλλων, ἢ πολεμῶν | his successor, arrayed alongside the Captain
ἐν σφενδόναις, καὶ ὑπὸ τοῦ Θεοῦ περιεζω- | of the Lord's hosts? What David, either by
σμένος δύναμιν εἰς πόλεμον, καὶ τοὺς δακτύ- | harping, or fighting with his sling, and girded
λους εἰς παράταξιν γυμναζόμενος; (PG 35, | by God with strength unto the battle and with
p. 492, ln. 16–25) | his fingers trained to war?... (trans. NPNF 2nd
| series vol. 7 p. 222)

Gregory's lack of use of the Joshua-Jesus typology is striking since immediately after discussing Moses' making the sign of the cross, he moves to Joshua as Moses' successor receiving the revelation from the Captain of the Lord's hosts, referring to the story in Josh 6 immediately before the conquest of Jericho.

Gregory makes use of the same imagery again in his *Orations* ("To his Father" 12:2).[606] The context is in asking why his father appointed him to serve along with him during his lifetime.

---

606 There are other references to this in his *Orations* as well, specifically 13:2 (*PG* 35 p. 836) 32:16 (*PG* 36 p. 192), and 45:21 (*PG* 36 p. 652). R. Martin Pope in his above-referenced commentary on the *Hymns* of Prudentius, writes in a note (see the translated text above *ad loc.*): "The idea that Moses defeated the Amalekites because his arms were outstretched in the form of a cross is found also in one of the hymns (lxi.) of Gregory Nazianzen." I am not sure to what he is referring here and cannot find this reference in the 61st hymn (perhaps I am looking at the wrong collection or the numbering is incorrect?) There are a number of collections of Gregory's hymns (*Carmina*), but as far as I can tell, none of the 61st hymns in these collections has this reference. I did find a reference in his *Carmina (Poematica Historica)* De Seipso (1):

Χριστὲ ἄναξ, ὃς ἁγναῖς ποτ' ἀειρομέναις | Lord Christ, for your servant Moses, who raised
παλάμῃσι Σταυροτύποις Μωσῆος ἐπ' οὔρεϊ | his pure arms on the mountain in the type of a
σοῦ θεράποντος, Ἔκλινας Ἀμαλὴκ ὀλοὸν | cross, you turned away the destructive strength of
σθένος (*PG* 37 p. 969–970). | the Amalekites.

The claim that Christ himself turned away the Amalekites is interesting, but, again, there is no reference to the role of Joshua and his name in the battle.

Ἢ τοῦτο εἰδὼς καὶ ἀκούων, ὅτι καὶ μετὰ Ἀαρὼν ἐκείνου τοῦ πάνυ ἐχρίσθησαν Ἐλεάζαρ καὶ Ἰθάμαρ οἱ υἱοὶ Ἀαρών; τὸν γὰρ Ναδὰβ καὶ Ἀβιοὺδ ἑκὼν ὑπερβήσομαι, δέει τῆς βλασφημίας· καὶ Μωϋσῆς ἀνθ' ἑαυτοῦ τὸν Ἰησοῦν ἀναδείκνυσιν ἔτι ζῶν ἀντὶ νομοθέτου καὶ στρατηγοῦ, τοῖς ἐπὶ τὴν γῆν τῆς ἐπαγγελίας ἐπειγομένοις; Καὶ τὸ μὲν γὰρ τοῦ Ἀαρὼν καὶ τοῦ Ὤρ ὑποστηριζόντων τὰς χεῖρας Μωϋσέως ἐπὶ τοῦ ὄρους, ἵν' ὁ Ἀμαλὴκ καταπολεμηθῇ τῷ σταυρῷ, πόρρωθεν σκιαγραφουμένῳ καὶ τυπουμένῳ, δοκῶ μοι παρήσειν ἑκών, ὡς οὐ σφόδρα οἰκεῖον ἡμῖν καὶ πρόσφορον· οὐ γὰρ συννομοθέτας ᾑρεῖτο τούτους Μωϋσῆς, ἀλλ' εὐχῆς βοηθούς, καὶ καμάτου χειρῶν ἐρείσματα. (*PG* 35 p. 844–845)

Why is it that, while yet able to establish and guide many, and actually guiding them in the power of the Spirit, you support yourself with a staff and prop in your spiritual works? Is it because you have heard and know that even with the illustrious Aaron were anointed Eleazar and Ithamar, the sons of Aaron—for I pass over Nadab and Abihu, lest the allusion be ill-omened—and Moses during his lifetime appoints Iesu in his stead, as lawgiver and general over those who were pressing on to the land of Promise? The office of Aaron and Hur, supporting the hands of Moses on the mount, where Amalek warred down by the Cross prefigured and typified long before, I feel willing to pass by, as not very suitable application to us: for Moses did not choose them to share his work as lawgiver, but as helpers in his prayer and supporters for the weariness of his hands. (trans. *NPNF* 2nd series vol. 7 p. 245)

The fact that a Greek-speaking (and writing) Church Father like Gregory, in the 4th century, skips over the possibility of invoking the typology at this most obvious of opportunities would seem evidence that he found such a correlation wanting in some way; it is very hard to believe that he simply wasn't familiar with it.

Ephrem of Syria

An extreme example of a Church Father who does not work with the Joshua-Jesus typology is Ephrem of Syria (b. 306, Nisibis – d. 373, Edessa). Like his older contemporary Aphrahat, Ephrem writes in Syriac. Although he makes a number of extremely anti-Jewish comments in his homiletical and liturgical writings,[607] his commentaries on Genesis and Exodus give the impression that he is well versed in Judaic commentaries and even rabbinic aggada and targum.[608]

---

607 For a discussion of the anti-Jewish attitude in Ephrem, see: Christine Shepardson, *Anti-Judaism and Christian Orthodoxy: Ephrem's Hymns in Fourth Century Syria* (North American Patristics Society: Patristic Monograph Series 20; Washington D.C.: The Catholic University of America Press, 2008).

608 For a monograph-length presentation of this argument, see Elana Narinskaya, *Ephrem: A 'Jewish' Sage: A Comparison of the Exegetical Writings of St. Ephrem the Syrian and Jewish*

Ephrem's lack of interest in or knowledge of the Joshua-Jesus typology can be seen most clearly in his commentary on Exodus (17.2). Commenting on the defeat of Amalek, he writes:

ܒܬܪ ܗܠܝܢ ܐܬܐ ܥܡܠܝܩ ܠܡܩܪܒܘ ܥܡܗܘܢ. ܘܢܦܩ ܝܫܘܥ ܠܐܘܪܥܗ ܘܡܘܫܐ ܣܠܩ ܠܛܘܪܐ. ܘܚܘܛܪܗ ܕܐܠܗܐ ܒܐܝܕܗ. ܚܘܛܪܐ ܕܝܢ ܐܠܐ ܐܢ ܒܙܒܢ ܚܝܠܐ ܘܬܕܡܪܬܐ. ܠܐ ܐܚܝܕ ܗܘܐ ܠܗ ܡܘܫܐ. ܕܬܕܥ ܕܐܪܙܐ ܗܘܐ ܕܨܠܝܒܐ ܕܒܗ ܘܒܚܝܠܗ ܟܠ ܬܕܡܪ̈ܢ ܗܘܝܢ ܗܘܐ. ܣܠܩܘ ܕܝܢ ܥܡ ܡܘܫܐ ܐܗܪܘܢ ܘܚܘܪ ܕܐܚܬܗ، ܐܝܟ ܕܐܡܪܝܢ ܒܥܠ ܚܬܗ ܕܡܘܫܐ. ܒܪܡ ܐܝܕܘܗܝ، ܕܝܢ ܕܡܘܫܐ ܬܩܦ ܗܘܐ ܐܝܣܪܝܠ ܘܚܪܒ ܗܘܐ ܠܡܪ̈ܚܢܘܗܝ ܕܥܡ̈ܡܐ. ܕܓܙܡܘ ܘܐܬܘ ܠܡܩܪܒܘ ܥܡ ܥܡܐ ܘܒܡܬܡܟܟܘܬܗܝܢ ܬܩܦܝܢ ܗܘܘ ܥܡ̈ܡܐ ܠܡܙܟܐ ܠܐܝܠܝܢ ܕܒܟܠ ܙܒܢ ܥܠ ܡܪܝܐ ܘܥܠ ܡܘܫܐ ܡܪܛܢܝܢ ܗܘܘ.	After this, Amalek came to battle with them. And Yeshua went out towards them and Moses went up the mountain with the staff of God in his hand. This staff Moses only held if it was a time for mighty works and marvels, so that you would know that it is a symbol of the cross, for through it and its power marvels come to pass. With Moses, Aaron and Hur went up; [Hur] was, as they say, the brother-in-law of Moses.[609] When the arms of Moses were raised Israel would win, and would massacre those venturesome ones of the nations who threatened and came to make war with the nation. But when [his arms] were down, the nations had the advantage against those who grumbled constantly against the Lord and against Moses.

Traditions (Studia Traditionis Theologiae: Exploration in Early and Medieval Theology 7; Turnhout, Belgium: Brepols Publishers, 2010).

609 This is the tradition recorded in Josephus (*Ant.* 3:54):

κελεύει τόν τε ἀδελφὸν Ἀαρῶνα καὶ τῆς ἀδελφῆς Μαριάμης τὸν ἄνδρα Οὖρον ὄνομα στάντας ἑκατέρωθεν αὐτοῦ διακρατεῖν τὰς χεῖρας.	[Moses] called both his brother Aaron and the husband of his sister Miriam – named Hur – to stand on either side of him in order to support his arms.

Oddly, Elana Narinskaya (*Ephrem*, 118, 214–215) claims this reference in Ephrem as evidence of Ephrem's knowledge of rabbinic tradition and his vague source of "as they say (ܐܝܟ ܕܐܡܪܝܢ)" as "very clearly indicating his (Ephrem's) reliance on oral Haggadic tradition" (118). Although I believe Narinskaya makes a compelling case in general of Ephrem's knowledge of Rabbinic aggada (including about Hur in a later section of Ephrem's commentary,) in this case, considering Josephus' referencing of this tradition, it is very possible that this was Ephrem's source, or that through Josephus the tradition entered Christian tradition earlier than Ephrem. Narinskaya is aware of this source in Josephus, as she references it later (215), commenting: "This source is supported by Josephus and other Rabbinical sources as well." I am not sure that the "they" are necessarily the rabbis, especially since Rabbinic tradition, as early as the Targum of 1 Chronicles 2:50, has Miriam as Hur's mother, not his wife. (That Hur is Miriam's son is also claimed in *Pirqei de-Rabbi Eliezer* 44 and *Exodus Rabbah* 48.4, despite Narinskaya's mistakenly footnoting them as supporting the tradition in Ephrem.)

ܟܡܘܫܐ ܕܝܢ ܒܪܝܡ ܐܝܕܘܗܝ، ܘܒܚܘܛܪܐ ܕܙܩܝܦ
ܗܘܐ ܥܠ ܣܛܪܗ ܒܓܠܝܐܝܬ ܢܝܫܐ ܕܙܩܝܦܐ
ܡܬܚܙܐ ܗܘܐ ܒܗ. ܝܫܘܥ ܠܐܐ ܒܦܩܥܬܐ
ܘܡܘܫܐ ܒܛܘܪܐ. ܟܕ ܚܙܐ ܥܡܐ ܕܐܢܝܚ
ܐܝܕܘܗܝ، ܙܘܥܐ ܒܗܘܢ̈ ܪܡܐ ܠܡܗܦܟ ܩܕܡ
ܒܥܠܕܒܒܝܗܘܢ̈. ܘܐܦ̈ ܐܪܝܡ ܐܢܝܢ ܐܬܚܝܠܘ
ܠܡܐܙܠ ܥܠ ܣܢܐܝܗܘܢ̈܀

When Moses was raising his arms with the staff standing straight at his side, the sign of the cross was seen clearly upon him. Yeshua wearied himself in the valley and Moses on the mountain. When the nation saw him rest his arms, it sent tremors into them, making them desire to run away from their enemies. But when he raised them, they felt strengthened to advance against their enemies.

Like all of the Christian commentators before him, Ephrem makes use of the odd image of Moses stretching out his arms to defeat Amalek by drawing attention to the cross-like form his arms would make. Although his emphasis on the staff is unique to him, Ephrem's point that the sign of the cross is what defeats the Amalekite army is standard fare in Christian exegesis.

What makes Ephrem unique, however, is that unlike his fellow Syriac or Syriac-influenced scholars (Aphrahat and Theodoret), Ephrem makes no mention whatsoever of the significance of Joshua having the same name as Jesus.[610] Perhaps, as argued by Elana Narinskaya, Ephrem was so steeped in "Jewish exegesis" that he was either unfamiliar or unimpressed with this similarity, although his use of the cross imagery here seems to belie this point. Is it possible that he simply wasn't familiar with the work of his predecessors, like Justin, who made use of this correlation?[611] Unfortunately, it would take someone with significantly more expertise in Ephrem and the literature of the Church Fathers to answer this question, but as an outlier, Ephrem's exegesis leaves some intriguing questions.

610 Narinskaya (*Ephrem*, 117–121) makes this point by comparing Ephrem's exegesis to that of Theodoret. However, she does not mention Aphrahat, which would strengthen her case that Ephrem's approach is unique (although see the next sub-section on Pseudo-Macarius). Nor does she mention that even Theodoret's exegesis falls short of the full Joshua-Jesus correlation as it appears in Justin, Tertullian, and Origen, which would add nuance to the point that the Syriac-speaking world (even for those who wrote in Greek) was something a little different.

611 Although this unlikely suggestion seems possible for Ephrem, it seems impossible as an explantion for Gregory Nazianzen, referenced above, who also uses the Moses correlation with the Joshua one in his invoking of the Amalek story.

Pseudo-Macarius

Pseudo-Macarius is believed to have been a Syrian church-father active in the 5[612]th century.[612] Like the other Syriac scholars surveyed here,[613] he is either unaware or unconcerned with seeing Joshua as prefiguring Jesus. This can be seen in his short discussion of Joshua in Homily 50.

Ἰησοῦς ὁ τοῦ Ναυῆ ὅτε ἀπῆλθεν εἰς Ἰεριχώ, περιεκαθέσθη ἑπτὰ ἡμέρας μηδὲν δυνάμενος ποιῆσαι τῇ ἰδίᾳ φύσει, ἀλλ' ὅτε ὁ θεὸς ἐκέλευσε, τὰ τείχη ἀφ' ἑαυτῶν κατέπεσε.

Iesu, son of Nau, when he arrived at Jericho, surrounded it for seven days without the power from his own strength to do anything. But when God called out, the walls fell on their own.

καὶ ὅτε εἰσῆλθεν εἰς τὴν γῆν τῆς ἐπαγγελίας, λέγει αὐτῷ ὁ κύριος· ‹ἄπελθε εἰς πόλεμον›. ἀπεκρίθη Ἰησοῦς· ‹ζῇ κύριος, οὐ μὴ ἀπέλθω ἄνευ σοῦ›.

And when he came to the land of promise, the Lord said to him: "Go to war." Iesu answered: "As the Lord lives, I will not set forth without you."[614]

καὶ τίς ἐστιν ὁ ἐπιτάξας τῷ ἡλίῳ στῆναι ἄλλας δύο ὥρας ἐν τῇ συμβολῇ τοῦ πολέμου; ἡ φύσις αὐτοῦ μόνη ἢ ἡ συνοῦσα αὐτῷ δύναμις;

And who was it that commanded the sun to remain another two hours [in its place][615] during the pitching of the battle? Was it his power alone or the power of He that stood with him?

καὶ Μωϋσῆς ὅτε συνέβαλε τῷ Ἀμαλήκ, εἰ μὲν ἐξέτεινε τὰς χεῖρας εἰς τὸν οὐρανὸν πρὸς τὸν θεόν, ἐπάτει τὸν Ἀμαλήκ· εἰ δὲ ἔκλινε τὰς χεῖρας, ὁ Ἀμαλήκ περιεγίνετο.

And Moses, when he engaged Amalek [in battle], if he extended his arms into heaven toward God, it defeated Amalek. But if he lowered his arms, Amalek would prevail.

The image of Joshua here, even at the moment of his greatest miracle, is that of a mere human guided totally by the divine. He cannot conquer Jericho without a miracle; he will not fight the native Canaanites without God by his side. Even the stopping of the sun was all God doing and Joshua's. Pseudo-Macarius totally ignores the observation made by Justin and Origen that it is Joshua who com-

---

612 At one point, the fifty homilies were attributed to the 4th century Egyptian monk, Macarius. However, modern scholarship rejects this unanimously. See Kallistos Ware's preface and the translator's introduction in: Pseudo-Macarius, *The Fifty Spiritual Homilies and the Great Letter* (trans. George A. Maloney; The Classics of Western Spirituality; New York: Paulist Press, 1992).
613 Although he writes in Greek, from the simplicity of his writing, and especially the word order, I imagine his first language was Syriac. In his translator's introduction, Maloney (7) claims that it is clear that Pseudo-Macarius was educated in Latin as well, as evidenced by a number Latinisms employed in the *Homilies*.
614 There is no source for this in the Hebrew Bible as far as I know. It is reminiscent of Barak's statement to Deborah (Judg 4:8) and, perhaps, Moses' statement to God (Exod 34:9), but that is all.
615 I do not know the source for Pseudo-Macarius's assertion that the miracle lasted two hours. Justin claims 36, but I know of no source for this either.

mands the sun to stop. Although God is the one with the power to actually stop the sun, the book of Joshua points out that the very fact that God "obeyed" a command by a human is unprecedented. Hence, it was probably not by accident that Pseudo-Macarius rewrites this miracle with Joshua as a meek bystander, waiting for divine intervention.

Moses does not fare much better in Pseudo-Macarius' retelling. This is especially marked since the story under discussion is none other than the account of the defeat of Amalek—the story that was the seed of the Joshua-Jesus typology. Pseudo-Macarius ignores any link between Iesu as general and the power of his name, but this is not surprising. All the Syriac-influenced scholars did so, even Theodoret. What stands out about Pseudo-Macarius' treatment is that he does not even see Moses' stretching out his hands as a sign of Moses using the power of the cross-symbol; even Ephrem makes recourse to this exegesis. Instead, Pseudo-Macarius imagines Moses' arms going straight up in supplication to God, not perpendicular to his body in imitation of a cross. For whatever reason, Pseudo-Macarius has no interest in using Jesus-related imagery to explain these Pentateuchal narratives. He is, instead, content to demonstrate that the various protagonists were helpless and totally dependent on God's grace for their success.

Summary

Looking at the creation of the Joshua-Jesus typology and its subsequent ebb and flow, the following overall pattern emerges. The typology seems to have come into being in the second century C.E., specifically in literature that was polemical in nature. The author of Barnabas, followed by Justin and Tertullian, realized that making Joshua—the successor of Moses—into a Jesus figure would go far in establishing the legitimacy of Jesus to those looking for Old Testement predictions and antecedents.

As time went on, and Judaism and Christianity grew farther apart, many polemicists found this typology to be less important. Some gave it quick mention; others gave it no mention at all. Although Lactantius and, specifically Zeno, found the aspect related to the recircumcision of the Israelites in Joshua's time to be fruitful in debating the importance of physical vs. spiritual circumcision, this was actually the exception rather than the rule at that point.

One striking development of the typology appeared in the work of Origen. Unlike most other uses of the typology, Origen is not interested only in polemic. Although he does seem to relish the idea of Moses suffering in comparison to Joshua, the greater part of Origen's *Homilies on Joshua* is dedicated to using the typology for the spiritual and ethical improvement of his readers and listeners. Origen seems to be the only one who tried to explore the purely spiritual potential of making the Joshua-Jesus correlation a key part of Christian thinking and exegesis.

Only Eusebius seems to have absorbed Origen's message, and it is just the existence of the correlation per se—and the implication it has for the prophecy of Moses—that is interesting to him. He does not have the same interest in the overall hermeneutic use of the typology that spurs Origen to interpret verse after verse in the Old Testament in an allegorical fashion.

Although the typology lives on in Greek exegesis in a limited way, and even gets mention in some (not all) Latin exegetes, it never actually makes inroads in the world of the Syriac Church Fathers. Whether this was due to some disconnection between the worlds of these thinkers, or whether, like Ephrem, they were steeped in a different hermeneutic tradition, in these works Joshua remains simply Joshua, the leader of Israel after Moses. The fact that he had the same name as Jesus was a rhetorical benfit at best (Aphrahat); to some it seems not to have mattered.

All in all, the Joshua-Jesus typology seems to have had its most powerful run as a polemic during the early period of Christian-Jewish argument. The attempt of Origen to turn it into a lasting piece of Christian exegesis can be seen as, mostly, a failure. His *Homilies on Joshua* are an interesting and powerful work, but one that receives little attention and no traction in later exegetes. Once the disconnection between Jews and Christians reaches a certain level, interest in this type of a polemic ceases, and so does interest in the typology. However, the creation of the typology does leave a fingerprint in the work of the Church Fathers (especially the Greek writers, but also many Latin ones,) and receives some mention.

Finally, as will be seen in the chapter on rabbinic literature, it is my contention that the Joshua-Jesus typology, and the polemical use to which it was put, was noticed by the rabbis. Although they never reference the Christian typology as such, this does not mean that they were ignorant of it or saw it as irrelevant. As will be shown, they responded in their own way.

Chapter 6 – Rabbinic Joshua(s)

Joshua is not a particularly prominent figure in rabbinic exegesis.[616] Although he receives ample mention, considering the amount of biblical material available regarding this figure, his place in rabbinic literature is secondary. When taken as a whole, rabbinic literature does not seem to have one main homiletical approach to Joshua as a character. Some of the comments about Joshua are negative and some are positive; some compare him favorably with other biblical characters and some unfavorably.

Nevertheless, within the cacophony of rabbinic voices, a few trends/images may be uncovered. This chapter will explore the main images of Joshua found in rabbinic literature and will attempt to put these images in context and, when possible, suggest an etiology for them.[617]

---

616 Cf. Elßner, *Josua*, 129–168. For this section there is almost no overlap at all between the sources I look at and those of Elßner. Since Elßner's interest is in the ethics of war, he discusses the Rabbinic sources that differentiate between different types of war (obligatory, optional, etc.) and ones that describe peace missions sent by Joshua before his conquest (j. *Shebi'it* 6:1 and *Lev. Rab.* 17:6), in line with the halakhot of war described by the rabbis, as well as the implications of Josh 11:19–20, which states that none of the locals were willing to make peace with Joshua except the Gibeonites. I will not discuss any of these sources as they focus on war and halakha, and not on the character of Joshua or his image. If these latter sources have anything to say about Joshua, they demonstrate that he follows halakha as the Rabbis understand it, *not* that he is a lover of peace. As such, they would fit in with the Joshua-as-Torah-Scholar or Joshua-as-Rabbi imagery discussed below.

617 Two notes on methodology are appropriate here. First, I explore the various Rabbinic texts pericope by pericope and do not attempt to take into account their positions in the various documents, as per Neusner's methodological suggestion. For a description of his method, see: Jacob Neusner, *Midrash as Literature: The Primacy of Documentary Discourse* (Eugene, OR: Wipf and Stock Publishers, 1987). Whether a documentary-type analysis would yield better fruit will have to be left to others to explore. My own view is more in line with scholars like James Kugel, that a pericope driven analysis often yields more fruit than a document-driven one. See: James L. Kugel, "Two Introductions to Midrash" *Prooftexts* 3 (1983): 131–155; repr. in *Midrash and Literature* (ed. Geoffrey Hartman and Sanford Budick; New Haven: Yale University Press, 1985), 77–103. For a good test case, see the work of Burt Visotzky on *Leviticus Rabbah*, where he challenges many of the conclusions of Neusner's documentary method as applied to the work: Burton L. Visotzky, *Golden Bells and Pomegranates: Studies in Midrash Leviticus Rabbah* (Tübingen: Mohr Siebeck, 2003).

Second—and somewhat related—I have not attempted to isolate the various sources and graph where and when they originated and what effect geography and time had on their development. Although this could theoretically yield some interesting results that could shed light on the intellectual and religious climate of various Jewish communities from this period, ne-

Joshua the Rabbi

Perhaps the least surprising image of Joshua is that of a rabbi. The fact that rabbinic culture would choose to see in one of its inherited heroes someone made in their own image is eminently understandable. In addition, even certain biblical passages give precedent for painting Joshua in the colors of a Torah scholar. Two passages in particular stand out.

Exod 33:11	וְדִבֶּר יְהוָה אֶל מֹשֶׁה פָּנִים אֶל פָּנִים כַּאֲשֶׁר יְדַבֵּר אִישׁ אֶל רֵעֵהוּ וְשָׁב אֶל הַמַּחֲנֶה וּמְשָׁרְתוֹ יְהוֹשֻׁעַ בֶּן נוּן נַעַר לֹא יָמִישׁ מִתּוֹךְ הָאֹהֶל.	And Yhwh spoke to Moses face to face, as a man speaks with his fellow. Then he would go back to the camp, but his attendant, Joshua son of Nun, the lad, would not step forth from the tent.
Josh 1:7–8	רַק חֲזַק וֶאֱמַץ מְאֹד לִשְׁמֹר לַעֲשׂוֹת כְּכָל הַתּוֹרָה אֲשֶׁר צִוְּךָ מֹשֶׁה עַבְדִּי אַל תָּסוּר מִמֶּנּוּ יָמִין וּשְׂמֹאול לְמַעַן תַּשְׂכִּיל בְּכֹל אֲשֶׁר תֵּלֵךְ. לֹא יָמוּשׁ סֵפֶר הַתּוֹרָה הַזֶּה מִפִּיךָ וְהָגִיתָ בּוֹ יוֹמָם וָלַיְלָה לְמַעַן תִּשְׁמֹר לַעֲשׂוֹת כְּכָל הַכָּתוּב בּוֹ כִּי אָז תַּצְלִיחַ אֶת דְּרָכֶךָ וְאָז תַּשְׂכִּיל.	Just be very strong and brave to make sure to perform everything according to the Torah which Moses my servant commanded you. Do not veer from it to the right or the left in order to be wise in all that you do. Let this Torah scroll not leave your mouth, and you should read from it day and night, so that you succeed in keeping everything written in it. Then your ways shall succeed and then you shall be wise.

In the first passage, from Exodus, Joshua is described as a young man that spends all his time in the Tent of Yhwh. Even the great Moses must leave the tent from time to time, to speak with the people and communicate Yhwh's word—but not Joshua.

In the second passage, from Yhwh's opening speech in the book of Joshua, we learn that the secret of Joshua's success, at least as envisioned by Yhwh, will be his attachment to Torah study. Echoing the phrase from the passage known as the *Shema* (Deut 6:7), Joshua must have the words of the Torah on his lips morning and night. If he does this, Yhwh promises that all of his actions will be wise and successful. Although these two passages are exceptional when it comes to describing Joshua, they give the rabbis a foothold which they can use to create

---

vertheless, such a study would require much more detailed analysis and sorting and will have to wait for a different venue.

a more "rabbinic" Joshua—one that spends his time studying Torah and contemplating God.

Joshua as an Essential Link in the Chain of Tradition

To the rabbis, Joshua plays an essential role as a link in the chain of Torah tradition from Moses to the people. The classic depiction of this comes in the opening words of Mishna *Abot* (1:1):

משה קבל תורה מסיני ומסרה ליהושע ויהושע לזקנים וזקנים לנביאים ונביאים מסרוה לאנשי כנסת הגדולה.	Moses received the Torah at Sinai and passed it on to Joshua, and Joshua to the elders, and the elders to the prophets, and the prophets passed it on to the men of the Great Assembly.

This description is expanded in the *Abot de-Rabbi Nathan* (b, ch. 1):

משה קבל תורה מסיני לא מפי מלאך ולא מפי שרף אלא מפי מ[לך] מ[לכי] ה[מלכים] הקדוש ברוך הוא שנאמר אלה החקים והמשפטים והתורות... משה מסר ליהושע שנאמר ויהושע בן נון מלא רוח חכמה כי סמך משה את ידיו עליו. יהושע מסר לזקנים שנאמר ויעבדו העם את ה' [כל ימי יהושע וכל ימי הזקנים אשר האריכו ימים אחרי יהושע...] אשר האריכו ימים אבל לא שנים. זקנים מסרו לשופטים...	Moses received the Torah at Sinai, not from an angel or a seraph but from the King of kings, the Holy One, bb"h (=blessed be He), as it says (Lev 26:46): "These are the statutes, rules, and laws..." ...Moses passed it on to Joshua, as it says (Deut 34:9): "And Joshua son of Nun was filled with wisdom, since Moses places his hands upon him." Joshua passed it on to the elders, as it says (Judg 2:7): "And the nation served the Lord [all the days of Joshua and all the days of the elders who survived during the days after Joshua...]" – they survived for days [after Joshua] not years. And the elders passed it on to the Judges...

Observing how the list begins, one notes how Joshua's unique place in the transmission of Torah stands out. Not only is he the only recorded direct student of Moses, at least in these sources, but he is the only source of tradition mentioned by name as an individual other than Moses himself. All the other carriers of tradition are groups, some of which span hundreds of years. It would seem, therefore, that in the eyes of the rabbis, the "Joshua epoch" of Torah was unique.

The way the Rabbis demonstrate this point is through a two-step midrash. First, the verse says that Joshua was filled with wisdom. Although the text does not say it here explicitly, wisdom is identified with Torah in a number of midrashim.[618]

אמר ר' בניה: "העולם [ומלואו] לא נברא אלא בזכות תורה, י"'י בחכמה יסד ארץ."	R. Baniah said: "The world and all that is in it was only created due to the merit of Torah, 'God created the world with wisdom' (Prov 3:19)."	*Genesis Rabbah* (Theodor-Albeck) *"Bereishit"* 1.
...ואומר י"'י בחכמה יסד ארץ וג', ואין חכמה אלא תורה, שנ' י"'י קנני ראשית דרכו וג', שהוא ר]אשית ד]רכו...	...and it says: 'God created the world with wisdom' (Prov 3:19)," and wisdom only refers to Torah, as it says: 'God formed me the beginning of his ways, etc.' (Prov 8:22), for it [Torah] was the beginning of his ways...	*Midrash ha-Torah of R. Tanḥuma*, Opening (p. 33); in *Qitei Midrashim from the Genizah* – Jacob Mann.

Hence, when the spirit passes on to Joshua, this means that the Torah passed on to Joshua.

The second implicit midrashic understanding is the Rabbis' identification of the placing of the hands of Moses on Joshua as the confirmation of a rabbinic title on his student; an official description of the implicit rabbinization of Joshua.

Considering the prominent place given to Joshua as the chief purveyor of Moses' Torah, as well as the similar position granted him in some biblical verses, one can't help feeling somewhat puzzled at the source in the Babylonian Talmud (*Eruvin* 54b) which discusses Moses' teaching habits and skips over Joshua entirely as if he didn't exist.

כיצד סדר משנה? משה למד מפי הגבורה, נכנס אהרן ושנה לו משה פירקו. נסתלק אהרן וישב לשמאל משה. נכנסו בניו ושנה להן משה פירקן, נסתלקו בניו, אלעזר ישב לימין משה ואיתמר לשמאל אהרן... נכנסו זקנים ושנה להן משה פירקן, נסתלקו זקנים, נכנסו כל העם ושנה להן משה פירקן. נמצאו ביד אהרן ארבעה, ביד בניו שלשה, וביד הזקנים שנים, וביד כל העם אחד.	How was the teaching (mishna) organized? Moses learned from the Almighty. Then Aaron entered and Moses taught him the material. Aaron moved away and sat to the left of Moses and in came his sons and Moses taught them the material. His sons moved away, Elazar sat on the right of Aaron and Itamar on the left of Aaron... Then the elders entered, and Moses taught them the material. Then the entire nation entered and Moses taught them the material. So Aaron will have heard the material four times, his sons three, the elders two, and the people once.

---

618 I thank William Gilders for pointing this out.

נסתלק משה, ושנה להן אהרן פירקו. נסתלק אהרן שנו | At this point Moses would leave, and Aaron
להן בניו פירקן. נסתלקו בניו, שנו להן זקנים פירקן. | would go over the material. Aaron would
נמצא ביד הכל ארבעה. | then leave and his sons went over the material. His sons left and the elders went over the material. Hence, everybody would have been presented the material four times.

מכאן אמר רבי אליעזר: "חייב אדם לשנות לתלמידו | From here R. Eliezer said: "A person must
ארבעה פעמים. וקל וחומר, ומה אהרן שלמד מפי | teach his students four times. This can be pro-
משה, ומשה מפי הגבורה – כך, הדיוט מפי הדיוט – | ven *a fortiori*: If Aaron, who learned from
על אחת כמה וכמה." | Moses—who himself learned from the Almighty—required this, how much more so does the average person!"

The basic elements of this account are not surprising. The Rabbis generally pictured Moses receiving the Oral Law from God at Sinai, so the fact that they speculate about its transmission is expected. The idea that *mishna* should be repeated (*shana*) in one's study was a standard trope for a culture steeped in memorization of large swaths of legal "texts."[619] Even the prominence of Aaron is not surprising—he is a significant biblical figure and important to the rabbis as well. What is surprising is that Joshua is not mentioned at all as being part of this process.

As the above source comes from the Babylonian Talmud, there is no way that its authors were unfamiliar with the extremely well known mishnaic dictum that "Moses received the Torah from Sinai and gave it to Joshua." So why is he skipped over? This question is difficult to answer, as the sources are silent on the subject. However, as will be seen in a later section, there seems to be some interest in this later rabbinic period to shrink Joshua's importance, perhaps as a reaction to the rise of his importance in Christian circles as a prefiguration of Jesus. Although I have no evidence that this factor is at play here—this might be a case where the original midrash is based on biblical passages that included Aaron, his sons and the elders but not Joshua—nevertheless, the possibility should be considered in light of some of the clearer examples that will be explored in later sections.

---

619 For more discussion on the rabbis as an oral culture, see: Martin S. Jaffee, *Torah in the Mouth: Writing and Oral Tradition in Palestinian Judaism, 200 BCE – 400 CE* (New York: Oxford University Press, 2001).

Joshua as a Decider of Halakha

Another way Rabbinic literature "rabbinizes" Joshua is by envisioning him functioning in a classic rabbinic role. This has little to do with Joshua per se or something specifically rabbinic about his character. Rather, the Rabbis picture all of their past heroic figures as rabbis, since this was a comfortable and familiar image to them.

An example of this phenomenon can be found in *Sifrei Numbers* 140 (Kahana ed.), commenting on the passage in Numbers (27:18) in which Moses is told to appoint Joshua as his successor.

'וסמכת את ידך עליו' – א[מר] לו: "משה, תן	'And place your hand upon him' – [God] said to him:
לו תורגמן ליהושע שואל ודורש ומורה הורייות	"Moses, give a public expositor to Joshua so that he
בחייך, כשאיתיפטר מן העו[לם] לא יהו יש[ראל]	can hold discussions and offer decisions in your life-
אומ[רים], 'בחיי רבך לא היית מדבר ועכשיו את	time so that when you leave this world Israel will not
מדבר'?"	say (to him) 'you never said anything while your mas-
	ter was alive, but now you speak?'
ר' נתן או[מר]: "העמידו מן הארץ והושיבו על	R. Nathan says: "[Moses] lifted Joshua up off the
הספסל.	ground and placed him on the bench,
דבר אחר: כיון שהיה יהושע נכנס היה	Another matter: Whenever Joshua would enter the
משתיק התורגמן עד שנכנס וישב במקומו.	room, [Moses] would quiet the expositor until he
	came in and sat in his spot.[620]
שנאמר: 'ונתת מהודך עליו' – מהודך, ולא כל	As it says: 'and you shall give him some of your glory'
הודך, נמצינו למדין פני משה כחמה ופני יהושע	– some of your glory, but not all of your glory. We can
כלבנה."	learn from this that Moses' face was like the sun and
	Joshua's like the moon."

The concern of this midrash—something that will be seen in other sections as well—revolves around the question of how the competence of a new leader (Joshua) can be demonstrated during the lifetime of the previous leader (Moses) without the upcoming leader behaving in a fashion that implies competition. The answer the midrash suggests is that the current leader must create these opportunities for his successor. The *Sifrei* understands God's command to Moses to place his hands upon Joshua as to give Joshua some access to the infrastructure Moses uses, and then take a step back and allow Joshua to shine, at least a little bit.

For the rabbis, this does not mean that Joshua should prophesy in public, perform miracles, or even lead the battles. Rather, the *sine qua non* of leadership, for the rabbis, is the ability to teach Torah and make authoritative decisions of halakha. Not only this, the rabbis picture Moses sitting on a bench before his stu-

---

620 This gloss appears as if it cuts right into the middle of R. Nathan's statement.

dents, who were sitting on the ground. They imagine Moses having a public expositor—a requirement for crowds when there is no microphone—just as in the
local synagogues.

In the first suggestion of the midrash, Moses is said to have given a public
expositor to Joshua so that his Torah could be disseminated to the people as
well. R. Nathan suggests that Moses added the public gesture of allowing Joshua
to sit by his side on the bench. R. Nathan seems to take issue with the idea that
Joshua would have his own expositor, as that would make him almost an equal
to Moses, but a seat next to Moses while Moses was teaching would, according to
R. Nathan, get the point across effectively.[621] A third suggestion claims that
Moses made the expositor be silent when Joshua came in the room, forcing everyone into reverential silence as Joshua took his seat.[622]

According to all the interpretations, the bottom line seems to be that for
Joshua to show his bona fides, he must be accepted by the people as a Torah
scholar. The only way they could know whether Joshua's Torah credentials
were solid would be through Moses. Moses' approval of Joshua in a Torah-teach-
ing context would demonstrate to the people that he (Joshua) was legitimate.

A more extreme version of this motif appears in a handful of midrashim that
describe a period of time when Joshua actually becomes greater than Moses. For
example, in a short text called *Midrash Peṭirat Moshe*, the death of Moses is described. However, before Moses is willing to accept death, the midrash records
that he fights off the angels coming to take him to heaven, forcing God to
come and take Moses' life. God, however, doesn't use force to get Moses to relin-
quish his life, but trickery (*Batei Midrashot* vol 1., ed. Shlomo Aharon Wertheim-
er, [revised ed.; Jerusalem: Ktab Yad Wasepher, 5749], p. 286).

---

621 The import of the sun and moon analogy will be taken up in a different section.
622 The theme of Moses treating Joshua with respect comes up in other midrashim as well,
although not with the focus of training Joshua to be a decider of halakha.

אמר לו הקדוש ברוך הוא למשה: "משה, רצונך שתחיה
ולא תמות?" אומר לו: "הן". אמר לו: "תן לי מפתחות
החכמה." מיד נתן לו ונשאר שלא ידע מאומה, וכשבאו
ישראל לדין לא ידע להשיב, וישב יהושע לדון. אמר
משה: "יהושע נערי ישב לדין ואני נשארתי טפש? טוב
מותי מחיי!" ובקש המיתה, ונטל הקדוש ברוך [הוא]
בעצמו את נפשו לשמים וקבר אותו בעצמו...

The Holy One, bb"h, said to Moses: "Moses, do you wish to live and not die?" [Moses] responds: "Yes." [God] said to him: "Give me the keys of wisdom." Immediately, Moses gave [them] to him, and ended up knowing nothing. When Israel came for judgment and [Moses] had no idea what to respond, Joshua sat down to judge. Moses said [to himself]: "Joshua, my lad, sat down to judge and I remain here dumbfounded?!" He then requested death, and the Holy One, bb"h, himself took his soul to heaven and buried him (Moses) himself.

The midrash appears to be a parable describing the benefit of death at old age, when a person's senility begins to set in. Moses himself, in this midrash, quickly decides that there is no point in continuing to live past his own usefulness. The parable describes Moses as jealous of Joshua who, faced with a leader who has forgotten his Torah, takes the bull by the horns and takes over Moses' position as chief judge of Israel.

This same midrash appears in a greatly expanded form in *Midrash Tanḥuma* (ed. Buber, *Parshat Va-Etḥanan* 6).[623]

א"ל הקדוש ברוך הוא למשה: "כל צער זה שאתה
מצטער למה?" אמר: "רבונו של עולם, מתיירא אני
מחבלו של מלאך המות." א"ל: "איני מוסרך בידו."

The Holy One, bb"h, said to Moses: "What is all this suffering you are expressing?" [Moses] said: "Master of the World, I fear the assault of the Angel of Death." [God] said to him: "I will not place you in his hands."

אמר לפניו: "רבונו של עולם, [יוכבד] אמי שהקהו שיניה
בשני בניה בחייה, יקהו שיניה במיתתי." אמר לו: "כך
עלתה במחשבה, וכך מנהגו של עולם, דור דור
ודורשיו, דור דור ופרנסיו, דור דור ומנהיגיו, עד עכשיו
היה חלקך לשרת, [ועכשיו הגיע חלקו של יהושע
תלמידך לשרת]."

[Moses] said before Him: "Master of the World, [Jochebed,] my mother, whose teeth were blunted by her two sons in her lifetime, shall her teeth be blunted upon my death?"[624] [God] replied: "Thus it appears proper and this is the way of the world; every generation has its scholars, every generation has its entrepreneurs and every generation has its leaders. Up until now it was your place to serve; [now the time has come for Joshua, your student, to serve.]"

---

623 The same midrash appears in *Deuteronomy Rabbah*, ad loc.
624 The meaning of this idiom is unclear.

אמר לפניו: "רבונו של עולם אם מפני יהושע אני מת, אלך ואהיה תלמידו." א"ל: "אם אתה רוצה לעשות כך לך עשה."

[Moses] said before him: "Master of the World, if Joshua is the reason I must die, I will go and be his student." [God] responded: "If you want to do this, go do it."

עמד משה והשכים לפתחו של יהושע, והיה יהושע יושב ודורש, ועמד משה וכפף קומתו, והניח ידו על פיו, ונתעלמו עיניו של יהושע ולא ראה אותו, כדי שיצטער וישלים עצמו [למיתה], והלכו ישראל אצל פתחו של משה, ומצאוהו בפתחו של יהושע, והיה יהושע יושב ומשה עומד.

Moses got up early and went to the opening of Joshua's [tent.] Joshua was sitting there and teaching. Moses got up and stood bending forward and placed his hand upon his mouth. He was hidden from Joshua's eyes and he did not see him, in order to make Moses suffer and make his peace [with dying.] Israel went to the tent of Moses but they found him at the tent of Joshua, with Joshua sitting and expounding and Moses standing.

אמרו לו ליהושע: "מה עלתה לך שמשה רבינו עומד, ואתה יושב?" כיון שתלה עיניו וראהו, מיד קרע את בגדיו וצעק ובכה, ואמר: "רבי רבי אבי אבי ואדני!"

They said to Joshua: "What's come over you? Moses our teacher is standing and you are sitting and expounding?!" Once Joshua lifted his eyes and saw him, he immediately tore his clothing, screamed and cried, and said: "My teacher, my teacher, my father, my father and master!"

אמר ישראל למשה: "משה רבינו למדנו תורה." אמר להן: "אין לי רשות." אמרו לו: "אין אנו מניחין אותך." יצתה בת קול ואמרה להם: "למדו מן יהושע." קיבלו עליהן לישב וללמוד מפי יהושע.

Israel said to Moses: "Moses, our master, teach us Torah." He said to them: "I do not have permission." They said to him: "We will not let you out of it." A heavenly voice spoke out to them saying: "Learn from Joshua." They accepted this and sat to learn from the mouth of Joshua.

ישב יהושע בראש, ומשה מימינו, ואלעזר ואיתמר משמאלו, ויישב ודורש בפני משה.

Joshua sat at the head, with Moses on his right and Elazar and Itamar on his left, and he sat and taught before Moses.

אמר ר' שמואל בר נחמני אמר ר' יונתן: בשעה שפתח יהושע ואמר "ברוך שבחר בצדיקים ובמשנתם", נטלו מסורות החכמה ממשה וניתנו ליהושע, ולא היה יודע משה מה היה יהושע דורש.

R. Samuel bar Naḥmani quoted R. Jonathan: When Joshua began to speak and recited [the blessing]: "Praised is the One who chose the righteous and their teachings," the stores of wisdom were taken from Moses and given to Joshua, and Moses did not understand what Joshua was teaching.

אחר שעמדו ישראל, אמרו לו למשה: "סתם לנו את התורה." אמר להם: "איני יודע מה אשיב לכם." והיה משה רבינו נכשל ונופל.

After Israel rose, they said to Moses: "Go over the teaching." He said to them: "I don't know what to tell you." Moses our teacher felt like a failure and collapsed.

באותה שעה אמר: "רבונו של עולם, עד עכשיו בקשתי חיים, ועכשיו הרי נפשי נתונה לך."

At that moment, he said: "Master of the World, until now I requested life, but now my soul is given to you."

In this story, motivated by the fear of death, Moses strikes a bargain with God to allow him to live as a subordinate to Joshua. Even though God appears to agree to Moses' terms, in fact, God sabotages Moses' attempt by adding on humiliations. First, God makes it so that Joshua doesn't even notice Moses standing there. This works only for a short time, though, since once the people point Moses out to Joshua, Joshua collapses in a panic and begs Moses' forgiveness. Next, God makes Moses lose his intelligence and knowledge base, so that Moses does not even understand Joshua's lecture and cannot function as a post-lecture summarizer, the job of the senior student. It is at this point—as in the version found in *Peṭirat Moshe*—that Moses gives in and begs for death.

Two features of this version of the story are worth noting. First, Joshua's collapse appears to mimic that of Elisha in the biblical account of the death of Elijah, in which Elisha calls him father (2 Kings 2:12). On one hand, by utilizing this imagery, the rabbis paint a picture of an exceptionally loyal Joshua, who has no desire to see his teacher die or be mocked. On the other hand, like Elisha, Joshua remains a confident successor who, when told he must, has little problem taking over the lecture. Second, it is worth noting the seating arrangement, with Moses in the top student slot, a compliment Joshua ostensibly pays to Moses, but which, due to their relative positions, can only be seen as an ironic, if unintended, slight.

The overall point of this version of the midrash seems to be the same as that of the version in *Peṭirat Moshe*, to serve as a parable about accepting death. The reluctance of Joshua to take this position and his strong positive feelings towards his mentor are emphasized here in a way they are not in the former version. Nonetheless, both of these rabbinic traditions see a confident Joshua, ready to take his place as leader. This contrasts strongly with texts like those in *Assumptio Mosis* or *L.A.B.* in which Joshua reacts with terror when he hears of Moses' immanant demise.

One final variation on this theme appears in *Deuteronomy Rabbah* (ed. Lieberman; *Parshat Va-Etḥanan* 6) as a gloss on God's words רב לך "it is enough for you" (Deut 3:26).

"רבו הוא לך, ביזה כולה בזוז לך, ואם אתה נוטל הכל, לית את שבק ליהושע תלמידך כלום. גאלת את ישראל ממצרים, הנהגתם בים והורדת להם המן ואת התורה, הנהגתם במדבר מ' שנה, ואת מבקש ליכנס לארץ לחלקה להם, אין אתה מניח ליהושע כלום."

[God said to Moses:] "Too much has accumulated for you, you are taking all the booty for yourself, and if you take it all you will leave your student, Joshua, with nothing. You redeemed Israel from Egypt, you brought them through the sea, you brought down the manna for them as well as the Torah, you led them through the wilderness for forty years, and now you are requesting to bring them into the land and divide it among them? You will leave Joshua with nothing!"

א"ל: "יכנס יהושע ויחלק הארץ להם ויהיה מנהיגם ואני נכנס עמהם כסגן."

[Moses] replied: "Let Joshua enter and divide up the land for them and he will lead them and I will enter as his assistant."

א"ל: "רב הוא לך, הוי יהושע יושב ודורש ומנהיג את ישראל ומלמדן ואתה יושב ורואה אותו, הוי רב לך."

[God] replied: "This is too much for you; Joshua will sit and expound and lead the Israelites and teach them while you sit and watch him – it will be too much for you."

This version, instead of emphasizing Moses' failed attempt to live as a secondary figure during Joshua's reign, presents the argument that if Moses were to do Joshua's job he would have accomplished "too much" for any one human. Additionally, there seems to be some special place for Joshua in the cosmic scheme, and Moses trying to take over his job would challenge the overall divine plan. In this sense, Joshua's position as Moses' successor and the man who would conquer the Promised Land seems to have been preordained according to this source.

One final point to notice in this description is that although Moses and God are focusing on the conquest of the land and its division among the tribes, God cannot help but throw in that if Moses were to survive and live a life as a secondary figure to Joshua, he would have to suffer through watching Joshua teach Torah – the ultimate jab, apparently, for the person who brought Torah to the world. In these midrashim, Joshua is firmly entrenched as a Torah personality, but one whose identity as a Torah scholar cannot be disentangled from his position as Moses' student and successor.

Joshua the Law-Maker

For the Rabbis, there is nothing more paradigmatically rabbinic than making laws. As part of imagining Joshua the rabbi, the sages of the Babylonian Talmud impute to him at least ten different laws that they believe he enacted. The full list appears in the seventh chapter of b. *Baba Qama* (80b-81a; MS Munich 95).

תנו רבנן עשרה תנאין התנה[625] יהושע:		Our Rabbis taught: Joshua instituted ten laws.[626]
שיהו מריעין בחורשי[ן].	א. 1.	That plowing animals be allowed to graze.
ומלקטין עצים משדותיהן.	ב. 2.	That wood may be collected from people's fields.
ומלקטין עשבים בכל מקום חוץ משדה תלתן.	ג. 3.	That grasses may be collected from anywhere, except from a field of fenugreek.
וקוטמין נטיעה בכל מקום חוץ מגרופיות של זית.	ד. 4.	That shoots may be cut anywhere, except from those of olive-trees.
ומעיין היוצא כתחילה מסתפקק בני העיר ממנו.	ה. 5.	That new springs may be used by the citizens of the city.
ומחכין בימ[א] של טבריא ובלבד שלא יפרוס קלע ויעמיד את הספינה.	ו. 6.	That one may fish with a hook in the Sea of Galilee, as long as one does not spread a net and park the boat.
ונפנין לאחורי הגדר אפי[לו] בשדה מליאה כרכום.	ז. 7.	That one may defecate behind a fence, even in a field full of saffron.
ומהלכין בשבילי רשו[ת] הרבים עד שתרד רביעית שנייה.	ח. 8.	That one may walk on private paths until the second rains fall.
ומסתלקי[ן] בצדי הדרכים מפני יתידות הדרכים.	ט. 9.	That one may travel on (private) sidewalks in order to avoid the road-pegs.
והתועה בין הכרמים מפסיג ועולה מפסיג ויורד.	י. 10.	That one who is lost in an orchard may cut his way through whether going up or down.
ומת מצוה קנה מקומו.	יא. 11.	That a dead body owns its spot.[627]

A number of elements stand out about this list. The first may be the utter banality of it. The key element of the disparate rules in the list has to do with navigating between private and public property. On one hand, halakha grants rights to people to own and control their own land. On the other hand, halakha worries that allowing too much control can be disruptive to the public. This series of laws is an attempt to forge a kind of compromise between these two values. Therefore, these rules legislate limits to private property rights at the point where trespassing on the part of the public is minimal and the nuisance of enforcing the owner's rights would be overwhelming.[628]

---

625 Literally, the term means "conditions," an unusual term for rules; one would have expected the term "*taqqanot*."

626 The list seems to include 11 rules. Probably two of the above were considered to be one by the author of the *baraita*, but as I am not sure which two to combine, I have left it at 11. Maimonides seems to combine rules eight and nine (*Mishneh Torah*, "*Nizqei Mamon*" 5:3), but other options (like combining numbers two and three) seem reasonable as well. Alternatively, one could have been added later but, if so, I do not know which one.

627 This refers to the rabbinic rule that if one finds a dead body which nobody claims, such that it has no family burial plot, the body must be buried on the spot where it is found.

628 The exception is number six, which actually limits people's fishing and parking rights in public property, in this case a public body of water.

Why are these rules being imputed to Joshua of all people? I would suggest that the above *baraita* wishes to see the history of "Jewish" or "Israelite" Israel as having been a country of *nomos* (law) from the beginning. In an ordered, civilized country, ruled by law, these types of conflicts that feature the clash between the public and private domain need to be directed and contained by a cogent system of law. Assuming Israelite Israel was never a barbaric nation—leaving Judg 17–21 out of the equation—then such laws must have been implemented from the beginning. If so, the laws must have been implemented by Joshua himself after the conquest. It makes sense that such practical concerns would fit best in the post-conquest context, rather than in the wilderness period. That is how I understand the origin of the claim that Joshua made these laws; Joshua is the conqueror of the land in the Bible, and the rabbis make him the "rabbi of the land" as well. Thus, the rabbis successfully maintain Joshua's connection to the land but recast it in an image more resonant with their focus on halakha. Insofar as the origin of the laws themselves, they are probably reflective of actual or ideal practice as experienced or imagined by the author of the *baraita*.

Joshua the Writer of Liturgy

One major part of rabbinic practice is liturgy. This refers not only to the prayer service but also to the myriad of blessings—many about food—that the rabbis inherited or legislated as part of their religious behavior.

One of these blessings is imputed to Joshua by the Babylonian Talmud in chapter 7 of *Berakhot* (48b; MS Munich 95).

אמ[ר] רב נחמן: "משה תיקן ברכת הזן לישראל בשעה שירד להם מן, יהושע תקן[629] להם ברכת הארץ כיון שנכנסו לארץ, דוד ושלמה תקנו עד בונה ירושלים..."	Rav Naḥman said: "Moses established the blessing of '*ha-zan*' (He who sustains) for Israel when the manna began to fall. Joshua established for them the blessing of '*ha-aretz*' (the land) once they entered the land. David and Solomon established until '*boneh yerushalayim*' (builder of Jerusalem)..."

Rav Naḥman is discussing the set of blessings that are said after eating a meal containing bread. The reason he assumes/argues that the authors of these blessings were figures from such early antiquity—as opposed to most blessings, which are assumed to be from the Men of the Great Assembly (Ezra and his presumed

---

629 Unlike in the earlier source, this is the more standard verb for creating a new halakhic rule. The root has the connotation of "fix."

associates) and later—is that the Rabbis assume that saying the grace after meals is a biblical commandment, based on the verse in Deuteronomy (8:10) "you will eat, and be satiated, and praise YHWH your God." The rabbis give this phrase normative force, i.e., when you eat and are satiated, you must praise God. This praising of God is accomplished, according to the rabbis, by reciting the grace after meals.

The problem is that if the first three blessings of the grace after meals are Torah law, they should have been written by Moses. But the second blessing talks about the land of Israel, and the third about Jerusalem and the Temple— Moses could not have written blessings like this, and people could not have been saying them! Rav Naḥman solves this problem by arguing that the obligation to add the second and third blessing only kicked in when reality made it possible. Therefore, Joshua would have been the one to institute the second blessing about the land, since he was its conqueror. David would have written about Jerusalem and Solomon about the Temple.

With this explanation, it becomes clear why Joshua was chosen as author of the second blessing in the grace after meals. He was the earliest leader who would have had the opportunity to do so, and since it is a biblical commandment, he would have had no choice but to institute it as soon as possible. The Rabbis appear to be thinking of biblical figures in terms of practical rabbinic activity. Additionally, since, as argued above, Joshua is "the rabbi of the land," he would be the perfect person to write this blessing.

Excursus: Did Joshua write *Aleinu?*

One interesting, post-Talmudic, development is the popular claim that Joshua is the author of the *Aleinu* prayer. It was once thought that this tradition went all the way back to the Geonic period in Babylon, since it seems to be referenced by R. Hai Gaon in his commentary on the *Aleinu* prayer and in a responsum of his found in the *Sha'arei Teshuvah* (43). Nevertheless, modern scholarship has demonstrated that the commentary is a pseudonymous work (i.e. forgery) by Moses de Leon (c. 1250 – 1305), author/editor of the Zohar, a forgery pseudonymous work.

In addition to having authored the commentary in R. Hai Gaon's name, De Leon also seems to have added a line about Joshua's authorship into an authentic responsum of Hai Gaon in *Sha'arei Teshuvah* (43), a book De Leon is known to have "touched up."[630] The fact that the line is an addition is rather clear. I will indent the addition below and quote it in its present context.

ושישאלתם לענין עירובין וידים בשלמא שלמה המלך תקן עירובין וידים.	You asked about [the passage that claims that] Eruvin and hand washing were established by King Solomon. It is true that King Solomon established Eruvin and hand washing.
יהושע תקן עלינו לשבח ולאו הוא מתקנת רבנן אלא יהושע תקנו כשנכנסו ישראל לארץ שיאמרו זה התיקון להבדיל בין משפחות האדמה וגויי הארצות ושכבר קבלו עליהם אלוה ועל כך תקן לפני מלך מ״ה הקדוש ברוך הוא שמשתחוים מה שלא היו משתחוים בח״ל.	Joshua established *Aleinu le-Shabei'aḥ*, this was not a rabbinic enactment but Joshua established that when Israel entered the land they should say this *tiqqun* to divide between the families of the land and the nations of the earth, those who already accepted God upon themselves.[631] Therefore, [Joshua] established before the King of kings, the Holy One, bb"h, that they bow, since they did not bow outside the land.
אבל עירובין וידים שלמה המלך תקנם....	But Eruvin and hand[-washing] were established by King Solomon...

The questioners asked about the Talmud's attribution of the rules of *Eruv* and hand-washing to King Solomon (b. *Eruvin* 21b), and the bulk of R. Hai's responsum is aimed at explaining this passage. Out of nowhere, Hai throws in Joshua and Aleinu. Before and after this out-of-the-blue reference the same line is repeated. A better example of a *Wiederaufnahme* (resumptive repetition) masking a later insertion could hardly be envisioned.

Although De Leon is responsible for making the idea of Joshua as author of Aleinu look more antique than it really is, he is not responsible for inventing the idea in the first place. It would seem that this idea began among early Ashkenazic qabbalists and migrated to Spain, as did so many other qabbalistic speculations originating among the Ḥasidei Ashkenaz. A clear articulation of this tradition as it appeared among the Ḥasidei Ashkenaz can be found in the Siddur of R. Elazar of Worms (132, "*malkhiyot*"), one of the leaders of this movement.[632]

---

630 For more on De Leon's forging of these (and other) documents, see the article by Elliot Wolfson and the bibliography cited there; Elliot R. Wolfson, "Hai Gaon's Letter and Commentary on *Aleynu*: Further Evidence of Moses De Leon's Pseudepigraphic Activity," *JQR* 81.3–4 (1991): 365–410.

631 Another way to translate this line would be "already accepted a god upon themselves." The first translation assumes the referent is Israel and the second assumes it is gentiles.

632 The tradition can also be found in the *Sefer ha-Maḥkim*, the *Arugot ha-Bosem*, and the *Siddur Ḥasidei Ashkenaz* in their discussions of the *Aleinu* prayer.

ויהושע איש האלהים יסדו כשנכנס לארץ הקדושה, וראה
כי חוקות הגוים הבל הם ואלילים תהו בלא יוכלו להציל
עובדיהם, התחיל לפרוש כפיו השמימה וכרע על ברכיו
באימה, ואמ' בקול רם בניגון המשמח הלב לכוין עלינו
לשבח.

Joshua, the man of God, composed it when he entered the holy land and saw that all the statutes of the nations were nothing and their gods emptiness, unable to save their followers, he began to spread his hands heavenwards and kneeled upon his knees in awe, and called out in a loud but melodious voice that gladdened the heart the *Aleinu le-Shabei'aḥ*.

ומפני ענוותו הגדולה אשר היה בו, כאשר למד ממשה ענו
מכל האדם אשר יסד מזמור שיר ליום השבת משה, אך
"ליום" מפסיק פן יבינו מי עשאו, כך היה יהושע ענו,
ויסד עלינו לשבח בשמו הושע למפרע, עלינו לשבח,
שלא שם, ואנו כורעים, הוא אלהינו...

And because of his great humility, when he learned from Moses, the humblest of all humanity, who established (Psalm 90) *Mizmor Shir le-yom ḥa-Shabbat* [forming the acronym] Moshe, however "*le-yom*" separated [the words of the acronym] so that people would not know who it was, the humble Joshua followed suit, and established the *Aleinu le-Shabei'aḥ* with his [original] name (Hoshea) Hwš', but backwards. *'Aleinu le-shabei'aḥ..., še-lo sam..., we-annu kor'im..., ḥu eloheinu...*

From this presentation, one can understand how Joshua became associated with this prayer. The two main themes of the prayer are distinguishing between Israel and its God and the nations and their gods, and the future establishment of God's kingdom on earth, with all the nations bowing to God's will. In that sense, the prayer is a combination of implied piety with an undercurrent of violence. R. Elazar envisions Joshua having this very combination of feelings upon his crossing over into the Holy Land and encountering the native Canaanites. The forced name acronym is a standard feature of *Ḥasidei Ashkenaz* exegesis.

Joshua the Torah Scholar as a Heuristic Model

In Tosefta *Sanhedrin* (ch. 4), there is a discussion of the biblical requirement for the king of Israel to have his own Torah scroll. In halakha 8, R. Shimon ben Elazar offers a *derasha* on the term "*mishneh ha-Torah*" (Deut 17:18), in which he claims that this means that the king must have two Torah scrolls, one to be kept in his home and one for him to carry around everywhere.[633]

Having made this extreme demand on the king, the Tosefta ends this halakha with a moralistic lesson (4:8):

---

633 Except, the halakha states, to the bathroom or the public bath (the Rabbis don't miss these kinds of details.)

והלא דברים קל וחומר ומה אם מלך ישראל שלא עסק
אלא בצורכי ציבור נאמר בו והיתה עמו וקרא בו כל ימי
חייו שאר בני אדם על אחת כמה וכמה!

Cannot an *a fortiori* argument be made here? If regarding the king of Israel, who is busy serving the community, it is written "it should be with him and he should read from it all the days of his life" – would this not apply even more to the average person?!

In keeping with this theme, the next halakha (4:9) offers a similar moralistic lesson, but this time not from the passage about the king but from a passage about Joshua.

כיוצא בו אתה אום' ויהושע בן נון מלא רוח חכמה כי סמך
משה את ידיו עליו וגומ' וכן הוא אום' ומשרתו יהושע בן
נון נער לא ימוש מתוך האהל וכן הוא אום' לא ימוש ספר
התורה הזה מפיך שאר בני אדם על אחת כמה וכמה.

Similarly, you say (Deut 34:9): "And Joshua son of Nun was filled with the spirit of wisdom, for Moses had placed his hands upon him, etc." And it says (Exod 33:11): "but his attendant, Joshua son of Nun, the lad, would not step forth from the tent." And it says: (Josh 1:8): "Let this Torah scroll not leave your mouth." [If this advice is necessary for Joshua] – would it not apply even more to the average person?!

Joshua was a leader of the people, like the king. Furthermore, Joshua was a man of God—one who spent all his time in the Tabernacle and was granted the spirit of wisdom from Moses himself. Even so, God tells him that he must study the Torah day and night. The Tosefta's argument is that if such extreme devotion to Torah study was necessary for a great man like Joshua, how much more necessary must it be for the average person?

The above is a very light example of painting Joshua in rabbinic colors. The author(s)/editor(s) of the Tosefta already have the model of a Torah-studying leader from the biblical descriptions of the king and of Joshua. All they need to do is shine a little light on these examples to make them stand out a bit and receive some emphasis. The rabbinizing of Joshua in this context seems to have little to do with any interest in the character of Joshua, but exemplifies taking an opportunity to use any verse about Torah study in the Bible as a way of encouraging their readers to take this activity—so central to the Rabbis' own religious experience—that much more seriously. In other words, it isn't that there is something about Joshua that causes the rabbis to use him as an exemplar of Torah study; it is more about the verse itself.

This heuristic midrash appears to be representative of the early use of Rabbinic Joshua as it appears in one of the Tannaitic midrash collections as well,

Sifrei Numbers 141.[634] The midrash functions as a gloss on Numbers 27:23, which has Moses place his hands on Joshua in the first of the transfer-of-authority rites recorded in the Pentateuch.

The idea of Joshua the Torah scholar par excellence continues into the later midrashim as well. For example, in the Geonic collection *Pitron Torah* (*Parshat Elleh ha-Devarim*, pp. 233–234), the merit accrued to Joshua due to his constant Torah study is described.

ד[בר] א[חר]: באי זה זכות היה הק[דוש] עם יהושע כשם שהיה עם משה? שלא זז מן התורה כל ימיו שנ[אמר]: "לא ימוש ספר התורה וג'.". ומנין שהיה עמל בתורה? שנ[אמר]: "ומשרתו יהושע בן נון נ[ער] לא ימוש מ [תוך] האהל],", לפיכך כת[וב]: "ויהי ה' את יהושע."	Another matter: Due to what merit was the Holy One with Joshua the same as he was with Moses? Since [Joshua] did not stop learning Torah all his days, as it says (Josh 1:8): "Let not this Torah leave your lips, etc." How do we know he worked hard in his Torah study? As it says (Exod 33:11): "And his attendant Joshua, a lad, never left the tent," therefore, it says: "God was with Joshua."

Joshua here is held up as an example of what a success story a person can be if only he (the Torah student is virtually always male in rabbinic literature) were to study Torah all of his days.[635] Insofar as the mechanics of the *derasha* are concerned here, the first part of the derasha seems to add little to the simple mean-

---

634 It has been well established over the past century of rabbinic scholarship that the midrashei halakha are collections, probably from the early Amoraic period, which only collect statements of the Tannaim. The dating was argued by Jacob N. Epstein and is accepted by many leading scholars on midrash, like Menachem Kahana. The later dating of the work by Hanokh Albeck, who believed the collections to be post-Talmudic, has been rejected by most scholars, although there are some who still accept it, like Moshe David Herr (personal communication). For more on midrashei halakha and a fuller introduction to the various postions on how they work and when and how they were edited, see: Menachem Kahana, "The Halakhic Midrashim," in *The Literature of the Sages: Part 2* (ed. Shmuel Safrai, Zeev Safrai, Joshua Schwartz and Peter J. Thompson; Compendia Rerum Iudaicarum ad Novum Testamentum; Netherlands: Royal Van Gorcum and Fortress Press, 2006), 3–106.

635 A similar tradition can be found in the *Samaritan Book of Joshua* (ch. 24).

وكان يجتمع مع العزر فى كل جمعة يوما واحد, ومع أهل الرياضة يوما لمذاكرتهم, ومع الروسا يوما لتفقد احوالهم, وفى شغله هو يوما والنظر فى اموره, وثلث ايام لا يفارق كتاب الله ليل ونهر.	And he (Joshua) would get together with Elazar one day every week, and with people of training one day, in order to deliberate with them, and with the chiefs one day, in order to inspect their strength, and one day for his own job and consideration of his affairs, and for three days he would not leave the book of God night and day.

According to this tradition, Joshua spent three days of every week studying Torah.

ing of the verse, which says that God tells Joshua not to let the Torah leave his lips day and night and the rabbis say that this means he learned Torah all his days.

The second part seems more of a jump as the verse says he remained in the tent with God, and the rabbis say that he worked hard in his Torah study. The rabbis seem to imagine the tent as a sort of beit midrash.[636] The mechanics of this *derasha* are based upon a *gezeira shava*, in which the two verses make use of the same word, *yamush* (ימוש). Just as God told Joshua that the Torah should never "leave" his lips, so too when Joshua avoided "leaving" the tent, it means he didn't stop learning Torah.

Joshua as an Example of a Great Torah Scholar

In the Babylonian Talmud, there is an expression that appears once or twice (depending on the manuscript) which holds Joshua up as the paradigmatic example of a great Torah scholar. It appears as part of a *reductio ad absurdum* argument, in which the opponent says something along the lines of "I wouldn't agree with you even if Joshua son of Nun himself were to tell me you are right."[637]

The example that occurs in all manuscripts of the Babylonian Talmud appears in *Ḥullin* 124a. The pericope in the Talmud discusses a two part mishna. According to the rabbinic laws of impurity, an olive-size worth of impure animal flesh can communicate impurity. The first part of the mishna states that if one touches a string of flesh or a hair that protrudes from the flesh, even if that string (or hair) does not have an olive's worth of flesh but the piece of flesh it protrudes from does, the person or object touching this string can become impure.

The second part of the mishna records a debate about what kind of impurity a person can receive if he or she holds two pieces of impure flesh, each of which is half an olive size. All agree that the person cannot receive the impurity of

---

636 It is worth noting that the rabbis use the same imagery of tent as *beit midrash* in their exegesis of Jacob the "tent-dweller" (Gen 25:27). See, for example *Exod. Rab. 1.1* "*Shemot*" 1, which interprets this phrase as Jacob first learning all the Torah of his father, Isaac, and then going to learn in the tent *beit midrash* of [Shem and] Eber; the latter is the interpretation of Rashi as well. I assume the rabbis are picking up here on the plural *ohalim*, which requires them to find multiple *batei midrash* for Jacob to have studied in.

637 The phrase continues as an expression into the medieval period (at least amongst the Arabic-Jewish philosophers,) and is used by Avraham son of Maimonides in his "Essay on the Midrashim of the Sages" and by Yadiya Bedarshi (Ha-Penini) in his "Letter of Defense."

touching, but R. Ishmael believes the carrier can receive the impurity of carrying whereas R. Akiva believes the person cannot receive even this impurity.[638]

The Talmudic pericope deals with a controversial comment of R. Yoḥanan, and the question about how he meant it and regarding which part of the mishna did he mean it. The pericope begins by quoting R. Yoḥanan as a gloss on the first part of the mishna.[639]

א[מר] עולא א[מר] ר[בי] יוחנן: "לא שנו אלא שפלטתו
חיה אבל פלטתו סכין בטל.".

Ulla said in the name of R. Yoḥanan: "This was only taught if [the flesh] was cut by an animal, but if it was cut by a knife, there is no concern [that it communicates impurity.]"

א[מר] ליה] רב נחמן לעולא: "א[מר] ר[בי] יוחנן אפי[לו]
תרטא?" א[מר] לי[ה]: "אין." "ואפי[לו] כינפיא." א[מר]
לי[ה]: "אין." א[מר] לי[ה]: "האלהים! אפי[לו] אמרה ר
[בי] יוחנן לי מפומיה לא ציתנא ליה!"

Rav Naḥman said to Ulla: "Did R. Yoḥanan mean this even if [the flesh] was the size of a *tirṭa?*"[640] [Ulla] responded: "Yes." [Rav Naḥman continued]: "Even if it is the size of a sieve?" [Ulla] responded: "Yes." [Rav Naḥman] responded: "My God! Even if R. Yoḥanan said it to me himself I would not listen to him!"

כי סליק רב אושעיא אשכחיה לר[בי] אמי. אמרה לשמעת
[א] קמיה דר[בי] אמי. א[מר] לי[ה]: "הכי א[מר] עולא
והכי אהדר ליה רב נחמן. א[מר] לי[ה]: "ומשום דרב
נחמן חתניה דבי נשיאה הוא מזלזל בשמעתא דר[בי]
יוחנן!?"

When Rav Oshaya went up [to Israel], he met with R. Ami. He told [R. Ami] the entire conversation: "Ulla said such and such and Rav Naḥman responded such and such." [R. Ami] responded: "Just because Rav Naḥman married into the president's family, does he think he can speak disparagingly about a statement of R. Yoḥanan?!"

זמנין אשכחי[ה] וקא[מר] לה אסיפא...
א[מר] לי[ה]: "מר אסיפ[א] מתני לה? ואלא עולא אריש
[א] אמרה ניהליה!" א[מר] לי[ה]: "אין." א[מר] לי[ה]:
"אי אמרה יהוש[ע] בן נון מפומי[ה] לא ציתנא ליה."

Later on, [Rav Oshaya] met up [with R. Ami again,] and he was teaching [R. Yoḥanan's statement] as being a gloss on the second part of the mishna. [R. Oshaya] said to him: "Does the master understand this gloss as relating to the second half of mishna, where Ulla believed that it was stated as a gloss to the first part?" [R. Ami] replied: "Yes." [R. Oshaya] responded: "Even if Joshua son of Nun himself said this to me, I would not accept it!"

The anecdote is probably meant to be humorous. It begins with Rav Naḥman, the Babylonian sage, scandalously discarding a statement by R. Yoḥanan, the great-

---

638 Unless, as the mishna points out, the person sticks the two pieces together with a toothpick; in such a case R. Akiva would agree with R. Yishmael

639 The text below follows MS Munich 95.

640 Probably a standard slice of meat.

est of the Galilean sages, as interpreted by his colleague Ulla, claiming that he (Naḥman) wouldn't believe it even if R. Yoḥanan himself said it to him with his own mouth. The younger Rav Oshaya brings this tidbit to the great Galilean sage R. Ami, when he moves from Babylonia to the Galilee. R. Ami reacts with appropriate astonishment.

However, some time later, Rav Oshaya hears R. Ami's own interpretation of R. Yoḥanan's statement and quickly decides that this version of R. Yoḥanan, if correct, makes the statement even harder to believe than that of Ulla. At this point, history is replayed. Like Rav Naḥman, he questions R. Ami about how seriously he meant what he just said. After R. Ami confirms that he did indeed mean to say what Rav Oshaya thought that he did, Rav Oshaya responds with an even more bombastic reply than the scandalous one of Rav Naḥman. All Rav Naḥman meant to say was that he was so sure that what Ulla said was wrong that even if R. Yoḥanan were to come to Babylonia[641] and tell this to him in person, he would not accept it.

Rav Oshaya, however, ups the ante. He claims that R. Ami's interpretation of R. Yoḥanan is, in fact, so absurd, that even if the great leader and prophet, Joshua, himself were to come back from the dead and tell him that this statement was true, he (Oshaya) would discount it. A statement such as this, although obviously meant rhetorically, is a way of communicating that R. Ami's position is not just wrong, but is existentially impossible. I would guess that Joshua was chosen here because of his proximity to Moses. Most probably, it would have felt too "blasphemous" to say "even if Moses himself told me," so Oshaya picks the next best thing, Moses' protégé.

Although this does demonstrate that Joshua could be used as a type of Torah scholar *par excellence*, nevertheless, it says little about any rabbinic view of Joshua's character per se, or about any specific interest in promoting him as a central figure. The use seems to be nothing more than a ripple-effect from Moses to his student.[642]

A similar statement appears in the Jerusalem Talmud as well (*Yebamot* 4:11). The topic under discussion is whether, when figuring out the age of a fetus and its viability, months need to be complete in order to be counted.

---

641 And, most probably, back from the dead.
642 There may be another example of this usage of Joshua, in the third chapter of *Berakhot* (24b). As there are textual problems with this example, however, it would require too much technical discussion to go into here.

אמר רבי מנא: "שמעית בשם שמואל 'היא הכרת העובר
היא לידתו.' ולית אנא ידע מן מה שמעת." אמר ר' בא בר
כהן קומי רבי יוסי: "רבי ירמיה אמרה." אמר ליה רבי
חזקיה: "לא אמרה רבי ירמיה." ואיקפד רבי יוסי לקיבליי.
אמר ליה: "שכן אפילו יהושע שהיה קושר למשה לא אמר
כן ואת אומרת כן!" חזר ואמר: "אין דאמרה אלא כאינש
דשמע מילה ומקשי עליה."

Rabbi Maneh said: "I heard in the name of Samuel, '[When counting months], the same rule applies for when the fetus is formed as it does for when it is born (i.e., that the months must be complete).' But I don't remember from whom I heard this." Rabbi Ba bar Kohen said before Rabbi Yossi: "Rabbi Jeremiah said it." Rabbi Hezekiah said to him: "Rabbi Jeremiah did not say it." Rabbi Yossi was upset with him and said: "Even Joshua, who was tied to Moses (alternatively: who would tie things for Moses), would not have said such a thing, but you say such a thing?!" [Rabbi Hezekiah] replied: "I only meant it like a person who hears something surprising and pushes back."

In this story, Rabbi Ba bar Kohen claims that a certain legal position was taken by Rabbi Jeremiah and Rabbi Hezekiah blurts out that it isn't true. Their mutual teacher, Rabbi Yossi, rebukes Rabbi Hezekiah, pointing out that it is impossible to know that someone never said something. To illustrate his point, Rabbi Yossi uses the paradigmatic student as his example. Even Joshua, who was Moses' attendant and went everywhere with him, would not have the temerity to make such a claim.

The rhetorical force of using Joshua here is two-fold. First, the Torah praises Joshua's attachment to Moses, so he is a good example of the loyal and ever-present student. Second, Joshua is a great leader from the past; he is not only a great student but a great leader who was a student. Thus, if even Joshua would never have been bold enough to speak on his teacher's behalf, shouldn't someone like R. Hezekiah be even more careful and not make such sweeping claims? R. Hezekiah agrees and says that he wasn't taking a position, just giving mouth to his bewilderment at R. Jeremiah having taken such a position.

Joshua's Era as a Time of Great Torah Knowledge

Another way that the rabbis emphasize Joshua as a Torah scholar is by idealizing the era in which he lived as a time of great Torah knowledge. There is already some biblical precedent for this, since Neh 8:17 describes the Sukkot festival during the time of Joshua as the last time the people kept the holiday properly.

וַיַּעֲשׂוּ כָל־הַקָּהָל הַשָּׁבִים מִן־הַשְּׁבִי סֻכּוֹת וַיֵּשְׁבוּ בַסֻּכּוֹת כִּי
לֹא־עָשׂוּ מִימֵי יֵשׁוּעַ בִּן־נוּן כֵּן בְּנֵי יִשְׂרָאֵל עַד הַיּוֹם הַהוּא
וַתְּהִי שִׂמְחָה גְדוֹלָה מְאֹד.

And the assembly who returned from captivity built booths and dwelt in the booths, for the the Children of Israel had not done this from the days of Yeshua bin Nun until that very day, and there was exceedingly great rejoicing.

This text implies that proper Torah observance during the period of Joshua was at an all-time high. It is worth considering whether this verse is not merely a prooftext to the idea that Joshua's generation was a time of great Torah knowledge, but may even be one of the primary sources for it.

The example I found in Rabbinic literature for the notion of Joshua's era being a special time for Torah knowledge comes from b. *Shabbat* 104a.

אמרו ליה רבנן לר[בי] יהושע בן לוי: "אתו דרדקי האידנ
[א] לבי מדרשא ואמרו מילי דאפי[לו] בימי יהושע בן נון
לא איתמר כוותיהו...[643]"

The rabbis said to R. Yehoshua ben Levi: "School-children came to the *beit midrash*, and they said things [so fantastic] that even in the days of Joshua son of Nun nothing comparable had been stated..."

The content of what the schoolchildren said is not important for the purposes of this chapter.[644] The significant point is that when these rabbis wanted to give an example of the time period of ultimate Torah learning, they use the period of Joshua. Again, one would think that an even stronger example would have been the period of Moses. However, I would argue that Joshua is chosen instead of Moses for the same reason as he was in the examples from the previous section. Implying that these children knew Torah better than Moses may have felt too "blasphemous" even if it was only meant as an expression. Joshua is the closest example to Moses one can use without actually invoking the law-giver himself.[645] In a personal communication, William Gilders suggests a slightly different interpretation of why Joshua's generation was chosen. The time of Joshua is the period when the Torah given through Moses was first put into effect in the

---

643 The above text is from MS Oxford Opp. Add. Fol. 23; there are some slight differences between the manuscripts, but none that change the meaning or have any relevance to the point being made here.

644 They gave a midrashic interpretation of the alphabet, associating each letter with a word and even finding meaning in the shape of the letters.

645 Considering the above, the famous example from b. *Menaḥot* 29b, which implies that R. Akiva was greater even than Moses, must be seen as a radical exception, highlighting the significance of that particular piece of aggada, as well as the figure of R. Akiva in rabbinic mnemohistory.

Land. This interpretation ties in with an issue that will be taken up in the upcoming addendum: the rabbinic use of the "Age of Joshua."

Addendum: The Age of Joshua in Rabbinic Thinking

A more prevalent use of the "age of Joshua" in rabbinic discourse is to present the period of the conquest as the *sine qua non* of ancient times. This finds some expression in the list of rules Joshua enacted, discussed above, but is most prominent in the various laws surrounding walled cities.

The most well-known example of the walled city laws appears in the laws regarding the recitation of *Megillat Esther.* The rule is an outgrowth of a counterintuitive interpretation of chapter 9 in the book of Esther that describes the celebration of the Jews. In this section, the reader is told that whereas most Jewish communities completed their victories on the first day of the war, the 13th of Adar, and celebrated on the 14th of Adar, the Jews of Shushan took two days to complete their victory and celebrated on the 15th. At this point, Mordechai writes a letter to all the Jews (Esth 9: 20–22) asking them:

...לְקַיֵּם עֲלֵיהֶם לִהְיוֹת עֹשִׂים אֵת יוֹם אַרְבָּעָה עָשָׂר לְחֹדֶשׁ אֲדָר וְאֵת יוֹם חֲמִשָּׁה עָשָׂר בּוֹ בְּכָל שָׁנָה וְשָׁנָה. כַּיָּמִים אֲשֶׁר נָחוּ בָהֶם הַיְּהוּדִים מֵאוֹיְבֵיהֶם וְהַחֹדֶשׁ אֲשֶׁר נֶהְפַּךְ לָהֶם מִיָּגוֹן לְשִׂמְחָה וּמֵאֵבֶל לְיוֹם טוֹב לַעֲשׂוֹת אוֹתָם יְמֵי מִשְׁתֶּה וְשִׂמְחָה וּמִשְׁלֹחַ מָנוֹת אִישׁ לְרֵעֵהוּ וּמַתָּנוֹת לָאֶבְיוֹנִים.	...to promise to keep the 14th of the month of Adar and the 15th of the month of Adar each and every year. The same days that the Jews rested from their enemies and the month which was turned for them from sadness to happiness and from mourning to holiday – to make them days of feasting and happiness, sending foodstuff to friends and gifts to the poor.

Although a simple reading would suggest that Mordechai was declaring a two-day holiday for everyone, the rabbis assume that Mordechai's intent was that Purim should be celebrated for only one day but that some communities would celebrate on the 14th and some on the 15th. Part of the celebration of this holiday would be the reading of the *Megillah* itself, which is the context for the debate in the Tosefta (*Megillah* 1:1).

כרכים המוקפין חומה מימות יהושע בן נון קורין בחמשה Cities that were walled from the time of Joshua
עשר.[646] ר' יהושע בן קרח' אומ': "מימות אחשוורוש." son of Nun read on the 15th. R. Joshua ben
אמ' ר' יוסה בן יהודה: "היכן מצינו לשושן הבירה Qorḥa says: "From the time of Ahashuerosh."
שמוקפת חומ' מימות יהושע בן נון? אלא משפחה R. Yossa ben Yehudah said: "Where did we
ומשפחה מדינה ומדינה עיר ועיר הסמוכין לכרך ונראין hear that Susa the capital was walled from
עמו, הרי הן כיוצא בו." the time of Joshua son of Nun? Rather, 'each
family, each state, each city' (Esth 9:28) –
whatever is near a city and seen with it is considered part of it."

If one were to take the verse at its most literal, then only Jewish communities in Susa should celebrate on the 15th. The rabbis seem to believe that position to be a non-starter and assume that the rule must apply to cities like Susa in some respect. In that sense the second two positions seem to make more sense than the first. R. Joshua ben Qorḥa's position is that cities that were walled, like Susa, at the time the war was fought should celebrate the 15th. R. Yossa ben Yehudah, on the other hand, seems to believe that the matter should be determined anew in every generation. Whatever city is, in fact, walled, as Susa was back in the days of Ahashuerosh, should celebrate the 15th.

The oddest position is that of the unnamed first tanna—the position adopted by the Mishnah as well.[647] If one is going to choose a specific time in history by which to define cities, the position of R. Joshua ben Qorḥa seems the most intuitive, as he advocates for the time of the events being celebrated. The walled cities in the time of Joshua may not have even existed during the time of the battle over Susa almost a millennium later. This position is truly a conundrum. The best answer I can suggest is that the rabbis view history, and especially halakha, through the prism of their own narrative. In this narrative, a walled city from the time of Joshua is synonomous with "walled city" in general, its hoary antiquity being what gives the city its significance, not whether it happened to have a wall at some later date.

Furthermore, there is something essential to the midrashic approach in the idea of walled city being defined by Joshua's era. In Rabbinic literature, there is often the sense that a question is best answered from the master-context of Scripture as a whole. Hence, if one were to aske, "Where in Scripture are walled cities of special significance?" The answer would be, "In the book of Joshua."

---

646 This first line is the position taken in the Mishnah (m. *Megillah* 1:1).
647 In general, whether the Tosefta is best understood as quoting from the Mishnah and then adding alternative positions or whether the Mishnah lifts its lines from the Tosefta is a debate among modern scholars of rabbinic literature, and is of no real relevance to what is being discussed in this section.

Thus, Joshua's period defines "walled city" for other contexts in Scripture. Considering this, it may be more than just 'hoary antiquity' that is the issue, but the paradigmatic role of a Scriptural example in relation to other texts in Scripture.

The benchmark nature of Joshua's period of time in determining the status of a given city shows itself clearly in other halakhic passages as well. For example, in the Mishnah ('*Arakhin* 9:6–7), the issue of houses sold under duress is discussed; specifically, the distinction made in the Pentateuch (Lev 25:29–34) between urban houses and suburban houses.

עיר [שגנותיה] [648] חומתה ושאינה מוקפת חומה מימות יהושע בן נון אינה כבתי ערי חומה.	A city where the gardens are the wall and which was not walled from the time of Joshua son of Nun is not considered a house from a walled city.
ואילו הן בתי ערי חומה: שלש חצירות שלשני שני בתים מוקפות חומה מימות יהושע בן נון...	These are considered houses from a walled city: [Any city that has] three courtyards with two houses each and was walled from the time of Joshua son of Nun...
...ואלו הן בתי חצרים: שתי חצרות של שני שני בתים, אף על פי <ש>מוקפין חומה מימות יהושע בן נון, הרי אלו כבתי החצירים.	...And these are considered suburban houses: [Any city that has only] two courtyards with two houses each, even if it was walled from the time of Joshua son of Nun, these are considered suburban houses.

The interpretation offered by the Mishnah of what is considered urban and what suburban contains two very different factors. The first factor mentioned is the type of wall; this is to be expected. The second factor mentioned is the size of the city, how many courtyards it has and how big those courtyards are (i.e., they must serve at least two houses apiece). This factor is also to be expected. The third factor, however, seems unrelated; according to this mishna, the city must have been walled going back to the days of Joshua. Why this should be is not stated. As mentioned above, one can speculate that, similar to the Platonic view of the paradigmatic "real," the rabbis believe that a real city is a city conquered by Joshua and listed in the Bible.

In the *Sifra* (*Behar* 4.4), the rabbis attempt to derive this rule from the verses in Leviticus.

---

648 This is the reading of MS Kaufmann, in the standard printings the word is גגותיה, "its roves."

[יכול אפי'[לו] 'ואיש כי ימכור בית מושב עיר חומה' –   'If a man buys a dwelling place (lit. house of
עיר – 'בית מושב' ת"ל: הקיפוה חומה מיכן ולהבא?   settlement) in a walled city' – perhaps this
חומה המוקפת חומה מימות יהושע בן נון, ולא   would apply even if it is walled in some future
שהקיפוה מיכאן ולהבא...   period? The verse teaches us 'dwelling place' –
a city walled from the time of Joshua son of
Nun, not one that is walled in some future
date...

The nature of the midrash is difficult to ascertain. The Babylonian Talmud (b.
Megillah 3b) suggests that the phrase *"beit moshav"* implies that it was first
built and then inhabited. This would only have occurred at the time of Joshua,
who can be said to have killed all the original inhabitants and then settled
the Israelites in their cities. Again it would seem that the time of the conquest
functions for the rabbis as paradigmatic Israel, and that the above two laws
make use of this category of "real city" in order to determine the details of various halakhot in rabbinic times.

Insofar as the mechanics of the *derasha* here, William Gilders, in a personal
communication, suggests that the word *moshav* (dwelling or settlement) may
have been understood as a redundancy—a house (*bayit*) is by definition a dwelling. To explain the redundancy they argue that the new connotation of the word
"moshav" is the focus not on dwelling by on settlement. This would bring to
mind the age of Joshua, when Israel was first "settled." The verse would then
be teaching that a house in a walled city is only defined as such if it is in a
city that was "settled" in the time of "settlement," i.e., the time of Joshua.

Moses' Protégé

The most common image of Joshua in rabbinic literature is that of Moses' pupil.
That this would be the dominant image of Joshua is hardly surprising. The central feature of Rabbinic Judaism is halakha; with Moses as the law-giver, it would
be virtually impossible to have greater credentials as a "student of halakha" than
literally being the student of Moses—the ultimate halakhic authority.

The Model Student

In some texts, Joshua is treated as the paradigmatic good student. For example,
in *Abot de-Rabbi Nathan* (b, ch. 18), the following gloss is offered on Joshua ben
Peraḥiah's dictum that one should have a teacher.

דבר אחר: 'עשה לך רב' – לחכמה, זה יהושע בן נון,
שנאמר: 'ויהושע בן נון מלא רוח חכמה'.

Another matter: 'Get yourself a teacher' of wisdom, this is Joshua son of Nun, as it says (Deut 34:9): "And Joshua son of Nun was filled with the spirit of wisdom."

In this gloss, Joshua is the example of a student who found himself a teacher—the best teacher—and ended up a wise man. One can imagine that this example was intended to inspire young students to aim high; perhaps they could achieve wisdom like the great Joshua some day?

Joshua Degrades Himself in his Service to Moses

Certain midrashim, in order to emphasize the great respect Joshua showed Moses, actually picture Joshua degrading himself before his master. In *Midrash Tannaim* on Deuteronomy (34:9), the following midrash appears.

'[אוצר נחמד ושמן בנוה חכם] וכסיל אדם יבלענו' –זה
יהושע בן נון שעשה עצמו ככסיל לפני משה רבינו והיה
מטריח עליו ללמוד בכל שעה עד שלמד כל התורה כולה
ולכך זכה לשררות אחריו שנ אמר "וישמעו אליו בני
ישראל ויעשו."

'[Precious treasure remains in the house of the wise,] but the fool devours it' (Prov 21:20) – this is Joshua son of Nun who made himself into a fool before our master Moses, and would nag him to study [with him] all the time until he (Joshua) learned the entire Torah. Therefore, he merited to rule after him, as it says: "And the Children of Israel listened to him and followed [him]."

According to this midrash, Joshua, in order to get Moses to teach him as much Torah as possible, acts as if he doesn't understand anything. By doing this, Joshua forces Moses to study with him more—the verb (ט.ר.ח) actually means to bother or weary. The strategy is a successful one and brings Joshua great Torah knowledge so that he can legitimately follow Moses as the leader of Israel.

This same midrash appears in later collections in different forms. For example, in the Geonic quasi-mystical midrash collection called the *Alphabet of Rabbi Akiva* (Eisenstein, *Otzar ha-Midrashim*, 410), the midrash appears in much shorter form.

'[אוצר נחמד ושמן בנוה חכם] וכסיל אדם יבלענו' –זה
יהושע בן נון שעשה עצמו ככסיל אצל משה רבו.

'[Precious treasure remains in the house of the wise,] but the fool devours it' (Prov 21:20) – this is Joshua son of Nun who made himself into a fool when by his master Moses.

Shorn of the explanation offered in *Midrash Tannaim*, that Joshua was trying to get Moses to teach him more Torah, this is a rather shocking description of Joshua. Although one certainly imagines that he demonstrated respect for the great Moses, why would he treat himself like a fool? One could suggest that this midrash is just inexplicable shorthand for the midrash as it exists in the earlier version, or one could imagine that this was some sort of extreme demonstration of deference to Moses.[649]

Even odder is the version found in the medieval collection, *Yalqut Shim'oni* (Proverbs 959).

'אוצר נחמד ושמן בנוה חכם' – זה משה, 'וכסיל אדם	'Precious treasure remains in the house of the
יבלענו' – זה יהושע, שלא היה בן תורה והיו ישראל קורין	wise' – This is Moses; 'But the fool devours
אותו כסיל, ובשביל שהיה משרת משה זכה לירושתו	it' – This is Joshua, who was not learned in
שהיה מכבדו ופורס הסדין על הספסל ויושב תחת רגליו.	Torah and all of Israel used to call him 'fool.'
לפיכך אמר הקדוש ברוך הוא 'איני מקפח שכרך' ועליו	But since he was the attendant of Moses, he
נאמר, 'נוצר תאנה יאכל פריה'.	merited inheriting him, for he would give him
	(Moses) honor, and spread a cloth over
	[Moses'] bench and sit by his feet. Therefore,
	the Holy One bb"h said: "I will not make
	your reward little," and regarding him [scrip-
	ture] states (Prov 27:18): 'One who tends a
	fig-tree will eat of its fruit.'

According to this midrash, it wasn't that Joshua was faking his foolishness in order to learn Torah or to honor Moses in the comparison, but he actually began his career as an ignoramus, scorned by all Israel. But because he gave Moses such respect, he inherited the position, ostensibly learning the requisite Torah while seating at Moses' feet. This text is an extreme example of the importance of serving Torah scholars, a value referenced—not surprisingly—in a number of rabbinic texts.

The principle that serving a scholar is even greater than learning from one is found in what appears to be its most extreme form in a *Midrash/Pereq Tzedaqot* (1:6–7; Eisenstein, *Otzar ha-Midrashim*, 499).

---

649 Methodologically speaking, the former suggestion seems problematic, since there would be no way of knowing that this was the meaning if one hadn't already known the text from *Midrash Tannaim*.

ו) גדול שימוש תורה יותר מלימודה שכן מצינו ביהושע
שנאמר 'ויען יהושע בן נון', 'תלמידו של משה' אין כתיב
כאן 'אלא משרת משה'.

6) The service of Torah is greater than the learning of it. For we find with Joshua that [scripture] states, 'And Joshua son of Nun' – it doesn't say 'student of Moses' but rather 'attendant of Moses.'

ומה שירות היה משרתו, היה נוטל את הדלי ואת
הבלנרים ומוליכו לפניו לבית המרחץ.

With what service would he attend him? He would carry his bucket and his bathing equipment and carry them before [Moses] on his way to the bathhouse.

ז) ד[בר] א[חר]: 'משרת משה' – מה שירות היה משרתו?
היה משכים בכל יום ובורר את הגס הגס שבמן ואומר:
'זה לרבי משה זה לרבינו משה'.

7) Another matter: 'Attendant of Moses' – with what services would he attend him? He would wake up early every morning and choose the thickest pieces of manna and he would say: 'This is for my master, Moses, this is for our master Moses.'

In this source there is no discussion whatsoever of the Torah Joshua learned. Instead, this midrash sees Joshua's claim to prominence stemming from his extreme servility to Moses. Quite literally, Joshua would go out of his way to choose the best food for Moses—a difficult task considering that the only food available was manna—and would carry Moses' bathing equipment for him to the bathhouse.

The set of sources analyzed in this section seems to be in some tension with the sources that emphasize Joshua's prowess as a Torah scholar. Nevertheless, they do fit in with a different trend that will be explored in a later section, namely to increase the prowess of Moses at the expense of Joshua.

The Relationship between Moses and Joshua

One way the Rabbis describe the link between Moses and Joshua is to explain why Joshua was chosen. For example, *Sifrei Numbers* (140), commenting on Numbers 27:18, in which Moses is told by YHWH to choose Joshua as his successor, writes:

'קח לך' – את שבלבך. 'קח לך'. 'קח לך' – מה שבדוק לך, ועליו 'Take for yourself'[650] – he that is in your heart.
מפורש 'נוצר תאנה יאכל פריה [ושומר אדניו יכבד].' 'Take for yourself' – he that has been looked
over by you. Regarding this the verse states
(Prov 27:18): 'He who guards a fig tree will
get fruit, [and he who protects his master will
be honored.]'

According to this reading of the verse, God is telling Moses that he (Moses) already knows who is to be picked as his successor. It is the person that already waits in Moses' heart and the person over whom Moses has already looked and of whom he has already approved. This reading moves the choosing of Joshua from God to Moses, placing God in the capacity of *confirming* Moses' (unspoken) choice, whereas the simple meaning of the biblical verse implies that God chose Joshua directly and is informing Moses of the choice.

The midrash continues by offering a proof-text from a verse in Proverbs; this proof-text adds a different nuance to the reasoning behind Moses' preference for Joshua. The verse states that one who honors his teacher will receive honor in return. Moses has been honored by Joshua throughout the wilderness period; it is time for Joshua to receive the position of honor to which Moses can appoint him. Hence, Joshua was chosen as the next leader due to Moses' preferring Joshua and grooming him for leadership, which was, in turn, due to Joshua's respectful service to Moses throughout his (Moses') tenure as leader.

Another example of the midrash developing the image of Joshua as being groomed by Moses appears in the very next passage of *Sifrei Numbers* (141), commenting on Numbers 27:22.

ויקח את יהושע – לקחו בדברים והודיעו מתן שכר פרנסי He took Joshua – he took him with words, telling
ישראל לעולם הבא. him the reward granted to leaders of Israel
in the World to Come.
ויצוהו כאשר צוה ה' את משה – מה צוה הקדוש ברוך And he commanded him, as God commanded
הוא את משה בשמחה כך צוה משה ליהושע בשמחה Moses – just like the Holy One, bb"h, commanded Moses gladly, so too Moses commanded Joshua gladly.

Although the *darshan* here is aware that Moses was commanded to choose Joshua and groom him for leadership, he describes the carrying out of this command as being in line with Moses' own instincts. Just as God was happy with Moses, Moses was happy with Joshua. Furthermore, Moses finds himself in the position of feeling the need to coax Joshua, taking him aside and speaking to him about the glory and reward of service to the people. The placement of the two *derashot*

---

650 The midrash picks up here on the use of the ethical dative, which is why I am translating it.

one after the other, although required by the context, does paint a portrait of a fatherly older man with his arm around his young successor, expressing his feelings of contentment and satisfaction with who was chosen to succeed him and letting him in on the perks of the job.

The theme of Moses' warm feelings for Joshua comes up as well in the general context of how Moses treats Joshua. In the *Mekhilta de-Rabbi Ishmael* (*Parshat Be-Shalaḥ, Masekhta de-Amalek* 1), a gloss is offered on Exod 17:9, where Moses appoints Joshua head of the army defending Israel against Amalek.

ויאמר משה אל יהושע: "בחר לנו אנשים" – מכאן שהיה עושהו כמותו.	Moses said to Joshua: "Choose men for us" – From here we see that [Moses] treated [Joshua] as an equal.
ילמדו כל אדם דרך ארץ ממשה, שלא אמר ליהושע "בחר לי אנשים" אלא "בחר לנו אנשים" – עשאו כמותו. מכאן שיהא תלמיד חביב לפני רבו כמותו.	All people should learn proper etiquette from Moses, for he did not say to Joshua "choose men for me," but "choose men for us" – making him an equal. From here [we learn] that a student should be appreciated by his teacher as much [as the teacher appreciates] himself.

The *Mekhilta* makes use of the technique of interpreting ethical datives in a literal manner to make the point that Moses says "us" instead of "me." This is understood by the *darshan* to mean that Moses saw himself in partnership with Joshua, at least insofar as this war was concerned.[651] The author of this *derasha*, however, cannot believe that Moses really saw himself in partnership with Joshua. Therefore, he understands Moses' use of this expression as etiquette. Hence, the *Mekhilta* draws a general lesson from this speech about teacher-student relationships. If Moses, the greatest man in history, treated his student with such courtesy, should not all teachers do the same with their students?

This same understanding of the verse appears in *Abot de-Rabbi Nathan* (A, ch. 27), but with an added element of reciprocity.[652]

---

651 In truth, this is hardly a *derasha*, and may very possibly be the meaning of the ethical dative in this case. Either way, since the rabbis pick up on it, it can be fairly categorized as rabbinic exegesis, if not full-blown midrash.

652 In between the two *derashot* is one about treating one's fellow with honor, that features Aaron, but as this midrash is not relevant to this chapter, I omit it.

ומנין שכבוד רבו יהא חביב עליו ככבוד שמים? שנאמר: "ויען יהושע בן נון משרת משה מבחוריו ויאמר 'אדני משה כלאם.'" שקלו כנגד שכינה.

And how do you know that the honor of one's teacher should be to [the student] on par with the honor of heaven? For it says (Num. 11:28): "And Joshua son of Nun, Moses' attendant, from his young men, said: 'My Lord, Moses, lock them up!'" He treated him as equal to the Divine Presence.

The midrash here plays off the use of the term "lord" ('*dn*) for Moses. The same word is often used as a replacement for the Tetragrammaton. Although when referring to God, the vowels, as a rule, reflect a plural form instead of the singular form used here, nevertheless the use of the term in any form is sufficient for midrash, especially here since vowels are not reflected in the written text, and a vowel-adjustment is a standard midrashic technique.

By adding this *derasha* to the previous one about Moses treating Joshua with respect, *Abot de-Rabbi Nathan* creates a parity between teacher and student, where the teacher must treat the student with respect above his station (as if he were a teacher,) and the student must treat the teacher with respect above his station (as if he were divine.)

It appears to me that even though these *derashot* treat the behavior and relationship of Joshua and Moses, they really tell us very little about the Sages' view of the two characters. These verses were chosen because of their heuristic value and their usefulness to illustrate points of concern to the rabbis, all of whom needed to navigate this type of teacher student relationship. In fact, in the context of *Abot de-Rabbi Natan*, these stories were brought to illustrate the dictum of R. Elazar ben Shamua, who stated that "the honor of one's student should be as dear to you as your own honor, and the honor of your fellow as much as the honor of you teacher, and the honor of your teacher as the fear of heaven."[653] There is little one can say about Joshua here other than that the rabbis saw him as a loyal student who was well treated by his master Moses.

The reciprocity theme appears as well in the *Sifrei's* understanding of Numbers 11:28 – 29. In the story, Eldad and Medad are prophesying in the camp, and a young lad warns Moses of this. Joshua yells out that Eldad and Medad should be locked up, and Moses, in a fatherly manner, tells Joshua not to be jealous on his (Moses') account. In fact, Moses tells Joshua, he would be happy if all Israel were prophets. *Sifrei Numbers* (91) offers two glosses that play off the relationship between the two men.

---

653 רבי אליעזר בן שמוע אומר: "יהי כבוד תלמידך חביב עליך כשלך, וכבוד חבירך כמורא רבך, ומורא רבך כמורא שמים."

'ויָרץ הנער ויגד למשה' – יש אומרים זה יהושע. כענין 'And the lad ran and told Moses' – there are
שנאמר "ומשרתו יהושע בן נון נער." ר' שמעון אומר: those who say that this was Joshua. For it is
"הרי הוא אומר 'ויען יהושע בן נון משרת משה מבחוריו stated (Exod 33:11): "and his attendant, Josh-
ויאמר: "אדני משה כלאם!'"' הא לא היה ראשון יהושע." ua son of Nun, the lad." R. Shimon says:
"But it says [subsequently] 'and Joshua son of
Nun, attendant of Moses, from among his
young men, responded: "Moses, my master,
lock them up!"' So the first person could not
have been Joshua."

ויאמר לו משה: "המקנא אתה לי?'" – אמר לו: "יהושע, 'And Moses said to him: "Are you jealous on
בך אני מקנא, לואי אתה כיוצא בי ולואי כל ישראל כיוצא my behalf?'" – [Moses] said to him: "Joshua,
בך, ומי יתן כל עם ה' נביאים." I am jealous for you. Would that you could
turn out to be like me, and would that all of Is-
rael could be like you. If only someone would
make all God's nation into prophets!"

In the first gloss, although R. Shimon argues that it is an impossible reading of
the verse, a suggestion is put forward that the lad who ran to tell Moses about
Eldad and Medad was none other than Joshua himself. Although this reading
is certainly inspired by the use of the word lad (נער), a word used to describe
Joshua in a different section of the Pentateuch, nevertheless, the suggestion
does paint a portrait of Joshua in a panic running to inform Moses about what
seems to him to be competition.

In this context, the *Sifrei*'s treatment of Moses' fatherly response seems all
the more poignant. Moses tells Joshua that he has no reason to be jealous on
Moses' behalf. If anything, Moses confesses, he himself is jealous on Joshua's behalf. Like all "Jewish believers" who keep Torah, Moses knows that he is the
greatest man that will ever live. However, he tells Joshua, he finds little comfort
in this. In fact, he actively wishes that things were different and that Joshua
could become as great as Moses. Although he continues along this theme with
the wish that the people could be as great as Joshua, for the purposes of this
chapter, this statement of Moses both underlines the closeness of the two individuals, but, at the same time, the distance that will always remain between
them.

The strong bond between Moses and Joshua, touched upon in the previous
examples, is a theme that the rabbis make use of in other places as well. For example, the Jerusalem Talmud (j. *Yebamot* 4:11) uses Joshua as a paradigmatic example of a close student who, nevertheless, does not take liberties with his master.

The context of this comment is in the Jerusalem Talmud's discussion of the
rule recorded in the Mishna that a woman may not marry or separate from her
levir (her deceased husband's brother, whom she must marry if she and her hus-

band had no children) until three months after her husband's passing. The reason for this waiting period is in order to determine if she is pregnant, as a pregnant woman would not be eligible for levirate marriage. The Mishna continues by applying the waiting period for any second marriage, so that paternity can be established. This Mishna kicks off the Talmudic discussion to determine the point at which it is actually possible to see that a woman is pregnant (j. Yebamot 4:11):[654]

אמר רבי מנא: "שמעית בשם שמואל היא הכרת העובר היא לידתו, ולית אנא ידע מן מה שמעת." אמר רבי בא בר כהן קומי רבי יוסי: "רבי ירמיה אמרה." אמ' ליה רבי חזקיה: "לא אמרה רבי ירמיה." ואיקפד רבי יוסי לקיבליה. אמר ליה: "שכן אפילו יהושע שהיה קושר למשה לא אמר כן ואת אומרת כן!" חזר ואמר "אין דאמרה אלא באיניש דשמע מילה ומקשי עליה..."	R. Manneh said: "I heard in the name of Shmuel that the same method of counting months is used for recognizing a pregnancy and determining the possibility of live birth, but I don't know from whom I heard this." R. Ba bar Kohen said before R. Yossi: "It was R. Yermiya that said this." R. Ḥizqiya retorted: "R. Yermiya never said this." R. Yossi got angry at him. He said to him: "Even Joshua, who was very connected to Moses, never spoke this way, but you speak this way!" [R. Ḥizqiya] backtracked and said: "It is true that he said something like this, but only in the context of suggesting a possibility he was about to refute..."

In this anecdote, R. Ba bar Kohen relates that R. Yirmiya had been the author of a certain statement R. Yossi was trying to remember. At this point, R. Ḥizqiya, apparently a younger colleague or student, retorts that R. Yirmiya never said this, which brings the ire of R. Yossi to the fore. R. Yossi believes that it was inappropriate for the younger and outranked scholar to speak so dismissively to R. Ba bar Kohen. To illustrate, R. Yossi brings Joshua as his example. His point seems to be that although Joshua was a very close disciple of Moses, and a very great man in his own right, he never allowed either of these factors to get the better of him. There is no record, R. Yossi implies, of Joshua ever speaking to Moses with anything but reverence. This point causes R. Ḥizqiya to back down, and he stammers out a more respectful and more nuanced disagreement.

In this case, similar to what was seen in the Babylonian Talmud in the previous section, Joshua is being used as a typological example, this time of the

---

654 The fact that the rabbis of the Talmud don't take into consideration the fact that the woman knows much earlier, since her body changes and she stops menstruating, is not taken into account. This is part of the generally paternalistic nature of both Talmuds, in which women's knowledge is rarely (but not never) consulted or relied upon, even if the knowledge is firmly in her domain.

great student. As there was no greater student than Joshua, one should take his modesty and restraint as a guide. Significantly, in contrast to the use of Joshua in the Babylonian Talmud, in this example the focus is on Joshua and his character, as opposed to a back-door way of getting to Moses (as was seen in some examples above). It would be impossible to understand the above quip as focusing on Moses since the quip would make no sense. "Of course Joshua didn't talk back to Moses," R. Ḥizqiya could have retorted, "who would talk back to Moses? But (to paraphrase Lloyd Bentsen), R. Ba bar Kohen, you are no Moses." R. Yossi's point must be focused on the character of Joshua: "If Joshua, who was the greatest student did not act this way with his teacher, you, Ḥizqiya, certainly should not act that way with yours!"

King Joshua and King Moses

The question of whether Joshua should be seen as the first king of Israel or whether there is something essentially different in his rule from that of Saul is a question interpreters have grappled with from early times. As was seen in the chapter on Samaritan Joshua, the Samaritans understand him as the first king of Israel. In contrast, it seems that the biblical authors, although making use of some elements of kingship in the account of Joshua, attempt to guide the reader in the opposite direction.[655] This can be seen by the fact that Saul is listed as a king of Israel, and the language is even used by the Book of Judges in reference to Abimelech, but never by the book of Joshua about Joshua.[656]

This tension between Joshua's monarch-like power over Israel on one hand, and his official position as leader and conqueror but not king on the other, was picked up by the rabbis. Although not a dominant theme in rabbinic literature, as opposed to Samaritan literature, Joshua the King makes his appearance in midrash. Two clear examples of this come from different sections of the same passage in the *Mekhilta of Rabbi Ishmael* (*Parashat be-Shalaḥ, Masekhta de-Amalek* 2), commenting on Exod 17:14.

---

[655] This idea is explored in the second chapter of the book, which treats the early development of the character of Joshua as part of a diachronic study of his character in the Bible.

[656] Another argument, pointed out to me by my teacher and colleague, Jacob Wright, is that the laws in Deuteronomy discuss Israel looking for a king after the land was conquered, precluding the possibility that Joshua the conqueror was Joshua the king, and pushing for Saul and the account of his anointment as being the story of the coronation of the first Israelite monarch.

"ושים באזני יהושע' – "מגיד שאותו היום נמשח יהושע   'And place [it] in the ears of Joshua' – "this
דברי ר' יהושע.   teaches that on that day Joshua was anointed"
– the words of R. Joshua.

The interpretation of this passage offered by R. Joshua appears, at first, rather jarring. There is no mention or even hint in the passage itself about kingship. Nevertheless, R. Joshua's interpretation stems from a basic assumption that the leadership of Moses and Joshua was a type of kingship. He is not learning this from the verse, but assuming this as the basis for his interpretation. What he does learn from the verse is that if God tells Moses that the Amalek scroll should be read to Joshua, this means that Joshua was already understood to be Moses' successor. Hence, one can only assume, R. Joshua argues, that Joshua son of Nun was anointed as heir apparent already on that very day.

The assumption that Joshua was a king is tied in conceptually with the view that Moses was a king. This appears in midrashic form in connection with a number of verses in the Torah. The most important verse, perhaps the one that creates the midrashic paradigm for all the others, is Deut 33:5. A short example of this theme can be found in *Midrash Tannaim* ad loc.

ד]בר] א]חר[: "ויהי בישׁ]ורון[מלך" – זה משה רבינו.   Another matter – "there was a king in Jeshurun" – this is our teacher Moses.

Although other interpretations are offered—most significantly the understanding of king as a reference to God—since the verse says that there was a king in Jeshurun, and the Torah presents the poem as one recited by Moses, the rabbis believe that understanding the verse as referring to Moses to be the most reasonable. Since Moses was the sole leader of Israel throughout the wilderness period, to whom else could it refer?

Despite the inconsistent use of the king imagery for Moses in Rabbinic literature, it seems that the rabbis were aware enough of the midrashic gloss on Deut 33:5 to make it usable when a given exegete saw fit. This midrash is, most probably, also the origin for the idea that Joshua was a king. The logic is simple: If Moses was a king, and Joshua was his successor, then Joshua must have been a king as well.

We already saw, in the *Mekhilta of R. Ishmael* passage quoted above, that R. Joshua believes Joshua to have been anointed as king. This assumption continues into a later passage in this same section of the *Mekhilta*—one not attributed to any particular rabbi (*Parashat be-Shalaḥ, Masekhta de-Amalek* 2, on Exod 17:14):

מנין לכל הבקשות כולן שבקש משה לראות הראהו
הקדוש ברוך הוא?

From where does one learn that everything Moses requested to see was shown to him?

שנאמר: "ויראהו ה' את כל הארץ מן הגלעד עד דן" – זו
ארץ ישראל.

For it says (Deut 34:1): "And God showed him all the land, from Gilad to Dan" – this is the land of Israel.

בקש לראות בית המקדש והראהו, שנאמר: "את
הגלעד", "ואין גלעד אלא בית המקדש...

He asked to see the Temple, and it was shown to him, as it says: "and Gilead." Gilead refers to the Temple...

מנין שהראהו אף שמשון בן מנוח?... ומנין שהראהו
לברק?...

From where does one learn that [God] also showed him Samson son of Manoaḥ?... From where does one learn that [God] showed him Barak?...

ומנין שהראהו יהושע <u>במלכותו</u>? שנאמר: "ואת ארץ
אפרים", ולהלן הוא אומר: "למטה אפרים הושע בן נן."

From where does one learn that [God] showed him Joshua <u>in his kingship</u>? For it says: "And the land of Ephraim," and later it says (Num. 13:8): "From the tribe of Ephraim, Joshua son of Nun."

ומנין שהראהו גדעון,... ומנין שהראהו דוד <u>במלכותו</u>?...

From where does one learn that [God] showed him Gideon?... From where does one learn that [God] showed him David <u>in his kingship</u>?...

The *Mekhilta* here offers a midrashic expansion of the people and places Moses was permitted or granted to see by God before his death. The list assumes that Moses was granted sight into the future, not just into the land as it stood during his lifetime. The list of people quoted in this midrash is somewhat random, since it is tied to whatever hermeneutic associations the rabbis could build on the verses in Deuteronomy 34. Nevertheless, one element of the hermeneutic is significant, which is that Joshua is referred to as having been a king.

Joshua's kingship is not what one would have expected Moses to be seeing. Insofar as the simple outline of biblical history, what Joshua accomplishes is the conquest of the land. This, in fact, is what Moses merits seeing in other versions of the above midrash. For example, in *Sifrei Deuteronomy* (*Ve-Zot ha-Brakha*, 357),[657] the following similar midrash is recorded:

---

657 An almost identical midrash is included in the *Midrash Tannaim* to Deuteronomy ad loc.

'ואת ארץ אפרים' – מלמד שהראהו ארץ אפרים יושבת
על שלותה, וחזר והראהו מציקים המחזיקים בה. דבר
אחר: 'ואת ארץ אפרים' – מלמד שהראהו יהושע בן
נון עושה מלחמה בכנענים, נאמר כאן: 'ואת ארץ
אפרים' ונאמר להלן 'למטה אפרים הושע בן נון'.

'And the land of Ephraim' – this teaches that [God] showed him the land of Ephraim sitting in tranquility, and then he showed him the tormentors that took it over. A different interpretation: 'And the land of Ephraim' – this teaches that [God] showed him Joshua son of Nun <u>making war against the Canaanites</u>. For it says here: "And the land of Ephraim," and later it says (Num. 13:8): "From the tribe of Ephraim, Joshua son of Nun."

The reading of the *Sifrei* seems more in line with what one would have expected, since it reflects what there is "to see" about Joshua in his biblical role. This highlights the significance of the *Mekhilta's* suggestion that Moses wants to see King Joshua. The uniqueness of the *Mekhilta's* midrash can be seen by looking at another parallel, this time from the sister work on Exodus, the *Mekhilta of R. Shimon bar Yoḥai* (*Rashbi*) on the same passage (Exod 17:14).

...ומנ' שהראהו יהושע בן נון? שנ[א]מר]: "ואת ארץ
אפרים", ואו[מר]: "למ[ט]ה אפרים הושע בן נון".

... From where does one learn that [God] showed him Joshua son of Nun? For it says: "And the land of Ephraim," and it says (Num 13:8): "From the tribe of Ephraim, Joshua son of Nun."

Considering this text, what stands out the most about the *Mekhilta of R. Ishmael* text is not simply its reference to Joshua as king, but that he is the only leader referred to this way other than David.[658] This is important, as it demonstrates that Joshua's position is unique among the "judges" and was more akin to how the rabbis viewed Moses, than how they viewed Gideon or Samson. Again, this should be seen as distinct from the way the Samaritans eventually approach the question, making Joshua the first king, but assuming the founding of a continuous monarchy from that point forward.[659]

Joshua as a Powerful Personality

One image of Joshua that does not focus on his relationship with Moses or his status as Moses' successor is the description of Joshua as a strong person. Since Joshua in the biblical accounts is described as a warrior and conqueror,

---

658 The *Mekhilta of Rashbi*, understandably, does refer to David as the king.
659 See chapter four of this book on Samaritan Joshua for more details.

the imagery of Joshua as tough is hardly surprising. In fact, these midrashim stay relatively close to the texts they interpret.

The idea that Joshua had a strong personality is stated almost explicitly in *Sifrei Numbers* (Pinḥas, 140) in a gloss on Num 27:18, where Moses is told to appoint Joshua as his successor.

'איש אשר רוח בו' – שיכול להלוך כנגד רוחו של כל אחד 'A man with spirit in him' – He can stand
ואחד. against the spirits of everyone else.

This midrash focuses on Joshua being strong-willed. The power of his spirit lies in the fact that his will cannot be overcome by any amount of pressure from the collective wills of others. One would imagine that the scout account, in which Joshua and Caleb stand against all of Israel, may have played a part in informing this view of Joshua.

Another example, also from *Sifrei Numbers* (Be-ha'alotkha, 96) is a gloss on Num. 11:28, in which Joshua reacts to the information that Eldad and Medad are prophesying in the camp by blurting out that Moses should restrain them.

'אדני משה כלאם' – אמר לו: "רבוני משה כלם מן העולם 'My master, Moses, *kal'a* them' – [Joshua] said
לבני אדם שבשרוני בשורה רעה זו." to him: "My teacher, Moses, eliminate (*kala*) them from the world, these men who have brought me such disturbing news."
ד[בר] א[חר]: "אוסרם בזיקים ובקולרות, כמה שנאמ[ר]: Another interpretation: "Tie them up with
ונתתם אותו אל בית הכלא'." ropes and chains, as it says (Jer 37:18): 'And they placed him in the prison (*kele*').'"

The inspirations for these glosses seem to have been Joshua's forceful outburst as well as Moses' calm dismissal of his attendant's fears. Clearly, Joshua wanted to do something bad to Eldad and Medad and Moses had to allay his concerns, but the exact meaning of k-l-' is unclear. The first suggestion interprets it as being related to k-l-y/h,[660] a root which means destruction. Although the interpretation seems forced—the third letter of the root is not a *yod* but an *aleph*—the hermeneutic attractiveness of it is that it takes Joshua's reaction to its most extreme. Joshua actually wants to execute Eldad and Medad for prophesying on Moses' turf. In this reading, Joshua is the ultimate hot-headed young loyalist.

The second interpretation follows the simple meaning of the text. Joshua does, apparently, wish to restrain Eldad and Medad in some way. However, even this interpreter adds a little color to the story by imagining that Joshua spe-

---

660 I prefer to use *yod* instead of *hey* for third-weak roots in which the letter *hey* functions purely as a place-holder for the *yod* that has fallen off.

cifically suggested tying them up or putting them in chains. Although this would be meant to accomplish the same thing as a prison cell—removing the presumptuous prophets from the population that might listen to them—the stark imagery of the two men in chains adds some punch to the suggestion.

The imagery of Joshua's aggressive impulses also receives midrashic extension in the *Mekhilta of R. Ishmael*'s gloss on Exod 17:13 (*Be-Shalaḥ, Masekhta de-Amalek* 1), which reports that Joshua weakened the Amalekite enemies.

׳ויחלוש יהושע את עמלק ואת עמוׂ.ׂ – רבי יהושע אומר:	'And Joshua weakened Amalek and his people'
׳ירד וחתך ראשי גבורין שעמו העומדים בשורות המלחמה.ׂ	– R. Joshua says: "He went down and chopped off the heads of the powerful warriors that were standing with him on the lines of battle."
ר׳ אלעזר המודעי אומר: ׳בו לשון נוטריקון ויחל ויזע וישבר.ׂ	R. Elazar of Modin says: "It is an acronym for 'and he began, and he tore, and he broke.'"

The impetus for both comments here is the unusual word *ḥ-l-š*, which means weaken. Why does it say that Joshua weakened Amalek, and not that he killed them or vanquished them? R. Joshua suggests that Joshua did not destroy the enemy army but thinned out their ranks by killing their most powerful warriors. R. Joshua is possibly inspired here by the account of David and Moab in 2 Sam 8:2 where David thins out the ranks of the Moabites, either by killing two out of three warriors or by killing the largest ones (depending on how one understands the phrase "two rope lengths to kill.") He may also have been inspired by the fact that according to Joshua 11:21–22, Joshua was a giant killer (also like David.) However R. Joshua derived this, the effect of the gloss is to paint Joshua as both physically powerful, and ruthlessly strategic.

R. Elazar of Modin's interpretation keeps Joshua in battle-mode (as opposed to R. Joshua's suggestion of targeted killings,) but understands the term *ḥ-l-š* as a *noṭriqon*, a type of rabbinic acronym. He makes it stand for three words – and he began'*va-yeḥal*', and he tore '*va-yiḇza*'' and he broke '*va-yiš̌bor*'. Even as a *noṭriqon*, this seems forced. The second word, the most graphic of the three, does not contain any letters from the desired root. The first two letters of the root (*ḥ* and *l*) are in the unnecessary (in this context) verb '*va-yeḥal*,' to begin. Only the verb *va-yiš̌bor*, to break, both illustrates Joshua's successful campaign and contains a letter (*š̌*) from the root in question. Perhaps the forced nature of the midrash points strongly towards R. Elazar of Modin's desire to paint Joshua as a brutally successful conqueror. Apparently, the idea of Joshua simply weakening the enemy doesn't do the great warrior justice.

Interestingly, in a later part of the *Mekhilta of R. Ishmael*'s analysis of this same verse, the reader is treated to the merciful side of Joshua (*Parashat be-Shalaḥ, Masekhta de-Amalek* 1, on Exod 17:13):

לפי חרב' – רבי יהושע אומר: "לא נוולם אלא דנם   'To the sword' – R. Joshua says: "He did not
ברחמים."   desecrate their bodies, but judged them with
   mercy."

Understanding the phrase about putting one's enemies to the sword as a sign of
mercy is a difficult feat. However, R. Joshua's point is not that Joshua let his enemies live –he did not– but rather that he forbade his army to destroy or otherwise humiliate the bodies of the fallen Amalekites. Instead, R. Joshua dealt mer-
cifully with them; ostensibly this would mean that he buried them.

Inspiration for this idea may have come from Joshua 10:26 – 27, in which
Joshua, having hung the enemy kings as a symbol of their defeat, takes them
down in the evening and places their bodies in a cave. In this sense, Joshua
has respected the bodies of his enemies, by not allowing them to decompose
publicly. In addition, he has followed the laws of the Torah of Moses, which explicitly forbids leaving a hung body out past the evening, since "קְלְלַת אֱלֹהִים תָּלוּי,"
a hanging body is a curse to God (Deut 21:23).

Joshua in the Eyes of the Enemy

One particularly unusual midrashic invocation of Joshua as a powerful or aggressive military personality is found in *Midrash Abba Gurion* 3 (*Sifrei de-Agga-
deta al Esther*, Buber ed.). The context of this midrash is the reading of the history book to Ahashverosh, in which he learns the details about Israelite/Jewish
history and how aggressive and bloodthirsty the Jews "really were" (in the estimation of his advisors.) The relevant passage describes the defeat of Amalek
(Haman's ancestors) by Moses and Joshua. According to this version of the
story, the Amalekites attack Israel after consulting with the wicked prophet Balaam.

מה עשה אותו משה? היה לו תלמיד אחד, ושמו יהושע בן   What did Moses do? He had one student, Josh-
נון, אכזרי בלא רחמנות, ואמר לו משה: "בחר לנו   ua son of Nun was his name, a cruel person
אנשים." איני יודע אם בכשפים בא עליהם, מה עשה   with no mercy. Moses said to him: "Choose
משה? נטל אבן וישב עליה, ואיני יודע מה היה לוחש עד   for us men." (Exod 17:9). I do not know if he
שרפו ידיהם של עם עמלק ונפלו לפניהם הרוגים, שנאמר   (Joshua?) came at them with witchcraft. What
"ויחלוש יהושע את עמלק."   did Moses do? He picked up a stone and sat
   upon it, and I do not know what (magic incan-
   tation) he whispered until the hands of the
   Amalekites grew weak and they fell before
   them (the Israelites) dead, for it says, "Joshua
   weakened Amalek."

באו לארץ סיחון, גבורי עולם היו, ואיני יודע במה הרגום,   They came to the land of Sihon, and these
באו למלכי מדין, אף אותם איבדום.   where great warriors of old. I do not know how they killed them. They came to the kings of Midian and destroyed them as well.

מה עשה תלמיד של משה שהכניסם לארץ ז' עממים,   What did the student of Moses do? He brought
איבדם מן העולם ונטל ארצם מידם, ואיבד ל"א מלכים   [the Israelites] into the land of the seven na-
ולא ריחמן.   tions and removed them from this world and took their land from them. He destroyed thir-ty-one kings and had no mercy upon them.

The description of Joshua from the vantage point of the enemy has an almost comical effect. The idea that Joshua was a monster, Moses an evil wizard, and the Amalekites, Amorites, and Canaanites people to be pitied, would probably strike the average reader of Rabbinic texts as comic relief. However, the descrip-tion does pick up on a reality of the biblical description of Joshua. He annihilat-ed all of his enemies without mercy.[661]

Joshua as a Great Man among Great Men

In certain places, the rabbis speak of Joshua simply as one of the great iconic figures of the past. The strongest statement to this effect comes from the *Mekhilta of R. Ishmael* (*Be-Shalaḥ, Masekhta de-Va-Yissa* 3), where, while discussing the manna, a gloss on Psalms 78:25 is offered.

'אכל איש צדה שלח להם לשובע' – זה יהושע בן נון   ''yš (a man) ate his portion, He (God) sent them
שירד לו מן כנגד כל ישראל.   (manna) for sustenance' – this ['yš] is Joshua son of Nun, on whose behalf the manna fell as it did for all of Israel.

The *darshan* picks up on the fact that the first part of the verse has the singular "man" but the second half has the plural "them." Although the simple meaning of man is "each man," the *darshan* interprets the term to be a reference to one man. Surprisingly, instead of picking Moses as this man, he picks Joshua. The message of the midrash is that a righteous person like Joshua had merit equal to the entire nation of Israel, and the manna would have fallen just for him if need be.

The midrashic maneuver of making one righteous man equal to the entire nation is not unique here, but is also used in a different place for—not surpris-

---

661 Although this may not have brought out serious moral qualms in the ancient reader, it is this aspect of Joshua that makes the study of his book so challenging for modern readers.

ingly—Moses. For example, in *Mekhilta of Rashbi* (15:13), the following midrash appears.

וכבר היה ר[בי] יושב ודורש שילדה אשה מיש[ראל] רבוא | Rabbi was sitting and offering the *derasha* that
ששים בכרס אחת, ונענו תלמידיו באותה השעה ואמרו: | an Israelite woman once gave birth to 600,000
"מי גדול צדיק או כל אדם?" אמ[ר] להן: "צדיק." | from one womb. His students had asked him at
אמרו לו: "במה?" אמ[ר] להן: "מצינו שילדה יוכבד | that time, saying: "Who is greater, one right-
אמו של משה את משה ששקול כנגד כל יש[ראל], וכן | eous person or all of [the rest of] humanity?"
מצינו שהיה משה שקול בכל יש[ראל]? בשעה שאמ[רו] | He said to them: "The righteous person."
שירה, שנא[מר]: 'אז ישיר משה ובני יש[ראל].' | They said to him: "How do you know?" He
said to them: "We see that Jochebed, the moth-
er of Moses, gave birth to Moses who was compared to all of Israel." Where do we find Moses
compared to all of Israel? At the time they sang
the song, as it says (Exod 15:1): 'then Moses
and all of Israel sang.'

This midrash comparing Moses to the people of Israel, although written in a somewhat playful tone, with its reference to a woman with 600,000 children in her uterus,[662] is actually less surprising than the midrash about Joshua cited above. There is almost no compliment too great for Moses in the mind of the rabbis, but placing Joshua on this pedestal is unusual. Perhaps, again, we are encountering the phenomenon of Moses' greatness (or spirit) rubbing off on his student, Joshua.[663]

Another place where Joshua seems to be placed on an extreme pedestal of greatness comes from the discussion of the students of Hillel in *Abot de-Rabbi Nathan* (b, ch. 28).

שמונים זוגות של תלמידים היו לו להלל הזקן. שלשים | Hillel the elder had eighty pairs of students.
מהם היו ראוים שתשרה עליהם שכינה. ושלשים מהם | Thirty of them were fit to have the divine pres-
היו ראוין שתעמוד להם חמה כיהושע בן נן. ועשרים | ence alight upon them. Thirty of them were
מהם בינונים. | worthy of having the sun stop on their behalf
like Joshua son of Nun. Twenty of them were
just average.

---

662 R. Shlomo Ben Aderet (Rashba), in his book on Aggadah, commenting on the version of this midrash that appears in *Song of Songs Rabbah*, believes the introduction to be a joke, meant purely for entertainment or to wake up dozing students.

663 It is possible that this line of thought, that a great person is equal to all of the average people, may be inspired by the rhetoric of Saul about himself and his son Jonathan in 1 Sam 14:40. The rabbis use this kind of rhetoric as well in comparing members of their own ranks. See, for example, the statements about the relative greatness of R. Eliezer ben Hyrkanus and R. Elazar ben Arakh in m. *Abot* 2:8.

The hyperbole surrounding the greatness of Hillel's students is clear. The three categories of students are interesting. The members of the second group, of interest in this chapter, are said to have been so great that they would have been worthy, like Joshua, to stop the sun. Perhaps Joshua is being used here, not due to something about him per se, but due to the impressiveness of the miracle. There is another possibility, however.

It is possible that the members of the first group, who were worthy to be visited by the divine presence, are being compared to Moses himself. As a comparison to Moses would be pushing the boundaries, perhaps the implication was being made, but without using his name. If this is true, it may be that if the first group were like Moses, then the natural choice for comparison with the group which was slightly less great than the first would be Joshua, the student of Moses, who was himself slightly less great than his master. It is difficult to know which of the two interpretations best explains the use of Joshua in this context; perhaps it was a combination of both factors.

Although the above are examples of the rabbis praising Joshua on his own, usually praise of Joshua is found in the context of comparing biblical heroes or just listing great heroes who share a certain characteristic.[664] For example, in the Bible Joshua is often found alongside Elazar. In *Sifrei Numbers* (*Pinḥas* 141), commenting on the ceremony where Joshua will stand before Elazar the priest to receive his commission (Num 27:21), the midrash discusses the relationship between the two men.

ולפני אלעזר הכהן יעמוד, שהיה יהושע צריך לאלעזר He will stand before Elazar the priest – for Josh-
ואלעזר צריך ליהושע. ua needed Elazar and Elazar needed Joshua.

According *Sifrei Numbers*, Joshua and Elazar are in a symbiotic relationship. This interpretation seems to be a way to solve the tension regarding the power dynamics between these two characters. In certain places Joshua is painted as being clearly in charge, in other cases the command seems joint, and in some places Elazar even seems to be on top. The verse being glossed here in Numbers is an example where Joshua must stand before Elazar, perhaps implying the more significant status of the high priest to the military leader. Therefore, the sages jump in at this spot to clarify that even if Joshua here needs Elazar for

---

664 This latter strategy is extremely reminiscent of what the church father Aphrahat does in his *Demonstrations*; see the chapter on Joshua in the Church Fathers for more discussion.

his swearing-in ceremony, Elazar will need Joshua as well—a symbiotic relationship.[665]

Another biblical character with whom Joshua has an ambiguous relationship is Caleb. Although Joshua becomes the leader of Israel, his early rise is tied in with that of Caleb in the scout story. If anything, Caleb comes off better in that account for two reasons. First, Joshua was already Moses' attendant so proper behavior was expected of him. Second, the first reaction is Caleb's alone; Joshua only joins in later. Considering the problematic nature of claiming Caleb to have been greater than Joshua, the *Mekhilta of R. Ishmael* (*Parshat Bo, Masekhta de-Pasha* 1) jumps into the fray.

כיוצא בדבר אתה אומר: "ויהושע בן נון וכלב בן יפונה	Similarly, you say (Num 14:6): "Joshua son of
וג'." – שומעני כל הקודם במקרא הוא קודם במעשה?	Nun and Caleb son of Jephuneh." I may have
ת[למוד] ל[ומר]: 'זולתי כלב בן יפונה ויהושע בן נון' –	thought that whoever is mentioned first in
מגיד ששנ' שקולים כאחת.	scripture is the more impressive one in his
	deeds? [Therefore, another verse] comes to
	teach (Num 32:12): "Except for Caleb son of Je-
	phuneh and Joshua son of Nun." This tells us
	that they were equal to each other.

In this example, point out that the order of the names of the two characters are reversed in two different verses, the midrash draws a lesson from the Torah about the behavior of the two characters. The two men were equal in their opposition to the corrupt scouts and the panicking people; there is no reason to believe one was superior to the other.[666]

One example of Joshua being compared favorably with another biblical character occurs in *Numbers Rabbah* (*Parshat Bemidbar* 1) which compares Joshua favorably with Saul.

---

665 See the chapter on the Samaritan book of Joshua for another way of dealing with this tension.

666 One can see the strategy employed by the midrash here to be a kind of smoke and mirrors. The reason one would suspect that Caleb was being presented as the more impressive scout is because he speaks first, not because his name is listed first. By drawing the reader's attention to the latter "problem," his or her attention is drawn away from the former, more serious problem.

את מוצא כל מי שנדבק בדבר המקום אהבו לעולם שכן
אתה מוצא ביהושע שנדבק בעמלק ועשה בו כתורה
שנאמר: "ויחלש יהושע וגו'." אמר לו המקום:
"משבטך אני מעמיד פורע לעמלק לעולם," 'מני אפרים
שרשם בעמלק,' שאול שנדבק ולא נמצא נאה בפיקודו
אלא 'ויחמל שאול והעם' החזירו לאחריו וניטלה הימנו
מלכותו.

You find that anyone who clings to a matter the Omnipresent loves forever. For you find by Joshua that he clung to Amalek and accomplished that which he was commanded to, as it says (Exod 17:13): "And Joshua weakened [Amalek] etc." The Omnipresent said to him: "I will raise an avenger from your tribe against Amalek forever," [as it says] (Judg 5:14): 'From Ephraim whose roots are in Amalek.' Saul, who clung but did not implement the command well, but instead 'Saul and the nation had compassion' (1 Sam 15:9), [God] pushed him back and the kingship was taken from him.

The actual details of the midrash are very difficult to understand. It is unclear how the author is using the word cling (נדבק) or what/who his referent is when he describes a future avenger from Ephraim. However, one matter is clear. The *darshan* compares Joshua's success against Amalek, as evidenced by God's glowing remarks about Joshua after the battle, and Saul's perceived failure, which led to his family being removed from the throne. The *darshan* is picking up on a biblical theme that I outlined in chapter 2: Joshua as a northern, non-royal alternative to the southern first king of Israel, Saul. Where Saul failed, Joshua succeeded.

Joshua also appears in midrashic lists of great people. These lists are generally centered on some special term used for only some people in a biblical verse and noticed by the *darshan*. Two examples, both from *Abot de-Rabbi Nathan* (b, ch. 43), include Joshua in the list.

The first example focuses on the term עבד ('*bd*), meaning slave or servant.

[שמנה עשר] אלו נקראו עבדים.

These [eighteen] were called servants.

אברהם נקרא עבד שנאמר: 'והרביתי את זרעך בעבור אברהם עבדי.'	א.	1. Abraham was called servant, as it says (Gen 26:24): 'And I will increase your seed on account of Abraham my servant.'
יעקב נקרא עבד שנאמר: 'ואתה אל תירא עבדי יעקב.'	ב.	2. Jacob was called servant, as it says (Isa 44:2): 'And you, my servant Jacob, do not fear.'
ישראל נקראו עבדים שנאמר: 'כי לי בני ישראל עבדים.'	ג.	3. The Israelites were called servants, as it says (Lev 25:55): 'For the Israelites are my servants.'
משיח נקרא עבד שנאמר: 'הן עבדי אתמך בו.'	ד.	4. The messiah was called servant, as it says (Isa 42:1): 'Here is my servant whom I uphold.'
מלאכים נקראו עבדים שנאמר: 'הן בעבדיו לא יאמין.'	ה.	5. The angels were called servants, as it says (Job 4:18): 'He doesn't even have faith in his servants.'
משה נקרא עבד שנאמר: 'לא כן עבדי משה.'	ו.	6. Moses was called servant, as it says (Num 12:7): "My servant, Moses, is not like that.'

יהושע נקרא עבד [שנאמר: 'וימת יהושע בן נון עבד ה'.'	ז. 7.	Joshua was called servant, [as it says: 'And Joshua son of Nun, servant of God, died.'
כלב נקרא עבד] שנאמר: 'ועבדי כלב עקב היתה.'	ח. 8.	Caleb was called servant,] as it says (Num 14:24): 'and my servant, Caleb, since he...'
דוד נקרא עבד שנאמר: '(ועבדי דוד) [ודוד עבדי] נשיא להם לעולם.'	ט. 9.	David was called servant, as it says (Ezek 37:25): '[My servant, David], will be their prince forever.'
ישעיהו נקרא עבד שנאמר: 'ויאמר ה' כאשר הלך עבדי ישעיהו.'	י. 10.	Isaiah was called servant, as it says (Isa 20:3): 'And God said: "Just like my servant Isaiah walked..."'
אליקים נקרא עבד שנאמר: 'וקראתי לעבדי לאליקים.'	יא. 11.	Eliakim was called servant, as it says: (Isa 22:20): 'And I will call my servant, Eliakim.'
איוב נקרא עבד שנאמר: 'השמת לבך אל עבדי איוב.'	יב. 12.	Job was called servant, as it says (Job 2:3): 'Have you noticed my servant Job.'
דניאל נקרא עבד שנאמר: 'דניאל עבד אלהא חייא.'	יג. 13.	Daniel was called servant, as it says (Dan 6:21): 'Daniel, the servant of the Living God.'
חנניה מישאל ועזריה נקראו עבדים שנאמר: 'שדרך מישך ועבד נגו עבדוהי די אלהא עילאה.'	טז.–יד. 14– 16.	Hannaiah, Mishael, and Azariah were called servants, as it says (Dan 3:26): "Shadrach, Meshach and Abed-Nego were servants of the Most High God.'
נבוכדנצר נקרא עבד ולא הוה שוה לו שנאמר: 'אל נבוכדנצר מלך בבל עבדי.'	יז. 17.	Nebuchadnezzar was called servant, but he wasn't deserving of it, as it says (Jer 25:9): 'To Nebuchadnezzar, King of Babylon, my servant.'
זרובבל נקרא עבד שנאמר: 'בעת ההיא נאם ה' אקחך זרובבל בן שאלתיאל עבדי.'	יח. 18.	Zerubabel was called servant, as it says (Hag 2:23): 'At that time—the Word of the Lord—I will take Zerubabel son of Shealtiel, my servant.'

When looking at the examples of those people in history that were called "servant of God," the list seems random. Most of them are heroic figures from Israel's past, like Abraham, Jacob, Moses, Joshua, Caleb, David, Daniel and his three friends, and Zerubabel. But there are a number of outliers as well. Isaiah is a prophet, the messiah is a future figure, Israelites are a mass group, Eliakim is an unknown, Job is a gentile, angels aren't even human, and Nebuchadnezzar is a villain. Also, the selection process is hard to understand. If Isaiah, why not other prophets? If David, why not Solomon or Josiah?

I imagine that the simple answer is that the list represents *all* the biblical figures referred to as servant of God. In this sense, the reason Joshua is in this rabbinic list is because the Bible in fact calls him the servant of God. The reason the Bible does this is probably because "servant of YHWH" is the appellation of Moses, and many passages in Rabbinic texts about Joshua were written with the intent of modeling him upon Moses.

The second example focuses on the word מלא (*ml'*), a term that often means "to fill," but can also have the connotation of "complete" or "fulfill." (*Abot de-Rabbi Nathan* b, ch. 43):

ששה אלו נקראו מלאים.		These six were called filled.
הקדוש ברוך הוא נקרא מלא, שנאמר: 'הלא את השמים ואת הארץ אני מלא'.	א.	1. The Holy One, bb"h, was called filled, as it says (Jer 23:24): 'Do I not fill the heavens and the earth?'
יהושע נקרא מלא, שנאמר: 'ויהושע בן נון מלא רוח חכמה'.	ב.	2. Joshua was called filled, as it says (Deut 34:9): 'And Joshua son of Nun was filled with the spirit of wisdom.'
כלב נקרא מלא, שנאמר: 'ועבדי כלב עקב היתה רוח אחרת עמו וימלא אחרי'.	ג.	3. Caleb was called filled, as it says (Num 14:24): 'And my servant Caleb, since he had a different spirit and followed (*ml'*) after me.'
בצלאל נקרא מלא, שנאמר: 'וימלא אותו רוח אלהים בחכמה'.	ד.	4. Bezalel was called filled, as it says (Exod 35:31): 'And He filled him with the spirit of God, with wisdom...'
אהליאב נקרא מלא, שנאמר: 'מלא אותם] חכמת לב'.	ה.	5. Oholiab was called filled, as it says (Exod 35:35): 'Filled their hearts with wisdom.'
חירם נקרא מלא, שנאמר: 'מלא חכמה] וכליל יופי'.	ו.	6. [Hiram was called filled, as it says (Ezek 28:12): 'Full of wisdom] and perfect in beauty.'

Again the collection of great people on the list lacks any real theme. Joshua and Caleb are ancient Israelite heroes, Bezalel and Oholiab were artists, Hiram was the king of Tyre[667] and God is God. The best explanation for the list is simply that this word, *ml'* was used for these six "characters" and that there is nothing else intrinsically connecting any of these to each other.

Joshua as a Competitor with Moses

The *Mekhilta de-Rabbi Ishmael* (*Be-Shalaḥ, Masekhta de-Amalek* 2) describes a dejected Moses falling apart over God's decision not to allow him to enter Israel.

ר' אלעזר המודעי אומר: "זה אחד מארבעה צדיקים שנתן להם רמז; שנים חשו ושנים לא חשו. משה נתן לו רמז ולא חש, יעקב נתן לו רמז ולא חש, דוד ומרדכי נתן להם רמז וחש.	R. Elazar of Mod'in said: "This is one of four righteous men who received a hint [about the future]. Two of them noticed and two of them did not notice. "Moses received a hint and did not notice; Jacob recieved a hint and did not notice. David and Mordechai received hints and did notice."

---

667 The verse in Ezekiel is not actually referring to Hiram king of Tyre, who assisted Solomon in building the Temple, but to the king of Tyre in his day. However, the rabbis, not knowing any other king of Tyre, conflate the two.

משה מניין? 'ושים באזני יהושע' – אמר: 'יהושע מנחיל
ישראל את הארץ'.

From where do we know that Moses [received a hint but did not notice it]? [The verse states (Exod 17:14)]: "Place in the ears of Joshua," [God] said (Deut 3:28): "Joshua will give them the land as inheritance."

ובסוף משה עומד ומתחנן, שנא[מר]: 'ואתחנן אל ה' בעת
ההיא לאמר...' היה עומד ומבקש כל אותן הבקשות אמר
משה לפניו: "רבונו של עולם, כלום נגזרה גזרה שלא
אכנס לה? 'לכן לא תביאו את הקהל הזה' – במלכות.
אכנס לה כהדיוט." אמר לו: "אין המלך נכנס כהדיוט..."

In the end, Moses stood up and begged (Deut 3:23): 'And he begged God at that time, saying...' [Moses] was standing and begging for all of these requests. Moses said to him: "Master of the world, is there a command that I may not enter [the land]? [You said] (Num 20:12): 'Therefore, you will not bring this people' – as the king, but I will enter it as a commoner." He said to him: "A king may not enter as a commoner..."

ר' חנניה בן אידי אומר: "משה היה בוכה על עצמו ואומר
'כי אתם עוברים [את הירדן' – אתם עוברים] ואני איני
עובר."

R. Ḥanina ben Iddi says: "Moses was crying about himself, saying 'you will cross the Jordan' (Deut 11:31) – you will cross, but I will not cross."

אחרים אומרים: 'היה משה מוטה על רגליו של אלעזר
ואמר לו אלעזר בן אחי בקש עלי רחמים כשם שבקשתי
על אהרן אביך...'

Others say: "Moses threw himself on the feet of Elazar and said to him: 'Elazar, my nephew, request mercy for me the way I did for Aaron your father...'"

The theme dealt with in these midrashim is the pain Moses feels at his having been rejected. The tension can be felt most poignantly in the way God speaks to Moses in one of the Deuteronomy verses (3:26–28) quoted above, where God responds to Moses' pleading:

וַיֹּאמֶר יְהוָה אֵלַי: "רַב לָךְ אַל תּוֹסֶף דַּבֵּר אֵלַי עוֹד בַּדָּבָר
הַזֶּה. עֲלֵה רֹאשׁ הַפִּסְגָּה וְשָׂא עֵינֶיךָ יָמָּה וְצָפֹנָה וְתֵימָנָה
וּמִזְרָחָה וּרְאֵה בְעֵינֶיךָ כִּי לֹא תַעֲבֹר אֶת הַיַּרְדֵּן הַזֶּה. וְצַו אֶת
יְהוֹשֻׁעַ וְחַזְּקֵהוּ וְאַמְּצֵהוּ כִּי הוּא יַעֲבֹר לִפְנֵי הָעָם הַזֶּה וְהוּא
יַנְחִיל אוֹתָם אֶת הָאָרֶץ אֲשֶׁר תִּרְאֶה."

YHWH said to me: "It is enough. Do not speak to me about this again. Go up to the summit of the mountain and lift your eyes west, north, south, and east, and see with your eyes, for you will not cross this Jordan. Command Joshua, strengthen him and encourage him, since he will cross before this nation and give them their inheritance in the land which you will see."

The differing fates of Moses on one hand and Joshua and the Israelites on the other could hardly have been expressed more clearly. The midrash implies that this verse was God's attack against Moses' blind spot. Further, it suggests that Moses should have picked up on the fact that it would be Joshua and not him leading the conquest from the very beginning; why else was the job of destroying Amalek handed over to Joshua and not Moses? Joshua would have the opportunity and Moses would not, since Joshua would be the one fighting the battles in the Promised Land. This was the hint, and Moses missed it, forcing God to eventually shout it out to him in the rough manner recorded in Deuteronomy.

The theme of Moses begging appears as well in *Midrash Peṭirat Moshe*[668] (Eisenstein, *Otzar ha-Midrashim*, 368 – 369). In this version, Moses does not only pray to God or throw himself before Elazar the priest, but between these two requests he begs intervention from the earth, the sky, the sun and the moon, Mount Sinai, the rivers, and Joshua.[669] Here is the last section:

הלך משה אצל יהושע בן נון והתחנן לו ואמר לו: "בני זכור כמה חסד עשיתי עמך לילה ויומס, עמוד לי במדת רחמים לפני הקדוש ברוך הוא אולי ירחמני על ידך ואראה את א[רץ] י[שראל]." באותה שעה היה יהושע בוכה ומספק כף על כף ועמד להתפלל.	Moses went to Joshua son of Nun and begged him. He said to him: "My son, remember the kindness I did for you night and day. Stand with me with the attribute of mercy before the Holy One, bb"h, perhaps he will have mercy on me on your behalf and I will be able to see the land of Israel." At that moment Joshua was crying and slapping hand upon hand he stood up and prayed.
בא [ש]מאל[670] ותפש את פיו ואמר לו: "מפני מה אתה דוחה דברי הקדוש ברוך הוא? הרי נאמר 'הצור תמים פעלו כי כל דרכיו משפט'?!"	Samael came and grabbed his mouth and said to him: "Why are pushing against the words of the Holy One, bb"h? Does [scripture] not say (Deut 32:4): 'The Rock, his works are perfect, for all his ways are just'?!"
מיד הלך יהושע אצל משה ואמר לו: "רבי, הרי [ש]מאל אינו מניח אותי להתפלל עליך!" וכששמע הדבר היה נותן קולו בבכי, אף יהושע בכה במר[ר] נפש.	Immediately, Joshua went to Moses and said to him: "My master, Samael will not allow me to pray for you!" When [Moses] heard this, he put forth his voice and wept. Joshua also wept with bitterness of spirit.

The above story contains an ironic twist. Moses begs Joshua, of all people, to allow him to enter Israel; this despite that fact that Joshua happens to be his successor. It is striking that Moses does not see Joshua as competition. It does not

---

668 There are a number of midrash collections by this name. This one was published as part of "Appendix 1" in the back of Alexander Kohut's edition of Abu Mansur Al-Dhamari's commentary on the Pentatuch, called *Notes on a Hitherto Unknown Exegetical, Theological, and Philosophical Commentary on the Pentateuch* (New York: Ginsburg, 1892), XV.

669 This is reminiscent of the Elazar ben Dordiya story in b. *Abodah Zarah* 17a, except that Moses is not a classic "sinner" in the way Elazar—the man who left no harlot unvisited—was. This makes the story about Moses that much more ironic.

670 Eisenstein changes the spelling here to סמאל; I assume this was to ensure the reader not mistake the word for the Hebrew *smol*, meaning left.

seem to cross Moses' mind that Joshua may not wish to pray for him, and he is correct. Joshua does attempt to pray for Moses, and Samael actually has to forcibly hold Joshua's mouth shut and lecture him not to attempt to flout God's command. This lecture is the only thing that can stop Joshua's prayer—one that ostensibly would have been answered (otherwise why send Samael to stop him)—and Joshua and Moses end their encounter by weeping together over Moses' fate.

Unfavorable Descriptions of Joshua

Moses Criticizes Joshua

Although the majority of rabbinic descriptions of the Moses-Joshua relationship are positive, this does not stop the rabbis from entertaining other possibilities. The rabbis were masters of polysemous homiletical interpretation, and were happy to consider exegesis reflecting the opposite approach to the more standard interpretations.[671] Nevertheless, the image of Moses strongly rebuking Joshua is exceedingly stark.

The midrash appears in the *Mekhilta of R. Ishmael* (*Parshat be-Shalaḥ, Masekhta de-Amalek* 1), commenting on Exod 17:9, where Moses tells Joshua to fight the Amalekites.

וצא הלחם בעמלק – רבי יהושע אומר: "אמר לו משה	Go out and make war with the Amalekites – R.
ליהושע: 'צא מתחת הענן והלחם בעמלק'." רבי אלעזר	Joshua says: "Moses said to Joshua: 'Get out
המודעי אומר: "אמר לו משה ליהושע: יהושע למה	from under the cloud and make war with Ama-
אתה משמר את ראשך? לא לכתר! צא מן המחנה	lek!" R. Elazar of Modin says: "Moses said to
והלחם בעמלק!".	Joshua: 'Joshua, what are you saving your head for? Is it not the crown?! Get out of the camp and make war with Amalek!'"

---

[671] For a discussion of polesemy and midrash see Susan A. Handelman, *The Slayers of Moses: The Emergence of Rabbinic Interpretation in Modern Literary Theory* (Albany: State of New York University Press, 1982). See also the back and forth between Handelman and David Stern debating the extent and nature of this polysemy: David Stern, "Moses-cide: Midrash and Contemporary Literary Criticism," *Prooftexts* 4 (1984) 193–213; Susan A. Handelman, "Fragments of the Rock: Contemporary Literary Theory and the Study of Rabbinic Texts—A Response to David Stern," *Prooftexts* 5 (1985): 73–95; David Stern, "Literary Criticism or Literary Homilies? Susan Handelman and the Contemporary Study of Midrash," *Prooftexts* 5 (1985): 96–103. For a somewhat different perspective, see: Jose Faur, *Golden Doves with Silver Dots: Semiotics and Textuality in Rabbinic Tradition* (University of South Florida Studies in the History of Judaism 213; Atlanta: Scholars Press, 1999 [orig. 1986]).

Both Rabbi Joshua and Rabbi Elazar of Modin understand Moses' command to Joshua to "go out and make war" as a criticism, implying that Joshua was shirking his responsibilities before Moses rebuked him.[672] Their disagreement lies in determining of what exactly Moses accuses Joshua. R. Joshua suggests that Moses accused Joshua of cowardice. Why else would he remain in the safety of the cloud of glory instead of leaving the cloud and leading the attack?[673] R. Elazar of Modin suggests that Joshua did not want to fight since he had aspirations for something higher. Joshua wished to stay alive long enough to enter Israel and inherit the crown! Moses, in his quip, disabuses Joshua of this notion and sends him off to serve his actual function; for the time being, at any rate, Joshua will be the great general of Israel, not its king.

Joshua Punished for Speaking in Front of Moses

In a different context, the Talmud (b. *Eruvin* 63a-b) quotes R. Levi taking Joshua to task for speaking out of turn.

אמר רבי לוי: "כל דמותיב מלה קמיה רביה – אזיל לשאול בלא ולד, שנאמר: 'ויען יהושע בן נון משרת משה מבחריו ויאמר: "אדני משה כלאם!"' וכתיב 'נון בנו יהושע בנו.'"	R. Levi said: "Anyone who calls out a word in the presence of his master will go to the grave without offspring, as it says (Num 11:28): 'And Joshua son of Nun, the servant of Moses, one of his young men, said: "My master Moses, restrain them!"' and it says (1 Chron 7:27): 'Nun his son, Joshua his son.'"

The reproach offered by R. Levi is more than a little extreme. Joshua, in the scene, is a young man who blurts out advice as he as afraid that Eldad and Medad are challenging Moses by prophesying in the camp. Moses himself seems to take Joshua's advice as a demonstration of Joshua's over-eagerness

---

672 This is an excellent example of how the rabbis read earlier parts of the Pentateuch assuming knowledge of later sections; how, otherwise, could the reader accept that Joshua was shirking? This is the first mention of Joshua in the entire book. One would have thought that the reader should first be introduced to the character of General Joshua; only then would it seem reasonable to assume that a command to Joshua to attack should imply some shirking on his part.

673 R. Joshua assumes that Joshua is in the cloud since the reader knows from later in Exodus that Joshua never leaves the Tabernacle, where the cloud of glory is found. Although the simple reading of the Pentateuchal narrative is that the Tabernacle had not yet been built, so Joshua could not have been there, this is not a significant problem for the rabbinic homileticist, who is often willing to reimagine the sequence of events to make a point.

as opposed to an example of rudeness. Even if the comment was inappropriate, saying that Joshua is the paradigmatic example of a rude student who is punished with lack of offspring seems exceedingly harsh.

R. Levi's comment is an outlier and was probably not meant to paint Joshua as the problematic student *par excellence*; the rabbis generally give this position to Gehazi, the student of Elisha whom he eventually curses with leprosy (2 Kings 5:25 – 27).[674] Instead, I would suggest that R. Levi could not resist the opening given by the verse in Chronicles that makes it sound as if Joshua had no offspring (the Bible never says one way or the other.)[675] "Why would the great Joshua not merit having children?" R. Levi may have asked himself. "What did he do wrong?" Hitting upon the verse in Numbers, in which Joshua blurts something out before his teacher, R. Levi may have seen an opening for an object lesson to overenthusiastic or rude students.

Midrashic literature has little problem with internal contradiction and complex discussion of characters. Rather than see R. Levi's *derasha* as an attempt to knock Joshua down, I suggest it should be seen as an opportunity taken to creatively interpret Chronicles and teach an important lesson (from the teacher's perspective at least) to overeager students.

Moses and Joshua Compared unfavorably with Abraham

In general, the rabbis are uncomfortable with anything or anyone competing with Moses. However, this is not a real red line, there are exceptions. For example, in the first midrash quoted in the "Joshua as Competitor with Moses" section, Rabbi Elazar of Modi'in compares Moses and Jacob unfavorably with David and Mordechai. Another example comes from *Midrash Tannaim* (Deut 34) where both Moses and Joshua are compared unfavorably to Abraham.

ר' חנינה בר יעקב אמ[ר]: "חביבה ראייתו שלאברהם	R. Ḥanina bar Jacob said: "The vision of Abra-
משלמשה ומשליהושע. אברהם 'קום התהלך בא[רץ] לא	ham is preferable to that of Moses and of Josh-
[רכה] ול[רחבה].'. ומשה ראה אותה בכל צרכה ויהושע	ua. For Abraham [it says] (Gen 13:17): 'Arise
כיבשה ולא ראה אותה."	and walk about the land lengthwise and width-
	wise.' Moses saw it with all its necessities and
	Joshua conquered it but did not see it."

---

674 See, for example, m. *Sanhedrin* 1:2 (Gehazi has no place in the World to Come) and b. *Sanhedrin* 100a (Gehazi was punished because he called Elisha by his name).

675 As will be seen later, in a different passage, the rabbis do suggest that Joshua had offspring (at least daughters).

In Genesis 13, Abraham is told to look at the land, and then he is told to walk around upon it. As a contrast, Moses was only allowed to look upon it, and Joshua to walk upon it. Therefore, argues the *darshan*, Abraham's experience was superior to those of Moses and Joshua.

In truth, neither Joshua nor Moses is the focus of this midrash, whose main point is to praise Abraham as having been granted a relationship to the land that neither Moses nor Joshua ever attained. Nevertheless, two aspects are worth noting. First, Joshua is less great than Abraham, because he only conquered the land but never saw it. Second, Joshua is paired with Moses, as if the two of them were equal—each is pictured as having had one half of the relationship to the land that Abraham had. Still, since the midrash wants to compare Abraham to other prophets with a relationship to the land, Joshua is the logical choice for "the other conqueror."

Joshua Compared Unfavorably with Ezra

A starker example of a relatively negative evaluation of Joshua comes from a midrash in *Mishnat Rabbi Eliezer* (6, p. 123), which compares Joshua unfavorably with Ezra.

ר' הלל אומ[ר]: "הרי הוא אומ[ר], 'ויעשו כל הקהל השבים מן השבי [סכות] וישבו בסכות כי לא עשו מימי ישוע בן נון כן בני ישראל.' חזרנו על כל המקרא ולא מצינו בן נון ישוע, אלא לומ' לך, שאלו היה יהושע קיים בימי עזרא, לא היה ראוי להקרות לפניו אלא ישוע, לפי שעזרא גדול הדור היה. הא למדת, שחכם שבדורך הרי הוא כמשה בדורו."

R. Hillel says: "Scripture states (Neh 8:17): 'And the entire congregation of those who returned from captivity observed [Sukkot] and they dwelt in booths, for the Children of Israel had not done so since the time of Yeshua son of Nun.' We have searched through all of scripture and have not found that Nun had a son Yeshua. Rather, this [strange form of Yehoshua's name] comes to teach that if Yehoshua had been alive during the time of Ezra, he would only have been fit to be called Yeshua, since Ezra was the great one of his generation. Thus you learn that the wise person of your generation should be considered by you as Moses was in his generation."

The bottom line in this passage—that the leader of one's generation should be venerated even if said leader is less great than previous leaders—is not surprising. The idea was famously expressed in the Talmudic dictum (b. *Rosh Ha-Shanah* 25b) "Jephthah in his generation is equal to Samuel in his generation." What is surprising in this text is that Joshua is described as being less than Ezra. Although it is not perfectly clear why the shortened form of Joshua's name is insulting, R. Hillel assumes that it demonstrates that when compared to Ezra, Joshua is something less.

However, this may be best understood not as an insult to Joshua, but as a compliment to Ezra. Early on in Rabbinic literature (and perhaps even in biblical or pseudepigraphic literature) Ezra is pictured as a second Moses. R. Yossi (t. *Sanhedrin* 4:7) states explicitly that if it weren't for Moses, the Torah could have been given to Joshua. Considering this, the above midrash may simply be expressing the same idea, that Joshua student of Moses would have been Joshua student of Ezra, had he lived in that period of time.

Joshua Punished for Accidentally Cancelling a Night of Procreation

One final criticism against Joshua appears in the context of the discussion of Joshua's lack of producing children (b. *Eruvin* 63b – MS Munich).[676]

...א"ר חנינא בר פפא: "לא נענש יהושע אלא מפני שביטל ישראל לילה אחד מפריה ורביה שנ[אמר], 'ויהי בהיות יהושע ביריחו וישא עיניו וירא והנה וגו' ויאמר, "אני שר צבא יי עתה באתי".'[677] אמ' לו: 'אמש בטלתם תמיד של בין הערבים ועכשיו בטלתם תלמוד תורה.' א"ל: 'על איזה מהם באתה?' א"ל: "'עתה באתי'." מיד 'וילן יהושע בלילה ההוא בתוך העמק.' וא"ר יוחנן: 'מלמד שלן בעומקה של הלכה,' וגמירי דכל זמן שארון ושכינה שרויין שלא במקומן אסורין ישראל בתשמיש המטה."	...R. Ḥanina[678] bar Pappa said: "Joshua was punished because he caused the Israelites to be unable to engage in procreative activities for one night, for it says (Josh 5:13): 'and it was when Joshua was in Jericho that he lifted his eyes and looked, and behold..., and he said: "No, for I, the minister of war for the Lord, have now come."' [The angel] said to [Joshua]: 'Yesterday you caused the cancellation of the afternoon daily sacrifice and now you are causing the cancellation of Torah study.' [Joshua] replied: 'On account of which violation have you come?' [The angel] replied: 'I have come [on account of] "now."' Immedi-

---

676 This was referenced earlier in the section on Joshua as a student of Moses, where he is criticized for speaking out of turn, and in the addendum on anti-Christian polemic, where the rabbis suggest that he did have children (perhaps only daughters).

677 At this point, only in MS Oxford Opp. Add. fol. 23, comes an aside about whether it should have been permitted for Joshua to respond to the angel, out of fear that it could have been a demon. Whether this tangent is a later gloss that found its way into this manuscript or it is an older line that was preserved only in this manuscript I cannot say, but either way the section is not relevant to the discussion in this chapter.

678 This is the name as it appears in MS Munich 95. The printed editions and MS Oxford Opp. Add. fol. 23 read "Abba," MS Vatican 109 and MS Cambridge T-S F2 (2) 65 read "Ḥiyya." I see no reason to prefer any one name over the other.

ately, Joshua went and lay down in the valley ('*emeq*)' (Joshua 8:9). And R. Yoḥanan said: 'This teaches that he lay in the depths ('*amuqah*) of halakha.' And tradition has it that whenever the ark and the divine presence were not in their place, it was forbidden to the Israelites to engage in conjugal relations."

The train of causality in this midrash is difficult to follow. Apparently, Joshua is accused of having spent the entire day, on the day the angel appears, without learning any Torah. Joshua recognizes that the problem is serious, since the chief of God's army himself has come to rebuke him, and he immediately dives into the deep study of halakha. However, as the ark seems to have remained with Joshua during this study period, the people back in the camp were forced to abstain that night from reproductive activities, as they were forbidden to do so when the ark was on the move or out of its usual place. Hence, by trying to fix one problem, Joshua unwittingly causes another. This latter offense is considered sufficiently egregious as to warrant an extreme punishment: Joshua will never reproduce.

The picture painted here of Joshua is one of a leader playing catch up. He caused a problem the day before (apparently the daily afternoon offering was not brought), he caused another problem on the day of the arrival of the angel (Torah was not learned), and in attempting to fix this latter problem he ends up causing yet another one. As all of these problems require heavy interpretation of the relevant verses, even beyond the usual midrashic methods, it would seem that the author is at great pains to paint Joshua in less than favorable colors. However, it should also be noted that the apparent sins of Joshua are unwitting and rather minor. Perhaps, at the same time as he is critiquing Joshua, the author is also pointing the reader towards the impossibility of a leader like Joshua ever succeeding given the enormity of the task and the shoes of the leader (Moses) he had to fill.

Moses vs. Joshua as Anti-Christian Polemic

Moses is the key figure for Rabbinic Judaism, and his position of incomparable primacy is generally defended, despite some exceptions detailed in the previous section. It appears that at a certain point, the rabbis began to feel that the position of Joshua was becoming a threat to the position of Moses as greatest prophet and leader of Israel. Most likely, this fear did not appear out of nowhere, but stemmed from the use of Joshua among Early Christian interpreters as a *type* of Jesus.[679] As such, early Christian exegetes argued for the primacy of Joshua over Moses, as an early instantiation of the primacy of belief in Jesus over the Torah of Moses. As detailed in the chapter on early Christianity, much of the early use of this paradigm was in polemical works such Justin's *Dialogue with Trypho* or Tertullian's *Adversus Iudaeos*.

Moses Stops the Sun

Although many of the arguments put forward about Joshua's primacy were idiosyncratic to the belief structure of the early Christians,[680] one seemed to have biblical support. After Joshua performs the miracle of stopping the sun, the biblical texts puts this miracle in (mytho-)historical context (Josh 10:14).

וְלֹא הָיָה כַּיּוֹם הַהוּא לְפָנָיו וְאַחֲרָיו לִשְׁמֹעַ יְהוָה בְּקוֹל אִישׁ כִּי יְהוָה נִלְחָם לְיִשְׂרָאֵל.	There was never a day like this before or afterwards when YHWH listened to the voice of a man, for YHWH was fighting for Israel.

This verse implies that this miracle was absolutely unique in its power and impressiveness, and that no other prophet in history—including Moses—can make a claim to something analogous. This point did not escape the notice of the early Christian interpreters. For example, Origen, in his *Homilies on Joshua* (1.5), explicitly identifies Joshua and Jesus (both Iesu.) He then goes on the "prove" that Joshua was a greater prophet than Moses, prefiguring Jesus and his oversha-

---

679 The idea that the Rabbis were in conversation with early Christian thinkers and that the two groups were mutually fructified and affected by each other's interpretations has come into its own over the past two decades. See, for example: Isaac Kalimi, *Early Jewish Exegesis and Theological Controversy: Studies in Scriptures in the Shadow of Internal and External Controversies* (Jewish and Christian Heritage Series 2; Assen, Netherlands: Van Gorcum, 2002); Burton L. Visotsky, *Fathers of the World: Essays in Rabbinic and Patristic Literatures* (Tübingen: Mohr Siebeck, 1995), Daniel Boyarin, *Border Lines: The Partition of Judaeo-Christianity* (Divinations: Rereading Late Ancient Religion; Philadelphia: University of Pennsylvania Press, 2004); Peter Schäfer, *The Jewish Jesus: How Judaism and Christianity Shaped Each Other* (Princeton: Princeton University Press, 2012); and, although covering a somewhat later period of time, Israel J. Yuval, *Two Nations in Your Womb: Perceptions of Jews and Christians in Late Antiquity and the Middle Ages* (trans. Barbara Harshav and Jonathan Chipman; S. Mark Taper Foundation imprint in Jewish studies; Berkeley: University of California Press, 2006.) Although this section does not directly engage these works, these pioneering studies dominate the field and strongly inform my own thinking on these subjects.

680 See the chapter on Church-Fathers for more details.

dowing of Moses. One of Origen's proofs comes from the story of the stopping of the sun (1:5):[681]

Moyses non dixit: "Stet sol" nec maximus imper-avit elementis, sicut Iesus fecit. "Stet" inquit, "sol super Gabaon et luna super vallem Aelom," et praeterea addit Scriptura et dicit quia: "Numquam sic audivit Deus hominem."	Moses did not say: "Let the sun stand still." Nor did he command the greatest elements as Joshua did. Joshua says: "Let the sun stand still over Gibeon and the moon over the valley of Aiyalon." Scripture adds to this: "Never in this way did God listen to a man."

Although I do not know to which Christian writers, if any, the Rabbis were privy, it is reasonable to assume that the rabbis were aware of this exegesis and were responding to it when they made the surprising assertion that Moses also stopped the sun.

The earliest example of this aggadic claim comes from *Sifrei Deuteronomy* (*Parshat Ha'azinu*, 306).

'האזינו השמים ואדברה' – היה רבי יהודה בן חנניה אומר: "בשעה שאמר משה 'האזינו השמים ואדברה' היו השמים ושמי השמים דוממים, ובשעה שאמר 'ותשמע הארץ אמרי פי' הייתה הארץ וכל אשר עליה דוממים.	'Let the heavens give ear and I will speak' (Deut 32:1) – R. Yehudah ben Ḥananiah used to say: "At the time when Moses said 'let the heavens give ear and I will speak' the heavens and the heavens of the heavens were still,[682] and when he said 'and let the land hear the words of my mouth' the land and everything on it was still.
ואם תמיה אתה על הדבר, צא וראה מה נאמר ביהושע: "ויאמר לעיני ישראל: "שמש בגבעון דם וירח בעמק אילון", וידום השמש וירח עמד... ולא היה כיום ההוא לפניו וג' – '. נמצינו למדים שהצדיקים שולטים בכל העולם כולו."	If this matter seems surprising to you, go and see what is stated by Joshua (Josh 10:12 – 14): 'and he said before the eyes of Israel: "Sun in Gibeon be still, the same for the moon in the Ayalon valley," and the sun stood still and the moon halted... and there was never a day like this before etc.' – We learn from this that the righteous are in control of the entire world."

R. Joshua son of Ḥananiah suggests a midrashic gloss on the verse in Deuteronomy which begins Moses' song. Moses poetically calls upon the heavens and the earth to give ear to the words he is about to utter. R. Joshua son of Ḥananiah interprets this opening to mean that Moses literally stopped them from moving by commanding them to stop moving while he sang his song. The *Sifrei* then imag-

---

681 For more on Origen's exegesis, see the previous chapter on the Church Fathers.
682 This word could also mean silent or it could have both connotations at the same time.

ines that an interlocutor might object by claiming that a person commanding the heavens is not possible, that it is too radical a claim. The *Sifrei* answers this interlocutor by quoting the story of Joshua stopping the sun in the battle over Gibeon.

What stands out about the *Sifrei*'s answer is that it ignores the import of the closing phrase describing the miracle. "There was never a day like this before..." Yet, R. Joshua son of Ḥananiah is claiming just that; he says that this exact miracle happened before in the time of Moses. What's more, whereas Joshua freezes the sun during a battle, in order to facilitate Israel's victory, Moses seems to do it simply for dramatic effect, so that he can have heavenly witnesses to his song predicting the future.

The *Sifrei* drives home the mundane nature of Moses' action by stating that we learn from Joshua (and Moses?) that the righteous control the world. The righteous is a large category, one that includes more than just Moses and Joshua. Since the righteous control the world, it stands to reason that other great figures of the past could have stopped the sun as well, in other words, such a miracle should not be considered a big deal for the righteous. This turns Joshua's miracle on its head.

It is possible that R. Joshua ben Ḥananiah came up with his gloss as a literal interpretation of Moses speaking to the heavens and the earth, since it would be a sign of respect for Moses if they would stop and listen. Certainly, the *darshan* could have been inspired by the miracle of Joshua, which put this possibility in his head, without having any polemical intent. To quote Jon Levenson, "We cannot easily distinguish between a response to a Christian challenge and the natural unfolding of Jewish theology and biblical interpretation."[683] Nevertheless, it seems more likely that R. Joshua ben Ḥananiah did intend to make at least a minor polemical point by granting Moses a power that the Bible ascribes only to Joshua.

Furthermore, whatever R. Joshua ben Ḥananiah's intent, the editor of the *Sifrei* almost certainly has a polemical meaning in mind. By making Joshua's greatest moment into something that is standard fare for the righteous, he undermines one part of Joshua's claim to a special place among Israelite leaders and prophets. The most obvious reason for a 3rd century rabbi to wish to deprive Joshua of his special position would be that early Christian exegesis had identified Joshua with Jesus and used this miracle to prove that Joshua/Jesus was the greatest of the prophets, even greater than Moses.

---

683 Levenson, *Inheriting Abraham*, 7

On the other hand, one could argue that an anti-Christian polemic is unnecessary to explain why a rabbi would wish to aggrandize Moses at the expense of anybody, including Joshua. Moses is considered to have been the greatest of prophets in Rabbinic tradition. Therefore, it would only be logical that Moses would have been the one to accomplish the greatest miracles. In fact, as William Gilders pointed out to me in conversation, the Rabbis use this very same kind of argument when comparing Moses' miracle in the midrash explaining how it is that Moses brought up Joseph's iron casket from the Nile (a non-biblical account assumed by the midrash) to that of Elisha raising the axehead (2 Kings 6:5; *Mekhilta of R. Ishmael, Be-Shalaḥ-Va-Yehi, petiḥtah*; b. *Soṭah* 13a).[684]

והרי דברים קל וחומר ומה אלישע תלמידו של אליהו	Cannot [the reasonability of the claim that
הציף הברזל ק"ו למשה רבו של אליהו.	Moses raised the axehead] be demonstrated a fortiori. If Elisha, the student of Elijah, made iron float, certainly Moses, the teacher of Elijah could do so.

Although I grant that the midrash on Moses stopping the sun fits into the general rubric of aggrandizing Moses, a number of elements stand out. First, the correlation with the early Christian claim that Joshua was greater than Moses, and the use by Origen of this sun-stopping as a prooftext encourages one to consider the possibility of a polemic. Second, the midrash tries to downplay the importance of the miracle, claiming that any righteous person could have accomplished it, despite the fact that such a claim contradicts an almost explicit biblical verse. Third, as will be seen, the theme of Moses stopping the sun becomes an exceedingly popular one, but the prooftext keeps changing. This implies, I believe, that the rabbis thought it important to establish this fact, and were worried that their prooftexts could be assailed. For this reason, generations of rabbis attempted to ground this "fact" in new prooftexts.

This midrash appears in a different form—including numerous prooftexts—in the Babylonian Talmud, in the second chapter of *Avodah Zarah* (25a).[685] The pericope begins with the quoting of a *baraita*.

תאנא: "כשם שעמדה לו חמה ליהושע כך עמדה לו חמה	It was taught: "Just as the sun stood for Joshua
למשה ולנקדימון בן גוריון."	so too did it stand for Moses and for Naqdimon ben Gurion."

---

684 For a thorough analysis of this midrash and how it was created, see James L. Kugel, *In Potiphar's House: The Interpretive Life of Biblical Texts* (Boston: Harvard University Press, 1994).
685 The text is from MS Paris 1337.

According to this text, this miracle was performed not only by Moses and Joshua, but even by the famous wealthy man from Second Temple times, Naqdimon ben Gurion. This alone brings the significance of the miracle down tremendously in a similar way to what was done in the previous version. In other words, by invoking Naqdimon or "the righteous," one doesn't really bolster Moses as much as one undermines the significance of the miracle. As great a man as Naqdimon was said to have been, he is hardly Joshua or Moses, at least from the perspective of mnemohistory, and comparing either of them to him would not be "complimentary."

The pericope continues with an attempt to prove that Moses did, in fact, stop the sun (b. *Avodah Zarah* 25a):

יהושע קרא, נקדימון בן גוריון גמרא. משה מנא לן?	For Joshua there is a verse. For Naqdimon ben Gurion there is a [traditional] teaching. From where did we learn this for Moses?
אמר רבי אלעזר: "אתיא 'אחל' 'אחל'."	Rabbi Elazar said: "We learn this through [a *gezeira shava*] 'I will begin' 'I will begin'." It says here (Deut 2:25): "I will begin to place fear of you…" and it says there (Josh 3:7): "I will begin to make you great."
כתי' הכא: "אחל תת פחדך..." וכתי' התם: "אחל גדלך."	
ר' יוחנן אמר: "אתיא 'תת' 'תת'."	R. Yoḥanan said: "We learn this through [a *gezeirah shava*] 'place' 'place'." It says here (Deut 2:25): "I will begin to place" and it says there (Josh 10:12): "On the day Yнwн placed the Amorite…"
כתיב הכא: "אחל תת" וכתיב התם: "ביום תת יי' את האמורי."	
ר' שמואל בר נחמני אמר: "מגופיה דקרא: 'אשר ישמעון שמעך ורגזו וחלו מפניך' – אימתי 'ורגזו וחלו מפניך'? בשעה שעמדה לו חמה למשה."	R. Samuel bar Naḥmani said: "[We learn it] from the verse itself (Deut 2:25): 'That they will hear the tidings of you and shake and be afraid in your presence' – when will they 'shake and be afeared in your presence'? When the sun stopped before Moses."

The Talmud claims that the miracles of Joshua and Naqdimon are well known. (The latter claim seems rather ironic.) However, the Talmud requests a biblical proof for Moses' stopping the sun. Three different Amoraim offer biblical proofs, two of which are far-fetched even for midrash. I will begin with the second *derasha*, that of R. Yoḥanan, as it is the one that "works" best, technically speaking.

R. Yoḥanan's uses a *gezeira shava*, choosing the word "to give" or "to place" (תת) as his key element. The verse about Moses is part of God's speech encouraging Moses before the battle with Siḥon king of the Amorites. The verse reads "I will begin to place (תת) fear and dread of you upon the nations." The verse about Joshua appears as part of the account of the defeat of the southern coalition and the stopping of the sun. This verse (Josh 10:12) states that on the day when God placed (תת) the Amorites into Joshua's hands, Joshua called out to the sun to stop.

Noting the use of the verb "to place" in both contexts (and in the same unusual form), R. Yoḥanan takes only a minimal step, midrashically speaking, and argues that God was promising Moses to place the Amorites in his hands the same way he placed/will place them in Joshua's hands, by stopping the sun so that Israel can win its victory in one very long battle.

R. Elazar, on the other hand, although also offering a *gezeira shava*, offers one that seems less "midrashically intuitive." Like R. Yoḥanan, R. Elazar connects a statement God made to Moses (the same one used by R. Yoḥanan) with one God made to Joshua, since both statements include the phrase "I will begin" (אחל). As described above, the statement to Moses was made as part of God encouraging Moses before the battle with Siḥon king of the Amorites. The statement to Joshua was made as an encouragement before Joshua crossed the Jordan River.[686]

R. Elazar assumes that the Moses language was specifically chosen to be reminiscent of the Joshua language as opposed to the other way around. However, even this seems insufficient as an explanation for R. Elazar's *derasha*, for the miracle that the verse about Joshua introduces is the miracle of crossing the Jordan, not the miracle of stopping the sun. At the point in the Pentateuch from which the verse about Moses is taken, the crossing of the Red Sea had already occurred, and there would be little reason to cross a body of water to fight Siḥon. (There are small rivers that could have been crossed, but such is never referenced.) Even if one assumes that R. Elazar preferred to stick to war miracles, the first war miracle Joshua will accomplish is the overturning of the walls of Jericho.[687]

I suggest that, as was the case for the editor of *Sifrei Deuteronomy*, underlying R. Elazar's *derasha* is polemical intent to give Moses the miracle of stopping the sun, so that no claim could be made that Joshua was greater than Moses in

---

686 Theoretically, even assuming one accepts R. Elazar's *gezeira shava*, a number of options remain for how to understand the connection between passages. The simplest possibility would be that the speech to Joshua is being modeled upon the speech to Moses. Joshua may be afraid that God will not be with him the way God was with Moses, so God allays his fears by promising this in the same language God used with Moses. Another possibility is that each leader is being offered the power of the other. Moses is calmed by God before a battle (Joshua's strength) and Joshua is being calmed before performing a miracle (Moses' strength). Nevertheless, these are not the options chosen by R. Elazar.

687 R. Elazar could have offered the following *derasha*, for instance: just like Joshua overturned the walls of Jericho miraculously so did Moses overturn the walls of Ḥeshbon miraculously.

this regard.[688] The reason this miracle is singled out over other miracles—Jericho, for instance—may simply be that the book of Joshua itself does this, by underlining the significance of this miracle as opposed to any other. Although this does not prove that the driving force behind R. Elazar's derasha is anti-Christian polemic—it could be "internal" rabbinic anxiety about the status of Moses—it fits well with the larger pattern established above. The Rabbis seem particulary interested in demonstrating that Moses was greater than Joshua and that there was nothing true of Joshua that was not also true of Moses, and specifically with regard to the miracle of stopping the sun.

The third *derasha* is also an example of a forced reading, even midrashically speaking. Instead of using a *gezeira shava*, R. Samuel bar Naḥmani tries to learn about Moses stopping the sun from a *diyyuq* (deduction) from Deut 2:25 itself. The verse says that the Amorites would be in fear and trembling of Moses. Why should they fear and tremble before Moses even before the attack? It must be because of a frightening miracle he performed. Although this seems like a regular midrashic deduction, one is forced to ask how R. Samuel bar Naḥmani knows what miracle Moses performed? It seems that he, like R. Elazar, was coming into this already knowing what the answer had to be. I would even speculate that all three of these rabbis were aware of a tradition based on Deut 2:25 that Moses stopped the sun, and each is attempting to recreate what the specifics of this tradition were. The multiple attempts at propping up Moses at Joshua's expense underline the "urgency" of the challenge to Moses' supremacy posed by Josh 10:14.

Unlike *Sifrei Deuteronomy*, which attempted to sweep the problem of Josh 10:14 under the rug with a creative twist, the Babylonian Talmud explicitly refer-

---

688 Implicit in my methodology is that I believe that one must factor in how powerful the "hook" of any midrash is with the question of "message." (By hook I mean the textual bump upon which the exegesis is built.) My own belief is that the stronger the hook, the less reason there is to look for a veiled message or polemical intent, since the midrash could simply be an example of expanding the Torah. However, the less any given hook seems to explain a midrash, the more probable it becomes that there is some sort of a message or polemic behind the midrash. That said, I accept the point made by Gilders (in his notes on this chapter) that "a good hook can still serve as the basis for a message or polemic." For the question of how important the hook should be in understanding midrash, see, for example: Daniel Boyarin, *Intertextuality and the Reading of Midrash* (Bloomington: Indiana University Press, 1990). See also the reviews and critiques of his approach: David Blumenthal, "A Review of Daniel Boyarin: *Intertextuality and the Reading of Midrash*," *CCAR Journal* (Summer/Fall 1995) 81–83; Martin Jaffee, "The Hermeneutical Model of Midrashic Studies: What it Reveals and What it Conceals," *Prooftexts* 11 (1991): 67–76.

ences the problem in the passage immediately following the *derasha* of R. Shmuel bar Naḥmani cited above (b. *Avodah Zarah* 25a):

מיתיבי: "ולא היה כיום ההוא לפניו ואחריו לשמוע יי'י
בקול איש"?! איבעיתימא: שעות הוא דלא הוה נפישן
כולי האי. ואיבעיתימא: אבני ברד לא הוו, דכתי[ב]: "ויהי
בנוסם מפני ישראל הם במורד בית חורון ויי'י השליך
עליהם אבנים גדולות מן השמים."

There is a problem: [The verse states] "And there was no day like this before or after where YHWH listened to a human's voice" (Josh 10:14)?! One could answer: It never lasted this long. One could also answer: There were no hail-stones [for Moses or Naqdimon], for it says: "And it was when they were running away from the Israelites, and they were on the Beit Horon descent, and YHWH threw upon them great stones from the sky."

The problem is clear. The verse says the miracle was unique, yet the midrash claims that Moses did it. The answers the Talmud offers undermine the uniqueness of the miracle. It isn't that only Joshua ever demonstrated control of the planets – Moses and Naqdimon did that as well. It is that some of the details of Joshua's miracle were unique; either it lasted longer than Moses' or the combination with the hailstone miracle was unique.[689] In both the Babylonian Talmud's iteration as well as that of the *Sifrei*, Joshua loses his special place as the only prophet/leader to ever stop the sun.

A third version of the tradition that Moses stopped the sun can be found in *Midrash Tanḥuma* (Warsaw ed., *Be-Shalaḥ* 28),[690] in a gloss on Exodus 17:12.

'ויהי ידיו אמונה עד בא השמש' – שהיו מחשבים את
השעות באסטרולוגיא. העמיד גלגל חמה מה עשה משה?
ולבנה וערב את שעותיהן, שנאמר: 'שמש ירח עמד זבולה
וגו',', וכתיב: 'נתן תהום קולו רום ידיהו נשא.'

'His hands were a source of faith until the sunset' – [The Amalekites] were trying to figure out [propitious] hours astrologically. What did Moses do? He stood the sun and moon still, mixing their hours, as it says (Hab 3:11): 'sun and moon stood still, each in its exalted place,' and it says (Hab 3:10): 'the depths give voice, he places his hands high.'

Although attached to the verse in Exodus, the key to the midrash are the two verses in Habakkuk. At the end of verse ten is a reference to someone with his hands extended and in the next verse there is the apparent freezing of the sun and moon in space. The *darshan* associates the arms raised in Habakkuk with the arms of Moses being raised. From there the jump to compare the context

---

689 The combination, but not the hailstones themselves, as Moses did bring hailstones as part of the ten plagues against the Egyptians (Exod 9:23).

690 The Buber edition does not contain a section on the Amalek story.

of Moses' arm-raising to the context of the next verse in Habakkuk is also a small one. Habakkuk describes hands reaching out leading to the stopping of the heavens, and if this is a reference to Moses, then when Moses had his hands outstretched, it must have been in order to stop the heavens.

Unique to *Tanḥuma* is the explanation for why Moses would need to perform this miracle. The midrash suggests that the miracle was performed not in order to extend the battle time (as Joshua did) or even in order to strike fear into the hearts of the enemy. Instead, the purpose was tactical and was meant to remove any possible benefit the Amalekites could have had due to their knowledge of astrology and, ostensibly, the times in which they could succeed against Israel, when God would be unable or unwilling to assist.[691]

Although *Tanḥuma* seems less easily traceable to anti-Christian polemic in this instance than the other two midrashim, there is actually a second element at play in this midrash that does bring up the specter of polemic. The oldest versions of the Joshua-Jesus typology use the battle with Amalek as one of their key elements. Specifically, the idea is floated that Joshua was chosen to defeat Amalek since Moses could not do it himself. For example, Justin Martyr (*Trypho* 90:5) writes:

οὐ γάρ, ὅτι οὕτως ηὔχετο Μωυσῆς, διὰ τοῦτο κρείσσων ὁ λαὸς ἐγίνετο, ἀλλ' ὅτι, ἐν ἀρχῇ τῆς μάχης τοῦ ὀνόματος τοῦ Ἰησοῦ ὄντος, αὐτὸς τὸ σημεῖον τοῦ σταυροῦ ἐποίει... | Really it was not because Moses prayed that the people were made victorious, rather because at the battlefront was the name of Joshua/Jesus while he [Moses] made the sign of the cross...

This idea that Moses stretching out his arms was really his making the sign of the cross becomes standard fare in Christian interpretation of the passage in Exodus. It would not be surprising, therefore, to see that the rabbis felt that this interpretation needed to be neutralized by offering another reason why Moses had his arms outstretched. In this sense, the *derasha* cited here in *Tanḥuma* accomplishes two polemical tasks at once: it neutralizes the cross symbolism of Moses stretching out his arms and it neutralizes the unique miracle of Joshua (stopping the sun) by giving it to Moses as well.

---

691 This midrash is reminiscent of the midrash regarding Balaam (b. *Berakhot* 7a), that the way he became successful at cursing and blessing was by learning the moments in which God is angry and exploiting this.

Moses the Giant Killer

There may be another, more subtle example of Moses being painted in Joshua's colors. In the Babylonian Talmud (b. *Berakhot* 54b), a list of places where miracles occurred to Israel's ancestors is provided; a blessing thanking God needs to be recited if anyone finds him- or herself in any of these places. One of the places mentioned is the rock which Og king of Bashan wished to throw upon the Israelites. The Talmud relates the story.

גמרא – 'אבן שבקש עוג מלך הבשן לזרוק על ישראל' גמירי לה.	'The stone which Og attempted to cast upon the Israelites' – this is a tradition.
איזיל ,אמר: "מחנה ישראל כמה הוי – תלתא פרסי ואיעקר טורא בר תלתא פרסי ואישדי עלייהו ואיקטלינהו."	[Og] said: "How big is the Israelite camp? Thirty parasangs? I will go and lift a thirty-parasang mountain and throw it upon them and kill them."
אזל עקר טורא בר תלתא פרסי ואייתי ואייתי על רישיה, קודשא בריך הוא עליה קמצי⁶⁹² ונקבוה ונחית בצואריה; הוה בעי למשלפה, משכי שיניה להאי גיסא ולהאי גיסא ולא מצי למשלפה,	He went and lifted a thirty-parasang mountain and rested it on his head. The Holy One, bb"h, brought locusts upon it and they ate a hole in it and it fell around his neck. [Og] tried to lift it off himself but his teeth stretched in each direction and he was unable to remove it.
וכדרבי שמעון בן והיינו דכתיב: 'שני רשעים שברת.' לקיש, דאמר רבי שמעון בן לקיש: "מאי דכתיב 'שני רשעים שברת'? אל תקרי 'שברת' אלא 'שרבבת.'"	This is the meaning of the verse (Ps. 3:8): 'You broke the teeth of the wicked.' And this is in accordance with R. Shimon ben Laqish, for R. Shimon ben Laqish said: "What is the meaning of the verse 'you broke the teeth of the wicked'? Do not read 'you have broken' (*shibarta*) rather 'you extended (*shirbavta*).'"
משה כמה הוה? עשר אמות. שקיל נרגא בר עשר אמין שוור עשר אמין, ומחייה בקרסוליה וקטליה.	How big was Moses? Ten cubits. He picked up an ax ten cubits long and jumped ten cubits. He hit [Og] in the ankle and he died.⁶⁹³

The story itself is a lampoon of Og the scary giant. As big as he was, and the story makes him monstrously big, he ends up with a mountain wrapped around

---

692 MS Florence leaves out the locusts and has God make the hole directly.
693 This final piece of the midrash is quoted verbatim in *Tarikh al-Ṭabari*. See: Abu Jafar al-Ṭabari's *History of the Prophets and Kings: Volume 3 – The Children of Israel* (trans. William Brinner; Albany: University of New York Press, 1991), "The Geneology of Moses b. Amram," 81–84. This plus the fact that the passage can be read independently of the story implies that "the ending" was either an independent passage added to an independent story or that the story was written with the already existing ending in mind.

his head like a doughnut and is quickly dispatched by Moses. The ankle theme may be an allusion to the famous story of Achilles' heel, but used for comic effect.

Two things stand out. First, the famous biblical giant killers are Caleb and, especially, Joshua. Joshua's prowess as a giant killer is emphasized at the end of the conquest account (Josh 11:21–22).

וַיָּבֹא יְהוֹשֻׁעַ בָּעֵת הַהִיא וַיַּכְרֵת אֶת הָעֲנָקִים מִן הָהָר מִן חֶבְרוֹן מִן דְּבִר מִן עֲנָב וּמִכֹּל הַר יְהוּדָה וּמִכֹּל הַר יִשְׂרָאֵל עִם עָרֵיהֶם הֶחֱרִימָם יְהוֹשֻׁעַ. לֹא נוֹתַר עֲנָקִים בְּאֶרֶץ בְּנֵי יִשְׂרָאֵל רַק בְּעַזָּה בְּגַת וּבְאַשְׁדּוֹד נִשְׁאָרוּ.	At that time, Joshua came and removed all the giants from the hill country – from Hebron, from Debir, from Anab, and from the entire hill country of Judah and from all the hill country of Israel, including their cities, Joshua destroyed them. No giants were left in the land of the Israelites; they remained only in Azza, Gath, and Ashdod.

I suggest that by making Moses a giant killer (the Bible does assume Og was large; see Deut 3:11) another feature unique to Joshua, or, at least, emphasized with Joshua and some other biblical characters—Caleb and David were giant killers as well but *not* Moses—disappears. Perhaps, as part of the polemic with Christianity, every matter with which Joshua excelled had to be given to Moses as well. Even if this was not the conscious intent of the authors of the story, this fact still sits well with the general trend to aggrandize Moses with the great actions of others, especially Joshua. In other words, perhaps due to the persistent Christian claim of Joshua/Jesus being greater than Moses, the Rabbis absorbed the polemical need to buttress the standing of Moses in every way possible. In this sense, the focus of the Rabbis in this midrash is less to shrink the image of Joshua (or Caleb), neither of whom are referenced here, than it is to strengthen the position of Moses as greatest Jewish hero (not just prophet) of the past.

One more element worth noting is the huge size of Moses himself. If Moses was ten cubits tall, then he was a giant as well. This same claim about an Israelite hero of the past having giant stature was made in the Samaritan book of Joshua about Joshua. In Joshua's letter to Shaubak, in chapter 29, he writes:

ليس انا جبار بل رب الجبابرة معى وطولى من الارض خمس اذرع ملكى.	I am no giant, but the master of giants is with me, and my height from the ground is five royal cubits.

Perhaps this represents a motif of making the great leaders of the past not only great in deed but great in appearance, specifically size. The two traditions share this motif, but I would not suggest any direct borrowing or polemical intent in this instance.

Moses Greater than Joshua

Another theme in Rabbinic midrash and aggadah regarding Joshua and Moses that might stem from anti-Christian polemic is the push to "remind the readers" that Moses was greater than Joshua. One example is the relative comparison of Moses and Joshua to the sun and moon respectively. This analogy seems to have its beginning in a statement of R. Nathan in *Sifrei Numbers* (*Pinhas* 140, Kahana ed.) quoted above.

ר' נתן או[מר]: "העמידו מן הארץ והושיבו על הספסל...	R. Nathan says: "[Moses] lifted Joshua up off the ground and placed him on the bench...[694]
שנאמר: 'ונתת מהודך עליו' – מהודך, ולא כל הודך,	as it says: 'and you shall give him some of your glory' – some of your glory, but not all of your glory. We can learn from this that Moses' face was like the sun and Joshua's like the moon."
נמצינו למדין פני משה כחמה ופני יהושע כלבנה."	

As discussed above, the original import of R. Nathan's statement appears to be that a balance had to be struck during Moses' lifetime between Joshua having a public face as a Torah-scholar on one hand and Moses maintaining his unique position as the source of Torah on the other.[695] However, his imagery of sun and moon soon took on a life of its own.

In the Babylonian Talmud (b. *Baba Batra* 75a) there is a statement of R. Ḥanina that echoes that of R. Nathan. R. Ḥanina is focusing on a verse in Isaiah (5:4).

וּבָרָא יי עַל כָּל מְכוֹן הַר צִיּוֹן וְעַל מִקְרָאֶהָ עָנָן יוֹמָם וְעָשָׁן וְנֹגַהּ אֵשׁ לֶהָבָה לָיְלָה כִּי עַל כָּל כָּבוֹד חֻפָּה.	YHWH will create over the whole seat of Mount Zion and over its places of assembly a cloud by day and smoke and the shining of a burning flame by night—for over all the glory there will be a canopy.

---

694 I am skipping over the gloss discussed above as it is not relevant to this section.

695 Whether the rabbis knew that the moon's light was simply a reflection of sun light (they probably did not know this) I am uncertain, but the imagery works fortuitously well for R. Nathan's point. As the Rabbinic saying goes, "He prophesied but did not know what he was prophesying."

The Talmud asks why there should be fire in the canopy. To this R. Ḥanina offers a response (b. *Baba Batra* 75a):

אמר רבי חנינא: "מלמד שכל אחד ואחד נכוה [חופתו][696] מחופתו של חבירו, אוי לה לאותה בושה, אוי לה לאותה כלימה!"[697]	R. Ḥanina said: "This teaches that each person's [canopy] is burned by the canopy of his fellow. Woe to this humiliation, woe to this degradation!"
כיוצא בדבר אתה אומר: 'ונתתה מהודך עליו' ולא כל הודך. זקנים שבאותו הדור אמרו: 'פני משה כפני חמה, פני יהושע כפני לבנה', אוי לה לאותה בושה, אוי לה לאותה כלימה!	Similarly, it says: 'and you shall give him some of your glory' – but not all of your glory. The elders of that generation would say: 'Moses' face is like the face of the sun and Joshua's face is like the face of the moon.' Woe to this humiliation, woe to this degradation!

The passage deals with competition between scholars, even scholars who are friendly with each other, living under the same "canopy." R. Ḥanina believes that the scholars inevitably burn each other, ostensibly with their Torah, with a distinct disadvantage going to the lesser scholars. Although it is inevitable, it is a shame, he says. The Talmud then brings up the case of Joshua and Moses as a comparison. According to this passage, it isn't simply that a later audience can learn from the verse that Moses was like the sun in comparison with Joshua's moon, but that during their lifetimes the elders of Israel would actually make this comparison. The passage then throws in the same woe, although it is unclear whether the shock is the fact that Moses so outshone Joshua or that the people would say this while they were around.

Either way, what this passage demonstrates is that the difference between Moses and Joshua isn't a neutral fact, but should be seen as embarrassing for Joshua. Such a shockingly insulting passage to Joshua may be better understood as a dig intended to knock Jesus, as the two individuals were identified with each other in some Christian hermeneutical traditions.

Excursus – Further Anti-Christian Polemics Surrounding Joshua

Although not particularly important insofar as Joshua's character is concerned, there are some examples of possible interreligious polemic worth noting, as they

---

696 Added based on MS Munich 95

697 This is the most common text; MS Vatican 115 and Oxford Opp. 249 (369) offer a slightly different text in which the canopies of the lesser individuals are burned by the canopies of the greater individuals.

may go a long way towards demonstrating that the Rabbis were aware of Christian appropriation of Joshua and concerned about it.

Joshua Marries Rahab

The first example of possible polemic is the midrash which says that Joshua married Rahab (b. *Megillah* 14b – MS New York-Columbia X 893 T 141).

אמ[ר] רב נחמן אמ[ר] רב: "חולדה מבני בניו שליהושע בן נון היתה. כתיב הכא: 'אשת שלום בן תקוה בן חרחס' וכת[יב] התם: 'ויקברו אתו בגבול נחלתו בתמנת סרח' וכת[יב] 'בתמנת חרס.'"	Rav Naḥman said in the name of Rav: "Huldah was a descendent of Joshua son of Nun. It says here (2 Kings 22:14): 'The wife of Shalom son of Tikvah son of Ḥarḥas,' and it says there (Josh 24:30), 'and they buried him on the edge of his inheritance in Timnat Seraḥ,' and it says (Judg 2:9), 'Timnat Ḥeres.'"
אותיביה רב עינא סבא לרב נחמן ואמרי לה רב [עניא]⁶⁹⁸ סבא לרב נחמן: "שמונה נביאים והם כהנים יצאו מן רחב הזונה, ואלו הן: ברוך בן נריה, שריה, מחסיה, ירמיה, חלקיה, חנמאל, שלום. ר' יהודה אומ[ר]: 'אף חולדה מבני בניה שלרחב היתה.' כת[יב] הכא: "אשת שלום בן תקוה", וכת[יב] התם: "את תקות חוט השני הזה וג'."	Rav Eyna the elder brought a contradictory source to Rav Naḥman – some say it was Rav Anya the elder to Rav Naḥman: "Eight prophets who were priests descended from Rahab the harlot, these were: Baruch ben Neriah, Sariah, Mahasiah, Jeremiah, Hilkiah, Hanamel and Shalom. R. Yehudah says: 'Even Huldah was a descendent of Rahab.' It says here: "The wife of Shalom son of Tikvah," and it says there (Josh 2:18), "the line (*tiqvah*) of scarlet thread...""
אמ[ר] ליה: "עניא סבא!" ואמרי לה "פתיא אוכאמא! מיני ומינך תסתיים שמעתא: דאיגיירא רחב ונסבה יהושע."	[Rav Naḥman] responded: "Poor old man!"⁶⁹⁹ Some say [Rav Naḥman] responded: "Dark pot! Between yours and mine we can solve the matter: Rahab converted and Joshua married her."
ומי הוה ליה זרעא ליהושע? והא כת[יב]: 'נון בנו יהושע בנו'? בני לא הוה ליה בנתא הוי ליה.	But did Joshua have offspring? Doesn't it say (1 Chron 7:27): 'Nun his son, Joshua his son'? He had no sons, but he did have daughters.

In this back and forth between Rav Naḥman and Rav Eyna, two different midrashim are placed in tension with each other. There is one midrash, that of Rav

---

698 The reading of this word in this manuscript is unclear. The above reading is based on MS Paris – Alliance Israelite University III A 46.

699 A play on his name – Eyna to Anya; this may also explain the confusion about his name at the beginning of the pericope, as a later copyist may not have understood the sarcasm behind Rav Naḥman's metathesis and thought that the man's name was actually Anya.

Naḥman, that makes Joshua the ancestor of Huldah the prophetess. This midrash is based on the bizarre name of one of Huldah's ancestors, Ḥarḥas.[700] The rabbis suggest that this name is actually an allusion to Joshua, and his city Timnat Ḥeres, also known as Timnat Seraḥ. The second midrash, the Tannaitic source quoted by Rav Eyna, has R. Judah claiming that Huldah is a descendent of Rahab. Although Rav Eyna sees this as a contradiction to Rav Naḥman, Rav Naḥman himself says that the tension is easily solved by assuming that Joshua and Rahab were married and were jointly the ancestors of Huldah.

On the surface, one can see this Talmudic pericope as based purely on the technicalities of the midrash. However, it should be pointed out that claiming Joshua married Rahab, or that Joshua was married at all, puts the rabbis in a contradictory stance to that of certain early Christian writers.

Concerning Joshua's being married, the Syriac church father, Aphrahat, makes a strong claim regarding Joshua's virginity in his 18th demonstration "Against the Jews and on Virginity and Sanctity" (18.7):

ܝܫܘܥ ܒܪ ܢܘܢ ܐܚܒ ܒܬܘܠܘܬܐ ܘܥܡܪ	Yeshua son of Nun loved virginity and dwelt in
ܒܡܫܟܢܐ ܐܬܪ ܕܩܕܝܫܐ ܡܬܫܡܫ ܗܘܐ...	the tent, a place where the Holy one was served...
ܐܠܐ ܚܘܐ ܠܝ ܐܘ ܡܠܦܢܐ ܥܠ ܝܫܘܥ ܒܪ ܢܘܢ	But show me, oh master, regarding Yeshua son
ܕܢܣܒ ܐܢܬܬܐ ܘܐܘܠܕ ܒܢܝܐ...	of Nun, that he took a wife and had children...

Aphrahat, listing parallels between the great leaders of the Israelite past and Jesus, points to the characteristic of virginity, and claims a number of leaders to have been unmarried, including Joshua. He challenges his Jewish opponents to prove that Joshua had a wife. It is possible that that is exactly what R. Naḥman intended to do. The Talmud is aware of the controversial nature of Rav Naḥman's *derasha*, as the voice of the editor raises the objection that Joshua had no offspring according to the midrashic reading of First Chronicles (analyzed above in a previous section). However, the Talmud quickly answers by suggesting that the midrash only said he had no sons, but he may have had daughters. Needless to say, if Joshua married Rahab and had daughters, he was not a virgin.

The other possible polemical use of the above quoted Talmudic passage focuses not on Joshua but on Rahab. The Gospel of Mathew (1:5) has Rahab marrying Salmon and giving birth to Boaz, thereby making her an ancestor of David as

---

700 The unusual nature of the name may also account for the confusion in the manuscripts. Some read Ḥeres, clearly influenced by the name of Joshua's city, and some read Ḥarḥam, due to the lithographic confusion between a *samekh* and a final *mem*.

well as Joseph, Jesus' "father." The rabbis, in turn, make her an ancestress of eight different people, including priests, but not of David. Also instead of being the wife of Salmon and progenitor of the "father" of Jesus, she becomes the wife of Joshua and the progenitor of Shalom, among others. It seems rather striking that both texts reference a man named Shalom. This appears to be a Rabbinic recasting of the Christian tradition, with the Rabbis saying "yes there is a tradition like this about Rahab, but not the way you (Christians) present it."

Both traditions emphasize the same basic irony. The Christians are saying that the famous harlot became the progenetress of the messianic line and the rabbis are saying that she became the progenetress of prophets and priests. The latter is especially poignant, from a halakhic perspective, since it is forbidden for a priest to marry a harlot, and a priest born of a harlot would be disqualified.

Joshua Stops the Sun in Order to Avoid Breaking Shabbat

According to Rabbinic halakha, it is permissible for an army to do battle on Shabbat. However, going back to Second Temple times, one can see that whether this was permissible or not was a matter of dispute.[701] It is no surprise, then, that in the late rabbinic work *Pirqei de-Rabbi Eliezer*, a work which is steeped in Pseudepigraphical literature from Second Temple times, this tradition makes its appearance again.[702]

In chapter 51, there is a listing of miracles. The sixth in the list deals with Joshua stopping the sun.

המופת הששי מיום שנבראו שמים וארץ השמש והירח	The sixth wonder: From the day the heavens
והכבבים וכל המזלות היו עולין להאיר על הארץ ואינן	and the earth were created, the sun the moon
מערערין זה עם זה, עד שבא יהושע ועשה מלחמתן של	and the stars and all the constellations rose
ישראל, והגיע ערב שבת וראה בצרתן של ישראל שלא	to give light upon the earth and [their sched-
יחללו את השבת, ועוד שראו חרטומי גוים כובשים	ules] were never in conflict until Joshua came
במזלות לבא על ישראל, מה עשה יהושע? פשט ידו לאור	and fought the wars of Israel. The eve of the
השמש ולאור הירח והזכיר עליהם את השם ועמד כל	Sabbath came along and he saw the pain Israel
אחד במקומו ששה ושלשים שעות עד מוצאי שבת, שנ'	was under, that they might violate the Sabbath

---

701 See, for example, 1 Macc 2:35 – 41, in which many Judeans die rather than fight on the Sabbath until the Maccabees make a rule that fighting on the Sabbath is permitted.
702 For more on the pseudepigraphical sources in *Pirqei de-Rabbi Eliezer*, see: Rachel Adelman, *The Return of the Repressed: Pirqe de-Rabbi Eliezar and the Pseudepigrapha* (JSJsup 140; Leiden: Brill, 2009).
703 These three words לא יהיה כן do not appear in the biblical text.

וידום השמש וירח עמד עד יקום גוי אויביו ויעמד השמש" —additionally, he saw that the gentile sorcerors
בחצי השמים ולא אץ לבא כיום תמים." וראו כל מלכי would conquer the constellations and send
הארץ ותמהו שלא היה כמהו מיום שנברא העולם, שנ' them against Israel. What did Joshua do? He
"ולא היה כיום ההוא לפניו ואחריו לא[703] יהיה כן לשמוע spread out his arm into the light of the sun
ה' בקול איש כי ה' נלחם בישראל." and the light of the moon and pronounced
the name of God. Each one stood in its place
for 36 hours until the Sabbath passed, as it
says (Josh 10:13): "And the sun froze and the
moon stood still until a nation was avenged
upon its adverseries. And the sun stood in
the middle of the sky and did not set for an entire day." Now all the kings of the land saw this
and were shocked, since nothing like this had
ever happened before, as it says (Josh 10:14):
"and there was never a day like this before
nor will there ever be one since where God listened to the voice of a human, for God fought
on behalf of Israel."

The benefit of having Joshua do the miracle in order to enable Sabbath observance may be clear to any halakhically minded person. It also may seem an ironic
triumphalism to outsiders, since Sabbath observance is only significant to keep-
ers of Torah, the fact that God would do a miracle unprecedented in all of human
history would go far in emphasizing the correctness of the Jewish, Sabbath-ob-
servant lifestyle. However, there may have been a polemical benefit to this claim
as well.

The fact that the siege of Jericho took seven days, and that each day the people would march around the city carrying shofars and blowing them, might be
taken to imply that Joshua and the Israelites must have violated the Sabbath
in the siege of the city. This fact did not go unnoticed by the Church Fathers.
For example, in his *Adversus Iudaeos* (4:8-9), Tertullian writes:

Denique adeo non in vacatione septimi diei haec In fact, to such a degree is this festival not to be
sollemnitas celebranda est, ut Iesus Naue eo celebrated through rest on the seventh day, that
tempore quo Hiericho civitatem debellabat prae- Iesu son of Nau, at the time he was subduing
ceptum sibi a deo diceret, uti populo mandaret, the city of Jericho, said that [he received] a
ut sacerdotes arcam testamend dei septem die- command to him from the deity to require the
bus circumferrent in circuitu civitatis, atque ita people that the priests should go around in cir-
septimi diei circuitu peracto sponte ruerent cuits with the ark of the testimony for seven
muri civitatis. days; as soon as the circuit of the seventh
day would be accomplished, the walls of the
city would immediately collapse.

Tertullian learns from the Jericho episode that Joshua was hinting to the people that resting on the Sabbath was not really God's ultimate intention. This was demonstrated by the fact that God himself, by commanding the people to circle the walls for seven days straight, was forcing the people of Israel to violate the Sabbath.

In his thirteenth demonstration ("On the Sabbath"), Aphrahat makes the same claim (13.12):

ܝܫܘܥ ܓܝܪ ܒܪ ܢܘܢ ܠܐ ܐܢܝܚ ܐܢܘܢ ܒܫܒܬܐ ܟܕ ܥܒܕ ܗܘܐ ܩܪܒܐ ܒܐܝܪܝܚܘ ܐܝܟ ܕܐܡܪ ܫܠܝܚܐ ܝܕܝܥܐ ܕܐܠܘ ܝܫܘܥ ܒܪ ܢܘܢ ܐܢܝܚ ܗܘܐ ܐܢܘܢ ܬܘܒ ܠܐ ܡܬܡܠܠ ܗܘܐ ܥܠ ܝܘܡܐ ܕܫܒܬܐ. ܐܠܐ ܡܟܝܠ ܩܝܡܐ ܗܝ ܫܒܬܐ ܕܐܠܗܐ.	Indeed, Yeshua son of Nun did not let them rest on the Sabbath when he was making war on Jericho, as the renowned apostle said (Heb 4:8 – 9): "For if Yeshua son of Nun had allowed them to rest there would not have been talk again about the Sabbath day. Rather, from that time on the Sabbath of God existed."

Although the text in *Pirqei de-Rabbi Eliezer* does not respond directly to the question of Sabbath observance and the siege of Jericho, claiming that God actually stopped the sun specifically for the purpose of allowing Israel not to violate the Sabbath in the middle of a battle that had already commenced would go a long way towards implying that Israel must have kept the Sabbath during their siege of Jericho and that the problematic behavior of carrying the rams horns must have a halakhically acceptable explanation.[704]

Joshua Receives the "Yod" from Sarai

In a number of places in rabbinic literature (*Gen Rab., Lekh Lekha* 47; also *Lev. Rab., Metzora* 19:2) the rabbis call attention to the changing of Joshua's name and Sarah's name.

704 For example, the area was not a public thoroughfare, they put up an *eruv*, they carried the horns in an unusual way, or with two people holding it at the same time – there is no shortage of technical ways out of this problem for those inclined to look for them.

'ר אמר – [ולא תקרא את שמה שרי כי שרה שמה]

יהושע בן קרחה יוד שנטל הקדוש ברוך הוא משרי היה

טס ופורח לפני הקדוש ברוך הוא, אמר לפניו רבון כל

העולמים בשביל שאני קטן מכל האותיות הוצאתני משם

הצדקת, אמר לו הקדוש ברוך הוא לשעבר הייתה בשמה

שלנקבה ובסוף האותיות, עכשיו אני נותנך בשם זכר

ובראש האותיות ויקרא משה להושע בן נן יהושע.

'Her name will no longer be Sarai, but Sarah is her name' (Gen 17:15) – R. Joshua ben Qorḥa said: "The *yod* that the Holy One, bb"h, took from Sarai was flying and floating before the Holy One, bb"h. [The yod] stated before Him: 'Master of the worlds, is it because I am the smallest of all letters that you took me out of the righteous woman's name?!' The Holy One, bb"h, replied: 'In the past you were in a woman's name and the last letter, now I will place you in a man's name and the first letter.' – 'And Moses called Hoshea son of Nun, Yehoshua' (Num 13:16)."

As it appears in *Genesis Rabbah* in the name of R. Joshua ben Qorḥa, the midrash is relatively early. The hermeneutic is relatively tight, as the argument is simply that God didn't waste the letter he removed from Sarah's name, but saved it for Joshua. (That this was noticed by a man named Joshua is a humorous irony.) The reason Abraham does not receive a *derasha* like this is because his name change was simply the addition of one letter, *hey*, into his name.

It is difficult to know whether there is polemical intent in this midrash, but a certain passage in Justin Martyr's *Dialogue with Trypho* (113) may be evidence that it is.

1. Ὃ δὲ λέγω τοιοῦτόν ἐστιν. Ἰησοῦν, ὡς προέφην πολλάκις, Αὐσῆν καλούμενον, ἐκεῖνον τὸν μετὰ τοῦ Χαλὲβ κατάσκοπον εἰς τὴν Χαναὰν [ἐπὶ τὴν] γῆν ἀποσταλέντα, Ἰησοῦν Μωυσῆς <ἐπ>εκάλεσε. Τοῦτο σὺ οὐ ζητεῖς δι' ἣν αἰτίαν ἐποίησεν, οὐκ ἀπορεῖς, οὐδὲ φιλοπευστεῖς· τοιγαροῦν λέληθέ σε ὁ Χριστός, καὶ ἀναγινώσκων οὐ συνίης, οὐδὲ νῦν, ἀκούων ὅτι Ἰησοῦς ἐστιν ὁ Χριστὸς ἡμῶν, συλλογίζῃ οὐκ ἀργῶς οὐδ' ὡς ἔτυχεν ἐκείνῳ τεθεῖσθαι τοὔνομα.

1. What I am saying is this: Iesu (Joshua), as I have said many times, was called Ausei (Hoshea); when with Caleb he was sent to scout out the land of Canaan, Moses renamed him Iesu. You (Jews) do not search out for the reason he did this, nor are you fond of inquiring. Accordingly, Christ has escaped your notice, and when reading you do not perceive, and not even now, hearing that Iesu is our Christ, do you do nothing to discover that he was given this name purposefully, not accidentally.

2. ἀλλὰ διὰ τί μὲν ἓν ἄλφα πρώτῳ προσετέθη τοῦ Ἀβραὰμ ὀνόματι, θεολογεῖς, καὶ διὰ τί ἓν ῥῶ τῷ Σάρρας ὀνόματι, ὁμοίως κομπολογεῖς· διὰ τί δὲ τὸ πατρόθεν ὄνομα τῷ Αὐσῆ, τῷ υἱῷ Ναυῆ, ὅλον μετωνόμασται τῷ Ἰησοῦ, οὐ ζητεῖς ὁμοίως.

2. Rather, you theologize about why one *alpha* was added into Abraham's name, and you speak boldly about why one *rho* was added into Sarah's name, but you do not search out in a like fashion why from the name of Ausai, the son of Nau, given by his father, the entire thing was changed to Iesu.

Justin's point seems to be that the change of Ausai to Iesu is much more extensive than merely adding a letter, as was done to Abraham and Sarah, and still the

Jews only notice these two but not Joshua. Now Justin is wrong about the mechanics here, due to his apparent lack of knowledge of the Hebrew text of the Pentateuch. (There may be a Hellenistic midrash, however, with which Justin was familiar.) Nevertheless, it is unknown whether there was a midrashic explanation of Joshua's name in Justin's time or not. Whether R. Joshua ben Qorḥa's midrash was in response to Justin or whether Justin was simply ignorant of Rabbinic lore surrounding the name of Joshua is difficult to say (the two men were roughly contemporary.)

Undoing the Significance of Joshua's "Second Circumcision"

The early Church Fathers note the odd description in the Bible of Joshua circumcising the Israelites a second time. Obviously, they say, a man cannot be circumcised twice. Ignoring the simple meaning of the text, that the wilderness-born generationwas not circumcised and that this was the second time the Israelites were ritually circumcised as a group, the first time being by Moses in Egypt, Justin Martyr (*Dialogue with Trypho* 113.6 – 7) argues that what is being referred to here is circumcision of the heart. This second circumcision of Joshua is really an allegory for the future spiritual circumcision of the world by the second Joshua, i.e., Jesus.[705]

ἐκεῖνος λέγεται δευτέραν *περιτομὴν μαχαίραις πετρίναις* τὸν λαὸν *περιτετμηκέναι* (ὅπερ κήρυγμα ἦν τῆς περιτομῆς ταύτης ἧς περιέτεμεν ἡμᾶς αὐτὸς Ἰησοῦς Χριστὸς ἀπὸ τῶν λίθων καὶ τῶν ἄλλων εἰδώλων) καὶ θημωνιὰν ποιῆσαι τῶν ἀπὸ ἀκροβυστίας (τοῦτέστιν ἀπὸ τῆς πλάνης τοῦ κόσμου) ἐν παντὶ τόπῳ περιτμηθέντων *πετρίναις μαχαίραις*, (<τουτέστι> τοῖς Ἰησοῦ τοῦ κυρίου ἡμῶν λόγοις). ὅτι γὰρ λίθος καὶ *πέτρα* ἐν παραβολαῖς ὁ Χριστὸς διὰ τῶν προφητῶν ἐκηρύσσετο, ἀποδέδεικταί μοι.

Καὶ τὰς μαχαίρος οὖν τὰς πετρίνας τοὺς λόγους αὐτοῦ ἀκουσόμεθα, δι' ὧν οἱ ἀπὸ τῆς ἀκροβυστίας πλανώμενοι τοσοῦτοι καρδίας περιτομὴν περιετμήθησαν ἣν περιτνηθῆναι...

This one (Joshua) was said to circumcise the people of foreskins a second time with swords of stone (thus it was a sign of that circumcision with which Jesus Christ would circumcise us – from stones and other idols) and to make a gathering from all of the uncircumcised (that is from the vagabonds of the world) in every place circumcising them with stone swords (namely with the words of Jesus our Lord.) For rock and stone are allegories for Christ through the proclamation of the prophets, as has been demonstrated by me.

And so, by the stone swords the meaning of his words we hear [properly], by which those who were wandering have been circumcised from their uncircumcision with the circumcision of the heart...

---

705 See the section on Justin Martyr in the chapter on Church Fathers for more discussion of this interpretation.

I would like to suggest that this claim about the symbolic nature of Joshua's circumcision of the people and the suggestion that it improves upon the original circumcision of the Children of Israel that began with Abraham, is the backdrop for the idiosyncratic interpretation of Rav, quoted by Rabbah bar Rav Yitzḥaq, in the Babylonian Talmud (*Yebamot* 71b):

אמר רבה בר [רב] יצחק אמר רב: "לא ניתנה פריעת מילה לאברהם אבינו, שנאמר: 'בעת ההיא אמר ה' אל יהושע: "עשה לך חרבות צורים ושוב מל את בני ישראל שנית."'".	Rabba son of [Rav] Yitzḥaq said in the name of Rav: "*Periʿah*[706] was not given to our father Abraham, as it says (Josh 5:2): 'At that time, God said to Joshua: "Make for yourself flintstone blades, and turn and circumcise the Children of Israel a second time."'"
ודלמא הנך דלא מהול, דכתיב: "כי מולים היו כל העם היוצאים וכל העם הילודים במדבר!" א"כ, מאי 'שוב'? אלא לאו לפריעה. ומאי שנית? לאקושי סוף מילה לתחלת מילה, מה תחלת מילה מעכבת, אף סוף מילה מעכבין בו.	Perhaps [the verse] refers to those who were never circumcised, as it says (Josh 5:5): "For all that left [Egypt] had been circumcised, but all who were born in the wilderness[as they were leaving Egypt were not circumcised]"! If that were the case, to what does "again" refer? Rather, [the verse] must be discussing *periʿah*. And what does "a second time" mean? This is meant to connect the end of circumcision with the beginning of circumcision; just like the beginning of circumcision is an absolute requirement, so too the completion of circumcision is an absolute requirement.

In this text, Rav suggests that it is true that Joshua's circumcision improved upon that of Abraham, but not *spiritually*. Instead, the improvement is *physical*, with the peeling of the epithelium being added to the process. This is what God meant by doing it again, i.e., doing it properly, the new way. This may be seen as a backhanded slap against the "spiritual circumcision" interpretation.

The above examples show how fertile and rewarding a cross cultural and multi-disciplinary approach to studying this material can be. By reading the Rabbinic texts in conversation with the Church Fathers, the study brings insights to what may be behind some of the midrashim that would otherwise be lost. In other words, sometimes in order to understand the Rabbis one must read the Church Fathers. Elchanan Reiner's studies, analyzed next, demonstrate a similar concept.

---

706 *Periʿah* refers to the peeling of the epithelium.

An Early Joshua-as-Messiah Tradition in the Galilee

In his studies of the religious geography of the Galilee in the classic through Byzantine periods, Elchanan Reiner isolates a messianic theme surrounding a figure, or multiple figures, named Joshua.[707] What attracts Reiner's notice are the many places in the Galilee associated with Joshua bin Nun, including places that the biblical story places in the Mount Ephraim region such as Timnat Heres and Mount Ga'ash. Additionally, a synagogue in Tiberious is identified by local tradition as the synagogue that Joshua built or the synagogue built on the spot where Joshua prayed immediately after he and the Israelites crossed the Jordan. This, Reiner points out, would mean that local tradition believed that the Israelites crossed the Jordan near the Sea of Galilee and not opposite Jericho as the Bible states.[708]

Reiner also notes that the idea of a northern crossing of the Israelites is buttressed by a well-documented and very old (Rabbinic) tradition that Miriam's well is actually part of the Sea of Galilee.[709] Finally, in one tradition, that of R. Jacob ben Nathaniel, it is recorded that Joseph's tomb, which is said to be in Shechem in the Bible, is located in the Galilee. "In other words, Joshua, Joseph and Miriam—three names that... are highly suggestive when they appear together... are commemorated in a number of spots in the Galilee" (Reiner, "Towards a Typology," 97).

At this point, considering the earliest source for any of these traditions is fourth century (*Lev. Rab.*), one might be tempted to explain this phenomenon as Old Testament characters being moved to the north either to merge with or compete with their New Testament namesakes. Perhaps local Jews, responding either consciously or unconsciously to the religious geography of their Christian neighbors, associated their own heroes with the local holy places associated with Jesus, Joseph, and Mary.

However, Reiner argues that something else might be occurring here. He points to a tradition in the *Book of Jubilees* 34:4–8 that Jacob defeated and then built up Ga'ash, Arbel, and Timnat Heres in his battle against the Amorites

---

707 Elchanan Reiner, "From Joshua to Jesus," 233–271; Elchanan Reiner, "Towards a Typology," 94–105.

708 Reiner uses a number of sources for the local traditions. Some of the key sources are medieval travel books like the *Itinerary* of Benjamin of Tudela (c. 1170), the *Travels* of R. Petaḥiah of Ratisbon/Regensberg (c.1180), and *Book of the Settlement* of Jacob ben Nathaniel ha-Kohen (second half of the twelfth century).

709 This can be found in *Midrash Tanḥuma ha-Qadum* (ed. Buber; Ḥuqqat 50) and *Leviticus Rabba* 22:4.

of Shechem. The question is whether the Arbel referenced here is meant to be near Shechem or whether the battle is imagined to have been fought in the Galilee. Reiner argues for the latter and points to Galilean traditions that Simon, Levi, and Dinah, the three main protagonists of the Shechem story, were buried in the Galilee.[710] For this reason, Reiner speculates that the idea of Joshua crossing the Jordan near the Galilee and being buried there might date back to the second century BCE. If that is correct, the reason for this move must be something other than Jesus.

Reiner notes that it is not only Joshua and Jesus who are interchangeable in certain of the local geographic traditions, but there are other "Joshuas" as well. For example, a quasi-rabbinic figure named R. Joshua ben Perahiah becomes associated with Joshua's Galilean tomb.[711] Another Galilean Joshua can be found in the Baraita of Priestly Course (*mishmarot*), which refers to a certain priestly course as that of Yeshua of Arbel. This character is known from other works as Yehoshua ben ha-Nisraf (or Nishdaf in some texts), an odd appellative meaning "the burnt" (or "the blighted.").

In the seventh century apocalyptic work, *Sefer Zerubbabel*, Yeshua of Arbel is identified with the biblical character Yehoshua ben Yehozaddak, the high priest from the second temple period. A possible explanation for this identification can be found in both Talmuds. The Jerusalem Talmud (*Ta'anit* 4:5), pointing to the verse in which God describes Joshua ben Jehozadak as "a brand plucked from the fire" (Zech 3:2), says that this Joshua was the only surviver out of 80,000 who were burned during the destruction of the first temple. The Babylonian Talmud (*Sanhedrin* 93a) suggests that Joshua ben Jehozadak was the fourth man together with Hananiah, Mishael, and Azariah in the flaming furnace. Either way, this would "explain" (or foreground) the nickname "Joshua the burnt."

All four (or five) of these Joshuas appear in Galilean traditions as locals, and all seem to be associated with some sort of messianic yearning, as is the city of Arbel itself. Furthermore, it seems clear that Jesus is the catalyst for many of these accounts. One can see a number of similarities between the Galilean Joshua stories and that of Jesus. When Joshua died, the world shook and a heavenly voice called out in agony. According to the *Book of Sefer Zerubbabel*, on the an-

---

710 In my opinion, this is the most speculative of all of Reiner's points, and the most difficult to defend. Why couldn't the story envision a campaign in which Jacob fights from the Shechem region all the way up to Arbel? If that were the case, it would be impossible to know from this text alone whether the traditions had moved north by this period.

711 Reiner speculates that this may have been because Joshua ben Perahiah was known as the partner (*zug*) of Nitai of Arbel (m. *Abot* 1:6), and the tomb is in the vicinity of Arbel ("Transformation," 213 n.24).

niversary of Joshua's death (18 Iyyar), the earth will shake again and redemption will come—Joshua's second coming.

The character of Joshua ben Peraḥiah is entirely intertwined with that of Jesus in popular literature from the ancient to medieval period. In the *Toledot Yeshu*, he is known as Jesus' teacher. Both men are magicians and they do battle in the sky (*p-r-ḥ* means "to fly" among other things.) Both men escape to Egypt together in the time of King Yanai. Also, Jesus, according to this tradition, was executed in the Galilee. With all of these details and more, Reiner suggests that there must have been a local Galilean version of "the passion" to which elements of *Toledot Yeshu* attempt to respond polemically.

In short, there seems to have been a strong tradition in the Galilee about a messianic figure named Joshua/Jesus. Whether this tradition predates Jesus (as Reiner believes) or whether it is a result of Jesus (which seems more likely to me) is unclear. However, after Jesus' death and the beginnings of Christianity, this idea took off. Joshua bin Nun is moved from Mount Ephraim into the Galilee, and Joshua ben Jehozadak the high priest is moved from Jerusalem to the Galilee. Both become quasi-messiah figures from the town of future redemption, Arbel. Furthermore, Joshua himself is given many of Jesus' roles. Even a sort of Rabbinic anti-Jesus (I do not mean antichrist) was created in the person of R. Joshua ben Peraḥiah. Some of the local traditions were sympathetic to the Joshua-Jesus idea (*Book of Sefer Zerubbabel*) and some were antagonistic (*Toledot Yeshu*).

Eventually, with the advent of the crusades, this Jewish messianic-Joshua figure became too controversial and "shattered." Some of the sites became associated with different biblical figures (the tomb of Joshua becomes the tomb of Jethro, for instance.) Finally, Reiner argues in his second article, the bulk of the messianic traditions became swallowed up by the mystical figure of R. Shimon bar Yohai, who inherited some of Joshua's messianic stories, including his Yahrzeit (day of death.)

When taking the above together with two examples in the excursus from chapter 5 called "The Joshua-Jesus Typology in Early Jewish-Christianity" it seems that there was a strong Jewish element behind the idea of a messianic Joshua, including perhaps, Joshua the high priest. Although it still seems most likely that the typology originated with Christians, Reiner's research (and Stroumsa's) points to a complex web of interactions between Jews, Jewish Christians, and gentile Christians in the formation of the Joshua Jesus correlation, one that affected the hermeneutic traditions of all three groups.

Joshua as Inferior to Moses

Whether inspired by polemic with Christianity or not, there seems to be a number of midrashim, unrelated to anything specific in Christian theology or hermeneutics, that emphasize the greatness of Moses as compared with Joshua.

Moses and his Trumpets

One rather benign example of a rabbinic interpretation that places Moses above Joshua comes in a quasi-halakhic discussion surrounding the blowing of the trumpets described in Numbers 10. The *derasha* appears both in *Midrash Tanḥuma* (*Ba-ha'alotkha*, ed. Buber 18 [ed. Warsaw 10]) and *Numbers Rabbah* (*Ba-ha'alotkha* 15). The text below is from *Tanḥuma* (ed. Buber), and begins with a gloss on Num. 10:2, in which Moses is told to make "for himself" (the ethical dative) two silver trumpets.

'עשה לך' – לך אתה עושה, ולא לאחרים, אתה משתמש בהן, ואין אחר משתמש בהן,	'Make for yourself' – make them for you, but not for others, you may use them but others may not use them.
תדע לך שהרי יהושע תלמידו לא נשתמש בהן, אלא בשופרות, כשבאו להלחם ביריחו...[712] מה כתיב? "וירע העם ויתקעו בשופרות." מלמד שאפי' יהושע תלמידו לא נשתמש בהן.	Notice that even his student, Joshua, did not use them, instead he used the shofars. When they arrived to do battle at Jericho... what does it say? "And the people blew on the shofars" (Josh 6:20). This teaches that even Joshua, [Moses'] student did not use [the trumpets].
ולא תאמר ליהושע, אלא אפי' משה רבינו עצמו עד שהוא חי גנזו.	This is not only true of Joshua, but even our Master Moses himself buried them during his lifetime.
אמר ר' יצחק: "הרי שמשה אמר בשעה שהוא בא להפטר מן העולם, 'הקהילו אלי [את כל זקני שבטיכם ושוטריכם.]' והיכן היו החצוצרות, שלא היה אומר תקעו בהן ויתכנסו? אלא שעד שהוא בחייו גנזו."	R. Isaac said: "At the time when Moses was preparing to depart from this world, [he said] (Deut 31:28), 'Gather to me all the elders of your tribes and your officials.' Where were the trumpets, for he did not say blow the trumpets in order to gather them? Rather, while he was yet alive, he buried them."
אמר ר' יהושע דסכנין בשם ר' לוי: "לקיים מה שנאמר: 'ואין שלטון ביום המות'."	R. Joshua of Sikhnin said in the name of R. Levi: "This was to fulfill the verse, 'There is no rulership on the day of death'."

---

712 I skip here a long tangent attempting to prove that members of all seven nations took part in the battle over Jericho.

הוי עשה לך, ואין אחר משתמש בהן כל ימיך. This 'make for yourself' implies that no one may use them throughout your lifetime.

Although the hook is the ethical dative, the rabbis are picking up on the lack of mention of trumpets in other narrative contexts. What happened to the trumpets? The author of this midrash suggest that the trumpets were a demonstration of Moses' unique authority and place in history. Moses would be permitted to use the trumpets, but they were to be buried during his lifetime. Even the great Joshua, who was to win the battle of Jericho by a miracle performed by the blasting of the horns, would have to be content using the rams horn and not the silver trumpets.

The midrash may be free-standing, as it makes sense even without any polemical context. Nevertheless, it takes on added force if seen as part of the push to place Joshua firmly as a distant second to Moses.

Joshua Completes Moses' Miracle with the Hail Stones

Another example of the rabbis connecting Joshua to Moses in such a way as to make Joshua an extension of Moses as opposed to an independent player can be found in b. *Berakhot* (54b), which discusses the miracle of hail.[713] The Talmud is commenting on a list of places where miracles occurred where a blessing thanking God for these miracles needs to be recited.[714] One of the places mentioned is the "al-gabish stones on the descent of Beit Horon." The Talmud suggests a midrashic explanation for this mysterious place based on word-play.

מאי אבני אלגבי"ש? תאנא: אבנים שעמדו על גב איש What are stones of al-gabish? It was taught: וירדו על גב איש. Stones that stood due to a man (*al gab ish*) and fell due to a man.

---

713 Following the Vilna and Soncino printings; there are significant variants but the midrash is substantially the same in all of them.

714 This is the same list referenced above in the section about Moses killing Og.

עמדו על גב איש – זה משה, דכתיב: "והאיש משה ענו Stood due to a man – this is Moses, for it is
מאד", וכתיב: "ויחדלו הקלות והברד ומטר לא נתך written (Num 12:3): "The man Moses was
ארצה." ירדו על גב איש – זה יהושע, דכתיב: "קח לך very humble," and it is written (Exod 9:33):
את יהושע בן נון איש אשר רוח בו", וכתיב: "ויהי "The noises stopped and the hail and rain
בנוסם מפני בני ישראל הם במורד בית חורן וה' השליך did not hit the ground." Fell due to a man –
עליהם אבנים גדלות." this is Joshua, for it is written (Num 27:18):
"Take Joshua son of Nun, a man with spirit in
him," and it is written (Josh 10:11): "and it
happened when Israel was on the descent of
Beit Horon, that the Lord threw down large
stones upon them."

Other than the word play and the use of the term 'man' (*ish*) by both Moses and
Joshua, what the midrash picks up on is the similarity in miracles between
Moses and Joshua. Both prophets rain hailstones down on their opponents.
The similarity between these two figures and their miracles was very possibly
an intentional resonance original in the biblical text. However, the Rabbis take
this resonance one step further by suggesting that the hailstones of Joshua
were actually the very hailstones created by Moses.

To make this argument, they point out that the verse in Exodus ending the
seventh plague says that the stones didn't fall to the ground; does this mean they
were created but stored in heaven? The Rabbis answer in the affirmative, noting
that in the Joshua account it merely says that God threw them, i. e., they were
already there to be thrown.

Even though the *derasha* here is a classic example of the rabbis picking up
subtle word choices in the biblical text and stretching them out to their full effect, nevertheless, it seems reasonable to suggest that there is also an underlying
message being conveyed. Joshua's miracle of the hailstones is simply the culmi-
nation of Moses' miracle. Joshua does not create the hailstones, Moses does. In
this sense Joshua can be seen as, again, a secondary figure to Moses who makes
use of his master's accomplishments during his own tenure.

Joshua More Naïve than Moses

In an unfavorable comparison between Moses and Joshua, Joshua is painted as a
more naïve leader than Moses. *Midrash Tanḥuma* (*Nitzavim* 5), commenting on
Deut 29:10, in which Moses describes everyone gathered together, including
strangers, woodchoppers, and water-drawers, offers a midrashic gloss.

אמר ר' יצחק בן טבלי: "מלמד שבאו גבעונים אצל [משה ולא קיבלן, ובאו אצל] יהושע וקיבלן, שנאמר: 'ויעשו גם המה בערמה.' מהו 'גם המה?' מלמד שבאו אצל משה ולא קיבלן."

R. Isaac ben Ṭabli said: "This teaches that the Gibeonites came to Moses but he did not accept them, then they came to Joshua and he accepted them, as it says (Josh 9:4), 'and they also behaved with deceit,' what does it mean 'they also'? It teaches that they came before Moses but he did not accept them."

The midrash seems to work off of two verses. First, R. Isaac ben Ṭabli points out the odd word "also" in the description of the deceit of the Gibeonites. The word "also" implies that some sort of deceit had occurred in the past. The other passage is the verse in Deuteronomy to which the midrash is attached as a gloss. The verse makes mention of woodcutters and water-drawers. These are the exact jobs Joshua assigns to the Gibeonites after he learns of their deception. By placing the *derasha* of R. Isaac ben Ṭabli as a gloss on this verse, *Midrash Tanḥuma* implies that Moses was seeing the existence of this subgroup in the future, perhaps making a subtle comment on Joshua's failure to see their deception for what it was.

The midrash itself claims an earlier attempt by the Gibeonites to fool an Israelite leader, this time Moses. Unlike Joshua, Moses sees through their ruse and sends them off. They make another attempt after the passing of the shrewder Moses, and find his successor Joshua more easily deceived. The rhetorical strategy here is the exact inverse of that which was taken with regard to the stopping of the sun and the giants. Instead of granting Moses the great works of Joshua, Moses is cleared of one of Joshua's faults. The former strategy aggrandizes Moses to avoid Joshua shooting ahead of him in any way; the latter strategy aggrandizes Moses by making him successful in an area where Joshua failed.

Joshua the Forgetter of Torah

Another way the rabbis emphasize the significance of Moses in comparison with that of all other future "Torah" leaders, including Joshua, is by emphasizing that Moses was the *only* prophet granted revelation codified as law. Other prophets receive messages from God, not Torah itself, which was given once and for all time to Moses. One place this point is made—and in relation to Joshua specifically—is in an *aggada* about how Torah was forgotten immediately after the death of Moses (b. *Temurah* 16a).

אמר רב יהודה אמר שמואל: "שלשת אלפים הלכות נשתכחו בימי אבלו של משה." אמרו לו ליהושע: "שאל!" א"ל: "'לא בשמים היא.' " אמרו לו לשמואל: "שאל!" אמר להם: "'אלה המצות' – שאין הנביא רשאי לחדש דבר מעתה."

Rav Yehudah said in the name of Samuel: "Three thousand laws were forgotten during the mourning over Moses." They said to Joshua: "Ask [God]." Joshua responded: "'It is not in heaven' (Deut 30:12)." They said to Samuel[715]: "Ask." He said to them: "'These are the commandments' (Lev 27:34, Num 36:13) – for a prophet is not permitted to add anything new from this point on."

...אמר רב יהודה אמר רב: "בשעה שנפטר משה רבינו לגן עדן, אמר לו ליהושע: 'שאל ממני כל ספיקות שיש לך!' אמר לו: "רבי, כלום הנחתיך שעה אחת והלכתי למקום אחר? לא כך כתבת בי, 'ומשרתו יהושע בן נן נער לא ימיש מתוך האהל'?" מיד תשש כחו של [משה],[716] ונשתכחו ממנו שלש מאות הלכות, ונולדו לו שבע מאות ספיקות, ועמדו כל ישראל להרגו. אמר לו הקדוש ברוך הוא: 'לומר לך אי אפשר, לך וטורדן במלחמה,' שנאמר: 'ויהי אחרי מות משה עבד ה' ויאמר ה' וגו'.'"

...Rav Yehudah said in the name of Rav: "When Moses, our teacher, was to go up to the Garden of Eden, he said to Joshua: 'Ask me regarding any matter about which you are in doubt.' [Joshua] replied: 'My teacher, did I leave your side at any point to go somewhere else? Did you not write about me, 'and his servant Joshua son of Nun, the lad, never left the tent.'" Immediately, Moses became weak, and he (Joshua) forgot 300 laws and 700 doubts began to plague him. All of Israel wanted to kill him. The Holy One, bb"h, said to him: 'To tell you [the laws] would be impossible, go and distract them with war,' as it says (Josh 1:1), 'And it happened after Moses, servant of God, died, that God said [to Joshua]....'"

במתניתין תנא: אלף ושבע מאות קלין וחמורין, וגזירות שוות, ודקדוקי סופרים נשתכחו בימי אבלו של משה. אמר רבי אבהו: "אעפ"כ החזירן עתניאל בן קנז מתוך פלפולו, שנאמר: 'וילכדה עתניאל בן קנז אחי כלב.'"

In our Mishna it was taught: "1700 a fortioris, *gezeirah shavas*, and scribal deductions were lost during the mourning period of Moses." R. Abahu said: "Even so, Othniel son of Kenaz brought them back with his subtle learning, as it says (Josh 15:17): 'Othniel son of Kenaz, brother of Caleb, conquered it.'"

In this pericope, the Babylonian Talmud collects three separate midrashim about halakhot being forgotten at the very beginning of Joshua's tenure, even as the people were still mourning Moses. In the first midrash, the emphasis appears to be on the unique nature of Moses' prophecy. This is underscored by the responses both of Joshua and Samuel to the forgetting. They both assert that al-

---

715 MS Munich 95 doesn't have Samuel here, just the pronoun "to him," so in this version the people would be reiterating their request/damand to Joshua himself.
716 Corrected based on MS Vatican 119, MS Vatican 120, MS Florence II-I-7, and the commentary of Rashi; the other manuscripts have Joshua becoming weak, but this leaves the punishment unexplained, except, perhaps, as a general response of God to Joshua's hubris, but not for the specific offense of hurting Moses' feelings.

though they are prophets, the Torah—Moses' book—explicitly forbids any later prophet from introducing divine revelation into the halakhic system. The people and their prophets have been left by Moses to fend for themselves.

The third midrash offers a solution to this problem. Although the mishna also records a tradition of matters being forgotten after the death of Moses, R. Abahu offers a solution. All the information required to properly observe God's laws is contained in the Torah itself. All that is needed is simply for a scholar with sufficient skill and suppleness to tease out the details from the nuances of the Torah. Interestingly, this scholar is not Joshua, but the relatively obscure leader who "succeeds" Joshua, Othniel ben Kenaz. Although the simple reason this leader was chosen was ostensibly the verse about his conquering "Qiryat Sefer," the city of the book, the book equaling the Torah in this interpretation, nevertheless, it is striking that it is Othniel and not Joshua who succeeds.

The second midrash is the one most directly related to Joshua. In this version, the forgetting is not recorded in the passive voice, which is a way of spreading the blame to an unspecified "they." Instead, Joshua forgets the laws, which infuriates the people of Israel, who were relying on him. Furthermore, the forgetting was not due to a failure of memory or intelligence, or even a failure to sufficiently study or review the material. Joshua says very clearly that he was a perfect student and missed nothing from Moses' lectures. Rather, Joshua is punished for his hubris in stating that he knows everything Moses taught as well as Moses himself, thereby implying that he was the equal of his teacher and hurting his teacher's feelings. For this reason, Joshua is punished by God and forced to forget halakha.

There is a great irony in this punishment, since God seems to be "cutting off his nose to spite his face," proverbially speaking. If God wishes the people of Israel to properly observe God's laws, and God is unwilling to communicate the details to any other prophet than Moses—and Moses is dead—God effectively condemns the Israelites to improper observance of God's own laws. I suggest that for the Rabbis, observance accurate to divine original intent is a secondary value. More important is the maintanence of the Rabbinic tradition and the focus on the Pentateuch as the source of Jewish law. The significance of Joshua forgetting a number of laws pales in comparison with the possible implication of his statement that he was as great as Moses.

Finally, God's message to Joshua that he will never recover these laws so he might as well distract the Israelites before they tear him to pieces, is a slap in the face to Joshua. In essence, God has told him that despite his hours clocked in the Tent learning from God and Moses, he (Joshua) will never be the Torah scholar Moses was. He should go back to his first calling, as military leader, and earn his glory and reputation in that capacity.

Addendum: Stabilization – Joshua in the Image of Moses

To some extent, the polemic of Joshua vs. Moses picks up on a biblical theme (one that was explored in the diachronic study of the second chapter.) Joshua is the great conqueror of Canaan, Moses the redeemer of Israel from Egypt and receiver of the Torah at Sinai. Although each character has biblical passages supporting his unequaled greatness, it is clear that the Bible as a whole decided upon Moses as the ultimate leader.

One of the solutions the biblical texts themselves use to diffuse the tension is to paint Joshua in Mosaic colors. This same strategy is used in the early post-Talmudic age to incorporate some of the polemical rabbinic texts about Joshua into the overall Joshua-as-Moses'-apprentice-and-successor model. For example, in the Geonic work, *Pitron Torah* (*Parshat Elleh ha-Devarim*, p. 233), a point by point comparison between Moses and Joshua is made.

ראה שכל מה שנעשה למשה כן נעשה ליהושע. היאך?	See that everything that was done for Moshe was done for Joshua. How is this?
א. למש[ה] נאמ[ר] 'של נעליך מ[על] רגליך,', וליהושע נאמ[ר]: 'של נעליך מ[על] רג[ליך].'	a. Moses was told (Exod 3:5): "Remove your shoes from your feet" and Joshua was told (Josh 5:15): "Remove your shoes from your feet."
ב. משה בנה מזבח, שנ[אמר] 'ויבן משה מזבח וג'', ויהוש[ע] בנה מזבח, שנ[אמר] 'אז יבנה יהושע וג'.'	b. Moses built an altar, as it says (Exod 17:15) "and Moses built an altar" and Joshua built an altar, as it says (Josh 8:30): "Then Joshua built an altar."
ג. למשה העמיד חמה ולבנה, שנ[אמר] 'היום הזה אחל תת וג'', וליהושע העמיד חמה ולבנה, שנ[אמר] 'שמש בגבעון דום.'	c. The sun and moon were stopped for Moses, as it says (Deut 2:25): "On this day I will begin to place..." and the sun and moon were stopped for Joshua, as it says (Josh 10:12): "Sun in Gibeon halt."
ד. משה קרע את הים ויהושע קרע ירדן.	d. Moses split the sea and Joshua split the Jordan.
ה. משה הוכיח את ישר[אל] שנ[אמר]: "אלה הדברים וג'', ויהושע הוכיחן, שנ[אמר] "לא תוכלו לעבד את ה' כי אל[הים] קדושים הוא."	e. Moses rebuked Israel, as it says (Deut 1:1): "These are the things," and Joshua rebuked them, as it says (Josh 24:19): "You cannot serve God, since God is a holy God."
ו. למשה נא[מר] 'ראה החילותי תת לפניך' וליהוש[ע] נא[מר] 'ראה נתתי בידך וג'.'	f. To Moses it was said: "See that I have begun to place before you..." and to Joshua it was said: "See I have placed in your hands, etc."

Most of these parallels are, in fact, biblical parallels with which the biblical authors probably intended to paint Joshua as a second Moses. For the purposes of this chapter, however, Moses and Joshua both stopping the sun (#3) stands out. By the time this compilation was put together, the midrashic "fact" that Moses also stopped the sun had already been well-established.[717] The author of *Pitron Torah* took this as a given and then added the comparison between the characters into his list of examples of how Joshua was like Moses—most probably without any awareness that, in this case, for polemical reasons, the flow of influence was actually the reverse, with Moses being painted in Joshua's colors.

Summary

Any study of images of Joshua in Rabbinic literature is fraught with difficulties, most obviously the extremely contradictory nature of the diverse images. The work of the Church Fathers, develops a typology of Joshua as Jesus, but the Rabbinic descriptions of Joshua do not seem to work with one dominant image.

This inconsistency in interpretation brings to the forefront the scholarly debate about the nature of midrashic interpretive pluralism. Should one understand Rabbinic interpretation as driven by pre-existing cultural or religious values or as driven by the text? Should midrashic interpretation be seen as creative play, some sort of religious hermeneutic activity, or as earnest exegesis?

Despite this problematizing of rabbinic hermeneutics, there do seem to be some overarching features in the Rabbinic discussion of Joshua. First, the Rabbis do have at least one relatively unique image of Joshua: Joshua as rabbi and halakha scholar. Although this can be seen as a natural outgrowth of the biblical image of Joshua as Torah scholar, the culturally constructed nature of a Torah scholar equaling halakha scholar is deeply Rabbinic.

Second, for the Rabbis (as well as for the Samaritans,) Joshua will always remain at least a notch below his teacher Moses. As was seen above, having Moses stop the sun is only the most egregious example of putting Joshua in his place. Throughout the various images of Joshua, it can be seen that the overarching emphasis of the Rabbis is not on Joshua himself, but on Joshua in his capacity as the student and successor of Moses, and one that could never really fill the shoes of the great prophet and law-giver.

---

717 Note that number 6, which began as the midrashic hook for one of the proofs that Moses stopped the sun, developed into its own category in this example.

Conclusion

We have traiced the continuous reinvention of Joshua over time, tracing his image from its earliest stages into the biblical text as it exists now and on through his reception in a select number of later traditions. A mnemohistorical figure such as Joshua is situated in the nexus between two competing cultural values. Cultures that venerate a historical figure from their (perceived) past actively attempt to maintain continuity with this past. "We venerate Joshua," they say, "because he was a great Israelite hero and we are part of / the continuation of this group (Israel) and share its memories." If this were all the culture was attempting, however, there would be no need to retell the story differently or cast Joshua in a new mold. That the story of Joshua is retold and his image recast time and again reflects the second value, which is to make the heroes of one's mnemohistorical past relevant to one's cultural present. This book has explored the tension between maintaining continuity with the past and reconceptualizing the past to make it relevant.

Joshua begins his "career" as a local warrior in the area of Mount Ephraim and connected with a burial plot in the city of Timnat Heres. Over time, his story is extended, and he is remembered as the leader of the Joseph tribes during the period when these tribes settled the highlands. With the consolidation of the "Israelite" identity as a pan-tribal identity, Joshua receives the title of first leader of all Israel, including Judah. I speculate that this occurred soon after the destruction of the northern kingdom when , when the inhabitants of Israel had a strong incentive to see themselves as being part of Judah—or, more accurately, to see Judah as part of Israel—with a northern hero serving as the first ruler (i.e., before Saul or David). Finally, later in the Neo-Assyrian or Neo-Babylonian period, an account of Joshua as conqueror of cities with a campaign is formed. This expansion from local hero to national leader to "royal" conqueror reflects the expanding self-image of the northern Israelite tribes. As Israel's view of itself and its past expanded, so did that of their hero and leader, whose image reflected the image this group projected into their past.

Joshua did not remain merely a Northern Josephite or Israelite figure, however. As Israel and Judah were consolidating their identities, Judah also adopted Joshua as a heroic figure of the past. Most importantly, as the mythic past of this Israelite group solidified, the two ancient figures of Joshua and Moses met and their stories began to merge. Although it is possible that, at one stage, Joshua was envisioned by some as the redeemer of the Israelites from Egypt, eventually Joshua became understood as Moses' attendant and inheritor of the mantle of Israelite leadership. It is hardly surprising that the historiography unfolded this way. Moses is granted pride of place as the law-giver. Moreover, Moses' story occurs outside the Promised Land, whereas Joshua's occurs within it. Since the Israelites' story was about leaving Egypt and coming into the land, it is logical (although not necessary) that Moses' account should precede that of Joshua.

The creation of one timeline including Joshua and Moses caused a seismic shift in Israel's understanding of Joshua. Instead of a homegrown warrior, Joshua begins as the understudy to the great law-giver. This, in turn, opens the opportunity for later redactors to paint Joshua's story in Mosaic colors and even to see Joshua as Moses' understudy, spending his time in the Tent of Meeting in his youth, and studying the Torah day and night throughout his life. In the book of Joshua, a number of verses reference his meticulous care to follow God's commandments as related to Moses. Additionally, this editor (D) records the speeches to Joshua about being brave and strong, allowing the reader to wonder whether Joshua had not been exhibiting such traits before this. It seems that the D editor, being greatly interested in law and Moses, made sure to configure a Joshua who would be subservient to Moses in all ways. Whether this should be traced to the time of Josiah or the exilic period I cannot say.

In the priestly tradition, Joshua's appointment as Moses' successor becomes part of a dual appointment—with Elazar the high priest as his partner and perhaps even superior in some respects. Most probably, this priestly redaction represents a late post-exilic/early Second Temple period layer. Viewed through the prism of this kingless Temple-focused priestly group, any "leader" of Israel (or Judea) would (should?) be subservient to the high priest in Jerusalem.

Following this last priestly redaction, the biblical story of Joshua was more or less complete. Even though each source and redaction had their own unique image or images of Joshua in mind, the combined work presents the reader with a complex and multi-dimensional character. Joshua begins his career both as a warrior and a disciple of Moses. He remains loyal to God as a scout and spends most of his time in the Tent of Meeting where God makes his appearances. He is the powerful leader who fills Moses' shoes but also shares his administration with Elazar, consulting with him and the divine oracle left in Elazar's charge.

Joshua experiences periods of nervousness wherein he must be reassured and periods of great confidence wherein he reassures his people. He is a bold tactician and a shrewd consultant. He is also a religious figure; he works miracles, issues curses, prays on behalf of the people, learns Torah, sets up altars, and even makes a covenant. He ends his career as a revered elder statesman, making speeches and reviewing the obligations the people must fulfill to stay on good terms with their God. It is this multi-dimensional Joshua that later reception engages.

During the Hellenistic Second Temple period, the image of Joshua the warrior dominates. Ben Sira describes Joshua as the warrior for God, and the second book of Maccabees invokes the destruction of Jericho by Joshua. The first book of Maccabees uses Joshua imagery as inspiration for Mattathias and lists Joshua among the heroes of the past to whom God granted assistance, in Joshua's case making him a leader (judge) in Israel. During this period, with Judea as a quasi-independent polity under the Romans and then the Greeks, constantly witnessing military conflicts and participating in them, the idea of a prototypical warrior hero would have resonance. This is certainly true for the Maccabees, who would have seen such a figure as a role model for their own military struggles on behalf of the Judean God.

A related description of Joshua, soon after the destruction of the Temple comes from Josephus' *Antiquities of the Jews*. He also emphasizes Joshua's military character, but from a more Hellenistic angle. Joshua is envisioned studying tactics with Moses, receiving the proper training from his future position as *strategon*. Josephus also emphasizes Joshua's administrative talents. The overall picture of Joshua in *Antiquities* is that of a statesman—a position any good Roman would be proud of.

Philo presents a different image of Joshua. True to his interest in philosophy, Philo describes Joshua in terms reminiscent of Greek philosophical ideals. Joshua has an excellent and amiable disposition, he is virtuous and pious; he loves his teacher, Moses, and imitates his ways. The two discuss philosophy, among other things. Nevertheless, despite Joshua's good qualities, Philo seems to have little interest in Joshua. Most of Philo's discussions about Joshua are lead-ins to discussions about Moses, Philo's primary interest.

A similar approach is taken by *Assumptio Mosis*, but in a more extreme fashion. This work—or at least the narrative framing of this work—was designed as an extended discussion of the death of Moses. As such, its interest is in magnifying the greatness of Moses, and presenting his death as of cosmic importance. Picking up on the biblical references to Joshua as needing to strengthen himself, *Assumptio Mosis* portrays an almost cowardly Joshua, bawling at the knowledge of the imminent death of his teacher and panicking at the responsibilities, military and political, that will be his burden after the master's death.

Liber Antiquitatum Biblicarum, although sharing *Assumptio Mosis*' picture of a crying Joshua, shows Joshua rallying after putting on Moses' clothing, and becoming a great leader and orator. *L.A.B.* then describes Joshua's founding of religious sites and delivery of moving speeches. The entire conquest is referenced in less than a sentence. This unusual retelling of the Joshua story strongly implies that the military picture of Joshua was not resonant with the author of *L.*

A.B. or his community of readers. A more spiritually inspiring character was required, and the Joshua story was modified to fit this mold.

The Qumran community, a group very interested in prophecy and its fulfillment in their days, sees Joshua as a prophet who predicts the future. The Qumranites have only one section of the biblical text on which to build this image: Joshua's cursing of anyone who rebuilds Jericho and its fulfillment in the time of Hiel. Upon this short detail in the Joshua story, the (extant) account of Joshua in the *Apocryphon of Joshua* is built. Joshua not only predicts the future of Hiel, but also King David and the building of the Temple. Joshua's greatness lies in the fact that he was a predictor of the future, a significant quality for a Qumran hero.

Fourth Ezra also pictures a more religious version of Joshua, like *L.A.B.* and Qumran. In the brief reference to Joshua found in *4 Ezra*, Joshua is pictured as an intercessor on behalf of Israel in the style of Moses.

Surveying the above images, one may notice an interpretive strategy used by multiple sources. Considering the multifaceted presentation of Joshua in the biblical texts, the authors of the various Joshua references and retellings have a number of images to choose from. These authors find the images that fit best with the stories they are trying to tell, expand those images and overlook or contract the ones that do not fit as well. For Ben Sira he is a warrior, for Josephus a statesman, for Philo a philosopher, for the *Apocryphon* a prophet, and for *L.A.B.* an inspirational religious leader. All of these images can be traced to the biblical text, but the editor of the biblical texts wove these various images into the overall tapestry of biblical Joshua, while the later receivers of this text disentangle the individual images from the tapestry and work with the ones they find most relevant.

More than a millennium later than the retellings in *Antiquities* and *L.A.B.*, the Samaritan book of Joshua offers its own expanded version of the Joshua narrative. Although the Samaritans never canonized this book or any other book outside the Pentateuch, Joshua is still a venerated figure of memory for this community and his story is an important one. Unlike the Christians and diaspora Jews, the Samaritans remained attached to the land throughout their history. As such, Joshua the conqueror remained an important figure. The Samaritan Book of Joshua adds a number of rhetorical pieces to Joshua's repertoire, specifically prayers and speeches. It also adds an entire battle account, wherein Joshua loses and must be saved by Nabih, but the overall story of Joshua is very much in line with the biblical presentation (and that of Josephus). Joshua is the successor of Moses and the conqueror of the Promised Land.

Among the founders or predecessors of Christianity, the character of Joshua seems to have had little resonance; he is hardly mentioned in the New Testament. Soon after this, however, the early Church Fathers created a Joshua-

Jesus typology, which allowed Christians to see a predecessor of Jesus in Joshua. Since Joshua was the successor of Moses, this was seen as a hint that Jesus and the religion of Jesus would inherit the place of Moses and his Torah in this world. Additionally, Joshua was the leader who presented his followers with the Promised Land, pointing to the future mission of Jesus, who would present his followers with the ultimate Promised Land, the redemption.

For the Rabbis, as for the Christians, a conqueror of the land of Israel had little of interest to say. Many of the Rabbis no longer lived in this land and their focus was more on Torah study and Jewish law than anything else. For this reason, the Rabbis recast Joshua into a more Rabbinic role. Instead of just conquering the land, Joshua is now "the Rabbi of the land." The Rabbis envision him as having established the halakhot relevant to the land, and written the blessing in the grace after meals about the land. Picking up on the verse wherein Joshua is told to learn Torah day and night, the Rabbis describe Joshua as a Torah scholar par excellence.

Another concern of the Rabbis seems to have been polemical in nature. Like Philo, the Rabbis are primarily interested in Moses and Torah. For this reason they share a strategy with Philo (and *Assumptio Mosis*) to use Joshua as a means of expanding the discussion of Moses. However, by the time the Rabbis are writing, the competitor religion, Christianity, also has a position on Joshua, one that specifically paints him as having been *greater* than Moses. Inspired by a desire to counteract this interpretation, along with a general wish to magnify Moses as much as possible, the Rabbis discuss Joshua as a student subservient to his master Moses and, at the same time, escalate Moses' miracle working to include even the great things that Joshua did, like stopping the sun and killing giants. They also attempt to counteract "slander" against Joshua, like the claim that he never married or that he violated the Sabbath. This last point demonstrates that the various "Joshuas" are in conversation with each other as the cultures that venerate them attempt to navigate and negotiate their own identities vis-à-vis each other—a fact that can only be brought out in cross-cultural and mutli-disciplinary studies such as this.

All of the above versions of Joshua contend with the fundamental tension that undergirds this study. How does one both maintain continuity with the mnemohistorical past while simultaneously making that past relevant and meaningful to new realities and differing circumstances. Each of the above versions of Joshua does just this. Each tradition finds one or two strands in the biblical tapestry that forms Joshua, unravels it and then uses it as the core of a new version. Each of the "Joshuas" found in this study are unique in their ways of being Joshua, but are not unrecognizable as Joshua.

The basic contours of his character and place in Israelite historiography remained consistent throughout, once the biblical story was in place. Joshua was the student of Moses. Once the biblical story was in place, Joshua was brought the people into the land; God supported Joshua. These elements appear universally. By affirming the broad outline of the story, each tradition stakes its claim as successor of the Israelites and keeper of Israelite history and lore. And yet, as Jon Levinson writes in his monograph on the reception of Abraham, the differences are even more important than the similarities. The discontinuities between these traditions and their biblical antecedents demonstrate how these traditions differ from the parent tradition, and comparing the different receptions to each other demonstrates the core value differences between the religions and cultures, all of whom wish to be seen as the proper and legitimate successor to Israelite religion. In this sense, Joshua appears in these traditions not only as a figure of consensus and continuity but also as a figure of distinctiveness and divergence.

Bibliography

Adelman, Rachel. *The Return of the Repressed: Pirqe de-Rabbi Eliezar and the Pseudepigrapha*. Supplements to the Journal for the Study of Judaism 140. Leiden: Brill, 2009.

Ahituv, Shmuel. *Joshua: Introduction and Commentary*. Mikra LeYisrael. Tel Aviv: Am Oved, 1995 [Hebrew].

Alt, Albrecht. "Die Landnahme der Israeliten in Palästina." Pages 89–125 in *Kleine Schriften zur Geschichte des Volkes Israel* 1 München: Beck'sche Verlagsbuchhandlung, 1968.

Al-Tabari, Abu Jafar. *History of the Prophets and Kings: Volume 3 – The Children of Israel*. Translated by William Brinner. Albany: University of New York Press, 1991.

Anderson, Robert T. and Terry Giles. *Tradition Kept: The Literature of the Samaritans*. Peabody: Hendrickson, 2005.

Angel, Hayyim. "Moonlit Leadership: A Midrashic Reading of Joshua's Success." *Jewish Bible Quarterly* 37.3 (2009): 144–152.

Artus, Olivier. "Josué 13–14 et le Livre des Nombres." Pages 233–247 in *The Book of Joshua*. Edited by Ed Noort. Bibliotheca Ephemeridum Theologicarum Lovaniensum 250. Proceedings of the Colloquium Biblicum Lovaniense. Leuven: Leuven University Press, 2010.

Assis, Elie. "Divine Versus Human Leadership: Joshua's Succession." Pages 25–47 in *Saints and Role Models in Judaism and Christianity*. Edited by Marcel Poorthuis and Joshua Berman. Jewish and Christian Perspectives Series 7. Leiden: Brill, 2004.

—— *From Moses to Joshua and from the Miraculous to the Ordinary: A Literary Analysis of the Conquest Narrative in the Book of Joshua*. Jerusalem: Magnes Press, 2005. [Hebrew]

—— "A Literary Approach to Complex Narratives: An Examination of Joshua 3–4." Pages 401–413 in *The Book of Joshua*. Edited by Ed Noort. Bibliotheca Ephemeridum Theologicarum Lovaniensum 250. Proceedings of the Colloquium Biblicum Lovaniense. Leuven: Leuven University Press, 2010.

Assmann, Jan. *Moses the Egyptian: The Memory of Egypt in Western Monotheism*. Cambridge: Harvard University Press, 1997.

—— *Religion and Cultural Memory: Ten Studies*. Stanford: Stanford University Press, 2006.

Athas, George. *The Tel Dan Inscription: A Reappraisal and a New Interpretation*. Supplements to the Journal for the Study of the Old Testament. Sheffield: Sheffield Academic Press, 2003.

Attridge, Harold W. *The Epistle to the Hebrews: A Commentary on the Epistle to the Hebrews*. Hermeneia: A Critical and Historical Commentary on the Bible. Philadelphia: Fortress Press, 1989.

Auld, A. Graeme. *Joshua, Moses and the Land: Tetrateuch-Pentateuch-Hexateuch in a Generation since 1938*. Edinburgh: T&T Clark, 1980.

—— *Kings without Privilege: David and Moses in the Story of the Bible's Kings*. Edinburg: T&T Clark, 1994.

Note: The bibliography references all secondary literature cited in the book. Primary sources and standard editions of these sources are not cited. Non-standard editions or editions for which I relied on the translation or engaged the editor's comments or emendations are referenced.

—— *Joshua Retold: Synoptic Perspectives*. Old Testament Studies. Edinburgh: T&T Clark, 1998.

Avigad, Naḥman. "New Light on the Na'ar Seals." Pages 294–300 in *Magnalia Dei, The Mighty Acts of God: Essays on the Bible and Archaeology in Memory of G. Ernest Wright*. Edited by Frank Moore Cross, Werner E. Lemke, and Patrick D. Miller, Jr. Garden City, NY: Doubleday, 1976.

Avioz, Michael. *Josephus' Interpretation of the Books of Samuel*. The Library of Second Temple Studies 86. London: Bloomsbury T&T Clark, 2015.

Baden, Joel S. *J, E, and the Redaction of the Pentateuch*. Forschungen zum Alten Testament 68. Winona Lake: Eisenbrauns, 2009

Bakhos, Carol. *Ishmael on the Border: Rabbinic Portrayals of the First Arab*. Albany: State University of New York Press, 2006.

Barthelot, Katel. "The Image of Joshua in Jewish Sources from the Second Temple Period." *Meghillot* 8–9 (2010): 97–112 [Hebrew].

Becker, Uwe. *Richterzeit und Königtum: Redactionsgeschichtliche Studien zum Richterbuch*. Beihefte zur Zeitschrift für die Alttestamentliche Wissenschaft 192. Berlin: De Gruyter, 1990.

—— "Endredaktionelle Kontextvernetzungen des Josua-Buches." Pages 139–161 in *Die Deuteronomistischen Geschichtswerke: Redaktions- und Religionsgeschichtliche Perspektiven zur "Deuteronomismus": Diskussion in Tora und Vorderen Propheten*. Edited by Markus Witte, Konrad Schmid, Doris Prechel, and Jan Christian Gertz. Beihefte zur Zeitschrift für die Alttestamentliche Wissenschaft 365. Berlin: de Gruyter, 2006.

Beentjes, Pancratius C. *The Book of Ben Sira in Hebrew: A Text Edition of All Extant Hebrew Manuscripts and a Synopsis of All Parallel Hebrew Ben Sira Texts*. Supplements to Vetus Testamentum 68. Leiden: Brill, 1997.

Begg, Christopher T. *Judean Antiquities Books 5–7: Translation and Commentary*. Flavius Josephus: Translation and Commentary 4. Edited by John Mason. Leiden: Brill, 2005.

—— "The Demise of Joshua according to Josephus." *Harvard Theological Studies* 63 (2007): 129–145.

—— "Josephus' and Pseudo-Philo's rewritings of the Book of Joshua." Pages 555–588 in *The Book of Joshua*. Edited by Ed Noort. Bibliotheca Ephemeridum Theologicarum Lovaniensum 250. Proceedings of the Colloquium Biblicum Lovaniense. Leuven: Leuven University Press, 2010.

Bieberstein, Klaus. *Josua—Jordan—Jericho: Archäologie, Geschichte und Theologie der Landnahmeerzählungen Josua 1–6*. Orbis Biblicus et Orientalis 143. Freiburg: Universitätsverlag, 1995.

Blenkinsopp, Joseph. *The Pentateuch: An Introduction to the First Five Books of the Bible*. Anchor Bible Reference Library. New York: Doubleday, 1992.

Blum, Erhard. "Überlegungen zur Kompositionsgeschichte des Josuabuches." Pages 137–157 in *The Book of Joshua*. Edited by Ed Noort. Bibliotheca Ephemeridum Theologicarum Lovaniensum 250. Proceedings of the Colloquium Biblicum Lovaniense. Leuven: Leuven University Press, 2010.

Blumenthal, David. "A Review of Daniel Boyarin: *Intertextuality and the Reading of Midrash*." *CCAR Journal* (Summer/Fall 1995): 81–83.

Boling, Robert G. and G. Ernest Wright. *Joshua: A New Translation with Notes and Commentary*. Anchor Bible 6. Garden City: Doubleday, 1982.

Boyarin, Daniel. *Intertextuality and the Reading of Midrash*. Bloomington: Indiana University Press, 1990.

—— *Border lines: The Partition of Judaeo-Christianity*. Divinations: Rereading Late Ancient Religion. Philadelphia: University of Pennsylvania Press, 2004.

Brettler, Marc Zvi. "Jud 1,1 – 2,10: From Appendix to Prologue." *Zeitschrift für die Alttestamentliche Wissenschaft* 101 (1989): 433 – 435.

—— *The Book of Judges*. Old Testament Readings. London: Routledge, 2002.

Brown, John Pairman. "The Templum and the Saeculum: Sacred Space and Time in Israel and Etruria." *Zeitschrift für die Alttestamentliche Wissenschaft* 98 (1986): 415 – 433.

Budde, K. *Die Bücher Richter und Samuel, ihre Quellen und ihr Aufbau*. Giessen, 1890.

Burney, Charles Fox. *The Book of Judges with Introduction and Notes*. London: Rivingtons, 1918.

Butler, Trent C. *Joshua*. Word Biblical Commentary 7. Waco: Word Books, 1983.

Carleton Paget, James Nicholas. *The Epistle of Barnabas: Outlook and Background*. Wissenschaftliche Untersuchungen zum Neuen Testament 64. Tübingen: Mohr Siebeck, 1994.

Chapman, Stephen B. "Joshua Son of Nun: Presentation of a Prophet." Pages 13 – 26 in *Thus Says the Lord: Essays on the Former and Latter Prophets in Honor of Robert R. Wilson*. Edited by John J. Ahn and Stephen L. Cook. Library of Hebrew Bible/Old Testament Studies 502. New York: T&T Clark, 2009.

Collins, John J. "Syballine Oracles." Pages 317 – 472 in *The Old Testament Pseudepigrapha* 1. Edited by James H. Charelsworth. Garden City: Doubleday, 1983 – 1985.

Corley, Jeremy. "Joshua as Warrior in Ben Sira 46:1 – 10." Pages 207 – 248 in *Visions of Peace and Tales of War*. Edited by Jan Liesen and Pancratius C. Beentjes. Deuterocanonical and Cognate Literature Yearbook. Berlin: De Gruyter, 2010.

Crane, Oliver Turnbull. *The Samaritan Chronicle, or The Book of Joshua Son of Nun*. New York: John B. Alden, 1890.

Cross, Frank Moore. *Canaanite Myth and Hebrew Epic: Essays in the History of the Religion of Israel*. Cambridge: Harvard University Press, 1973.

—— "A Response to Zakovitch's 'Successful Failure of Israelite Intelligence'." Pages 99 – 104 in *Text and Tradition: The Hebrew Bible and Folklore*. Edited by Susan Niditch. Atlanta: Scholars Press, 1990.

Cumont, Franz. "ΙΧΘΥΣ." Pages 844 – 850 in *Pauly-Wissowa Encyclopädie der klassischen Altertumswissenschaft* IX.2, 1916.

Daniélou, Jean. *From Shadows to Reality: Studies in the Biblical Typology of the Fathers*. Translated by Dom Wulstan Hibberd. Westminster: The Newman Press, 1960.

Davies, Philip R. *The Origin of Biblical Israel*. Library of Hebrew Bible/Old Testament Studies 485. London: T&T Clark, 2007.

Dayan, Moshe. *Living with the Bible*. Illustrated by Gemma Levine. New York: William Morrow, 1978.

De Pury, Albert. "The Jacob Story and the Beginning of the Formation of the Pentateuch." Pages 51 – 72 in *A Farewell to the Yahwist? The Composition of the Pentateuch in Recent European Interpretation*. Edited by Thomas B. Dozeman and Konrad Schmid. Society of Biblical Literature Symposium Series 34. Atlanta: Society of Biblical Literature, 2006.

De Troyer, Kristin. *Rewriting the Sacred Text: What the Old Greek Texts Tell Us about the Literary Growth of the Bible*. Text-Critical Studies 4. Atlanta: Society of Biblical Literature, 2003a.

—— "Did Joshua have a Crystal Ball? The Old Greek and the MT of Joshua 10:15, 17, and 23." Pages 571–590 in *Emanuel: Studies in Hebrew Bible, Septuagint, and Dead Sea Scrolls in Honor of Emanuel Tov.* Edited by Shalom M. Paul, Robert A. Kraft, Lawrence H. Schiffman, and Weston W. Fields. Supplements to Vetus Testamentum 94. Leiden: Brill, 2003b.

De Vos, J. Cornelis. "Josua und Jesus im Neuen Testament." Pages 523–540 in *The Book of Joshua.* Edited by Ed Noort. Bibliotheca Ephemeridum Theologicarum Lovaniensum 250. Proceedings of the Colloquium Biblicum Lovaniense. Leuven: Leuven University Press, 2010.

DePalma Digeser, Elizabeth. *The Making of a Christian Empire: Lactantius and Rome.* Ithaca: Cornel University Press, 2000.

Dimant, Devorah. "*The Apocryphon of Joshua* – 4Q522 9 ii: A Reappraisal." Pages 179–204 in *Emanuel: Studies in Hebrew Bible, Septuagint, and Dead Sea Scrolls in Honor of Emanuel Tov.* Edited by Shalom M. Paul, Robert A. Kraft, Lawrence H. Schiffman, and Weston W. Fields. Supplements to Vetus Testamentum 94. Leiden: Brill, 2003.

—— "Between Sectarian and Non-Sectarian: The Case of *the Apocryphon of Joshua.*" Pages 105–134 in *Reworking the Bible: Apocryphal and Related Texts at Qumran.* Edited by Esther G. Chazon, Devora Dimant, and R.A. Clements. Studies on the Texts of the Desert of Judah 58. Leiden: Brill, 2005

Dozeman, Thomas B. "Joshua in the Book of Joshua." Pages 103–116 in *Raising up a Faithful Exegete: Essays in Honor of Richard D. Nelson.* Edited by K. L. Noll and Brooks Schramm. Winona Lake: Eisenbrauns, 2010a.

—— "The Beginning of a Book or Literary Bridge?" Pages 159–182 in *The Book of Joshua.* Edited by Ed Noort. Bibliotheca Ephemeridum Theologicarum Lovaniensum 250. Proceedings of the Colloquium Biblicum Lovaniense. Leuven: Leuven University Press, 2010b.

Dunn, Geoffrey D. *Tertullian.* The Early Church Fathers. London: Routledge, 2004.

—— *Tertullian's Aduersus Iudaeos: A Rhetorical Analysis.* Patristic Monograph Series 19. Washington D.C.: Catholic University of America Press, 2008.

Earl, Douglas S. *Reading Joshua as Christian Scripture.* Journal of Theological Interpretation Supplements 2. Winona Lake: Eisenbrauns, 2010.

Elßner, Thomas R. *Josua und seine Kriege in jüdischer und christlicher Rezeptionsgeschichte.* Theologie und Frieden 37. Stuttgart: W. Kohlhammer, 2008.

Eisenman, Robert H., and Michael Wise. *The Dead Sea Scrolls Uncovered.* Shaftesbury, Dorset: Element, 1992.

Eisler, Robert. *Orpheus the Fisher: Comparative Studies in Orphic and Early Christian Cult Symbolism.* London: Watkins, 1921.

Eshel, Hanan. "The Historical Background of the Pesher Interpreting Joshua's Curse on the Builders of Jericho." *Revue de Qumran* 15 (1991/1992): 409–420.

Falls, Thomas B. *St. Justin Martyr: Dialogue with Trypho.* Revised by Thomas P. Halton. Edited by Michael Slusser. Selections from the Fathers of the Church 3. Washington D.C.: Catholic University of America Press, 2003.

Farber, Zev I. "Timnat Heres and the Origins of the Joshua Tradition." Pages 301–311 in *The Book of Joshua.* Edited by Ed Noort. Bibliotheca Ephemeridum Theologicarum Lovaniensum 250. Proceedings of the Colloquium Biblicum Lovaniense. Leuven: Leuven University Press, 2010.

—— "Jerubaal, Jacob, and the Battle for Shechem: A Tradition History." *Journal of Hebrew Scriptures* 13 (2013): article 12.

Faur, José. *Golden Doves with Silver Dots: Semiotics and Textuality in Rabbinic Tradition.* University of South Florida Studies in the History of Judaism 213. Atlanta: Scholars Press, 1999 [original, Indiana Univ. Press, 1986].

Faust, Avraham. *Israel's Ethnogenesis: Settlement, Interaction, Expansion, and Resistance.* Approaches to Anthropological Archaeology. London: Equinox, 2006.

Feldman, Louis H. "Prolegemenon." Pages ix-clxix in *The Biblical Antiquities of Philo.* Translated by M.R. James. Reprint. Translations of Early Documents 1. New York: Ktav, 1971.

—— "Josephus's *Jewish Antiquities* and Pseudo-Philo's *Biblical Antiquities.*" Pages 59–80 in *Josephus, the Bible and History.* Edited by Louis H. Feldman and Gohei Hata. Detroit: Wayne State University Press, 1989a.

—— "Josephus's Portrait of Joshua." *Harvard Theological Review* 82.4 (1989b): 351–376.

—— *Studies in Josephus' Rewritten Bible.* Supplements to the Journal for the Study of Judaism 58. Leiden: Brill, 1998a.

—— *Josephus's Interpretation of the Bible.* Hellenistic Culture and Society 27. Berkeley: University of California Press, 1998b.

—— *Judean Antiquities 1–4: Translation and Commentary.* Flavius Josephus: Translation and Commentary 3. Edited by John Mason. Leiden: Brill, 2000.

—— "Philo's Interpretation of Joshua." *Journal for the Study of the Pseudepigrapha* 12.2 (2001): 165–168.

Ferguson, Everett. "Spiritual Circumcision in Early Christianity." *Scottish Journal of Theology* 41 (1988): 485–497.

Franke, John R. *Joshua, Judges, Ruth, 1–2 Samuel.* Ancient Christian Commentaries on Scripture, Old Testament 4. Downers Grove: Inter-Varsity Press, 2005.

Frankel, David. *The Murmuring Stories of the Priestly School: A Retrieval of Ancient Sacerdotal Lore.* Supplements to Vetus Testamentum 89. Leiden: Brill, 2002.

—— *The Land of Canaan and the Destiny of Israel: Theologies of Territory in the Hebrew Bible.* Siphrut: Literature and Theology of the Hebrew Scriptures 4. Winona Lake: Eisenbrauns, 2011.

Fritz, Volkmar. *Das Buch Josua.* Handbuch zum Alten Testament I/7. Tübingen: Mohr Siebeck, 1994.

Gadamer, Hans-Georg. *Truth and Method.* 2nd Revised Edition. Translated by Joel Weinsheimer and Donald G. Marshall. New York: Continuum, 1999.

Galil, Gershon. *The Book of 1 Chronicles.* Olam HaTanach. Jerusalem-Tel Aviv: Davidson-Atai, 1995 [Hebrew].

Galil, Gershon and Yair Zakovitch. *The Book of Joshua.* Olam HaTanakh. Tel Aviv: Davidson-Atai, 1996 [Hebrew].

Garfinkel, Yosef. "The Eliakim Na'ar Yokan Seal Impression: Sixty Years of Confusion in Biblical Archaeology Research." *Biblical Archaeologist* 53 (1990): 74–79

Gertz, Jan Christian. "The Literary Connection between the Books of Genesis and Exodus." Pages 73–87 in *A Farewell to the Yahwist? The Composition of the Pentateuch in Recent European Interpretation.* Edited by Thomas B. Dozeman and Konrad Schmid. Society of Biblical Literature Symposium Series 34. Atlanta: Society of Biblical Literature, 2006.

Ginzburg, Louis. *Legends of the Jews.* 7 volumes. Translated by Henrietta Szold. Philadelphia: Jewish Publication Society, 1909–1938.

Goodenough, Erwin R. *By Light, Light: The Mystic Gospel of Hellenistic Judaism*. New Haven: Yale University Press, 1935.

Guillaume, Phillipe. "Tracing the Origin of the Sabbatical Calendar in the Priestly Narrative (Genesis 1 to Joshua 5)." *Journal of Hebrew Scriptures* 5.13 (2005).

Halbwachs, Maurice. *On Collective Memory*. Translated and edited by Lewis A. Coser. Chicago: University of Chicago Press, 1992 [original French pub. 1941, 1952].

Hall, Sarah Lebhar. *Conquering Character: The Characterization of Joshua in Joshua 1–11*. The Library of Hebrew Bible/Old Testament Studies 512. New York: T&T Clark International, 2010.

Halpern, Baruch. *David's Secret Demons: Messiah, Murderer, Traitor, King*. Grand Rapids, MI: Eerdmans, 2001.

Handelman, Susan A. *The Slayers of Moses: The Emergence of Rabbinic Interpretation in Modern Literary Theory*. Albany: State of New York University Press, 1982.

—— "Fragments of the Rock: Contemporary Literary Theory and the Study of Rabbinic Texts— A Response to David Stern." *Prooftexts* 5 (1985): 73–95.

Havrelock, Rachel. *River Jordan: The Mythology of a Dividing Line*. Chicago: University of Chicago Press, 2011.

—— "The Joshua Generation: Conquest and the Promised Land." *Critical Research in Religion* 1.3 (2013): 308–326.

Heinemann, Joseph. "The Messiah of Ephraim and the Premature Exodus of the Tribe of Ephraim." *Harvard Theological Review* 68 (1975): 1–15. (Previously published in Hebrew, *Tarbiz* 40 (5731): 450–461.)

Hess, Richard S. *Joshua: An Introduction & Commentary*. Tyndale Old Testament Commentaries. Leicester, England: Inter-Varsity Press, 1996.

Holub, Robert C. *Reception Theory: A Critical Introduction*. New Accents. London: Methuen, 1984.

Horner, Timothy J. *Listening to Trypho: Justin Martyr's Dialogue Reconsidered*. Contributions to Biblical Exegesis and Theology 28. Leuven: Peeters, 2001.

Hurtado, Larry W. "'Jesus' as God's Name, and Jesus as God's Embodied Name in Justin Martyr." Pages 128–136 in *Justin Martyr and his Worlds*. Edited by Sara Parvis and Paul Foster. Minneaopolis: Fortress Press, 2007.

Hvalvik, Reidar. *The Struggle for Scripture and Covenant: The Purpose of the Epistle of Barnabas and Jewish-Christian Competition in the Second Century*. Wissenschaftliche Untersuchungen zum Neuen Testament 82. Tübingen: Mohr Siebeck, 1996.

Irenaeus. *On the Apostolic Preaching*. Translated (from the Armenian) by John Behr. Popular Patristics Series 17. Crestwood, NY: St. Vladimir's Seminary Press, 1997.

Iser, Wolfgang. *The Act of Reading: A Theory of Aesthetic Response*. Baltimore: Johns Hopkins University Press, 1978.

Jacobson, Howard. *A Commentary on Pseudo-Philo's Liber Antiquitatum Biblicarum, with Latin text and English translation*. 2 Volumes. Leiden: Brill, 1996.

Jaffee, Martin S. "The Hermeneutical Model of Midrashic Studies: What it Reveals and What it Conceals." *Prooftexts* 11 (1991): 67–76.

—— *Torah in the Mouth: Writing and Oral Tradition in Palestinian Judaism, 200 BCE-400 CE*. New York: Oxford University Press, 2001.

Japhet, Sara. "Conquest and Settlement in Chronicles." *Journal Biblical Literature* 98.2 (1979): 205–218.

Jauss, Hans Robert. *Toward an Aesthetic of Reception.* Translated by Timothy Bahti. Theory and History of Literature 2. Minneapolis: University of Minnesota Press, 1982.

Johnson, Luke Timothy. *The Acts of the Apostles.* Edited by Daniel J. Harrington. Sacra Pagina 5. Collegeville, MN: Liturgical Press, 1992.

Jones, C.P.M. "The Epistle to the Hebrews and the Lucan Writings." Pages 113–143 in *Studies in the Gospels: Essays in Memory of R. H. Lightfoot.* Edited by Dennis E. Nineham. Oxford: Blackwell, 1955.

Juynboll, Theodore William John. *Chronicon Samaritanum: Aribice Conscriptum cui Titulus est Liber Josuae.* Lugduni Batavorum, 1848. [Latin]

Kahana, Menachem. "The Halakhic Midrashim." Pages 2–106 in *The Literature of the Sages: Part 2.* Edited by Shmuel Safrai, Zeev Safrai, Joshua Schwartz, and Peter J. Thompson. Compendia Rerum Iudaicarum ad Novum Testamentum. Netherlands: Royal Van Gorcum and Fortress Press, 2006).

Kalimi, Isaac. *Early Jewish Exegesis and Theological Controversy: Studies in Scriptures in the Shadow of Internal and External Controversies.* Jewish and Christian Heritage Series 2. Assen, Netherlands: Van Gorcum, 2002.

Kallai, Zecharia. "The Settlement Tradition of Ephraim: A Historiographical Study."*Zeitschrift des Deutschen Palastina-Vereins* 102 (1986): 68–74.

Kartveit, Magnar. *The Origin of the Samaritans.* Supplements to Vetus Testamentum 128. Leiden: Brill, 2009.

Kirchheim, Raphael. *Karmei Shomron.* Frankfurt: Isaac Kaufman, 1851.

Knauf, Ernst Axel. "Buchschlüsse im Josuabuch." Pages 217–224 in *Les dernières rédactions du Pentateuque, de l'Héxateuque et de l'Ennéateuque.* Edited by Thomas Römer and Konrad Schmid. Bibliotheca Ephemeridum Theologicarum Lovaniensis 203. Leuven: Peeters, 2007.

—— *Josua.* Zürcher Bibelkommentare Altes Testament 6. Zürich: Theologicher Verlag, 2008.

—— "Die Adressatenkreise von Josua." Pages 183–210 in *The Book of Joshua.* Edited by Ed Noort. Bibliotheca Ephemeridum Theologicarum Lovaniensis 250. Proceedings of the Colloquium Biblicum Lovaniense. Leuven: Leuven University Press, 2010.

Knohl, Israel. *The Sanctuary of Silence: The Priestly Torah and the Holiness School.* Minneapolis: Fortress, 1995.

—— *The Bible's Genetic Code.* Israel: Dvir, 2008 [Hebrew].

Koch, Stefan. "Mose sagt zu 'Jesus'—Zur Wahrnehmung von Josua im Neuen Testament." Pages 541–554 in *The Book of Joshua.* Edited by Ed Noort. Bibliotheca Ephemeridum Theologicarum Lovaniensum 250. Proceedings of the Colloquium Biblicum Lovaniense. Leuven: Leuven University Press, 2010.

Kofsky, Aryeh. *Eusebius of Caesarea against Paganism.* Jewish and Christian Perspectives Series 3. Leiden: Brill, 2000.

Kohut, Alexander. *Notes on a Hitherto Unknown Exegetical, Theological, and Philosophical Commentary on the Pentateuch.* New York: Ginsburg, 1892.

Kratz, Reinhard G. *The Composition of the Narrative Books of the Old Testament.* Translated by John Bowden. London: T & T Clark, 2005.

Kugel, James L. "Two Introductions to Midrash." *Prooftexts* 3 (1983): 131–155. Repr. pages 77–103 in *Midrash and Literature.* Edited by Geoffrey Hartman and Sanford Budick. New Haven: Yale University Press, 1985.

—— *In Potiphar's House: The Interpretive Life of Biblical Texts.* Boston: Harvard University Press, 1994.

—— *The God of Old: Inside the Lost World of the Bible.* New York: Free Press, 2003.

Kurtzer, Yehuda. *Shuva: The Future of the Jewish Past.* Waltham, Mass.: Brandeis University Press, 2012.

Le Roux, Jurie H. "Andries van Aarde's Matthew Interpretation." *Hervormde Teleogiese Studies* 67.1 (2011): #1013 (10 pages).

Levenson, Jon D. *Inheriting Abraham: The Legacy of the Patriarch in Judaism, Christianity and Islam.* Princeton: Princeton University Press, 2012.

Lipschits, Oded. "On 'Servant of YHWH' and 'Servant of the King'." *Shenaton* 13 (2001–2): 157–171 [Hebrew].

Livneh, Atar. *The Composition Pseudo-Jubilees from Qumran (4Q225; 4Q226; 4Q227): A New Edition, Introduction and Commentary.* Ph.D. diss., University of Haifa, 2010 [Hebrew].

Lowy, S. *The Principles of Samaritan Bible Exegesis.* Studia Post-Biblica. Leiden: Brill, 1977.

Marcovich, Miroslav. *Iustini Martyris: Apologiae Pro Christianis.* Patrische Texte und Studien 38. Berlin: Walter de Gruyter, 2005 [original 1994].

Marhiv, Baruch and Shahar Yehoshua, eds. *Sefer Yehushua ha-Shomroni.* Holon: Betzel-El, 1976.

Martinez, Florentino Garcia. "The Dead Sea Scrolls and the Book of Joshua." Pages 97–110 in *Qumran and the Bible: Studying the Jewish and Christian Scriptures in Light of the Dead Sea Scrolls.* Edited by Nora David and Armin Lange. Leuven: Peeters, 2010.

—— "Light on the Joshua Books from the Dead Sea Scrolls." Pages 145–159 in *After Qumran: Old and Modern Editions of the Biblical Texts – The Historical Books.* Edited by H. Ausloos, B. Lemmelijn and J. Trebolle Barrera. Bibliotheca Ephemeridum Theologicarum Lovaniensium 246. Leuven: Peeters, 2011.

Masalha, Nur. *The Bible and Zionism: Invented Traditions, Archaeology and Post-Colonialism in Palestine- Israel.* London: Zed Books, 2007.

Mendels, Doron. *The Rise and Fall of Jewish Nationalism: The History of Jewish and Christian Ethnicity in Palestine within the Graeco-Roman Period, 200 BCE to 132 CE.* Anchor Bible Reference Library. New York: Doubleday, 1992.

Milstein, Sara J. *Reworking Ancient Texts: Revision through Introduction in Biblical and Mesopotamian Literature.* Ph.D Dissertation. New York University, 2010.

Mowinkel, Sigmund. *Zur Frage Nach Dokumenterischen Quellen in Josua 13–19.* Oslo: I kommisjon hos J. Dybwad, 1946.

Murphy, Frederick J. *Pseudo-Philo: Rewriting the Bible.* New York: Oxford University Press, 1993.

Na'aman, Nadav. "The 'Conquest of Canaan' in the Book of Joshua and in History." Pages 218–281 in *From Nomadism to Monarchy: Archaeological and Historical Aspects of Early Israel.* Edited by Israel Finkelstein and Nadav Na'aman. Jerusalem: Yad Itzhak ben Zvi, 1994.

—— "Saul, Benjamin, and the Emergence of Biblical Israel – Part 1." *Zeitschrift für die alttestamentliche Wissenschaft* 121 (2009): 211–224.

—— "Saul, Benjamin, and the Emergence of Biblical Israel – Part 2." *Zeitschrift für die alttestamentliche Wissenschaft* 121 (2009): 335–349.

Nelson, Richard D. "Josiah in the Book of Joshua." *Journal of Bibilical Literature* 100.4 (1981a): 531–540.

—— *The Double Redaction of the Deuteronomistic History.* Supplements to the Journal of the Study of the Old Testament 18. Sheffield: Continuum, 1981b.

—— *Joshua: A Commentary.* Old Testament Library. Louisville, Westminster John Knox Press, 1997.

Narinskaya, Elana. *Ephrem: A 'Jewish' Sage: A Comparison of the Exegetical Writings of St. Ephrem the Syrian and Jewish Traditions.* Studia Traditionis Theologiae: Exploration in Early and Medieval Theology 7. Turnhout, Belgium: Brepols Publishers, 2010.

Neusner, Jacob. *Aphrahat and Judaism: The Christian-Jewish Argument in Fourth-Century Iran.* USF Studies in the History of Judaism 205. Atlanta: Scholars Press, 1999 [original Brill 1971].

—— *Midrash as Literature: The Primacy of Documentary Discourse.* Eugene, OR: Wipf and Stock Publishers, 1987.

Newsom, Carol. "The 'Psalms of Joshua' from Qumran Cave 4." *Journal of Jewish Studies* 39 (1988): 56–73.

—— "4Q378 and 4Q379: An Apocryphon of Joshua." Pages 35–85 in *Qumranstudien.* Edited by H.J. Fabry, A. Lange, and H. Lichtenberger. Göttingen: Vandenhoeck & Ruprecht, 1996.

—— "Apocryphon of Joshua." Pages 237–288 in *Discoveries in the Judean Desert* 22: *Qumran Cave 4, v. 17: Parabiblical Texts Part 3.* Oxford: Clarendon Press, 1996.

Nickelsburg, George W.E. "Good and Bad Leaders in Pseudo-Philo's Liber Antiquitatum Biblicarum." Pages 49–66 in *Ideal Figures in Ancient Judaism: Profiles and Paradigms.* Edited by John J. Collins and George W.E. Nickelsburg. Society of Biblical Literature: Septuagint and Cognate Studies 12. Chico: Scholars Press, 1980.

Niessen, Friedrich. *Eine Samaritanische Version des Buches Yehošua und die Šoḇaḵ-Erzählung.* Texte und Studen zur Orientalistik 12. Hildesheim: Georg Olms Verlag, 2000.

Noort, Ed. "Josua 24,28–31, Richter 2,6–9 und das Josuagrab." Pages 109–130 in *Biblische Welten: Festschrift für Martin Metzger zu seinem 65. Geburtstag.* Orbis Biblicus et Orientalis 123. Freiberg: Göttingen Vandenhoeck & Ruprecht, 1992.

—— *Das Buch Josua: Forschungsgeschichte und Problemfelder.* Erträge der Forschung 292. Darmstadt : Wissenschaftliche Buchgesellschaft, 1998.

—— "Joshua: The History of Reception and Hermeneutics." Pages 199–215 in *Past, Present, Future: The Deuteronomistic History and the Prophets.* Edited by Johannes C. De Moor and Harry F. Van Rooy. Oudtestamentische Studien 44. Leiden: Brill, 2000.

—— "Der Reißende Wolf – Josua in Überlieferung und Geschichte." Pages 153–173 in *Congress Volume Leiden 2004.* Supplements to Vetus Testamentum 109. Leiden: Brill, 2006.

—— "Josua im Wandel der Zeiten: Zu Stand und Perspektiven der Forschung am Buch Joshua." Pages 21–47 in *The Book of Joshua.* Edited by Ed Noort. Bibliotheca Ephemeridum Theologicarum Lovaniensum 250. Proceedings of the Colloquium Biblicum Lovaniense. Leuven: Leuven University Press, 2010.

Noth, Martin. *Das Buch Josua.* Handbuch zum Alten Testament 7. Tübingen: Mohr Siebeck, 1938.

—— *A History of Pentateuchal Traditions.* Translated by Bernhard W. Anderson. Englewood Cliffs: Prentice Hall, 1972 (Original 1952).

O'Neil, J.C. "The Man from Heaven: SibOr 5.256–259." *Journal for the Study of Pseudepigrapha* 9 (1991): 87–102.

Origen. *Homilies on Joshua.* Translated by Barbara Bruce. Edited by Cynthia White. Fathers of the Church 105. Washington D.C.: Catholic University of American Press, 2002.

Persico, Tomer. "The Messianic Fervor that Revamped Gush Emunim." *Mussaf-Shabbat* (July 1, 2012): http://musaf-shabbat.com/2012/07/01/המשיחיות-שההחליפה-את-גוש-אמונים-תומר-פר/ [Hebrew].

Pitkänen, Pekka M. A. *Joshua*. Apollos Old Testament Commentary 6. Nottingham: InterVarsity Press, 2010.

Pope, R. Martin. *The Hymns of Prudentius*. Project Gutenberg, 2005. http://www.gutenberg. org/files/14959/14959-h/14959-h.htm

Pruzansky, Steven. *A Prophet for Today: Contemporary Lessons from the Book of Yehoshua*. Jerusalem: Gefen, 2006.

Pseudo-Macarius. *The Fifty Spiritual Homilies and the Great Letter*. Translated by George A. Maloney. The Classics of Western Spirituality. New York: Paulist Press, 1992.

Puech, Emile. "Fragments du Psaulme 122 dans un manuscript hébreu de la grotte IV." *Revue de Qumran 9* (1978): 547–554.

—— "La pierre de Sion et l'autel des holocaustes d'après un manuscrit hébreu de la grotte 4 (4Q522)." *Revue Biblique 99* (1992): 676–696.

—— "4Q522, 4QProphétie de Josué (4QapocrJosué^c?)." Pages 39–74 in *Discoveries in the Judaean Desert 25: Qumrângrotte 4. XVIII: Textes hébreux (4Q521–4Q528, 4Q576–4Q579)*. Oxford: Clarendon Press, 1998.

Qimron, Elisha. "Concerning 'Joshua Cycles' from Qumran (4Q522)." *Tarbiẓ 63* (1994): 503–508 [Hebrew].

Rabin, Hayim, Yehuda Elitzur, Hayim Gevaryahu, and Ben Tzion Luria, eds. *Studies in Tanakh by the Study Group in the House of David Ben-Gurion*. Jerusalem: Kiryat Sefer, 1971 [Hebrew].

Reed, Annette Yoshiko. "The Construction and Subversion of Patriarchal Perfection: Abraham and Exemplarity in Philo, Josephus, and the Testament of Abraham." *Journal for the Study of Judaism 40* (2009): 185–212.

Reiner, Elchanan. "From Joshua to Jesus: The Transformation of a Biblical Story to a Local Myth: A Chapter in the Religious Life of the Galilean Jew." Pages 233–271 in *Sharing the Sacred: Religious Contacts and Conflicts in the Holy Land: First-Fifteenth Centuries CE*. Edited by Arieh Kofsky and Guy G. Stroumsa. Jerusalem: Yad Izhak Ben Zvi, 1998.

—— "From Joshua through Jesus to Simeon bar Yohai: Towards a Typology of Galilean Heroes." Pages 94–105 in *Jesus Among the Jews: Representation and Thought*. Edited by Neta Stahl. Routledge Jewish Studies Series. London: Routledge, 2012.

Remnick, David. "The Joshua Generation." *The New Yorker* (Nov. 17, 2008): http://www.newyorker.com/reporting/2008/11/17/081117fa_fact_remnick.

Richter, Wolfgang. *Traditionsgeschichtliche Untersuchungen zum Richterbuch*. Bonner Biblische Beiträge 18. Bonn: Hanstein, 1963.

Rofé, Alexander. "Ephraimite versus Deuteronomistic History." Pages 462–474 in *Reconsidering Israel and Judah: Recent Studies on the Deuteronomistic History*. Edited by Gary N. Knoppers and J.G. McConville. Winona Lake: Eisenbrauns, 2000.

—— "Joshua son of Nun in the History of Biblical Tradition." *Tarbiz 73*:3 (2004): 333–364 [Hebrew].

Rokeah, David. *Justin Martyr and the Jews*. Jewish and Christian Perspectives Series 5. Leiden: Brill, 2002.

Römer, Thomas. *Israels Väter: Untersuchungen zur Väterthematik im Deuteronomium und in der Deuteronomistischen Tradition*. Orbis Biblicus et Orientalis 99. Freiberg: Universitätsverlag, 1990.

—— *The So-Called Deuteronomistic History: A Sociological, Historical and Literary Introduction.* London: T&T Clark, 2007.

—— "The Exodus in the Book of Genesis." *Svensk Exegetisk Årsbok* 75 (2010): 1–20.

—— "Book-Endings in Joshua and the Question of the So-Called Deuteronomistic History." Pages 87–101 in *Raising up a Faithful Exegete: Essays in Honor of Richard D. Nelson.* Edited by K. L. Noll and Brooks Schramm. Winona Lake: Eisenbrauns, 2010.

Römer, Thomas and Marc Zvi Brettler. "Deuteronomy 34 and the Case for a Persian Hexateuch." *Journal of Biblical Literature* 119 (2000), 401–419.

Sand, Shlomo. *The Invention of the Jewish People.* Translated by Yael Lotan. London: Verso, 2009.

Schaeffer, Francis August. *Joshua and the Flow of Biblical History.* 2nd U.S. edition. Wheaton: Crossway Books, 2004.

Schäfer-Lichtenberger, Christa. *Josua und Salamo: Eine Studie zu Autorität und Legitimität des Nachfolgers im Alten Testament.* Supplements to Vetus Testamentum 58. Leiden: Brill, 1995.

Schäfer, Peter. *The Jewish Jesus: How Judaism and Christianity Shaped Each Other.* Princeton: Princeton University Press, 2012.

Scheftelowitz, Isidor. "Das Fisch-Symbol im Judentum und Christentum." *Archiv für Religionswissenschaft* 14 (1911): 1–54, 321–392.

Schmid, Konrad. *Genesis and the Moses Story: Israel's Dual Origins in the Hebrew Bible.* Translated by James Nogalski. *Sifrut:* Literature and Theology of the Hebrew Bible 3. Winona Lake: Eisenbrauns, 2010.

—— *The Old Testament: A Literary History.* Translated by Linda M. Maloney. Minneapolis: Fortress Press, 2012.

Schnocks, Johannes. "Rezeption des Josuabuches in den Makkabäerbüchern." Pages 511–521 in *The Book of Joshua.* Edited by Ed Noort. Bibliotheca Ephemeridum Theologicarum Lovaniensum 250. Proceedings of the Colloquium Biblicum Lovaniense. Leuven: Leuven University Press, 2010.

Seeman, Don. "Martyrdom, Emotion and the Work of Ritual in R. Mordecai Joseph Leiner's *Mei Ha-Shiloah.*" *AJS Review* 27.2 (2003): 253–280.

Sharon, Ariel and David Chanoff. *Warrior: An Autobiography.* New York: Touchstone, 2001.

Shepardson, Christine. *Anti-Judaism and Christian Orthodoxy: Ephrem's Hymns in Fourth Century Syria.* North American Patristics Society: Patristic Monograph Series 20. Washington D.C.: The Catholic University of America Press, 2008.

Sider, Robert Dick. *Ancient Rhetoric and the Art of Tertullian.* Oxford: Oxford University Press, 1971.

Smend, Rudolf. "Das Gesetz und die Völker: Eine Beitrag zur Deuteronomischen Redaktionsgeschichte." Pages 494–509 in *Probleme Biblischer Theologie: Festschrift für Gerhard von Rad.* Edited by Hans Walter Wolf. München: Kaisar, 1971.

Smith, Yancy Warren. *Hippolytus' Commentary on Song of Songs in Social and Critical Light.* Ph.D. diss., Brite Divinity School, 2009.

Soggin, J. Alberto. *Joshua: A Commentary.* Translated by R. A. Wilson. The Old Testament Library. Philadelphia: Westminster Press, 1972.

Stenhouse, Paul. *The Kitab al-Tarikh of Abu 'l-Fath: Translated with Notes.* Studies in Judaica 1. Sydney: University of Sydney, 1985.

Stern, David. "Moses-cide: Midrash and Contemporary Literary Criticism." *Prooftexts* 4 (1984): 193–213.

—— "Literary Criticism or Literary Homilies? Susan Handelman and the Contemporary Study of Midrash." *Prooftexts* 5 (1985): 96–103.

Stroumsa, Gedaliahu Guy. "The Early Christian Fish Symbol Reconsidered." Pages 199–205 in *Messiah and Christos: Studies in the Jewish Origins of Christianity–Presented to David Flusser on the Occasion of his Seventy-Fifth Birthday*. Edited by Ithamar Gruenwald, Shaul Shaked, and Gedaliahu G. Stroumsa. Texte und Studien zum Antiken Judentum 32. Tübingen: Mohr Siebeck, 1992.

Theodoret of Cyrus. *The Questions on the Octateuch*. Greek text revised by John F. Petruccione. English translation with introduction and commentary by Robert C. Hill. Library of Early Christianity 1, 2. Washington, D.C.: Catholic University of America Press, 2007.

Tov, Emanuel. "The Rewritten Book of Joshua as Found at Qumran and Masada." Pages 71–91 in *Hebrew Bible, Greek Bible and Qumran: Collected Essays*. Texts and Studies in Ancient Judaism 121. Tübingen: Mohr Siebeck, 2008.

—— "Literary Development of the Book of Joshua as reflected in the MT, LXX and 4QJoshᵃ." Pages 65–86 in *The Book of Joshua*. Edited by Ed Noort. Bibliotheca Ephemeridum Theologicarum Lovaniensm 250. Proceedings of the Colloquium Biblicum Lovaniense. Leuven: Leuven University Press, 2010.

Tromp, Johannes. *The Assumption of Moses: A Critical Edition with Commentary*. Studia in Veteris Testamenti Pseudepigrapha. Leiden: Brill, 1993.

Van Aarde, Andries. "Jesus as Joshua: Moses en Dawidiese Messias in Matteus." *Scriptura* 84:3, (2003): 453–467 [Afrikaans].

—— "Jesus' Mission to All of Israel Emplotted in Matthew's Story." SBL 2005 (Philadelphia). http://www.sbl-site.org/assets/pdfs/aarde_jesus.pdf

Van Bekkum, Koert. *From Conquest to Coexistence: Ideology and Antiquarian Intent in the Historiography of Israel's Settlement in Canaan*. Culture and History of the Ancient Near East 45. Leiden: Brill, 2011.

Van der Meer, Michaël N. *Formation and Reformulation: The Redaction of the Book of Joshua in the Light of the Oldest Textual Witnesses*. Supplements to Vetus Testamentum 102. Leiden: Brill, 2004.

Van Goudoever, Jan. *Biblical Calendars*. Leiden: Brill, 1959.

Van Seters, John. "Joshua's Campaign of Canaan and Near Eastern Historiography," *Scandinavian Journal of the Old Testament* 2 (1990): 1–12.

Visotzky, Burton L. *Fathers of the World: Essays in Rabbinic and Patristic Literatures*. Tübingen: Mohr Siebeck, 1995.

—— *Golden Bells and Pomegranates: Studies in Midrash Leviticus Rabbah*. Tübingen: Mohr Siebeck, 2003.

Weinfeld, Moshe. "Historical Facts behind the Israelite Settlement Plan." *Vetus Testamentum* 38:3 (1988): 324–332.

—— *The Promise of the Land: The Inheritance of the Land of Canaan by the Israelites*. Berkeley: University of California Press, 1993.

—— *The Decalogue and the Recitation of "Shema": The Development of the Confessions*. Tel Aviv: Hakibbutz Hameuchad, 2001 [Hebrew].

Wénin, André. "Josué 1–12 Comme Récit." Pages 109–135 in *The Book of Joshua*. Edited by Ed Noort. Bibliotheca Ephemeridum Theologicarum Lovaniensum 250. Proceedings of the Colloquium Biblicum Lovaniense. Leuven: Leuven University Press, 2010.

Whitfield, Bryan. *Joshua Traditions and the Argument of Hebrews 3 and 4*. Doctoral Dissertation. Emory University, 2007.

—— "The Three Joshuas of Hebrews 3 and 4," *Perspectives in Religious Studies* 37 (2010): 21–35.

Wolfson, Elliot R. "Hai Gaon's Letter and Commentary on *Aleynu:* Further Evidence of Moses De Leon's Pseudepigraphic Activity." *Jewish Quarterly Review* 81.3–4 (1991): 365–410.

Wright, Jacob. *David, King of Israel, and Caleb in Biblical Memory*. Cambridge: Cambridge University Press, 2014.

Yerushalmi, Yosef Hayim. *Zakhor: Jewish History and Jewish Memory*. Samuel and Althea Stroum Lectures in Jewish studies. Seattle: University of Washington Press, 1982.

Yonge, Charles Duke. *The Works of Philo: Complete and Unabridged*. Peabody, Mass: Hendrickson Pub., 1993 [original 1854].

Yoreh, Tzemah L. *The First Book of God*. Beihefte zur Zeitschrift für die Alttestamentliche Wissenschaft 402. Berlin: De Gruyter, 2010.

Young, Frances Margaret. *Biblical Interpretation and the Formation of Christian Culture*. Cambridge: Cambridge University Press, 1997.

Younger, K. Lawson. *Ancient Conquest Accounts: A Study in Ancient Near Eastern and Biblical History Writing*. Supplements to the Journal for the Study of the Old Testament 98. Sheffield: Sheffield Academic Press, 1990.

Yuval, Israel J. *Two Nations in Your Womb: Perceptions of Jews and Christians in Late Antiquity and the Middle Ages*. Translated by Barbara Harshav and Jonathan Chipman. S. Mark Taper Foundation Imprint in Jewish Studies. Berkeley: University of California Press, 2006.

Zakovitch, Yair. "Humor and Theology or the Successful Failure of Israelite Intelligence: A Literary-Folklore Approach to Joshua 2." Pages 75–98 in *Text and Tradition: The Hebrew Bible and Folklore*. Edited by Susan Niditch. Atlanta: Scholars Press, 1990.

Zeitlin, Solomon. "The Assumption of Moses and the Revolt of Bar Kokba: Studies in the Apocalyptic Literature." *Jewish Quarterly Review* 38 (1948): 1–45.

Primary Sources

Modern Authors